Oracle Press

Oracle Fusion Applications Development and Extensibility Handbook

About the Authors

Vladimir Ajvaz is an Oracle expert and has been working with the Oracle E-Business Suite and, more recently, Oracle Fusion Applications for the past 15+ years. He worked at Oracle Corporation for many years, and was fortunate enough to work on some of Oracle's best teams across the globe where he gained in-depth knowledge of Oracle technologies. The practical experiences from numerous projects in a wide range of industries inspired Vladimir to coauthor *Oracle E-Business Suite Development & Extensibility Handbook*, which was his first book published by McGraw-Hill Education (Oracle Press). Today, he provides independent advice and consulting services to companies around the globe but also inspires and participates in the development of new enterprise-class products and services.

Anil Passi is an Oracle ACE, with implementation experience across various Oracle products that include Fusion Applications, Financial Accounting Hub, planning and modeling tools, Identity & Access Governance, and OFSAA. He is an independent IT advisor to various financial services organizations in Europe. Anil is also a cofounder of iTouchVision, a company specializing in public-facing multichannel SaaS CRM products. In addition, he cofounded a company named Focusthread that gives online trainings across various Oracle products.

Dhaval Mehta is a Group Development Manager for Fusion Applications in Oracle Corporation. Previously Dhaval worked on Oracle E-Business Suite applications development within Oracle Corporation. Dhaval has worked on building Oracle Sales Cloud applications from their inception to current releases.

About the Technical Editor

Gustavo Gonzalez is an Oracle ACE Director and Chief Technology Officer at IT Convergence, leading the decision of technology strategy for technology platforms, partnerships, and external relationships. Specializing in E-Business Suite, Oracle Business Intelligence, and Fusion Applications, with more than 15 years implementing and upgrading Oracle Applications for worldwide organizations, Gustavo has led early adopter programs for Oracle E-Business Suite and Oracle Fusion Applications. Based in Argentina, he enjoys traveling for business and leisure with his family around the world.

Oracle Press™

Oracle Fusion Applications Development and Extensibility Handbook

Vladimir Ajvaz

Anil Passi

Dhaval Mehta

New York Chicago San Francisco
Athens London Madrid Mexico City
Milan New Delhi Singapore Sydney Toronto

Cataloging-in-Publication Data is on file with the Library of Congress

McGraw-Hill Education books are available at special quantity discounts to use as premiums and sales promotions, or for use in corporate training programs. To contact a representative, please visit the Contact Us pages at www.mhprofessional.com.

Oracle Fusion Applications Development and Extensibility Handbook

1234567890 DOC DOC 109876543

ISBN 978-0-07-174369-3
MHID 0-07-174369-3

Sponsoring Editor
Paul Carlstroem

Editorial Supervisor
Janet Walden

Project Editor
LeeAnn Pickrell

Acquisitions Coordinator
Amanda Russell

Technical Editor
Gustavo Gonzalez

Copy Editor
Margaret Berson

Proofreader
Paul Tyler

Indexer
Karin Arrigoni

Production Supervisor
Jean Bodeaux

Composition
Cenveo Publisher Services

Illustration
Cenveo Publisher Services

Art Director, Cover
Jeff Weeks

To my wife, Milica, and our daughter, Anja—love you both.
—Vladimir Ajvaz

I dedicate this book to my wife Anjali and
two gorgeous sons, Nikhil and Anshu.
—Anil Passi

Dedicated to my lovely wife, Bhumi,
and our beautiful daughter, Aanya.
—Dhaval Mehta

Contents at a Glance

Contents

Acknowledgments

A big thanks to our families, friends, and colleagues who put up with us over the long period of writing. Industry insiders would appreciate the amount of effort that is consumed by this book—we are grateful for everyone who supported us along the way.

We'd like to thank Paul Carlstroem, Amanda Russell, Janet Walden, Jean Bodeaux, LeeAnn Pickrell, and the rest of the McGraw-Hill Education production team. Paul and Amanda were a great support during the challenging times and they gently nudged us toward the finish line. We really felt we were working as one team.

The book wouldn't have been possible without having access to Fusion Applications environments. We would like to thank Stuart Provan (Oracle Sales Director, UK Technology) who helped us obtain earlier versions of Fusion Applications through the partner program, and Tushar Thakker (founder of ORATraining.com) who provided us with the most recent software installations that were used for the best part of the book.

We'd also like to thank Dakshesh Patel for sharing his experiences on Fusion Applications implementation projects, especially in the area of extensions and reporting in SaaS-based HCM environments. Also, we are grateful to Gustavo Gonzalez for his efforts in reviewing, tech editing, and providing valuable feedback.

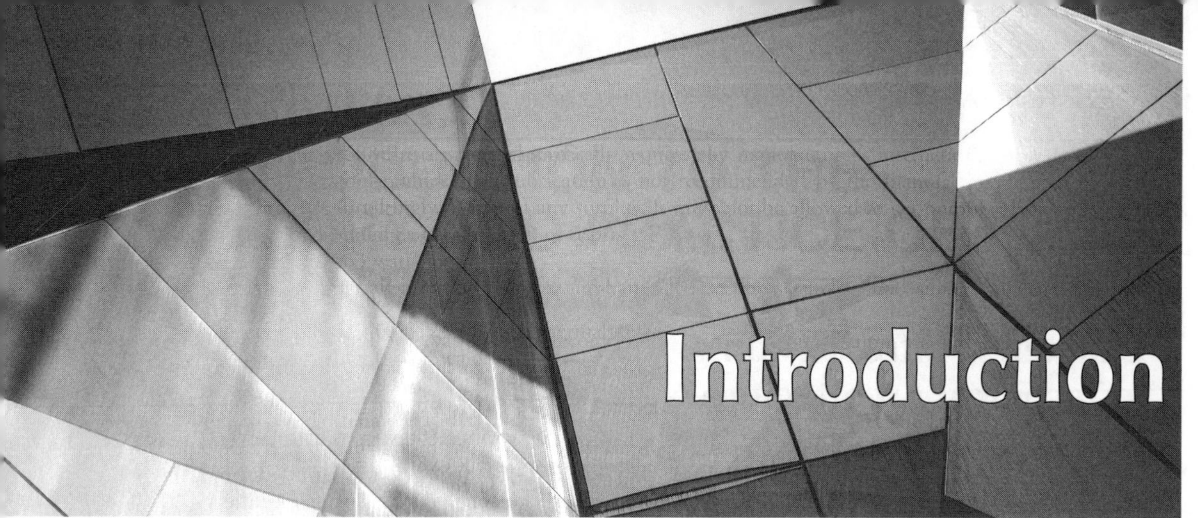

Introduction

Oracle Fusion Applications are designed from the ground up using primarily Oracle's latest middleware and database technologies. They feature hundreds of built-in business processes out of the box, which are based on the industry's best practices as well as a combination of features already available in E-Business Suite, PeopleSoft, Siebel, and JD Edwards enterprise applications.

Although feature-rich, enterprise-class products like Fusion Applications can rarely cater to every single business requirement in a reasonably large enterprise or organization, which often results in requirement gaps that are addressed through customizations and extensions. And this is what leads us to the main goals of the book, which are to provide key information and to be a consolidated reference for the most important customization and extension techniques available in Fusion Applications.

This book covers customization and extension approaches available in releases up to and including version 11.1.6. Most examples in the book are demonstrated using release 11.1.6, which was the latest release available to the authors at the time of writing it.

What the Book Covers

What follows next is a chapter-by-chapter breakdown of what's in the book.

Chapter 1: Introduction to Technical Architecture

In this chapter, you'll learn about the key technology components used in Oracle Fusion Applications. In addition to the technical architecture overview, you'll become familiar with extensions to Oracle Fusion Middleware components specific to Oracle Fusion Applications.

Chapter 2: Introduction to Customization

You'll explore the main types of changes you can perform to an out-of-the-box installation: personalizations, run-time customizations, application extensions, and design-time customizations and extensions. You'll also learn how to use sandboxes and customization manager tools to manage customizations and their deployment.

Chapter 3: Flexfields in Oracle Fusion Applications

In this chapter, you'll learn about the role of available types of flexfields in Fusion Applications, including descriptive, extensible, and key flexfields, along with examples to put the theory into practice.

Chapter 4: Security in Fusion Applications

In this chapter, you'll learn how Oracle Fusion Applications leverage Oracle Identity Management and Oracle Entitlement Server capabilities to provide secure access to an application's resources and data. You'll learn about the Authorization Policy Manager (APM) tool and how to use it, Role-based Access Control (RBAC), function and data security, Web services security, and how the Fusion Applications security model maps into the E-Business Suite model.

Chapter 5: Run-time Customization with Oracle Page Composer

You'll learn how to use Oracle Page Composer from both end-user and system administrator perspectives. You'll also learn about the different modes of run-time customizations, such as design mode, source mode, and select mode. You'll learn how to do field- and region-level customizations, task pane and navigator menu customizations, and how to change page layout and add new content on a page.

Chapter 6: Extending CRM with Oracle Application Composer

In this chapter, you'll learn how to use Oracle Application Composer for run-time customizations and extensions in CRM applications such as sales, marketing, customer center, and CRM common and sales catalog (order capture).

Chapter 7: Customizing with Oracle JDeveloper

In this chapter, you'll learn how to use Oracle JDeveloper to customize Fusion Applications for situations and use cases where the business requirement cannot be satisfied with run-time customization tools. You'll learn about setting up Oracle JDeveloper for customizing Fusion Applications, about the required roles for customization, how to identify artifacts to be customized from the run-time application, and how to deploy JDeveloper customizations.

Chapter 8: Building a New User Interface with ADF

In this chapter, you'll learn about the building blocks of a custom application and how to design it. This chapter shows you how to define and implement business logic and its components, application pages, and integration with UI Shell, security, and deployment.

Chapter 9: Business Process Management (BPM) in Fusion Applications

You'll learn about BPM processes available in the current product release. You'll also learn about BPM tools and techniques available to business analysts, process designers, and developers, and how they can work together to optimize BPM processes.

Chapter 10: Run-time and Design-time Customizations of SOA Components in Fusion Applications

In this chapter, you'll learn how to use run-time and design-time tools such as Oracle BPM Worklist, Oracle SOA Composer, and SOA Editor in JDeveloper to customize and extend SOA composites. You'll also learn about Approval Management Extensions (AMX) and how to create your own approval rules in Fusion Applications.

Chapter 11: Reports

In this chapter, you'll learn how to use BI Publisher to customize existing reports and design (develop) your own reports.

Chapter 12: Analytics in Fusion Applications

In this chapter, you'll be introduced to OBIEE and how it is leveraged in Fusion Applications. You'll also learn about Oracle Transactional Business Intelligence (OTBI) and its function and data security features along with several examples to provide further insight.

Chapter 13: Enterprise Scheduler Jobs and Processing

In this chapter, you'll learn about Enterprise Scheduler Services (ESS) architecture, how to schedule and monitor ESS jobs, the role of the Metadata Services (MDS) repository, and how to configure metadata security for custom ESS jobs.

Chapter 14: Custom Look and Feel with ADF Skinning

In this chapter, you'll learn how to apply corporate or any other branding to your Fusion Applications using the ADF skinning feature. This powerful technique will allow you to change the appearance of applications to suit your individual needs.

Chapter 15: Integration with Fusion Applications

In this chapter, learn how to implement the most common inbound and outbound integration patterns with Fusion Applications. You'll also learn about object workflow, business events, bulk export, file import, and the use of Web services for integration purposes. Additionally, you will follow step-by-step examples for some of the standard patterns presented in this chapter.

Intended Audience

This book is for consultants, developers, product implementers, technical managers, and other professionals who are either already working or intend to work on customizing, extending, and personalizing Oracle Fusion Applications. It covers a wide variety of topics and therefore potentially has a broad audience.

For example, some chapters like Chapter 3, "Flexfields in Oracle Applications," and Chapter 9, "Business Process Management (BPM) in Fusion Applications," can easily be followed by business analysts and functional consultants. Others, like Chapter 7, "Customizing with Oracle JDeveloper," and Chapter 8, "Building a New

User Interface with ADF," are aimed at technical developers. There are also chapters in the book, such as Chapter 10, "Run-time and Design-time Customizations of SOA Components in Fusion Applications," which contain a good mix of sections including both nontechnical and technical material explaining, for example, how to set up approval hierarchies using configuration tools, but also how to add and develop new artifacts into an existing SOA process using JDeveloper.

As far as technical content in the book is concerned, and there is plenty of it, we assume that you have a good knowledge of Oracle Fusion Middleware and Oracle Database technologies, tools, and development techniques. The aim of this book is not to teach you how to get started in the technologies that underpin Fusion Applications, but to provide guidance on how to use them in the context of product customizations and development of extensions. However, we do try to provide a gentle introduction to these technologies where possible in the book.

Two major options for deploying Oracle Fusion Applications are OnPremise or Software-as-a-Service (SaaS). This book assumes that you have unrestricted access to an OnPremise installation as the SaaS option restricts you from performing some of the tasks and techniques described in this book. If you are a reader with access to an SaaS environment only, we advise you to get in touch with your Oracle account manager or Oracle Support representative to become familiar with what customization and extension techniques are available to you and how they are different from the OnPremise deployment option.

CHAPTER 1

Introduction to Technical Architecture

This chapter will provide a bird's-eye view of the key technical components of Oracle Fusion Applications with emphasis on those that are typically relevant to designers and developers of extensions and customizations. Detailed deep-dive and technical insights will be provided in the subsequent chapters in this book, and the highlights provided in this chapter give a cursory glimpse of the technology components that are used to build Fusion Applications.

While reading this chapter, and of course the rest of this book, keep in mind that some of the key drivers that shaped the technical architecture of Fusion Applications were to have an efficient, productive, and predictable user experience, and to build an adaptable applications platform based on established standards such as Java, Service Oriented Architecture (SOA), Extensible Markup Language (XML), Business Process Execution Language (BPEL), and technology acceptance that is suitable for current and emerging trends such as cloud and mobile computing, social media, embedded business intelligence, predictive analytics, and so forth.

Fusion Applications (11.1.*X*) are built using Oracle Fusion Middleware 11*g* components, Oracle Database 11*g*, and Oracle Essbase, and the focus of this chapter is to outline the way those technologies are leveraged and exploited to build Oracle Fusion Applications.

Technical Architecture Overview

On the level of technology, Fusion Applications primarily use Oracle Fusion Middleware and Oracle Database as depicted in Figure 1-1. In addition to the standard Fusion Middleware components, you can see an extra technology layer called Fusion Middleware Infrastructure Components, which are specific to Fusion Applications to provide a common and reusable framework that can be applied to any Fusion Applications product.

In comparison to other Oracle Applications products such as Oracle E-Business Suite, there is a visible shift in the pronounced use of standard application middleware features such as Identity Management and SOA. However, Fusion Middleware Extensions for Applications (Applications Core or applcore) still feature prominently in the technology stack, and we will cover them extensively throughout the book as they are essential tools in the application designer's arsenal. The components, such as flexfields, UI templates, document attachments, and hierarchical trees, are some of the tools that promote common development standards across applications.

Fusion Middleware Components

It shouldn't come as a surprise that Oracle Fusion Middleware and its components provide the principal infrastructure foundation to Fusion Applications and its product families. Oracle has heavily invested in making Fusion Middleware a complete,

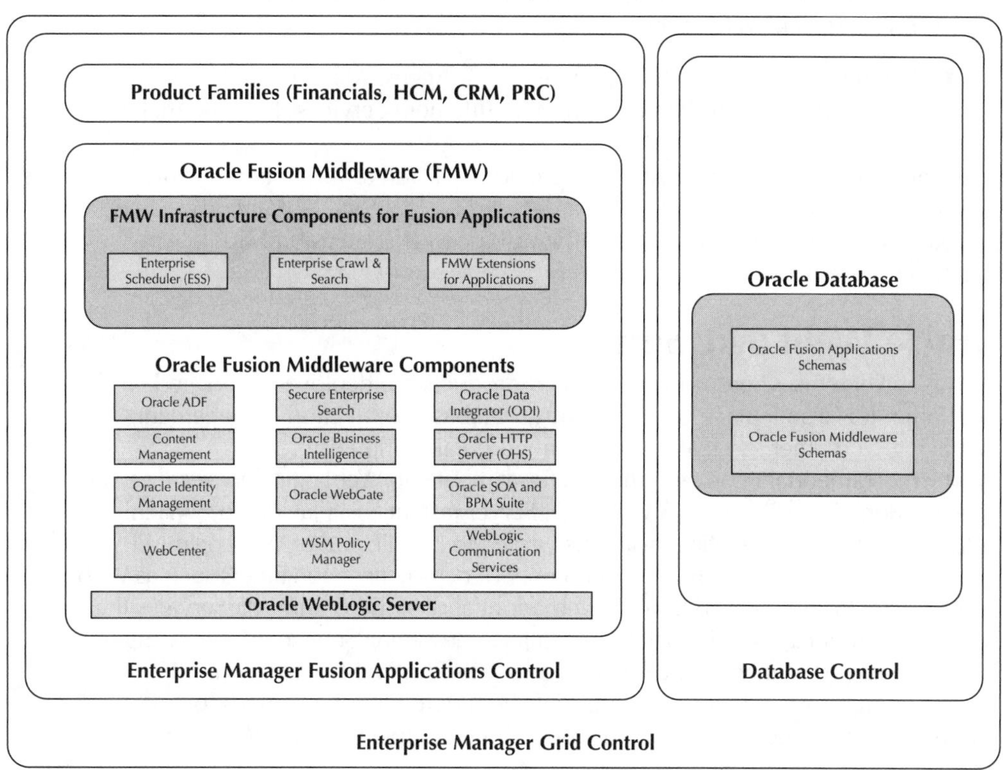

FIGURE 1-1. *Fusion Applications architecture overview*

open, and integrated set of components that fall into different categories and functional areas:

- Development Tools and Frameworks (JDeveloper, Applications Development Framework, Enterprise Pack for Eclipse)
- User Experience (WebCenter)
- Service Oriented Architecture (SOA Suite)
- Content Management
- Business Intelligence
- Data Integration

- Application Grid (WebLogic Server, JRockit, Oracle Coherence, Oracle HTTP Server, Web Cache)
- Identity Management (Directory Services, Access Management, Identity Federation, Identity Administration, Entitlement Services, Identity Analytics)

While our book touches on most of the previously listed topics in later chapters, we will now take this opportunity to have a detailed look at Oracle WebLogic Server, the foundation component on which all Java-based Oracle Fusion Middleware components are built.

Oracle WebLogic Server

WebLogic Server is where applications and products are deployed, managed, and monitored. It is also a place where security, database connection management, messaging, and other key features are configured and administered.

The most important concepts that are fundamental to WebLogic Server are server instance, domain, and cluster. A WebLogic Server instance is a Java Virtual Machine (JVM) process that is executing Java code written to Java EE and/or WebLogic API specifications. The server consists of a number of deployment containers such as Web Container that run deployed Java EE Web applications, JDBC and JMS Services that manage communication with database and Java Messaging Service resources, Security Services, Request Management Services, and Java Runtime Environment (JRE).

The domains are a logical grouping of WebLogic Server instances for administration and configuration purposes. There are two types of WebLogic Servers:

- Administration (Admin) Servers
- Managed Servers

Admin Server is a special type of WebLogic Server and is used for domain administration, configuration, and monitoring. There can only be one Admin Server within a domain. What distinguishes the Admin Server from other (managed) servers is that it performs some additional functions:

- Configuration management for all servers that belong to its domain. Stores the master copy of the domain configuration including the configuration of other servers (managed servers).
- Provides administration consoles to manage the domain and its servers; the consoles are HTML-based and can be accessed through a browser to perform administration, configuration, and monitoring tasks.
- Enables server and service migration as well as deployment of applications within the domain.

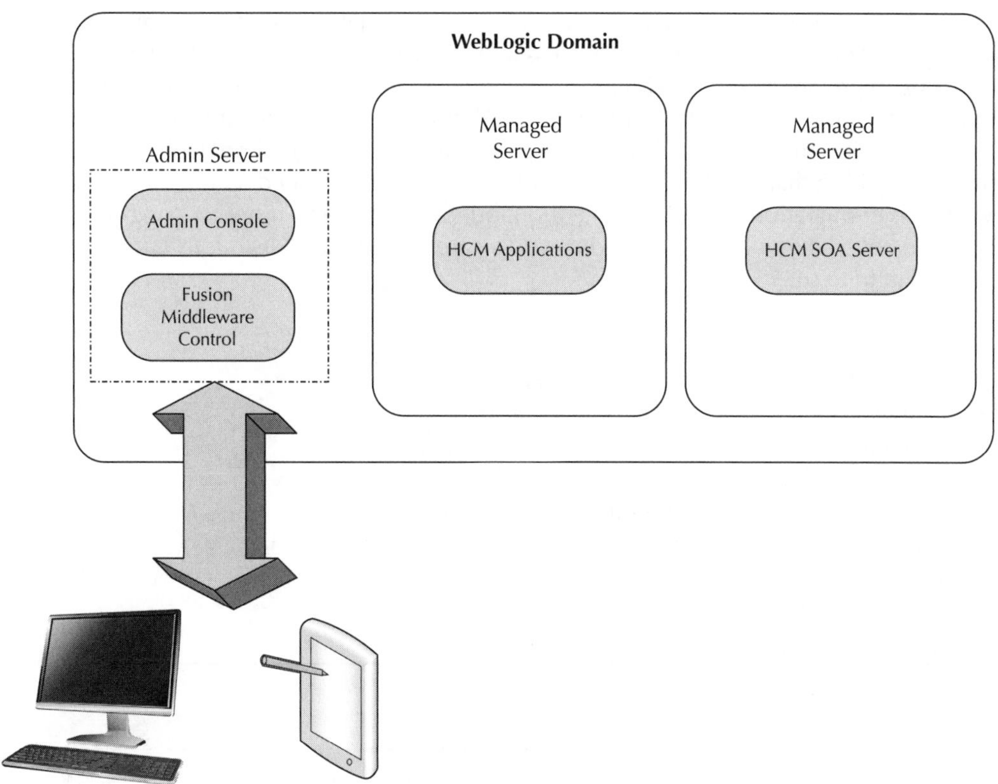

Managed servers, on the other hand, are running instances of WebLogic Server where Java EE applications are usually deployed, and they also host other resources required by applications. There is nothing preventing you from deploying an application to the Admin Server; however, that is not recommended in a production environment as all applications should be deployed to the managed servers within the domain. Managed servers are independent of each other unless they form a part of a cluster (discussed shortly); the number of managed servers is unlimited, and they can be added as necessary to either increase capacity or group similar applications together.

When managed servers are started, they connect to the Admin Server to synchronize its local copy of configuration files with the master copy on Admin Server. Every time the configuration changes, Admin Server notifies the managed servers and sends the changed configuration to them to keep the configuration in synch.

Managed servers within the domain can be grouped to form a cluster. A WebLogic domain can have many clusters, but each managed server can only belong to one cluster. One such example is Oracle Fusion Applications HCM Domain, illustrated in Figure 1-2.

One of the main benefits of clusters is application scalability since one can keep adding as many managed servers as necessary to increase the capacity. WebLogic clusters also provide high availability and reliability through deployment across more than one server. To most client applications, a WebLogic cluster will appear as a single server instance, and applications deployed to the cluster will be deployed to all servers within that cluster. Clusters enable some other advanced features such as whole server migration and server migration, but the details and inner workings of those are covered in the *Oracle Fusion Middleware System Administrator's Guide* rather than in this text.

NOTE

In Figure 1-2 you see a screen shot of Enterprise Manager Fusion Applications Control that shows HCMDomain configuration installed on an instance of Fusion Applications on a single node. Therefore, you only see one managed server per cluster, but additional managed servers as represented by elements with a dashed boundary in the diagram can be added on Host 2, for example.

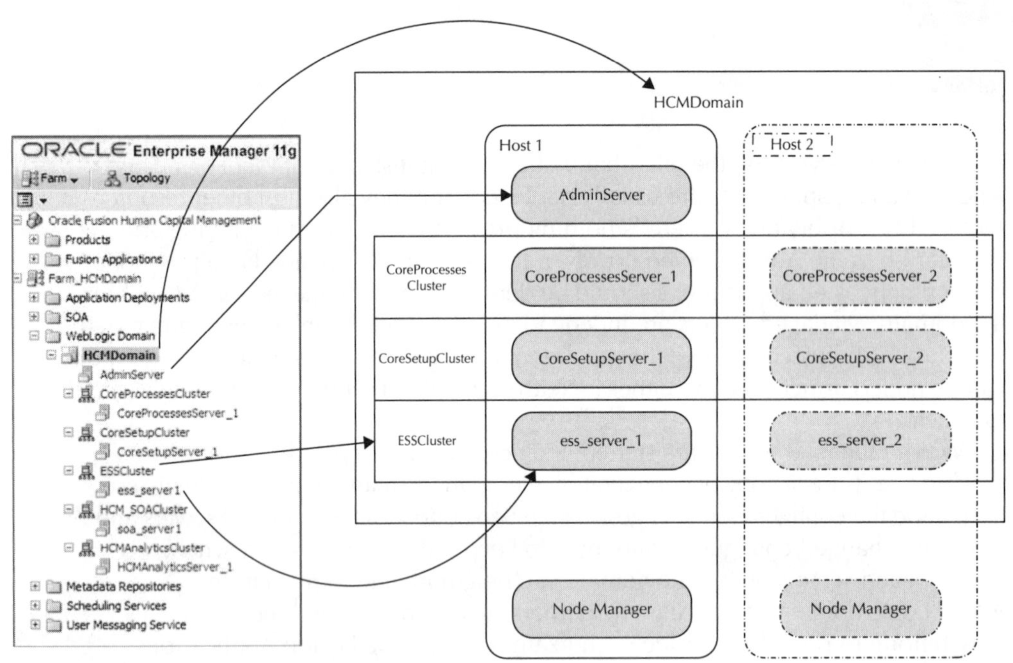

FIGURE 1-2. *Oracle Fusion Applications HCM Domain*

Each host can have a node manager, which is a WebLogic Server utility that allows system administrators to start, stop, and restart administration and managed servers from a remote location. The node manager is a process that is not tied to a particular WebLogic domain but to the physical machine, for example, a Linux or Windows host.

The WebLogic domain directory structure reflects the fact that the server configuration is segmented by domain where each domain has one set of configuration files. Among many configuration files, config.xml is the main configuration file located under the config directory as shown in Figure 1-3. This central configuration file is where the details about server instances, clusters, and other resources for the domain are provided.

In Fusion Applications, the applications from product families, such as Oracle Fusion Human Capital Management (HCM), are all deployed within a single domain, which is called HCMDomain in this case. In addition to the product family–related applications, Fusion Applications domains usually have two additional clustered servers: Oracle Enterprise Scheduler Service (ESS) cluster and SOA cluster. The ESS server hosts Enterprise Scheduler Application (ESS App), which manages and schedules jobs for that product family similarly to what concurrent request managers do in Oracle E-Business Suite, for those who are familiar with one of Oracle's earlier enterprise applications products. Equally, SOA servers host composite applications for the applications that belong to the particular product family.

Fusion Applications Product Families

In the previous section, we mentioned the Oracle Fusion HCM product family without introducing the concept of product families. Product families are simply collections of products associated with a particular business function, and they consist of one or many applications.

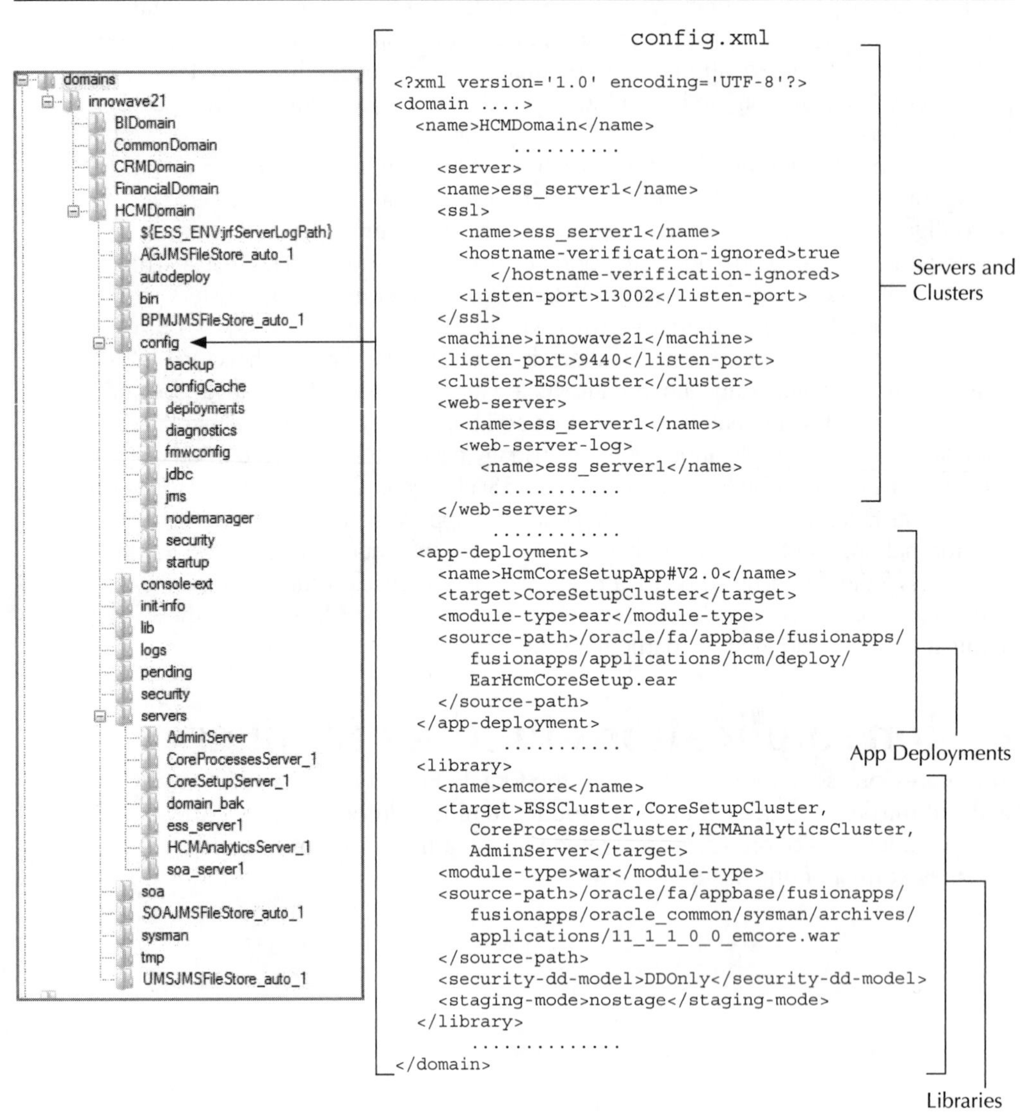

FIGURE 1-3. *WebLogic domain directory structure*

In Figure 1-4, you can see that the Oracle HCM product family consists of four Fusion Applications: HcmCoreSetupApp, HcmCoreApp, HcmEssApp, and HcmAnalyticsApp. Also, you notice that individual products can be part of many applications and that applications may extend across many products. The products,

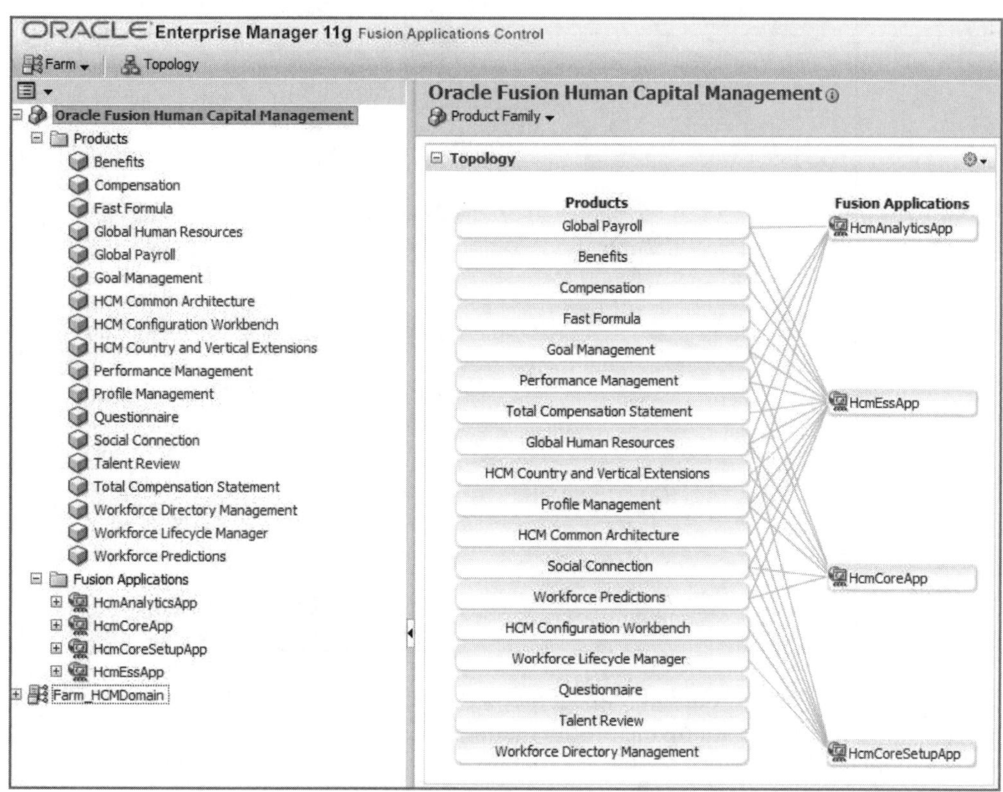

FIGURE 1-4. *Oracle HCM product family*

like Global Human Resources, which is shown next, are normally deployed as an Enterprise Archive File (ear) file on the middle tier.

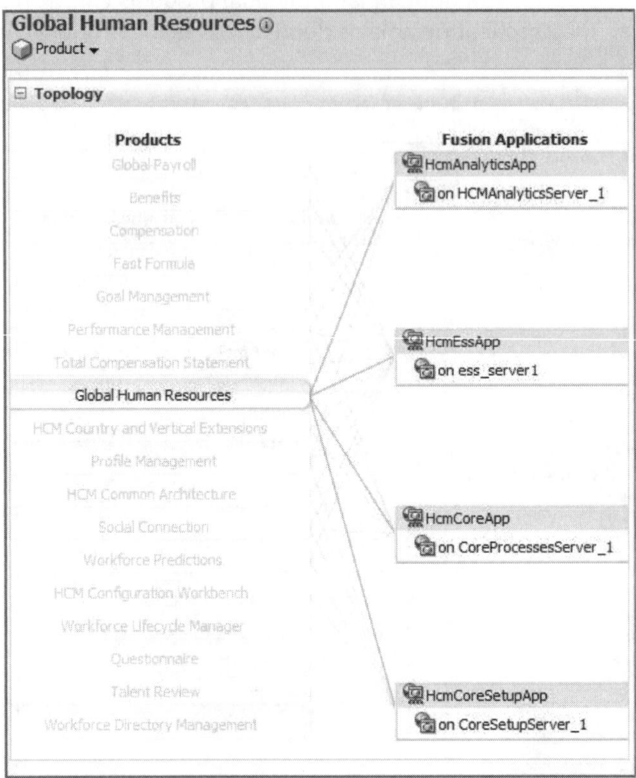

In addition to Human Capital Management, the current release of Fusion Applications features the following product families: Customer Relationship Management (CRM); Procurement; Governance, Risk, and Compliance (GRC); Project Portfolio Management (PPM); and Supply Chain Management (SCM).

Fusion Middleware Infrastructure Components for Fusion Applications

Most enterprises and organizations accomplish common business functions like accounting in similar ways; however, an enterprise application such as Oracle Fusion Financials has to provide a great deal of flexibility to accommodate requirements that are specific to a particular organization and business environment. Take the example of a Chart of Accounts, which is an accounting structure that is different from one company to another.

This drives the need for a specialized type of infrastructure that underpins the extensibility and other features specific to Fusion Applications that go beyond what Oracle Fusion Middleware offers out of the box. Oracle Fusion Applications borrows some of the best architectural concepts from its previous application product offerings such as flexfields from E-Business Suite, PeopleSoft tree hierarchies, effective dates, shared reference data (SetIds), and so on.

As shown earlier in Figure 1-1, the main components of Fusion Middleware Infrastructure for Fusion Applications are

- Oracle Fusion Middleware Extensions for Applications
- Oracle Enterprise Scheduler
- Oracle Enterprise Crawl and Search Framework (ECSF)

Since this book is almost entirely dedicated to extensions, customizations, and development techniques, in the next sections we'll provide only a brief description and summary of the Fusion Middleware Infrastructure for Fusion Applications components as they will be covered extensively in the subsequent chapters.

Oracle Fusion Middleware Extensions for Applications

Oracle Fusion Middleware Extensions for Applications are reusable common components that can be used in both standard (shipped by Oracle) or bespoke applications written by Fusion Applications developers. From a programming point of view, the extensions are packaged as a Java library that needs to be added to the project so that common components can be used in that project.

Following is a partial list of components that are commonly used in Fusion Applications along with a brief summary of their features:

- **Flexfields** Allow customers to configure Fusion Applications products to meet the business requirements without writing custom code. Similarly to Oracle E-Business Suite, a flexfield is a data field that is expandable and consists of segments. Generally, they either capture and store additional information about some business entity such as customers through the user interface, or they can provide a multipart key identifier for a business entity, such as account numbers so it can be uniquely identified. In Fusion Applications there are three types of flexfields: descriptive, extensible, and key.
- **UI Shell** Provides a default page template for all Fusion Application pages apart from login and the password preferences page. UI Shell provides predictable behavior of all pages, and it also enforces the use of standards such as Oracle Fusion Guidelines, Patterns, and Standards (GPS). UI Shell supports global search, navigation menus, and cross-application navigation.

- **Trees** Allow data to be organized in hierarchies and allow creating of tree hierarchies based on data. Fusion Applications developers design and deploy tree structures, while application users use trees, which are individual instances of those structures that can be used to group and roll up data.
- **Attachments** Provide a mechanism of attaching additional content to a business object. An example is a purchase order with, for example, a supplementary PDF attached to it. Users of applications can attach URLs, plain text, desktop, and repository files to the business objects. From a development point of view, attachments are declaratively added to the Fusion Applications UI pages. When added, they appear on the page as Attachment item (field), Attachment column in the table, or Attachments table.

Oracle Fusion Application developers spend most of their time working with different components of Fusion Middleware Extensions for Applications, which is also known as Applications Core or applcore. For example, if a developer needs to throw a Java exception in their code, he or she will do it with help of a Java class from the Applications Core (applcore) library:

```
import oracle.apps.fnd.applcore.messages.ApplcoreException;
...
Map<String, Object> tokens = new HashMap<String, Object>();
tokens.put("TEXT", "Exception text");
tokens.put("NUMBER", new BigDecimal(2001));
...
throw new ApplcoreException("XXAPP:::XXAPP_MESSAGE_NAME", tokens);
```

Other examples of Applications Core extensions are PL/SQL entities, FND services, Unique IDs, document sequencing, Set IDs, TL (translatable) tables, and WHO columns, and we will discuss them as they appear in detail in subsequent chapters.

Oracle Enterprise Scheduler (ESS)

In addition to being able to provide an efficient user experience through browser-based user interaction, enterprise systems like Fusion Applications are required to have the capability of running scheduled background processes for long-running, back-office, and reporting tasks. Users of Oracle E-Business Suite will undoubtedly be familiar with the concept of concurrent requests, and similar functionality is available in Fusion Applications through the Oracle Enterprise Scheduler component.

Unlike Concurrent Request Managers in Oracle E-Business Suite, Oracle Enterprise Scheduler has a mere role of time and resource controller for the job and its schedules; the responsibility of running the actual jobs is delegated to the client applications, which receive callbacks from the Enterprise Scheduler engine.

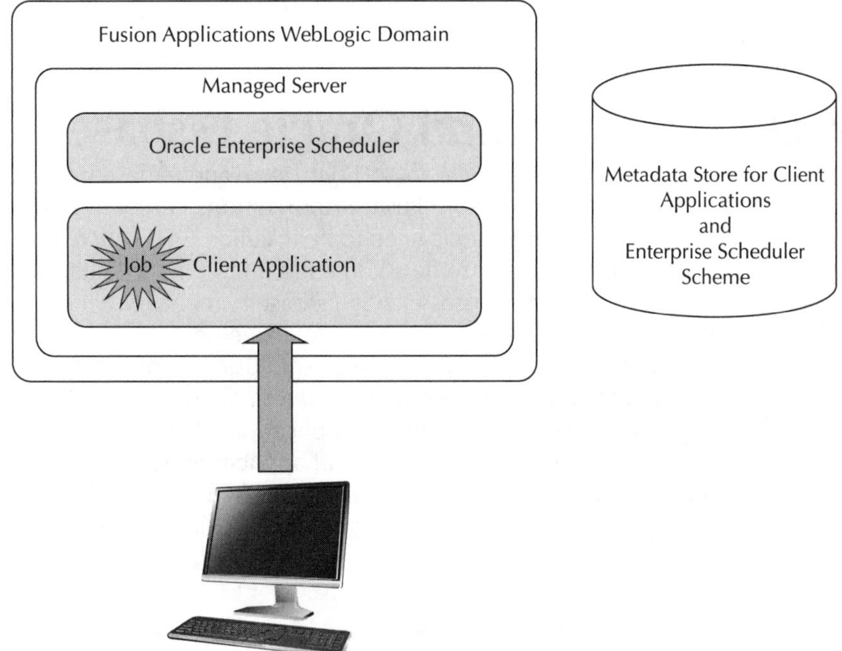

Each Fusion Applications Domain has a dedicated ESS cluster with an Ess-app .ear file deployed. The client server cluster runs a client application along with its UI, which allows the application user to submit and monitor jobs.

Developers use Oracle JDeveloper and Enterprise Manager (EM) Control to develop ESS client applications, job definitions, sets, and incompatibilities between the jobs. Business users can use ESS Submission Request Screen (SRS) UI and ESS Monitor UI to submit and monitor the jobs they own. The primary interface for System Administrators is EM Control, where they can define security, monitor the jobs for all users, define job schedules, perform ESS troubleshooting, and control other aspects of job execution such as stopping and resuming.

Oracle Enterprise Crawl and Search Framework (ECSF)

The ECSF redundant integrates with Oracle Secure Enterprise Search (Oracle SES) through Security and Crawler plugins to provide the ability to perform secure searches on ADF view objects, Fusion file attachments, and WebCenter tags. It exposes application programming APIs, which developers can use to design and incorporate search capability in their Fusion Applications. Developers use the View Object editor's Search page in JDeveloper to set search properties for business objects.

Searches are category- or keyword-based, and ECSF takes care of security and user access rights.

Oracle Database and Oracle Essbase

Oracle Fusion Applications use Oracle Database 11*g* to store and retrieve transactional data from applications. However, before Fusion Applications can be installed, Oracle Identity Management components need to be installed first, which also use Oracle databases for data storage and retrieval. In addition to Oracle Database 11*g*, the Fusion Applications environment uses Oracle Essbase to manage multidimensional data in analytic and performance management applications.

The transactional database, in the current release of Fusion Applications 11.1.*x*, keeps data for all product families and middleware in a single database. Oracle Fusion Applications Repository Creation Utility (Applications RCU) is used during the environment installation to create a repository of application-specific schemas and tablespaces for Oracle Database. The Applications RCU creates Oracle Database schema users that own appropriate middleware and application components as shown in Figure 1-5.

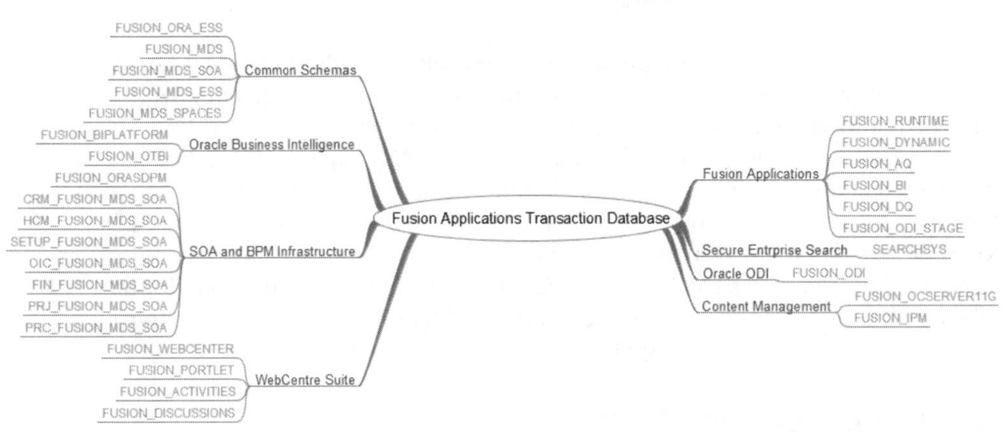

FIGURE 1-5. *Fusion Applications transactional database schemas in Oracle Database*

Enterprise Manager Controls (Administration Tools)

Oracle Enterprise Manager is certainly one of the most important tools for monitoring and management of applications, middleware, and Oracle databases. Fusion Applications are shipped with a special version of Enterprise Manager (EM) known as Fusion Applications Control (see the earlier Figure 1-4).

Fusion Applications Control enables end users and system administrators to monitor and administer a product family within the Oracle Fusion Applications environment. Information is presented in the form of dashboards to show real-time performance details about running ESS jobs, WebLogic server statuses, Service Oriented Architecture (SOA) processes, execution statuses, and so on. In addition to Fusion Applications Control, system administrators can separately install Oracle EM Grid Control, which provides even more centralized monitoring and management capability to monitor Oracle Database and Oracle Fusion Middleware components across the entire Oracle Fusion Applications environment.

Summary

In this chapter, we have glanced over most of the major technology components in Fusion Applications. Undoubtedly, Oracle Fusion Middleware with Fusion Applications–specific extensions functions as the principal technology toolset used to build, deploy, and run Fusion Applications.

Its technologies provide a platform to build a user interface with the Application Development Framework (ADF), orchestrate services with SOA Suite components, offer security and extensibility frameworks, integrate data with the Oracle Data Integrator tool, as well as provide tools such as Enterprise Crawl and Search, Enterprise Scheduler Service, and so on.

In addition to the middleware components, back-end technologies such as Oracle Database and Oracle Essbase are the primary places where Fusion Applications store and retrieve transactional and multidimensional data.

CHAPTER 2

Introduction to Customization

Oracle Fusion Applications provide robust and comprehensive features and functionality across all product areas. While out-of-the-box features satisfy a majority of customer requirements, there may be areas of the application that need change depending on how the business processes are followed for these functions. The process of customizing and extending Fusion Applications ranges from a simple change like moving UI fields around to complicated changes like modifying an SOA business process and adding brand new objects and user interfaces to applications.

Understanding Types of Customization

All Fusion Applications user interfaces are built using Oracle Application Development Framework. There are different tools available to customize different components of the application. These tools allow you to modify any existing artifact such as a page or a View object and allow you to create a brand new artifact and integrate with existing applications. There are mainly four types of changes you may need to do depending on your business needs: personalization, run-time customization, application extensions, and design-time customization and extensions.

Personalization

Personalization is a change or changes made by an end user to any application UI. These changes persist across user sessions and are visible every time the user logs in to the application. The changes are visible only to the user who made the change. Personalization is about changing the application behavior to the way an individual end user may like, making changes based on personal preferences. These changes are not applicable to all users in the enterprise and are done by the end users themselves. Some of these common changes include allowing the user to save the search criteria for future use, saving the UI table column width changes, persisting the show or hide state of a collapsible region, or allowing the user to rearrange certain aspects of the page. These changes are saved either implicitly when the user makes these changes in the UI, or they are done using Oracle Page Composer using the Edit Current Page option from the Personalization menu as shown in Figure 2-1.

Most of the end-user roles get access to the Personalization menu. Different pages in Fusion Applications allow certain types of personalization to be done, and this is defined by the default configuration of Fusion Applications. An administrator can customize what an end user can personalize for a given application using tools we will discuss in the following chapters.

FIGURE 2-1. *Edit Current Page option*

Run-Time Customization

Run-time customization consists of changes made by an administrator or a business user to any application UI. These changes persist across user sessions and are visible every time the user logs in to the application. The changes are visible to all the users in the enterprise. These customizations are done in a similar fashion to personalization, but these are driven by the business processes and enterprise policy concerning how the applications need to behave, rather than an end user's personal choice. Some of these common changes include changing the look and feel of the UIs; adding new content to the pages; changing the labels, display text, and other properties of fields; or rearranging the content on the page. These changes are done using Oracle Page Composer using the Customize Workarea Pages option from the Administration menu, as shown in Figure 2-2.

The Administration menu is enabled for most of the Fusion Applications work area pages. The menu is visible to only those users who have privileges to see the administrative options available. The Customize Workarea Pages menu entry is visible only to the users who have access to customize a given page. These options are not available to every end user in the enterprise. If you have a family administrator or implementation consultant role, you get access to this menu option.

Application Extensions

If you are using Fusion CRM Applications, you can use CRM Application Composer to customize and extend certain CRM business objects and their application pages. You use Application Composer to extend CRM applications when the default features do

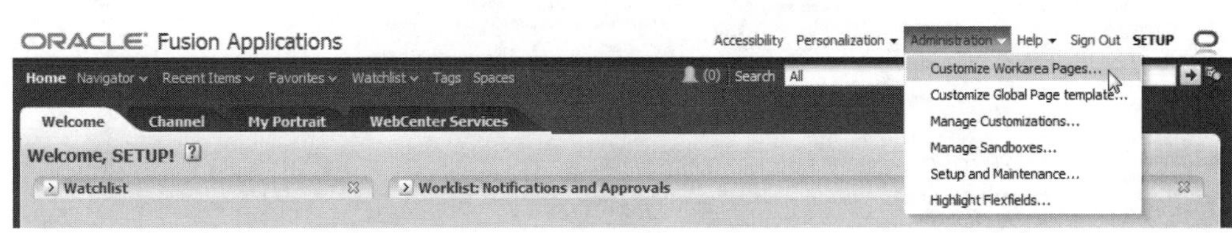

FIGURE 2-2. *The Customize Workarea Pages option*

not meet your business needs. You can use CRM Application Composer to extend the objects by adding brand new attributes, adding brand new custom objects and associating them to out-of-the-box objects, exposing custom objects on application UIs, and adding custom logic to change application behavior using Groovy scripts. The Application Composer also allows you to define business events on the objects and define business processes and workflows in response to those events. The changes made by Application Composer are visible to all the users in the enterprise. These changes are done with CRM Application Composer, using the Application Composer option from the Navigator | Tools menu as shown in Figure 2-3.

The menu is visible to only those administrative and business users who have access to Application Composer. The objects you can extend using Application Composer are predefined by Fusion Applications and you cannot customize that object list. Application Composer is very feature-rich. What you can do with each out-of-the-box object is defined by Fusion Applications and it cannot be customized. You can add as many custom objects as required and associate them to out-of-the-box objects exposed in Application Composer. We will discuss these features and when to use Application Composer in following chapters. Only CRM Administrators or implementation consultant roles get access to this tool.

Design-Time Customization and Extensions

Personalization, run-time customization, and CRM application extensions allow you to modify several aspects of the application behavior. If you need to make other changes that are not supported by those tools, or if you need to extend

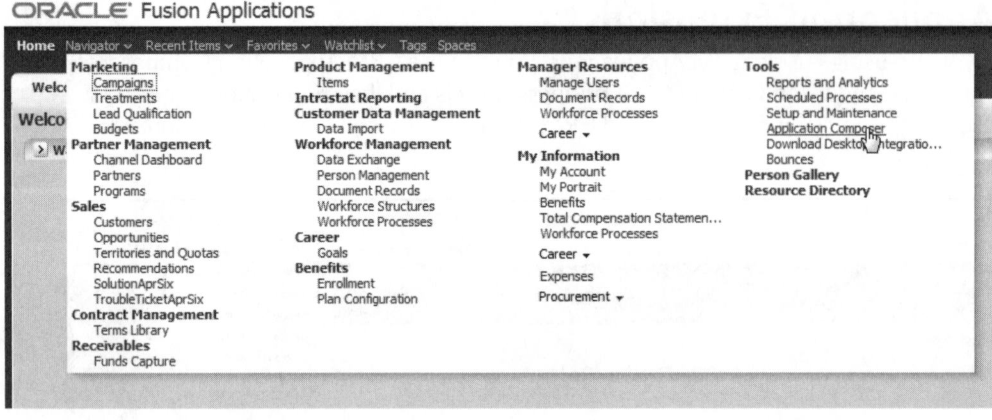

FIGURE 2-3. *The Application Composer option*

non-CRM applications, you will need to use Oracle JDeveloper to do design-time customizations to Fusion Applications. The design-time customization and extensions are done by developers who understand Oracle Application Development Framework. The customizations done in JDeveloper need to be deployed to a run-time Fusion Applications instance to make those changes available to users. These changes are visible to all users in the enterprise once deployed. Some of the design-time customizations include extending non-CRM applications, changing out-of-the-box business logic and validations for objects, changing application pages' behavior, building brand new applications and integrating them with Fusion Applications, and so on. To customize an artifact in JDeveloper, you choose the Oracle Fusion Applications Administrator Customization role when launching JDeveloper, as shown in Figure 2-4. You will need Fusion Applications Extensions for this specific role, and we will discuss how to set up JDeveloper for this in later chapters.

You can customize all UIs and their related application logic using JDeveloper.

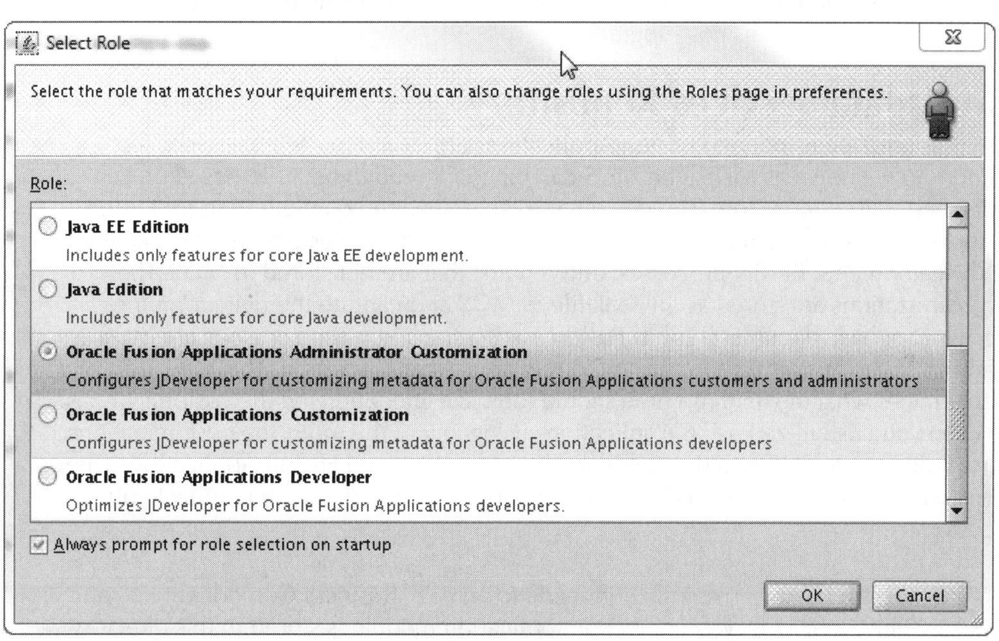

FIGURE 2-4. *Choosing the Oracle Fusion Applications Administrator Customization role*

Other Customizations

There are many other components that constitute Fusion Applications, like flexfields, identity management and security, business processes, SOA composites, business intelligence and analytics reports, enterprise scheduler jobs, and so on. There are different tools available to customize and extend these components. We will focus on UI customizations and extensions in this chapter. Details about customizing other components of Fusion Applications are covered in specific chapters for those components in this book.

Understanding Customization Run-Time Behavior

Customizations made to Fusion Applications UIs via Oracle Page Composer, CRM Application Composer, or directly done in JDeveloper are stored in a repository that is different from the base source code. This allows the customizations to live and progress independent of the source code. You can upgrade Fusion Applications without the fear of it overwriting your customizations or losing them and having to redo the customizations post-upgrade.

Metadata Services Repository

All customizations done to Fusion Applications are stored in Metadata Services Repository, known as MDS. The MDS can be configured to be a file-based or database-based repository. The default and recommended configuration for Fusion Applications is to use a database for MDS. There are some customizations, like the Navigator menu, BPMN processes, and reports, that are not stored in MDS. The customizations are stored as an XML file in MDS and capture the dèlta from the original or base document. All of Fusion Applications' run-time engines are MDS-aware, so the customizations are uniformly applied and honored. The XML file determines what the final run time should look like after applying the customizations. When you customize Fusion Applications using any of the tools, the customizations are written to the MDS Repository configured for deployed Fusion Applications. The customizations are stored in different directories depending on what artifact you customize.

- **persdef** Any customization made to an ADF Business Component like an entity object or view object or application module is stored in this directory.
- **oracle** Any customization made to an ADF UI artifact like a JSFF or JSPX or a pagedef file associated to the UI is stored in this directory. Any customization made to a Web service schema XSD file is also stored in this directory.

- **sessiondef** Any new artifact created using CRM Application Composer or JDeveloper, like a new view link or application module, is stored in this directory.

The MDS repository is integrated with WebLogic Scripting Tool (WLST) and you can use the commands to interact with the repository. You can upload, download, or delete documents in the MDS repository using the WLST commands. Incorrect or corrupt entries in the MDS repository can cause undesirable run-time behavior for Fusion Applications, and you should be extremely careful when directly interacting with the MDS repository to make any changes. You should use the customization tools available for all the changes and use direct MDS interaction only when you need to reverse or add a change not supported by any of the tools.

Customization Layers

The customizations made to Fusion Applications are applicable to all users in the enterprise. However, it is possible that some of the customizations are not necessary for all users and you may need to restrict only certain users who will see these customizations. Fusion Applications have built-in customization layers that allow you to achieve this separation of customization between sets of users. When you customize a page, you first choose the layer for which it should be customized. The customization XML is stored in MDS with the layer information from the tools used for customization. When a request comes for an artifact, the run-time engine checks the MDS repository for an XML file that matches the artifact and the given context or layer, and if there is a match, it applies the customization on top of the base artifact. If there is no matching customized document found for the artifact in the given context, the base artifact is returned and used for the run-time rendering. Figure 2-5 shows how the layers are applied at run time from the MDS repository. In this graphic, the Data Steward Dashboard is customized for the Customer Data Steward role layer. At run time, when a user with the Customer Data Steward role is logged in to the application, the MDS engine finds a match in the repository and applies the customization on top of the base Data Steward Dashboard document. If the same page is requested by a use that does not have the Customer Data Steward role, like a data steward manager, no customization is applied and the base document is used to show the page.

Similar to customizations, the end-user personalizations are also stored in the MDS repository. The personalizations done by end users are stored in the User layer. Since these changes are the same as any other customization but just stored in a different layer, the MDS engine simply applies these additional changes for a given user. Figure 2-6 shows how multiple layers are applied at run time from the MDS repository. In this illustration, a page is customized for the Customer Data Steward role layer by an administrator. The page is also personalized by User 1. At run time, when User 1 is logged in the MDS engine finds a match in the repository.

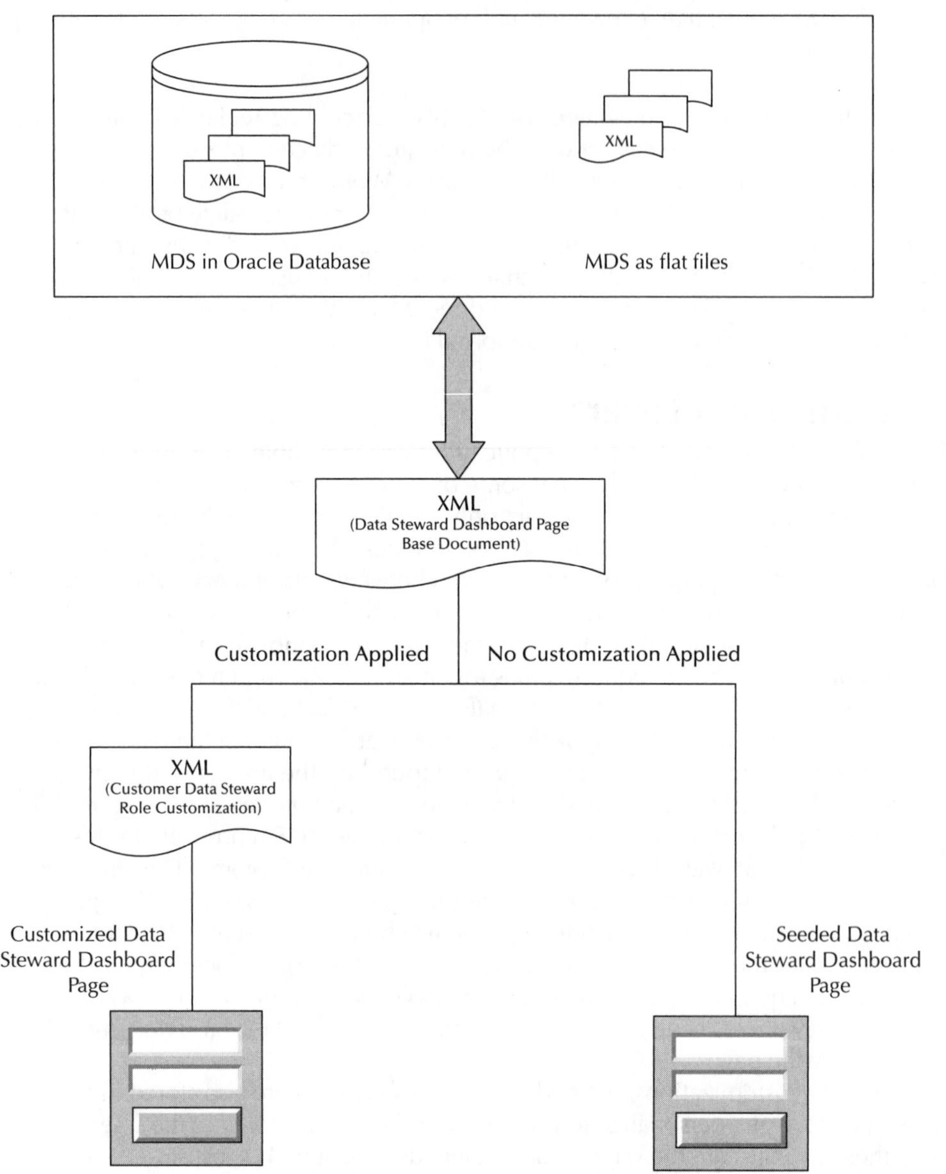

FIGURE 2-5. *Applying layers at run time from the MDS repository*

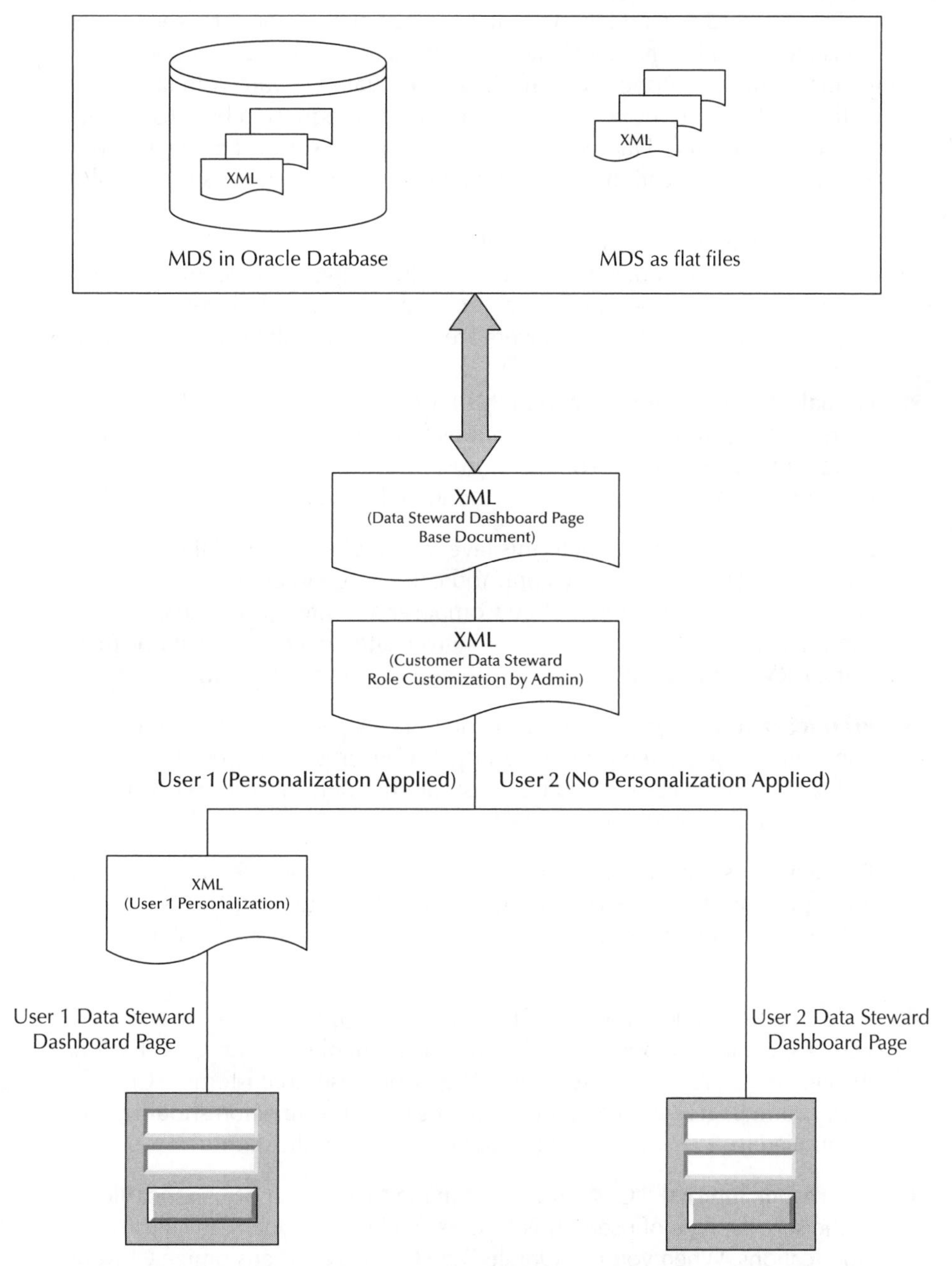

FIGURE 2-6. *Applying multiple layers at run time from the MDS repository*

It then applies the customization on top of the base page document for the Customer Data Steward role and then applies the personalization for User 1. If the same page is requested by another Customer Data Steward User 2 that does not have any personalization done, only the Customer Data Steward role layer customization is shown to the user. If the same page is requested by a user who does not have the Customer Data Steward role, like a data steward manager, no customization or personalization is applied and the base document is used to show the page.

Several customization layers are available for Fusion Applications. The layers available depend on what application you are customizing. The customization layers are hierarchical, which allows you to make changes at multiple layers without overwriting each other. The following layers are available for all Fusion Applications.

- **Global** Customizations made to this layer are applicable to all the users of the application. Customizations from this layer are added to the artifact's XML file for everyone. Any customizations made to ADF business components in JDeveloper must be done in the global layer.
- **Site** Customizations made to this layer are applicable to all the users for a particular site or deployment. You can choose to do administrator customizations using Oracle Page Composer at a site level if the change should be applicable to all users for a given site. Any customizations made using CRM Application Composer are done in the site layer too.
- **Product Family** Customizations made to this layer are applicable to applications for a given product family. This layer is not exposed to customers. This is Fusion Applications' internal-only layer for seeded customizations for shared regions.
- **Product** Customizations made to this layer are applicable to applications for a given product. This layer is not exposed to customers. This is Fusion Applications' internal-only layer for seeded customizations for shared regions.
- **Role** Customizations made to this layer are applicable to users with a specific enterprise role. This layer is available only for CRM Fusion Applications. When you use Oracle Page Composer to customize CRM application pages, you can pick what role the customization should be applied to. This layer is not available to other applications.
- **External or Internal** Customizations made to this layer are applicable to the specific type of users. This layer is available only for CRM Fusion Applications. When you use Oracle Page Composer to customize CRM application pages, you can pick if the change is for an internal user or an external user. If you choose internal, the changes are visible to users that

are internal to the deploying company, like the employees. If you choose external, the changes are visible to users that are external to the deploying company, like the partner users.

- **HcmCountry** Customizations made to this layer are visible for users for a given country. This layer is available only for HCM applications for country-specific localization purposes.
- **HcmOrganization** Customizations made to this layer are visible for users for a given HCM Organization. This layer is available only for HCM applications.
- **User** Any end-user personalization is saved in this layer. This layer is available only to end users and it is implicitly set when the user chooses the Personalize menu option. The Administrator cannot choose the User layer for other customizations.

Table 2-1 shows a summary of which customization layer is available for which tool and which applications can use that layer.

The MDS run time applies the changes on the base document starting from the lowest level up to the highest level in a given context. The global layer is the lowest or base, and the user level is highest in this hierarchy. The highest level is considered tip in a given run-time context. The customizations from the tip layer take precedence over all other layers. For example, if an administrator customizes a label on the UI at the site layer and also modifies it for a role layer, the customization from the role layer will be visible at run time. If the customizations made for each layer are not for the same attribute or property, they are merged and all customizations are visible at run time. All the tools ask you to pick the customization layer before you can start making any changes. It is recommended to use as low a level as possible for customizations so that it is easy to make more customizations and changes in the future when there are new business needs.

Understanding Customization Management

All the customizations must be fully tested in an isolated environment to make sure they do not break any existing functionality and customizations work as expected. Customizations are done by developers, administrators, or business users depending on what tool is being used for the customization. Once the customizations are done and tested locally in an isolated environment, they can be published in a central test environment where QA, project managers, and end users can perform testing and validations. Once everything is working to your satisfaction, the customizations will be published to a production environment.

Customization Layer	Available Tool	Available Application	Applicable Users
Global	JDeveloper	All	All
Site	Page Composer Application Composer	All	All
Product Family	Oracle internal only	All in given family	All
Product	Oracle internal only	Given product	All
Role	Page Composer	CRM	All users for given role
Internal or External	Page Composer	CRM	All internal or external users
HcmCountry	Page Composer	HCM	All users in country
HcmOrganization	Page Composer	HCM	All users in organization
User	Page Composer	All	Given single user

TABLE 2-1. *Customization Layers*

Using Sandbox

Sandbox is a virtual environment where the customizations can be made and tested in the deployed application. Sandbox allows you to isolate the customizations from the other users of the application. The customization XML files are stored in MDS, which is available only to the sandbox. If any other users want to see the customization, they can choose to use the sandbox and the customizations will be visible to that user. When you are satisfied with all the customizations and ready to make the changes available to everyone in the application, you publish the sandbox to the main line. Publishing the sandbox will merge the customizations from Sandbox to the main MDS repository.

Types of Sandboxes

Three types of sandboxes are supported:

- **Metadata** You will use this sandbox for most of the customizations. This type of sandbox supports making changes to application artifacts and metadata that is stored in MDS. Any personalization, customization, or extension can be done in a sandbox. This type of sandbox is available in JDeveloper also when you try to deploy the customizations from JDeveloper. You can download this type of sandbox and import it into any deployed Fusion Applications environment.
- **Security** You will use this sandbox when you need to customize data security. This is needed when using CRM Application Composer to make security changes to custom objects. When you create a security sandbox, the Fusion data security schema is duplicated for this sandbox. Any changes made to security policies will be applied to this copied schema. When you publish the sandbox, these security schemas are merged back to the main Fusion schema and will overwrite any previous customizations done to that. You should be careful when making changes and publishing a security sandbox because it may result in inconsistency in application if the security policies are corrupted during the process. You can download this type of sandbox and import into any deployed Fusion Applications environment.
- **Flexfield** You will use this sandbox to deploy flexfields for testing. This is a deployment-only sandbox and does not allow you to set up flexfields in the sandbox. When you use the flexfield setup UI, you always enable flexfields in main deployment. The flex setup changes are immediately saved to the main Fusion schema, but the run-time applications do not see the flexfields until they are deployed. You can use the sandbox to deploy the flexfields and test there. Once you are satisfied with testing and setup, you can deploy the flexfields to the main application. You do not create a flexfield sandbox manually; it is taken care of internally by the flex setup UI deployment process when you choose to deploy in a sandbox.

Multiple Sandbox Guidelines

Making customizations involves multiple people, and everyone will use sandboxes to make their changes. There are two types of sandboxes that will be created during the customization process:

- **Test sandbox** These sandboxes are created just for testing purposes. You create the sandbox, make some changes to see what it looks like, test it, and then destroy the sandbox. The changes made to such sandboxes are never visible to anyone. There will be multiple such test sandboxes depending on how many people are making and testing customizations.

- **Publish sandbox** These sandboxes are created to publish the customizations made to applications. You create the sandbox and make the changes that you are happy with that you made in your test sandboxes. You do more validation and testing in this sandbox and publish it to the main deployed application once satisfied.

Making customizations to an application means modifying an existing artifact or introducing a new artifact. This means that when you publish a sandbox, it is possible that there could be conflicts saving the changes to MDS for the artifacts that are modified. The Page Composer and CRM Application Composer tools do provide warnings and errors when such conflicts are detected. The sandbox manager will also detect such conflicts during publishing the sandbox and throw errors in such cases. You can choose to overwrite the conflict and force-publish a sandbox. There are mainly two types of conflicts that can happen when working with sandboxes:

- **Direct** This type of conflict happens when multiple users customize the same artifact, for example, if two users modify the same page or UI at the same time, in the same customization layer.
- **Indirect** This type of conflict happens when multiple users customize something that results in modifying the same metadata file. For example, modifying a translatable string shared by the same resource bundle or two users creating their own custom objects that will in turn modify the CRM Application Composer metadata file that tracks the custom objects.

To avoid such metadata conflicts, you need to follow these general guidelines on using the sandboxes:

- If multiple users share the same sandbox, they should operate on different, unrelated objects only. Care should be taken not to modify artifacts that are shared. If multiple users modify the same artifact concurrently, the second user's changes will not be saved and an error will be thrown during save.
- When the sandbox is shared by multiple users, the changes made by one user are visible to the other. Most of the changes are instantly visible to other users when saved. You can log out and log back in to get the latest sandbox updates for ADFbc customizations.
- When multiple sandboxes are used for test purposes, you can modify any artifacts. The sandbox is used by only one user and it is destroyed after testing the customization. Such changes are never published to the main deployed application.

- When multiple sandboxes are used for publishing, you should customize artifacts that are mutually exclusive and do not conflict directly or indirectly. If there are conflicts during publishing these sandboxes, you will get errors.

Managing Sandboxes

We will discuss how to create, use, and manage sandboxes in this section. The details about deploying flexfields to a sandbox will be covered in later chapters in this book.

Setup Sandbox

1. Go to the sandbox manager using the Manage Sandboxes option from the Administration menu as shown here.

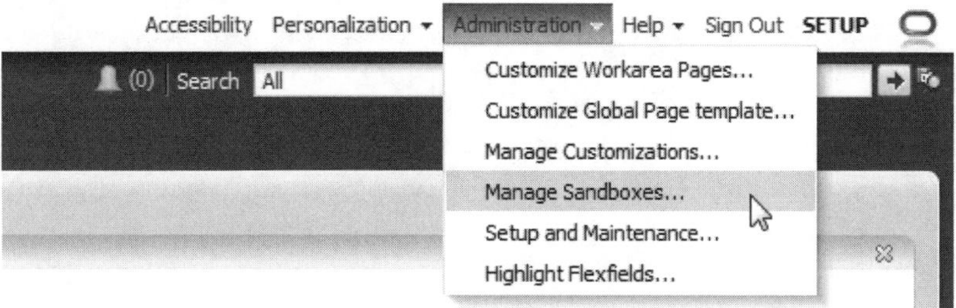

2. The Manage Sandboxes dialog allows you to create a new sandbox, make any existing sandbox active for the current user, publish a sandbox, import any sandbox, or view existing published sandbox details. The following illustration shows the Manage Sandboxes dialog.

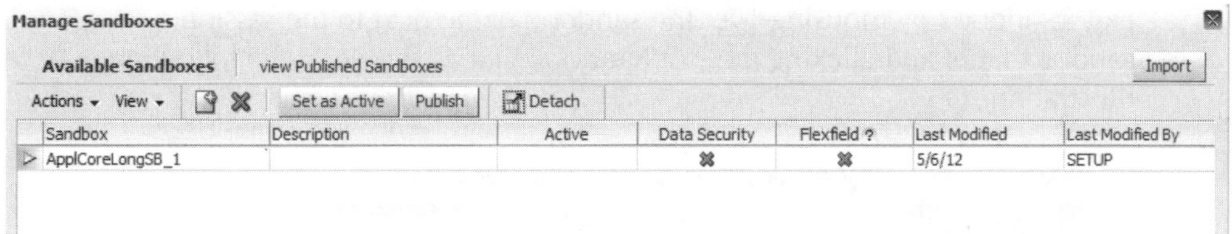

3. Click the Create icon or choose the New option from the Actions menu to create a new sandbox. Give a name and description to the sandbox as shown in the following illustration. If you want to create a data security sandbox, check the check box Create Data Security Sandbox and click the Save and Close button. When you create a new sandbox, all the MDS data with existing customizations is included in the sandbox.

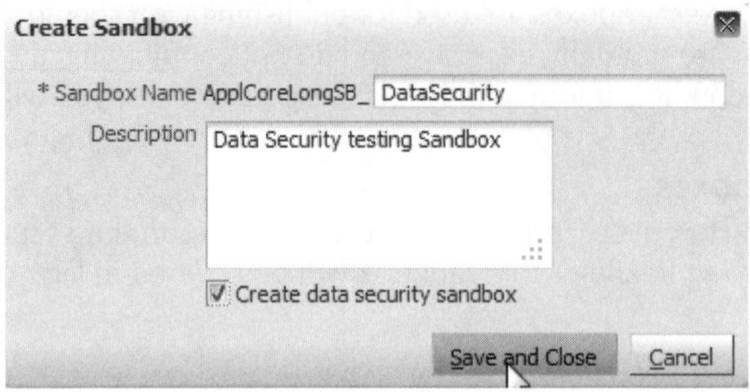

4. To use a sandbox, select the row for a sandbox you want to use and click the Set as Active button. The following illustration shows how to make sandbox 1 the active sandbox for the current logged-in user.

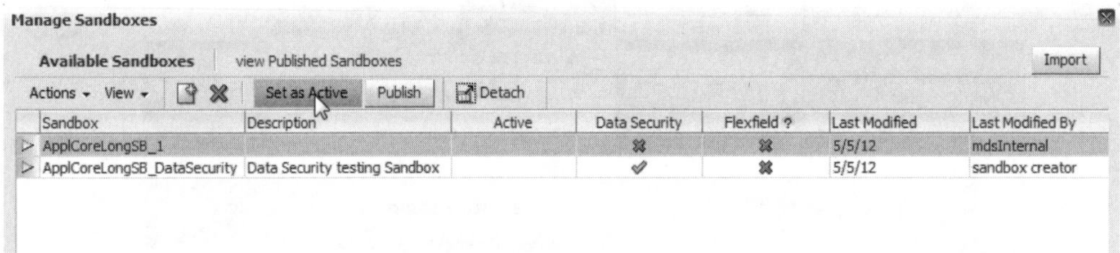

5. Once the sandbox is made active, any customization made via Page Composer or CRM Application Composer is isolated to this sandbox and will be visible to any user who chooses to use this sandbox by making it active for a given user session. Once a sandbox is made active for a given user, it remains activated for all future logins of that user. You can exit a sandbox by mousing over the sandbox name next to the session sandbox label and clicking the Exit Sandbox link as shown in the following illustration.

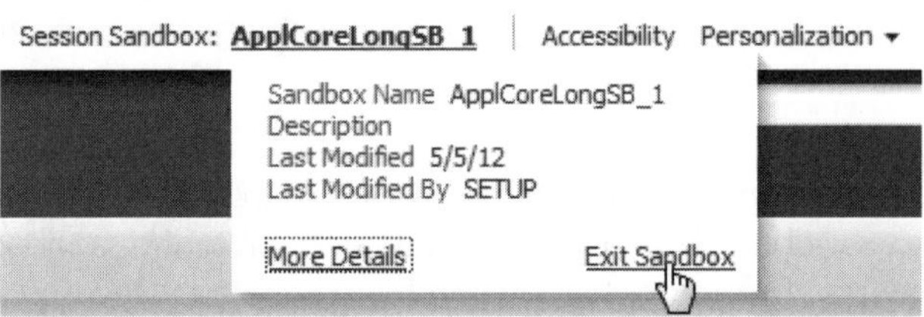

6. Click the Yes button in the Exit Sandbox dialog.

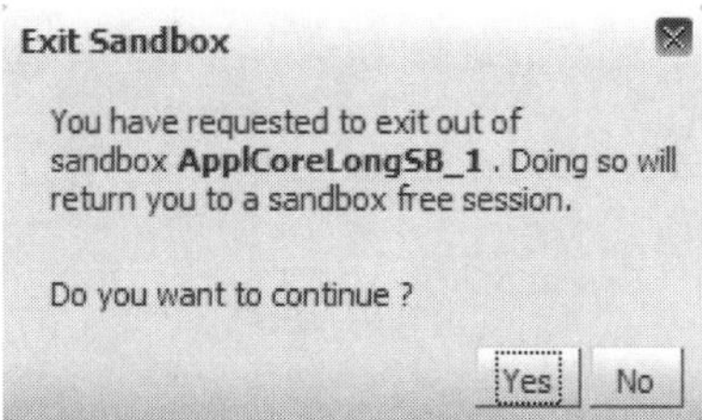

Migrate Sandbox Data

1. Mouse over the sandbox name next to the session sandbox label and click the More Details link as shown in the following illustration to see the details of customizations made in this sandbox.

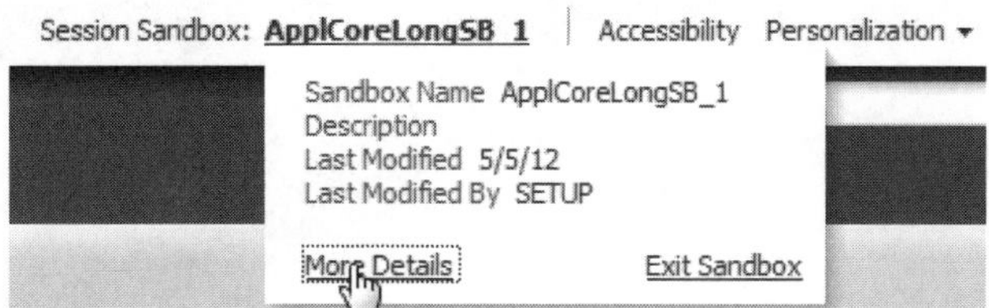

2. The Sandbox Details dialog shows all the customizations in the sandbox for all layers. The MDS tab shows the customizations stored in MDS, and the Data Security tab shows the customizations done to data security policies if this is a data security sandbox. You can filter the customizations made by layer name like User, Site, and so on, or by the layer value, like the name of the user who may have made the customization or site, and so on. Figure 2-7 shows the Sandbox Details dialog.

3. You can export all the customizations in a sandbox to a file so that it can be used to share with others and to import in a different environment. To export a sandbox, click on the Download All button in the Sandbox Details dialog as shown in Figure 2-7. Specify the location of the downloaded file to save the sandbox customizations.

4. To import a sandbox, go to the Manage Sandboxes dialog and click the Import button. Browse the downloaded file from where you want to import the customizations as shown in the following illustration. Once you import the sandbox, you will see all the customizations available to the user using the sandbox you imported.

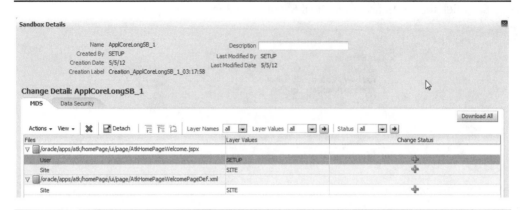

FIGURE 2-7. *Sandbox Details dialog*

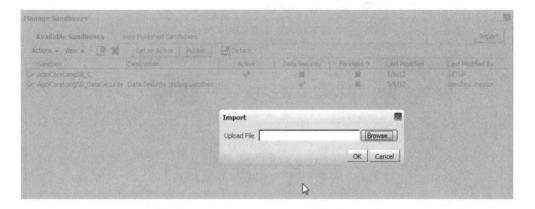

Publishing the Sandbox

1. You can publish the sandbox by going to the Manage Sandboxes dialog, selecting the sandbox to publish, and clicking the Publish button as shown in the following illustration.

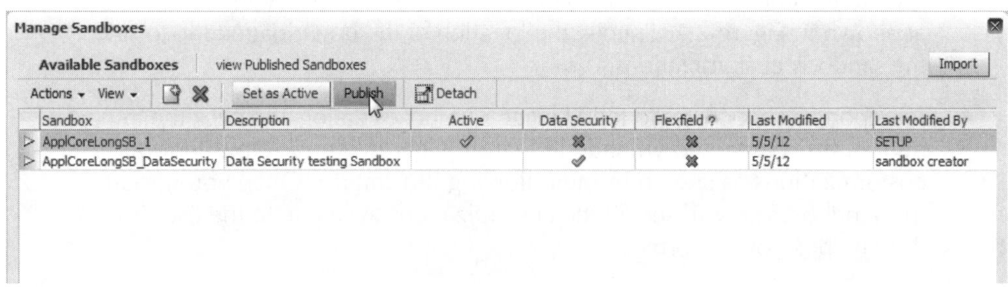

2. You can also publish the sandbox from the Sandbox Details dialog by clicking the Publish button, as shown in the following illustration.

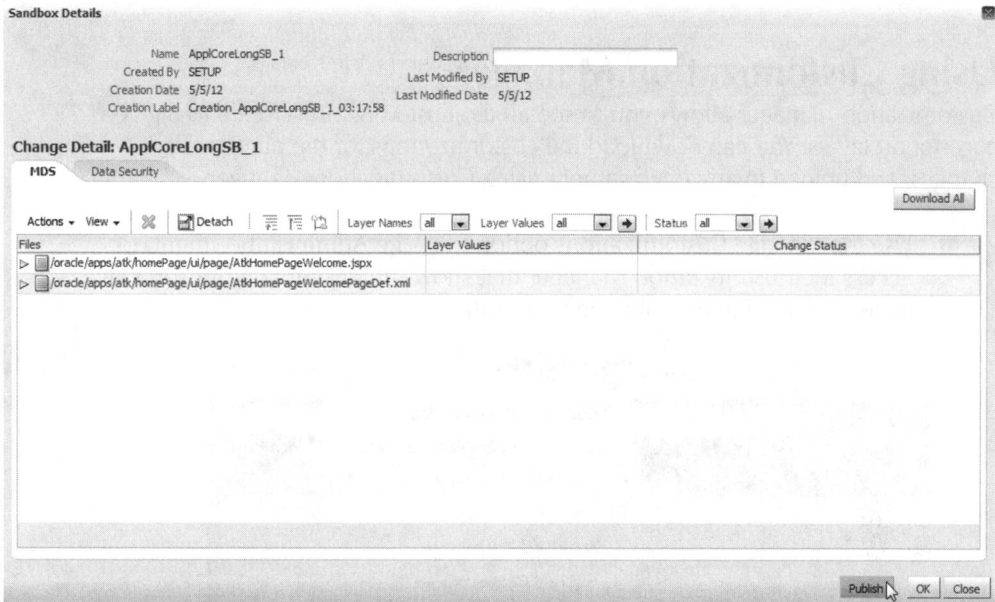

Development Lifecycle

Customization development needs several iterations before the final changes are published to main deployment. Following is a typical customization development lifecycle.

1. Decide what type of customization you need to do.
2. Decide the tool to be used for customization.
3. Create a sandbox for Page Composer and Application Composer.
    a. Make customizations in the sandbox for run-time tools.
    b. Test customizations within the sandbox.
    c. Publish the sandbox to a test environment.
4. Use JDeveloper for design-time customizations.
    a. Make customizations in JDeveloper.
    b. Test customizations locally in JDeveloper.
    c. Deploy customizations to a test environment.

5. Fix issues found during testing.
6. Download all customizations and upload to a production environment.

Using Customization Manager

Customization Manager allows you to see all the customizations made to a given page for all layers. You can download the customizations for the page, make changes, and upload to any environment using Customization Manager.

- Use the Manage Customizations option from the Administrator menu to access the Customization Manager that shows all customizations for a given page, as shown in the following illustration.

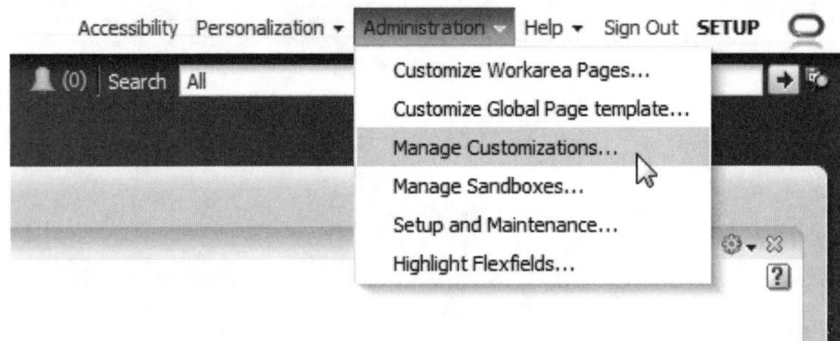

- The Customization Manager shows all the artifacts customized for a given page for all layers as shown in Figure 2-8. The Current Context column shows customizations applicable at run time for the current logged-in user's session. The All Layers column shows customizations that are applicable to other layers and may not be visible to the logged-in user's current session. You can switch the values for the current context or all layers to see more details of those customizations.
- You can download the customization for a given layer using the Download link next to the customization artifact in the Current Context or the All Layers column.
- You can upload modified customizations for a given layer using the Upload link in the Current Context or the All Layers column.
- You can delete customizations done to a given artifact on the page using the Delete link in the Current Context or the All Layers column.
- You can download all the customizations for a given page using the Download Customizations for All Layers link. You can view and modify these customizations if needed in the XML file directly.

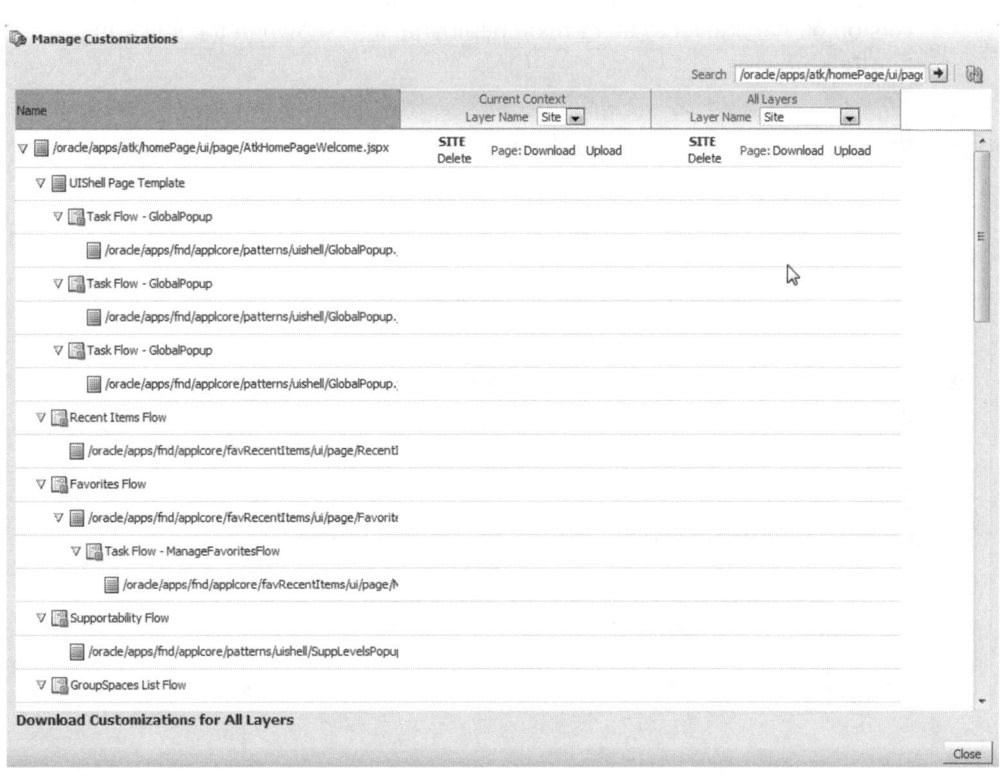

FIGURE 2-8. *Customized artifacts*

- If you know the full path of a page, you can use the search box in the Customization Manager dialog to search for a given page and see all the customizations for that page. You do not need to navigate to that page to see customizations.
- Using Customization Manager, you can restore the previous working version of customization done via Oracle Page Composer. When you are in Customize Page view, go to Manage Customizations from the Page Composer menu options as shown in the following illustration.

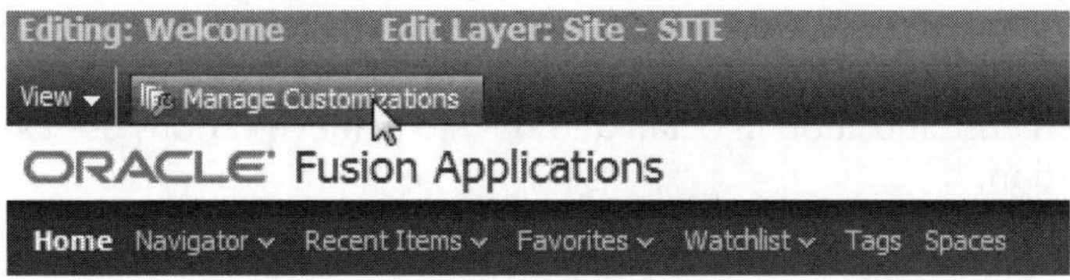

- You can click the Promote link for a given artifact to promote a previous version of that artifact to tip or main deployment as shown in the following illustration.

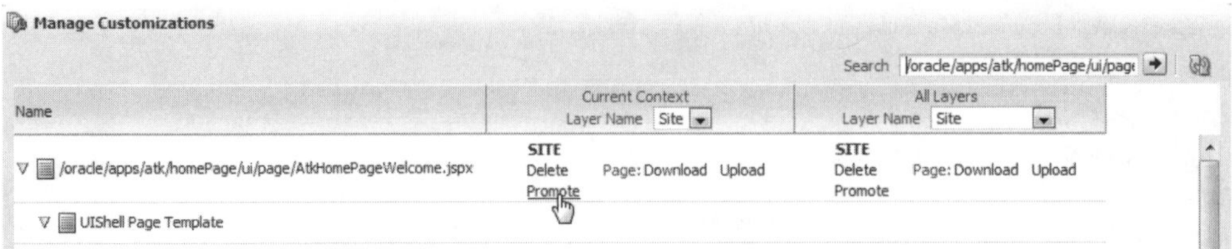

- You can choose what previous label or save point you want to promote to tip as shown in the following illustration.

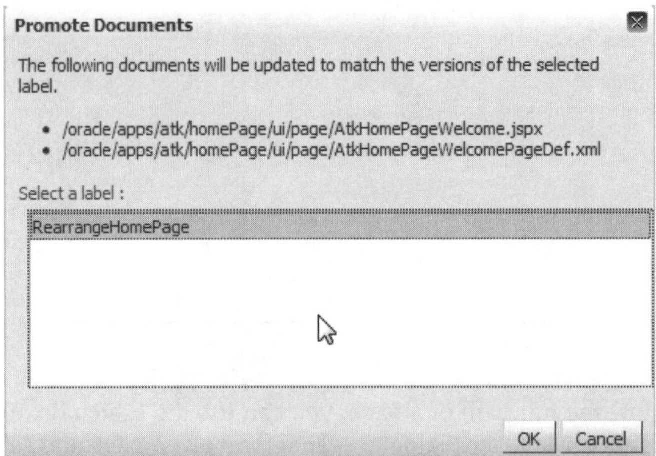

Summary

In this chapter, we discussed various customizations possible with Fusion Applications such as personalization, run-time customization, application extensions, and design-time customizations. We also talked about the tools to be used for each type of customization requirement, such as Oracle Page Composer, CRM Application Composer, and JDeveloper. We discussed how to plan, develop, view, test, and manage customizations using Sandbox Manager and Customization Manager. We will discuss each customization in detail and how to achieve various use cases for each customization.

CHAPTER 3

Flexfields in Oracle Fusion Applications

Flexfields are a user interface component within Oracle Fusion Applications. Broadly speaking, there are two types of flexfields. The first type of flexfields allows extra information to be captured in Oracle Fusion Applications. The second type of flexfields allows implementers to create user-defined composite data keys. These composite data keys can then be referenced and attached to the various transactional records in Oracle Fusion Applications.

The flexfields that allow extra information to be captured can be further subdivided into two types, which are *descriptive flexfield* and *extensible flexfield*. The flexfields that allow composite data keys to be created are known as *key flexfields*. In this chapter we will learn about the different types of flexfields, to understand how implementers can configure flexfields to meet their business requirements.

Descriptive Flexfields

Organizations that implement Oracle Fusion Applications often want to capture additional information specific to their enterprise through the various screens. The simplest way to achieve this is by the configuration of descriptive flexfields (DFFs), which provide a mechanism for capturing additional data in application tables through user-defined fields without the need to customize the underlying database schema or the user interface.

In other words, descriptive flexfields add extra information to a transaction record. Every data entry screen in Fusion Applications consists of a group of fields, and these fields capture the data entered by the user. Of course, most fields have a business purpose; for example, in the Purchase Order entry screen, the Supplier field captures the name of the supplier from whom you purchase the goods. Oracle develops the screens in a generic manner, with a generic set of fields, so that any company in the world can use them. However, different companies have different or additional needs to capture extra details about a transaction. For example, in purchasing, one company might require a Shipping Special Instructions field, whereas another company might require a Telephone Number of Purchaser field. To meet the requirements of different companies, Oracle Fusion Applications comes with a preseeded set of flexible fields. Descriptive flexfields allow you to customize your applications to capture data that would not otherwise be captured by your application. These fields can be used to capture values for additional fields as per business requirements. Given that these are generic fields, they are named ATTRIBUTE1..*n*, ATTRIBUTE_DATE1...*n*, ATTRIBUTE_TIMESTAMP1..*n*, or ATTRIBUTE_NUMBER1..*n* for character, date, date with timestamp, and number fields respectively.

Oracle Fusion Applications tables that support DFFs have a predefined number of ATTRIBUTE% columns. These additional attribute columns belong to the table in which extra information is being captured; therefore, there are a limited number of attributes that can be added to the user interface using descriptive flexfields. It also means that for each record, a value in a given DFF field can be entered just once. At design time, the Oracle Fusion Applications product development team typically creates approximately 20 attribute columns each for character, number, date, and timestamp columns. This imposes a limit on the number of extra fields that can be added to a standard Oracle Fusion Applications screen using a DFF.

The fields created using a DFF can be presented in various formats such as text box, text area, check box, or radio group on the page. At the time of creation, these fields can be configured as mandatory or optional. You can also configure the rule for defaulting values into these fields when a new record is created during user data entry.

The data captured in these segments can be validated at the point of data entry by means of value sets. Value sets are the validations that are attached to the flexfield segments to ensure that junk data does not get entered into the fields of the record. Value sets also allow you to present a list of values from which users can select a value into the flexfield segment.

There is also something known as *context* in descriptive flexfields. A context allows you to display different sets of fields depending on the context of the record. For example, in the Purchase Order entry screen, you may want to create a field named Shipping Special Instructions that can be entered for every single purchase order record. However, you may wish to create a set of context-sensitive fields that describe the nature of the goods being purchased. If the goods are of type "Hazardous Materials," then you may wish to show fields to capture information such as whether it is life-threatening material or it is flammable. However, if the purchase order is for buying material that requires cold storage, then you may wish to capture the Minimum Temperature Required and the Maximum Time this item should be kept in cold storage. In order to achieve this requirement, you will create two contexts besides the Global Context as shown in Figure 3-1.

The Shipping Special Instructions field will always be displayed regardless of the context selected because it belongs to the Global Context. However, the value selected in the DFF context field will decide whether cold storage–related fields are displayed or if hazardous materials–related fields are displayed.

The context field can be defined when configuring your descriptive flexfield. The value selected in the context field is typically stored in the ATTRIBUTE_CONTEXT column of the base table. The descriptive flexfield context can also be designed to automatically select the context value of the record from one of the existing fields in the user interface. This can be done by selecting a value in the field Derivation Value for the Context Segment.

Example of Configuring Descriptive Flexfields

Let us take an example for creating a descriptive flexfield for the Manage Common Lookup screen. A Common Lookup screen is delivered out of the box by Oracle Fusion Applications to create and maintain lookup codes in the application. In this

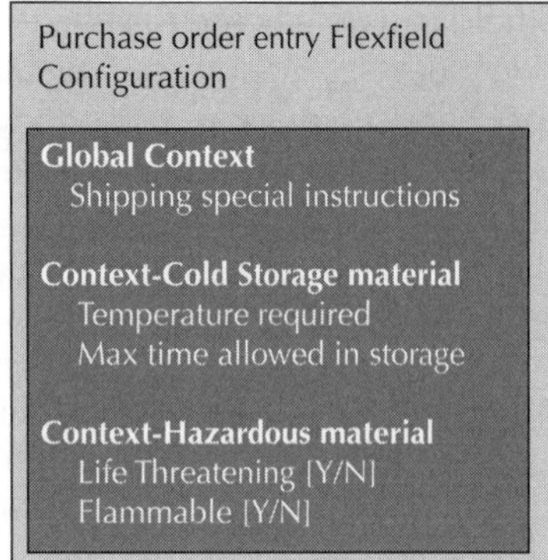

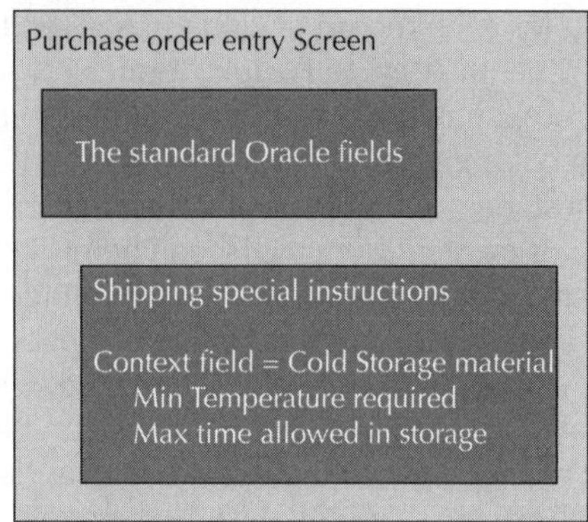

FIGURE 3-1. *Contexts in descriptive flexfields*

example, let us assume that we want to create the fields in the Common Lookup screen as per Table 3-1.

As shown in Table 3-1, for this example, we want to create one field that is visible for all the lookup values. A free text value can be entered into this field, thus allowing the teams to capture the contact person that is the owner for this lookup. Further, we want to display additional fields when the lookup type is XX_INVESTMENT_BOND_TYPES or XX_LOAN_TYPES. The fields that we wish to show for these lookups are different, as shown in Table 3-1.

In order to implement this requirement, the field Owning Team will be added to the Global Context of the Lookup DFF. Further, two new contexts will be created, which are Investment Bond Type Context and Loan Context.

To begin with, let us create two value sets to restrict the values users can enter for fields Bond Type and Loan Type. In order to create these value sets, log in to Fusion Applications as user XX_FA_IMPLEMENTOR. Chapter 4 shows the steps used for creating this user. After logging in, click the Navigator menu, and select Setup and Maintenance. In the Search: Tasks field in the left-hand pane, enter **Manage Value Sets** and click the Search button beside the Search: Tasks field. Click Go To Task as shown in Figure 3-2.

Next, click the Create icon in the Search Results section to create a value set. Enter the values in the fields as shown here.

Value Set Code:	XX_BOND_TYPES
Description:	XX Type of Bonds
Module:	Accounting Hub
Validation Type:	Independent

Value Data Type:	Character
Value Subtype:	Text
Maximum Length:	30

Click the Save and Close button. This will take you back to the Manage Value Sets screen. Search on value set code XX_BOND_TYPES and click the Search button. Next, click the Manage Values button, click the Create button, and enter Value = **GOVT**, Description = **Government Bonds**. Click Save and Close. Click Create again to add Value = **CORP**, Description = **Corporate Bonds** and click Save and Close. Repeat the same steps to create another value set named XX_LOAN_TYPE with the value set values being FIXED (Fixed Term Loan) and VARIABLE (Variable Term Loan).

Name of the Field	Validation Type	When Should the Field Appear	Database Column in FND_LOOKUP_VALUES
DFF Context	One of the existing contexts can be selected	During data entry	ATTRIBUTE_CATEGORY
Owning Team	Free text field	For all the lookup codes, regardless of the Lookup Type	ATTRIBUTE1
Bond Type	Radio group Corporate or Govt Bond	Visible for those records where the Lookup Type is XX_INVESTMENT_BOND_TYPES	ATTRIBUTE2
Number of Years	Numeric field	Visible for those records where the Lookup Type XX_INVESTMENT_BOND_TYPES	ATTRIBUTE3
Loan Type	Drop-down list Fixed or Variable interest rate	Visible for those records where the Lookup Type XX_LOAN_TYPES	ATTRIBUTE2
Is Early Repayment Allowed	A check box with values Y or N	Visible for those records where the Lookup Type XX_LOAN_TYPES	ATTRIBUTE3

TABLE 3-1. *Example for Adding DFF Fields to Common Lookup Screen*

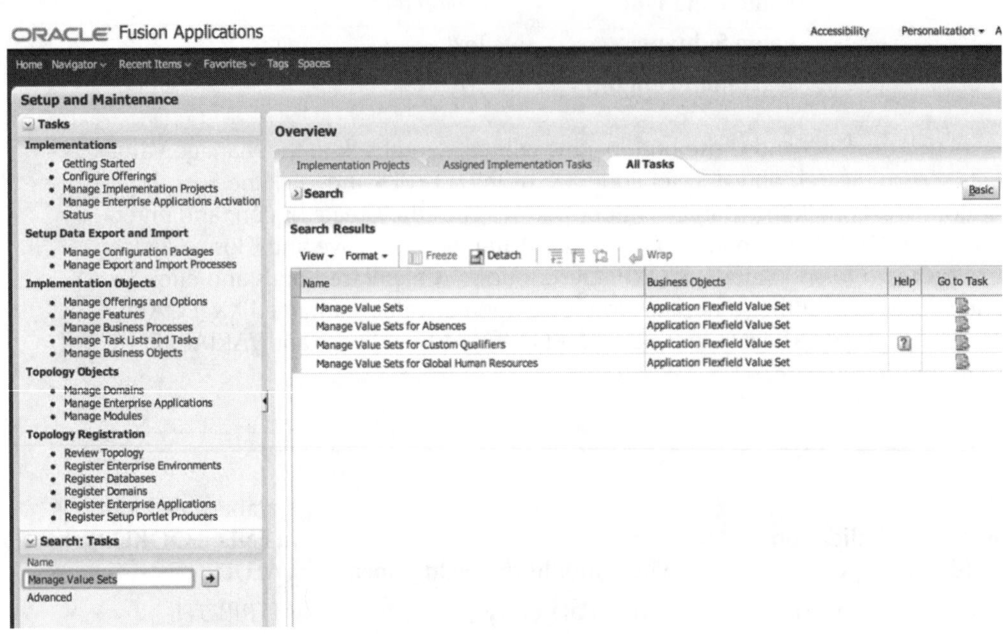

FIGURE 3-2. *Navigating to the Manage Value Sets screen*

Next, we can go to the flexfield configuration screen. Search for the task "Manage Descriptive Flexfields," click the Search button, and then click Go to Task. Here you will be presented with a screen to search the descriptive flexfields shipped out of the box by Oracle. Given that we know the name of the table, we can also run a SQL query as shown here to find the DFF name that we can search on to identify the desired lookup flexfield.

```
select descriptive_flexfield_code, table_name from FND_DF_TABLE_USAGES
where table_name like 'FND%LOOKUP%VALUES%'
```

This will return FND_LOOKUP_VALUES_B as the Descriptive Flexfield Code. Enter this value in the search field Flexfield Code. Alternately, search using wildcard **%LOOKUP%** in the Flexfield Code field. Click the Edit icon after selecting the record that has Flexfield name = Lookup values descriptive flexfield.

In the Edit Descriptive Flexfield screen, click the Create icon as shown in Figure 3-3 to create a segment "Owning Team" under Global Segments Context. At this stage, you can also set the Derivation Value field to LookupType, Default Type to Parameter, and Default Value to LookupType, so that the flexfield context is automatically defaulted to the Lookup Type at the time of data entry.

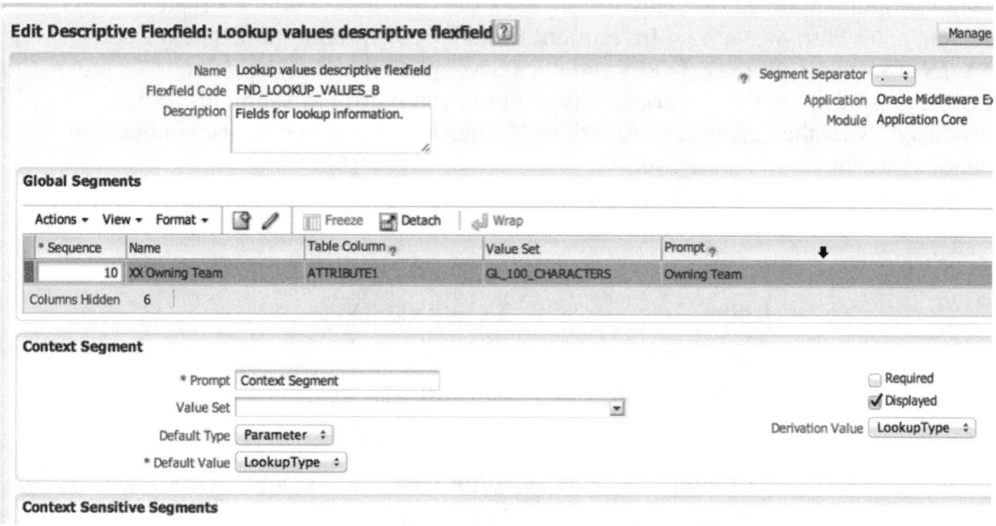

FIGURE 3-3. *Set the Derivation Value to Lookup Type and create a global segment.*

If you do not want to default the context, and you want the user to select the flexfield context during data entry, then you can enter a value in the Prompt field for Context Segment and check the Displayed check box, but leave the Default Type, Default Value, and Derivation Value fields blank.

In the Create Segment field for Global Context, enter the values as shown here:

Name:	XX Owning Team
Code:	XX_OWNING_TEAM
Data Type:	Character
Table Column:	ATTRIBUTE1
Value Set:	GL_100_CHARACTERS
Default Type:	Constant
Default Value:	IT Department
Prompt:	Owning Team
Short Prompt:	Owning Team
Display Type:	Text Box
Display Height:	1

Click Save and Close. Now click the Manage Contexts button to create the desired contexts. In the Manage Contexts screen, click the Create icon. In the Create Context screen, enter Display Name = **Investment Bond Types Context** and Context Code = **XX_INVESTMENT_BOND_TYPES** and click Save. Note that it is the value in Context Code that should match the Lookup Type field for the desired segments to be displayed. Now the Create icon for adding Context Sensitive Segments will become enabled, as shown in Figure 3-4.

Create the Bond Type segment as shown here.

Name:	XX Bond Type
Code:	XX_BOND_TYPE
Data Type:	Character
Table Column:	ATTRIBUTE2
Value Set:	XX_BOND_TYPES
Prompt:	Bond Type
Short Prompt:	Bond Type
Display Type:	Radio Button Group
Display Height:	1

Click Save and Close, click Create again, and repeat the process as shown next.

Name:	XX Number of Years
Code:	XX_NUMBER_OF_YEARS
Data Type:	Character
Table Column:	ATTRIBUTE3
Value Set:	HRX_IE_NUMBER_5
Prompt:	Number of Years
Short Prompt:	Number of Years
Display Type:	Text Box
Display Height:	1
Display Size:	5

Now, we need to repeat the steps for Context = XX_LOAN_TYPES, so that when the user enters lookup values for lookup type XX_LOAN_TYPES, then segments Loan Type and Early Repayment Allowed are displayed. In order to do so, click Save and Close, navigate back to the Manage Contexts screen, and click the Create icon to create a new context. In the Create Context screen, enter Display Name = **Loan**

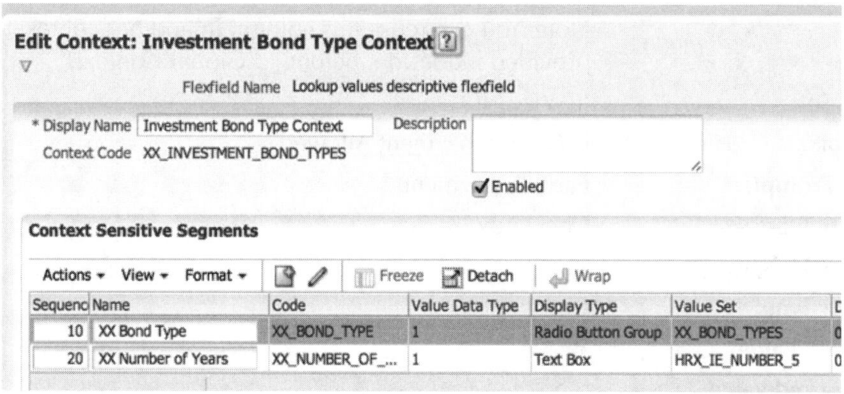

FIGURE 3-4. *Creating segments for context XX_INVESTMENT_BOND_TYPES*

Context and Context Code = **XX_LOAN_TYPES** and click Save. Add the segments as shown here and in the next table by clicking the Create icon in the Context Sensitive Segments region.

Name:	Type of Loan
Code:	XX_LOAN_TYPE
Data Type:	Character
Table Column:	ATTRIBUTE2 Note: You can reuse this column in another context provided it does not belong to Global Context.
Value Set:	XX_LOAN_TYPE
Prompt:	Loan Type
Short Prompt:	Loan Type
Display Type:	Drop-down List
Display Height:	1

Create a field Early Repayment Allowed of type Checkbox as shown here.

Name:	Early Repayment Allowed
Code:	EARLY_REPAYMENT_ALLOWED
Data Type:	Character

Table Column:	ATTRIBUTE3 Note: You can reuse this column in another context provided it does not belong to Global Context.
Value Set:	JE_YES_NO
Prompt:	Is Early Repayment Allowed
Short Prompt:	Early Repayment
Display Type:	Checkbox
Display Height:	1
Display Type:	Checkbox
Checked Value:	Y
Unchecked Value:	N
Display Size:	1

Click Save and Close and in the Manage Contexts screen, click Done. Click Save and Close in the screen titled Edit Descriptive Flexfield: Lookup values descriptive flexfield. Now, you are back in the Manage Descriptive Flexfields screen. Highlight the record for Lookup values DFF and click Deploy Flexfield as shown in Figure 3-5.

Upon successful completion of the deployment, you will see the screen with a confirmation message as shown in Figure 3-6.

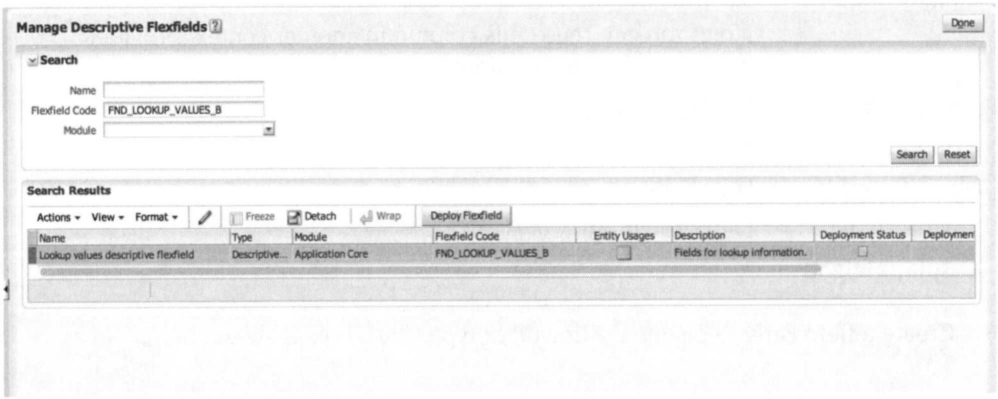

FIGURE 3-5. *Deploying a descriptive flexfield*

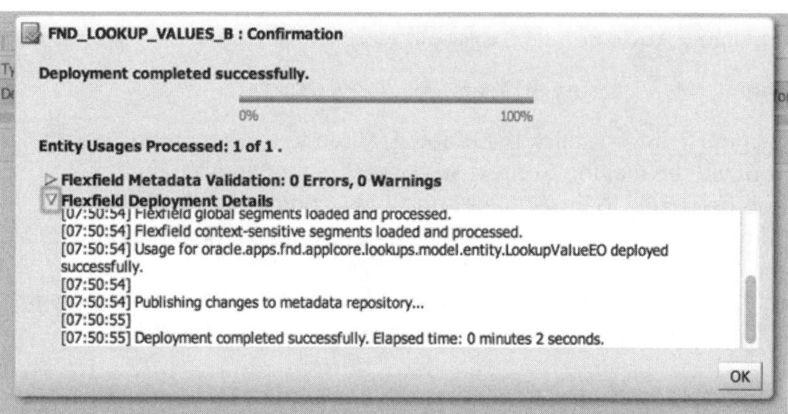

FIGURE 3-6. *Deployment confirmation*

Next, you can proceed with testing this flexfield:

1. Click OK, click Sign Out, and sign back in as XX_FA_IMPLEMENTOR.
2. Click Navigator menu | Setup and Maintenance, and then in the Search: Tasks field, enter **Manage Common Lookups** and click the right arrow. This will display the task Manage Common Lookups in the search results. Click Go To Task.
3. In the Search Results region, click the + sign to create a new lookup type. Enter the values as shown here:

   Lookup Type = XX_INVESTMENT_BOND_TYPES

   Meaning = Investment Bond Lookup Type

   Module = Accounting Hub
4. Click Save.
5. Next, we create the lookup codes. For ease of data entry, click the Detach icon in the Lookup Code region. A pop-up window will appear. Click the + sign to create a new lookup code.

   Lookup Code = US_XTR_30

   Display Sequence = 1

Enabled = Y

Start Date = Any date

Meaning = US Treasury 30 Years

As shown in Figure 3-7, click the triangular icon to the left of the Lookup Code field and you will see that the Context Segment is defaulted from the LookupType and the fields belonging to Investment Bond Type Context are displayed.

Using similar steps as previously, create a new lookup type named XX_LOAN_TYPES and create a lookup code as shown in Figure 3-8.

As a result of entering the data into flexfields, the net result of data entry in Figure 3-7 and Figure 3-8 produces data in the database table as shown in Figure 3-9.

Polymorphic View Objects to Support Descriptive Flexfields

As seen in Figure 3-9, the columns ATTRIBUTE2 and ATTRIBUTE3 in FND_LOOKUP_VALUES are being used for different purposes depending upon the value in ATTRIBUTE_CATEGORY. If you wish to expose ATTRIBUTE2 and ATTRIBUTE3 to the real-time analytic reports by setting their BI Enabled Flags in DFF segments, then it will not make sense for the end users to see ATTRIBUTE2 and ATTRIBUTE3 in the presentation layer of Oracle Business Intelligence Enterprise Edition (OBIEE). Therefore, once the BI Enabled flag is set, and the DFF has been deployed, then those DFF fields can be exposed to business users with their user-friendly names. The business user in this case will see the type of investment bond and type of loan as the available fields when developing real-time

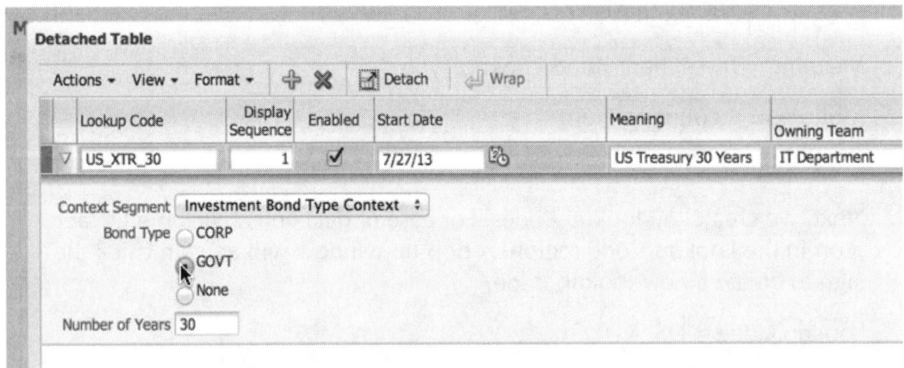

FIGURE 3-7. *Fields displayed when Investment Bond Type Context is displayed*

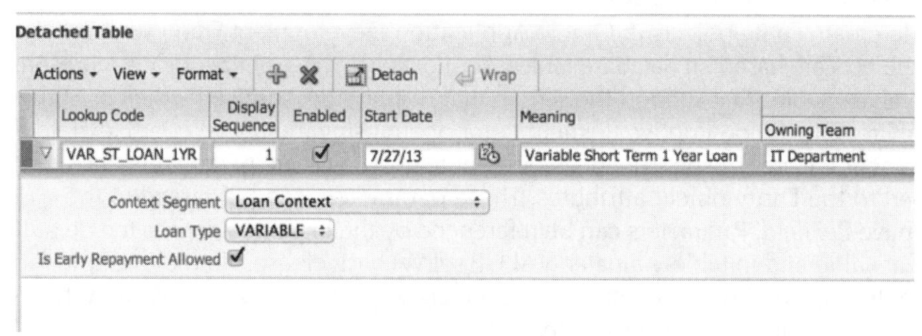

FIGURE 3-8. *Fields displayed when Loan Type Context is displayed*

analytic reports in Fusion Applications. When you deploy descriptive flexfields, then behind-the-scenes polymorphic view objects in ADF are generated, with user-friendly names for ATTRIBUTE2 and ATTRIBUTE3. During design time in ADF, the developer flags the column ATTRIBUTE_CATEGORY as a discriminator attribute using JDeveloper. The DFF deployment process looks at the possible values for this discriminator attribute, and generates one polymorphic view object for each possible value in ATTRIBUTE_CATEGORY. These ADF view objects are then exposed in real-time analytics reports by importing them into an RPD file using the OBIEE tool.

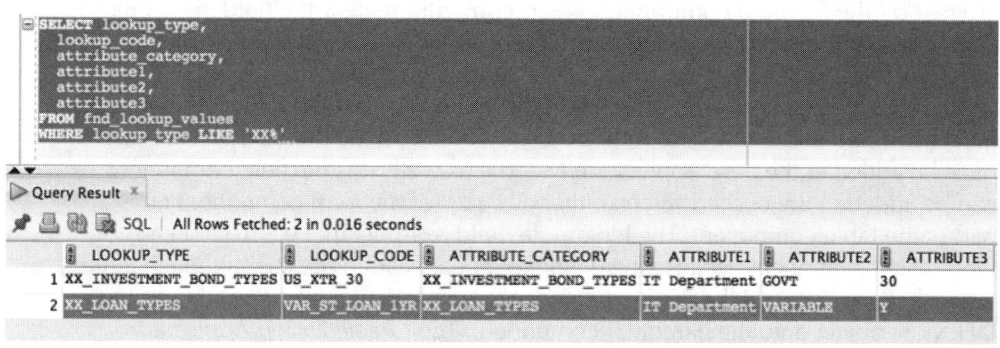

FIGURE 3-9. *Descriptive flexfield data stored in database table*

Descriptive Flexfield Parameters

You can create Entity objects in Oracle Application Development Framework (ADF). Entity objects are based on database tables. For flexfields, these entity objects represent the database tables that support the screen that displays descriptive flexfields. At the time of creating the descriptive flexfield component using the JDeveloper Flexfield Component wizard, the product development team can create parameters that are mapped to the Entity object attributes. These parameters can be passed to the descriptive flexfield. Parameters can be referenced by the logic that derives the default segment value and in table-validated VALUE set WHERE clauses. In the example for lookup descriptive flexfield configuration, the LookupType is a parameter used for defaulting the value for context segment.

Registration of New Flexfields for Your Custom Screens

A flexfield along with its table and column usage must be registered in the application. You can navigate to the Register Descriptive Flexfields task under the Setup and Maintenance menu to register new flexfields for your custom screens. In the registration screen, you can specify the flexfield code, flexfield name, application name, module, and BI Enabled flag. Further, you specify the table usages for your flexfield and the ATTRIBUTE columns that will be used by this flexfield. The registration of the flexfield can also be done using PL/SQL API FND_FLEX_ DF_SETUP_APIS.

After the registration process is complete, you need to create a user interface artifact in JDeveloper for your custom flexfield. To do so, you need to use the Flexfield Business component in Oracle ADF, where you will be asked to specify the flexfield code used during registration. Next you select the entity object for the table containing flexfield columns and define the flexfield parameters while mapping them to entity object attributes. Behind the scenes, the view object is created by the flexfield component. Next, you will create a flexfield view link between the master view object that references the base entity table and the descriptive flexfield view component. Note that your master view object will not contain the attribute columns used by the flexfield. The flexfield application module must be nested within the base Application Module and the flexfield view object must be added to the base Application Module as well. This flexfield component can be added to the desired screen either as a part of the form component or as a part of the table component. The lookup flexfield example that we have seen is of type Table Component because the flexfield appears within the user interface table for each record. To add the flexfield component, simply drag and drop the nested DFF view object onto the parent UI component. The *Oracle Fusion Applications Developer's Guide* contains the detailed steps for performing this exercise.

Extensible Flexfields

As you notice in Figure 3-9, descriptive flexfields have the following limitations:

- The number of attribute columns are limited in a table, which is decided at design time by the Oracle Fusion Applications product development team.
- One single record can be attached to just one single context value, which in the previous example was either an Investment Bond Context or the Loan Context. In some cases you may wish to attach multiple contexts to a single base record.

Both of these limitations can be overcome by using extensible flexfields, which are also known as EFFs. This is made possible because the data captured for the extensible flexfields is stored in another table that contains a foreign key to the base table. This allows the additional information to be captured in multiple records, using as many contexts as you desire. In other words, a screen that allows extensible flexfields to be configured will allow the implementers to define an unlimited number of additional segments.

It must be noted that while most of the Fusion Applications screens come integrated with descriptive flexfields, not as many screens have provisions for configuring the extensible flexfields. The simplest way to identify the objects that have predefined extensible flexfields is by running the following SQL query:

```
select name, descriptive_flexfield_code from fnd_DF_FLEXFIELDS_VL where
FLEXFIELD_TYPE ='EFF'
```

Over a period of time, Oracle will keep adding extensible flexfields for more and more screens. If you want a particular screen to contain an extensible flexfield, then you can either extend the screen yourself following the *Oracle Fusion Applications Developer's Guide* or raise an enhancement request with Oracle Support. The latter option is preferred because if Oracle adds an EFF to a screen in their core product, then it becomes available to all the Fusion Applications customers.

Every EFF involves at least two tables, the first table being the base table, for example PER_LOCATIONS for capturing location records in HCM, and the second table being an extension table, for example PER_LOCATION_EXTRA_INFO_F. The result from the previous SQL query can be used to identify the tables that are involved in an EFF by running another SQL query as shown here:

```
select table_name, table_type from FND_DF_TABLE_USAGES fd
where fd.descriptive_flexfield_code = 'PER_LOCATION_INFORMATION_EFF'
```

The following table shows the results of this SQL query, which will help you identify the tables for an EFF:

Table Name	Table Type
PER_LOCATIONS	BASE
PER_LOCATION_EXTRA_INFO_F	EXTENSION

For SaaS customers who do not have access to the SQL tool, you can navigate to Setup and Maintenance | Search Tasks, and search for Manage Extensible Flexfield. After the search, click Go To Task, and click the Search button to display all the seeded extensible flexfields that are available for you to configure. Click the Entity Usages icon as shown in Figure 3-10 to identify the database tables used by extensible flexfields.

The architecture of the EFFs can be explained using Figure 3-11.

At the very heart of an EFF is the *context*, which can be defined as either single- or multirow. There is not much difference between single-row EFF context and the descriptive flexfields. A multirow context allows you to capture multiple records as extra information. For example, against an HCM Location, you may want to

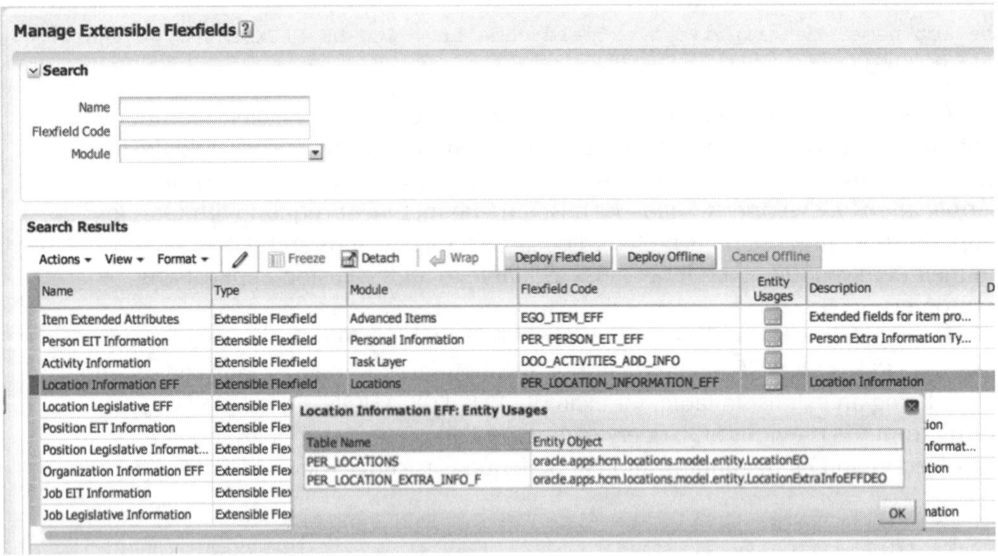

FIGURE 3-10. *Database tables used by extensible flexfields*

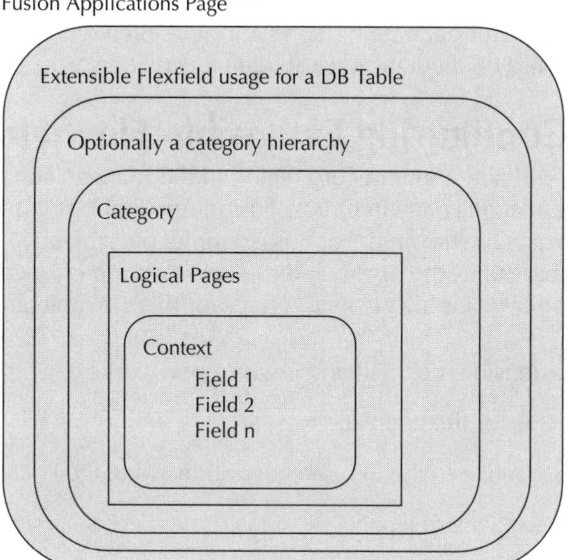

FIGURE 3-11. *Architecture of extensible flexfields*

capture the dates on which the Health and Safety inspection had taken place. You can mix and match the multirow and single-row contexts into an EFF. In the example of HCM Locations, a single record in PER_LOCATIONS can have multiple contexts (group of fields) applicable and each context can have multiple records entered by the users.

Extensible flexfields allow you to combine contexts into presentation groups known as *pages*, which help to bring different contexts to be presented together in the screen. Each ADF screen corresponds to one extensible flexfield category. A *category* is the grouping of related data items that are considered to belong together. You can associate any combination of contexts with a given category. It is the category of the EFF that provides a linkage back to the base table record, which decides the contexts that will be displayed for a given base table record. Some flexfields come predefined with category hierarchies, allowing different flexfield contexts to be made visible for different records.

When the Oracle Fusion product development team creates an EFF, they create one flexfield usage for each set of tables in the application that uses the EFF. In most cases you will see that EFFs have just one flexfield usage. But you can have more than one object in the application that can be extended using the same extensible flexfield. In such cases Oracle ships the EFF with multiple usages for the flexfield.

For example, in the case of an Items application, there might be different data levels, such as items and item revisions. In this case, you create one usage per data level. Defining separate usages for each set of tables allows implementers to reuse the same extensible flexfield configuration for all data levels.

Example of Configuring Extensible Flexfields

In this example, we will add a multirecord region to the Manage Locations screen in HCM. The Manage Locations page in Oracle Fusion Applications comes shipped with a predefined extensible flexfield. For this example, our objective is a to add a multirecord region that tracks the health and safety inspection checks performed on the site location in a year. At a high level the steps for this example are

1. Identify the extensible flexfield and create a new context for multirows.
2. Define segments for the context.
3. Associate the context to the EFF category on the Manage Locations page.
4. Add the context to the EFF page.
5. Deploy the flexfield and test.

Log in to Fusion Applications as XX_FA_IMPLEMENTOR and click Navigator | Setup and Maintenance. In the Search: Tasks field, enter **Manage Extensible Flexfields**, and Click Go to Task. In the Manage Extensible Flexfields screen, click the Search button. This will list all the EFFs in your Fusion Applications environment. Scroll down to select and highlight Location Information EFF and click the Pencil icon to edit.

In the Category section, select and highlight category HcmLocationsCategory. Click the Manage Contexts button and click the Create icon in the Manage Contexts Search Results region. Create a new context with the properties as shown here.

Display Name:	Health and Safety Inspection History
Code:	XX_H_AND_S_INSPECTION_HIST
Enabled:	Yes
Behavior:	Multiple Rows

Next, click the + icon in the Context Usages region and add Name = **Location Information EFF**, View Privileges = **None**, Edit Privileges = **None,** and click Save. It means that the context Health and Safety Inspection History is being used for

Location Information EFF. Next, click the Create icon in the section Context Sensitive Segments and create the segment as shown here.

Name:	Inspection Year
Code:	XX_INSPECTION_YEAR
Unique Key:	Yes
Data Type:	Character
Table Column:	LEI_INFORMATION1
Value Set:	JEES_YEARYYYY
Required:	Yes
Prompt:	Inspection Year
Short Prompt:	Inspection Year
Display Type:	Text Area
Display Height:	1
Display Size:	4

Create a segment to capture if inspection checks were a success as shown here.

Name:	Inspection Passed
Code:	INSPECTION_PASSED
Unique Key:	No
Data Type:	Character
Table Column:	LEI_INFORMATION2
Value Set:	JE_YES_NO
Required:	Yes
Prompt:	Inspection Passed
Short Prompt:	Inspection Passed
Display Type:	Drop-down List
Display Height:	1
Display Size:	1

Click Save and Close. After the segments have been created, the context will appear as shown in Figure 3-12. Click Save and Close again and then click Done.

In the region "Edit Extensible Flexfield: Location Information EFF," click the + sign and search and add the Health and Safety context to the category as shown in Figure 3-13.

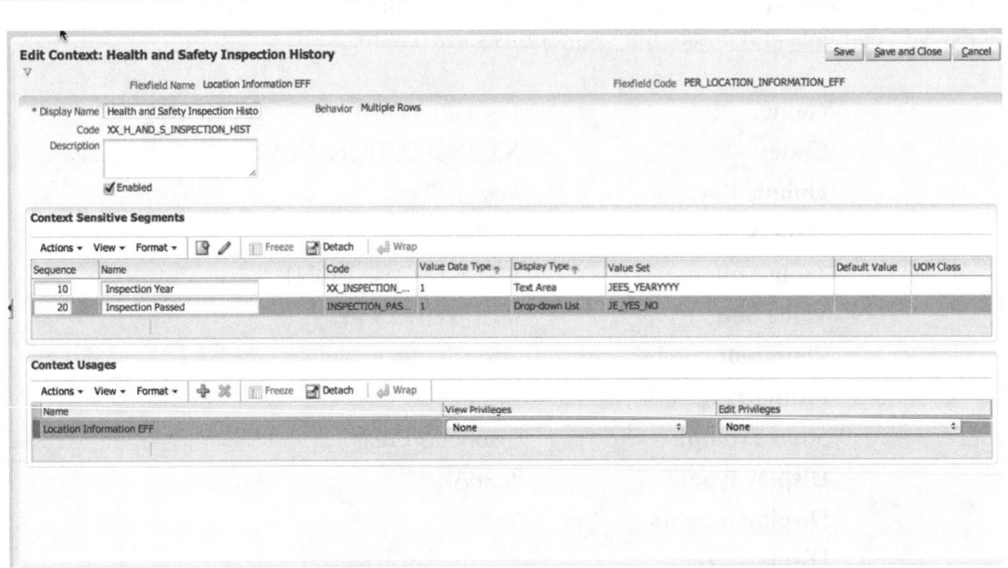

FIGURE 3-12. *Context for multirecord EFF region in Location screen*

Click the Pages tab and then click the + icon in the Associated Contexts Details region to add Associated Context "Health and Safety Inspection History" to the Location Information page. This is shown in Figure 3-14.

Click Save and Close, and deploy the Location Information EFF. Next sign out and sign back in to the application as XX_FA_IMPLEMENTOR user. In the Search: Tasks field, search for Manage Locations and click Go To Task. Click the Create icon to create a new Location, and there you should see the EFF configured for Health and Safety as shown in Figure 3-15.

The logic for adding subsequent regions for varying sets of contexts is the same as shown in this example. EFFs are a very powerful mechanism that allow you to capture as many additional attributes as you desire for your Fusion Applications screens that support EFFs.

Key Flexfields

Key flexfields (KFFs) in Oracle Fusion Applications allow businesses and other organizations to create user-definable, unique composite keys such as accounting codes, item codes, and many others. The key difference between descriptive or extensible and key flexfields is that KFFs provide user-defined, unique keys or identifiers for data entities.

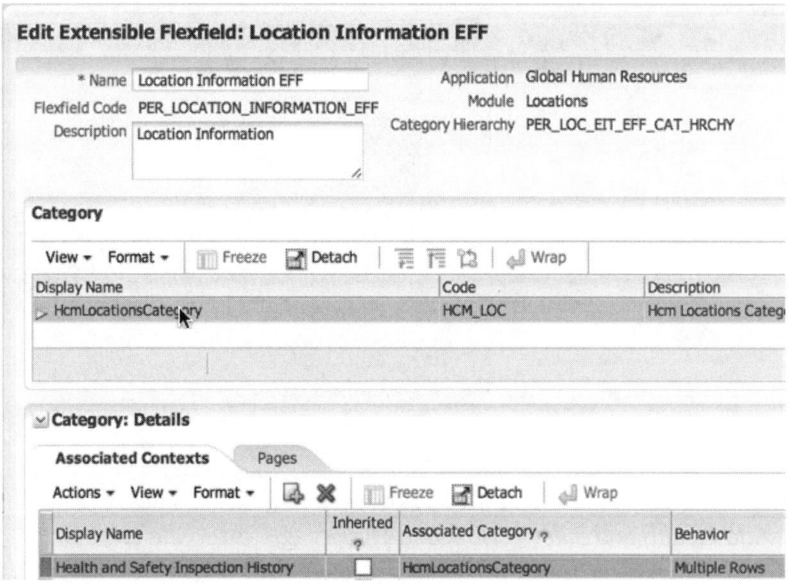

FIGURE 3-13. *Add the context that you created to Associated Contexts.*

To illustrate the difference between KFFs and DFFs, let's take a look at an example. Assume for a minute that there is no such thing as key flexfields and all you have on a screen or inside a table is a descriptive flexfield. Assume that the basic requirement is to be able to capture values in the following additional fields for a purchase order and invoices transaction:

Company name: GM

Cost Center: IT

Project: OFP (Oracle Fusion Project)

Expense Type: OCC (Oracle Consultant Cost)

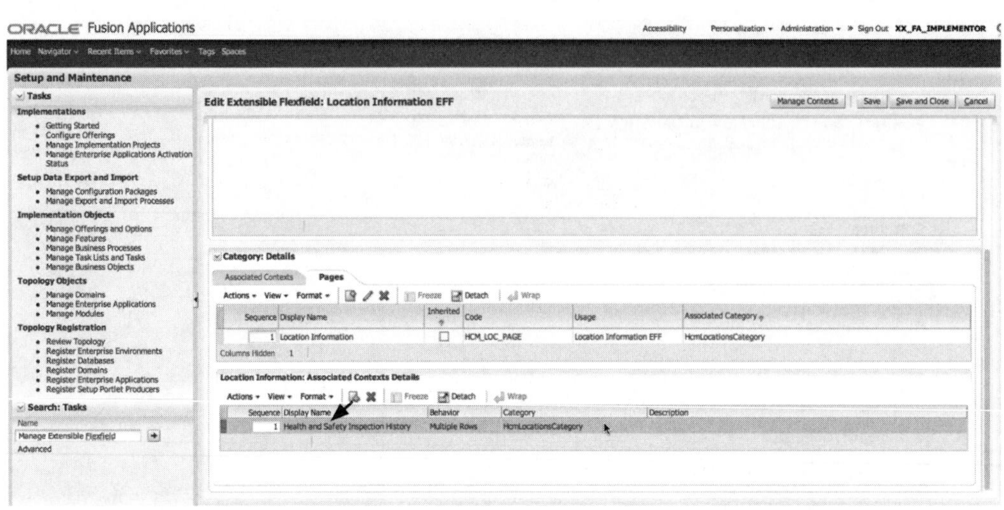

FIGURE 3-14. *Add Health and Safety Inspection History context to the Location Information page.*

If you had only DFFs available as a configuration option, when the business raises a purchase order to IT Consulting Company, the Purchase Order Distributions table PO_DISTRIBUTIONS_ALL would store values for the following columns in a record:

ATTRIBUTE1 : GM

ATTRIBUTE2 : IT

ATTRIBUTE3 : OFP

ATTRIBUTE4 : OCC

When an invoice is received from the consulting company, the payables clerk would capture the Invoice Line accounting as follows in AP_INVOICE_DISTRIBUTIONS_ALL:

ATTRIBUTE1 : GM

ATTRIBUTE2 : IT

ATTRIBUTE3 : OFP

ATTRIBUTE4 : OCC

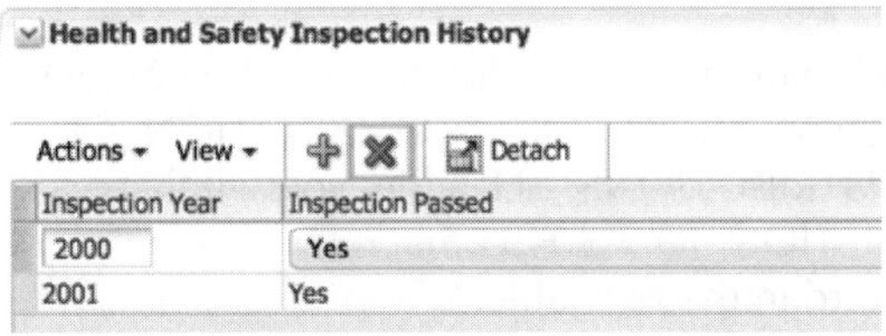

FIGURE 3-15. *EFF in the Location screen*

In other words, if DFFs were used for capturing the accounting details as in the example, then the four text values for fields (ATTRIBUTE1…4) would be physically duplicated in each module for the related transactions. Imagine further when this transaction flows to the Oracle General Ledger. Given the nature of DFF, the Oracle Database would again have to store the four columns physically into the table GL_JE_LINES. If so, the table GL_JE_LINES would have the following values in its DFF (descriptive flex) columns:

ATTRIBUTE1 : GM

ATTRIBUTE2 : IT

ATTRIBUTE3 : OFP

ATTRIBUTE4 : OCC

As you can see, such a design using a descriptive flexfield is flawed, as it causes duplication of data at various places. It is also possible that the same combination of GM-IT-OFP-OCC would be required against thousands of other purchase order records, and the text GM-IT-OFP-OCC would be duplicated across many tables and many records in each such table.

Clearly, the descriptive or extensible flexfield does not fit into this scenario. Let's now consider a new approach using a key flexfield. In this example, you have a table named GL_CODE_COMBINATIONS with the following columns:

- CODE_COMBINATION_ID
- SEGMENT1
- SEGMENT2
- SEGMENT3
- SEGMENT4

You capture a *single* record in the table GL_CODE_COMBINATIONS as shown in Table 3-2.

The preceding combination of four fields can now be uniquely identified by a value of 50493 in a column named CODE_COMBINATION_ID.

Now, in the PO_DISTRIBUTIONS_ALL table, you will have a column with the value CODE_COMBINATION_ID = 50493 that refers to the unique key combination of the record in the KFF table.

In the Oracle Fusion Payables, even though a clerk enters the values for four columns (one for each segment), the database stores only the reference value 50493 in the column CODE_COMBINATION_ID of the Payables Distributions table. Ditto for the entry in the GL_JE_LINES table in the Oracle Fusion Accounting Hub module: only the ID that references those four columns will be stored. Therefore, all the tables (Purchase Order Distributions, Payables Distributions, and General Ledger Journal Lines) will reference just the CODE_COMBINATION_ID. This concept of having a unique ID that maps to a combination of other values is called key flexfields.

Every key flexfield has a table dedicated to storing the unique combination for a group of fields. For the GL accounting key flexfield, there is a table named GL_CODE_COMBINATIONS. Another example is people groups in Oracle Fusion Human Capital Management. To capture some of the key attributes of a staff, you can define a people group flexfield. The combination of those staff attributes will be stored in the PER_PEOPLE_GROUPS table.

It is a standard practice used by Oracle to give generic names like SEGMENT1, SEGMENT2...SEGMENT*X* to these columns. These segment columns are generic columns so that each Fusion Applications customer can reference them by whatever name they like and by giving the desired prompt name to the key flexfield segment.

Oracle Fusion Applications delivers many KFFs out of the box, but implementers need to configure their segments as per business needs. You can also create new KFFs in Oracle Fusion Applications; however, this is a very rare requirement and is

Column Name	Column Value
CODE_COMBINATION_ID	50493 ** a unique number value
SEGMENT1	GM
SEGMENT2	IT
SEGMENT3	OFP
SEGMENT4	OCC

TABLE 3-2. *A Record in a Key Flexfield Table*

not covered in this book. The *Oracle Fusion Applications Developer's Guide* contains the steps for creating custom key flexfields.

Similar to DFFs and EFFs, key flexfields have something known as *structure*. This allows you to define a different combination of segments for each structure. After the structure has been created and segments have been added to that structure, next you create the instance of that structure. For example, when you configure a GL Chart Of Accounts key flexfield, you will define a structure and add GL Chart of Accounts Segments to that structure. Next, you define the instance of that structure. Within the instance, for each segment you can specify the name of Value Set and if the segment is displayed, and if the segment is required in that instance or is enabled for Business Intelligence. You can also assign default values for each segment per KFF Structure's instance. For example, the GL Chart of Accounts Structure's instance is assigned to a Ledger. The idea behind this approach is that you can define a global GL Chart of Accounts Structure, and create multiple instances of that structure, with one instance for each country. This will allow you to specify different value sets for a segment per structure instance.

Cross-Validation Rules

Cross-validation rules (CVRs) are used to prevent the creation of invalid segment combinations. For example, a Location key flexfield can have two structures, for example, one for each country, the United Kingdom (U.K.) and the United States (U.S.). For the U.S. flexfield structure, you can define a cross-validation rule that excludes COUNTY=NY and CITY=ABERDEEN. At the time of defining cross-validation rules, you also specify the accompanying error message that the end user will receive if he or she uses the wrong combination of values in segments.

Whenever any component of the Oracle Fusion Applications attempts to create a new segment combination, the flexfield engine checks all the cross-validation rules against that KFF structure to ensure that the combination is valid. If the combination fails to pass a rule, the error message associated with that rule is displayed to the end user. CVRs are applied to all users in Oracle Fusion Applications before a new segment combination is generated, but they are not applied to existing segment combinations that already exist in the KFF tables.

To create a cross-validation rule in Fusion Applications, navigate to the Manage Cross-Validation Rules, select a KFF structure, and then click the + sign. Give your rule a name, description, start date, and end date, and set the enabled flag if required. Click the icon shown in Figure 3-16 to create a Validation Filter, wherein you can select Segment & Value combination as shown in Figure 3-17.

You also need to create a Condition Filter by selecting Segment & Value combination. Next, enter the error message to be displayed when the cross-validation rule fires. When you create new flexfield combinations, the system first checks the

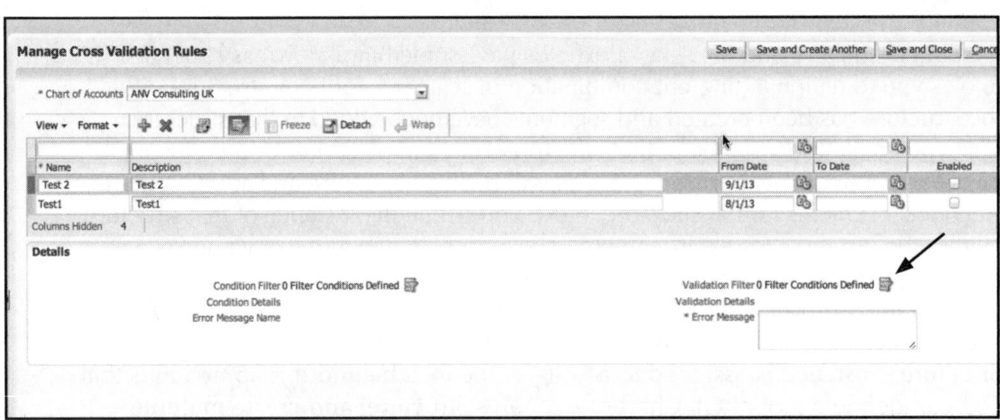

FIGURE 3-16. *Define filter condition.*

conditions filters that evaluate to true. Within those conditions, their corresponding validation filter is executed to validate if the combination is valid for the specified condition. If both the condition filter and validation filter evaluate to true, then the Error message is returned to the application.

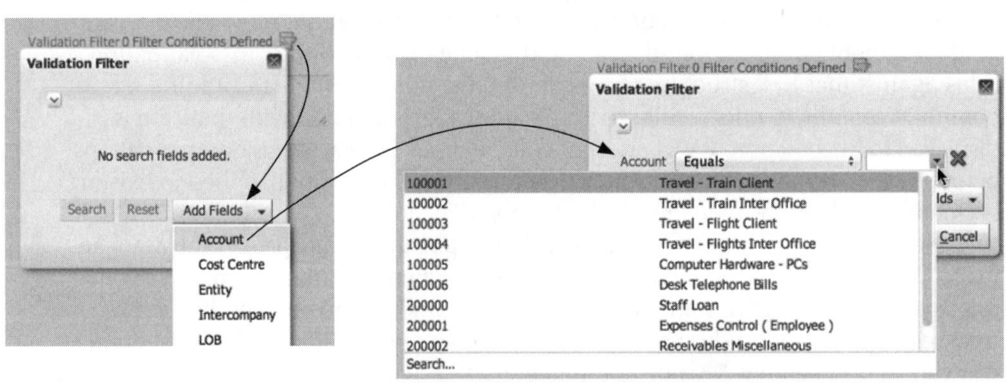

FIGURE 3-17. *Specify segment and value combination for filter condition.*

Deployment of Flexfields

A flexfield should be deployed in order for its configuration to become visible in the user interface. Deployment of a flexfield generates the ADF business component objects that help in displaying the flexfield at run time in the user interface. Flexfields can either be deployed globally for a Fusion Applications instance for its configuration to become effective for all the users, or the flexfields can be deployed into a sandbox.

When you deploy a flexfield as a sandbox, that flexfield-enabled sandbox automatically gets activated in your user session. When you sign back in to see the changes, the sandbox is active in your session. The status of the sandbox is managed by the Manage Sandboxes task that can be accessed from the Administrator menu of the Setup and Maintenance area. Here you can activate, access, or delete a flexfield-enabled sandbox. Whether you use deployment into mainline or deployment into sandbox, in either case you must sign out and sign back in before you can see changes you deployed in the run time.

The flexfields can also be deployed using a command-line tool in WebLogic Scripting Tool (WLST). Log in to your server Common Domain host. The script should be located under $APPLTOP. If you find multiple scripts, pick the one under the atgpf folder, for example:

```
.../common/bin/wlst.sh
connect('weblogic_fa','password for weblogic_fa','t3://HOST:PORT')
deployFlex('EGP_TRADING_PARTNER_ITEMS_DFF','DFF',forceCompleteEFF
Deployment=true)
```

To deploy all flexfields for the specified enterprise application, use `deployFlexForApp`. To deploy a single flexfield, use `command deployFlex`. To deploy flexfield changes that have been delivered using a flexfield Seed Data Framework (SDF) patch, use `command deployPatchedFlex`.

Summary

In this chapter you have seen how Oracle Fusion Applications allows implementers to extend the user interface without any programming effort. You should use descriptive flexfields when you wish to add some fields for each record. Extensible flexfields are useful when you wish to capture a large number of additional attributes or when you wish to capture additional information in multiple records for a single database record. Key flexfields are primarily used to capture unique combinations of segments.

CHAPTER 4

Security in Fusion Applications

The purpose of this chapter is to give you all the essential information so that you can understand and work on the key security aspects in Oracle Fusion Applications across various technology layers within this application suite. Every business application has a basic need for securing its resources and its data. Oracle Fusion Applications is no exception to those requirements.

At a very high level there are two key components in any security model. These are authentication and authorization. *Authentication* means that the application ensures that a person accessing a protected resource has been validated for their username and password. The objective of authentication is to verify that the user is actually who they say they are. Once Fusion Applications identifies the user through authentication, then *authorization* is how it decides what the user can do. For example, the authorization layer in Fusion General Ledger can decide these types of questions:

- Is the user authorized to access the Journal Entry screen?
- Should the user's activity in the Journal Entry screen be restricted to a set of ledgers?
- Should the user be allowed to enter the journals and also to post the journals?

In this chapter, we will begin by explaining the architecture at a high level, followed by an explanation of how usernames and passwords are validated. The key emphasis, however, will be on authorization, which is the security layer that decides the screens, Web services, and other components that the users can access and what data can they view or modify. Next we will see how data security has been implemented in some of the key modules within Fusion Applications. At the end of this chapter you will see some troubleshooting tips.

High-Level Overview of Technology Components

Figure 4-1 shows the high-level components in Fusion Applications Security. The actual technical stack has further Oracle components; however, the components listed in this figure will give you a fair idea about the architecture of Fusion Applications Security.

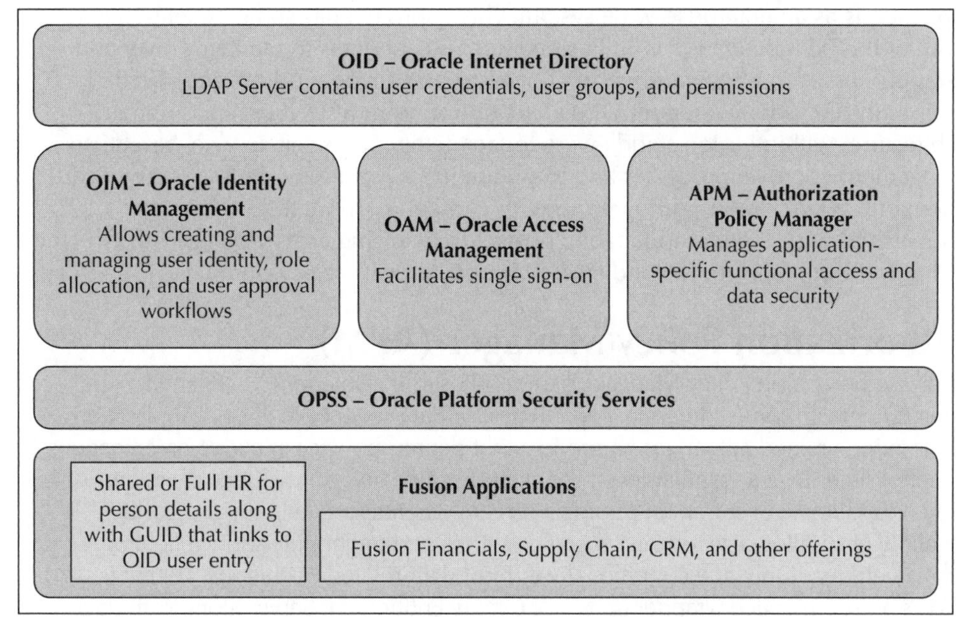

FIGURE 4-1. *High-level components in Fusion Applications Security*

Oracle Internet Directory

At the very back end of the security layers is OID (Oracle Internet Directory), where the user credentials are stored along with the user groups, permissions, and various other user login–related attributes. OID is Oracle's implementation of Lightweight Directory Access Protocol (LDAP). When you install Oracle Fusion Applications, a tool called Oracle Directory Services Manager (ODSM) gets installed as well, and it has a URL similar to http://hostname:port/odsm. ODSM allows you to interrogate the OID contents from a browser. Any kind of role that is created in Fusion Applications gets registered as a group within OID. The users who have access to that role get registered as the members of those groups in OID. Even though Fusion Applications provides user-friendly screens to create users, roles, permissions, and so on, behind the scenes these get registered into OID's LDAP-based repository.

Oracle Identity Manager

Oracle Fusion Applications also comes installed with OIM (Oracle Identity Manager). OIM allows a company to manage their users and their access to various roles centrally from a Web console. Corporations implementing Fusion Applications have an option to leverage the Identity Management suite installed as a part of Fusion Applications as an enterprise-wide system. This approach has some benefits, such as out-of-the-box integration with Fusion Human Resources to manage leaver and joiner processes to allow automatic allocation and revocation of roles. Further possibilities include leveraging OIM's integration with SOA (Service Oriented Architecture) within Fusion Middleware to facilitate various self-service–based user management approval processes and to streamline integration with the security card system of the corporation, integrating with canteen card facilities, staff gym membership, and so on as applicable, subject to licensing costs verified with Oracle for the usage of platforms beyond Fusion Applications.

Authorization Policy Manager (APM)

Oracle Authorization Policy Manager is a Web-based console for Oracle Entitlement Server (OES) with some additional capabilities for data security in Fusion Applications. OES is a fine-grained authorization product that defines policies allowing organizations to control security at a granular level. For example, a coarse-grained security might allow or disallow a user from accessing a screen, whereas a fine-grained security can allow or disallow users seeing specific buttons and might hide/show a field or make a field read-only and conditionally control data-related operations. Think of APM as a user interface wrapper on top of Oracle Entitlement Server along with data security–related features. At a very high level APM has the components listed in the following sections.

Resource Types in APM

A *resource type* represents the type of a secured object. Protected application components that share common characteristics can be represented by a particular resource type. Examples of resource types are ADF Task Flow, Enterprise Scheduler Service, Web services, and so on. APM allows you to define the possible actions that can be performed on a resource type. For example, a Web service can have an action of invoke and a page can have an action of view, customize, or grant.

Resources in APM

A *resource* represents a specific, secured target in a protected application. Each resource belongs to a defined resource type. Think of resource definition as registering a Fusion Applications artifact that is to be protected for access. For example, when defining a resource you will enter the Web service name or the path of the ADF screen. A resource points to an actual physical deployed code that delivers a piece of functionality.

Entitlements in APM

After you register the resource in APM, next you define entitlements for that resource. These entitlements are also known as privileges in Fusion Applications. Here you can bundle a group of resources and specify the actions that are allowed on each such resource within the privilege. This bundling of resources along with the permissible actions allowed on them is called an entitlement. For example, a resource of type Web service can have an action named invoke. When that entitlement is granted to a user via a role, then that user will be allowed to perform the specified actions on the resource as defined in the entitlement definition.

Duty Roles in APM

Using APM, you can create duty roles. Oracle Fusion Applications comes with a long list of seeded duty roles. A duty role gives a representation of the features in the product that can be controlled for their access. For example, the Journal Entry role and Journal Posting role can be two separate duty roles. An organization may want a single individual to be disallowed from performing both the functions of entry and posting on the journal, even though both the actions can be performed from the same journal entry screen. To handle this scenario, the Oracle Fusion Applications product team would create one duty role for each of these activities. Duty roles are also referred to as application roles because these are specific to an application. For example, a duty role that allows creation of new employee records has to belong to the HCM (Human Capital Management) application and cannot belong to the Financials suite in Fusion Applications.

Authorization Policy in APM

Next you define an Authorization policy in APM. When defining the Authorization policy, you specify which duty roles can perform what actions on which set of resources. You do so by attaching one or more resources to a duty role within the Authorization Policy definition. There are two ways to attach a resource to a duty role. You can either attach a resource directly to the duty role or you can attach an entitlement to the duty role.

Oracle Platform Security Services

OPSS is the short name for Oracle Platform Security Services, and it is based on the industry best practices for securing enterprise applications. OPSS supports Java Authentication and Authorization Service (JAAS) and Role-Based Access Control (RBAC) features. You can think of OPSS as a decision engine that resides between the Oracle Fusion Applications code and the security repository that includes LDAP server and APM. Given that each request made by the application is sent via OPSS to the identity management, it is the central integration point between the application logic and the security layer. OPSS also has an auditing feature to log which user requested access to which resource and at what timestamp. From the developer's standpoint, think of OPSS as a set of Java APIs that Fusion Applications calls to authenticate and authorize the actions being performed in the application. OPSS provides security policies that are external to application-specific code, hence it facilitates altering the security behavior of the application without changing the application code. OPSS can also be considered as an engine that is capable of interpreting the authorization policies defined in APM. The benefit of this approach is that when you change the security behavior of your application via APM, then there is no change required to the source code of the application.

Role-Based Access Control (RBAC)

Role-Based Access Control (RBAC) restricts access to the system based on the role of the user within the organization. Of course the desired roles have to be granted to the user in the first place. RBAC in Fusion Applications defines "who can do what on which set of data." In Fusion Applications the security based on RBAC has been implemented using a common framework across all its applications.

The terminology behind various types of roles can be confusing. Therefore, for simplicity in this chapter we will classify the roles into two types, that is, external roles and application roles. These roles can have further subclassifications as explained in Table 4-1.

Both application roles and job roles categorize the users into different groups. The job roles are categorized as per the company's organization structure, whereas application roles are driven by the capabilities within the product. For example, if Fusion Applications did not have a feature for Journal Posting, then there would be no point in defining an application role named "Journal Posting Duty." Therefore, application roles also reflect the application features. Someone on the Oracle design team recognized the need for the Fusion Applications product to have a Journal Posting feature that can potentially be separated from the Journal Entry feature, and therefore created these as two different duty roles.

Role Hierarchy

Both the external roles and the application roles support nesting of hierarchies. The hierarchical concept of roles is diagrammed in Figure 4-2. As evident from the example in this figure, the policies applied to the roles at a higher level are automatically inherited by the roles at a lower level. In other words, the policies added to the child roles get applied in addition to the policies for the parent roles.

Role Type	Also Known As	Comments
Job roles	Enterprise roles	These roles get mapped to one or duty roles, because a person who takes a job in a company is meant to perform several duties. The name of this role has the suffix _JOB. Some examples are Account Payables Manager Job, General Ledger Accounting Manager Job, and so on.
Abstract roles	Enterprise roles	These roles are associated with a user regardless of the job they perform within an organization. Therefore abstract roles are at a higher level spanning various jobs, and hence their name, abstract. Examples are Employee role, Temporary Staff role, and so on. An organization might decide to autoprovision the Expense Entry Duty role to all the Employees, and likewise may decide to autoprovision the Timesheet Entry Duty role to all the contract workers.
External roles	Enterprise roles	Job roles and Abstract roles are also called external roles as these are defined in Oracle Identity Manager, which is external to APM.
Duty roles	Application roles	These are the granular duties performed by the jobs. Examples are GL Journal Entry Duty, GL Journal Approval Duty, GL Journal Posting Duty, and so on. The name of this role has the suffix _DUTY. The duty role provides access to screens, reports, and dashboards via privileges and provides access to data behind the screens using data security.
Data roles	External roles	You can think of these roles as data wrappers around the job and abstract roles. The wrapper contains a WHERE condition on the database resources that the job or abstract roles have access to via their underlying duty roles. The duty roles have access to resources and the resources can reference a database view or a table, with the WHERE condition applied to those database objects. The data roles inherit from the job roles or abstract roles. For example, a data role named General Accountant ANV Common UK will inherit permissions from a job role General Accountant. Users who have access to this data role can only access journals that belong to ledger set ANV Common UK. This becomes possible because an extra WHERE condition for restricting ledgers to ANV Common UK will be appended to the SQL queries when ledger data is accessed via the data role General Accountant ANV Common UK.

TABLE 4-1. *Types of Roles in Fusion Applications*

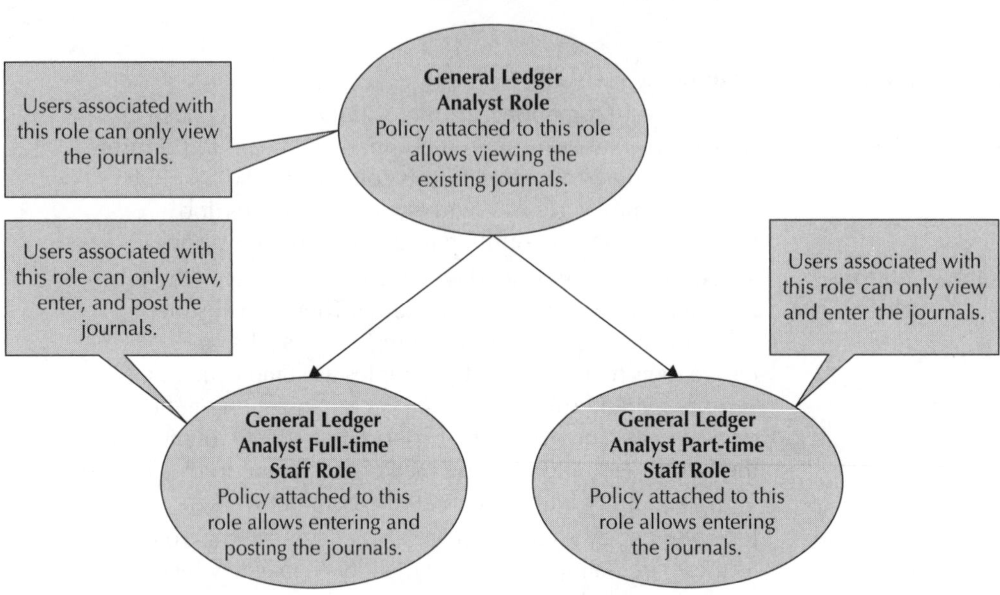

FIGURE 4-2. *Sample role hierarchy in Fusion Applications*

Authentication in Fusion Applications

In order to appreciate the authentication approach implemented in Fusion Applications, it is important to highlight how security works in traditional applications. In old-school enterprise software, the authentication process is local to the application itself, and in those systems it is not possible to integrate authentication with a central corporate authentication system. Local authentication means that the user logins and their passwords are stored within the application tables itself instead of being stored in a centralized corporate repository.

Companies these days use a variety of systems in their enterprise. Some of these systems are hosted within the company data center, whereas other systems could be hosted in the cloud. In order to keep the user experience seamless, it is advantageous to have the same username and password across various applications. Fusion Applications makes centralized authentication a possibility because it delivers an out-of-the-box integration with Oracle Internet Directory and Oracle Identity Management.

Technically, it is possible to use the Fusion Applications security platform for centralized corporate authentication. Alternatively, it is also possible to configure Fusion Applications to be authenticated from an existing centralized LDAP server such as Microsoft Active Directory, IBM Tivoli Directory Server, and so on.

Typically, Human Capital Management (HCM) systems are the starting point for registering new staff into the organization. Therefore you will find that creation of an Employee record in HCM usually triggers creation of new user records in Fusion Applications. In order to facilitate use cases where users have to be automatically created from an HCM record, Oracle Identity Management has a feature that allows organizations to define their username construction logic. For example, some organizations will create a username called TSMITH for Mr. Tom Smith, whereas in other organizations they might want to automatically create a username of SMITHT. If the users are automatically generated, then the password too can be automatically generated by the system. Again Oracle Identity Management allows implementers to write their own initial password creation logic.

Authorization in Fusion Applications

Permission to access a resource is called authorization. Authorization ensures that the user only has access to resources they have been granted access to. These grants are also known as privileges or entitlements. These grants are defined in APM. As you already know, APM is based on another Oracle Product named Oracle Entitlement Server (OES). In Fusion Applications, authorization check is a combination of function and data security. It must be noted that the data security feature is not a part of Oracle Entitlement Server. The Fusion Applications team added the data security feature to OES under the umbrella of APM.

Function security ensures that a user can access only those resources for which they have been granted permissions. The Data security controls access to the data. The authorization checks can either be enforced via APM or explicitly implemented by a developer declaratively or programmatically.

Function Security

Function security decides which user can perform which set of actions on which set of resources. A grant provides a role (or user) access for permission set (or individual resource). The permission set is a grouping of related permissions required to complete a task. For example, the resources to access a page and all related task flows may be grouped together into a permission set such that they can be granted together instead of granting each separately. This grouping of permissions is also known as entitlements.

The developer building the application has to secure the application in JDeveloper at design time using the menu option Application | Secure | Configure ADF Security. By doing so, all the resources within the application are protected by default. Once these pages are protected, the only way to access them at run time is to grant access to these components via RBAC. If the application contains a bounded task flow, then you protect the flow's entry point and then all pages within that ADF task flow are secured by the policy it defines. Also, top-level pages in an unbounded taskflow are secured by default.

The security policies (resources, permissions sets, grants, and application roles) are contained in the policy store, and security policies can be changed without any code change. These security policies can either be defined in an APM console that reads directly from the policy store, or they can be configured using JDeveloper in a file named jazn-data.xml. This file is created automatically when the application is secured. If the security policies are defined in jazn-data.xml, then those have to be loaded into the policy store by the developer or an administrator to enable further maintenance from APM.

Developers can also opt for explicit authorization checks by calling authorization APIs or declaratively.

An example of a programmatic check is shown here:

```
if(row.getSecurityHints().allowsOperation("ApproveJournal").hasPermission())
        // code for GL Journal approval
else
        // display error message
```

The declarative check can be performed via Groovy expressions as in the following examples:

```
#{bindings.<attrName>.hints.allows.<privilegeName>}
#{bindings.PersonId.hints.allows.UpdateEmployeeSalary}
```

There are many variants in which the Groovy expressions can be applied declaratively to the user interface objects. For the complete list, see the chapter "Implementing Oracle Fusion Data Security" in *Oracle Fusion Applications Developer's Guide*.

Authenticated and Anonymous Users

Some applications have a requirement that a portion of the application should remain accessible even for the users who have not logged in. For example, in a recruitment application for external candidates, the applicants should be able to register themselves to apply for the jobs. Similarly, a business may decide to expose the supplier registration form on the Web, thus allowing the vendors to submit requests to register themselves for selling certain services. In these cases, the users accessing the application may not be authenticated. In JDeveloper, to secure an ADF application, the developer can run the Configure ADF Security Wizard by using the menu option Application | Secure | Configure ADF Security. By running this wizard, the entire application becomes secure except for the data model layer. In other words, running the Configure ADF Security Wizard for an application in JDeveloper sets the flag for OPSS to be activated for that application. The name of this flag is AuthorizationEnforce in the adf-config.xml. Once the OPSS has been activated, the only way to make the user interface accessible without logging in is to grant permissions to a special role called anonymous-role. This makes it possible to write policies for the users who haven't logged in to the application yet. After the user logs in to the application, the anonymous-role remains and the authenticated-role gets attached to the user. This makes it possible to write policies for all authenticated users that have successfully logged in to the application. Additional roles that are applicable to the user get applied in addition to the anonymous- and authenticated-role.

Data Security

Data security defines "who can do what action on which set of data." From this definition, "which set of data" can be enforced by appending a WHERE clause. As for the action, you may not want certain roles to be able to modify the invoices. Another example of an action is to control whether users should not be allowed to delete approved invoices.

In order to secure an entity object, it is important at design time to select the permissible actions on that entity object. Thereafter, the table backing this entity object has to be registered in APM as a database resource. By doing so, an entry gets created in FND_OBJECTS. Once that database object has been registered, it then becomes possible to define WHERE clauses and different actions permissible on that database object. The permissions on those actions on the database objects can then be granted to the application roles. Typically there are two types of actions that can be performed. The first set of actions consists of select, update, and delete. Other actions are the custom actions that can be added at design time in Fusion Applications, with the WHERE clauses controlled at run time via the policies defined in APM.

Use Cases and Reference Implementation

In this section you will find some examples of how Fusion Applications leverages its security platform. Exactly the same concepts are applicable to any custom extension that you develop in your implementation project.

Creating a Super User in Fusion Applications

The purpose of this exercise is to demonstrate the basic steps required for setting up a super user. This super user login can be used during your implementation phase so that you can create one single user to perform most implementation-related activities. A user with these roles should be disabled after the implementation project is complete.

In order to explain the concept of hierarchies of roles, you will be creating two custom roles. The first role will be the XX FA Admin role, which will have security administrator–related access. The second role will be the XX FA Implementor role, which will inherit from the XX FA Admin role and will additionally inherit other seeded implementation-related roles. Next, the XX FA Implementor role will be attached to a user named XX_FA_IMPLEMENTOR. The end result will be that this user will have both the Admin-related and Implementation-related roles.

Log in to Oracle Identity Manager, which will have a URL similar to http://host:port/oim. After installation your DBA should have a login for OIM administrator named xelsysadm. This user is the default administrator for Oracle IDM in Fusion Applications. After logging in, you will see a screen that allows you to manage your own profile and tasks for the xelsysadm user. Click Administration in the top-right corner of the page so that you can define or amend the roles and users as per your business needs. In the Administration section, click Create Role.

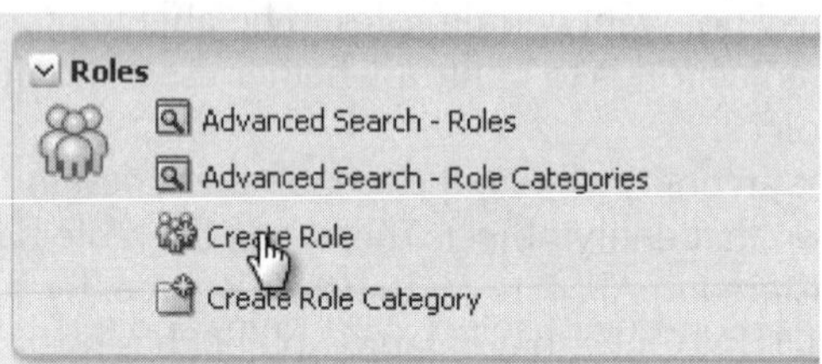

Create a new role named XX_FA_ADMIN by entering the values as shown here, and click Apply.

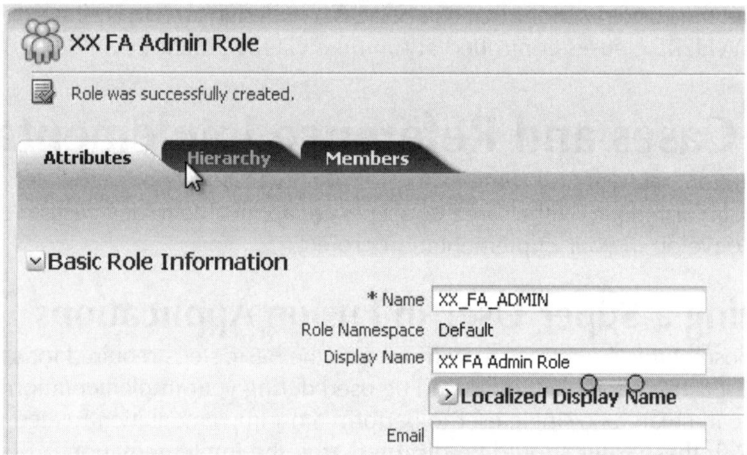

After the role has been created, the next step is to inherit existing roles. This can be done by clicking the Hierarchy tab. Next click the subtab titled Inherits From and then click Add as shown in the following illustration. Effectively here we are saying that this role will inherit the permissions that already exist for a seeded set of roles. These seeded roles are also known as the roles present in the reference implementation that is delivered out of the box with every install of Fusion Applications.

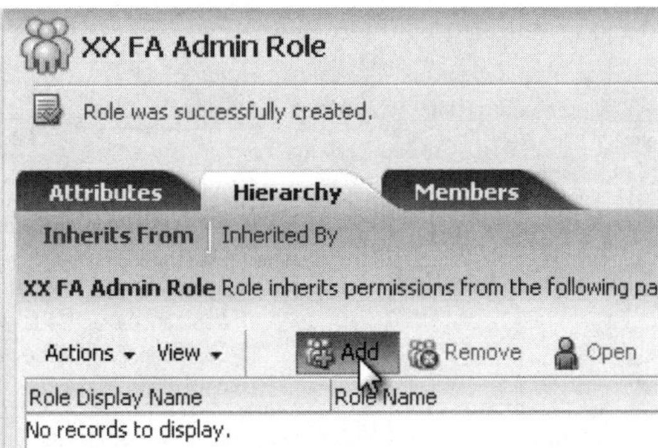

In the Search Roles drop-down, select OIM Roles and click the right arrow above the label Roles to Add as shown here. You will find all the OIM roles listed that are available to be inherited by the new role being created.

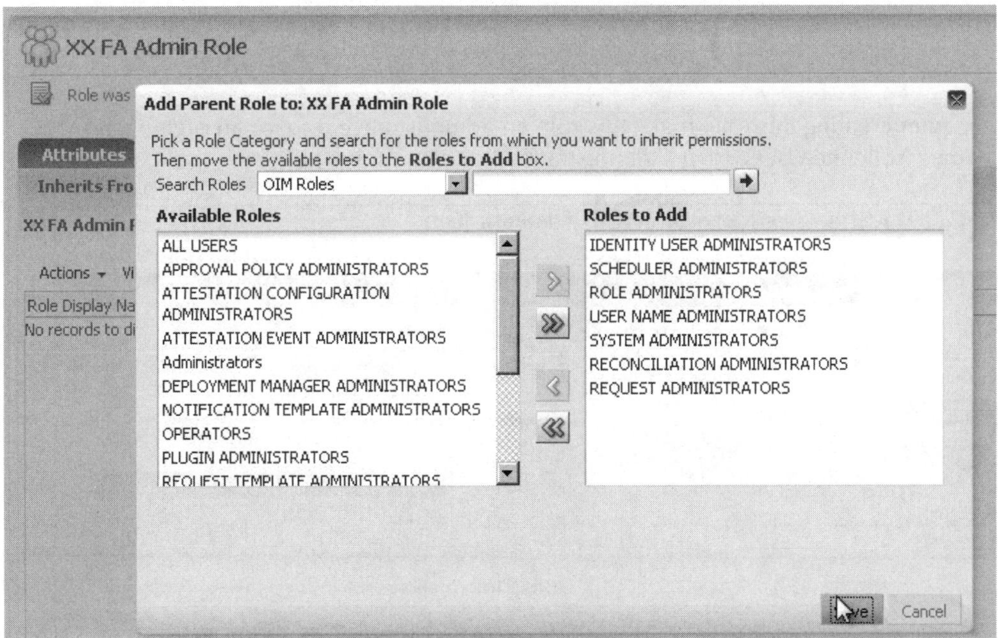

Repeat the steps performed for OIM Roles, so as to bring all the available roles from Common - Abstract Roles, Common - Job Roles as shown in the following illustration.

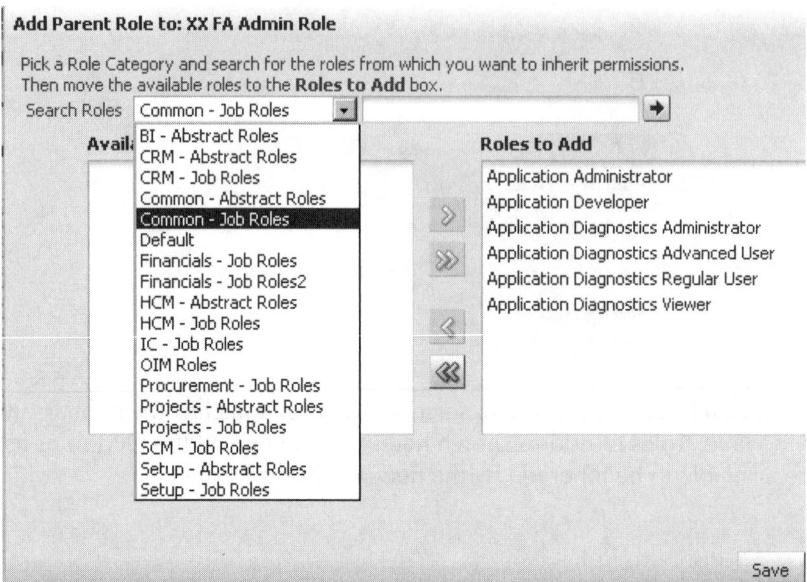

After creating this role, make this role an administrative role for an organization named Xellerate Users. Click Administrative Roles as shown here.

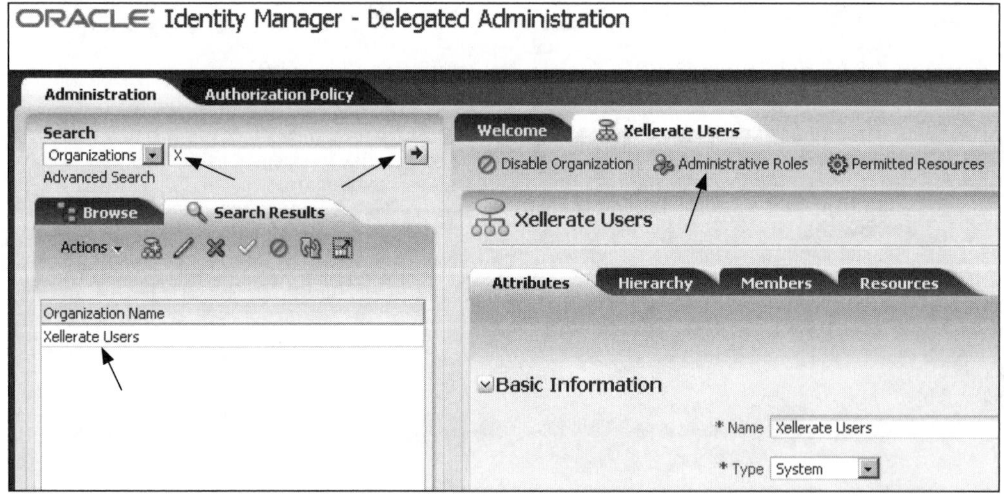

Assign the Write, Delete, and Assign privileges on the Xellerate Users organization to the XX_FA_ADMIN role.

Organization Detail >> Administrative Roles >> **Assign**

You can assign the following roles as administrators to this organization:

Organization Name: Xellerate Users

Filter By Role Name [ ] Find

Results 141-150 of 166 First | Previous | Next | Last

Role Name	Read	Write	Delete	Assign
cn=FusionGroups,cn=Groups,dc=paramlabs,dc=com.ASM_FUNCTIONAL_SETUPS_USER_ABSTRACT	☑	☐	☐	☐
cn=FusionGroups,cn=Groups,dc=paramlabs,dc=com.FBI_TRANSACTIONAL_BUSINESS_INTELLIGENCE_WORKER	☑	☐	☐	☐
cn=FusionGroups,cn=Groups,dc=paramlabs,dc=com.OBIA_BUSINESS_INTELLIGENCE_APPLICATIONS_WORKER	☑	☐	☐	☐
cn=FusionGroups,cn=Groups,dc=paramlabs,dc=com.AttachmentsAdmin	☑	☐	☐	☐
cn=FusionGroups,cn=Groups,dc=paramlabs,dc=com.AttachmentsUser	☑	☐	☐	☐
Monitors	☑	☐	☐	☐
Operators	☑	☐	☐	☐
XX_FA_ADMIN	☑	☑	☑	☑
OrclPolicyAndCredentialWritePrivilegeGroup	☑	☐	☐	☐
OrclPolicyAndCredentialReadPrivilegeGroup	☑	☐	☐	☐

Assign

First | Previous | Next | Last

Cancel

Next we create a custom Admin user. Give this user a desired password in the password field.

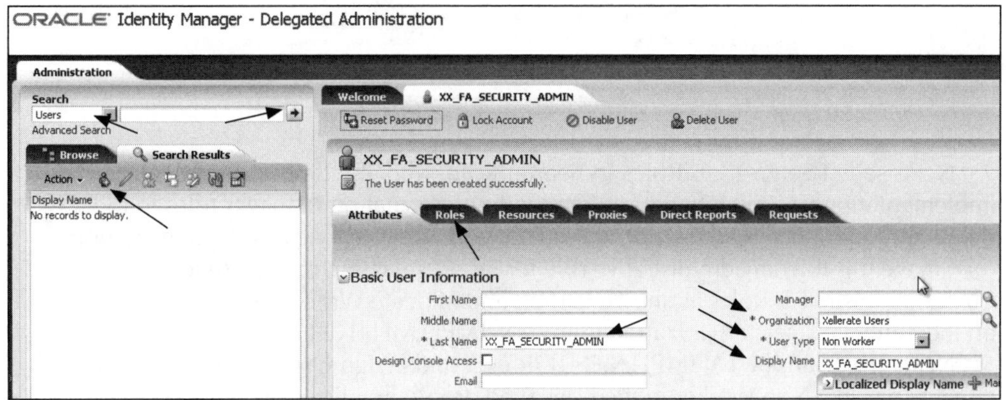

After creating the user, click the Roles tab, and attach the custom role XX_FA_ADMIN created in prior steps to this user.

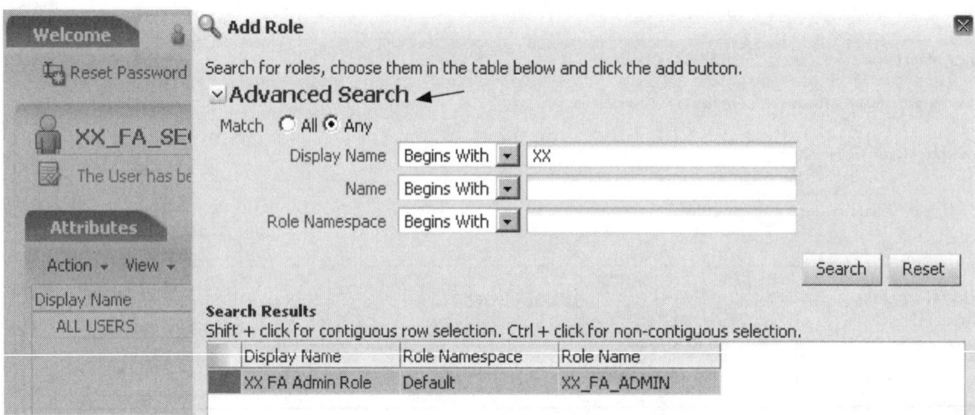

Now that you have created an Administrative user, you will be able to log in as this user. However, we need to create another role so that we can have a super user that has not only the administrative but also the implementation access. Click Create Role in OIM and create a role named XX_IMPLEMENTOR having a display name of XX Implementor. Click the Hierarchy tab, select Inherits From, and then click Add. Select Default in the Search Roles field and click the right arrow as shown here.

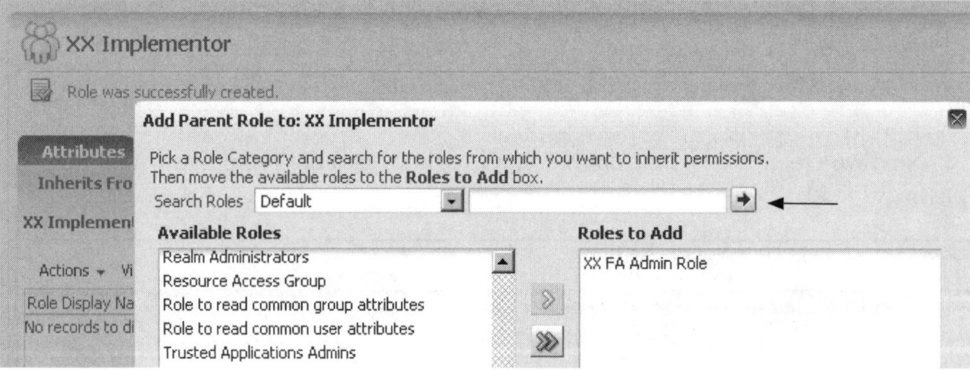

Next, select Setup - Job Roles in Search Roles and shuttle both Application Implementation Consultant and Application Implementation Manager roles to the right-hand side. Click Save to apply these changes. After creating this implementation role, make this role an administrative role for an organization named Xellerate Users. Click Administrative Roles as shown earlier, and allocate Write, Delete, and Assign on the Xellerate Users organization to the XX_IMPLEMENTOR role.

Next, create an XX_FA_IMPLEMENTOR user and assign Organization Xellerate Users and select Non Worker in the User Type drop-down list. Click the Roles tab for this user and assign the XX Implementor role to this user. Further, you can assign various other roles to this user. During implementation it is convenient to have a super user role that has access to all the areas within the application. Therefore you can add all the remaining roles to this user as well, as shown in Figure 4-3. In order to do so, select the first role, scroll down to the bottom, and then SHIFT-click the last role in the list. This will select all the roles, and now you can deselect the XX FA Admin role, as it has already been added by clicking CONTROL-click. It must be noted that the Oracle Fusion Applications security framework will create a distinct union of all the roles available to the user. When the user logs in, an entry is created in the

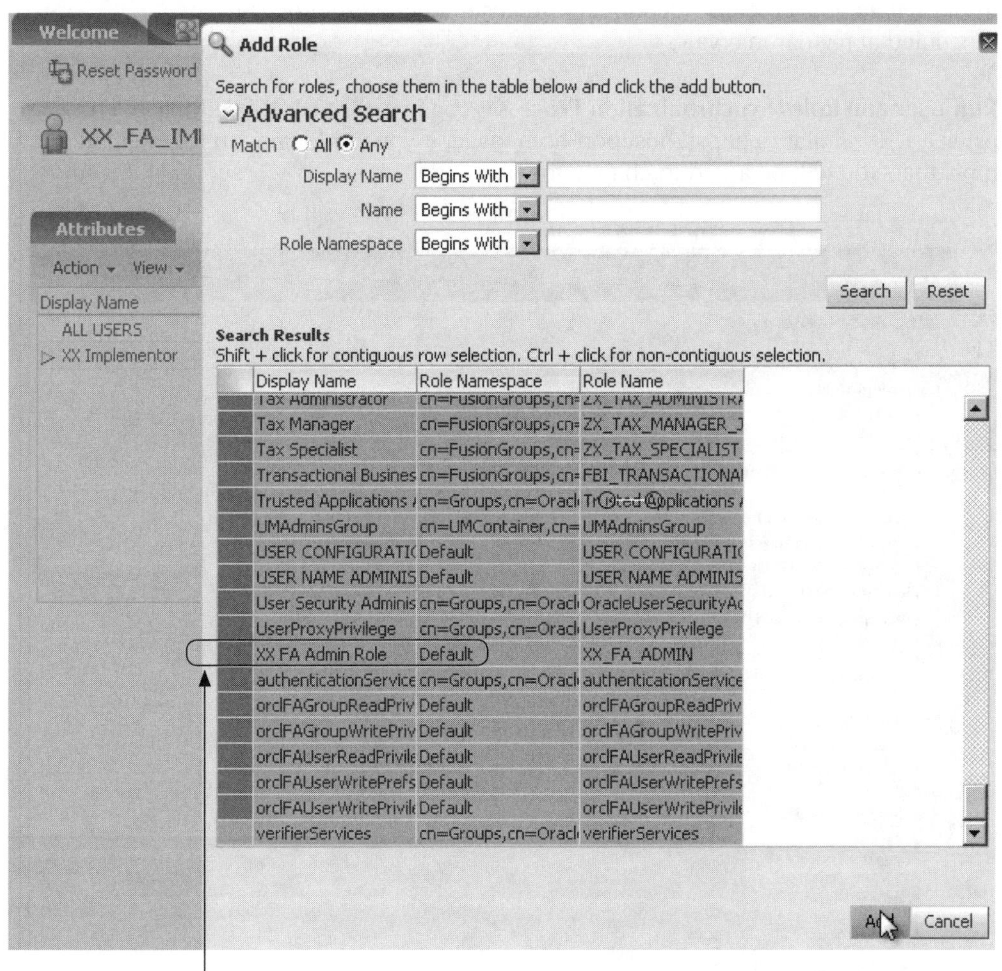

CONTROL-click to exclude this role as it has already been inherited by adding XX Implementor role.

FIGURE 4-3. *Assign all other roles to the XX_FA_IMPLEMENTOR user.*

fnd_session_roles table for each unique role applicable to user session. At run time, you can use the FND_SESSIONS and FND_SESSION_ROLES tables to interrogate roles that have been applied to a user.

Running the Synchronization Processes

As a standard practice, you should have two processes scheduled. These are Run User and Roles Synchronization Process and IDM Reconciliation Process. You do not need to run these processes if you have simply created a user and allocated existing roles to them. However, if you are creating new roles and making changes in APM, then it is recommended for you to ensure that these processes are scheduled at regular intervals.

Run User and Roles Synchronization Process Log in as XX_FA_IMPLEMENTOR using a URL similar to https://host:port/homepage. If you are logging in for the first time, then you will be asked to change the password.

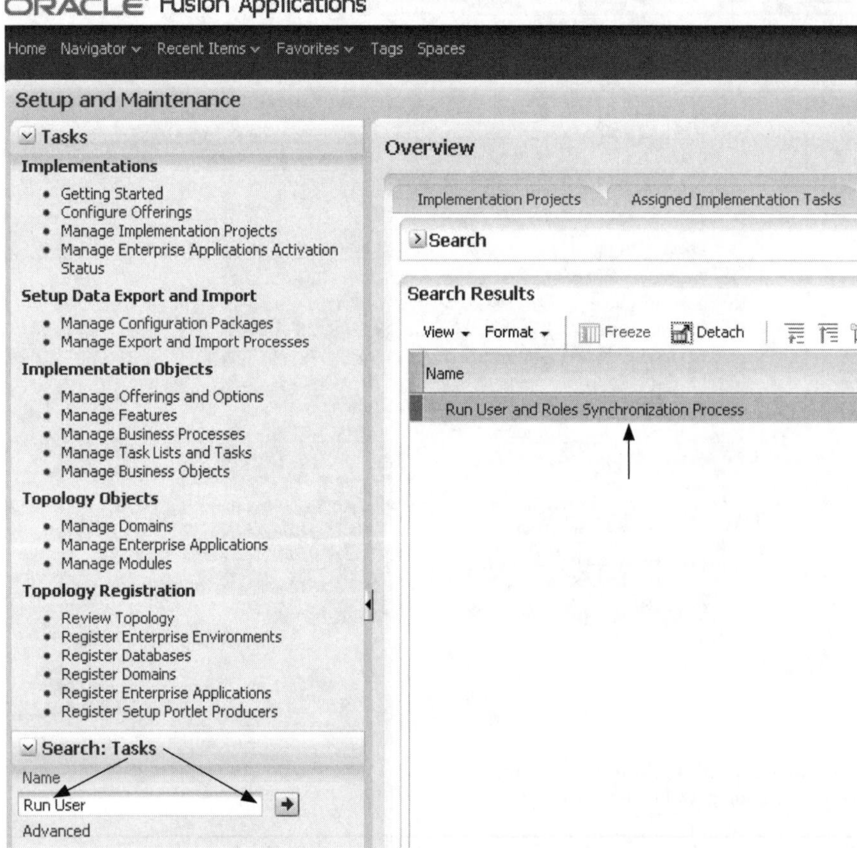

After logging in, search on Run User and Roles Synchronization Process as shown in the preceding illustration and click on Go to Task. This program takes no parameters. Click Submit.

Running LDAP Role Create and Update Reconciliation

In order to run LDAP Role Create and Update Reconciliation, first navigate to Oracle Identity Manager and log in as xelsysadm user. Click the Administration link and then click Advanced. Navigate to the System Management tab and search using wild card ***Recon*** as shown in Figure 4-4. Click Run Now, or alternatively, create a periodic schedule.

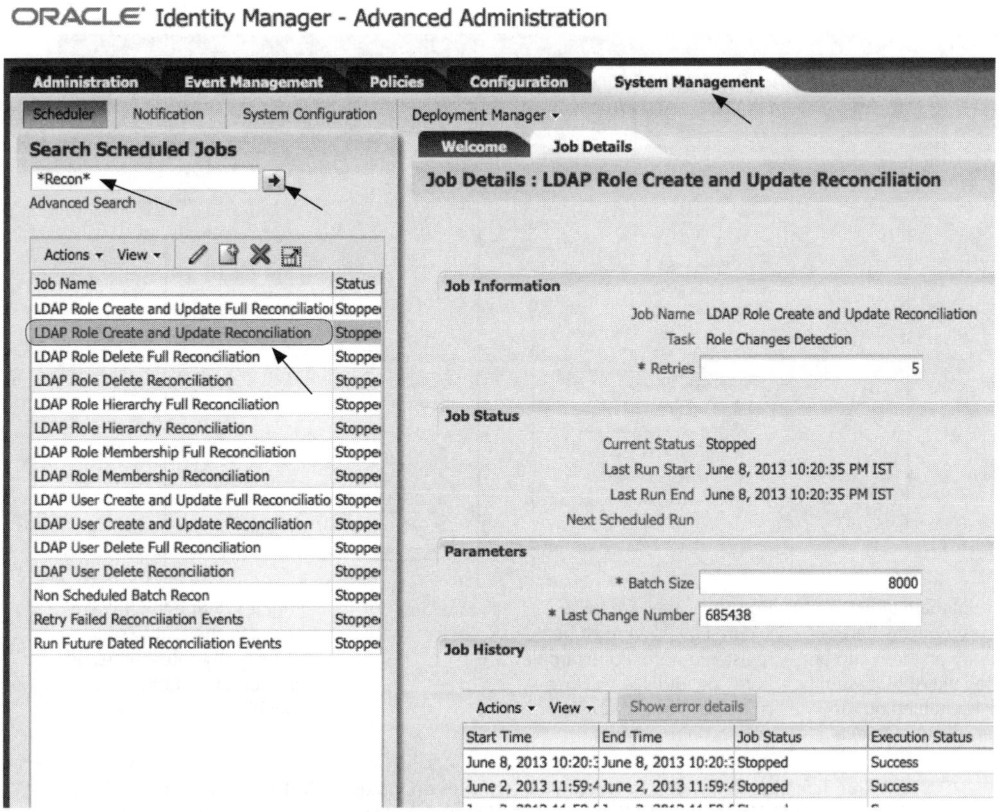

FIGURE 4-4. *LDAP Role Reconciliation program*

APM Components

APM has a URL similar to https://host:port/apm. Figure 4-5 shows the key components of APM. As mentioned previously, the APM product is based on Oracle Entitlement Server. However, the Fusion Applications team added a data security feature to OES. As shown in Figure 4-5, you can search for artifacts defined in APM by searching in

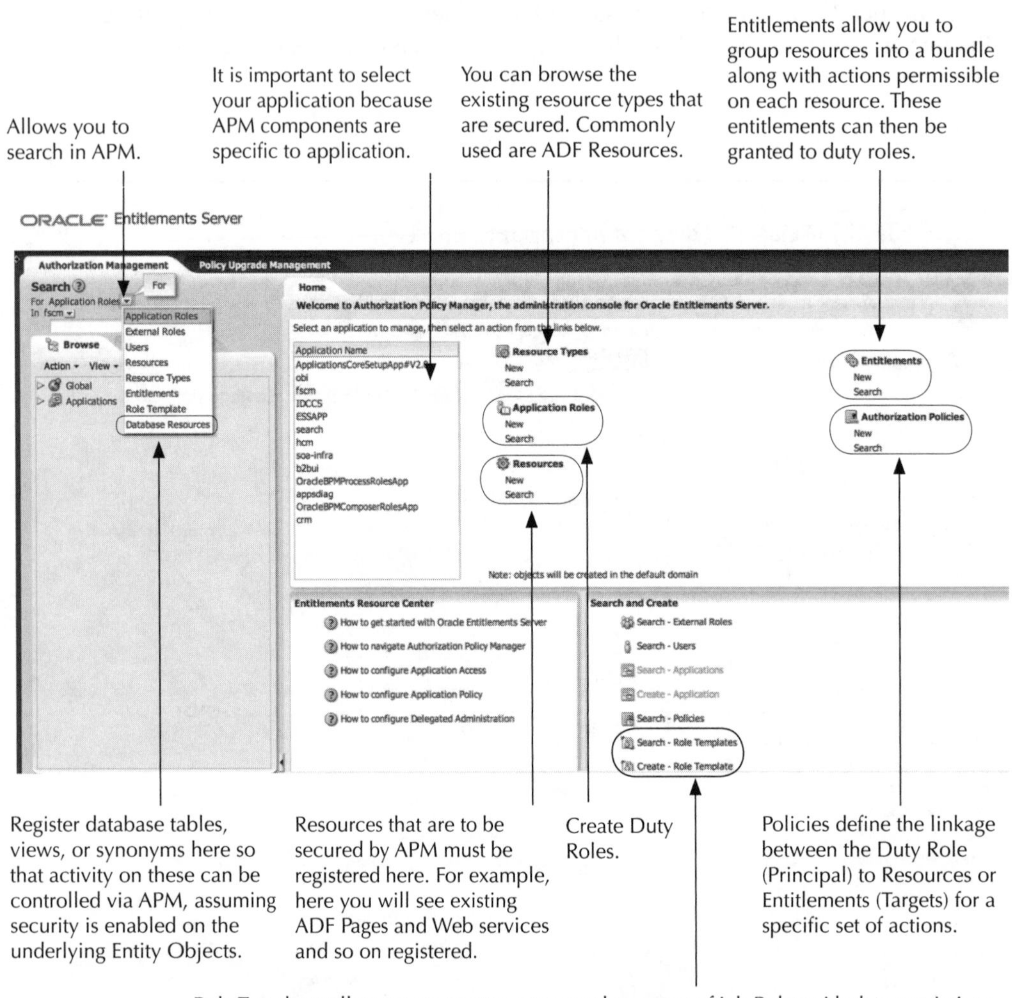

Allows you to search in APM.
It is important to select your application because APM components are specific to application.
You can browse the existing resource types that are secured. Commonly used are ADF Resources.
Entitlements allow you to group resources into a bundle along with actions permissible on each resource. These entitlements can then be granted to duty roles.
ORACLE Entitlements Server
Register database tables, views, or synonyms here so that activity on these can be controlled via APM, assuming security is enabled on the underlying Entity Objects.
Resources that are to be secured by APM must be registered here. For example, here you will see existing ADF Pages and Web services and so on registered.
Create Duty Roles.
Policies define the linkage between the Duty Role (Principal) to Resources or Entitlements (Targets) for a specific set of actions.
Role Templates allow you to create wrapper roles on top of Job Roles with data restrictions. For example, the Payables Manager USA and Payables Manager UK roles can be generated for the Payables Manager Job Role whenever a UK or USA business unit is created.

FIGURE 4-5. *APM home page that allows you to secure artifacts in Fusion Applications*

the left-hand pane. When searching for components in the left-hand pane, it is important that you first select the application. Application fscm contains the Financials and Supply Chain Management artifacts. This includes component offerings such as Fusion Accounting Hub, Fusion Payables, Fusion Payables, and so on. HCM is the Human Capital Management application and CRM is the Customer Relationship Management application.

Securing Your Custom User Interfaces in Fusion Applications

The approach taken for securing your custom user interface pages should be no different than the techniques applied by the Oracle Fusion Applications product development team. Let us take the example of a journal posting function in Fusion Accounting Hub. First, the developer building the application has to secure the application in JDeveloper at design time using the menu option Application | Secure | Configure ADF Security.

Next, jazn-data.xml can be amended to define the policies for securing the ADF artifacts.

As shown in Figure 4-6, jazn-data.xml can be used by the developer to easily edit and configure the role security for the ADF artifacts. In that figure you can see that the posting screen along with other journal posting–related artifacts are a part of an entitlement named GL_POST_JOURNAL_PRIV, and that privilege has been granted to two application roles, which are GL_JOURNAL_POSTING_DUTY and GL_JOURNAL_POSTING_PROGRAM_DUTY. You can also click the Application Roles tab to create new application roles and see the entitlements that have been added to this role. These application roles get mapped to the job roles, and the job roles are allocated to the users, thus allowing the users access to perform certain functions on the Fusion Applications components. The developer then deploys the jazn-data.xml to the policy store. Figure 4-7 shows the equivalent policy in APM after those have been deployed to the policy store.

Exploring the APM Contents on the Public Web Site

Security Reference Implementation is the definition of authorization roles and policies that get delivered out of the box by Oracle Fusion Applications. Besides the APM, you can also browse the contents of reference implementation in https://fusionappsoer.oracle.com/oer/index.jsp. When you navigate to that URL, you will be asked to log in to your Oracle account first, and then you can select the guest option. In the Search Criteria Type, select Role, and in the Logical Business Area field, select All Fusion Apps: Logical Business Area. Click the Search button and then select Fusion Accounting Hub or any other desired offering you wish to explore. Under the Documentation Tab, open up Security Reference Manual.

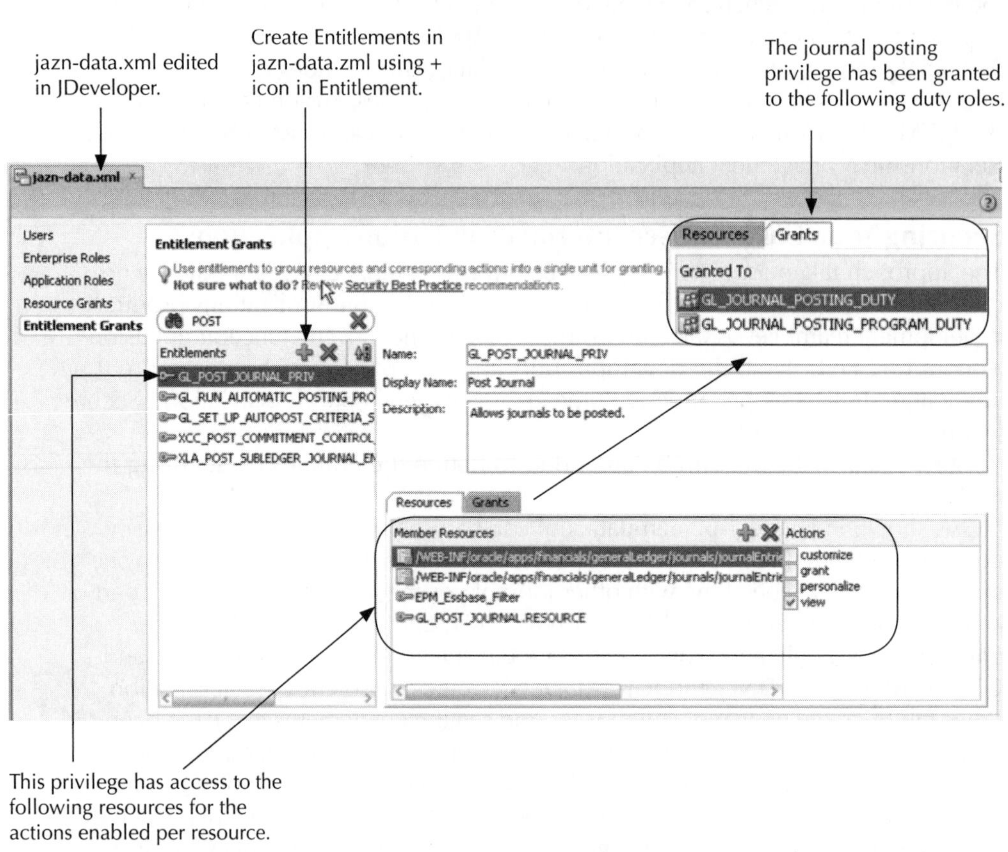

FIGURE 4-6. *Editing jazn-data.xml to grant security to roles in JDeveloper*

How Does Oracle Secure Database Resources in Fusion Applications?

The data security policy is to secure the data in Fusion Applications. For example, if you are given access to the Invoice Inquiry screen in Fusion Payables Manager, then you will not be able to see the data in that screen unless you have been granted access to the relevant business unit via data security. Similarly, if you are given

After jazn-data.xml has been deployed to the policy store, you can view and amend them from APM.

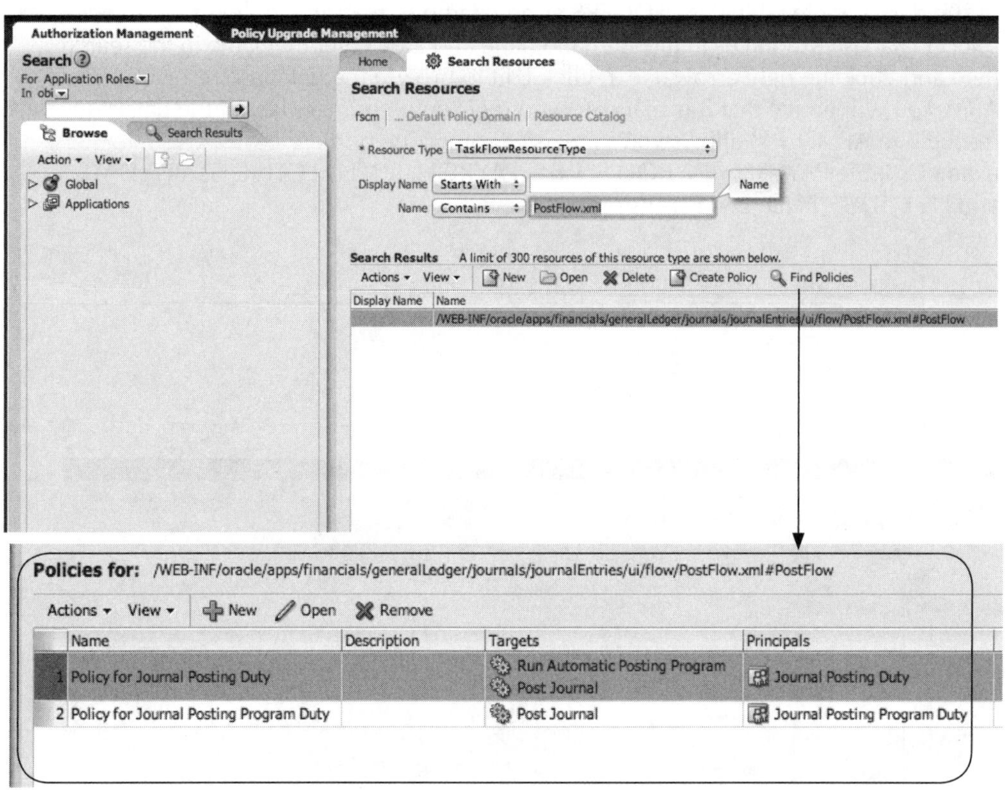

FIGURE 4-7. *Policy in APM after the jazn-data.xml has been deployed to the policy store*

access to the General Ledger Accounting Manager job role, you will still not be able to view or enter any journals or balances unless you have access to the ledger via the data security policy. In other words, with the job roles you may be able to see the screens but not operate on the data. This is so, because the function security is different than the data security. The data security is implemented in Fusion Applications by something called data roles, which are nothing but the wrappers around the job roles.

Oracle Fusion Applications delivers some out-of-the-box role templates that help in generating the data roles. In order to understand the data roles and templates, it is first important to understand how security is implemented on the database resources. At the very end of the chain, a database table contains the data that needs to be secured. This database table might have some database views as wrappers around it, or will be available as synonyms. Regardless, if this database object needs to be secured, then it must be registered in APM. Figure 4-8 shows the registration of standard Oracle table GL_LEDGERS as an example. To search on existing objects, select Database Resources in the left-hand pane and then enter the name in the search field and click the right arrow. Next, click Edit to browse the database resource in APM. You will notice that it is mandatory to register the primary key of the database resource in APM. APM allows you to register composite primary keys as well; for example, table PAY_ALL_PAYROLLS_F has PAYROLL_ID, EFFECTIVE_START_DATE, and EFFECTIVE_END_DATE as its primary keys.

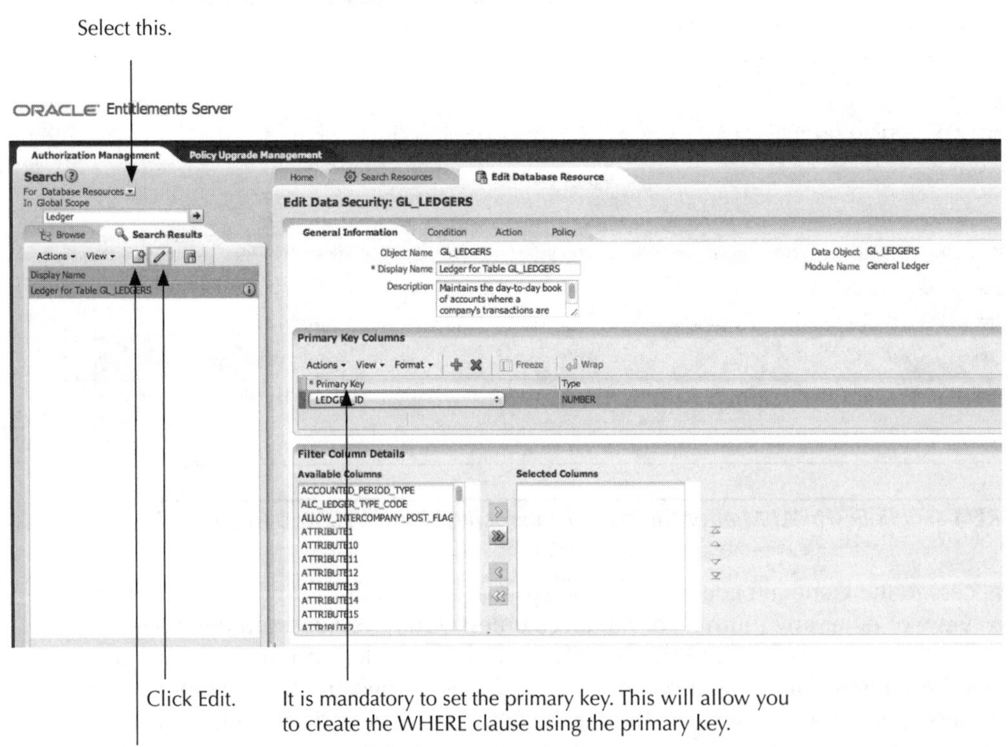

FIGURE 4-8. *Registered database resource in APM*

To create a set of WHERE clauses, you can click the Condition tab as shown in Figure 4-9. It must be noted that adding conditions here is of no relevance unless those conditions are applied to the database resource. Conditions that are defined are responsible for returning a set of rows at run time and these conditions are known as *instance sets*. You do not need to define a condition if you wish to return just a single row as per the primary key or if you wish to return all the rows. As noted from the conditions defined on GL_LEDGERS, &GRANT_ALIA.PARAMETER1..*n* are the parameters that are used by the SQL predicate, and values for these parameters can be assigned at run time. Conditions can also be defined as filters that get stored as XML expressions in the APM and are applied to the returned records at run time.

After defining the condition, you can define actions. Actions applicable on the entity objects are insert, update, and delete. However, you can define further actions on the database resource. Those additional actions must have a corresponding design-time implementation to make them effective. The Policy tab on the database

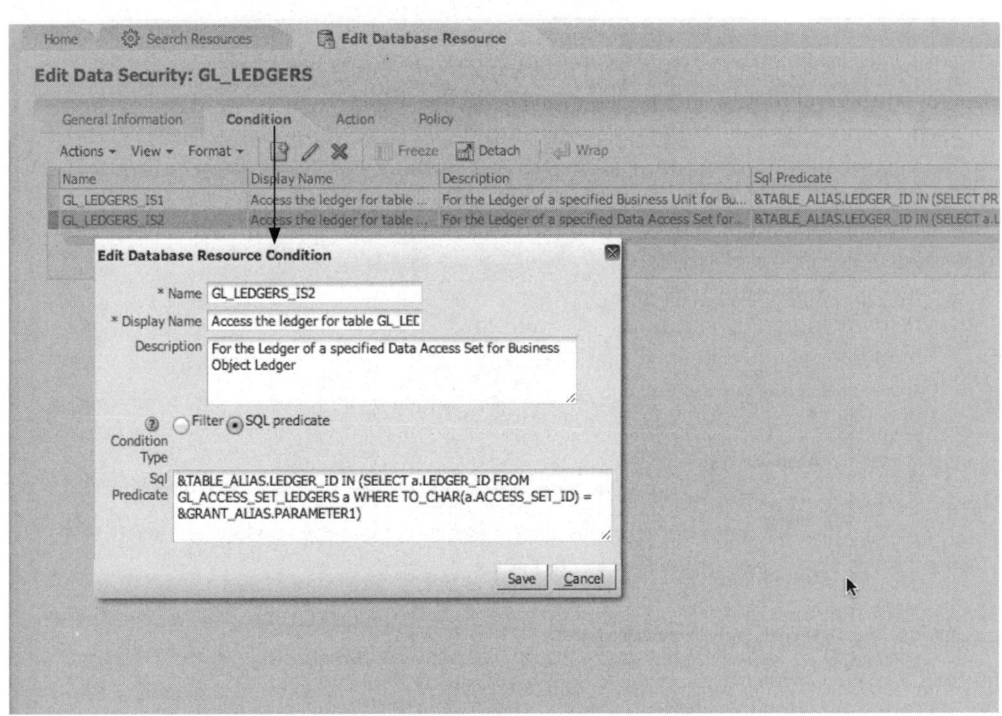

FIGURE 4-9. *The conditions can be defined as SQL predicates.*

resource is where job, action, and condition are stitched together for data security, as shown later in Figure 4-12. On the Policy tab, you specify that a job such as Payables Manager USA Operations will have permissions to update the table AP_INVOICES_ALL for the invoice records belonging to USA Operations, where USA Operations is a business unit.

The database resource name registered in APM must match the database object name backing the entity object. This can be seen by opening the relevant entity object in JDeveloper. For multilanguage-based entity objects, there is more than one table involved, in which case the database object name to be secured is decided as per the value in the entity object property named fnd:OA_BASE_TABLE. Alternately for non-multilanguage–based entity objects, you can use the custom property OA_DS_BASE_TABLE on the entity object to override the database resource name to be secured for that entity object. In order for the security policies defined on the database resources to become effective, their corresponding entity object must be secured as shown in Figure 4-10. This means that when you define actions in APM Security on

The data security policies defined in APM on the database resource will take effect only when their corresponding Entity object's actions have been secured by enabling the relevant check boxes in the security section.

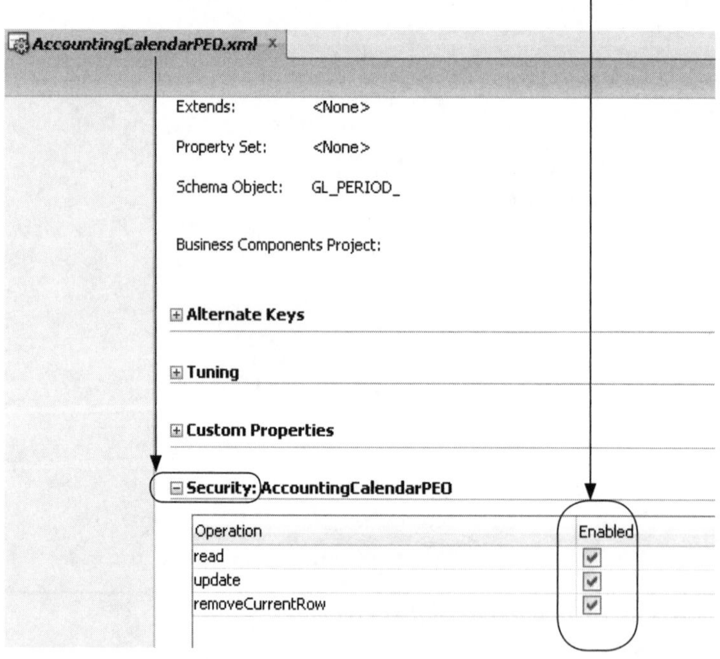

FIGURE 4-10. *Securing the actions in an Entity object*

a database resource, those actions should be named as read, update, or delete to correspond to the entity object security operations. It must be noted that the APM security takes effect only when Entity Object actions have been secured at design time in JDeveloper. Until the entity object has been secured, the security defined in APM for the database objects will not take any effect on the Fusion Applications. Therefore, one of the initial steps to secure data is to secure the entity object as shown in Figure 4-10.

Besides the standard actions, that is, read, update, and delete, it is also possible to define custom actions on a database resource. Figure 4-11 shows how the Oracle product team has defined the custom actions on a GL_LEDGERS. These custom actions are a design-time decision but their corresponding WHERE clause is decided in APM and applied at run time. In ADF it is possible to define something known as View Criteria against the view objects. The view objects are based on the entity objects. If the entity object has been secured, then its corresponding view object also gets secured. If you want the WHERE clause for a view object to be prepared at run time for a certain action, then the view object can be given a dummy view criteria name with a format as shown here:

FNDDS__<ACTION NAME>__<OBJECT NAME>__<OBJECT ALIAS>

The ACTION_NAME must be an exact match for the text APM action on that object as shown in Figure 4-11. For example, if you open the view object for this resource, you will find a dummy view criteria named FNDDS__GL_LEDGERS__GL_VIEW_ACCOUNTING_PERIOD_STATUS_DATA. At run time, if the view criteria name begins with FNDDS__, then Oracle will split the view criteria name by double underscores to identify the object name and the action name to fetch the

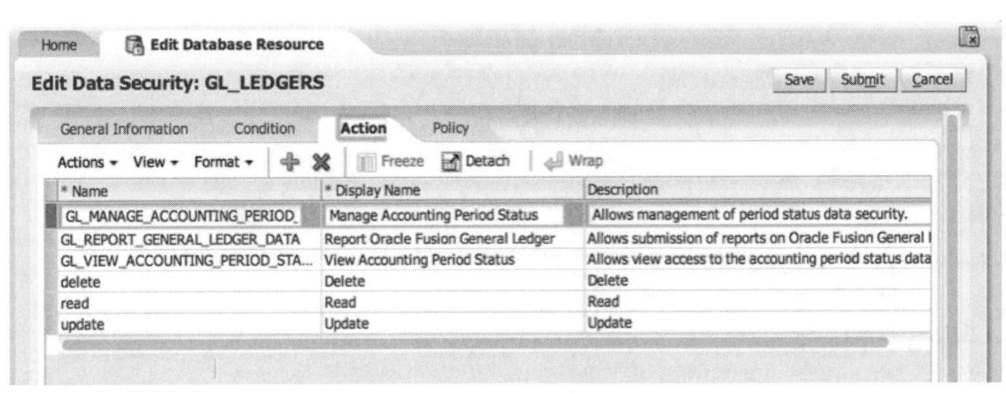

FIGURE 4-11. *Custom actions on a database resource*

applicable WHERE clause for that action. For this reason, the view criteria in JDeveloper is a dummy view criteria because the actual implementation of the WHERE clause is performed at run time via APM security. If you change the SQL predicate in the condition in APM, then you can alter the security behavior of actions on a database object without making changes to the underlying source code of Fusion Applications. As a good practice, you should define a new condition and attach it to an action in the database resource policy rather than modifying the existing condition itself.

On the Policy tab, Role, Actions, and Condition are joined together to define the data security for the database resource, as shown in Figure 4-12.

The reason the Oracle Product team introduced custom actions was to give granular control of the nature of operations that can be performed on data. For example, it may not be sufficient to grant a delete operation on invoices for a business unit. The implementation team might want to restrict deletion only for the nonapproved invoices, or the deletion should be allowed for invoices that cost less than xyz amount. In order to achieve this, the implementation team can define new conditions as SQL predicates and attach those conditions to the database resource for the desired custom action. Of course you will be reliant on the Oracle product team to have implemented that custom action at design time in the ADF application. Therefore even though APM will allow you to define new actions on the database resource, they will have no impact on the application because there is a dependency on the design-time implementation of those actions.

The OBJECT_ALIAS in the FNDDS view criteria name is optional and represents the alias used in the view object for the table name to which the SQL predicate is being applied. The value in OBJECT_ALIAS, if present, is used as a value for &TABLE_ALIAS shown previously in Figure 4-9.

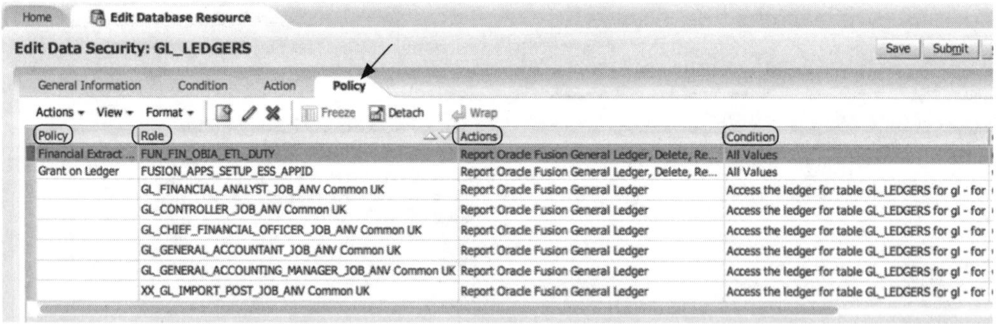

FIGURE 4-12. *Policies defined on the database resource*

Role Templates

During the implementation project, when it comes to granting roles to the users, you will be granting job roles that are specific to certain data sets. For example, in Fusion Payables you will have roles similar to Account Payables Manager US Operations, Account Payables Manager UK Operations, and for Fusion Accounting Hub for a company named ANV, you may allocate roles such as General Accounting Manager ANV Common UK, and so on.

When building the product, the Oracle Fusion product development team took some basic data granularity decisions at design time. This data granularity has been achieved by something called dimension. In Fusion Accounting Hub, one or more ledgers can belong to a GL access set. The product team made a decision to provide data security for GL-related job roles at the GL Access Set levels. Similarly, Fusion Payables provides security at the Business Unit level. In the case of Fusion Accounting Hub, the GL Access Set can be a dimension, whereas in Fusion Payables the Business Unit can be a dimension. It must be noted that there are also other security layers that have been implemented in those products. During large implementations, there will be many possible values for the dimensions such as Ledgers or Business Units. It can become quite a laborious process for the implementation team to define job roles manually for each such dimension value. To ease this process, Oracle Fusion Applications allows automatic generation of data roles that are wrappers around the job roles. This is achieved by means of a role template.

Figure 4-13 shows some of the role templates that exist out of the box in the product. APM allows you to define your own role templates as well, which is useful when you are developing custom modules and wish to leverage the security model framework delivered by Fusion Applications.

These role templates come predefined with some components. These components can be extended, or new role templates can be created in APM by the project implementation team to secure the data in custom applications that you are developing.

At design time, each Fusion Applications team decides the applicable dimensions for a set of job roles. For example, the Fusion Accounting Hub team decided that accountant's access to journals should be controlled by GL Access Sets, which in turn is based on GL Ledgers. In the example to follow, let us assume that there is a need to generate a data role for a job named XX_GL_IMPORT_POST_JOB that allows access to journal posting functions for a GL Access set named ANV Common UK for a company called ANV, as shown in Figure 4-14.

In order to generate the desired data roles, the role template delivered by Oracle has the following components as listed in Table 4-2.

Home | Search Role Templates | General Ledger Templat

Global | Role Templates

Search - Role Templates

Search

Name: Starts with

Display Name: Starts with

Group Id: Starts with

Search | Reset | Save...

Search Results

Actions ▾ View ▾ | New | Open

Display Name	Name
Financials Common Module Template for InterCOOrg	FinancialsFunInterCoOrg
Financials Common Module Template for SetID	FinancialsFunSetId
General Ledger Template for Ledger	FinancialsGlLedger
Global Human Resources Template for SetID	HcmPerSetId
Global Payroll Template for Business Unit Security	HcmPayBusinessUnit
Global Payroll Template for Payroll Security	HcmPayPayroll
HCM Common Architecture Template for SetID	HcmHrcSetId

FIGURE 4-13. *Role templates*

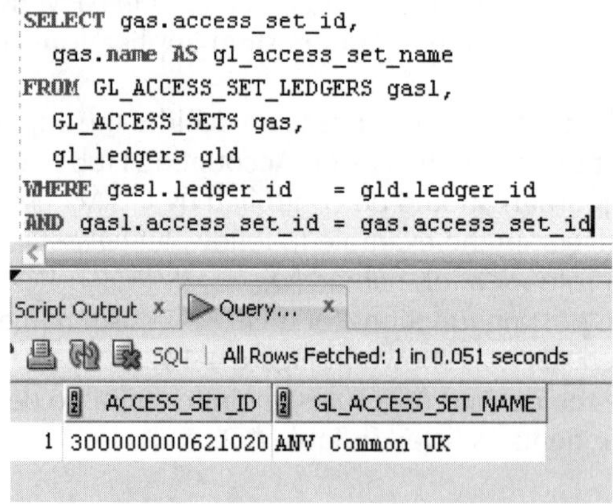
SELECT gas.access_set_id,
gas.name AS gl_access_set_name
FROM GL_ACCESS_SET_LEDGERS gasl,
GL_ACCESS_SETS gas,
gl_ledgers gld
WHERE gasl.ledger_id = gld.ledger_id
AND gasl.access_set_id = gas.access_set_id
Script Output
Query...
SQL
All Rows Fetched: 1 in 0.051 seconds
ACCESS_SET_ID
GL_ACCESS_SET_NAME
1
300000000621020
ANV Common UK

FIGURE 4-14. *GL Access set for which a job role is to be generated*

Role Template Component	Purpose
External Roles	Add here the job roles for which the data roles must be generated. The list of job roles secured for ledgers via Data Access Sets is shown in Figure 4-15.
Dimension	This is the data bifurcation level. In this example, as shown in Figure 4-16, the dimension is a GL Access Set and therefore the SQL statement is as follows, to get a list of all the GL Access Sets. `SELECT distinct access_set_id, name FROM gl_access_sets`
Naming	This section decides how the name of the data role is generated, that is, by concatenating the Job name and GL Access Set name.
Policies	This is where you define for each job role which database objects need to be secured and also pass the run-time parameter value for execution of the SQL predicate. This is shown in Figure 4-17. Note that one data role is generated for each job in the External Role tab for every record returned by the SQL statement in the Dimension tab. In other words, the number of data roles generated is the Cartesian product between the number of dimension values and number of external roles.

TABLE 4-2. *Components for Defining Data Role Templates*

Finally you can click Generate Roles, which will generate a data role for a Cartesian product of jobs entered in the External Roles tab and the dimensions returned by the SQL statements. This is shown in Figure 4-18.

Set ID to Share Reference Data As shown previously in Figure 4-13, Fusion Applications comes out of the box with various role templates. Some of those role templates refer to SetIDs, which allow sharing of reference data across organizations. This is made possible by partitioning the data into different sets of values. The principles are based on the role templates that we have seen in the previous section. You create reference data sets and attach those to the underlying master data or transaction.

One of the implementations for SetIDs is Payment terms in Fusion Payables. A large organization may wish to use a group of payment terms across a set of the business units. Assume a business requirement that a company with operations in the United States and the United Kingdom may want to use some payment terms

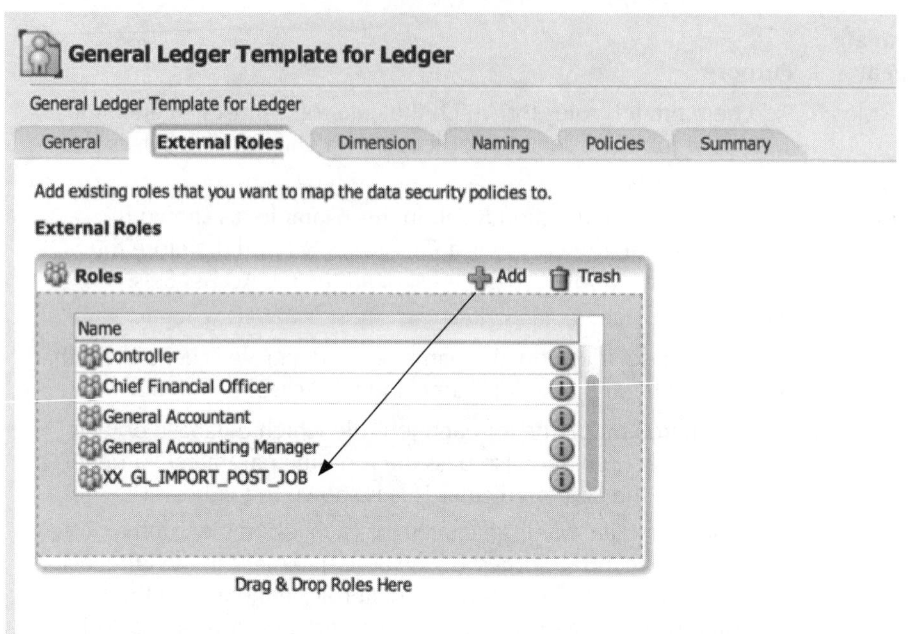

FIGURE 4-15. *Job roles for which the data roles are to be generated*

globally, and certain other payment terms locally per business unit. For globally applicable payment terms, you can create a reference data set named ANV Global Payment Terms as shown in Figure 4-19.

When you define a reference data set, it must then be associated with a predefined set of reference groups that have been delivered by Oracle out of the box. The reason is that security implementation related to reference sets has design-time implications for the entity objects. Therefore you will attach data set ANV Global Payment terms to reference group Payables Payment Terms as shown in Figure 4-19. Data roles can then be generated for each data set value for the applicable jobs in the Role Template. Figure 4-20 shows the data set becoming available to the dimension for payment terms. When creating payment terms, users can attach the payment terms to a reference set. This allows usage of the desired payment terms by the users that have access to data role for global payment terms.

As you have noticed, the concept for generating data roles based on SetIDs leverages the role template process described earlier in the chapter.

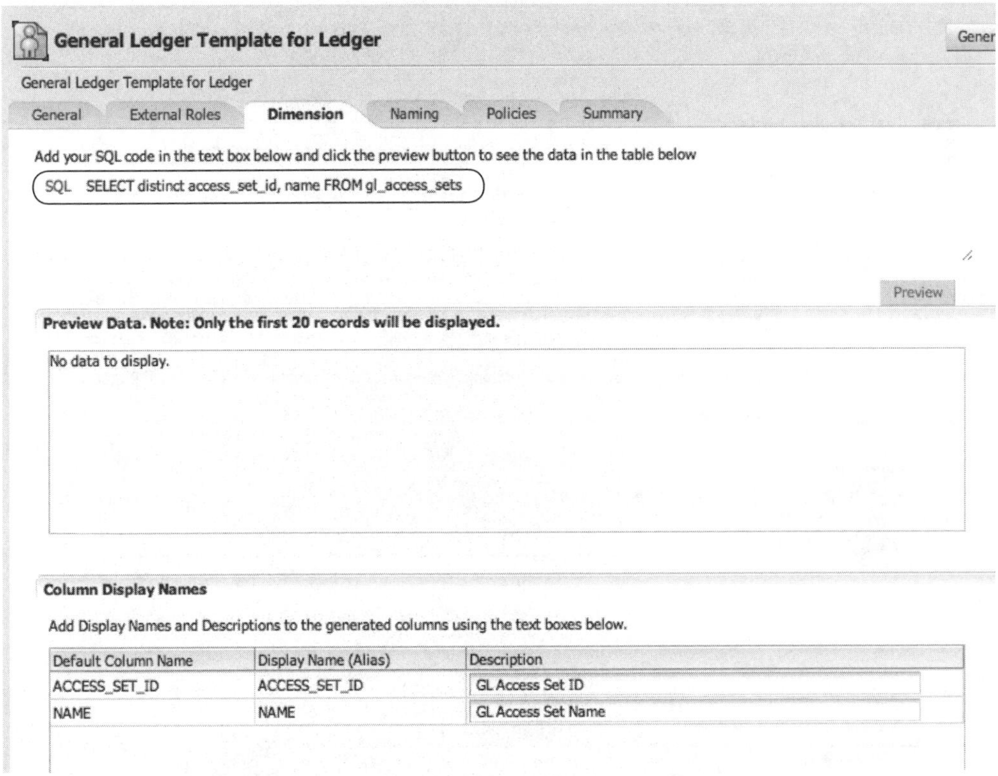

General Ledger Template for Ledger

General Ledger Template for Ledger

General | External Roles | **Dimension** | Naming | Policies | Summary

Add your SQL code in the text box below and click the preview button to see the data in the table below

SQL SELECT distinct access_set_id, name FROM gl_access_sets

Preview

Preview Data. Note: Only the first 20 records will be displayed.

No data to display.

Column Display Names

Add Display Names and Descriptions to the generated columns using the text boxes below.

Default Column Name	Display Name (Alias)	Description
ACCESS_SET_ID	ACCESS_SET_ID	GL Access Set ID
NAME	NAME	GL Access Set Name

FIGURE 4-16. *A data role will be generated for every job in an external role for each row returned by this SQL query.*

Integrating Oracle Fusion Data Security with Virtual Private Database (VPD) The Oracle Database has a feature called Virtual Private Database (VPD). VPD allows a WHERE clause to be appended to a table, view, or synonym. By doing so, the WHERE clause restricts the rows returned by a SQL query. A PL/SQL function is attached to the secured object that returns the WHERE clause that gets executed along with the SQL query. In Fusion Applications, if you wish to leverage the data security defined in APM on an object, then you need to call fnd_data_security.get_security_predicate() for that object.

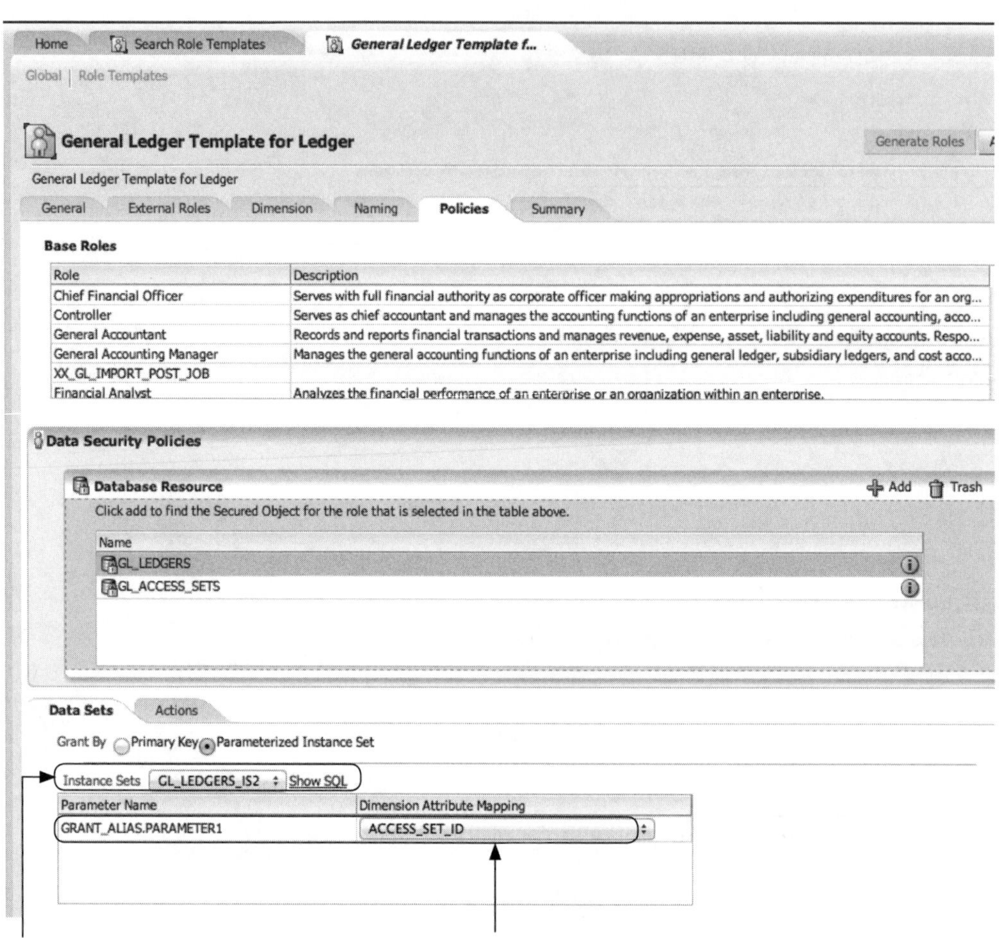

This Instance Sets is one of the conditions that is defined against database resource GL_LEDGERS.

Parameter value passed is the value returned by the SQL statement in the Dimension tab. Alternatively, the data set can be created using the primary key matched to the value returned by dimension SQL.

FIGURE 4-17. *Data security and actions applicable for job role*

The steps for implementing a custom VPD that leverages the APM are

1. Create a PL/SQL function and call fnd_data_security.get_security_predicate().

```
A sample piece of code that can be plugged into your VPD function is shown below
FUNCTION get_my_predicate RETURN VARCHAR2 IS
l _predicate varchar2(2000) ;
l_return_status varchar2(2000) ;
begin
  fnd_data_security.get_security_predicate
```

```
      (p_api_version       => 1.0,
       p_privilege         => 'XX_MY_ACTION_NAME_IN_APM',
       p_object_name       => 'XX_MY_TABLE',
       p_grant_instance_type  => 'SET',
       p_statement_type    => 'VPD',
       x_predicate         => l_predicate,
       x_return_status     => l_return_status,
       p_table_alias        => NULL );
  return l_predicate ;
  end ;
```

2. Attach this function to a VPD policy for table XX_MY_TABLE.
3. Ensure that XX_MY_TABLE is registered in APM.
4. Create an action named XX_MY_ACTION_NAME_IN_APM.

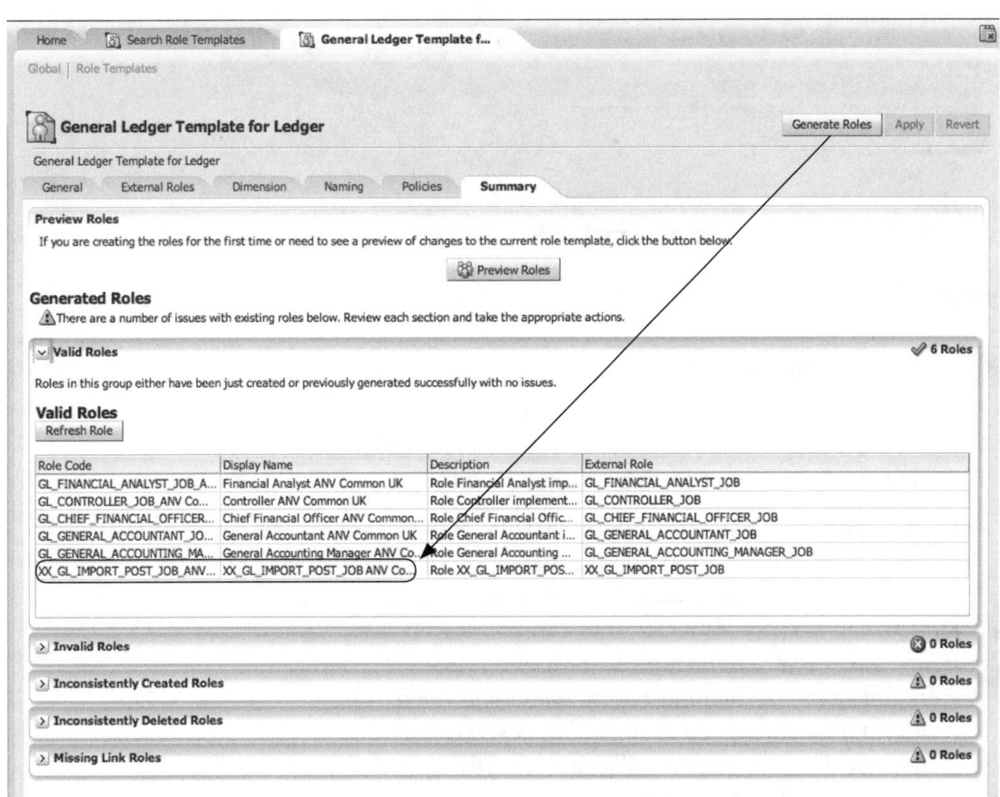

FIGURE 4-18. *The data roles generated for job roles and dimension values*

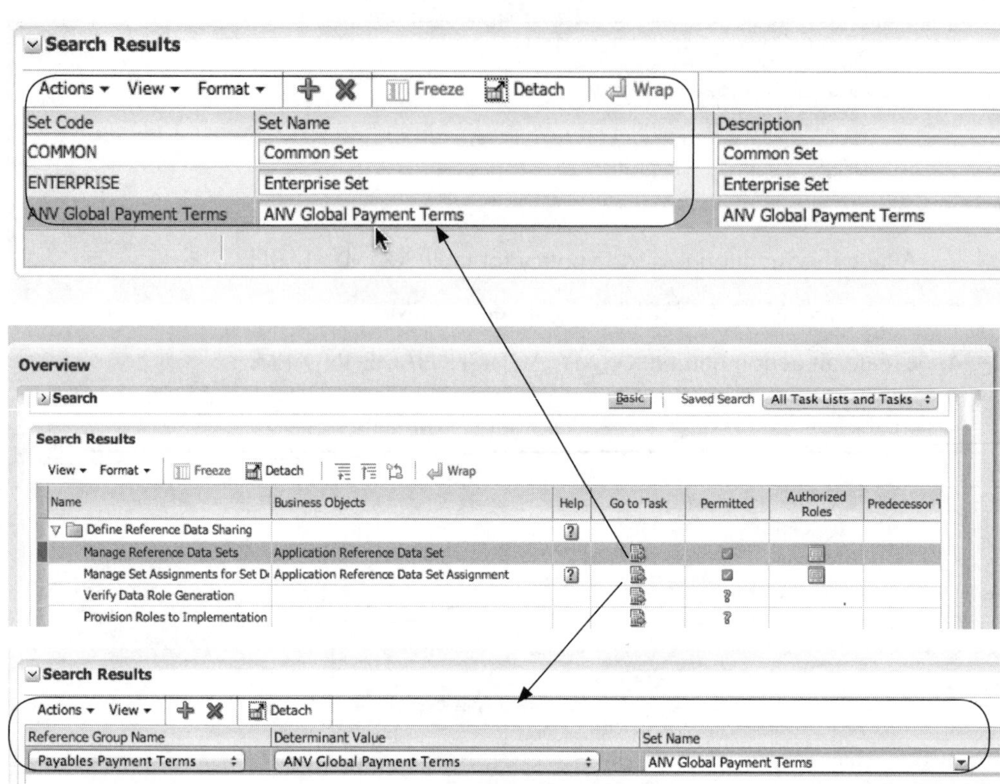

FIGURE 4-19. *Reference data sets*

5. Create the desired conditions using the tab as shown in Figure 4-20.
6. Attach the XX_MY_ACTION_NAME_IN_APM to the Condition for a role in the Policy tab of Database Resource.

NOTE

It must be noted that the data security does not work out of the box in BI Publisher when you build a custom SQL-based data model. The reason is that entity objects and therefore OPSS are completely bypassed and therefore the data security is not fetched for the database objects. Therefore you need to make joins to an object that is secured by a VPD policy to secure the results of your SQL.

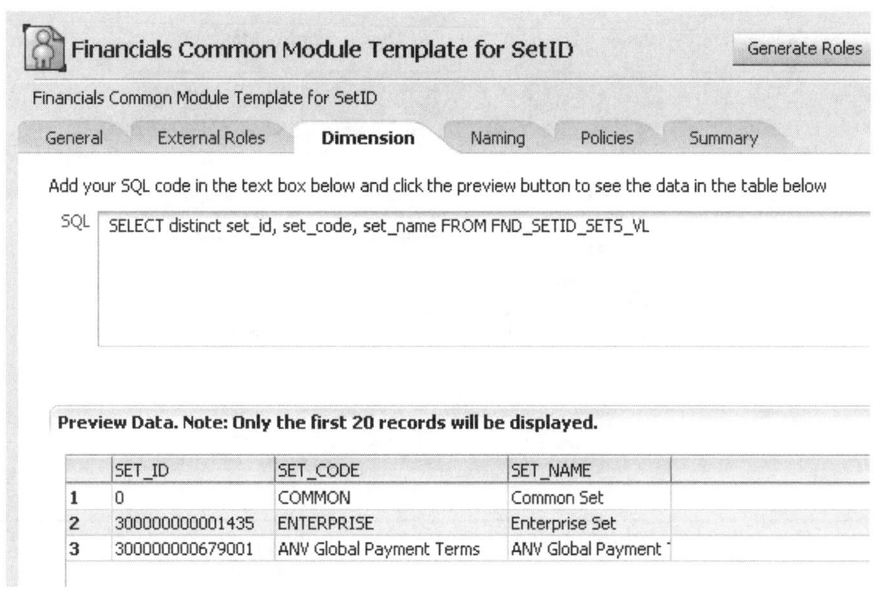

FIGURE 4-20. *Dimension values for SetIDs to generate data roles*

For HCM, Fusion Applications delivers a set of secured views that have VPD policies attached to them. These objects can be identified by running the following SQL query:

```
SELECT object_name FROM all_objects
WHERE object_name LIKE 'PER%_SECURED_LIST_V%'
AND owner       ='FUSION' AND object_type='VIEW'
```

You can join any one of these secured views in your SQL data model when building a BI Publisher for HCM. For non-HCM reporting requirements that are run off a SQL data model, it is a good practice to check if secured views have been delivered by Oracle. You can use the following SQL query to see the objects secured in the Fusion Accounting Hub module.

```
select * from ALL_POLICIES where object_name like 'XLA%'
```

On similar lines, you can use this VPD approach to secure objects used in PL/SQL-based Enterprise Scheduler Service programs.

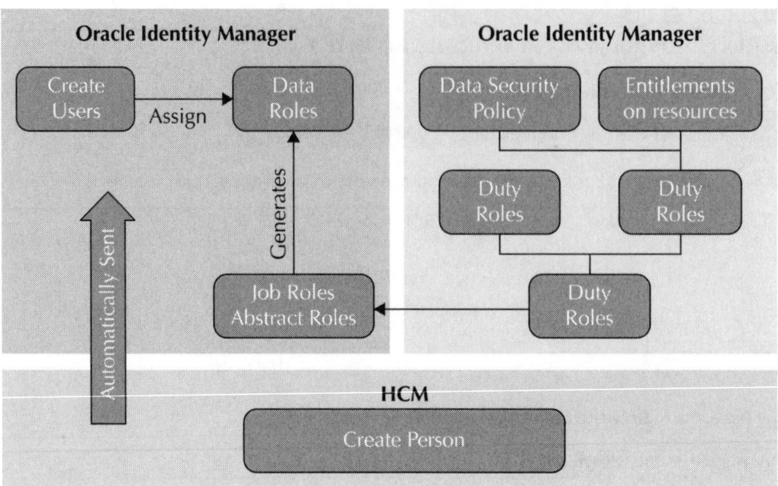

FIGURE 4-21. *Overall relationship among security components in Fusion Applications*

Overall Visualization of Relationship Among Security Components Figure 4-21 shows the overall relationship among the application roles, data roles, job roles, data security policies, and privileges/actions. The menus can be added by using a custom menu.

Auto Provisioning of Roles in HCM

HCM provides a functionality that allows roles to be provisioned automatically to the users when certain conditions are met. To enable a role to be automatically provisioned to users, you need to define a mapping between the role and a set of conditions. The conditions can be defined based on assignment attributes such as department, job, system person type, and so on.

The role mapping can support the following:

- Automatic provisioning of roles to users
- Manual provisioning of roles to users
- Role requests from users
- Immediate provisioning of roles

A role is provisioned to a user automatically if the following conditions are true:

1. At least one of the user's assignments satisfies all conditions associated with the role in the role mapping.
2. You select the Autoprovision option for the role in the role mapping as shown in Figure 4-22.

For example, you may want to automatically assign the Expense Manager ANV UK role to the Employee managers in the ANV UK Operations business unit. Automatic role provisioning occurs as soon as the user is confirmed to satisfy the role-mapping conditions, which can be when the user's assignment is either created or updated. The provisioning process also removes automatically provisioned roles from users who no longer satisfy the role-mapping conditions. Therefore, in this example, if the person is no longer a Manager, then the Expense Manager role will be automatically removed.

NOTE
The automatic provisioning of roles to users is a request to OIM to provision the role. OIM may reject the request if it violates segregation-of-duties rules or fails a custom OIM approval process. Segregation of duties is a functionality that can help prevent fraudulent activities by preventing provision of an invalid combination of roles to a user.

Create Role Mapping
Apply Autoprovisioning | Save | Save and Close | Cancel
* Mapping Name: ANV Auto Provisioning Mapping
* From Date: 9/8/13
To Date
Conditions
Business Unit: ANV UK Operations
Legal Employer
Department
Job
Position: Manager
Grade
Location
System Person Type: Employee
User Person Type
Assignment Type
Assignment Status
Resource Role
Party Type Usage
Manager with Reports
Associated Roles
View | Format | Freeze | Detach | Wrap

Role Name	Requestable	Self-requestable	Autoprovision
Expense Manager ANV UK	☐	☐	☑

FIGURE 4-22. *Automatically assigning the Expense Manager role to all Employee Managers*

Mapping to Oracle EBusiness Suite Components

The various security components in Fusion Applications map to Oracle EBusiness Suite as shown in Table 4-3. The Role-Based Access Control follows a positive approach rather than a negative approach toward role allocation. For example, Oracle EBusiness suite allows you to exclude certain form functions from a responsibility. However, Fusion Applications does not have a concept of exclusion of duty roles from a job role or a data role. As per the RBAC standards, if a user has access to a role, they should be able to use the features presented by that role.

The duty roles themselves are not attached to the menu item. When defining a menu item in Fusion Applications using the Manage Menu Customization task, you simply attach the menu item to a resource. If that resource is available to the user via their RBAC policies, then that user will be able to see that menu item.

Web Services Security in Fusion Applications

Oracle Fusion Web Services are set up with internal and external policies. All internal-facing Web services are protected by Authentication Only policies. These policies send and accept passwords in clear text, meaning unencrypted. They do not perform any encryption or signing, and they do not have high security. However, they are high performance because they don't do any expensive cryptography operations. They should be used only for back-end Web services in small internal private networks that are completely blocked off from the Internet and also blocked off from the enterprise intranet.

Oracle EBusiness Suite Component	Corresponding Fusion Applications Component
Responsibility	Data Roles
Top-level menu	Job Roles
Submenu	Duty Roles
Form Function	Privileges and Data Security Policies

TABLE 4-3. *EBS to Fusion Applications Comparison for Security Components*

External-facing Web Services

External-facing Web services are protected by WS11 Message protection policies. The service accepts an encrypted username and password token, or a signed SAML token, plus the entire message body must be signed and encrypted. The client sends an encrypted username and password or a signed SAML token. These policies are very secure; however, they are not high performance because they do expensive cryptographic operations.

External clients must complete the following steps.

1. Get the certificate of the service. The certificate is advertised in the Web Services Description Language (WSDL). To extract the certificate from the WSDL, perform the following steps.

   a. Save the WSDL to a local file.

   b. Search for the string X509Certificate inside the local file to locate the certificate. For example,

```
<dsig:X509Certificate> MIICHTCCAYagAwIBAgIETBwVYjA ... </dsig:X509Certificate>
```

   c. Copy this long string framed by the <dsig:X509Certificate> tags into a text file.

   d. Rename the file.

      - If you are using this certificate in a Microsoft client, you can rename this file with a .cer file extension and use it as a certificate file.
      - If you are using this certificate in a Java client, change the text file so that the certificate is framed by BEGIN and END. For example,

```
-----BEGIN
MIICHTCCAYagAwIBAgIETBwVYjA ...
-----END
```

2. Import the certificate of the service into your client's trust store. For Java clients, use `keytool -importcert` to import this file from the previous step into your client's keystore.

3. [For SAML only.] Generate a client certificate. If your client expects to perform ID propagation, the client needs to authenticate with SAML certificates. For this the client needs to have a client certificate for use as a SAML signing key.

4. [For SAML only.] Import the client certificate into the trust store of the service. Take the certificate in the previous step and import it into the default-keystore.jks file of the service.

Troubleshooting Web Services Grants

One of the common issues when invoking the Web service in Fusion Applications is the access denied error. Therefore, it is important to figure out the steps involved to know which privilege is required to invoke a Web service and how to assign the privilege to the user that will invoke the Web service. The quickest way to find this information is to navigate to the APM dashboard and open the resource screen as shown in Figure 4-7 and search for the Web service name using the CONTAINS clause in the Resource Name field. Next, click the button Find Policies and this will list the Duty roles that have entitlements to invoke this Web service. Alternatively, you can also search for the Web description service name in an Excel spreadsheet downloaded from My Oracle Support note 1460486.1, and in that spreadsheet, you will find the duty roles and their corresponding external roles. Once you have identified the duty role, then open the external role that the user has access to, click the Application Role Mapping tab, and map the identified duty role to this external role.

Summary

In this chapter we aimed to provide an introduction to how Fusion Applications secures various technical components across different technologies. We learned how Oracle Fusion Applications leverages Oracle Identity Management and Oracle Entitlement Server capabilities. We learned about the extra data security features added by Oracle Entitlement Server via the APM console. Using the concepts in this chapter, the developers should be able to secure their custom extensions by adopting the best practices used by the Oracle product development team for securing Fusion Applications product components.

CHAPTER 5

Run-time Customization with Oracle Page Composer

We talked about various types of customizations and tools available for that purpose in Chapter 2. We will discuss how to do run-time personalization and customizations and how to use Oracle Page Composer in this chapter. End users will use Oracle Page Composer to personalize the application pages, such as rearranging the content on the dashboard page. The administrator will use Oracle Page Composer to customize application pages at the appropriate layer for the enterprise, such as adding new content to the page or changing label or other properties of the components. The administrator can also use Functional Setup Manager to modify the Navigator menu for Fusion Applications.

What Can Be Customized

Oracle Page Composer is a run-time tool and you can customize Fusion Applications pages to do the following using Page Composer.

- Add or remove content from a page using the resource catalog
- Change the page layout
- Modify the component properties that are allowed to be changed such as label, mandatory, read-only, show/hide, and so on
- Rearrange and rename regions on a page
- Modify the task list

There are many other customization tasks that cannot be performed in the run-time environment of Oracle Page Composer. You will need to use either CRM Application Composer or JDeveloper to achieve these customizations.

- Making a page personalizable or customizable
- Editing embedded help text
- Changing ADF Business Components
- Changing ADF Task Flow behavior
- Adding a custom or extended attribute
- Changing mobile pages

Customization Modes

There are three different modes you can use Oracle Page Composer to customize application pages. These modes are available to users based on the access privileges for a given application page.

- **Design view** This mode is the most basic view of the page and provides WYSIWYG capability to customize the page. This mode is available to every user when they go to the Personalize Page option. This mode is available to administrators when they go to customize a page. Design view is mainly used to manage regions on the UI. Design view allows you to change page layout, add content on a given page, edit region properties, rearrange regions, or hide or show regions on the dashboard page. The following illustration shows the customization region when open in Design view mode in Page Composer.

- **Source view** This mode is an advanced mode in which the source hierarchy of the page is exposed to the user. Source view gives advanced users finer control over every component of the page. The mode is available to administrators only when they go to customize a page. This mode is not available in CRM applications. Using Source view, you can hide or show components on a page, edit components inside a task flow, edit component properties, and so on. The Source view is used when you cannot modify the components using Design view. The following illustration shows the customization region when open in Source view mode.

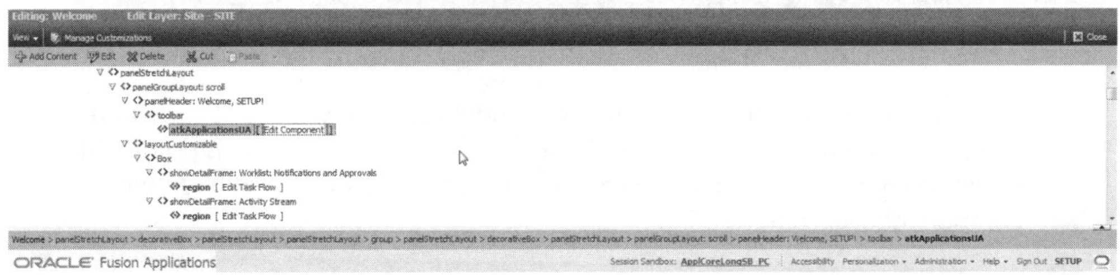

You can switch between Source view and Design view using the View menu in Change mode as shown here. You can also choose where you want to see the Source view on your window using the Source Position menu.

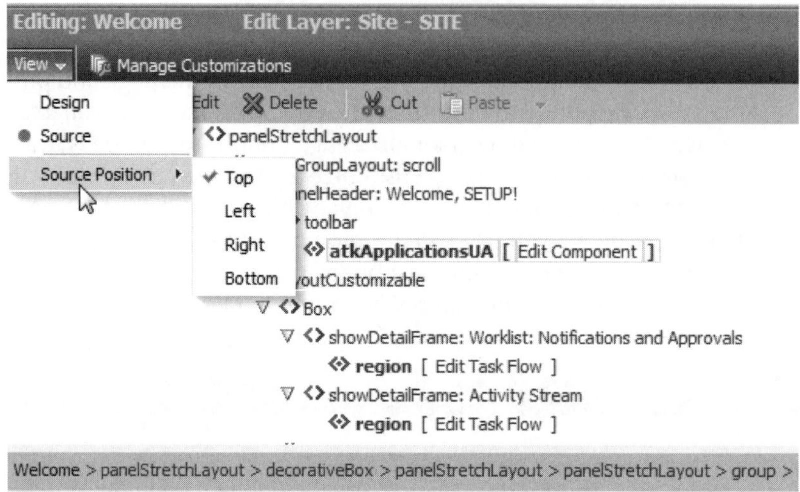

- **Select mode** This is an enhanced Design view mode available to only CRM applications. This mode is the replacement of Source view for CRM applications. A CRM applications administrator only has Select mode available for customizations. This mode allows modifying component properties. The following illustration shows the customization region when open in Select mode.

The Select mode also protects any component property with EL (Expression Language) and does not allow modifying such properties. You can point and select a given component in this mode and then choose to modify either the component or its parent container.

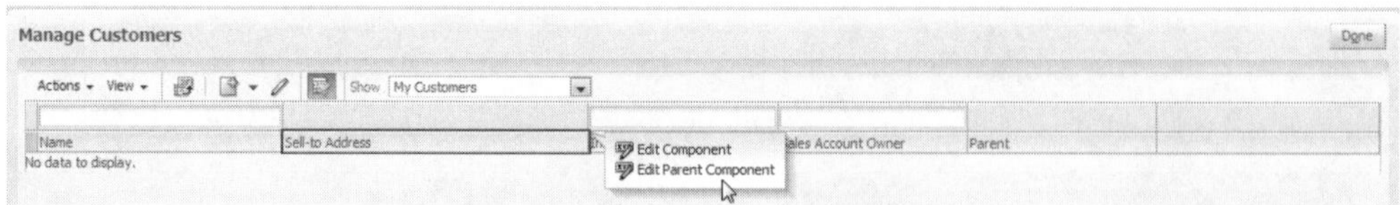

User Personalization

There are two types of end-user personalization in Fusion Applications.

Implicit Personalization

Implicit personalization is a change made by a user at run time and saved implicitly by the application, such as whether the user last expanded or collapsed a panel. All the changes made by the user persist for a given user session in Fusion Applications. However, not all changes are persisted across sessions because this has performance implications. Fusion Applications enable implicit personalization across sessions for show detail expand-collapse and resize, portlet expand-collapse, and all operations to panel and layout customizable components. Some of the Fusion Applications also enable implicit personalization on other components such as table column rearrange, show/hide, width, frozen, no-wrap, table filter show/hide, and Rich Text Editor mode. The components and properties enabled for implicit personalization are defined in the adf-config.xml file for a given application. This file can be customized using JDeveloper. Please read Fusion Applications product-specific documentation to understand which components are enabled for implicit personalization across sessions.

Composer Personalization

Users can make some explicit changes to application pages using Oracle Page Composer. These are changes made to a page using the Personalization menu. This option is available to every user, and what an end user can do is very limited. The user can only add or remove the content and move the regions around but cannot change the content inside the region. Every dashboard page in Fusion Applications is enabled for personalization. Some of the work area pages are also enabled for personalization. Which page is enabled is configured by Fusion Applications and this setting is defined by the isPersonalizableInComposer property for a given page. You can use JDeveloper to change this property for any page.

How to Change Page Layout

An administrator can modify the layout of the page that will be available to all users in the enterprise. We will modify the layout of the home page of Fusion Applications to rearrange the regions and make space to add new content.

1. Log in to the Fusion Applications home page with a user who has administration access.

2. Create a sandbox as explained in Chapter 2 and use it for this customization.

3. Click on the Administration menu and select the Customize Workarea Pages option. This opens up the page in Design view customization mode.
4. Click the Change Layout button at the top-right corner of the page and select the layout with three columns and narrow sides.

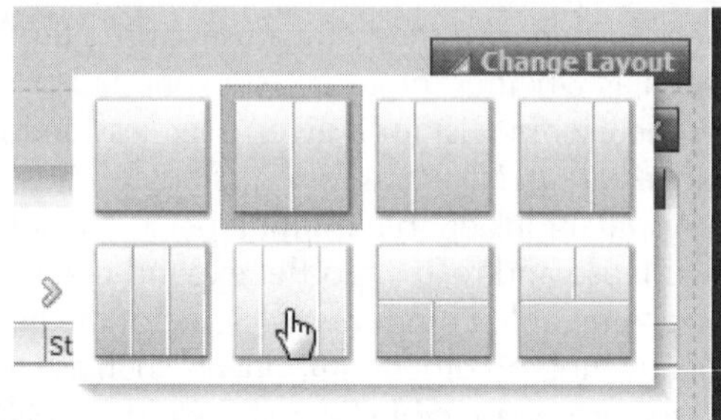

5. This changes the page layout and existing content remains in the first two columns.
6. You can use the Move Up or Move Down icon on the region to change its position in the layout.

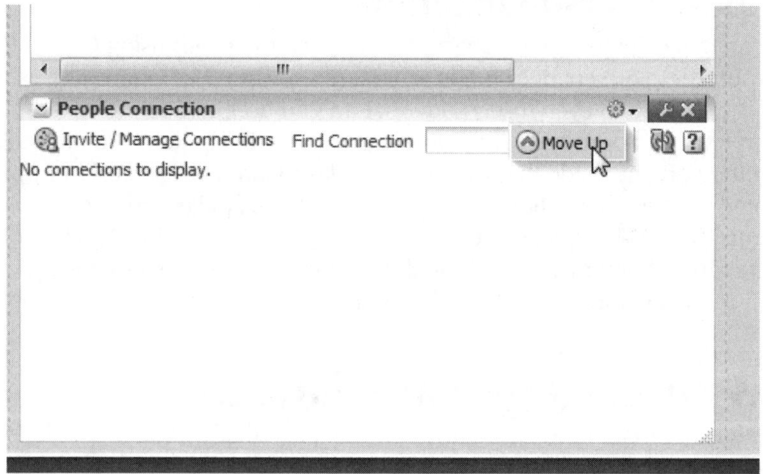

7. You can drag and drop a region to another region on the layout as well.

How to Add New Content on a Page

Using Page Composer, an administrator or user can add content that is available in the resource catalog to the page. There are several types of content that can be added using Page Composer.

- Oracle Web Center components like activity stream and message boards
- Fusion Applications common components like work list, notifications, and task lists
- Any portlets that are registered with Fusion Applications
- Analytical reports from the Fusion Applications BI repository
- Other ADF components such as a Web page, hyperlink, image, static text, or any HTML markup
- HCM components such as people connection, organization chart, and person search

In this section, we will discuss how to add some of this content to a page.

1. Click the Add Content button in the third column on the page layout.

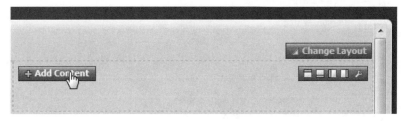

2. This will show a dialog where you can pick the content to be added on the region on the page. Click the Add link for Activity Stream as shown in the following illustration.

3. Click the Add link for Message Board. Click the Close button. This will add these two components on the page as shown here.

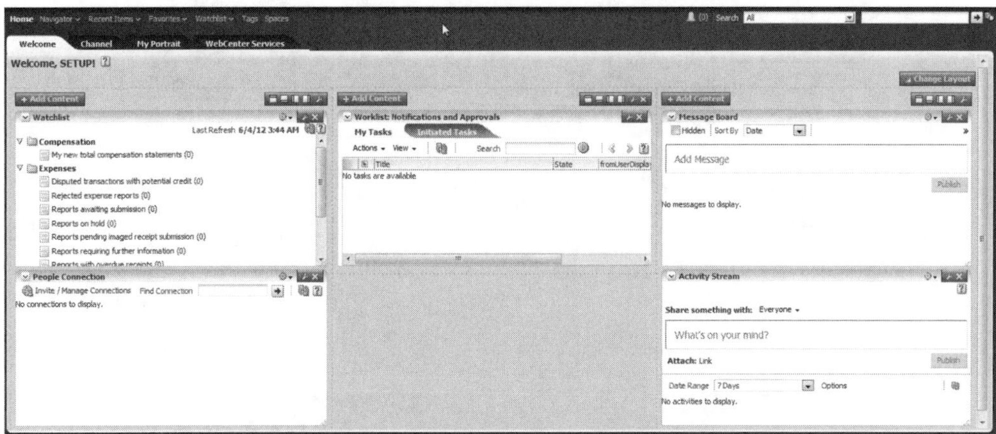

4. Click the Add Box Below button in the second column on the page layout. This will add another region where you can add new content.

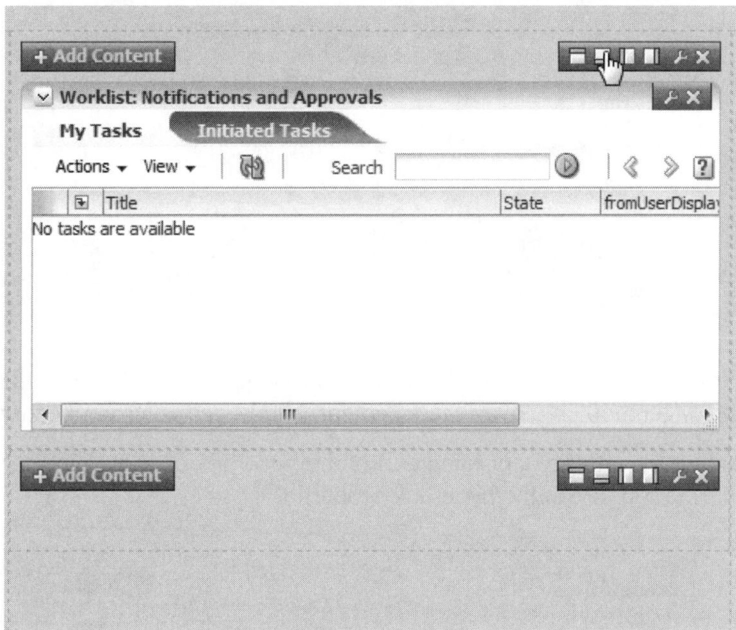

5. Click the Add Content button in this new region in the second column. Click the Components folder to see a list of available components that can be added on the page.

6. Click Add for Web Page, HTML Markup, and click three times for Hyperlink. Click the Close button. This will add these components on the page.

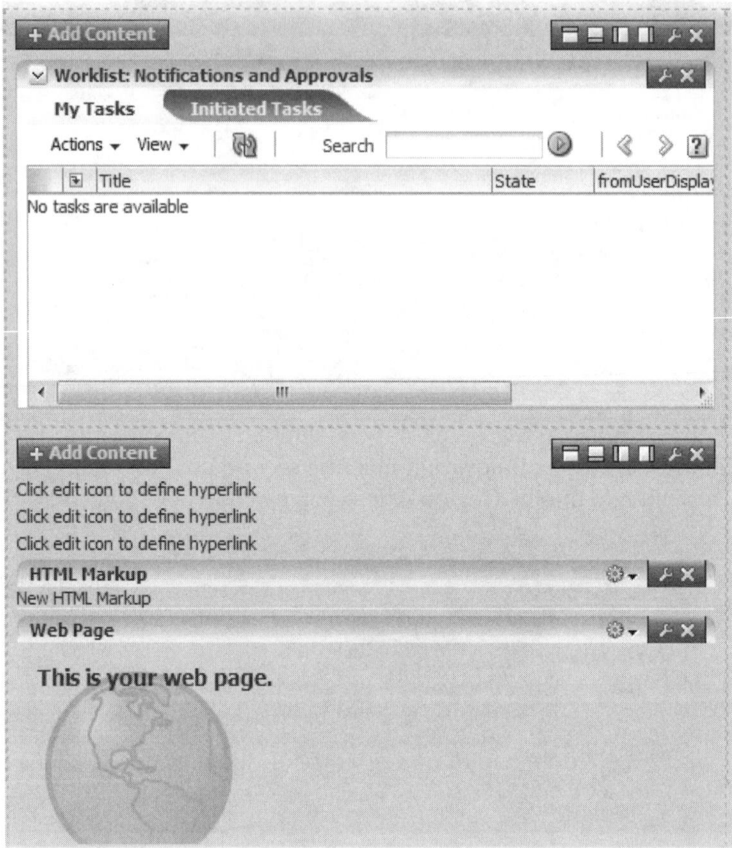

7. Now we will change the hyperlink to navigate to the Opportunity Management, Employee Management, and Receivables applications.

8. Hover toward the right-hand end of the hyperlink as shown in the following illustration to edit the hyperlink properties.

9. This will show the Hyperlink Component Properties dialog. To modify the text shown for the hyperlink, click the down arrow for the Text property and select the Expression Builder option.

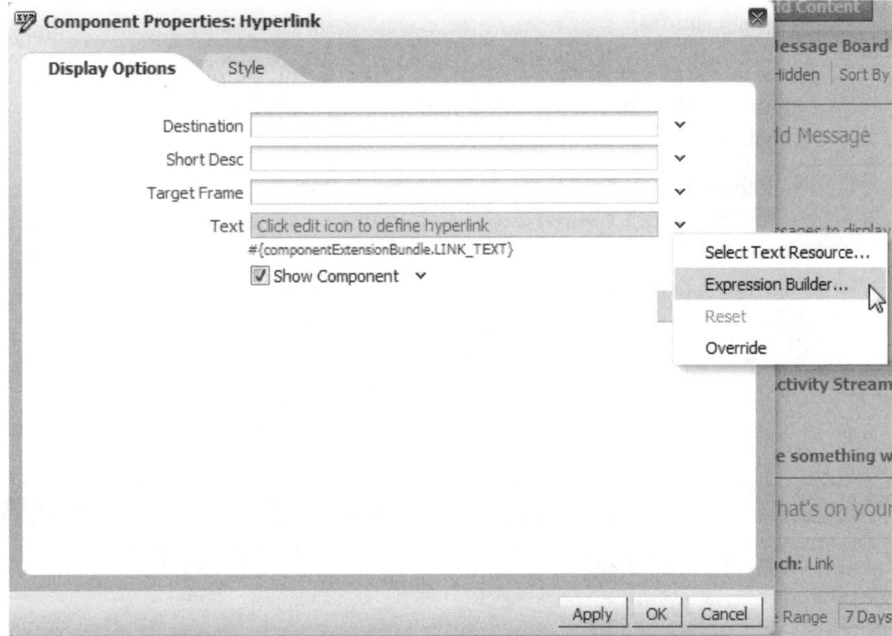

10. In the Edit Text dialog, change the text to Opportunity Management. Click OK.
11. Specify the Destination as the opportunity home page.

```
http://<CRM host>:<port>/sales/faces/mooOpportunityHome
```

12. Modify the style of hyperlink to set Color Red, Font Size Large, and Font Style Bold.
13. Modify the other two hyperlinks also to point to the Employee and Receivables home page.

```
http://<HCM host>:<port>/hcmCore/faces/PersonSearch
http://<FIN host>:<port>/receivables/faces/TransactionsWorkArea
```

14. After all these changes, you can click the hyperlinks to directly navigate to those home pages instead of using the Navigator menu. The page looks like the following illustration with these changes.

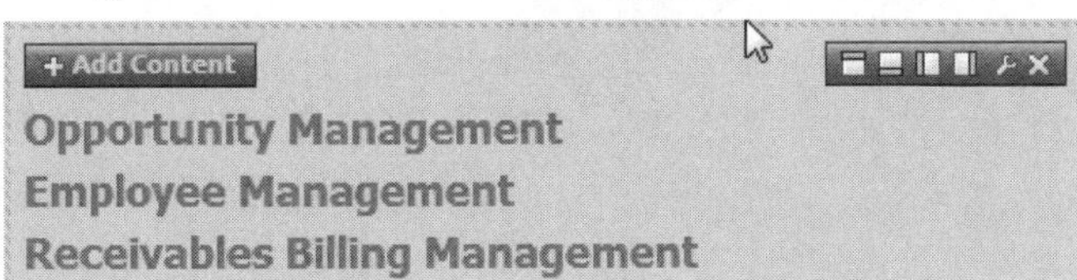

15. Click the Edit icon for the Web Page region and specify the source as http://www.bing.com/.

16. Use the Delete icon on the People Connection region to remove that from the first column.

17. Click the Add Box Below icon in the first column of the layout to add a region to move some content to. Drag and drop all three hyperlinks and the HTML Markup to this region.

18. Click the Edit icon for HTML Markup region. We will add iframe markup to get an RSS feed from Yahoo News using the free widget service rssinclude.com. Set the value attribute using Expression Builder to the following markup.

```
<iframe width="400" height="400" style="border:none;"
src="http://output49.rssinclude.com/output?type=iframe&amp;
id=486118&amp;hash=7ad36b404d0ffc5f6ab1cb034b22221f"></iframe>
```

19. Click the Close button on the top-right corner of the page from the Customization region. This shows the home page with all the content added.

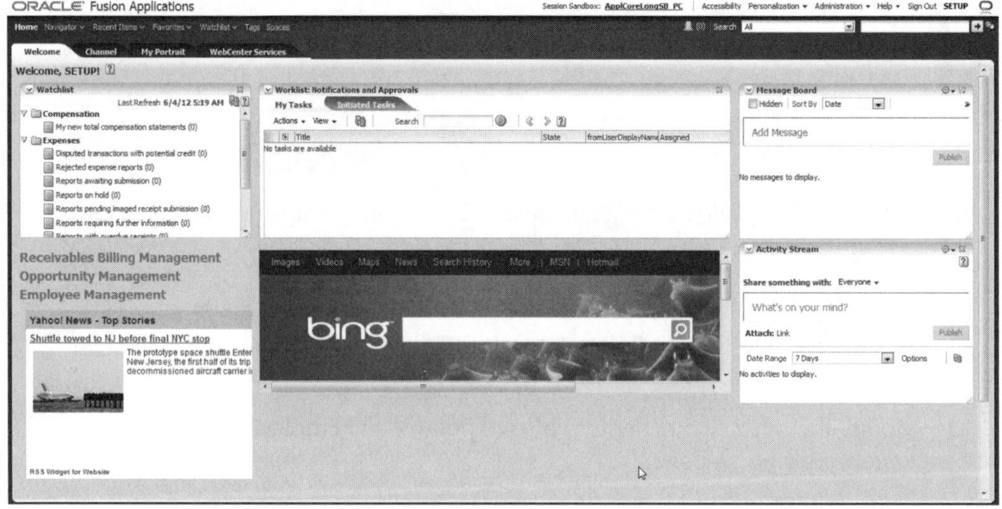

20. Click the Add Content button in the second column on the page layout. Click the Reports and Analytics folder to navigate to the BI repository to add a new report on the page.

How to Customize Fields

The most basic component on a page is a UI field component such as input text, output text, choice list, or a table with one or more columns. You can customize the field properties; for example, you can hide or show a field, make a field read-only or editable, make a field mandatory, and change the label. For table columns, you can customize properties like hide or show column, set width, change label, and make the column sortable. You can customize all these in both Source view and CRM Select mode. We will discuss how to achieve all these customizations in both modes in this section. To use Select mode, we will customize the Opportunity Management page, and to use Source view, we will customize the expense creation page.

How to Use Select Mode to Customize Fields

1. Log in to Fusion Applications with a user who has the Sales Administrator role. Go to the Opportunity home page using the Opportunities option in the Navigator menu under Sales. Click the Create Opportunity link from the Task pane. Create and use a sandbox from the Administration menu using Manage Sandboxes. Click Customize Opportunities Pages in the Administration menu to customize fields on the Create Opportunity page. Choose the customization layer as Job Role and value as Sales Representative.

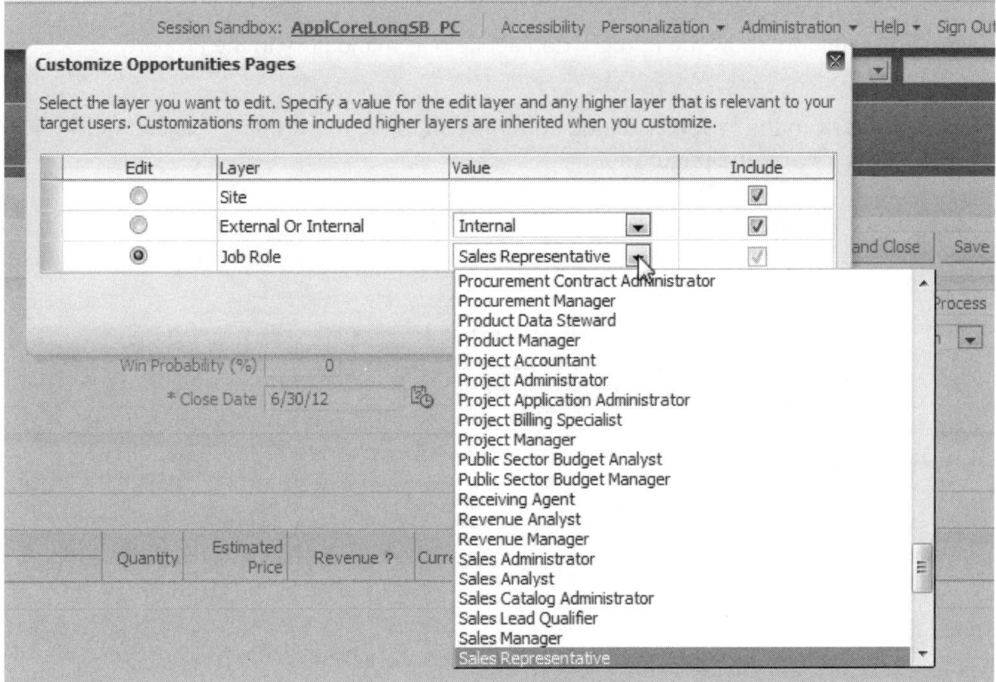

2. This shows the Create Opportunity page in Select mode for customization where you can select the fields you want to customize.
3. We will make the Primary Contact attribute mandatory for sales representatives. Select the Primary Contact field and click the Edit Component link that shows up. This will show the Change Property dialog for the Primary Contact attribute. Click the down arrow for a required field and select Expression Builder as shown in the following illustration.

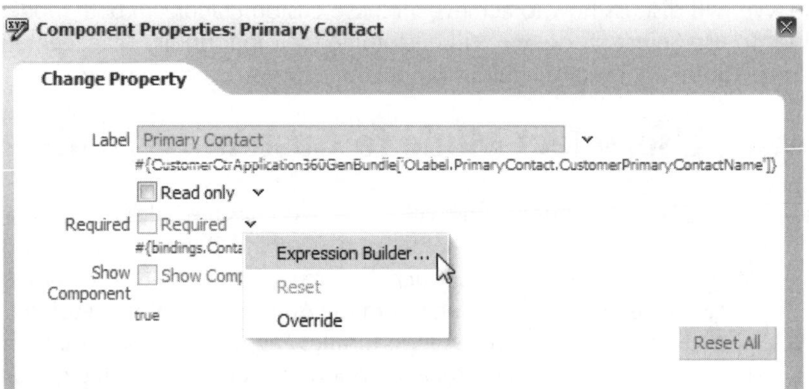

4. Change the expression to true and click OK.
5. This will now show the Primary Contact field as mandatory in the Property dialog.
6. Click OK in the Property dialog and this will make the Primary Contact field mandatory on the page.

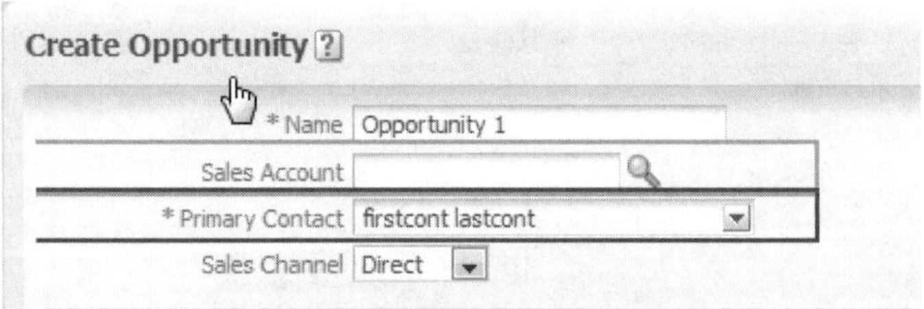

7. We will make the Close Date field read-only for sales representatives. Select the Close Date field and go to Edit Component. Check the Read Only check box.

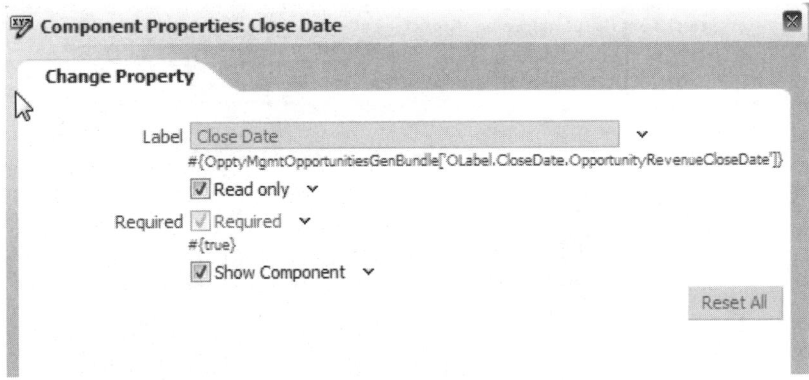

8. Click OK and this will make the Close Date field read-only on the UI.

9. We will now modify the Edit Opportunity page for other field and table column customizations. Go to the Edit Opportunity page by drilling down to any opportunity. Once in Select mode, go to the Edit Component dialog for the Competitors field. Click Select Text Resource from the drop-down menu for the Label property.

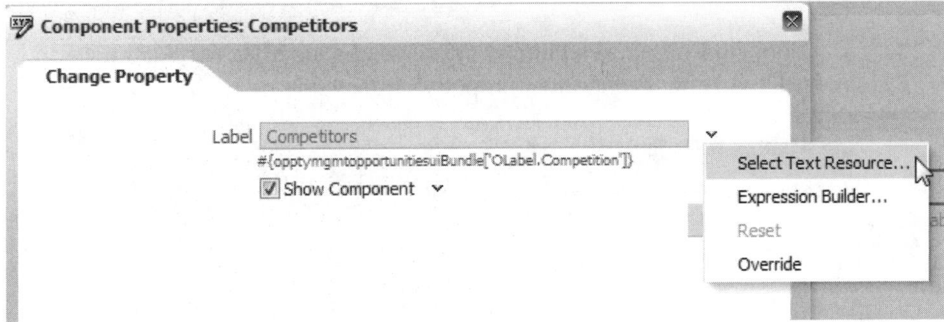

10. Provide details for the new label and give the Display Value as **Competing With**.

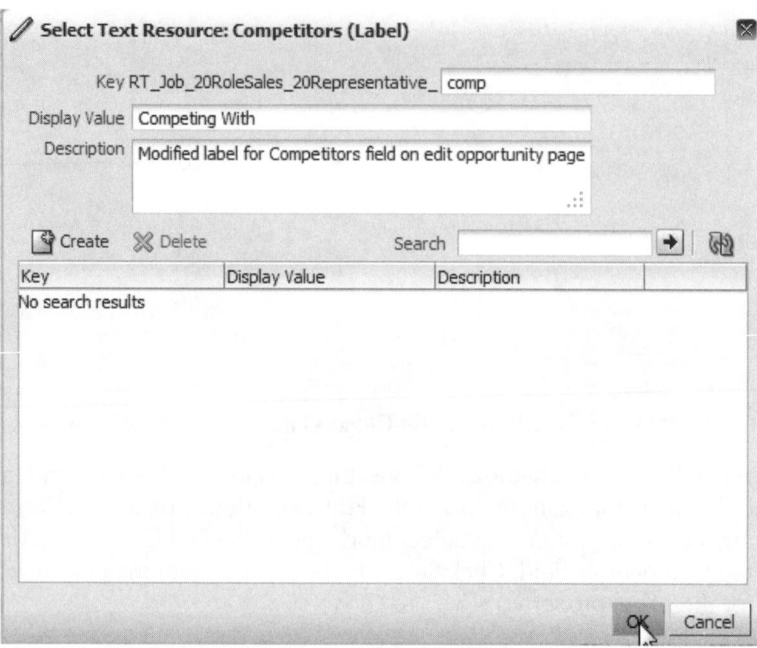

11. Go to the Edit Component dialog for the Enable Social Networking field and uncheck the Show Component property.

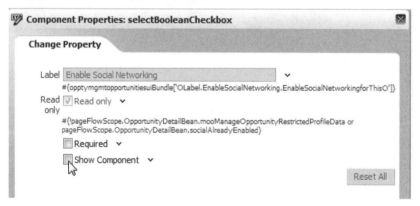

12. Select the Currency column from the Revenue Items table and go to Component Properties. Check the Sortable check box.

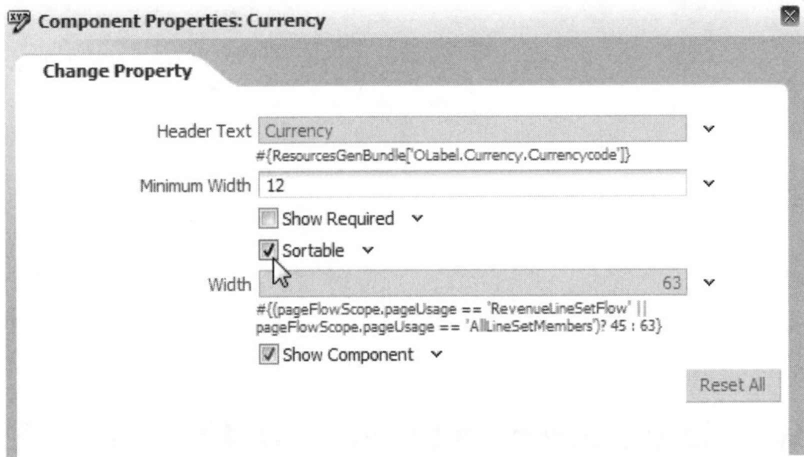

13. Select the Estimated Price column from the Revenue Items table and go to Component Properties. Change the width of the column to 100.

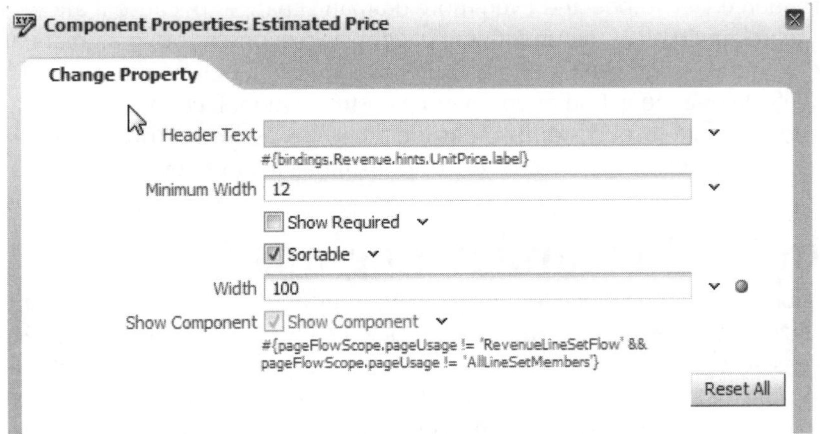

14. This will modify the Opportunity edit page with a new label and removed fields and modified look for the table as per the preceding customizations.

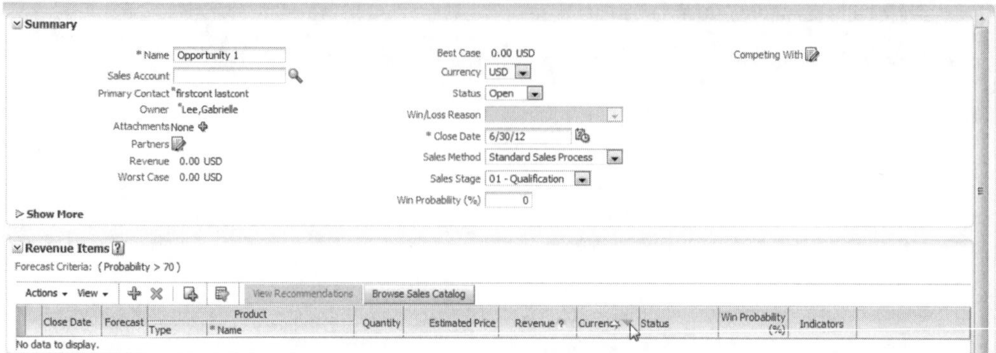

How to Use Source View Mode to Customize Fields

If you are using a non-CRM application such as HCM, SCM, or Financials, you will not see Select mode for customizing using Page Composer. These applications expose Source view mode for the pages that allow customization. You can do all the functions using Source view mode and even more dramatic changes because it allows you to see the full anatomy of the underlying page. It also exposes you to a great danger of making mistakes and getting into an unrecoverable situation where you will have to do MDS clean-up to get rid of your wrong customization. Details about using Source view for attribute-level customizations are the same, as we will discuss in the next section where you do regional-level customizations in Source view mode.

How to Customize Regions

A region is a building block for any page. Various fields on a given page are organized under regions to group the fields logically. The regions are organized as tabs or stacked on a given page. You can show or hide a given region or tab, rearrange the regions or tabs, rename a region or tab, or rearrange attributes within the region. You need to use Source view mode to do region customizations. The CRM Select mode supports only fields rearranged in a given region and does not support any other region customization.

1. On the Edit Opportunity page, select any attribute and click the Edit Parent Component link to customize a given region as shown in the following illustration.

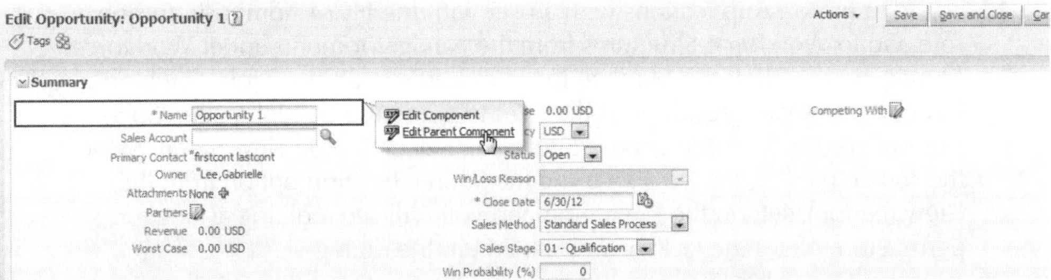

2. This shows the Edit Region Properties dialog where you can move any field up or down to rearrange them or show or hide a field. Make the changes as shown here.

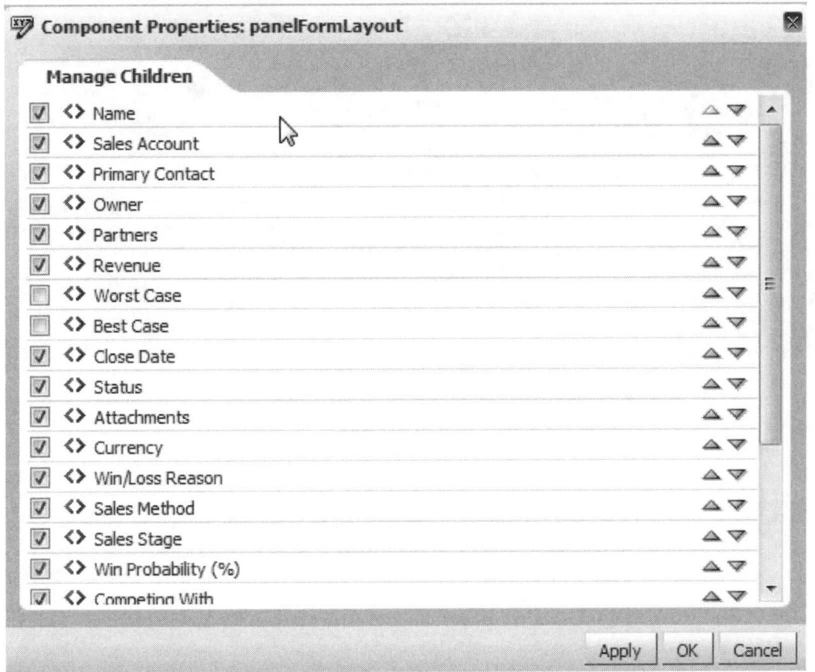

3. Click OK to save the changes and the page will change the layout as selected in the Edit Parent Component dialog.

4. Log in to Fusion Applications with a user with the HCM Administrator job role. Go to Workforce Structures from the Navigator menu under Workforce Management. Click the Manage Jobs tab and search for a job. Click on a job from the search results to drill down to get to the Edit Job page. Go to Customize This Page and choose Site Layer. Select Source view mode. Move the source pane to the left side using the Source Position option from the View menu. Click on the Job region and you will see a dialog asking for permission to edit the task flow. Click Edit in the dialog.

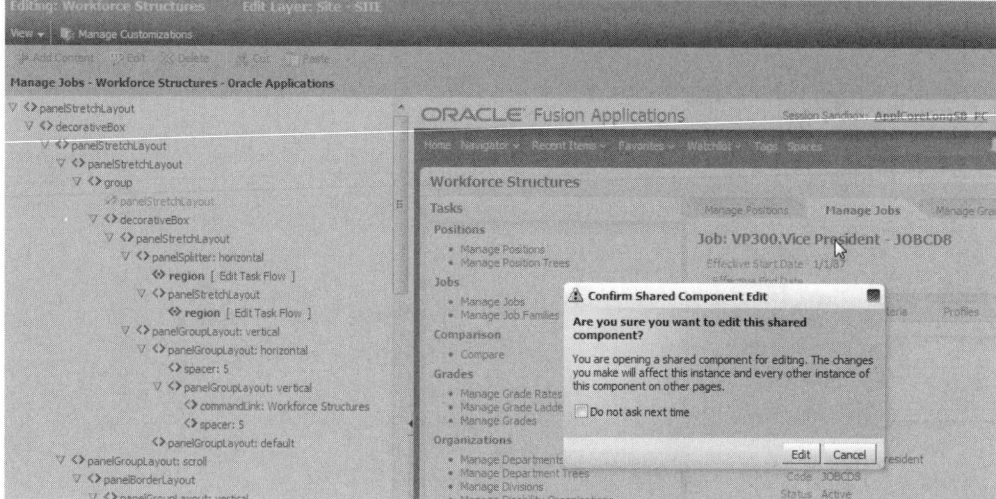

5. This will show the Job task flow Source view where you can visually see the regions and attributes on that page and customize it.

6. Select the Basic Details region and right-click to see options for customization as shown in the following illustration. You can delete using the Delete menu option or hide the region using the Hide Component menu option. You can use the Expand and Expand All Below menu options to expand the source view to see all components on the page. You can use the Show as Top menu option to make the current region as top in Source view so that it is easy to see the Source view for that part of the page and customize that particular region.

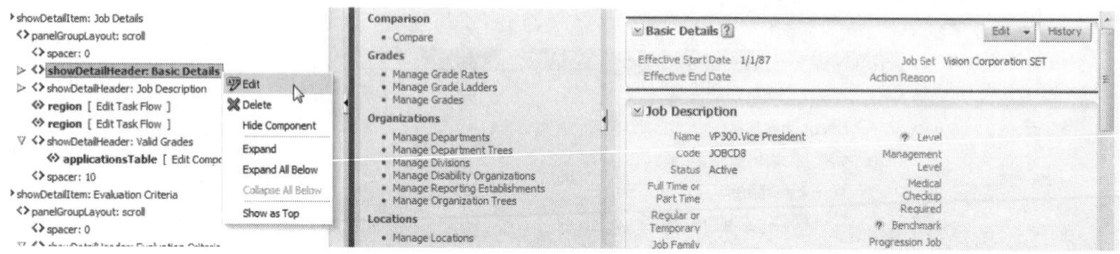

7. Click the Edit menu option to modify this region property. This shows the Component Properties dialog where you can modify display options. For this showDetailHeader region, modify the text property by adding a new text from resource bundle to "Basic Information."

8. Right-click on the Valid Grades region and click Cut from the Customization menu.

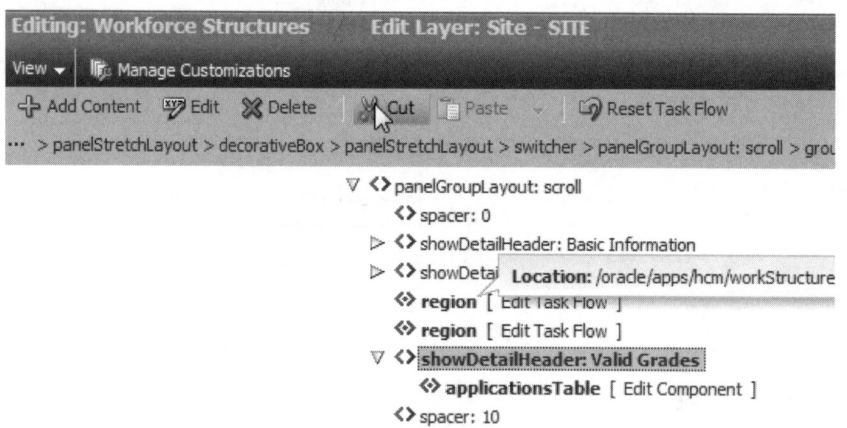

9. Now select the Job Description region and select the Paste Before option from the Customization menu. This will move the Valid Grades region above Job Description and below the Basic Information region.

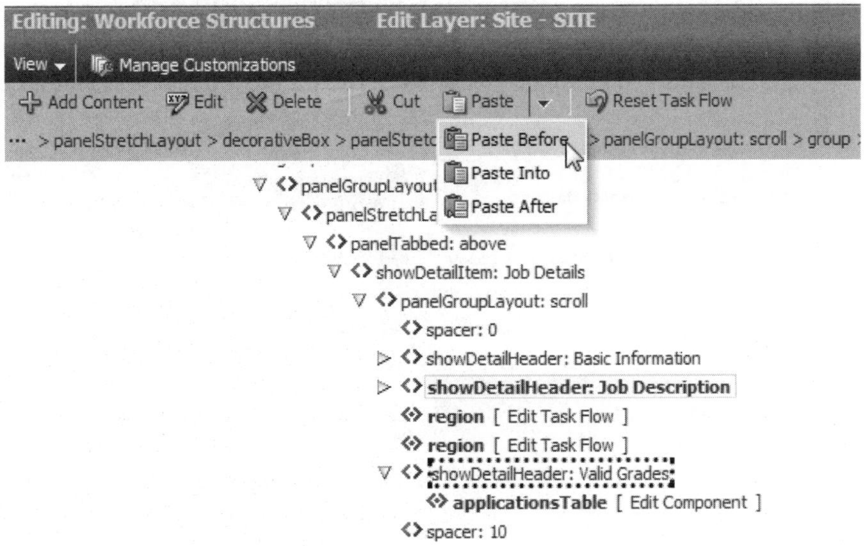

10. Now select panelTabbed: above region, right-click, and edit.

11. This opens up the Component Properties dialog where you can modify the properties of this tabbed region.

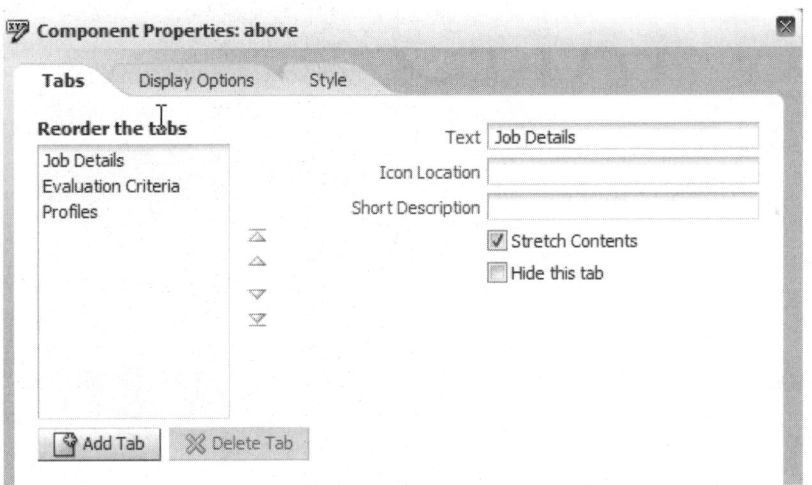

12. Move the Profiles tab to second place and rename to Applicable Profiles. You can add a new tab using the Add Tab button and remove the existing tab using the Delete Tab button.

13. You can use the Display Options tab in the Component Properties dialog to customize display options for the tabbed region. Modify the tab display option (Short Desc) to both in order to show tabs at the top and bottom of the page.

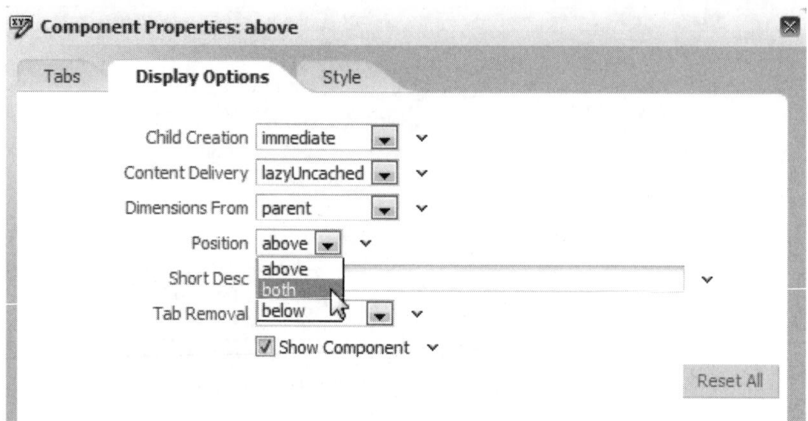

14. Save the changes and return to Design mode and you can see the changes on the run-time page.

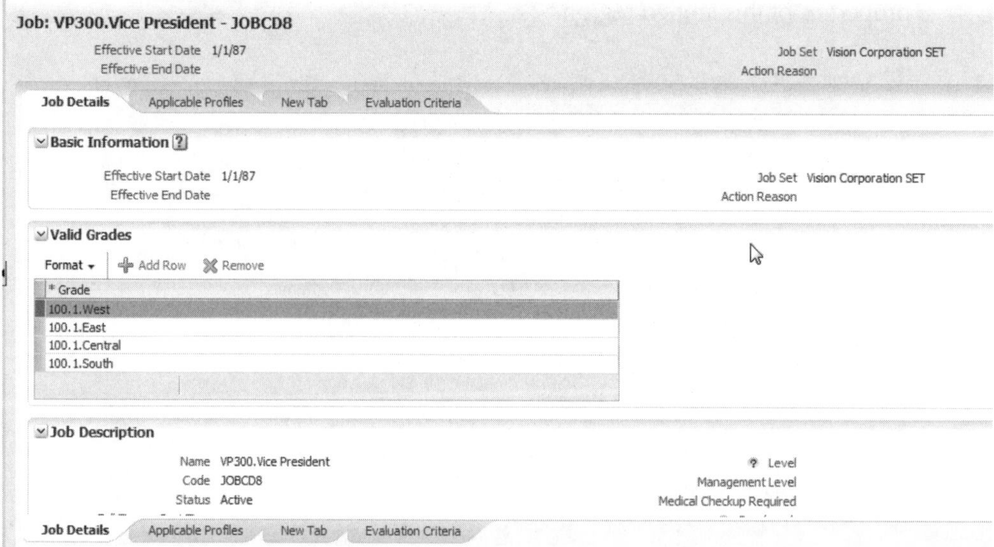

How to Customize the Task Pane

The Task pane is a standard region on any Fusion Applications page. The Task pane gives quick access to frequently used task flows or pages to users for a given work area. You can customize the Task pane using Source view. We will customize the Task pane for the Workforce Structures work area in this section. Navigate to the Workforce Structures work area page using the Navigator menu.

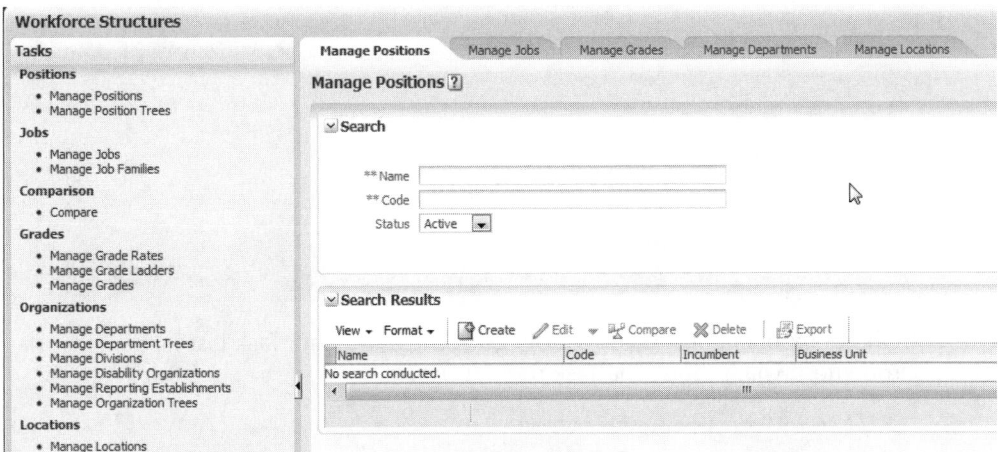

1. Once in Source view mode for customization, click the Task pane and edit the task flow. This will show the Task pane region. Click on the Edit Task Flow region under Tasks.

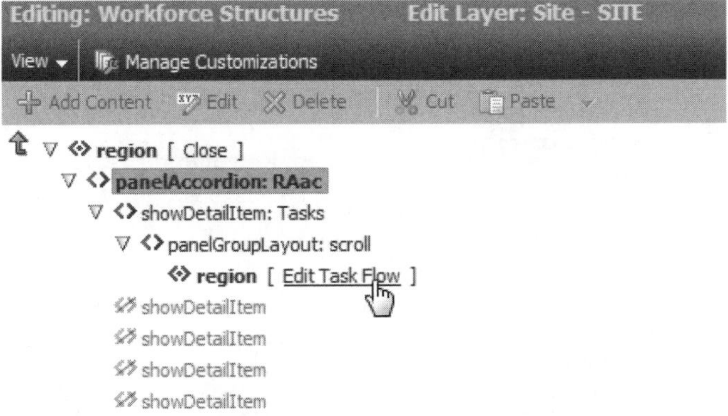

2. Select panelFormLayout for the Task pane and click Edit to open the Edit Task Pane dialog.

3. In the Component Properties dialog, go to the fourth tab, Task List Task Properties, which shows the Task pane structure.

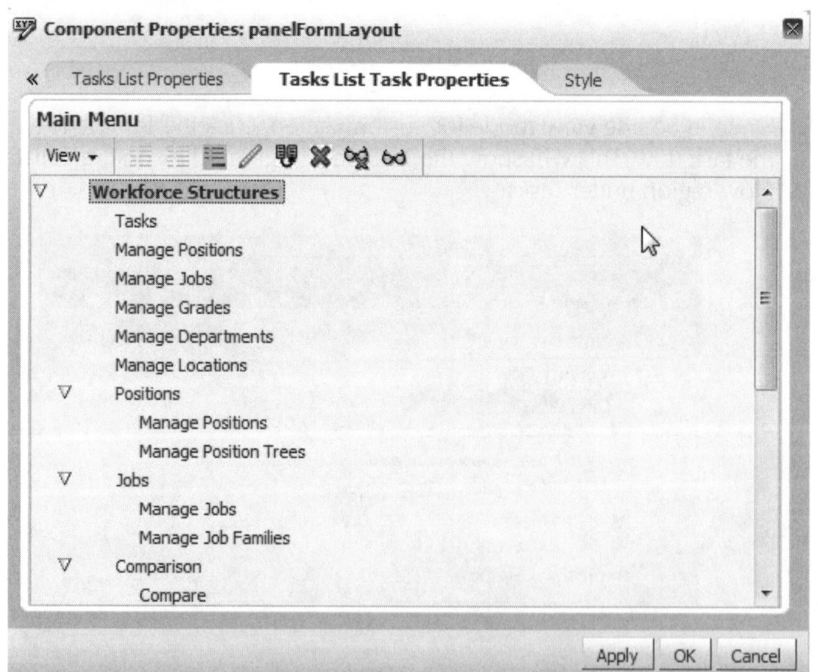

4. You can use the menu icons to customize the Task pane list. Use the Edit icon to modify the properties of a given task entry.

5. When you modify or define a new task, the following important properties must be specified, and the behavior of the task depends on the property specified.

   - **Web Application** Name of the application from the list of values.
   - **Focus View ID** focusViewId of the target page as specified in the adfc-config file of the Web application.
   - **Label** The name for the task entry.
   - **Destination** Specify this only if this is a direct URL link and not a navigation to Task Flow.
   - **Task Type** The value for this attribute controls the behavior of this task entry. You can specify this only for new tasks and cannot modify it for any existing task.
     - **defaultMain** This means the task flow will open in the Local Area tab.
     - **dynamicMain** This adds the task flow as the default tab in the local area.
     - **taskCategory** This adds the entry as a nonclickable Task pane category under which you can add more links.
     - **defaultRegional** This adds the task flow as another pane in the regional area.
   - **Taskflow ID** This is the fully qualified task flow name that you want to invoke when you click this Task pane entry.

6. You can use the Duplicate icon to copy a given Task pane entry. This will copy existing metadata for the task and you can modify to make changes.

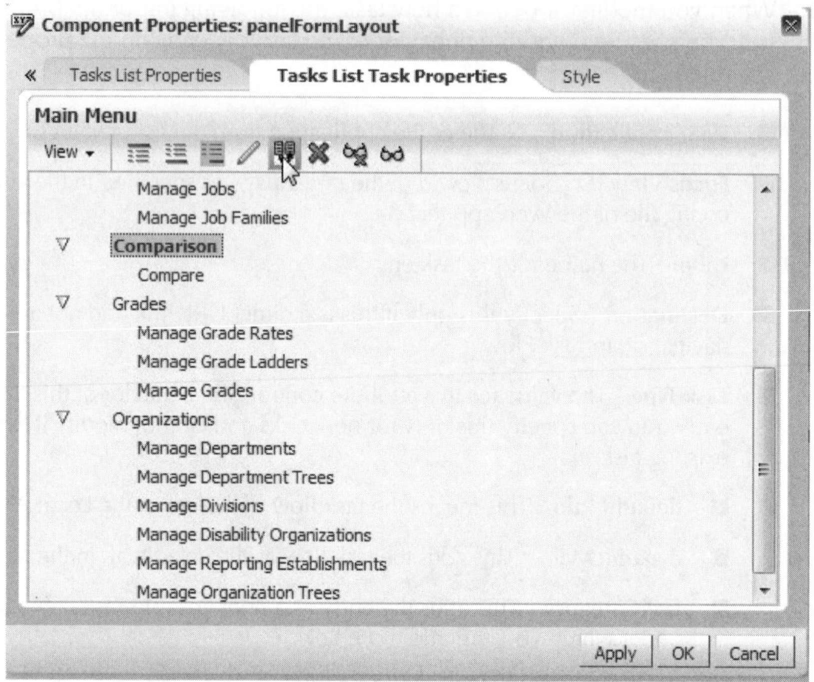

7. You can use the Delete icon to completely remove any entry. Select Locations and click Delete.

8. You can use the Show or Hide Glass icon to show or hide any task entry. Select the Manage Departments task and hide it.

9. You can use the Insert Before or Insert After or Insert Child icons to add a new entry in the Task pane. Select the Copy of Compare entry and add a child pane inside it. Give the destination as www.google.com. Rename the Copy of Compare entry to Web Sites. After saving all changes, the page will reflect the changes made.

How to Reset Customization

We have gone through many customization examples in this chapter. Page Composer provides a very easy way to reset the customizations and go back to the original state of the page. This is handy in case the customization went wrong, or you made a mistake and the results are not what you expect and you want to go back to the original state quickly. Each customization mode provides different ways to get back to the original state.

If you are customizing in Source view, there is a Reset Task Flow button in the Customization menu bar that resets the content of the task flow to its original state as shown in the following illustration.

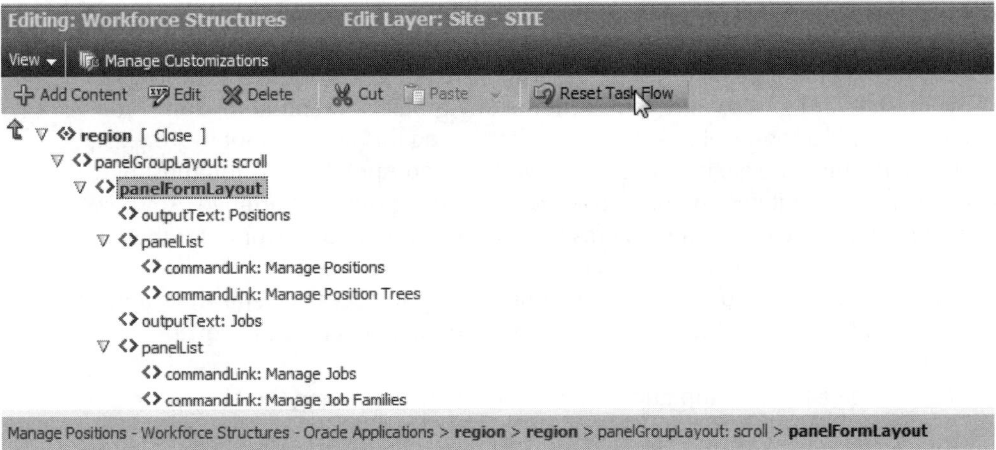

If you are customizing in CRM Select mode, you can see what properties are modified via a blue dot change indicator in the Component Properties dialog. The Reset All button allows you to reset the customizations and revert the component to its original state as shown here.

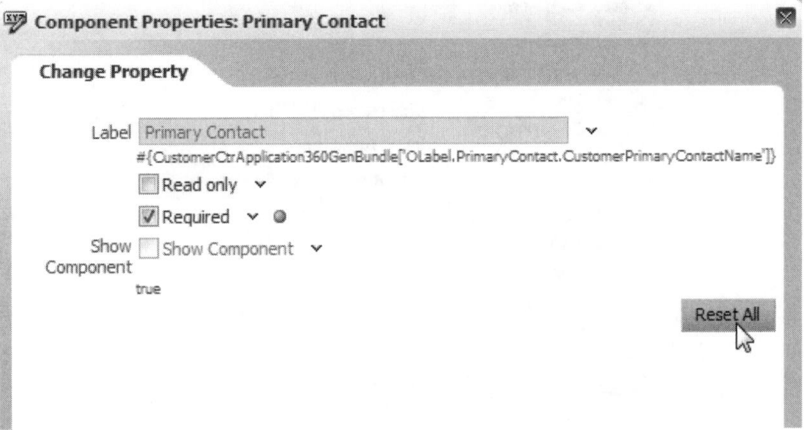

How to Customize the Navigator Menu

The Navigator menu in Fusion Applications is the main entry point to all the dashboard and work area pages. The Navigator menu is available in the global area of the UI Shell page and is accessible all the time. You can customize the Navigator menu using the Manage Menu Customizations task from Functional Setup Manager accessed by using the Setup and Maintenance link from the Navigator menu under the Tools category. Using this task, you can customize the Navigator menu such as adding or deleting a custom group, adding or deleting custom items, hiding or showing standard groups and items, editing any group or menu item, and so on. You cannot add a top-level linkable menu item using this task, cannot move existing nodes, and cannot delete items delivered with Fusion Applications. You must hide the standard menu items and copy over to a different group to rearrange. Any customization done to the menu items will honor the function security for the logged-in user. The menu items are visible only if the user has access to the page. We will use the Navigator menu to add a new group to access several work areas as a top node in the menu. The customizations are done only at the Site level.

1. Navigate to the Setup and Maintenance work area using the Navigator menu.
2. Search for the task Manage Menu Customizations and click the Go to Task button. This will launch the page to customize the Navigator menu. You use standard buttons to add groups or items to the menu.

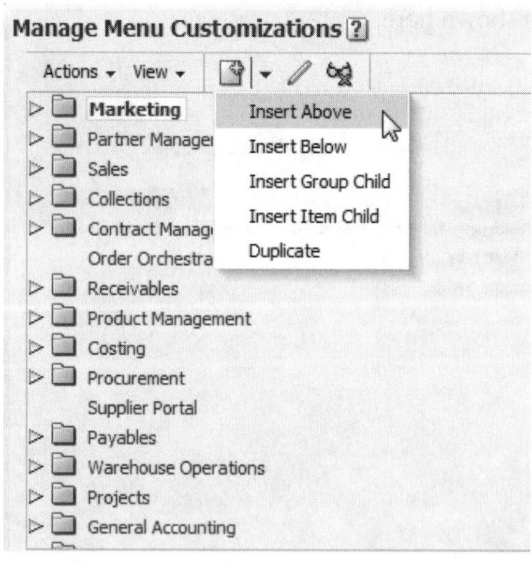

3. Select the Marketing node and click Insert Above. This will show the dialog to enter a group name. Enter Frequent as the name for the new menu group.

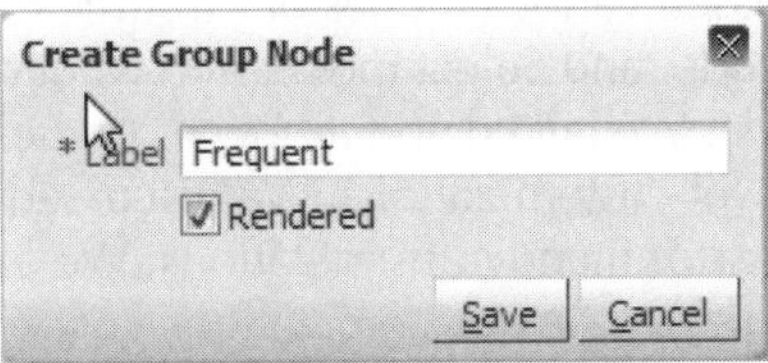

4. Select Frequent and Insert Item Child to add nodes under this new group.

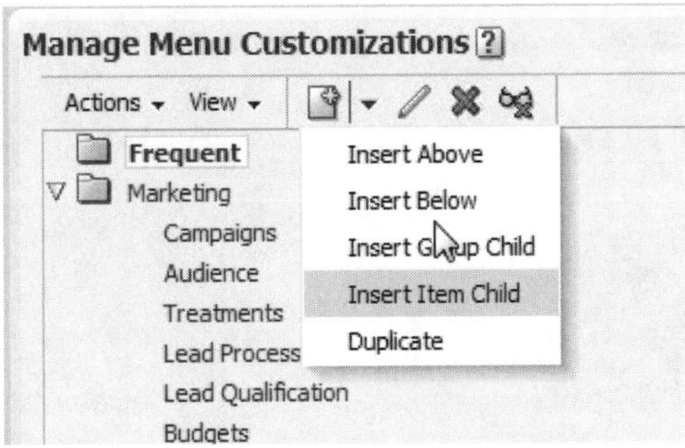

5. Use this option to add Leads, Opportunities, Customers, Setup and Maintenance, File Import, and Manage Users nodes under it. Look at existing standard nodes for these work areas to see what values should be specified.

6. Hide these nodes from the standard Navigator menu list using the Hide icon.

7. Save the changes and the Navigator menu now looks like the following illustration.

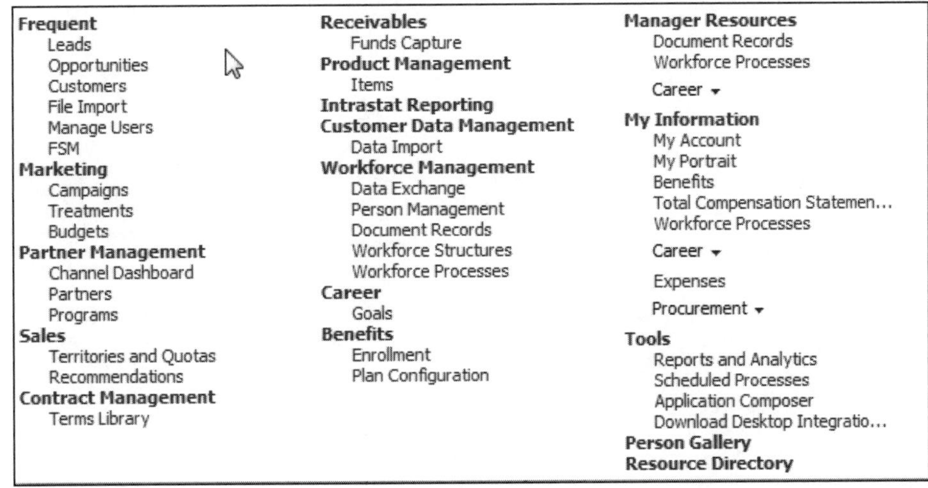

Summary

In this chapter, we discussed various modes of run-time customizations such as Design mode, Source mode, and Select mode, and what can and cannot be customized in each mode. We talked about how to do field-level customizations and how to do region-level customizations. We discussed how to do Task pane customization and Navigator menu customizations. We explained how to get back to the original state of a page when customizations go wrong by resetting the changes.

CHAPTER 6

Extending CRM with Oracle Application Composer

Oracle Application Composer is a tool available for run-time customization and extension for CRM application sales, marketing, customer center, CRM common objects, and sales catalog (order capture). You can extend standard objects for these applications that are enabled for customization as well as define new custom objects for these applications. Application Composer is available only to CRM products at this point. All CRM objects are not enabled for customization in Application Composer; please read the product-specific documentation for more details on which objects are enabled for Application Composer in CRM. Application Composer is a tool that allows business users, administrators, and developers to customize and extend CRM application objects in a run-time environment. You can modify the standard behavior of applications; for example, you can add new attributes to objects and expose them on the application UI, import and service artifacts, define business events and construct workflow with those events, and define additional validations and triggers to meet business requirements.

Application Composer Overview

You can access Application Composer with a user with the CRM administrator role using the Application Composer link from the Navigator menu under the Tools category as shown in Figure 6-1.

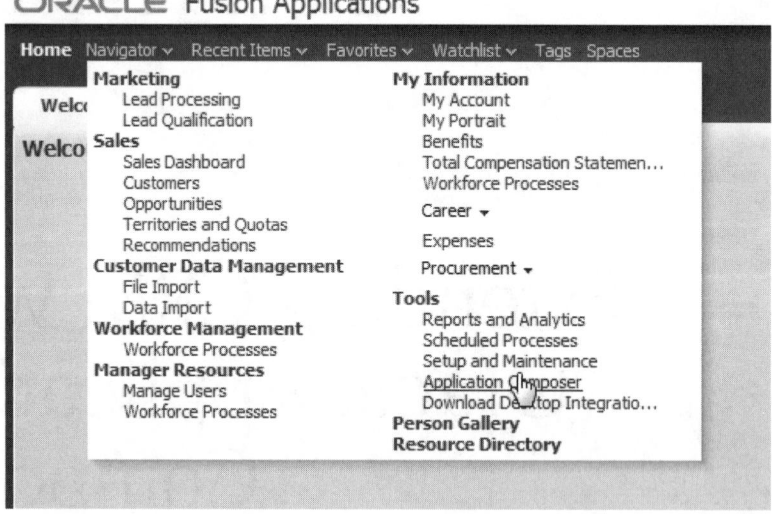

FIGURE 6-1. *Application Composer Navigator menu link*

The Application Composer home page gives you navigation access to every feature of Application Composer as shown in Figure 6-2.

Let's understand the meaning of each of these features and then we will go into details of how you go about using these features in the following sections.

- The application choice list shows the name of the CRM application context where you are customizing objects. You can switch the value to see objects for a specific application.
- **Standard Objects** allows you to manage out-of-the-box extensible objects for a given application.
- **Custom Objects** allows you to manage custom objects created by the deploying company for a given application.
- **Relationships** allows you to manage standard and custom relationships between objects for a given application.
- **Role Security** allows you to manage security rules for custom objects for given application.
- **Custom Subject Areas** allows you to manage custom subject areas for your custom objects for a given application.
- **E-Mail Templates** allows you to manage e-mail notification templates that can be used in the object workflows for a given application.

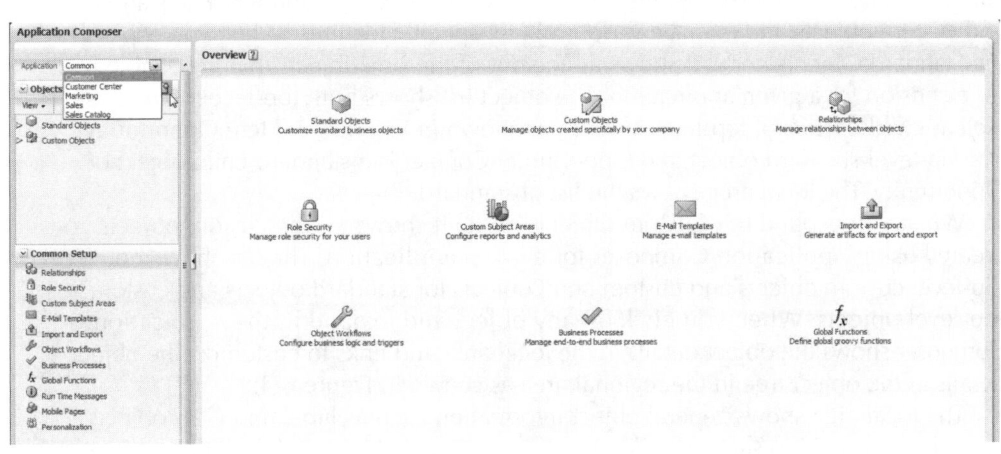

FIGURE 6-2. *Application Composer list of features*

- **Import and Export** allows you to manage the generation of import and export artifacts for your customizations to standard objects.
- **Object Workflows** allows you to define and manage business events and workflows in response to those events for standard and custom objects for a given application.
- **Business Processes** allows you to build and manage business processes for standard and custom objects for a given application.
- **Global Functions** allows you to build global functions written in Groovy language that can be used by customizations and extensions for standard and custom objects defined in scripting such as validations or triggers.
- **Run Time Messages** shows you messages logged by the Groovy scripting at run time, if there were any log messages in the script for a given application.
- **Mobile Pages** allows you to manage and configure extensions and customizations for mobile pages for a given standard or a custom object in a given application.
- **Personalization** shows you personalization done by an end user and allows the administrator to reset personalizations in a given application.

Understanding Object Structure in Application Composer

The Application Composer regional area allows you to explore and navigate standard and custom objects and manage various object-specific features. When you expand the Standard Objects node, it shows all the out-of-the-box objects that are enabled for extension for a given application. The object list shows both top-level objects as well as child objects of top-level objects, as shown in Figure 6-3. Here Opportunity is a top-level standard object and Opportunity Contact is a standard child object of Opportunity. The local area shows the list of standard objects.

When you expand the Custom Objects node, it shows all the custom objects created using Application Composer for a given application. The list shows both top-level custom objects and custom child objects for standard objects and custom top-level objects. When you click on any object and expand it, the Application Composer shows the object details in the local area and links to customize the object details in the object tree in the regional area as shown in Figure 6-4.

The local area shows general object information such as label and view objects and other information such as child objects and related objects. We will discuss how to manage these in later sections. The regional area object tree shows links to extend

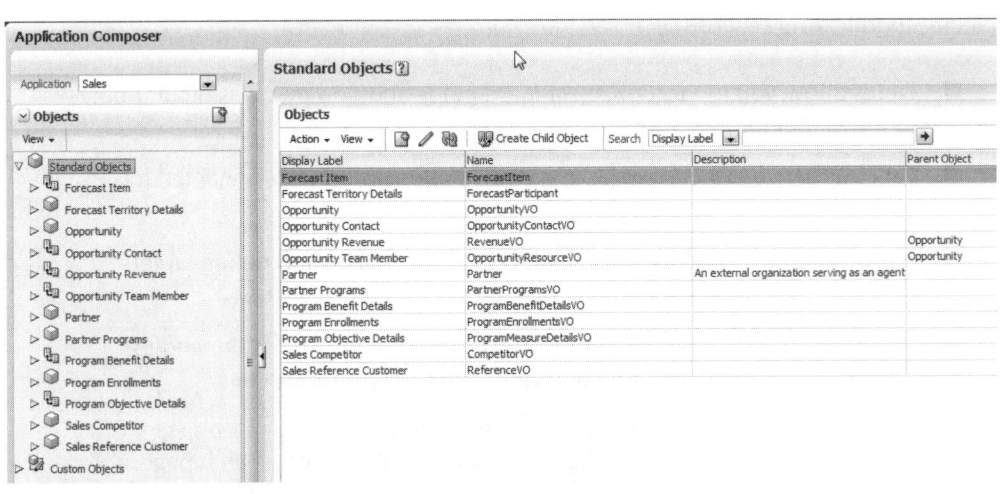

FIGURE 6-3. *List of objects in Application Composer*

the object. Links that show up for any given standard object depend on the features enabled for that standard object by the Fusion application out of the box. This cannot be customized. Read product-specific documentation to understand which features are enabled for which standard object. The custom objects support all the features in Application Composer. Following is a list of features supported in Application

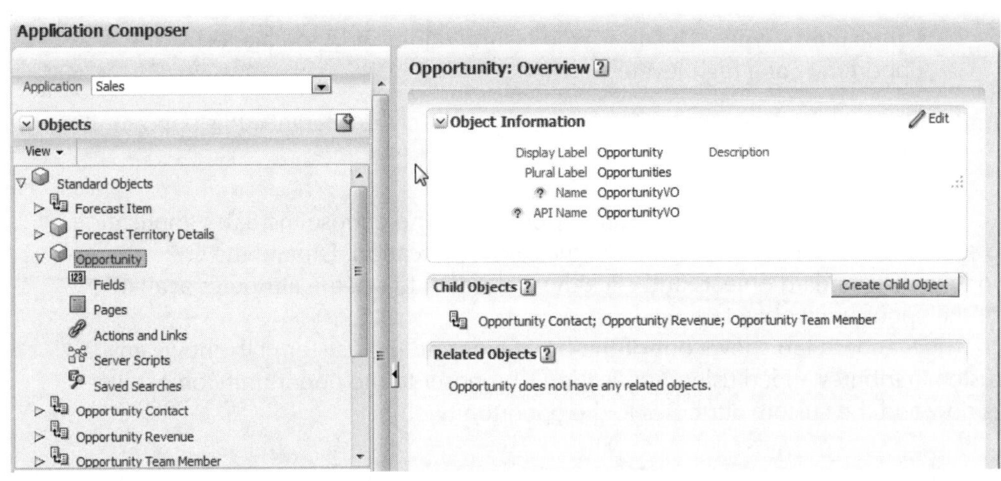

FIGURE 6-4. *Customization options for an object in Application Composer*

Composer for any object, and we will discuss in detail how to use all of these features in following sections.

- **Fields** allow you to customize standard fields and add new custom attributes to the model for the object.
- **Pages** allow you to customize and extend application pages enabled for extension for a given object.
- **Actions and Links** allow you to add buttons and links and define target actions for them on the application page for a given object.
- **Server Scripts** allow you to add field- or object-level validation, and to trigger and define object functions that can be used for scripts.
- **Saved Searches** allow you to define a new saved search for an object that will be visible to all users of the application on the object search page.

How to Add a New Field to an Object

Application Composer allows you to add a new attribute or field to a standard or custom object. When you add a new field, it gets added to the physical data model, to the object model such as EO, VO, and to Web services. You will use Application Composer to add new fields when the standard fields do not meet your business requirements. In this section, we will add three new attributes to an opportunity object.

1. **Top Opportunity** This field is auto-calculated if the opportunity revenue is > 100000.
2. **Opportunity Type** This is a fixed List of Values field to categorize the opportunity at a high level.
3. **Opportunity Reference** This is a text field to cross-reference this opportunity in a different system.

Create a sandbox, go to Application Composer, and choose the Sales application to see all standard objects available in the sales application. Expand the Opportunity node under standard objects and click the Fields link to see the attributes available for the opportunity object.

The Standard tab shows out-of-the-box fields and the Custom tab shows any custom attributes added using Application Composer to the opportunity object. Let us now add the custom attributes to the opportunity object.

1. Click the Create icon in the Custom tab. This will bring up the Create Custom Attribute dialog as shown in the following illustration where you first choose the type of custom field you want to add.

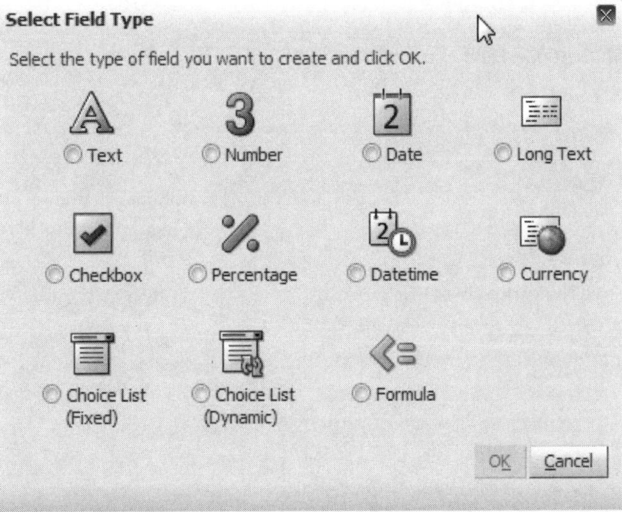

2. Most of the field types are self-explanatory. There are a few special field types supported by Application Composer that you can use based on your business needs.

   a. **Percentage type** allows you to capture percentage values for the field.

   b. **Currency type** allows you to capture amounts of data.

   c. **Dynamic Choice List** allows you to build a list of values where the list is from a related object.

   d. **Formula field** allows you to specify an expression that calculates the field value and cannot be updated by the end user. The value is automatically updated by the application based on the expression.

3. Select Formula and click the OK button to create the Top Opportunity field. Specify the display label as Top Opportunity and Depends On field as Revenue because this field will be recalculated every time revenue on opportunity is updated, as shown in the following illustration.

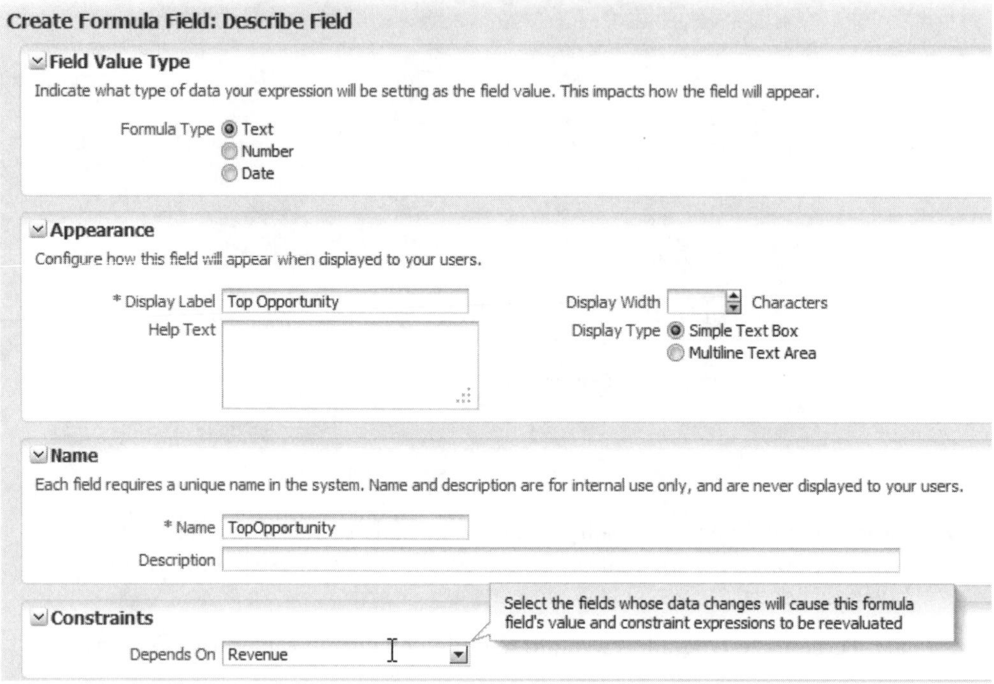

4. Click the Next button to configure the expression for this formula field. Specify the formula to return Y if revenue is 100000 as shown in the following code. Click Submit to create this formula field.

```
Revenue >= 100000 ? "Y" : "N"
```

5. Click Create again and select Choice List (Fixed) as field type and click OK to define the Opportunity Type attribute. On the Create Fixed Choice list page, click the Create icon for the Lookup Type field under the List of Values region. This will launch the FND lookup creation screen where you can define the lookup types and codes to be used by this fixed choice list. Define the values as Hardware, Software License, Support, Service, and Consulting, as shown in the next illustration.

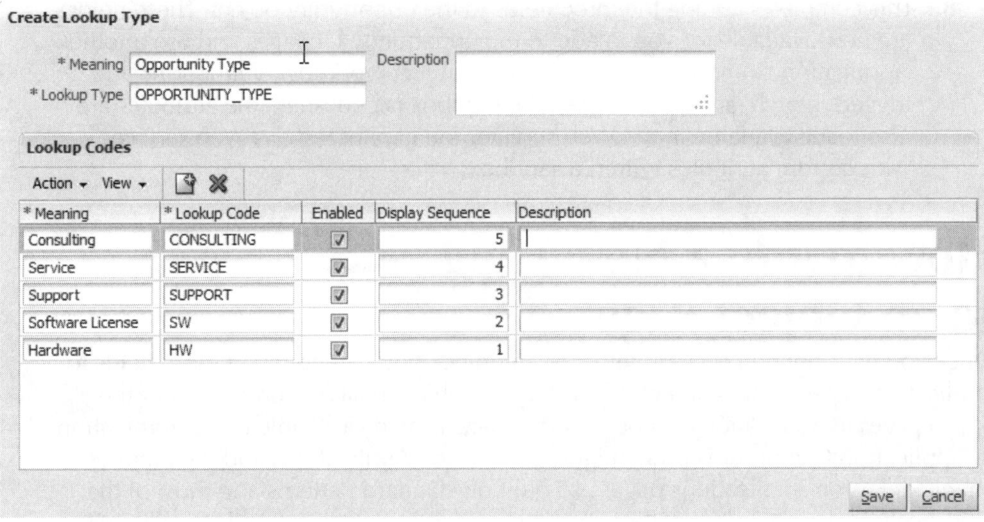

6. You can optionally specify a default value for this attribute to one of the lookups by picking it from the Fixed Value field under the Default Value region.

7. Click the Create icon again to create and select the Text field type. Give the label as **Opportunity Reference Number** and mark it as Indexed Field so that it can be used for efficient search as shown in the following illustration. Click Save and Close to create this field.

Create Text Field

Appearance

Configure how this field will appear when displayed to your users.

* Display Label Opportunity Reference Number

Help Text

Display Width Characters

Display Type Simple Text Box

Multiline Text Area

Name

Each field requires a unique name in the system. Name and description are for internal use only, and are never displayed to your users.

* Name OpportunityReferenceNumber

Description

Once this field is created, you cannot change your selection

The database column that stores values for this field is indexed for faster access

Constraints

Required

Updateable

Searchable

Indexed

Minimum Length Characters

Maximum Length 80 Characters

Default Value

Enter the value you want to set for the field when an object is created. Select Expression if you want to set the default dynamically.

Fixed Value

Expression

8. This completes adding the three fields to the opportunity object. These fields are now available for you to add to the opportunity UI pages and use in other Application Composer features such as object workflow, validations and triggers, search, and so on. When the sandbox is published, the attributes are also made available in the Web service. You cannot test the Web service with custom attributes within a sandbox.

How to Add a New Field to an Object Page

Once you have defined custom fields for an object, you can now add these fields to application pages for that object. Each standard object enables some or all of the object pages in Application Composer. What page is made available for customization in Application Composer is preconfigured by Fusion Applications and it cannot be changed. Fusion Applications pages are built on standard patterns and most of the object pages follow a similar pattern. Typically standard objects have a list or summary table page, create page, and edit summary form. If the object has any standard child object, the detail tabs for those child objects are also available in Application Composer. Click the Pages link under Opportunity object to see the application pages available for customization for opportunity object as shown in the following illustration.

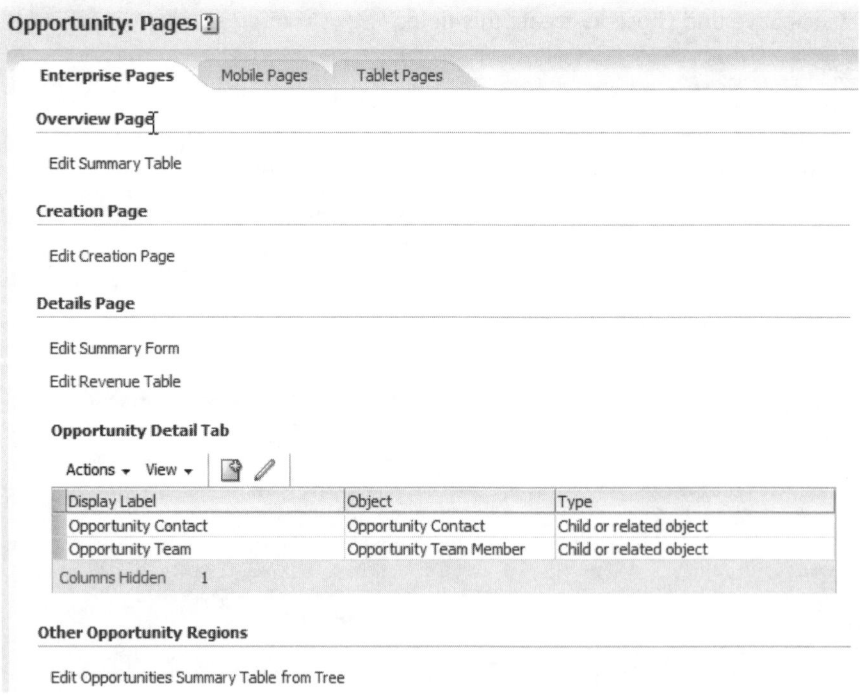

Opportunity: Pages

Enterprise Pages | Mobile Pages | Tablet Pages

Overview Page

Edit Summary Table

Creation Page

Edit Creation Page

Details Page

Edit Summary Form

Edit Revenue Table

Opportunity Detail Tab

Actions View

Display Label	Object	Type
Opportunity Contact	Opportunity Contact	Child or related object
Opportunity Team	Opportunity Team Member	Child or related object

Columns Hidden 1

Other Opportunity Regions

Edit Opportunities Summary Table from Tree

In addition to the application or enterprise pages, you can also customize the mobile and tablet pages for an object if they are enabled for those devices. We will now add the new attributes to the summary list table and edit page for the opportunity.

1. Click the Edit Summary Table link to add these attributes to the opportunity list table. Select the three custom attributes from the Available Fields shuttle to the Selected Fields shuttle. Move the two fields up as shown in the following illustration. Click Save and Close to save the customization.

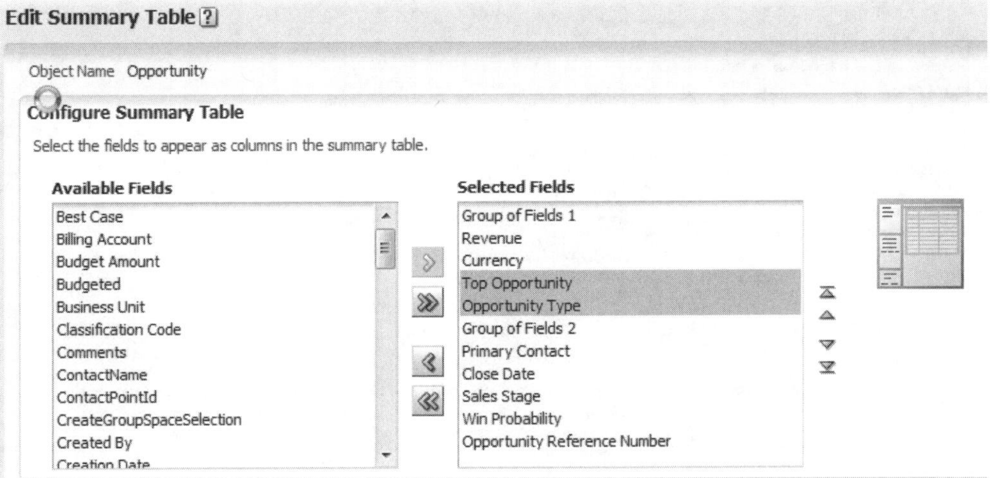

2. From the Navigator menu, select Opportunities under Sales to go to the opportunity home page. In the opportunity search result list, you can see new attributes.

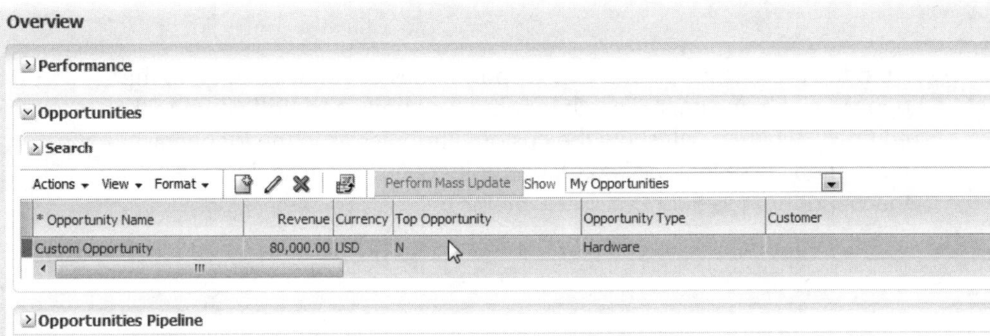

3. Go back to the opportunity pages in Application Composer and click the Edit Summary Form link to customize the opportunity edit page to add these attributes. Add Top Opportunity and Opportunity Type in the default summary region and Opportunity Reference Number field to the detailed summary region shown in the following illustration. You can use the Move Up or Down arrow to move the fields to the right place on the page. Click Save and Close to save the customization.

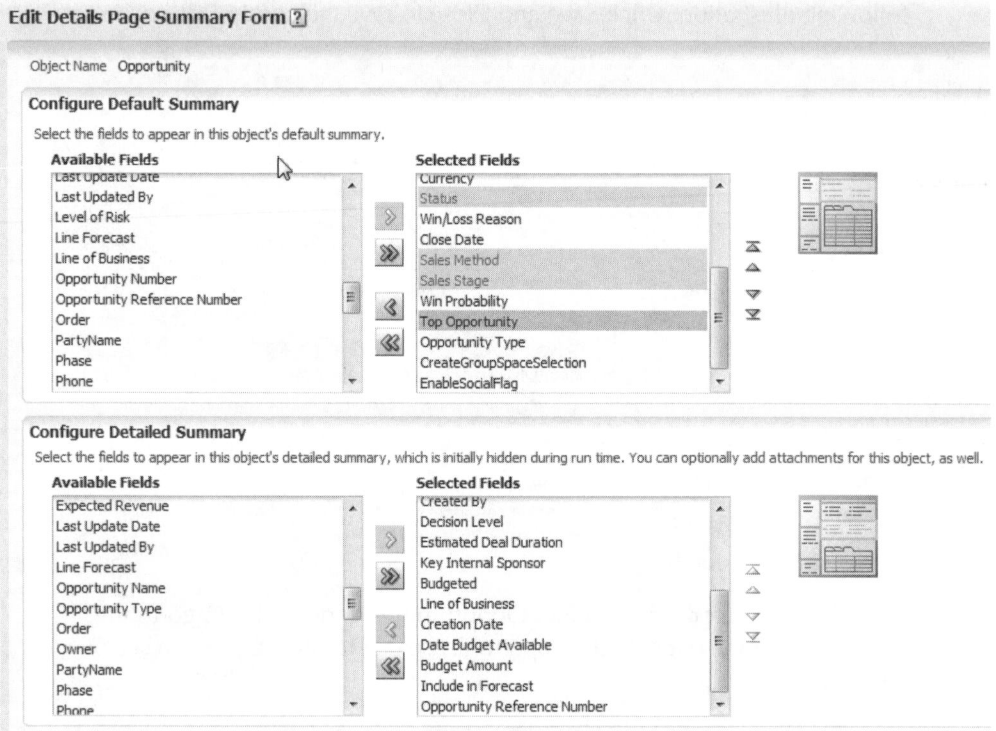

4. From the Navigator menu, select Opportunities under Sales to go to the opportunity home page. Search for an opportunity and drill down to the edit page where it will show the custom attributes as in the following illustration. Note that the Top Opportunity is "N" because the revenue for this opportunity is 80000.

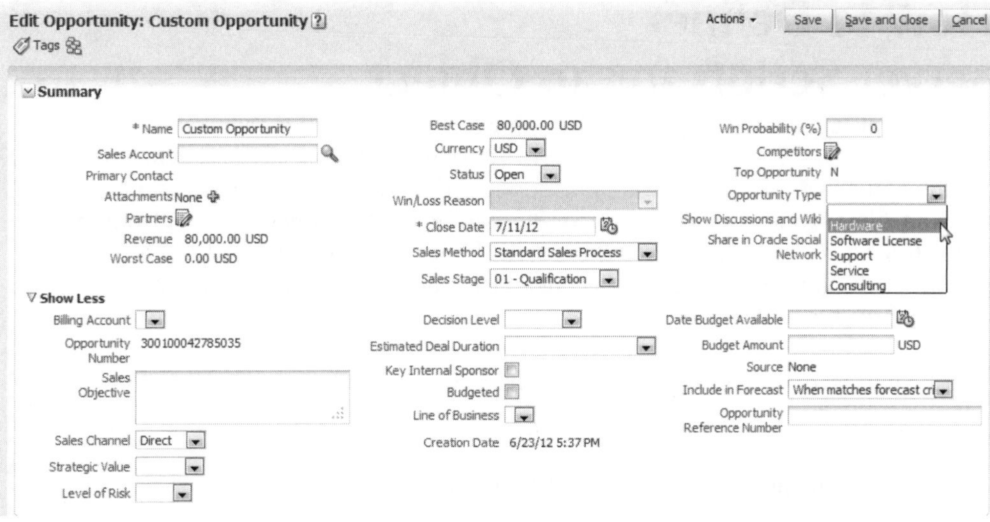

5. Update the opportunity reference number to MYSYS101 and update the revenue line for the opportunity such that the total revenue will be > 100000. This will now change the Top Opportunity formula field to Y.

6. Click Save and close to go back to the search page. Click the Advance button. Click the Add Fields button and you will see that the new custom attributes are available for search, as shown in the following illustration. You can add these attributes and use them for the search.

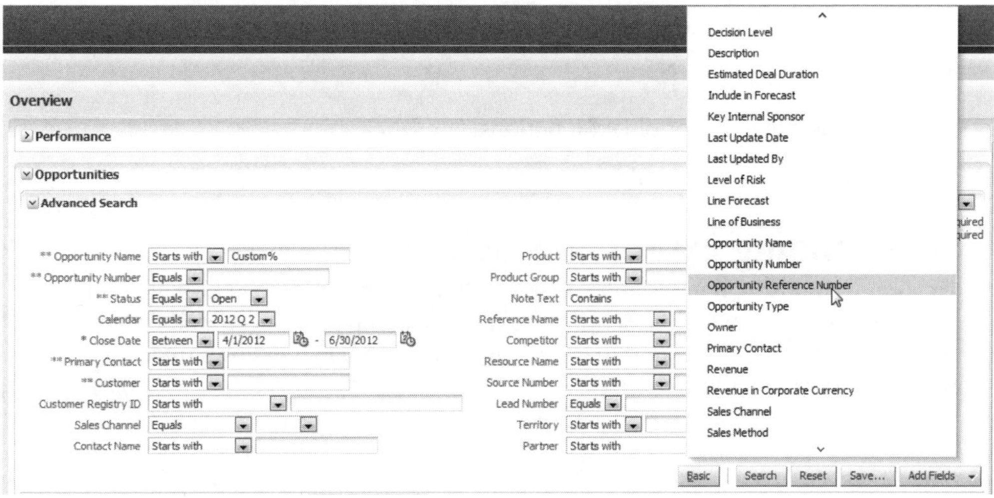

How to Define Server Scripts for an Object

Server scripts are a powerful feature that allows you to customize the business logic for a given object. The scripts are written in Groovy, which is a standard dynamic scripting language for Java platform and supported by ADFbc. The Groovy script can be a very simple one-line expression, or it could be multiple lines-n-long or multiple pages-n-long code for complicated business logic. There are many places in Application Composer where you may need to write a Groovy script. The scripts fall into three broad categories.

1. Field-level scripts allow you to do the following:
    a. Calculate a formula field's value
    b. Calculate a default value for a custom field
    c. Make a custom field conditionally required
    d. Make a custom field conditionally updateable
    e. Define a validation rule for any field
2. Object-level scripts allow you to do the following:
    a. Define a condition for an object workflow
    b. Define a validation rule for the object
    c. Define triggers to extend default processing for the object
3. Generic scripts
    a. Reusable code for object functions
    b. Utility code in global functions

Understanding Expression Builder

Application Composer provides an Expression Builder where you can visually write the script. You can also write the script code directly in the scripting editor. Every place where you can write a script has the ability to launch Expression Builder, as shown in the following illustration.

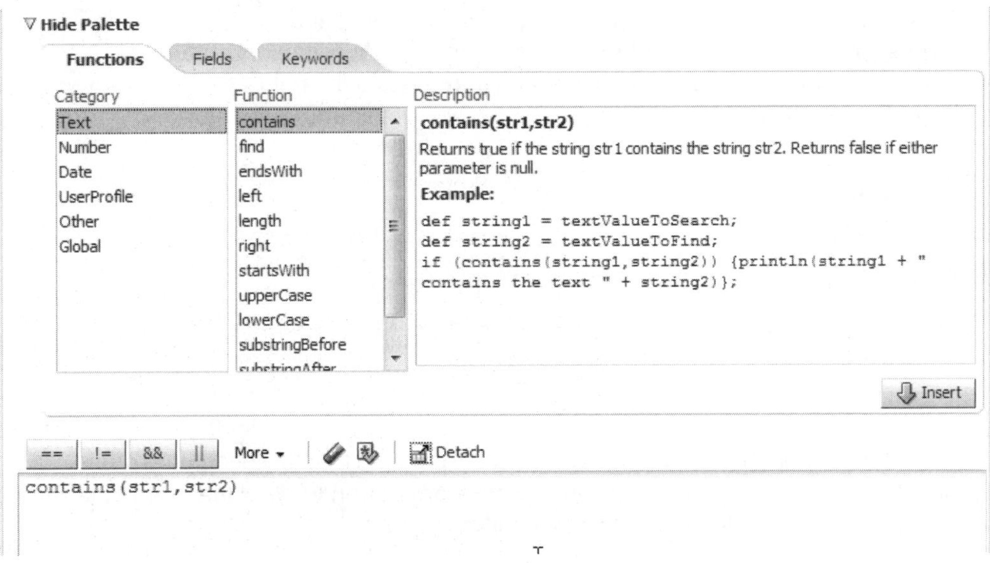

The Functions tab shows the standard Groovy functions available for scripting. You can select a function and click the Insert button to pull the expression into your script. The Fields tab shows all the fields available for the object and all the child collections available for a given row of the object. This list is generated based on the View object and its view links to child objects as defined by Fusion Applications out of the box and Application Composer. You can select a field and click the Insert button to pull that field into your script as shown in the following illustration. At run time, the value of that field is substituted for evaluation in the script.

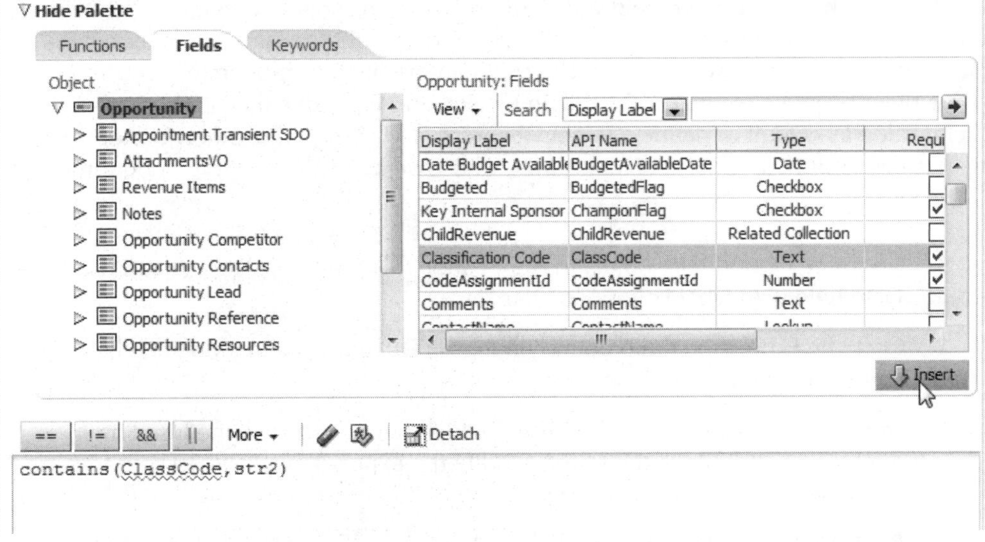

When you are writing the script in the context of a field and not an object, the Keywords tab shows you available keywords to inspect the value of that field as shown here. You use oldValue and newValue to reference the field's values before and after the modification was done.

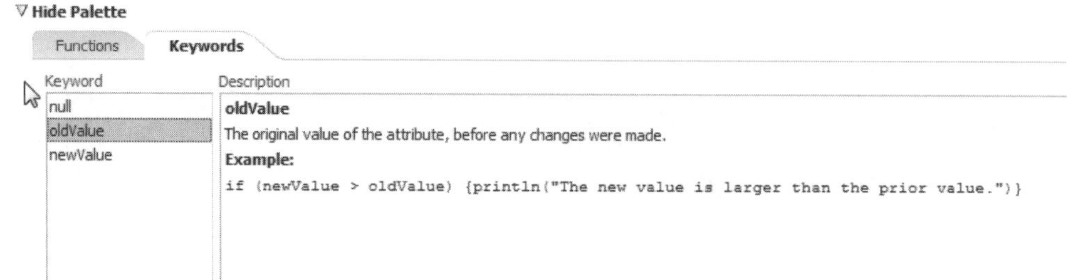

The script editor allows you to add standard operators to help speed up writing the script such as >, <, >=, <=. You can use the Erase button to clear the script editor and the Validate button to check the syntax of your script.

Calculate a Formula Field's Value

We defined a custom attribute Top Opportunity, which is a formula field. We defined a Groovy expression for this field that checks if the revenue of the opportunity is 100000 or more and returns the value of this field to Y or N based on this. You can put any other complicated logic in the formula field based on your business needs.

Calculate the Default Value for a Custom Field

When you create new data for a given object, the attributes do not have any value and the user must specify the field values on the UI or in service. When you define custom fields, you can specify a default value for the attribute that is put in the attribute when a new row is created. The user can modify the value in the UI or overwrite it by passing a different value in the service. You can either specify a fixed literal value as default or define a Groovy expression. Let us define a new custom field called Follow-up Date on Opportunity whose default value will be Opportunity Close Date + 30.

1. Go to the Opportunity object in Application Composer and define a new Date field with label Follow-up Date.
2. Click the Expression radio button under the Default Value region and click the Expression Builder icon.
3. From the Fields tab, select the Close Date attribute and click the Insert icon to pull that attribute in the script. Modify the expression to add 30 days to it as shown in the following example.

```
EffectiveDate == null ? today() + 30 : EffectiveDate + 30
```

4. Save the attribute and add it to the Create Opportunity page using the Pages link in Application Composer under the Opportunity object as shown in the following illustration.

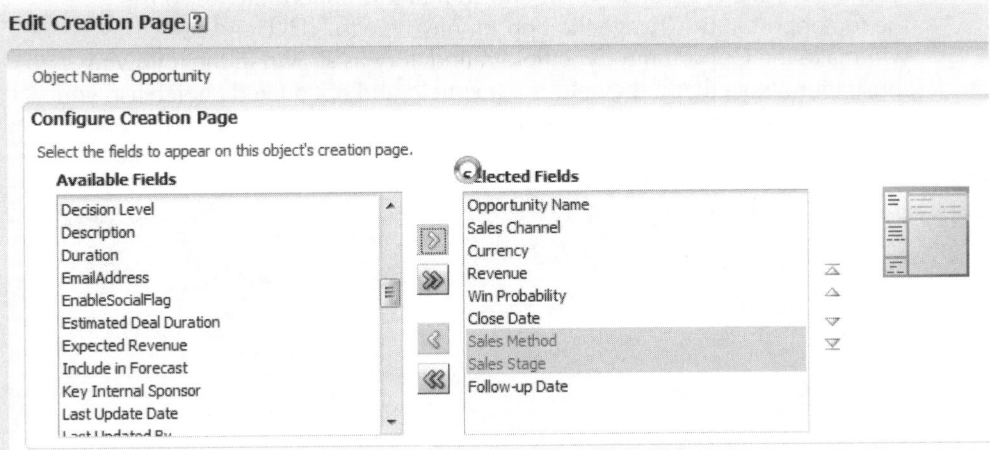

5. Navigate to the Opportunity home page and click Create Opportunity. This will show the Follow-up Date as today's date + 30.

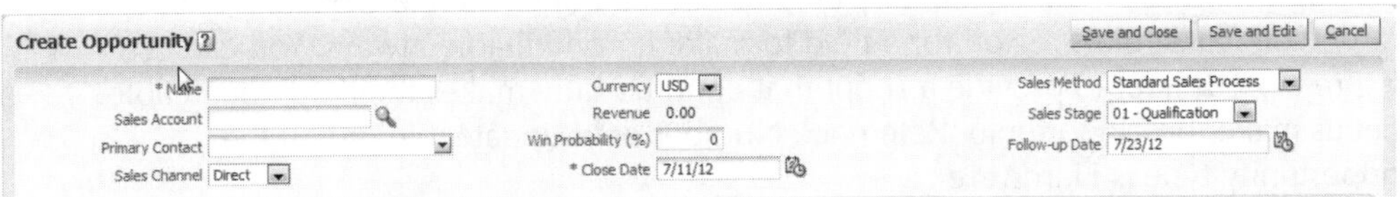

Make a Custom Field Conditionally Required

Custom fields are not required by default. You can make a custom field always mandatory by checking the required box under the Constraints region for a given field.

You can use the Expression Builder to define an expression to conditionally make this field required. We will make the Opportunity Type field mandatory for top opportunities.

1. Go to the Fields for Opportunity object in Application Composer. From the Custom attributes, click the Opportunity Type field to edit it. Click the Expression Builder icon next to the Required field under the Constraints region.

2. Select the Top Opportunity field and click the Insert button to pull the attribute into the script. Modify the script to compare the value to 'Y' as shown in the following example so that the required property will be set for top opportunities.

```
TopOpportunity_c == 'Y'
```

3. Go to the opportunity home page using Navigator and drill down to an opportunity that is not a top opportunity. The Opportunity Type field is not required at this point.

4. Now modify the revenue to > 100000 so that this opportunity becomes the top opportunity. Change the opportunity type to NULL and save. This will make the Opportunity Type field mandatory as shown in the following illustration. Note that if the field is a text field and not a fixed choice list, you will get a client-side mandatory error and not an error from the server side.

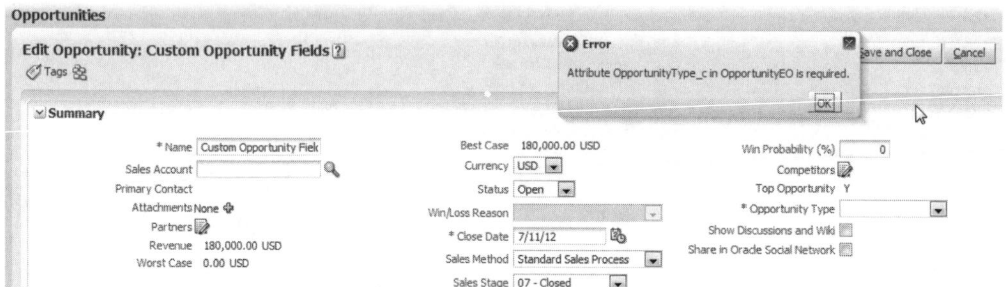

Make a Custom Field Conditionally Updateable

Whether a custom field is editable or not is controlled by its Updateable property. All custom fields are updateable by default. You can uncheck the Updateable box under the Constraints region for a field to make it noneditable always. You can use Expression Builder to provide a script that conditionally makes the field updateable. Let us make the Opportunity Reference Number field updateable only if the opportunity type is Hardware.

1. Go to the Fields for Opportunity object in Application Composer. From the Custom attributes, click the Opportunity Reference Number field to edit it. Click the Expression Builder icon next to the Updateable field under the Constraints region.

2. Select the Opportunity Type field and click the Insert button to pull the attribute into the script. Modify the script to compare the value to 'HW' as shown in the following example so that the Updateable property will be set for open opportunities.

```
OpportunityType_c == 'HW'
```

3. Select the Depends On field as Opportunity Type so that when you change status, the UI field reflects the new state as shown in the following illustration.

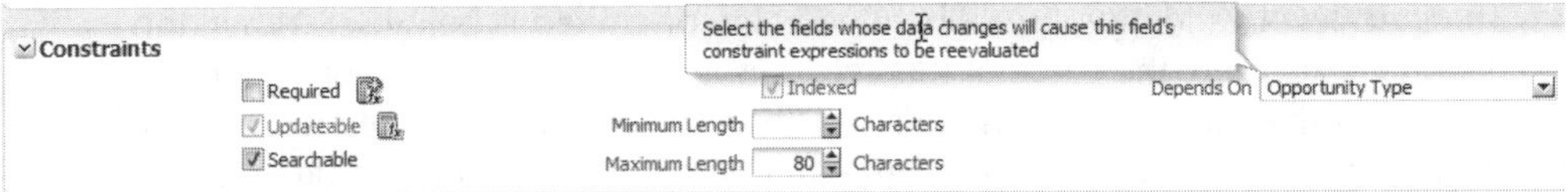

4. Go to an opportunity home page and edit an opportunity. You can modify the Opportunity Reference Number field if the opportunity type is Hardware.

5. Update an opportunity type to something else and the Opportunity Reference Number field is not editable.

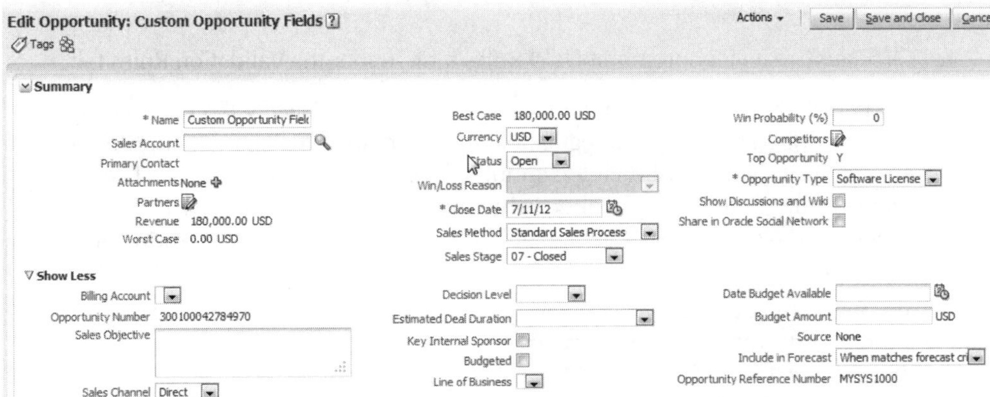

Define a Validation Rule for a Field

You can define a new field-level validation rule using Application Composer for both standard field and custom fields. To define a new validation rule, click the Server Scripts link for any object, as shown here.

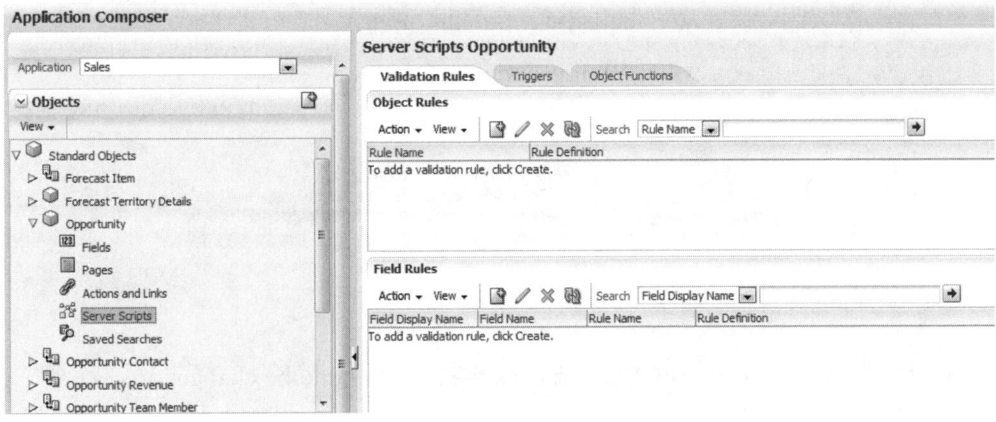

The field-level validation fires when the value on a field is being set. When the validation is executed, the value of the field is not yet set. The validation rule must return true for the success case and false for the failure case. If the rule returns true, the value of the field is set to its new value if all the field rules return true. If the rule returns false, the error message configured in the validation rule is thrown and the field value remains as it was before the validation was fired. You can use the oldValue keyword to access the old value of the field and the newValue keyword to access the new value of the field being set in the validation rule. You define a field-level validation rule when the rule is independent of values for other fields and should be executed only when setting the value for a given field. Let us define a validation rule to allow only alphanumeric values for the Opportunity Reference Number field.

1. Click the Create icon from the Field Rules table under the Validation Rules tab.
2. Select Field Name as Opportunity Reference Number. Specify the Rule Name. In the script editor, specify a regular expression to match alphanumeric values as mentioned in the following example. Specify the Error Message "The Opportunity Reference Number value must be alpha numeric without space or any other special character." The rule looks like the one shown in Figure 6-5.

```
import java.util.regex.Matcher
import java.util.regex.Pattern
def pattern = ~/[A-Za-z0-9]*/
pattern instanceof Pattern
return pattern.matcher(newValue).matches()
```

3. Click Save and Close to save the rule.
4. Go to the opportunity home page using Navigator and drill down to an opportunity edit page. Enter the Opportunity Reference Number as **ABC_123** and click the Save button. This will throw a field-level validation error message as shown in the following illustration

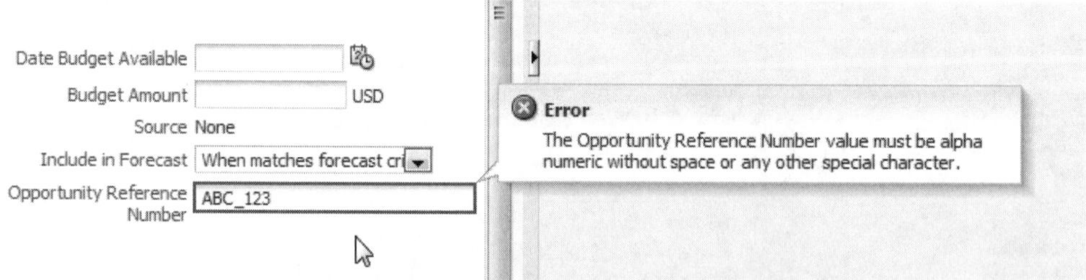

5. Modify the value to **ABC123** and click the Save button; the changes are saved without any errors.

Create Field Validation Rule

* Field Name: Opportunity Reference Number

* Rule Name: ORNAlphaNumericOnly

Description: Validate that the value is only alpha numeric without space or special characters

Rule Definition

Hide Palette

Functions | Keywords

Category	Function	Description
Text	contains	
Number	find	
Date	endsWith	
UserProfile	left	
Other	length	
Global	right	
	startsWith	
	upperCase	
	lowerCase	
	substringBefore	

== != && || More Detach

```
import java.util.regex.Matcher
import java.util.regex.Pattern

def pattern = ~/[A-Za-z0-9]*/
pattern instanceof Pattern
return pattern.matcher(newValue).matches()
```

Error Message

The Opportunity Reference Number value must be alpha numeric without space or any other special character.

FIGURE 6-5. *Defining a field validation rule*

Define a Validation Rule for an Object

The object-level validation rule fires during the validation phase of the entity row. The validation rule must return true for the success case and false for the failure case. If all the object-level validation rules return true, the object row will be saved to the database. If the rule returns false, the error message configured in the validation rule is thrown. You define an object-level validation rule when the rule is dependent on multiple fields so that the validation is correctly evaluated irrespective of the order in which field values are assigned. Let us define a validation rule that for an open opportunity, a sales account must be mandatory if it is a top opportunity.

1. Click the Create icon from the Object Rules table under the Validation Rules tab.

2. Give the rule name as **MandatorySalesAccount**. From the Fields tab, pick the necessary attributes and build the script as shown in the following example to return false when the sales account is null for the top open opportunity. Provide the error message "Sales Account is mandatory when Opportunity Status is Open and it is Top Opportunity," as shown in Figure 6-6.

```
if (StatusCode == 'OPEN' && TopOpportunity_c == 'Y') {
  if (TargetPartyId == null){
    return false;
  }
}
return true;
```

Edit Object Validation Rule
* Rule Name MandatorySalesAccount
Description For an open opportunity, sales account must be mandatory if it is a top opportunity
Rule Definition
Hide Palette
Functions Fields Keywords
Category Function Description
Text Number Date UserProfile Other Global
contains find endsWith left length right startsWith upperCase lowerCase substringBefore
== != && || More Detach
if (StatusCode == 'OPEN' && TopOpportunity_c == 'Y') {
if (TargetPartyId == null){
return false;
}
}
return true;
Error Message
Sales Account is mandatory when Opportunity Status is Open and it is Top Opportunity.

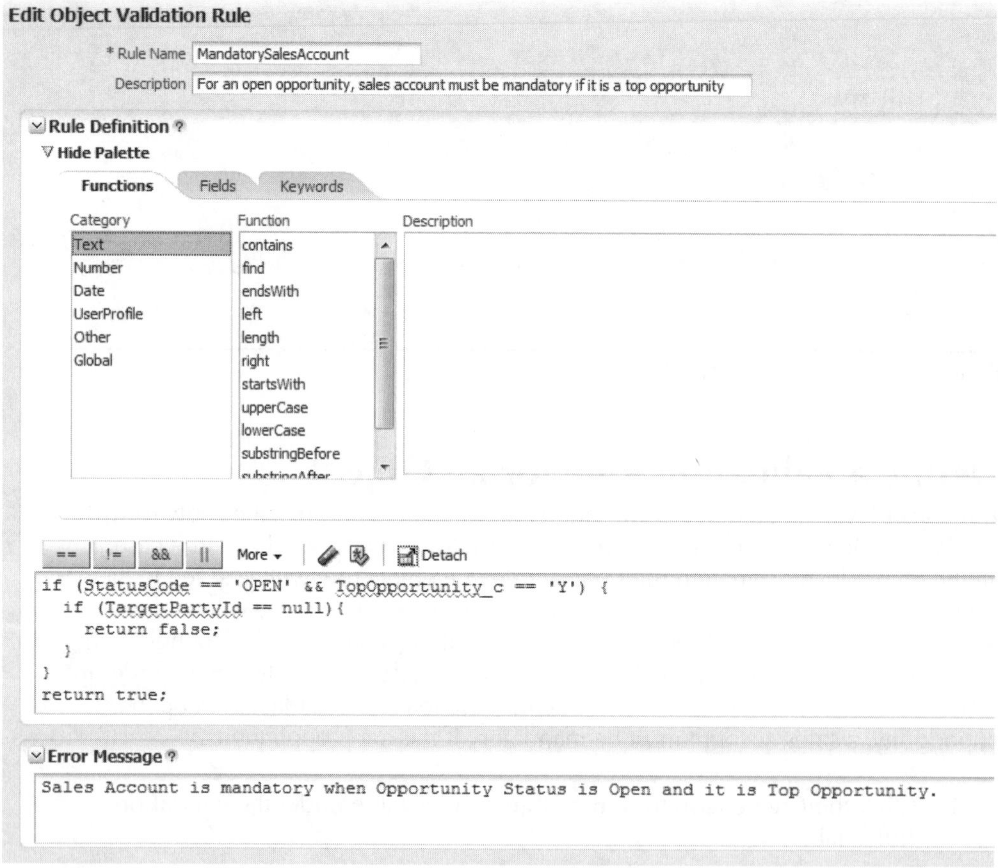

FIGURE 6-6. *Defining an object validation rule*

3. Click Save and Close to save the rule.

4. Go to the opportunity home page using Navigator and drill down to an opportunity edit page. Modify an open top opportunity and save without the sales account field. This will throw an object-level validation error message.

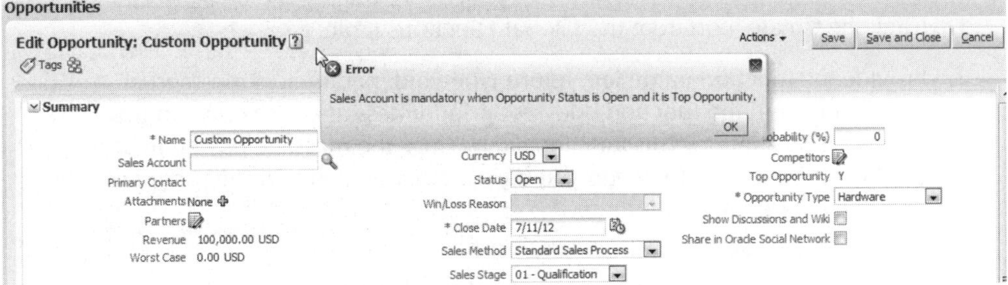

Reusable Code for Object Functions

We can define certain routines for a given object in object functions and call these routines from various scripts as applicable. You can define object functions from the Object Functions tab when you go to the Server Scripts link for any object.

1. Click the Create icon from the Object Functions tab.

2. Provide the function name **openOpportunity**, return type **void**, and the function body that sets the Opportunity Status field to OPEN as shown in the following illustration.

```
setAttribute("StatusCode", "OPEN")
```

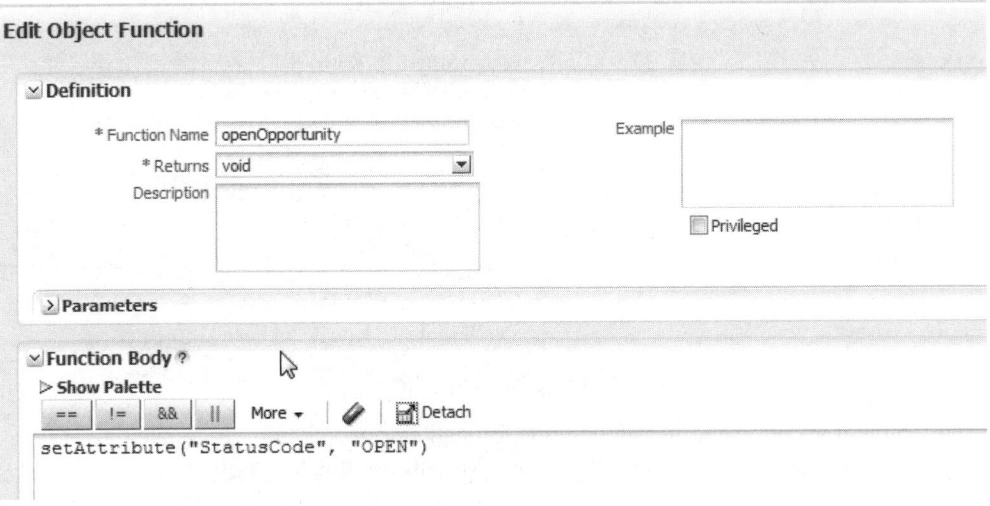

3. Click Save and Close to save the object function.

Utility Code in Global Functions

You can define a reusable utility script or code in global functions that you can access across all objects. You can define these functions via the Global Functions link under the Common Setup regional area pane.

1. Click the Create icon from the Global Functions table.
2. Provide the function name **log**, return type **void**, parameters message of type String, and the function body as "println(message)" as shown in the following illustration. This function simply logs the message passed in as a parameter. This is useful when you have a complicated and long script and you need to debug it at run time.

```
println(message)
```

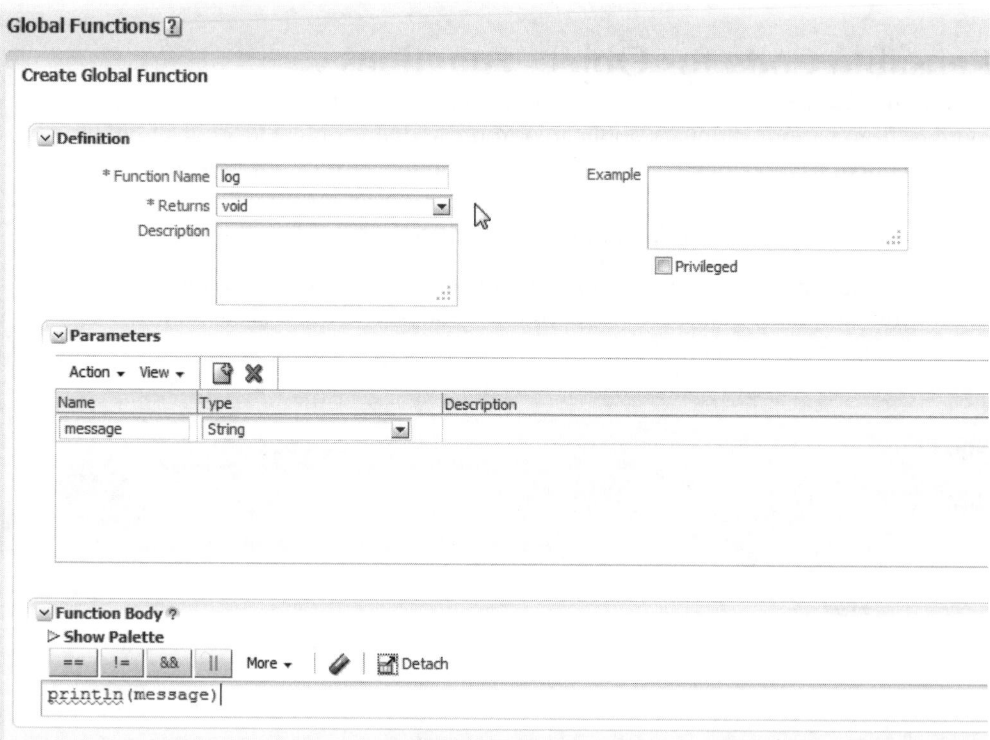

3. Click Save and Close to save the global function.
4. Similarly, define another global function getRegionForCountry to derive the world region based on country code. We will use this function in later

sections. The function takes countryCode as input parameter and returns the region for that country as String.

```
if(countryCode == 'US' || countryCode == 'CA'
|| countryCode == 'MX')
  return 'NA'
else if(countryCode == 'GB' || countryCode == 'FR'
|| countryCode == 'IT' || countryCode == 'DE'
|| countryCode == 'GR' || countryCode == 'SA'
|| countryCode == 'YE')
  return 'EMEA'
else if(countryCode == 'JP' || countryCode == 'SG'
|| countryCode == 'HK' || countryCode == 'PH'
|| countryCode == 'KP' || countryCode == 'KR')
  return 'APAC'
else if(countryCode == 'BR' || countryCode == 'RU'
|| countryCode == 'IN' || countryCode == 'CN')
  return 'BRIC'
else
  return 'OTHER'
```

Programmatically Access View Objects in Scripting

Application Composer provides a way to access a standard or custom view object instance to programmatically access the rows from that View object. This function is called newView and it takes the name of the View object as argument.

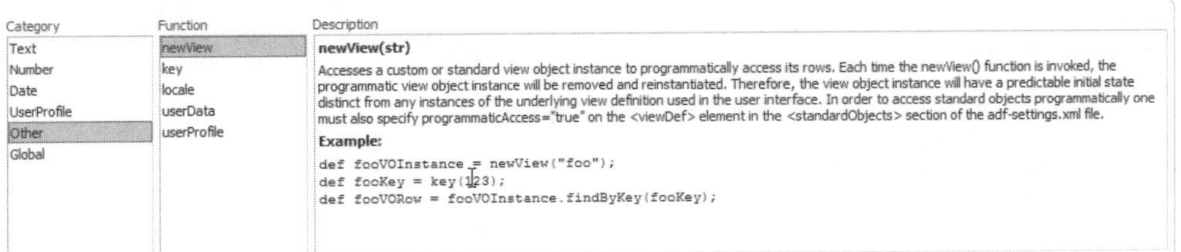

This is a very powerful function that allows you to access unrelated objects in scripting. To access standard view objects, you need to know the exact name of the view object made available for scripting via the newView function. View objects for custom and standard objects in Application Composer are available for scripting by default. Any other view objects made available for script are defined by Fusion Applications and you cannot customize that. Please read product-specific documentation to know which view objects are available for scripts in a given application. Once you get the view object instance using newView, you can write Groovy code to access the view object methods on that instance. You cannot apply all the methods on the View object class if security on scripting is enabled in your environment. Please read Application Composer documentation to get a complete list of trusted APIs available for scripting. In the following code snippet, we get the classification view object and find out classifications assigned to a given party for a given category.

```
def classificationVO = newView('CodeAssignment')
// Define the view criteria
def organizationTypeVC = classificationVO.createViewCriteria()
def organizationType = organizationTypeVC.createRow()
// find by PartyId
def organizationTypeCategory = organizationType.ensureCriteriaItem('OwnerTableId')
organizationTypeCategory.setOperator('=')
organizationTypeCategory.setValue(<party_id>)
// find by party
def organizationTypeCategory = organizationType.ensureCriteriaItem('OwnerTableName')
organizationTypeCategory.setOperator('=')
organizationTypeCategory.setValue('HZ_PARTIES')
// find by ORGANIZATION_TYPE
def organizationTypeCategory = organizationType.ensureCriteriaItem('ClassCategory')
organizationTypeCategory.setOperator('=')
organizationTypeCategory.setValue('ORGANIZATION_TYPE')
// filter by Status
def organizationTypeCategory = organizationType.ensureCriteriaItem('Status')
organizationTypeCategory.setOperator('=')
organizationTypeCategory.setValue('A')
// filter by ORGANIZATION_TYPE
def organizationTypeCategory = organizationType.ensureCriteriaItem('StartDateActive')
organizationTypeCategory.setOperator('ONORBEFORE')
organizationTypeCategory.setValue(adf.currentDate)
// filter by ORGANIZATION_TYPE
def organizationTypeCategory = organizationType.ensureCriteriaItem('EndDateActive')
organizationTypeCategory.setOperator('ONORAFTER')
organizationTypeCategory.setValue(adf.currentDate)
// apply this VC
organizationTypeVC.insertRow(organizationType)
classificationVO.appendViewCriteria(organizationTypeVC)
classificationVO.executeQuery()
while(classificationVO.hasNext()){
  def codeRow = classificationVO.next()
  println("class code = " + codeRow.getAttribute("ClassCode"))
}
```

Define Triggers to Extend Default Processing for Object

Triggers are defined to complement default processing for standard or custom objects. You write Groovy script in the trigger body to execute your additional logic that may alter the default behavior of the data processing. When you define triggers, they get executed at various points in the entity object lifecycle of a given entity row. You define triggers from the Triggers tab under server scripts for any object.

In this section, we will define a new attribute on an opportunity called Region and populate its value when the opportunity sales account is assigned based on the country of primary address of the customer on the opportunity.

1. Define a new Fixed Choice List attribute field for opportunity. Define the lookup codes with values as shown in the following illustration.

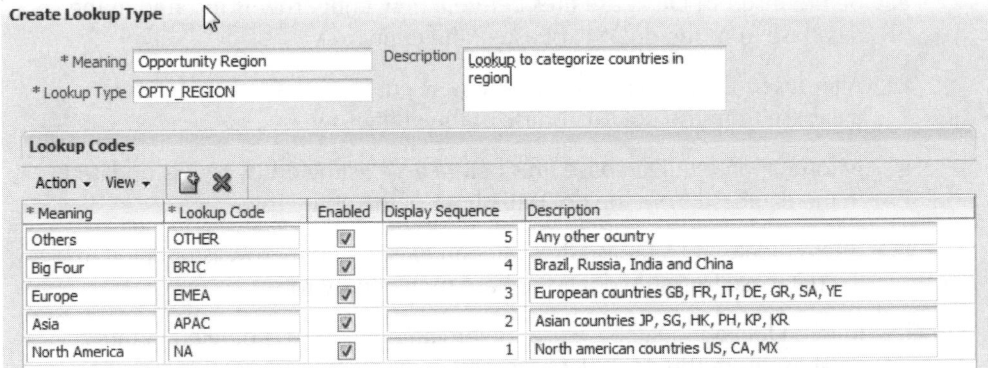

2. Add this attribute to the Opportunity Edit page.

3. Click the Create icon from the Triggers tab for server scripts under opportunity. This will show the Create Trigger page.

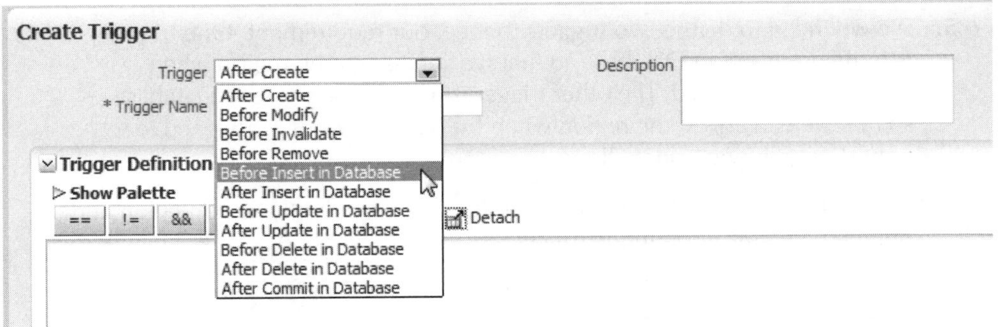

4. The Trigger field defines when this script will be executed in the entity row processing cycle. The following triggers are available in Application Composer for any object.

   a. After Create fires when a new entity row is created. Use this to set default field values programmatically.

b. Before Modify fires when the first persistent field is modified for an entity row on an existing, newly queried row.

c. Before Invalidate fires when the first persistent field is modified for a new or existing, newly queried entity row.

d. Before Remove fires when an entity row is deleted.

e. Before Insert in Database fires before a new entity row is inserted in the database from the doDML phase of the entity row.

f. After Insert in Database fires after a new entity row is inserted in the database from the doDML phase of the entity row.

g. Before Update in Database fires before an existing entity row is updated in the database from the doDML phase of the entity row.

h. After Update in Database fires after an existing entity row is updated in the database from the doDML phase of the entity row.

i. Before Delete in Database fires before an entity row is deleted in the database from the doDML phase of the entity row.

j. After Delete in Database fires after an entity row is deleted in the database from the doDML phase of the entity row.

k. After Commit in Database fires after the entity row is saved in the database.

5. We will need to define two triggers to meet our requirement. One trigger is in Before Insert in Database so that we can assign the region when opportunity is created. The other trigger is in Before Update in Database so that we can assign the region when the sales account is assigned to opportunity during update flow.

6. Define the trigger for Create Flow and name it CreateOptyAssignRegion and put the following code in the trigger.

```
// If the sales account is selected
if(TargetPartyId != null){
  // Get the organization party VO
  def organizationVO = newView('OrganizationParty')
  // Find the organization by PK
  def organizations = organizationVO.findByKey(key(TargetPartyId),1)
  // If found, execute logic to get country and set region
  if (organizations != null && organizations.size() > 0) {
    def organization = organizations[0];
    if(organization != null){
      // Get the country for primary address
```

```
            def country = organization.getAttribute("Country")
            // Use global function to get region for given country
            def region = adf.util.getRegionForCountry(country)
            // Set the region attribute in region field for opportunity
            setAttribute("Region_c", region)
        }
    }
}
```

7. Go to the opportunity home page using the Navigator menu. Click the Create Opportunity icon. Select sales accounts with addresses in the United States and click the Save and Edit icon.

8. The Edit Opportunity page will show the Region field as North America.

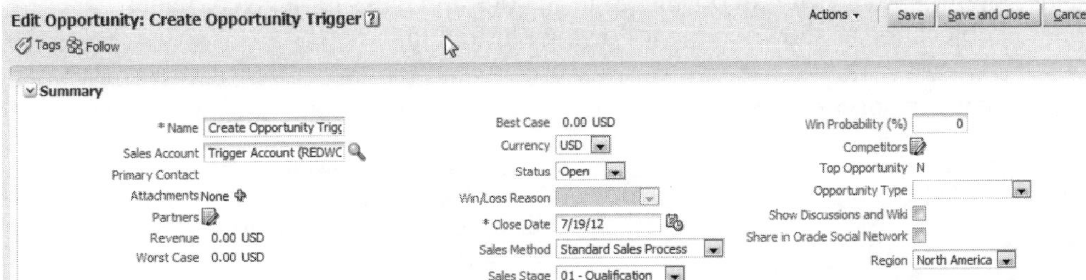

9. Define the trigger for update flow and name it UpdateOptyAssignRegion and put the following code in the trigger.

```
// If the sales account is changed to a different value
if(TargetPartyId != null && isAttributeChanged("TargetPartyId")){
  // Get the organization party VO
  def organizationVO = newView('OrganizationParty')
  // Find the organization by PK
  def organizations = organizationVO.findByKey(key(TargetPartyId),1)
  // If found, execute logic to get country and set region
  if (organizations != null && organizations.size() > 0) {
    def organization = organizations[0];
    if(organization != null){
      // Get the country for primary address
      def country = organization.getAttribute("Country")
      // Use global function to get region for given country
      def region = adf.util.getRegionForCountry(country)
      // Set the region attribute in region field for opportunity
      setAttribute("Region_c", region)
    }
  }
}
```

Go to the above opportunity and change to sales accounts with addresses in India and save the opportunity. Drill down to the opportunity again and the Region field will now show Big Four.

How to Define Buttons and Links on Object Pages

Application Composer allows adding buttons and links to certain pages for standard and custom objects. You can define buttons to take action on an object or do navigation to a different page or a Web site. You can define links to navigate to a Web site. Which standard object allows buttons and links is configured by Fusion Applications. Please read product-specific documentation to know the details. To define buttons and links for an object, go to Actions and Links for a given object from the object tree as shown in the following illustration.

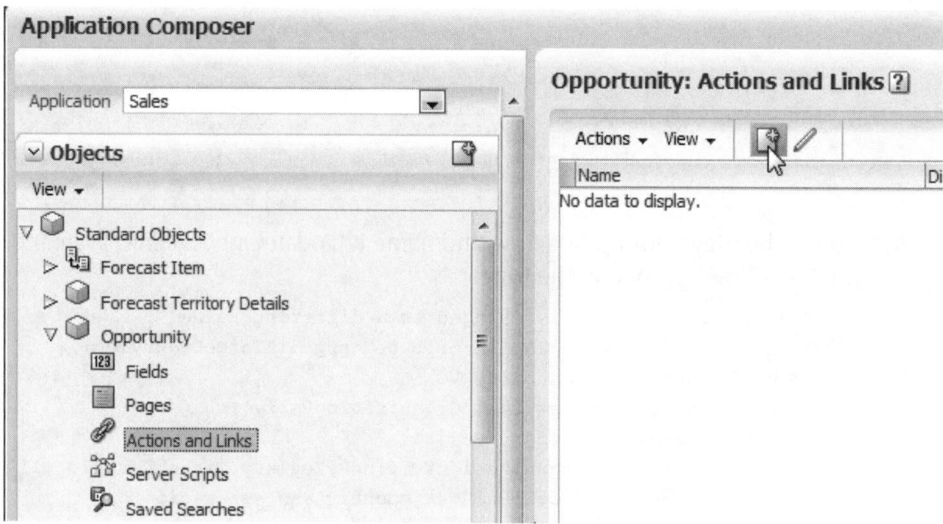

1. Go to Actions and Links for Opportunity object and click the Create icon to define a new button for opportunity.

2. Give the name as **Open Opportunity**, choose Script for Source, and select a method name as our object function defined earlier, **openOpportunity**.

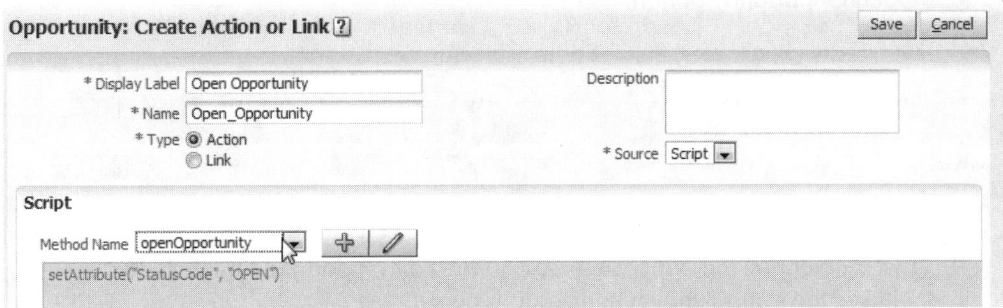

3. Go to the pages for opportunity and go to the summary page. Add this button to the summary table.

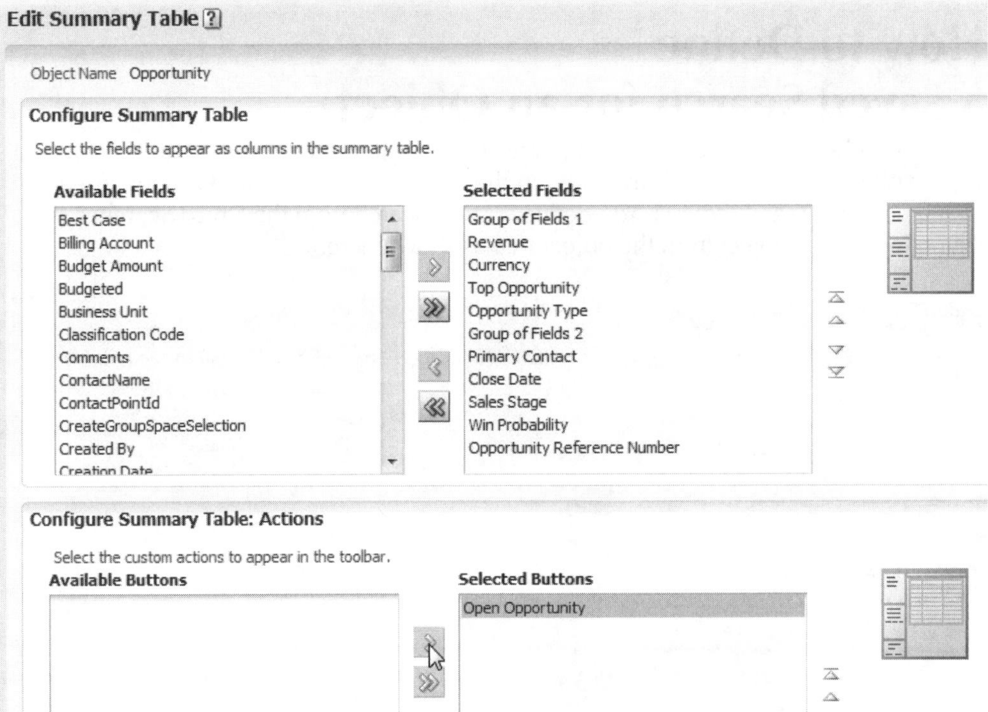

4. Go to the opportunity home page using the Navigator menu and search for any closed opportunity. Select the opportunity from the results and click the Open Opportunity button.

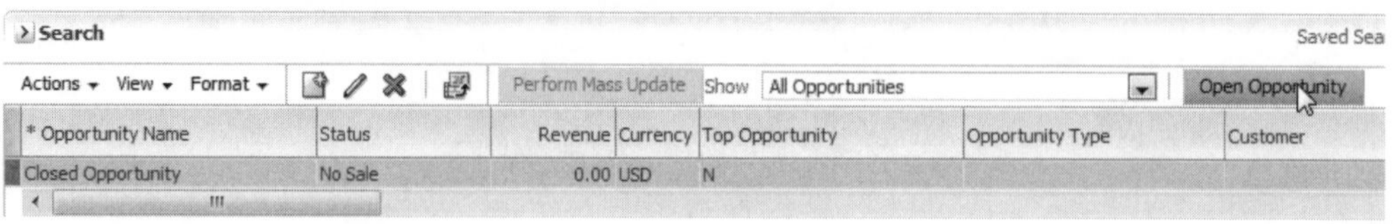

5. This will reopen the opportunity. Go to the Edit Opportunity page and you will see the status is now changed to Open.

6. You can define a link to any Web site or URL and add to the summary table in similar fashion.

How to Define a Saved Search for an Object

Application Composer allows defining a saved search that is available to all users for a given object. Saved search is available in the object search page and is configured with predefined search criteria. You define a saved search from the Saved Searches region for a given object from the object tree as shown here.

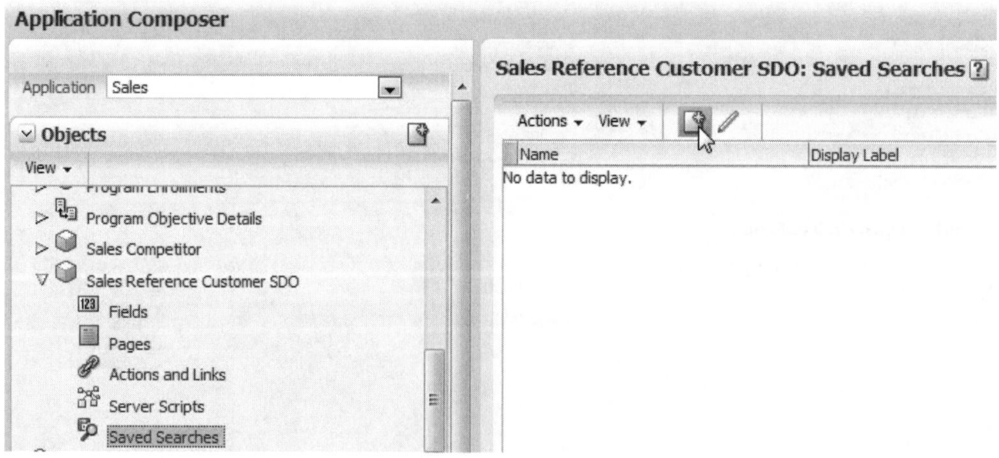

1. Go to the saved search for Sales Reference Customer object and click the Create icon to define a new saved search.
2. Name it **Large References**, define the search condition as Size = LARGE, and save the search.

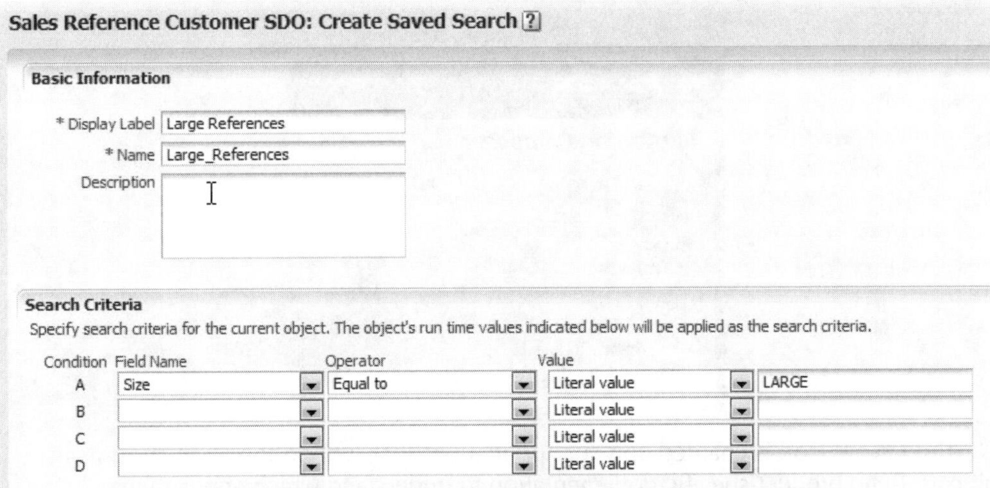

3. Go to the opportunity home page using the Navigator menu. Click the Manage Sales References link from the Task pane. Notice a new saved search.

How to Define a Top-Level Custom Object

You can define a top-level custom object for an application using the Create icon in the Objects pane in the regional area as shown here.

This Create icon is enabled only for applications that support top-level custom objects. Read product-specific documentation to understand which applications support top-level custom objects. This is configured with Fusion Applications and cannot be customized. You can also create a new top-level custom object using the Create button from the local area custom object list table.

1. Click the Create icon to define a custom top-level object and provide the details as shown in the following illustration. The Record Name is a mandatory attribute created by the Application Composer for the object internally. It represents the name of a single instance of the object.

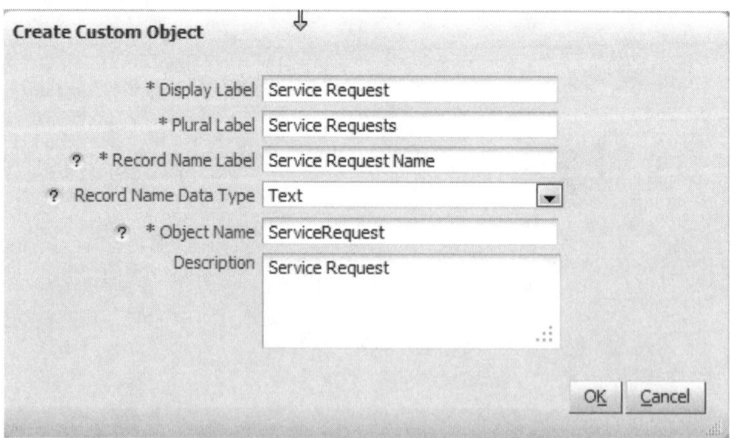

2. Once the custom top-level object is created, click the Fields link to define additional attributes for this object. The Standard tab shows default fields created by Application Composer for the object as shown in the following illustration. The default fields include the system attributes like RecordName, CreatedBy, CreationDate, LastUpdateDate, LastUpdatedBy, and Id which is a system-generated primary key attribute for the object.

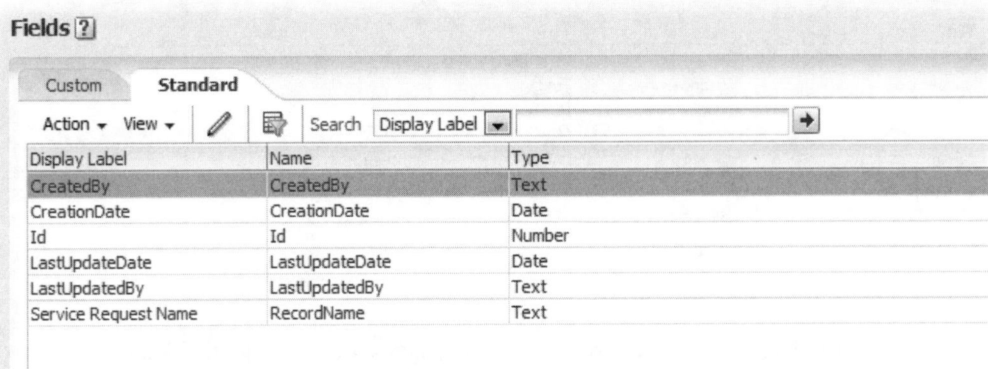

3. Go to the Custom Fields tab and define the following custom attributes for the service request object as shown in the upcoming illustration.

   - **Severity** Fixed choice list field with lookup that accepts values 1, 2, 3, 4. Provide default value 3.
   - **Status** Fixed choice list field with lookup that accepts values Open, Closed, Support Working, and Customer Working. Provide the default value Open.
   - **Summary** Text field to explain the summary of service request. Mark it indexed field.
   - **Details** Long text area to explain and update the progress.
   - **Justification** Text field to capture details when priority changes.
   - **Priority** Number field to capture internal work priority for this request.

- **Reported Date** Date field defaulted to today() function and index-enabled and noneditable to capture the date reported.

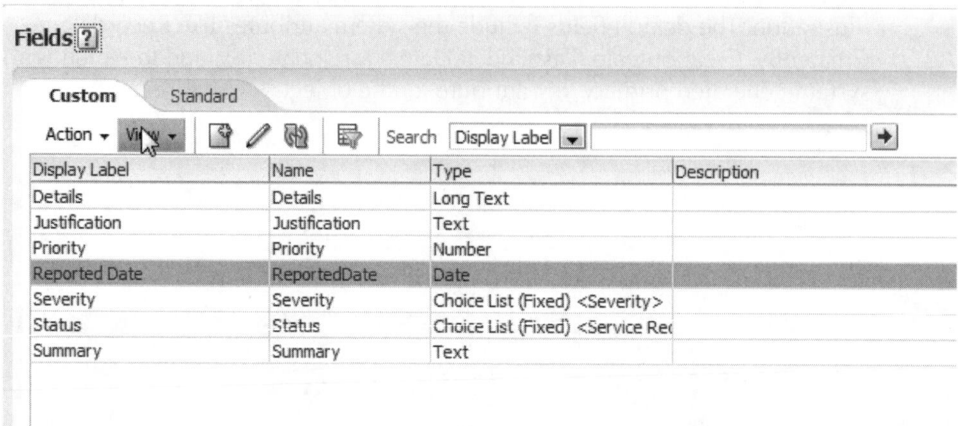

4. Click the Pages link to generate work area pages for this object. Click the Create Work Area link to start the generation wizard.
5. The first step is to configure the Navigator menu and regional search for the work area page. Select Menu Category as Customer Data Management, give the menu label as **Service Request**, and optionally choose where this particular menu entry shows under this category along with other standard menu items. Enable the regional search and select reported date, name, status, and severity and mark name and reported date as "at least one is required" so that the search is efficient, as shown in Figure 6-7.
6. Click the Next button to configure the local area search region. Include all the attributes for search as shown in Figure 6-8.
7. Click the Next button to configure overview and creation pages. Select the drill-down column from the summary table as Service Request Name and show reported date, severity, status, summary, and priority in the summary table. Enable create, edit, and delete actions. Expose the Service Request Name, Severity, Summary, and Details fields only on the creation page as shown in Figure 6-9.

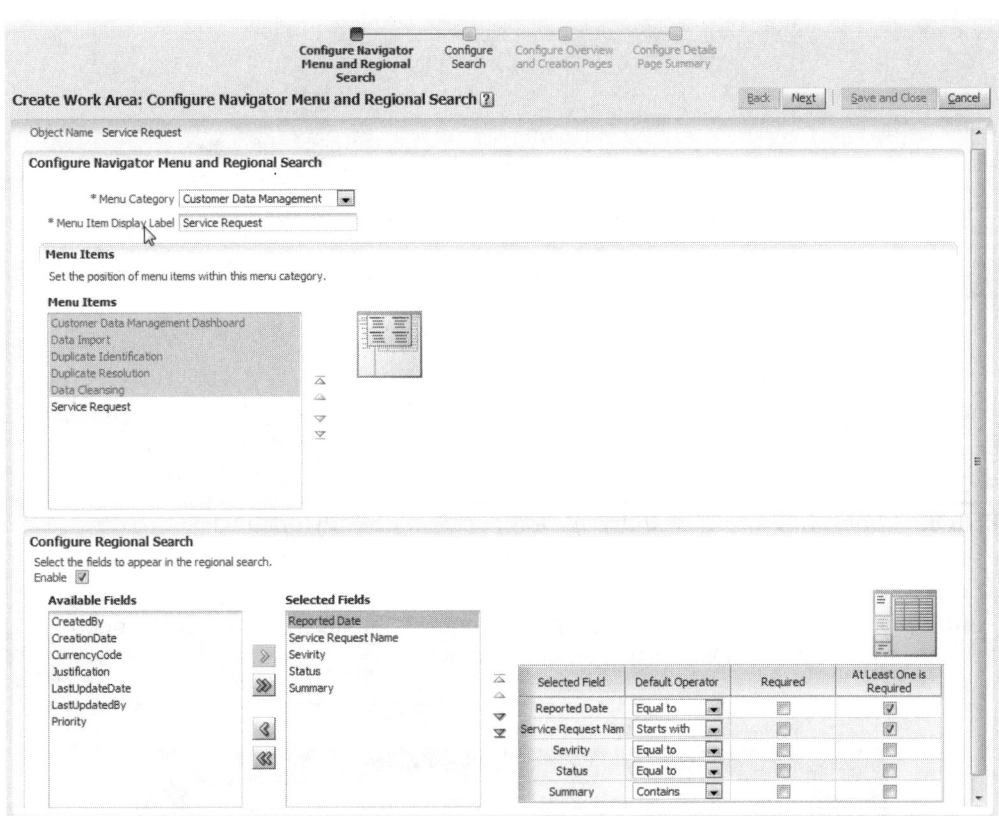

FIGURE 6-7. *Configuring the Navigator menu and regional search for a custom object work area*

8. Click Next to complete the details page for this object as shown in Figure 6-10.
9. Click Save and Close to complete the configuration and see the pages generated as shown in Figure 6-11.

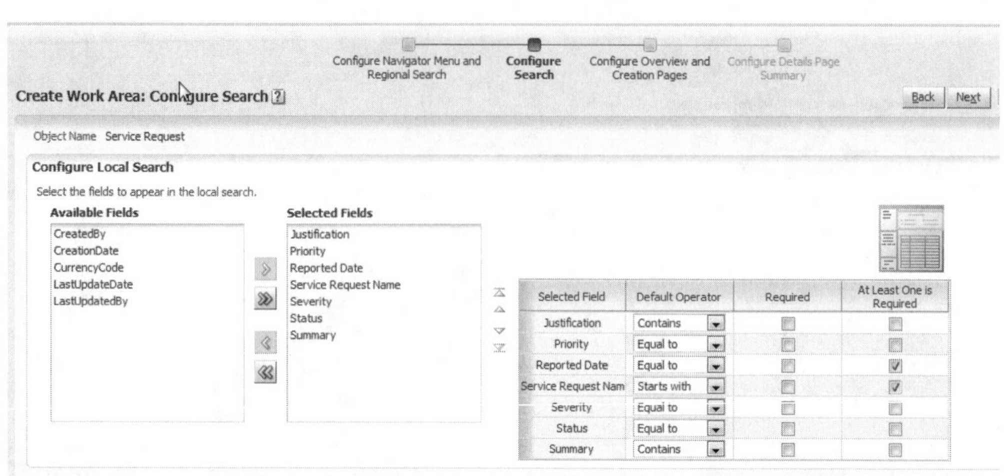

FIGURE 6-8. *Configuring a local search page for a custom object work area*

10. Go to the work area using the Service Request link from the Navigator menu under Customer Data Management as shown here.

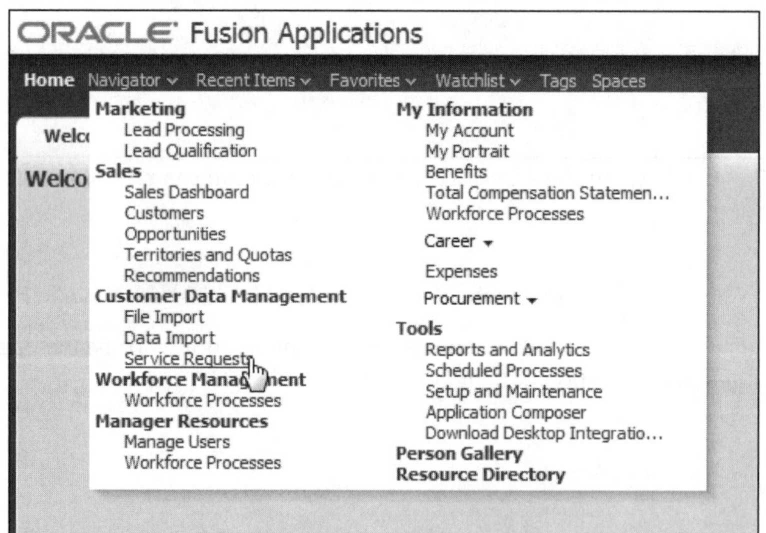

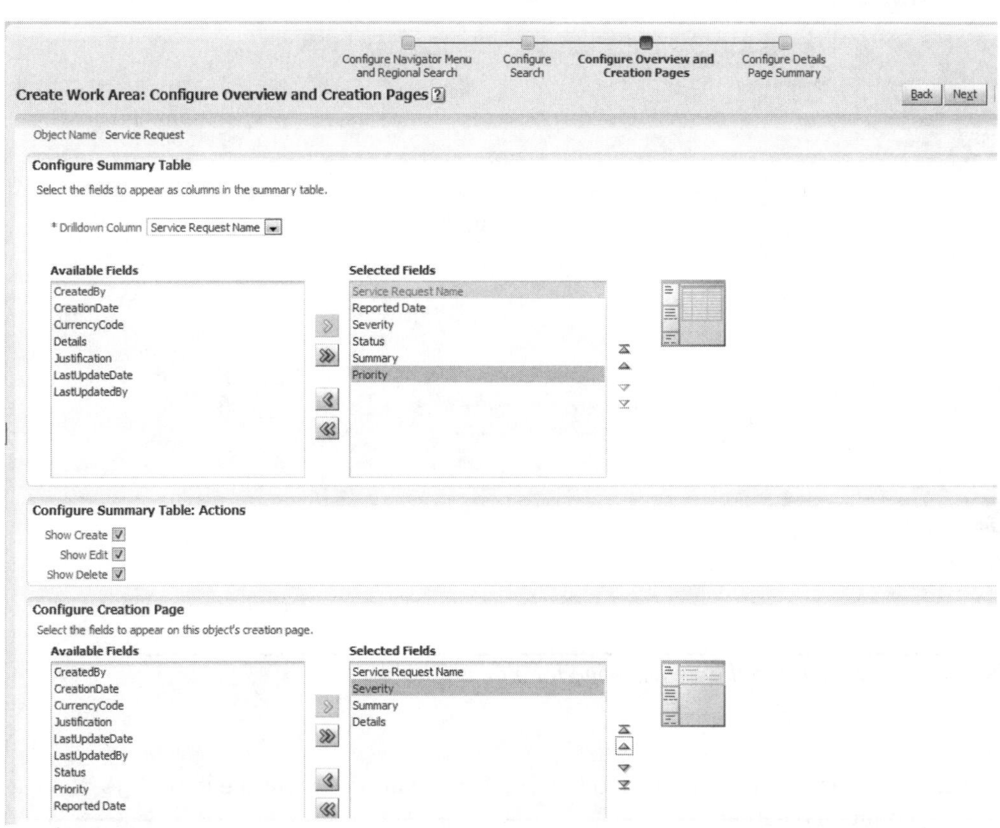

FIGURE 6-9. *Configuring overview and create page for a custom object*

11. When you go to the service request work area using the link, you see the regional search area and local search area as configured earlier here.

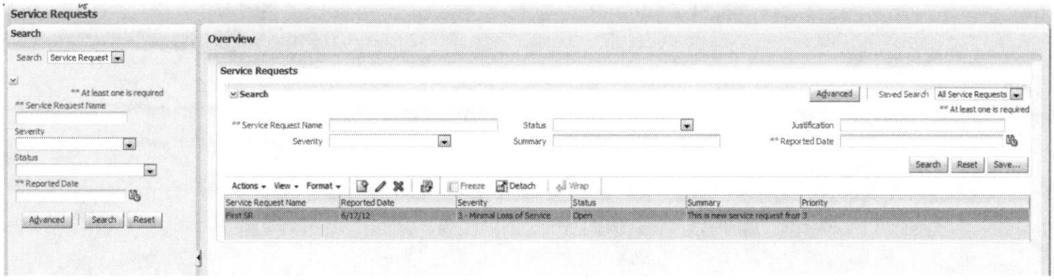

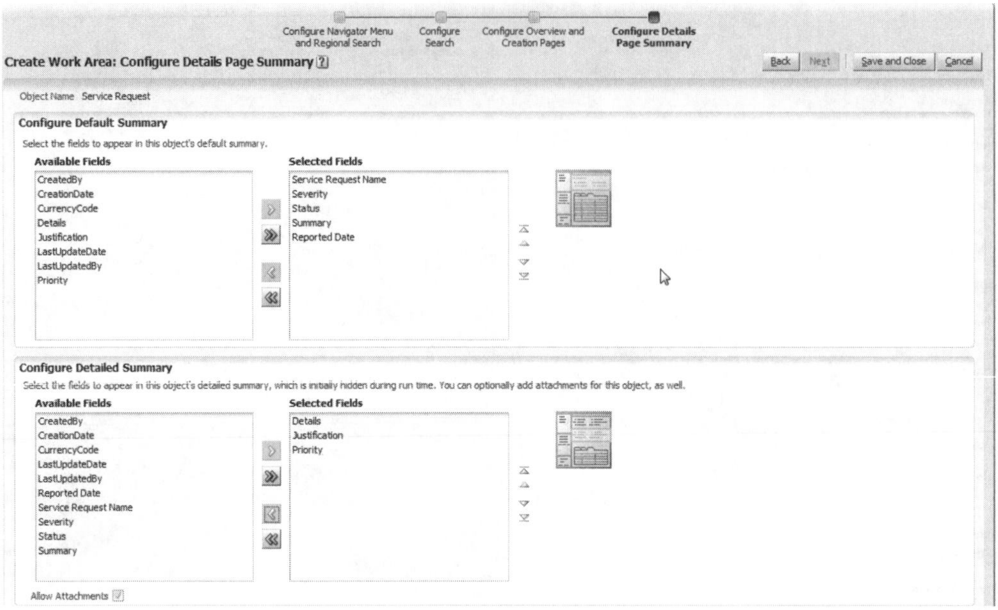

FIGURE 6-10. *Configuring the details page for a custom object*

12. Click the Create icon to go to the Create page and you will see it as configured earlier.

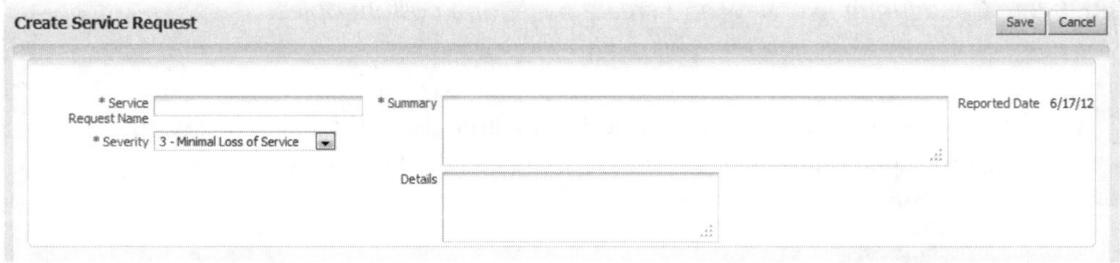

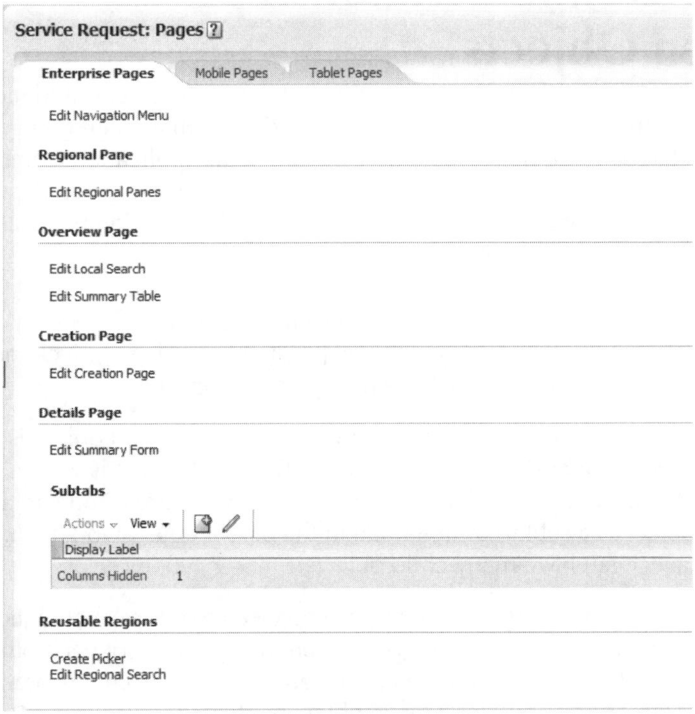

FIGURE 6-11. *Custom object generated work area pages*

13. Click on the Service Request Name from the summary page to go to the Details page and you will see it as configured earlier, as shown here.

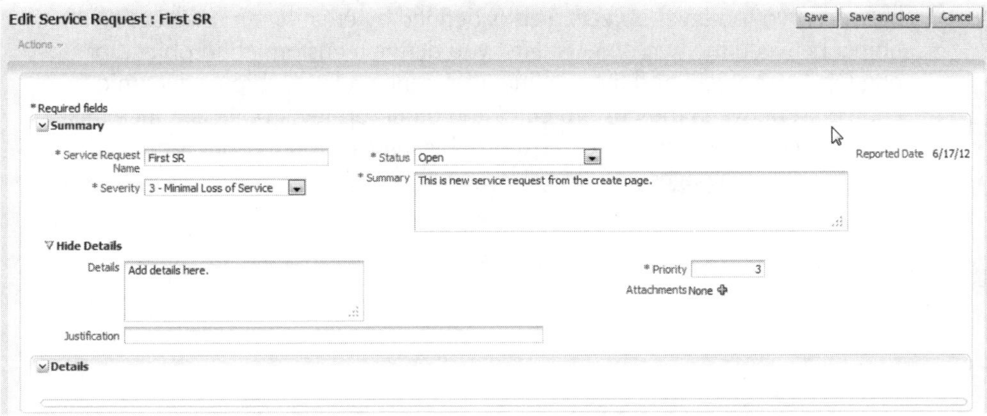

How to Define Relationships Between Objects

A relationship defines a foreign key association between two objects and indicates how the data is connected for the two objects. The data from a related object can be shown as a subtab or a tree node in the object work area. Application Composer allows defining these relationships between objects within the same application. There are various types of relationships exposed in Application Composer as discussed in the following section.

- A *standard relationship* is defined between two standard objects by Fusion Applications. This is predefined by the product for a given object and visible on the object overview page in Application Composer.
- A *parent-child relationship* is created when a custom child object is created for a standard or custom top-level object. The child object is always in the context of its parent and does not have its own work area. You can add the child object as a subtab or tree node in the parent object work area. A top-level object can have many child objects.
- A *reference relationship* can be created between two top-level objects in Application Composer. The two objects are independent of each other but may have relations between them. You can show data from a related object in a subtab or tree node for a given object work area.
- A *choice list relationship* is created when you define a dynamic choice list field for a given object. This is a reference relationship created implicitly by Application Composer when you define a dynamic choice list field for one object by pulling data from other objects to define the choice list.
- A *many-to-many relationship* can be defined in Application Composer between two top-level objects. This is defined by creating an intersection object between the two objects. First you define a custom child object for one top-level object and then define a reference relationship or dynamic choice list between the custom child and other top-level objects. Once this relationship is defined, you can expose this intersection in both top-level object work area pages.

You can view all relationships for a given application from the Relationships page from the Common Setup pane in the regional area as shown in the following illustration.

To define a new reference relationship, click the Create icon in the list. Specify the source object, target object, and the name of the relationship and click Save and Close to define the relationship.

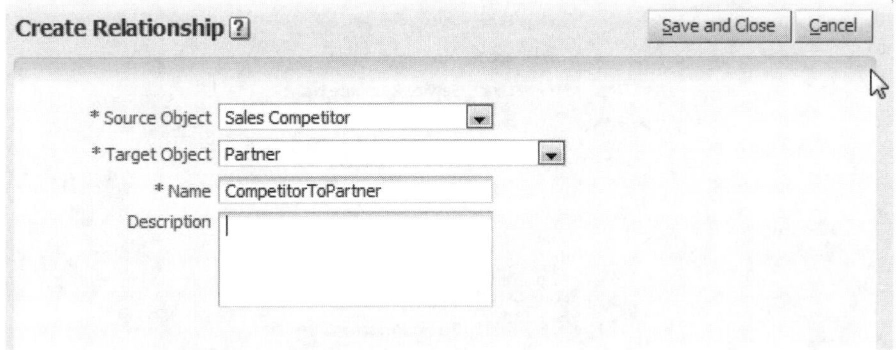

You define a parent-child relationship by creating a new custom child object for a given object. We will discuss this in the following section.

How to Define a Custom Child Object

You can create a custom child object for a standard or custom object in Application Composer. This is a pure child object for other objects and it cannot exist without the parent object. Once you define the child object:

1. Click on the standard object or custom object link in the regional pane on the left side to see a list of objects. We will define a custom child for the custom object we created earlier. You can select the object and click the

Create Child Object button to create a custom child for the selected object as shown here.

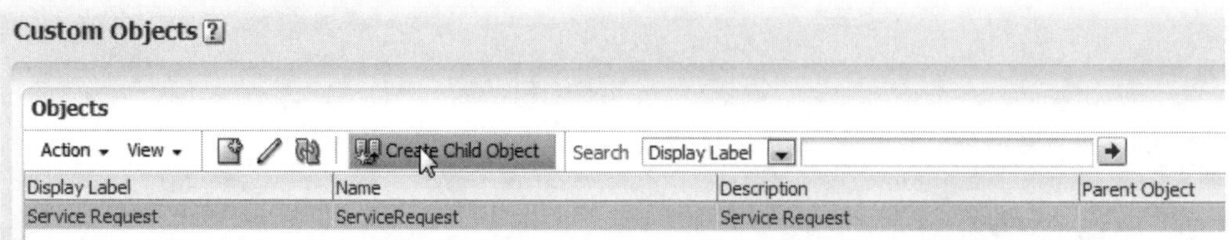

2. You can also go to the object overview page by clicking on the object and then click the Create Child Object button from the Child Objects region.
3. In the Create Custom Child Object dialog, provide the object name as **Service Response**.

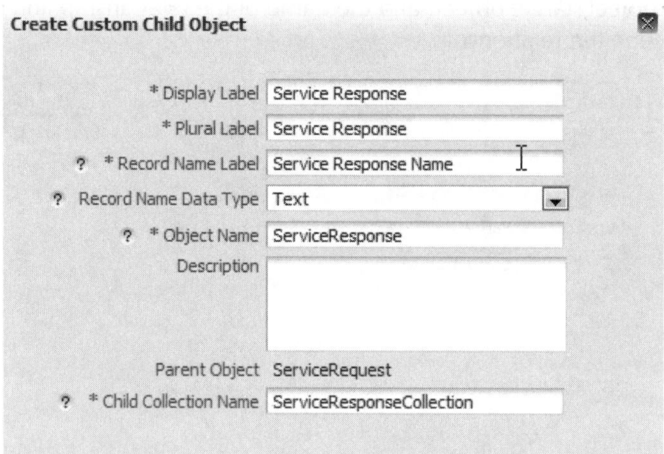

4. Add a new field Response Date to this object and give the default value as today() using Expression Builder.

How to Define Subtab Content

Application Composer allows you to add the content from related objects to the subtab for a top-level object. The subtab for the standard object detail page is enabled on selected objects by Fusion Applications. Please read product-specific documentation to understand which objects allow subtabs. You can add content to a subtab for any top-level custom object. You can define a subtab from the details page for a given object. Let us now add the custom child object content to the service request page.

1. Go to the pages for the custom object Service Request from the object tree. It shows the list of work area pages for this object.

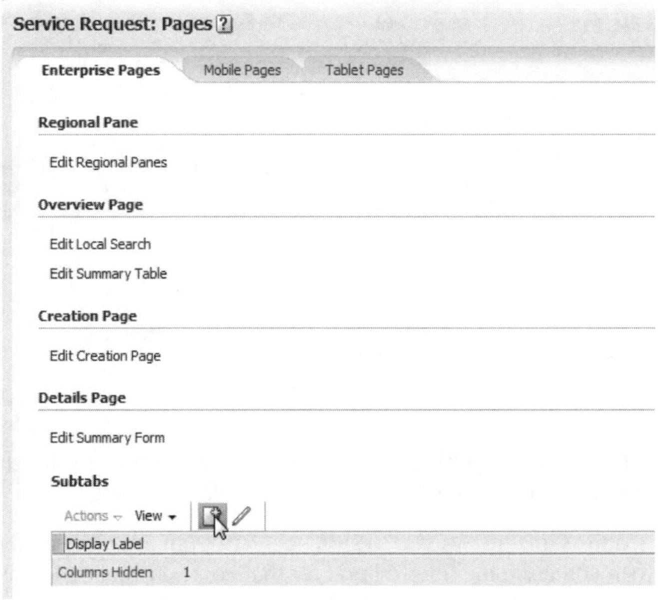

Service Request: Pages

Enterprise Pages | Mobile Pages | Tablet Pages

Regional Pane

Edit Regional Panes

Overview Page

Edit Local Search

Edit Summary Table

Creation Page

Edit Creation Page

Details Page

Edit Summary Form

Subtabs

Actions View

Display Label

Columns Hidden 1

2. Click the Create icon under the Subtabs list for the Details page. This will show the Create Subtab page. You can choose the type of content you want to add on the subtab from among four options.

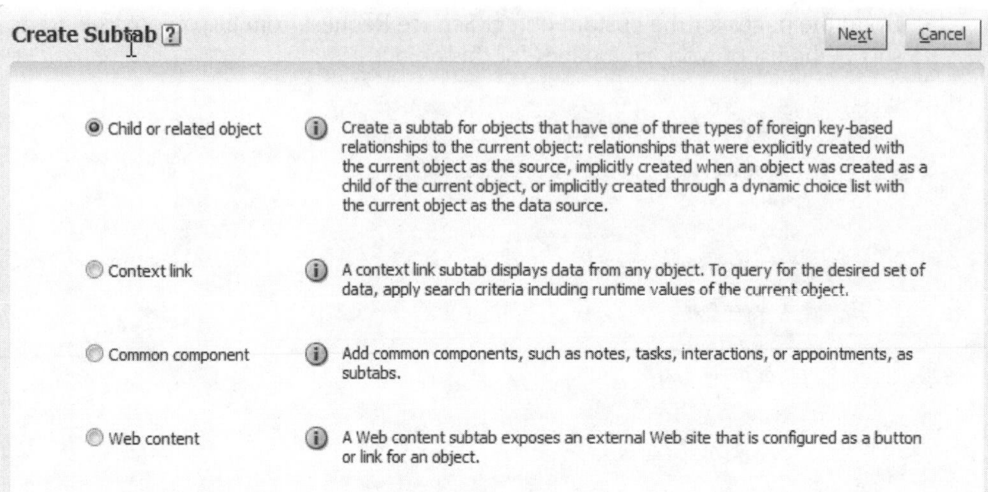

- **Child or related object** allows you to show content for the child object of a given top-level object of any related object for this top-level object.
- **Context link** allows you to show content from any unrelated object. You can configure the filter criteria for that context object and pass the run-time values from the current object.
- **Common component** allows you to add notes, tasks, interactions, and appointments to your custom object.
- **Web content** allows you to add an external Web site as subtab for the object.

3. Go to the Create Subtab page again and select the Common Component option and click the Next button. This will show the Edit Common Components subtab page. Select all options and click Save and Close.

4. Navigate to the service request home page using the Navigator menu and drill down to a service request. The Edit page will show the new subtabs.

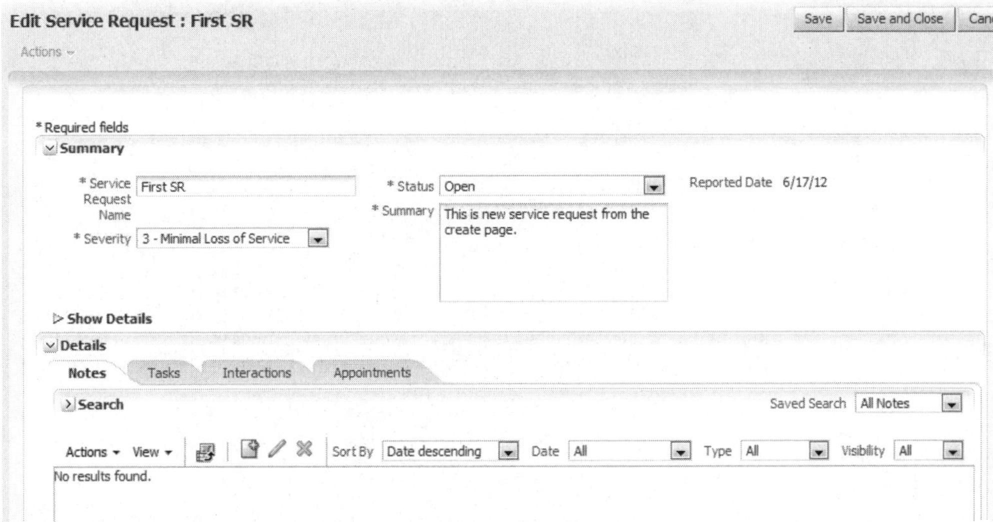

5. Go to the Create Subtab page again and select Child or Related Object and click the Next button. This will show the Select Child or Related Object page. Select the Data Object as the Service Response and give it the label **Service Response**. Configure the summary table and detail form by selecting attributes you are interested to see on those pages. Enable the Show Create and Show Delete options from the Configure Summary Table actions. The page looks like Figure 6-12. Click Save and Close to add the subtab to the Details page.

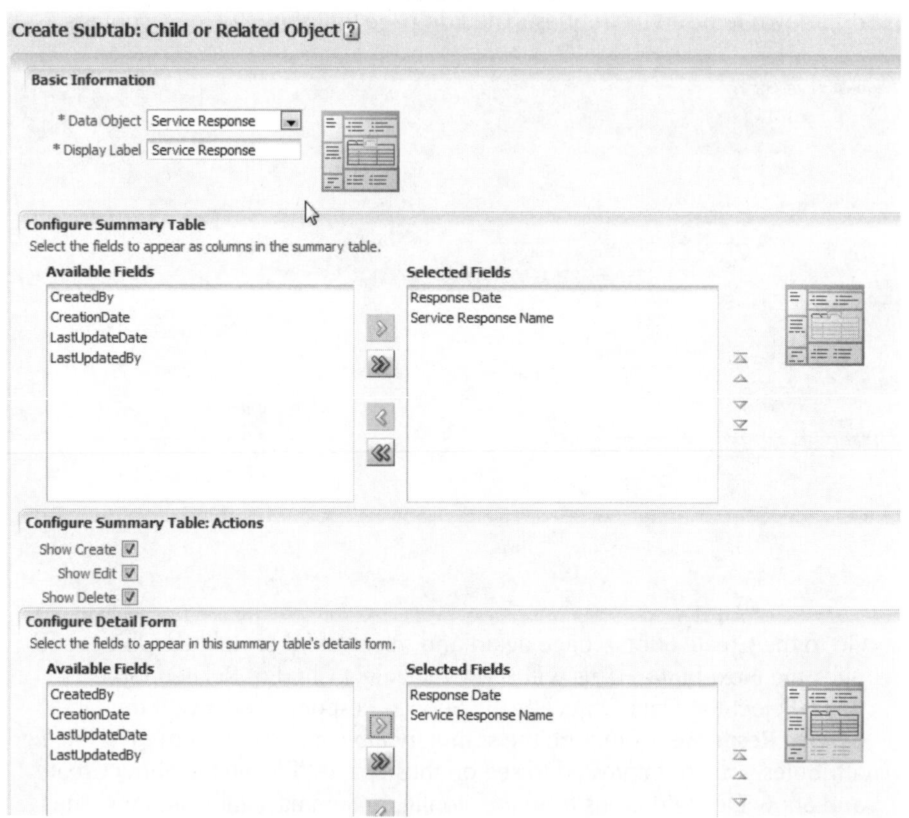

FIGURE 6-12. *Adding a custom child service response subtab on the edit service request page*

6. Navigate to the service request home page using the Navigator menu and drill down to a service request. The Details page will show the Service Response tab as shown in Figure 6-13. You can use the Create and Delete buttons to manage the responses.
7. Similarly, you can add a context link and Web content.

FIGURE 6-13. *Service response custom child subtab on run-time page*

How to Define Tree Node Content

CRM applications have an object tree for Sales Account and Partner objects where the tree nodes show details about the object. Except for common components, you can add all the content as tree nodes as you do for subtab. For these two objects, subtab is not available and you can add the content as a tree node.

1. Go to the pages for the Partner object under the Sales application. This will show you existing tree nodes for the Partner object under the Details page section as shown here.

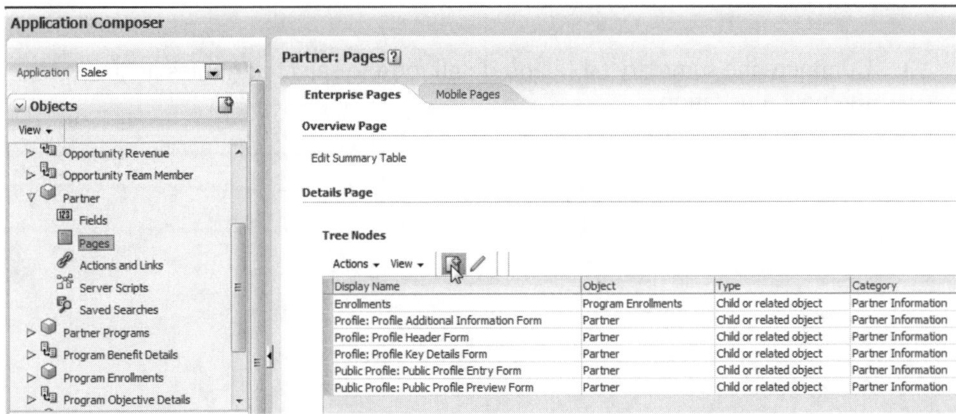

2. Click the Create icon to navigate to the Define Tree Node page. Select Context Link as option and click Next. On the Create Tree Node: Context Link page, select Partner Programs in the Data Object drop-down and set the Search Criteria as Program Name starts with Test as shown here.

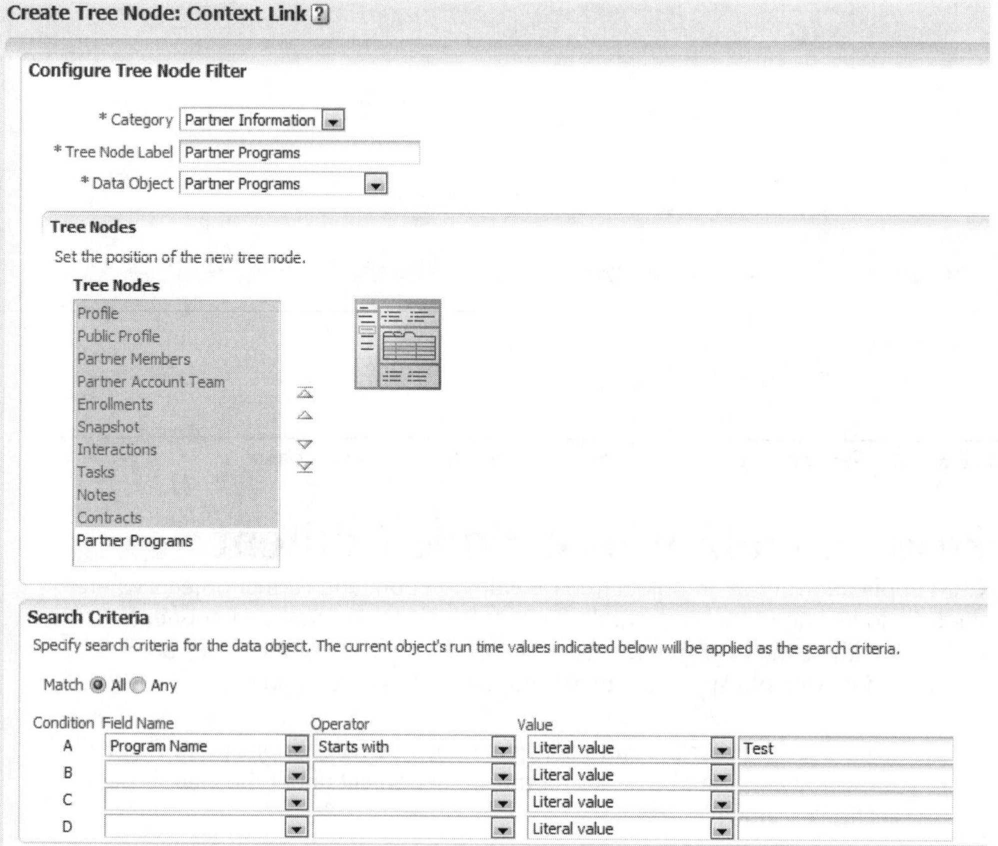

3. Configure the summary table and detail form to select attributes as shown in the next illustration.

Configure Summary Table

Select the fields to appear as columns in the summary table.

Available Fields	Selected Fields
End Date	Program Name
Item Description	Program Description
Last Update Date	Program Status
Last Updated By	Program Type
Objectives Description	
Primary Contact	
Program Manager	
Start Date	
Term Autorenewal	
Term Expiry Warning	
Term Grace Period	

Configure Summary Table: Actions

Show Create ☐

Show Edit ☐

Show Delete ☐

Configure Detail Form

Select the fields to appear in this summary table's details form.

Available Fields	Selected Fields
Last Update Date	Agreement Description
Last Updated By	Benefit Description
Primary Contact	Description
Program Description	Eligibility Description
Program Manager	Start Date
Program Name	End Date
Program Status	Item Description
Program Type	Objectives Description
ApprovalStatus	Term Autorenewal
Term Expiry Warning	Term Grace Period
Approval Comments	

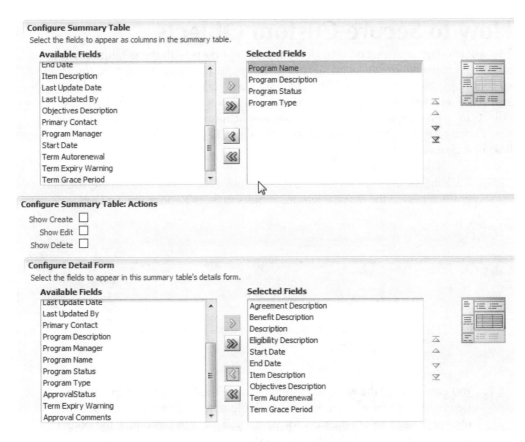

4. Click Save and Close to configure the node. Navigate to the Partners home page using the Partners link under Partner Management in the Navigator menu. Drill down to a partner and it shows the new Partner Programs node with details per the criteria given as shown in the following illustration.

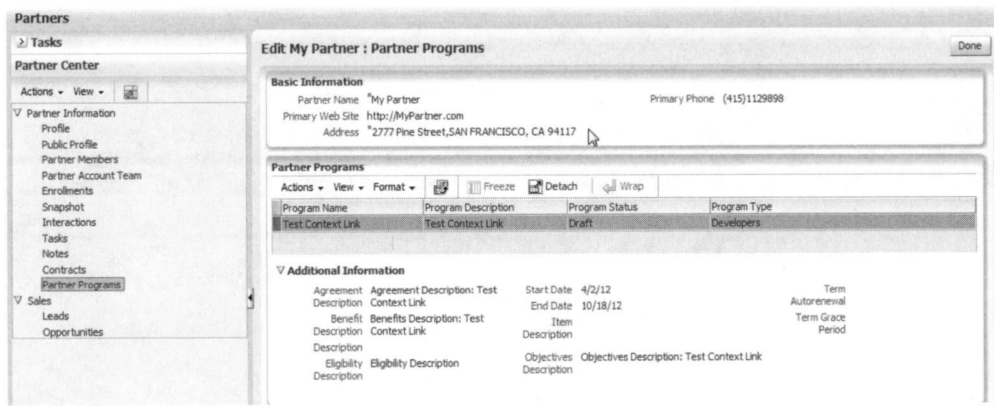

How to Secure Custom Objects

The custom objects are secured by default, and only users with the default duty role for a given application will get access to those objects. This holds true for the top-level custom object and custom child object for standard objects. Please read product-specific documentation to know the default duty roles that give access to custom objects for a given application. You can use Application Composer to customize this default behavior and give access to users with other CRM duty roles using the Security link for a given object.

1. Click the Security link for Service Request object as shown next, where you can grant access to the Service Request object to Sales Representative Duty.

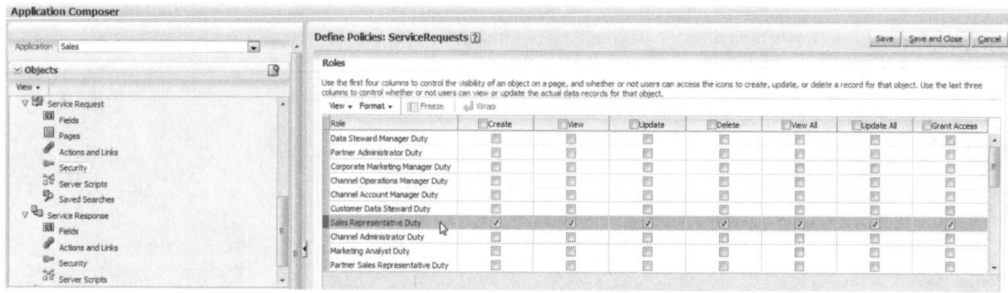

2. You can also use the Role Security page from the Common Setup pane to define security for a given duty for multiple objects. From the Role Security overview page, select the duty for which you want to customize the object security and click the Define Policies button.

3. On the Define Policies page, you can see all custom objects for a given application and then define the security access to a given duty for any or all objects as shown here.

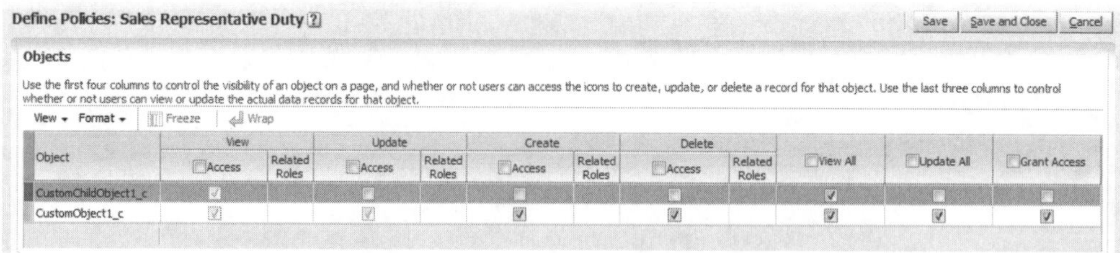

4. You can define both function and data security policy for an object for a given duty role using the check boxes provided for various access levels.
    a. Function Security
        i. **View Access** enables object work area pages for the user.
        ii. **Create Access** enables a create action for the user.
        iii. **Update Access** enables an edit or update page for the user.
        iv. **Delete Access** enables a delete action for the user.
    b. Data Security
        i. **View All** access gives users the ability to view all data for a given object. If this access is granted, the user automatically gets view function security access.
        ii. **Update All** access gives users the ability to update all data for a given object. If this access is granted, the user automatically gets update function security access.
        iii. **Grant Access** controls the Manage Permissions button on the object's summary table. A user with this button can select a record and define data security access level for other users for the selected record.

How to Define E-Mail Templates

E-Mail Templates allows you to define the structure and body of the notification content. You can manage E-Mail Templates outside a sandbox only. Click the E-Mail Templates link from the regional pane Common Setup or from the Overview page in the Application Composer home page. This will launch the Manage E-Mail Templates page where you can search, create, edit, copy, or delete templates for a given application. We will define a new template for Opportunity that can be used to send notifications when an update is made to an opportunity that is marked as top opportunity.

1. Click the Create icon to define a new template. This will launch the Create E-Mail Template page.
2. Select Opportunity from the Object drop-down.
3. Give it the name **TopOpportunity** and provide a description of the template.

4. Specify the E-Mail Subject that looks like Updated Opportunity <opportunity name> - <opportunity number> at run time when e-mail notification is sent. You can do this either by specifying the fields from the opportunity object in the E-Mail Subject field directly, or by picking the field and clicking the Insert button as shown in the following illustration.

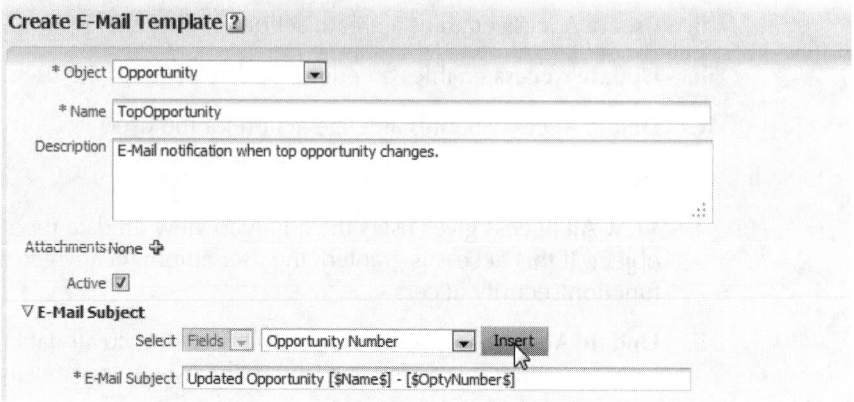

5. Now specify the E-Mail body similarly to constructing the message using fields from opportunity attributes. The content of the E-Mail will be "The opportunity [$Name$] - [$OptyNumber$] for customer [$PartyName$] in stage [$SalesStage$] and status [$StatusCode$] is updated. Please review the details and take appropriate action," as shown here.

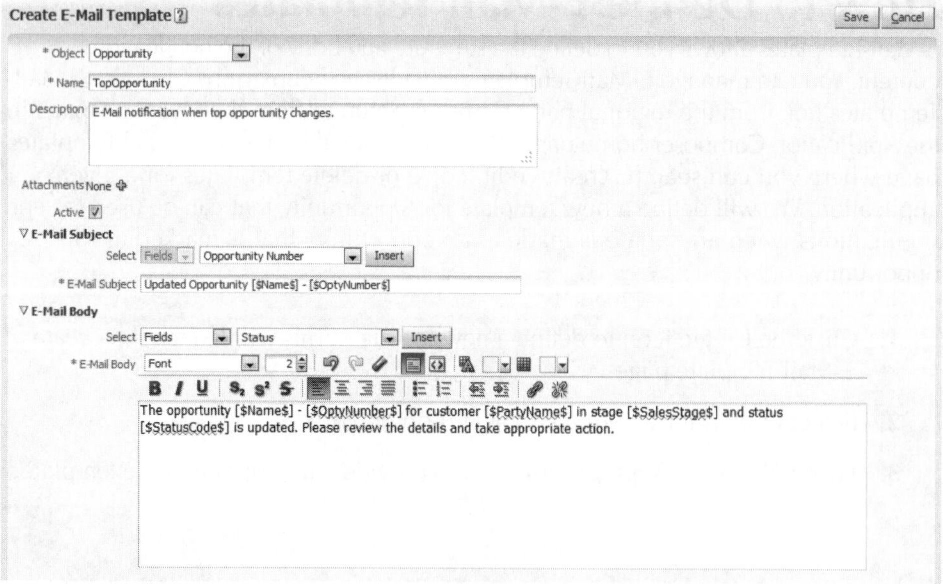

6. Click Save to save the template and use it for object workflow.

How to Define Object Workflow

Object Workflow is an orchestrated process executed based on a set of triggering conditions defined for a given object. To define an object workflow, you go to the Object Workflows page using the Common Setup pane from the regional area.

1. Click the Create icon to go to the Create Object Workflow page. To define a workflow, the following properties must be specified.

    a. The object for which you want to define the workflow.

    b. Event Point when the workflow should be triggered. You can choose either Create or Update as Event Point.

    c. Event Condition in addition to Event Point. The workflow will be triggered only when the Event Condition specified using a Groovy script is satisfied. Mention the condition to trigger the workflow only under certain circumstances instead of every time a record is created or updated.

    d. Actions define the outcome of workflow execution when the specified event point and conditions are satisfied. There are five types of actions supported in Application Composer.

        i. **Field Updates** allows you to update other fields for objects in response to the event. Which fields are available for update is configured by Fusion Applications.

        ii. **E-Mail Notification** allows you to send e-mail in response to an event. You can use e-mail templates to send the notification and include field values from the object in the body.

        iii. **Task Creation** allows you to automatically create a work list task in response to the event.

        iv. **Outbound Message** allows you to invoke an external Web service in response to the event. This external Web service will receive the data from Fusion CRM Applications in response to the object event. This external service endpoint URL will be registered when you define the outbound message action, and this service schema must conform to the object schema as defined by Oracle applications. Please read product-specific documentation to understand exact details about service for a given object or custom object for a given application.

        v. **Business Process Flow** allows you to invoke a business process in response to the event.

2. We will define a workflow to send notification when top opportunity is updated as shown here.

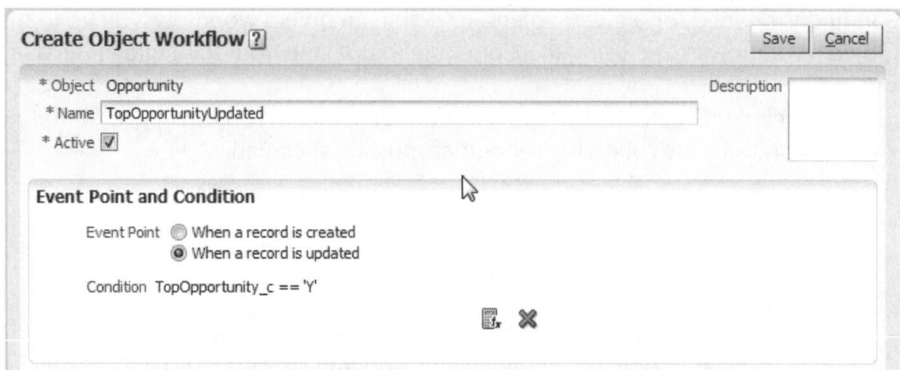

3. Click the Create icon for the E-Mail Notification section under the Actions region to send e-mail notification using the template we created earlier as shown in Figure 6-14. The Recipient Type allows you to specify who should get the notification when the object workflow is executed.

   a. **E-mail fields on record** allow you to select an attribute from the object that specifies the e-mail to be used. The attributes available for this list are configured by Fusion Application standard objects.

   b. **Relative users on record** allow you to select users associated to the object such as who created or last updated the record or resource on the object team like the opportunity team. The attributes available for this list are configured by Fusion Applications standard objects.

   c. **Roles** allow you to pick CRM application roles and all users will get notification for the specified role.

   d. **Specific users** allow you to pick any user from the Fusion Applications to send notification.

   e. **Specific e-mail addresses** allow you to specify one or more hard-coded email addresses that will get notification. For our exercise, specify your e-mail address to send notification.

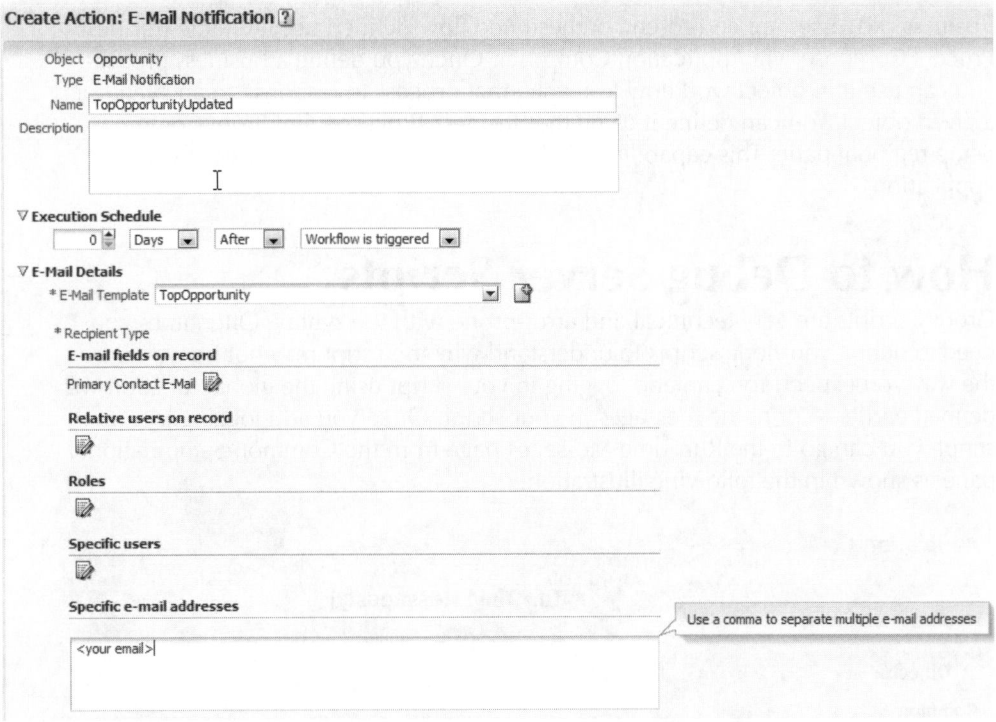

FIGURE 6-14. *Define E-Mail Notification action for object workflow*

4. Go to the opportunity home page and update any top opportunity. This will send the notification content as shown in the following illustration.

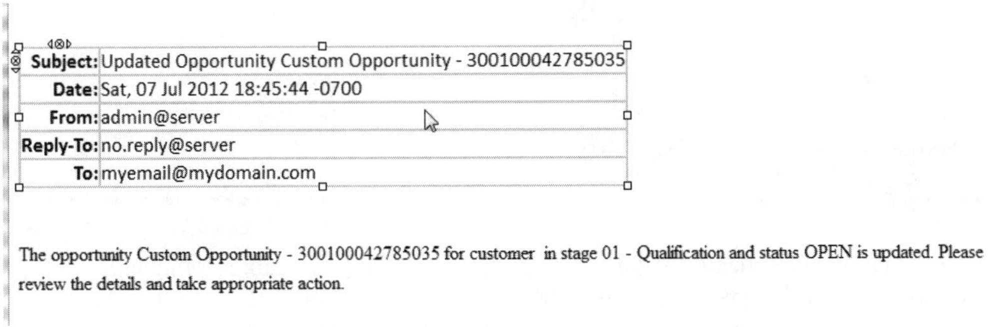

5. You can define multiple actions for the object workflow event.

How to Define Business Processes

Business processes are end-to-end orchestrated flow defined using Oracle Business Process Composer via Application Composer. Once you define a business process, you can use it in object workflow to invoke that process in response to an event for a given object. You can define it using the Business Processes link from Common Setup regional pane. This capability will be available in future releases of CRM applications.

How to Debug Server Scripts

Groovy scripts are very technical and error-prone with the syntax. Oftentimes you need to debug your long scripts to understand why the script may not be working the way you expect. You can add logging in your script using the global function we defined earlier to print the messages in your script. Once you add logging in your script, you can go to the Run Time Messages page from the Common Setup regional pane as shown in the following illustration.

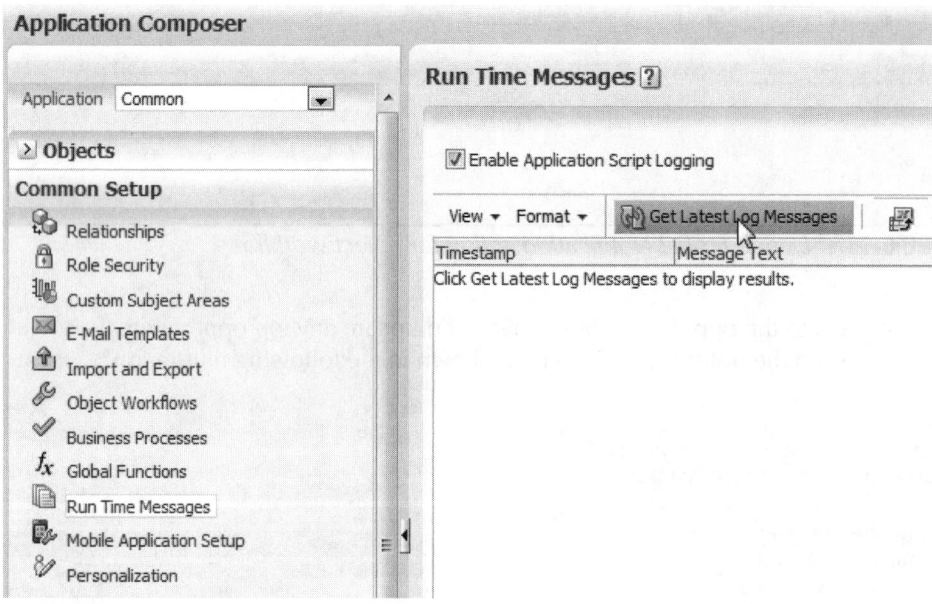

You first need to enable logging by clicking the check box Enable Application Script Logging for the given application. Make sure to select the right application first. The application must be selected where your code will be executed at run time and not where you have defined the object. For example, if you define a script on a

Trading Community Organization Profile object and want to debug it for the Create Customer flow in the Customer Center, you need to enable logging on the Customer application and not on the Common application. Once you enable logging for the given application, you can go to the application page and execute the flow that will trigger the script. Once flow is executed, you can come back to the Run Time Messages page for that application and click the Get Latest Log Messages button to get the logging that you added in your script.

How to Extend Import and Export

Oracle CRM applications allow import and export for standard objects using the file import, bulk import, and file export utilities. You can expose the custom attributes and custom objects on those interfaces. Please read product-specific documentation to understand which objects support import and export and how to execute those. To expose the custom attributes and objects to import and export interfaces, you need to be outside of the sandbox. Go to the Import and Export page from the Common Setup in the regional area and click the Generate button to expose the custom attribute and objects that are published for the given application in these interfaces as shown in the following illustration.

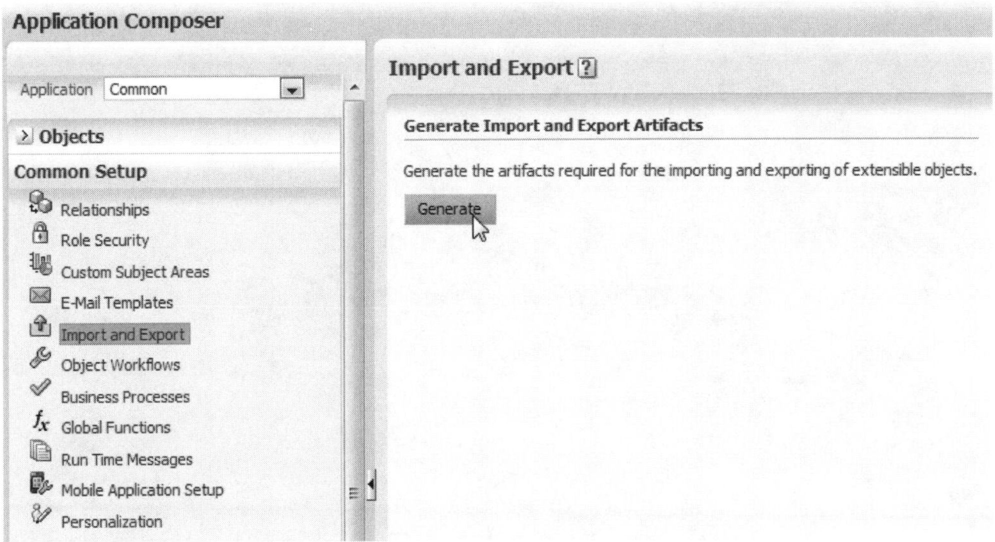

Summary

In this chapter, we discussed the capabilities of Oracle Application Composer for CRM applications. We talked about how to extend standard objects to add new attributes and expose those attributes on application pages, how to define a saved search for those objects, and how to define validations and triggers on the objects and how to debug these scripts. We also discussed how to define custom top-level and child objects, how to secure them, and how to define relationships between standard and custom objects. We described how to define business events and object workflows in response to those events. We talked about how to expose the extensions to import and export interfaces and how to build business process for objects.

CHAPTER 7

Customizing with Oracle JDeveloper

As discussed in Chapter 2, you use Oracle JDeveloper to customize Fusion Applications for cases where the business requirement cannot be satisfied with run-time customization tools. It is recommended that you do not use Oracle JDeveloper for customizations of CRM applications and use CRM Application Composer instead as much as possible. For non-CRM applications, JDeveloper is the only tool available in current releases to customize and extend standard behavior. In this chapter, we will discuss steps to set up a development environment and a few sample use cases for customizations using Oracle JDeveloper.

How to Set Up a Development Environment

To customize Fusion Applications using JDeveloper, you will need Fusion Applications extensions with JDeveloper for the given version of Fusion Applications. You can download the necessary version of JDeveloper and the extension from the Oracle eDelivery Web site. Select Oracle Fusion Applications as product pack and the platform where you want to use JDeveloper as shown in Figure 7-1 and click Go.

Select the release you want to download the JDeveloper for and click Continue. Download Oracle Fusion Applications Companion 11*g*, Oracle JDeveloper 11*g*, Oracle Application Development Framework 11*g* Part 1 to 3, and Oracle Fusion Applications Technology Documentation Library 11*g* as shown in the following illustration.

Download	Oracle Fusion Applications Companion 11g (11.1.1.5.3)	V28727-01	1.2G
Download	Oracle JDeveloper 11g and Oracle Application Development Framework 11g (11.1.1.5.3) (Part 1 of 3)	V28726-01 Part 1 of 3	1.7G
Download	Oracle JDeveloper 11g and Oracle Application Development Framework 11g (11.1.1.5.3) (Part 2 of 3)	V28726-01 Part 2 of 3	1.1G
Download	Oracle JDeveloper 11g and Oracle Application Development Framework 11g (11.1.1.5.3) (Part 3 of 3)	V28726-01 Part 3 of 3	1.3G
Download	Oracle Fusion Applications Technology Documentation Library 11g Release 1 (11.1.1.5)	V27924-01	769M
Download	Oracle Fusion Applications Technology Documentation Library 11g Release 1 (11.1.2)	V29127-01	792M

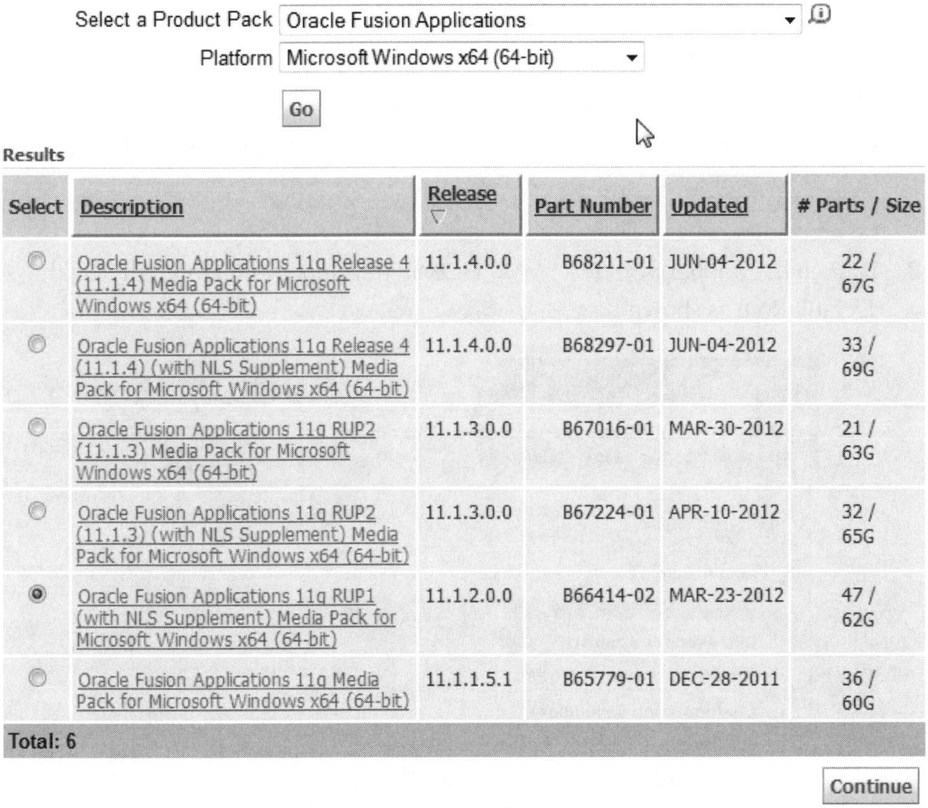

Select a Product Pack: Oracle Fusion Applications

Platform: Microsoft Windows x64 (64-bit)

Go

Results

Select	Description	Release	Part Number	Updated	# Parts / Size
○	Oracle Fusion Applications 11g Release 4 (11.1.4) Media Pack for Microsoft Windows x64 (64-bit)	11.1.4.0.0	B68211-01	JUN-04-2012	22 / 67G
○	Oracle Fusion Applications 11g Release 4 (11.1.4) (with NLS Supplement) Media Pack for Microsoft Windows x64 (64-bit)	11.1.4.0.0	B68297-01	JUN-04-2012	33 / 69G
○	Oracle Fusion Applications 11g RUP2 (11.1.3) Media Pack for Microsoft Windows x64 (64-bit)	11.1.3.0.0	B67016-01	MAR-30-2012	21 / 63G
○	Oracle Fusion Applications 11g RUP2 (11.1.3) (with NLS Supplement) Media Pack for Microsoft Windows x64 (64-bit)	11.1.3.0.0	B67224-01	APR-10-2012	32 / 65G
●	Oracle Fusion Applications 11g RUP1 (with NLS Supplement) Media Pack for Microsoft Windows x64 (64-bit)	11.1.2.0.0	B66414-02	MAR-23-2012	47 / 62G
○	Oracle Fusion Applications 11g Media Pack for Microsoft Windows x64 (64-bit)	11.1.1.5.1	B65779-01	DEC-28-2011	36 / 60G
Total: 6					

Continue

FIGURE 7-1. *Select the Fusion Applications release you want to download.*

Follow the detailed instructions in *Oracle Fusion Applications Developer's Guide* to set up the JDeveloper environment for customization. The steps outlined here will serve as guidelines to complete the setup.

1. Install JDeveloper using the downloaded Oracle JDeveloper 11*g* based on your platform. If you are installing on Windows, make sure the path used to install JDeveloper does not have any space(s) in it.

2. Set the following environment variables before you launch JDeveloper:

```
set PATH=<path to python 2.3 or higher>\bin:%PATH%
set MW_HOME=<path to JDeveloper installation directory>
set JAVA_HOME=%MW_HOME%\jdk160_24
set PATH =%JDK_HOME%\bin:%PATH%
set JDEV_USER_HOME=<path to JDeveloper installation directory>\jdeveloper\mywork
set FADEV_VERBOSE=true
set USER_MEM_ARGS=-Xms256m -Xmx1024m -XX:MaxPermSize=512m
-XX:CompileThreshold=8000
```

3. Launch JDeveloper from the $MW_HOME/jdeveloper/ directory. Choose the Default Role as shown here.

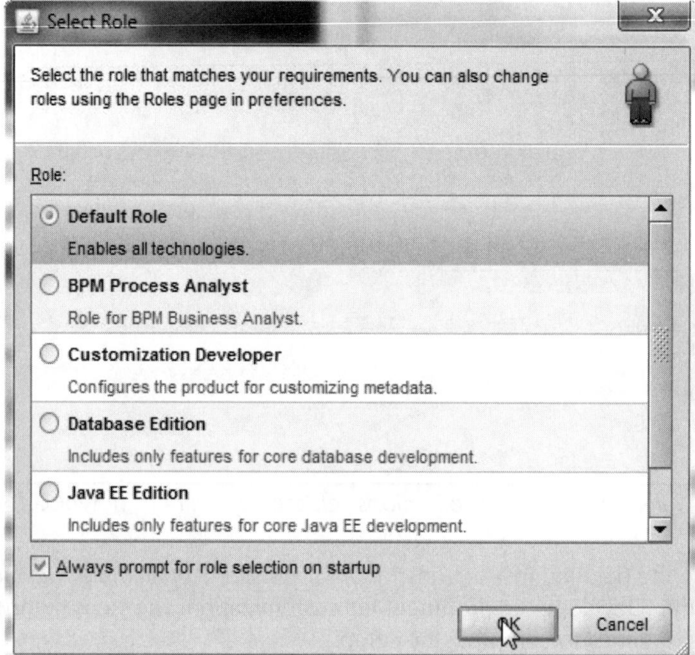

4. Once JDeveloper opens up, use the Help menu and go to Check for Updates.

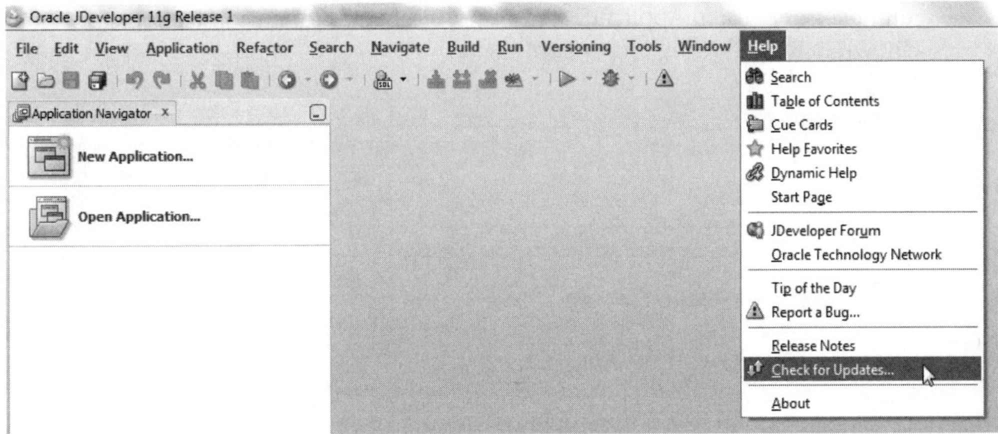

5. Create a new update center for Fusion Applications as shown in the following illustration. The location of the fusion_apps_updatecenter.xml file is in the fusion_apps_extensions folder when you unzip the Oracle Fusion Applications Companion 11*g* zip file that you downloaded earlier.

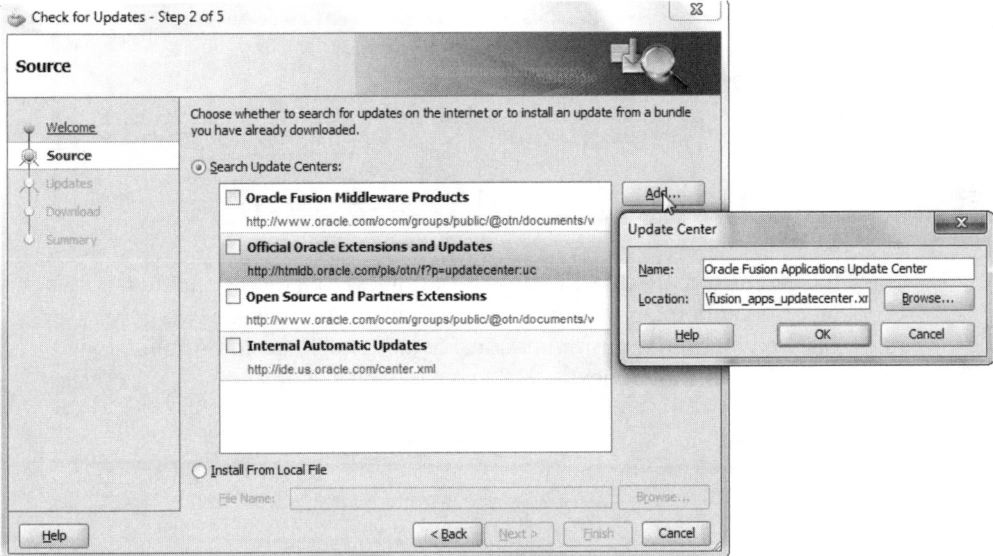

6. Select this new Update Center and click Next. Select Fusion Apps Development Environment from the available updates, and this will choose all necessary Fusion Application Extensions required for customizations as shown in the following illustration.

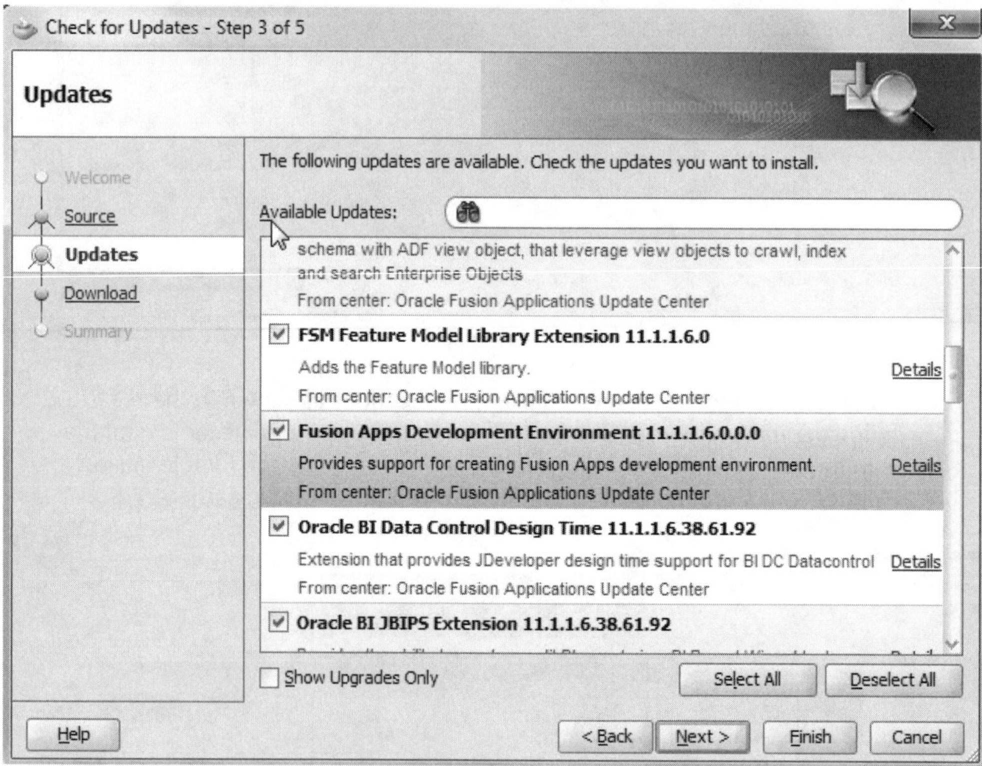

7. Once the extensions are downloaded, restart JDeveloper to configure the WebLogic Server domain for your customizations. You will see two new roles that we will use for customizations. Select Oracle Fusion Applications Developer Role as shown next.

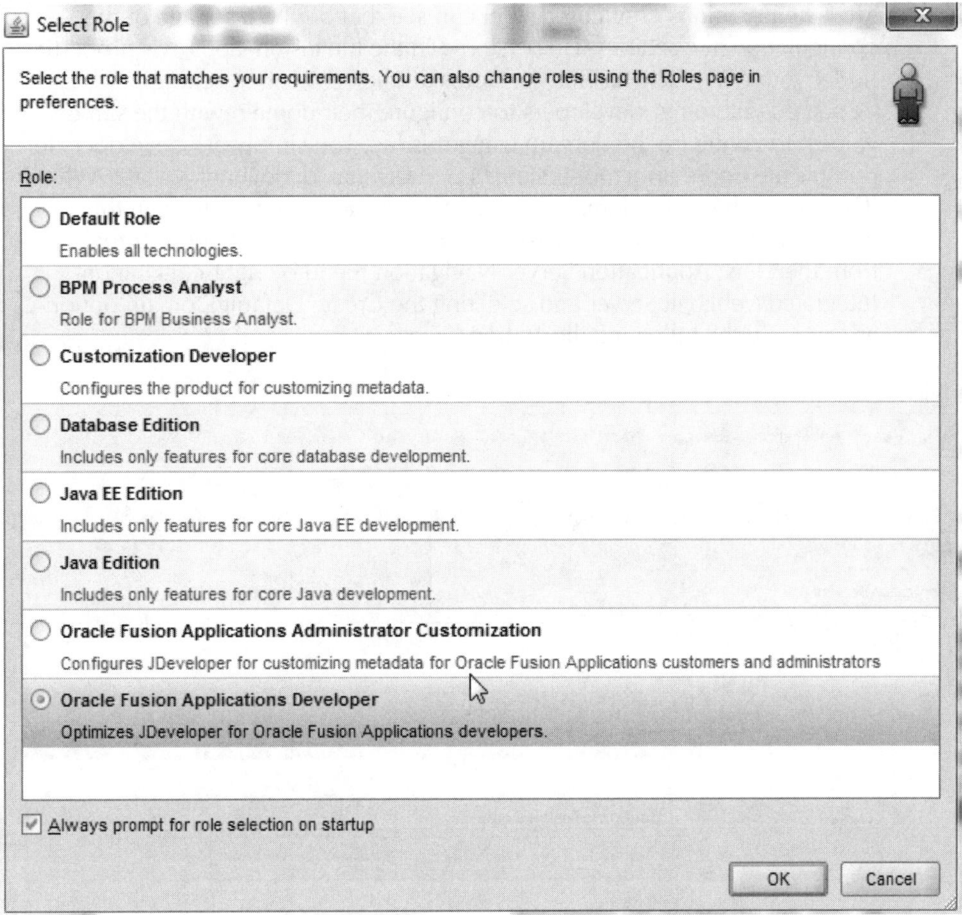

8. Once JDeveloper opens up, it will ask you to configure the WebLogic Server for your customizations.

9. Click Yes to configure the server. Select Default Integrated Server on Step 1 of configuration. Provide details for Fusion database and LDAP server during the configuration setup. The default password for WebLogic domain is weblogic1 and you can change that during the setup.

10. After the domain is configured, you can see that on the last page of the configuration, the settings will be stored in the file fusion_apps_wls.properties under your MW_HOME. This file stores all the connection settings and can be shared with other developers to configure their domain with the same values. To configure the domain using this file, you simply ask developers to put this file under directory system11.1.1.xx.yy.zz/o.jdevimpl.rescat2. When JDeveloper starts, the domain is configured to point to the values in this file. After that, you can manually create the integrated WebLogic domain from the View: Application Server Navigation menu by right-clicking on IntegratedWebLogicServer and selecting the Create Default Domain option as shown in the following illustration.

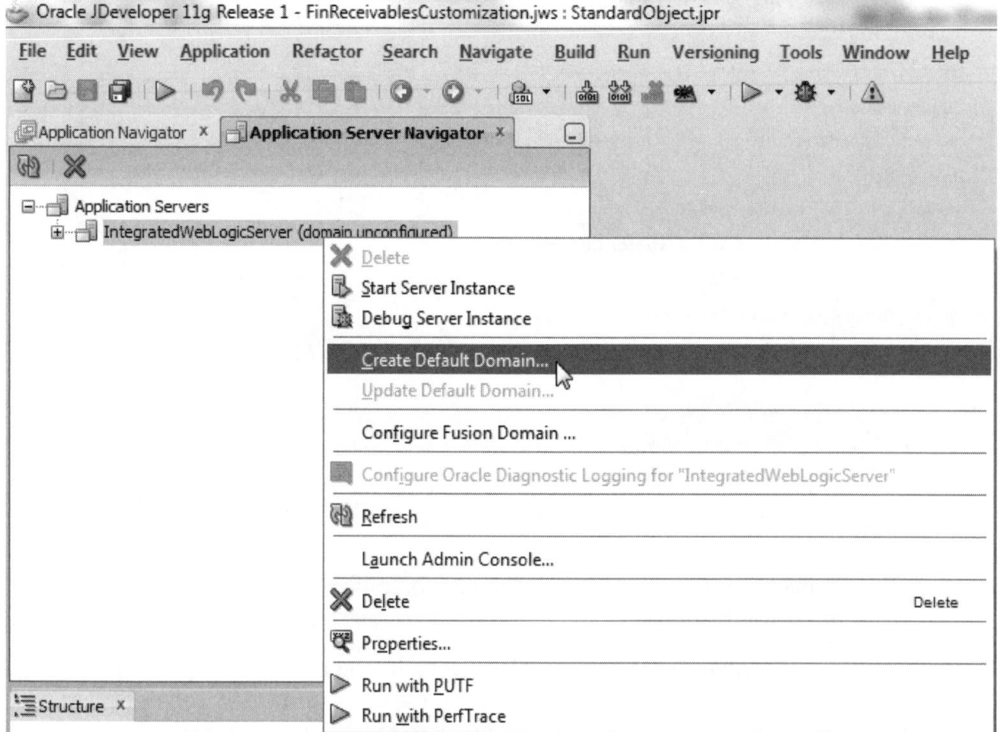

How to Determine Application Artifacts for Customization

To customize any application page or behavior on the page, you first need to know and understand the anatomy of how Fusion Applications are built and how you can identify the artifacts involved on that page for customization. In the Oracle E-Business

Suite application, there was an "about this page" link that used to give information on the page and underlying business objects used for the page. In Fusion Applications, there is no such single place to identify the name of the page and business objects behind that page at this point, and that makes it very difficult and tedious to find out which artifacts you should customize. Let us first understand the typical application page and how it is built.

- Every page in Fusion Applications is built as a bounded task flow (TF). The bounded task flow is built using page fragments (JSFF). The navigation is defined in the TF between two JSFF or between JSFF and another TF declaratively. Identifying this TF is key to finding out the artifact you need to customize.
- The entry points to a given application such as dashboard or a work area are built as JSF pages (JSPX) and are directly accessible from the Navigator menu or the UI Shell global menu. You can look at the menu file associated with the page to find out the TF that constitutes the landing page or the Task pane or Regional area pane links.
- Every page is built using ADF Application Module (AM) Data Controls, which consist of View objects (VO) that are built on top of Entity objects (EO). Once you identify the page, you can look at the associated pageDef binding for the page to identify associated AM, VO, and EO objects that are used to construct the page.
- If your page is a setup task invoked using the Setup and Maintenance application, you can identify the TF by going to the Manage Task Lists and Tasks page. This page is accessible to the administrator from the Task pane under Implementation Objects in the Setup and Maintenance work area. Navigate to this page and search for the task you are interested in customizing. Click on the task name to drill down to see the details. It will show the name of the TF behind that setup task as Program Name.

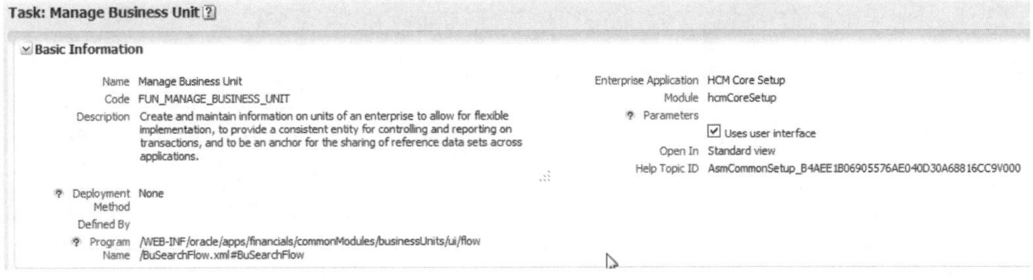

Now that you know how to identify the underlying task flow and the application details for a given page at run time, we will discuss how can you locate those artifacts in JDeveloper to do customizations. We will import the deployed Enterprise Achieve (EAR) file in JDeveloper so that we can find the artifacts to customize.

1. To identify the artifacts to customize in a given application, you first create a customization application in JDeveloper. To create a customization application, launch JDeveloper and select the Oracle Fusion Applications Developer role.

2. Once JDeveloper is launched, choose the File | New menu option to open the New Gallery and select Fusion Applications Customization Application as shown in Figure 7-2.

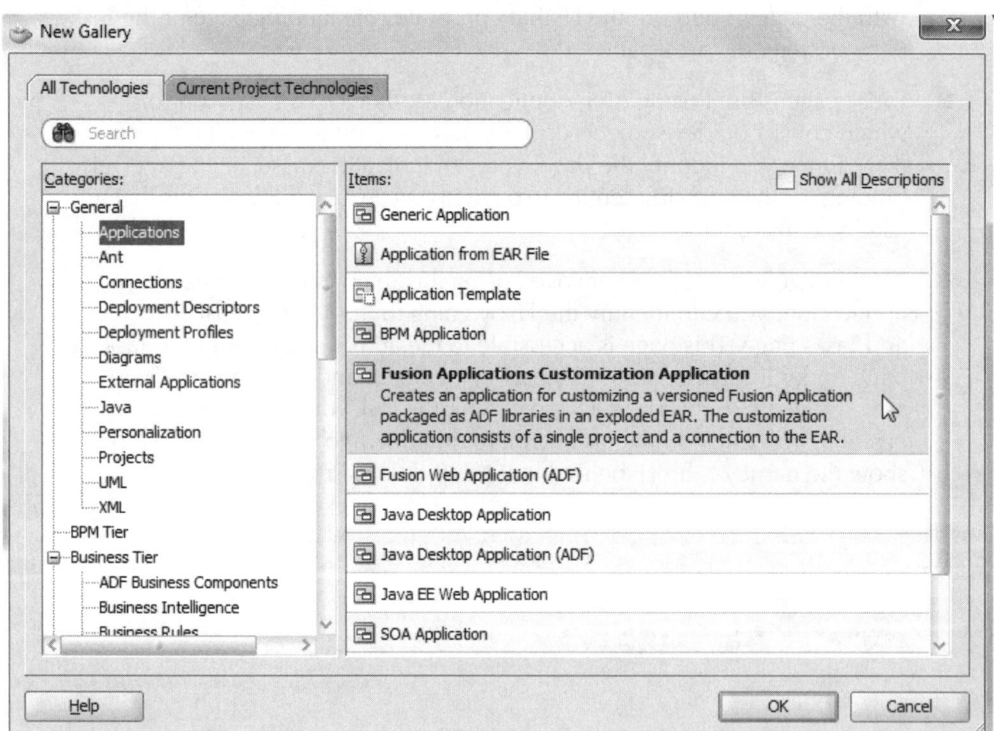

FIGURE 7-2. *Creating a Fusion Applications customization workspace*

3. On the Create Customization Application dialog, provide the details for your new customization application as shown in Figure 7-3. You must specify the deployed application ear or the location to the exploded EAR directory for the application that you want to customize.

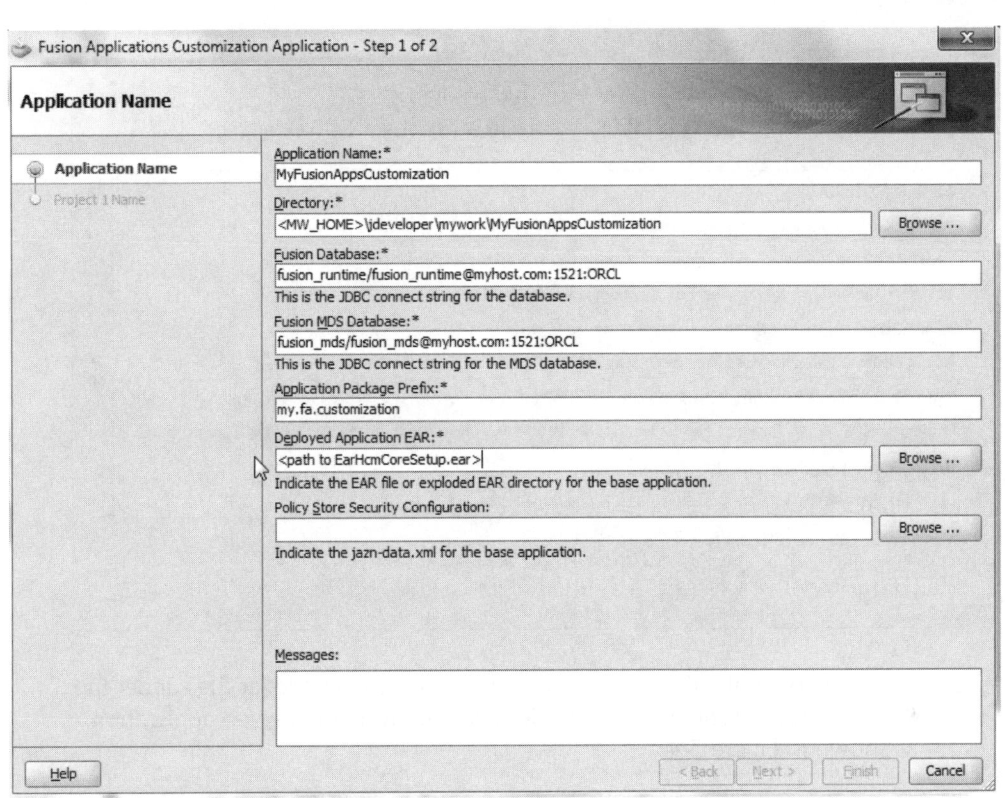

FIGURE 7-3. *Customization application properties*

4. Give the name of the project as StandardObjectCustomization and complete the application creation.

   ```
   You use JDeveloper with the Oracle Fusion Applications Adminis-
   trator Customization role as shown in the following illustration
   to customize any artifact.
   ```

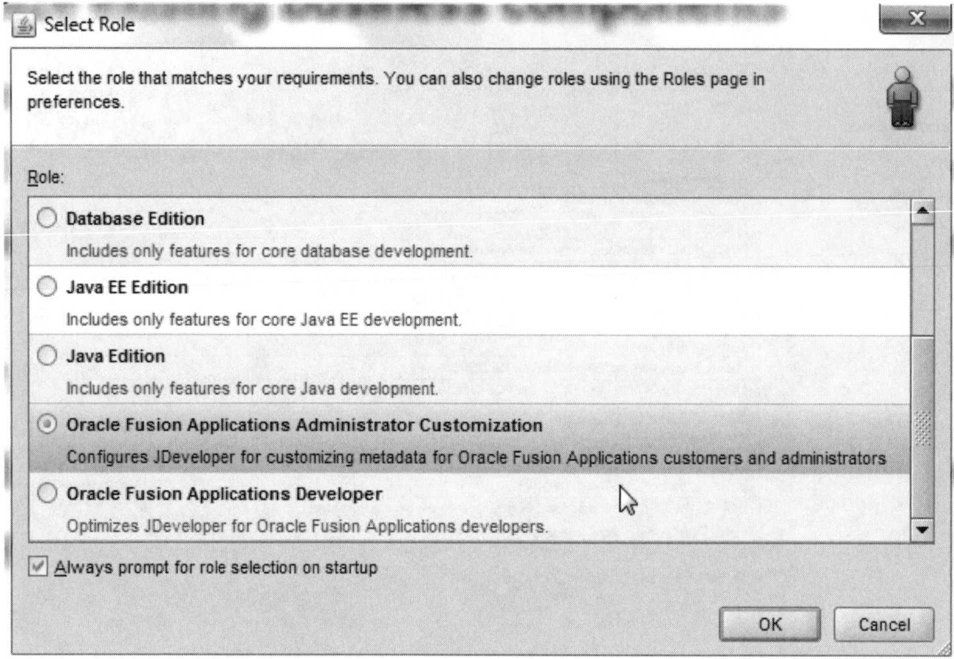

5. Once you open the JDeveloper, you can see customizable jar files under the Resource Palette and available customization layers for a given application as shown in Figure 7-4.

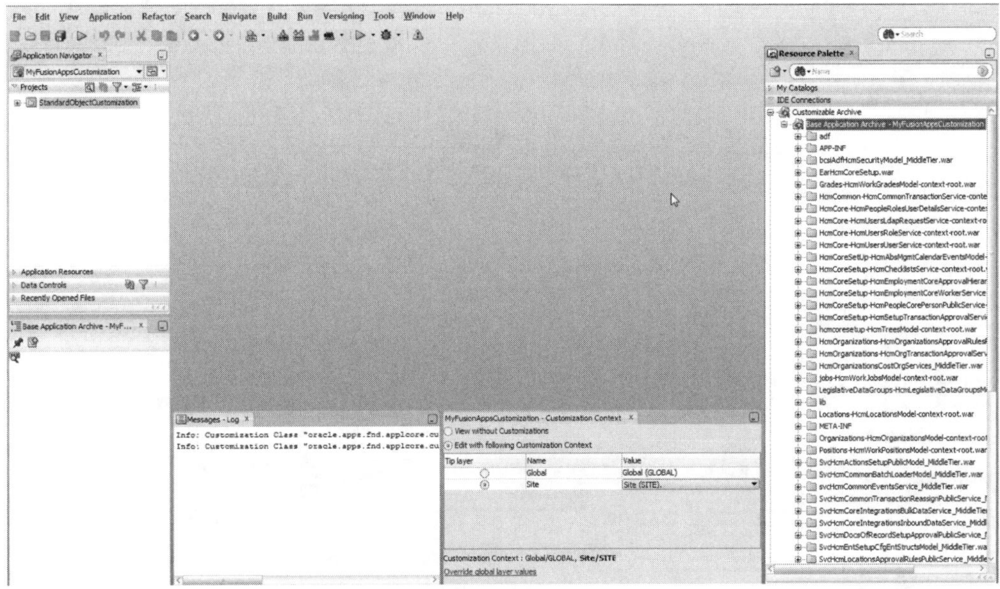

FIGURE 7-4. *Customizable jar files for a given application in JDeveloper*

6. Search for the task flow you have identified inside which you need customizations. You can use the Resource Palette search window to search by name. Search for BuSearchFlow. Double-click the BuSearchFlow.xml file to open the task flow in JDeveloper as shown in Figure 7-5.

7. The Manage or Create/Edit action in this task flow invokes another task flow, BuMaintainFlow. Search for this in the Resource Palette and open the task flow as shown in Figure 7-6.

8. The page used for create/edit of BU is BuProperties.jsff as seen in the task flow. Search for this page and open the BuPropertiesPageDef file to inspect what ADFbc is used on this page as shown in Figure 7-7.

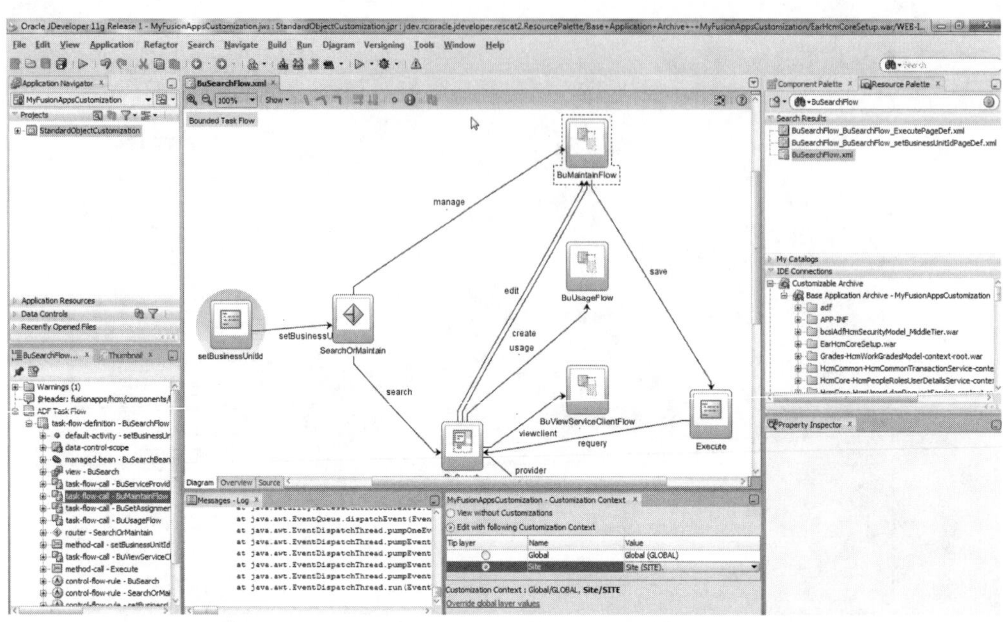

FIGURE 7-5. *Business Unit search task flow*

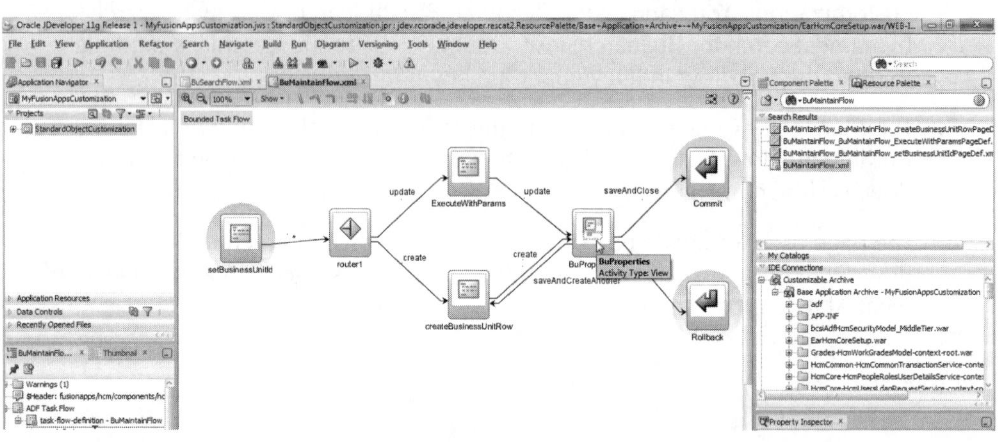

FIGURE 7-6. *Business Unit manage task flow*

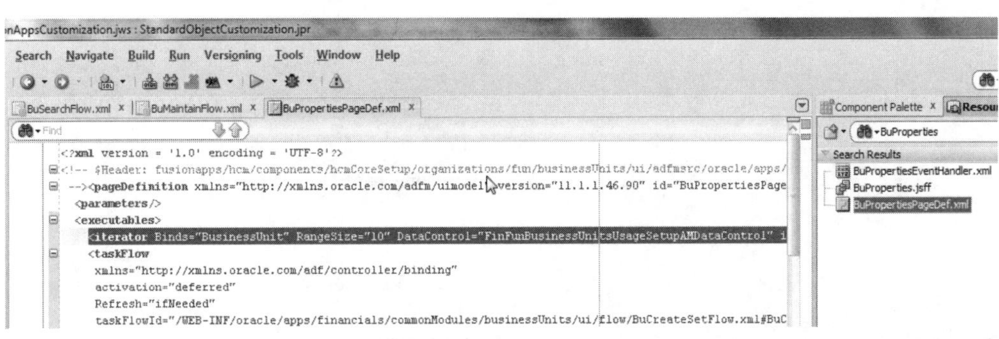

FIGURE 7-7. *Business Unit manage page definition file*

9. The pageDef shows that the page is using FinFunBusinessUnitsUsageSetupAM and BusinessUnit view instance in the AM. Search for FinFunBusinessUnitsUsageSetupAM and open to find the VO definition for the BusinessUnit instance as shown in Figure 7-8.

10. The AM shows that the VO definition is BusinessUnitSetupVO. Search for this VO in the Search Palette. Right-click on the VO and you should see the Customize menu option as shown in Figure 7-9. If you do not see that option or see a message in jdev log that reads "Customizations are disabled for the node 'BusinessUnitSetupVO.xml' because it is not part of the project contentset," choose GLOBAL layer for customization context.

FIGURE 7-8. *Application module for Business Unit setup page*

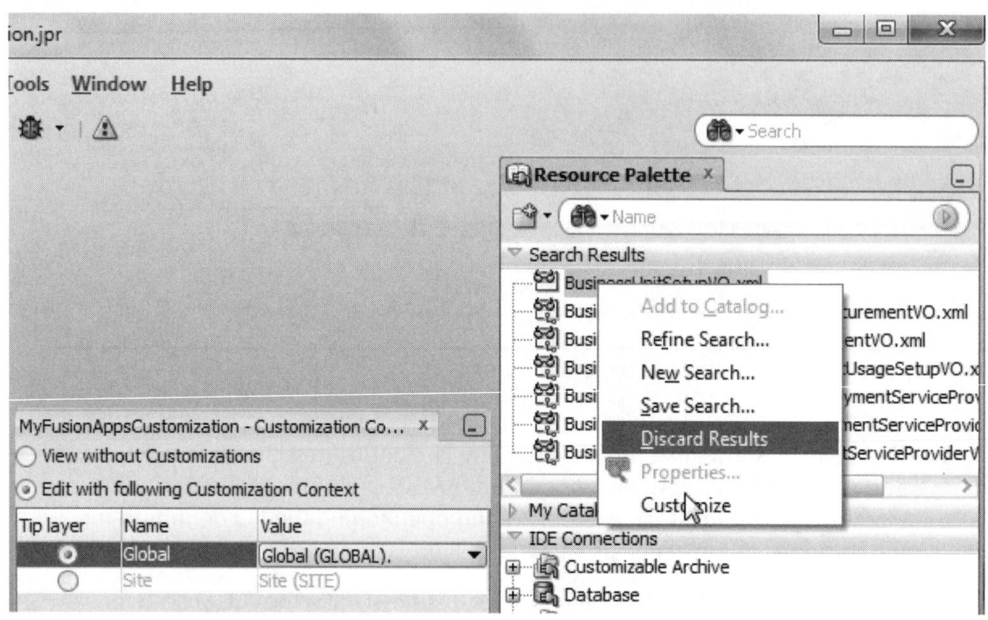

FIGURE 7-9. *Setting the customization layer*

How to Customize Existing Business Components

In this section, we will discuss two use cases to customize standard ADF business components. We will modify an out-of-the-box list of values (LOV) for a field to add more filters to it, and we will add a new business rule to an entity object.

How to Modify LOV

We will modify the Business Unit setup UI Manager Field LOV to show only Employees and not show contingent workers in the LOV.

1. Right-click on BusinessUnitSetupVO and choose Customize. This will ask you to add ADF Library AdfHcmOrgBusinessUnitsModel.jar to your project. Click the Add Library button to add the library to your customization project.

2. Once the VO is added for customization, you can edit in the JDeveloper VO editor. Go to Manage LOV and find the data source for this LOV as shown in Figure 7-10.

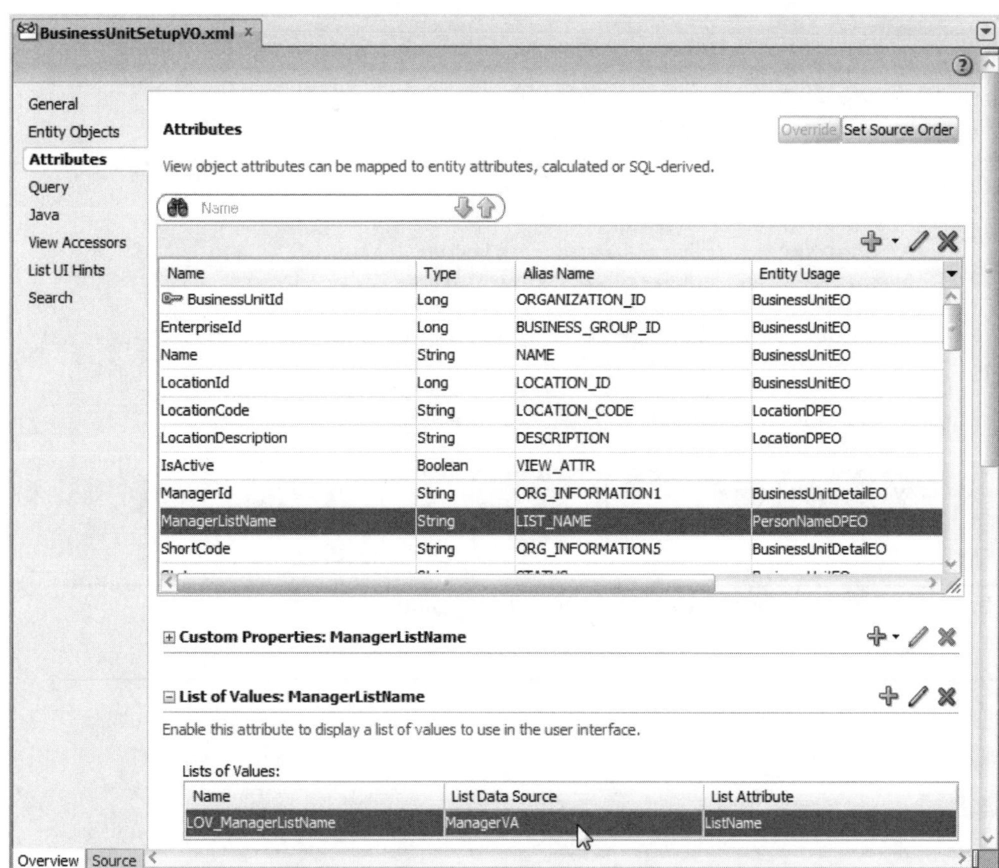

FIGURE 7-10. *Manager field List of Values for Business Unit Setup VO*

3. The LOV list data source points to ManagerVA. Go to the View Accessors tab in the VO and edit ManagerVA as shown in Figure 7-11.

4. Select AllEmployees view criteria and add it to the select list to filter the LOV to return only employees for Manager Field as shown in Figure 7-12.

5. This completes the customization use case of modifying the LOV to filter the data shown. You can view the customizations in Application Navigator as shown in Figure 7-13.

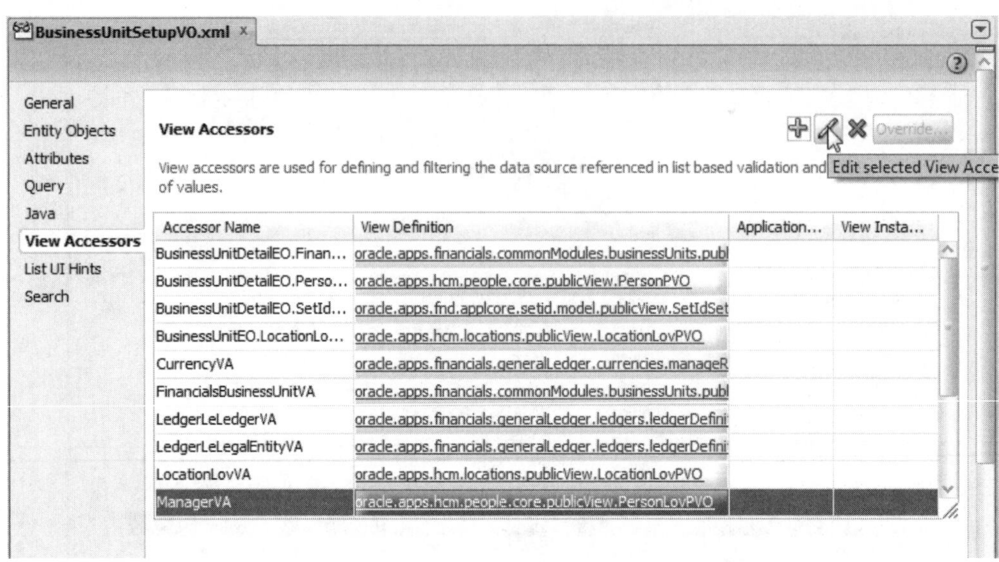

FIGURE 7-11. *View Accessors tab for manager list of values*

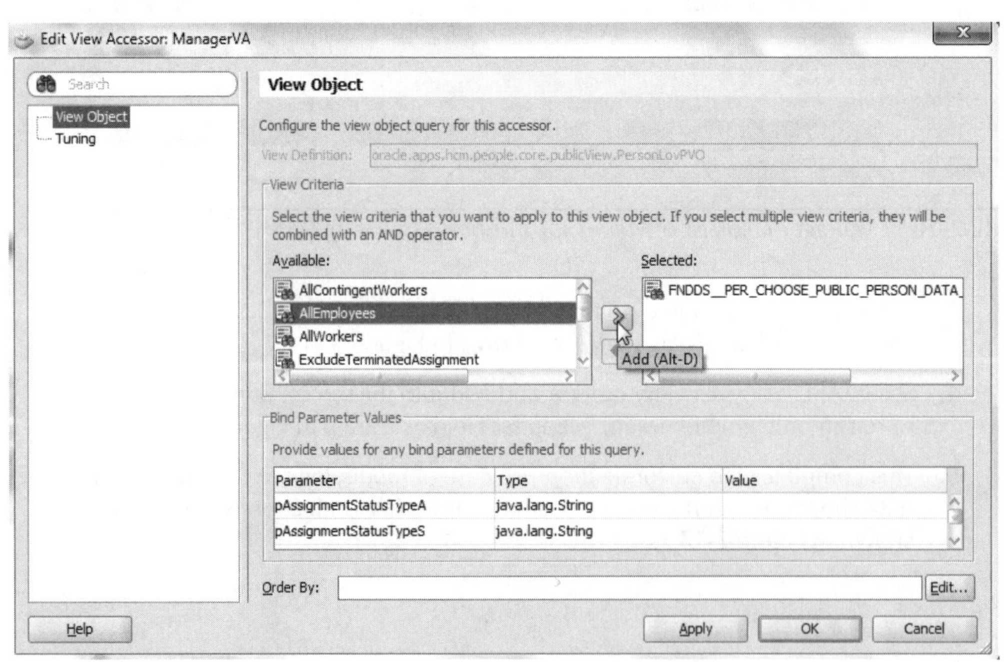

FIGURE 7-12. *Modifying manager LOV data source to show only employees*

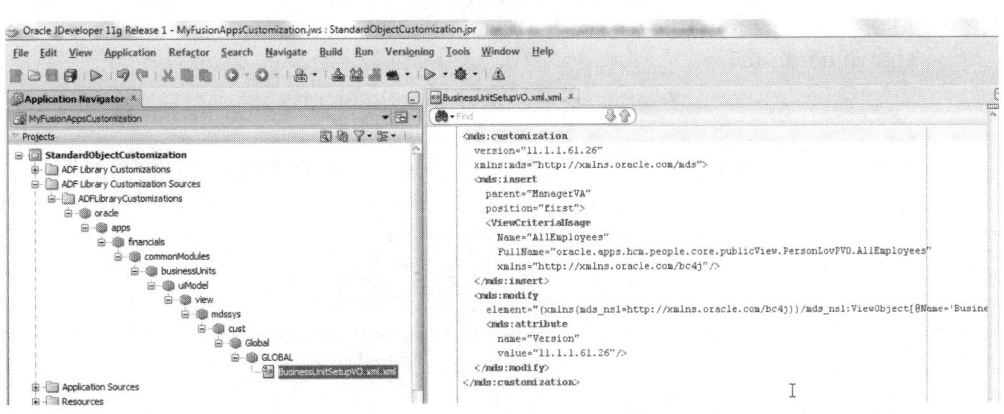

FIGURE 7-13. *Customized file for Business Unit Setup VO*

How to Add New Validation

Fusion Applications enforce a lot of business rules and validations out of the box. They cover most of the common scenarios, but many times you have a requirement to enforce certain business rules that are not enforced as standard behavior. You will need to modify the entity objects to add, remove, or modify existing rules. In this section, we will add a new validation on a business unit that it cannot be inactivated if there is a business function assigned to the business unit.

1. Search for BusinessUnitEO in the Resource Palette, right-click, and choose the Customize menu option. This will open the EO in the JDeveloper editor.
2. To check if there is a business function associated with the business unit, we will use BusinessUnitUsageSetupVO and view criteria SearchGenFinTxnBF in that VO. Go to the View Accessors tab in the EO and click the Create New View Accessor button as shown in the following illustration.

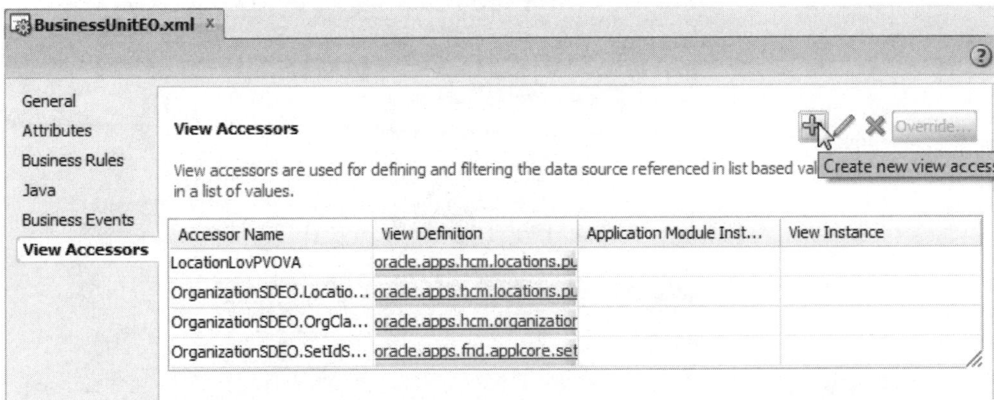

3. Select the VO and name it BusinessUnitUsageValidate. Click the Edit icon to use the necessary View Criteria (VC) for this view accessor definition as shown here.

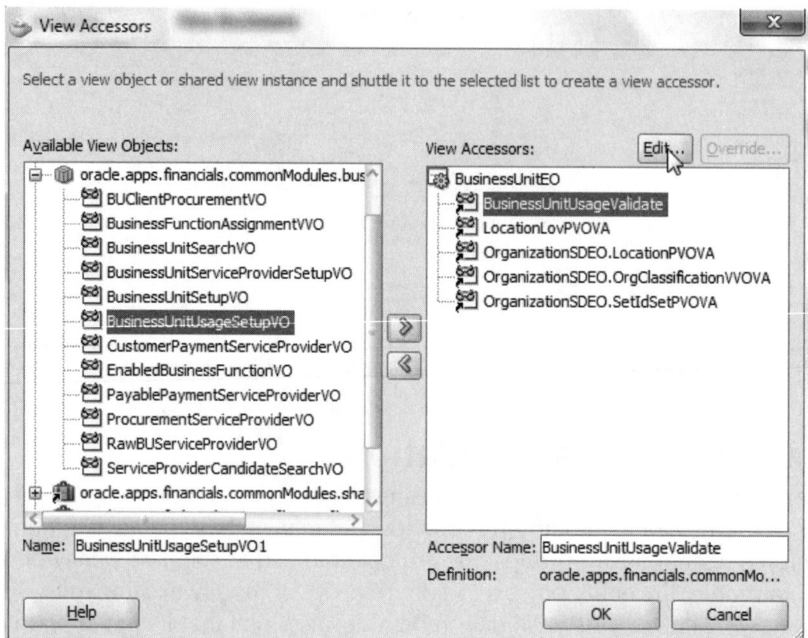

4. Select SearchGenFinTxnBF view criteria and supply the value for the bind variable via OrganizationId attribute.

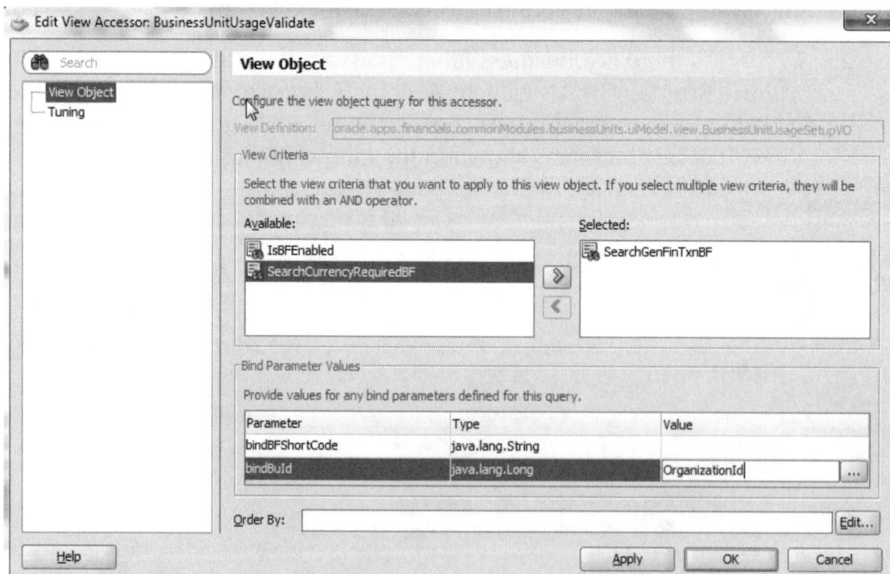

5. Now go to the Business Rules tab and click the Create New Validator icon to define a new validation rule using the view accessor.

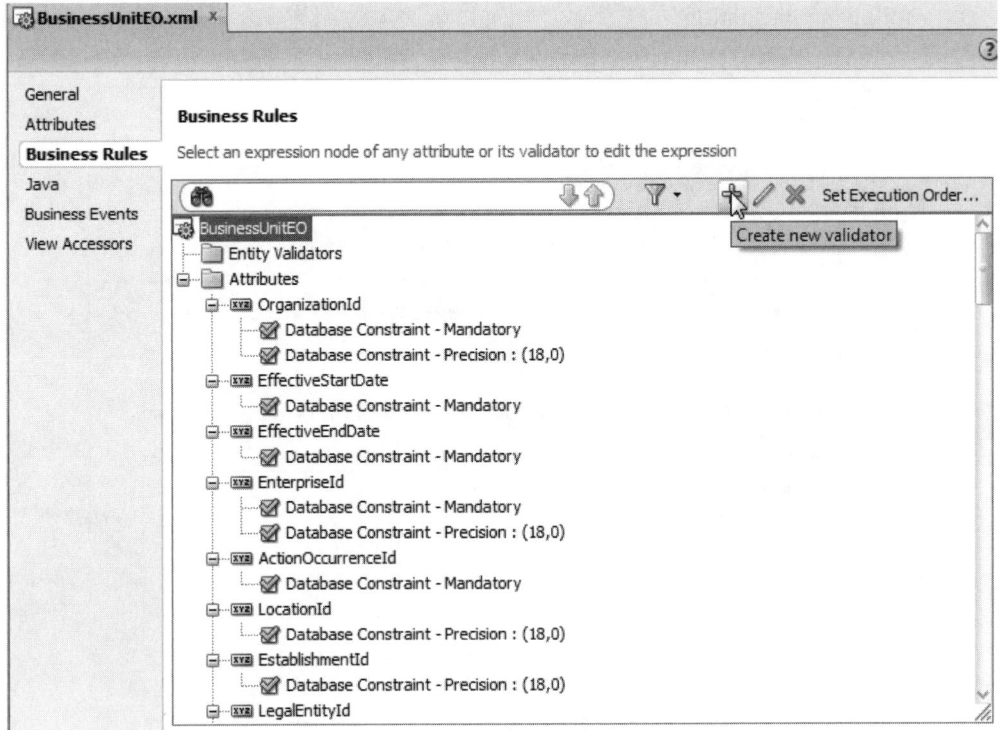

6. Select the Script Expression from the Rule Type drop-down, and enter the script such that it returns false when a row is found in View Accessor, or else returns true indicating there are no business functions, as shown in the following illustration.

```
if(BusinessUnitUsageValidate?.hasNext())
  return false;
return true;
```

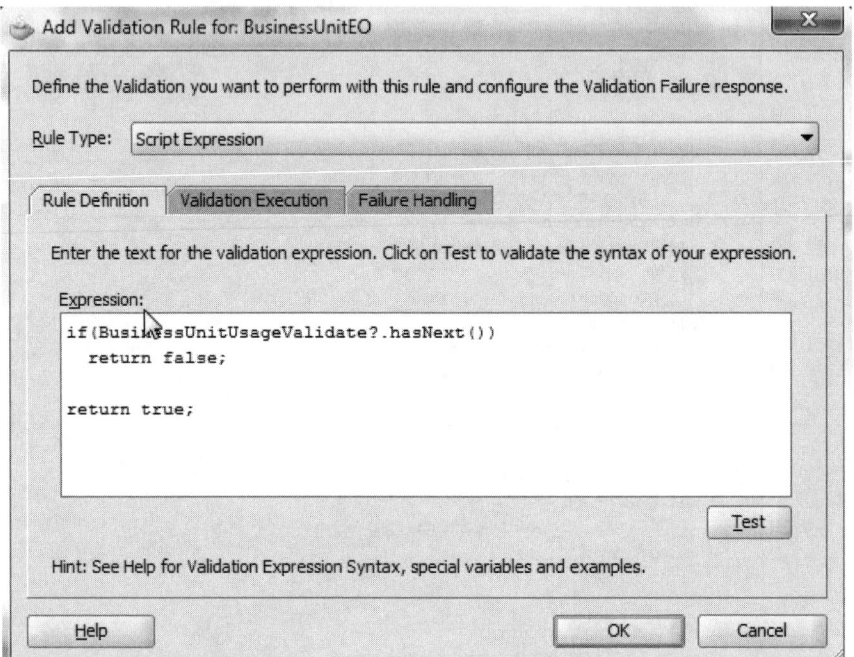

7. Now go to the Validation Execution tab and give the conditional execution expression such that the validation is executed only when Status == 'I'. Also, execute the validation rule only when the Status attribute is changed by selecting that attribute as shown in Figure 7-14.

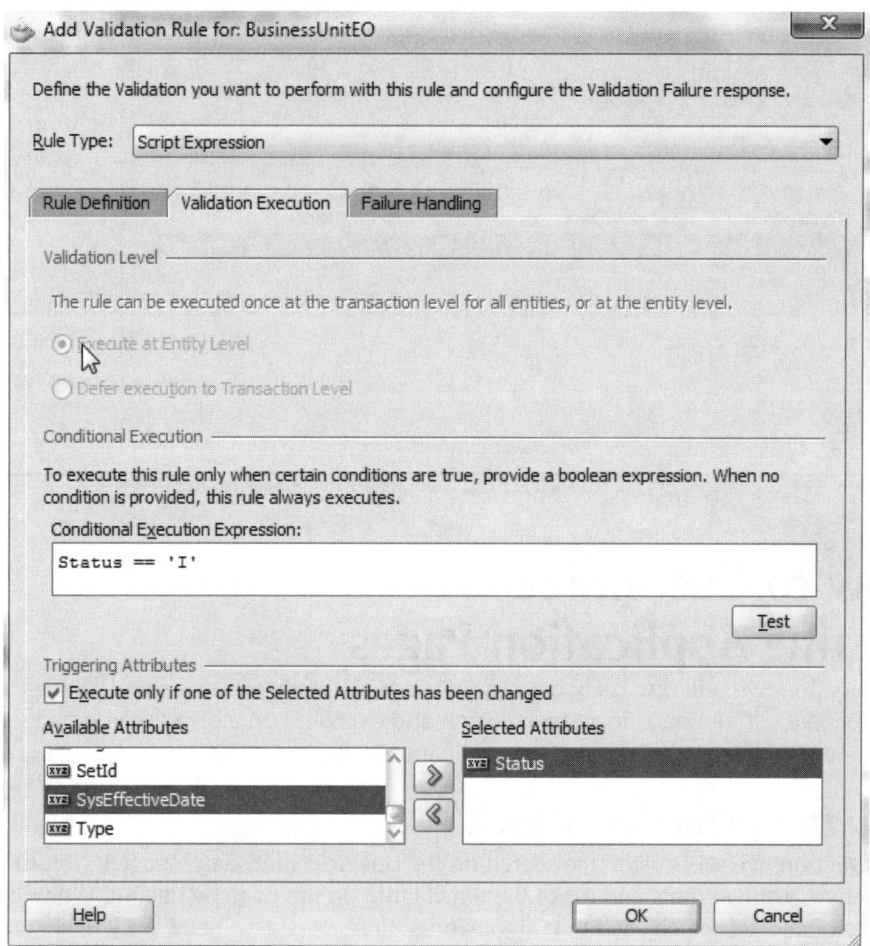

FIGURE 7-14. *Specifying validation execution condition*

8. Go to Manage Messages tasks in FSM and define a new error message. Now go to the Failure Handling tab on the validation window and click Browse to select the Existing Message icon. Choose your newly defined message as shown in Figure 7-15.

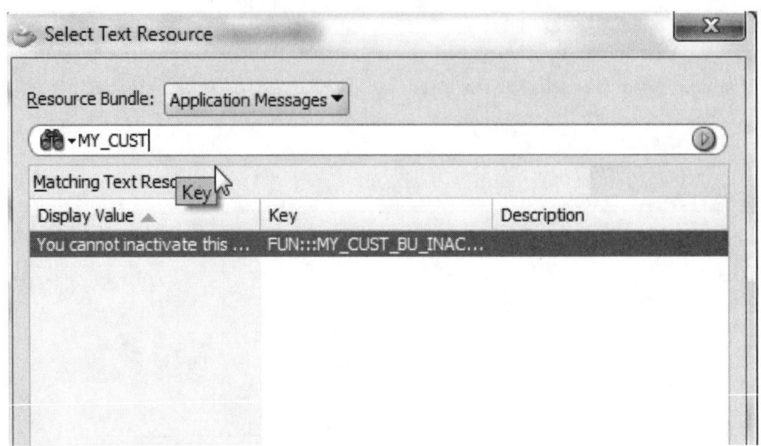

FIGURE 7-15. *Specifying an error message for a validation rule*

How to Customize Existing Application Pages

In this section, we will discuss two use cases on how to customize a standard page behavior. We will define a new saved search and expose it on a given search page and we will add a new attribute to an application page.

How to Customize Search

In this section, we will customize search on the business unit search page to return only active business units and make them available on the page by default. We will add another saved search to search all business units.

1. Open BuSearchPageDef to find out what VO and VC are used for the search region on this page as shown in Figure 7-16.
2. Open the BusinessUnitSetupVO in customization mode. Go to the Query tab and edit the ManageBusinessUnitsSearch view criteria. Modify the view criteria to change the Status field Operand to Literal and value of "A" as shown in Figure 7-17.

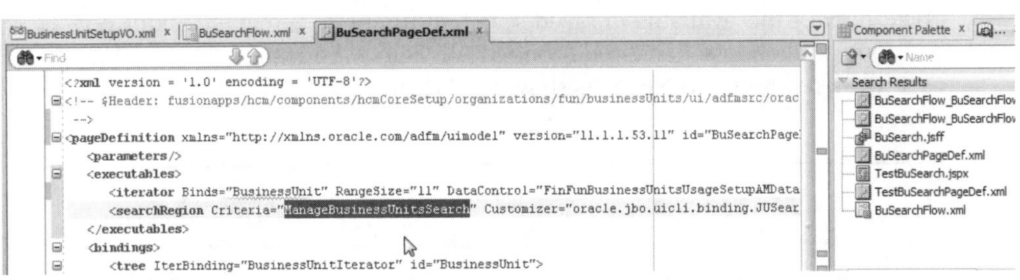

FIGURE 7-16. *Page definition file for the business unit search page*

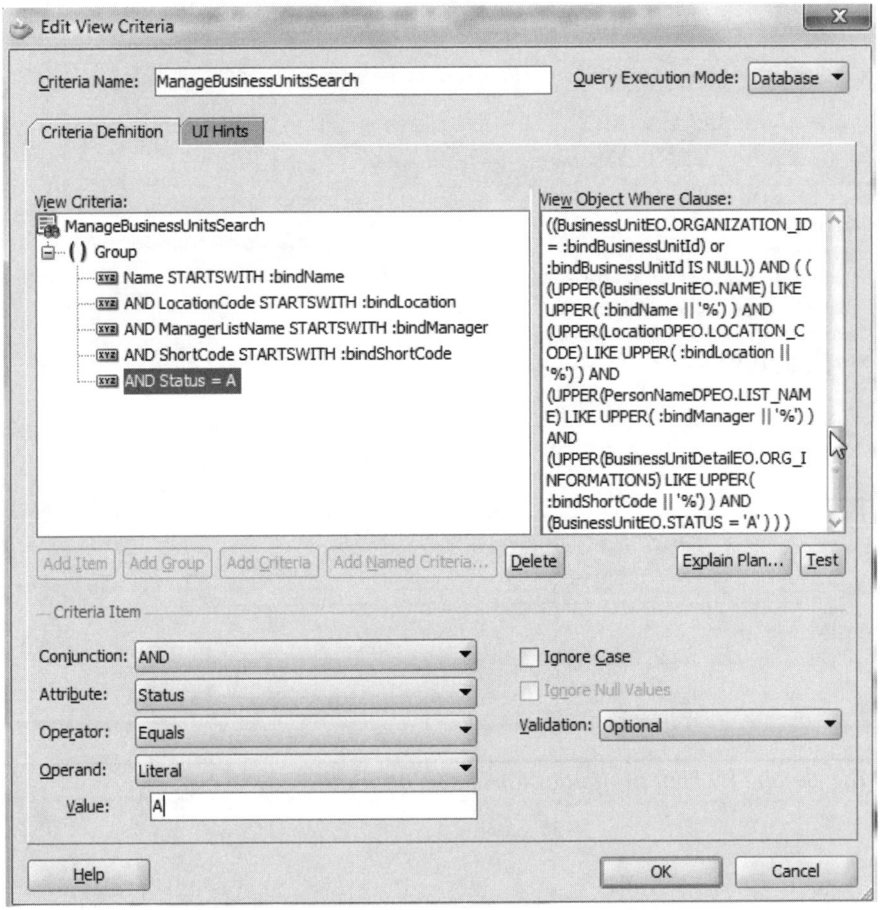

FIGURE 7-17. *Customizing out-of-the-box search criteria*

3. Go to the UI Hints tab in the View Criteria editor and check the Show in List box to make this available in saved search at run time. Select the ShortCode attribute and choose Rendered Mode to All. Select the Status attribute and set Rendered Mode to Never as shown in Figure 7-18.

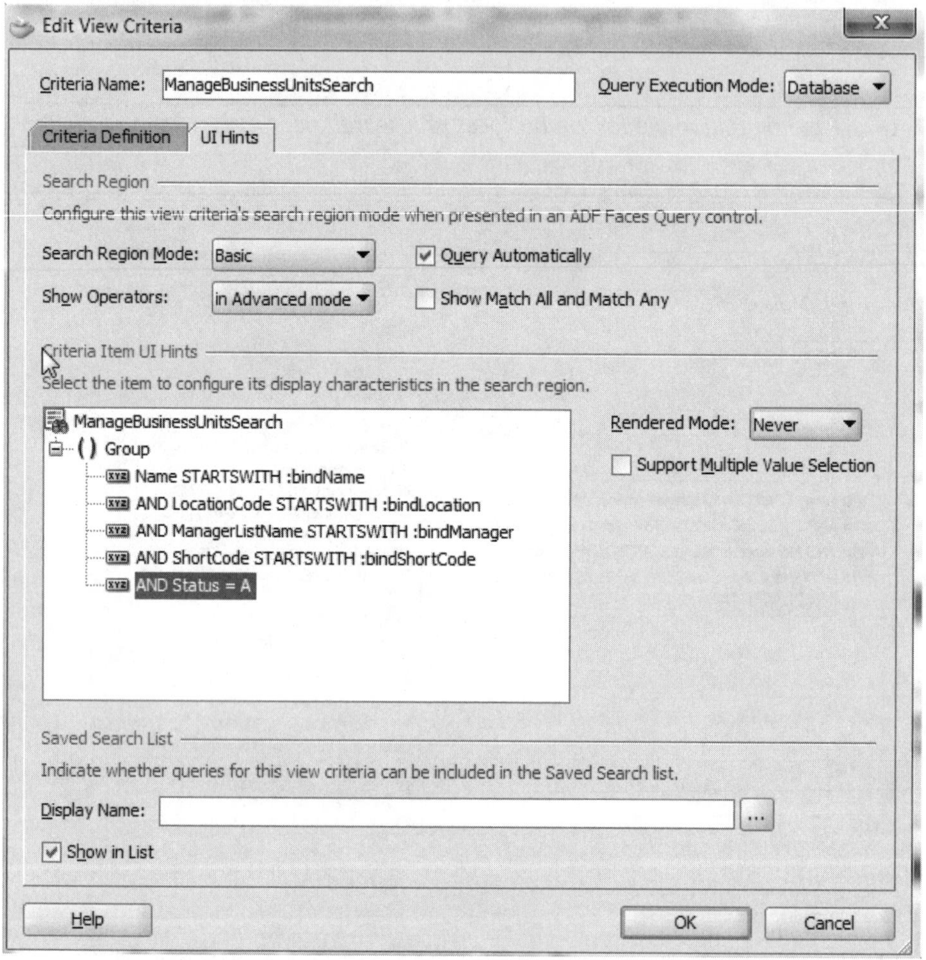

FIGURE 7-18. *Setting UI Hint properties for search attributes*

4. Click the Create New View Criteria button and define a new VC to return all business units as shown in Figure 7-19.

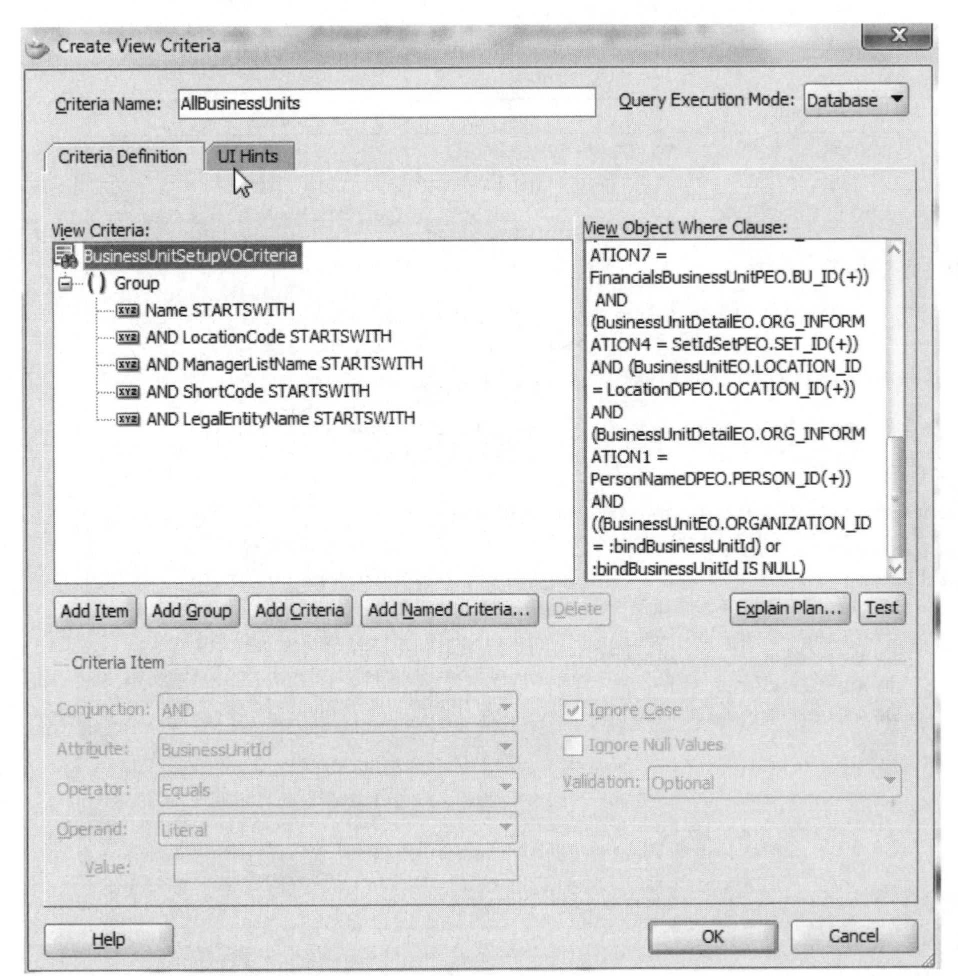

FIGURE 7-19. *Adding new view criteria*

5. The view criteria created is available in saved search by default. Go to the UI Hints tab and check Query Automatically shown in Figure 7-20. Uncheck the Show Match All and Match Any box. This saved search will be available on run-time UI and the user can select it from the Saved Search list of values on the Manage Business Units page.

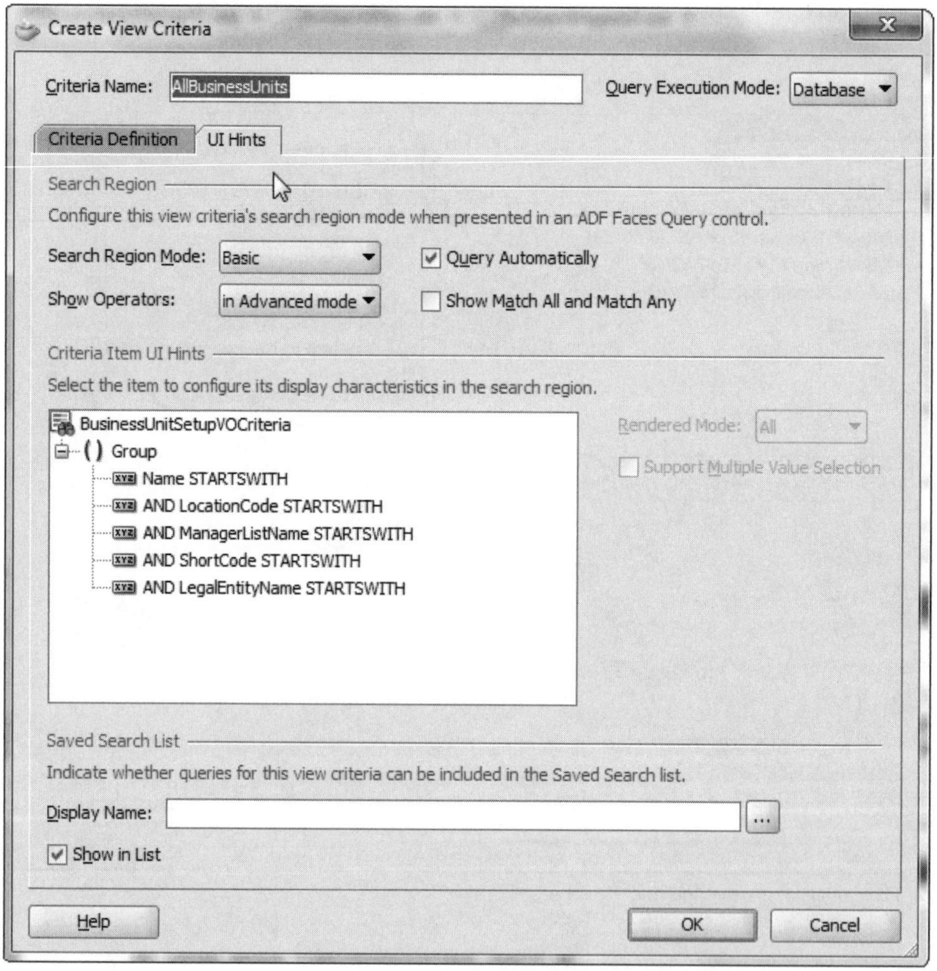

FIGURE 7-20. *Configuring new view criteria for saved search*

How to Add a New Attribute to a Page

In this section, we will add a new attribute that indicates the number of transaction business functions assigned to the business unit and expose it on the business unit search page.

1. Open BusinessUnitEO in customization mode and click the Create New Attribute button from the Attributes tab.
2. Name the attribute NumberOfTxBusFuncAssigned and provide an expression to calculate the number of rows in the view accessor BusinessUnitUsageValidate that we created earlier to check transaction business functions assigned for this business unit as shown in Figure 7-21.

   ```
   BusinessUnitUsageValidate.count("BusinessUnitId")
   ```
3. Open BusinessUnitSetupVO in customization mode and click Add Attribute from Entity as shown in Figure 7-22.
4. Select the newly added attribute from the BusinessUnitEO to this VO as shown in Figure 7-23.

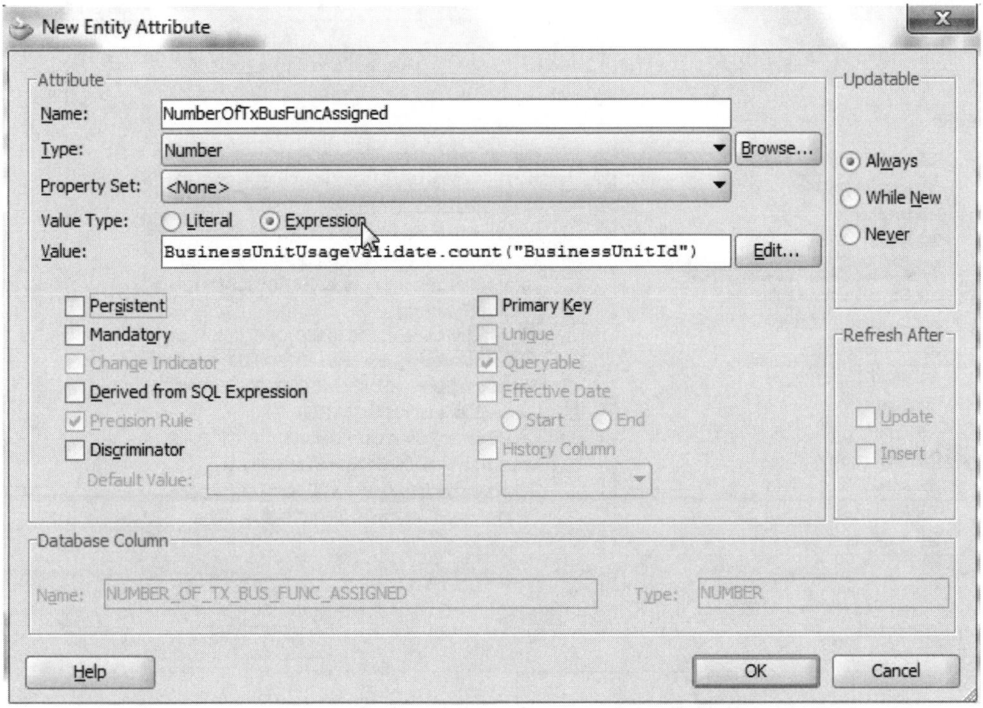

FIGURE 7-21. *Creating a new attribute in the EO*

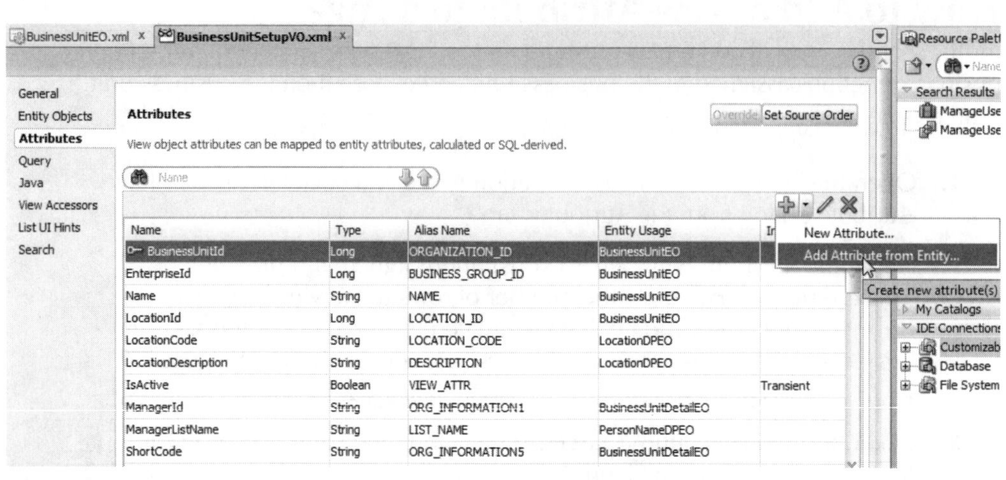

FIGURE 7-22. *Adding a new attribute in the VO*

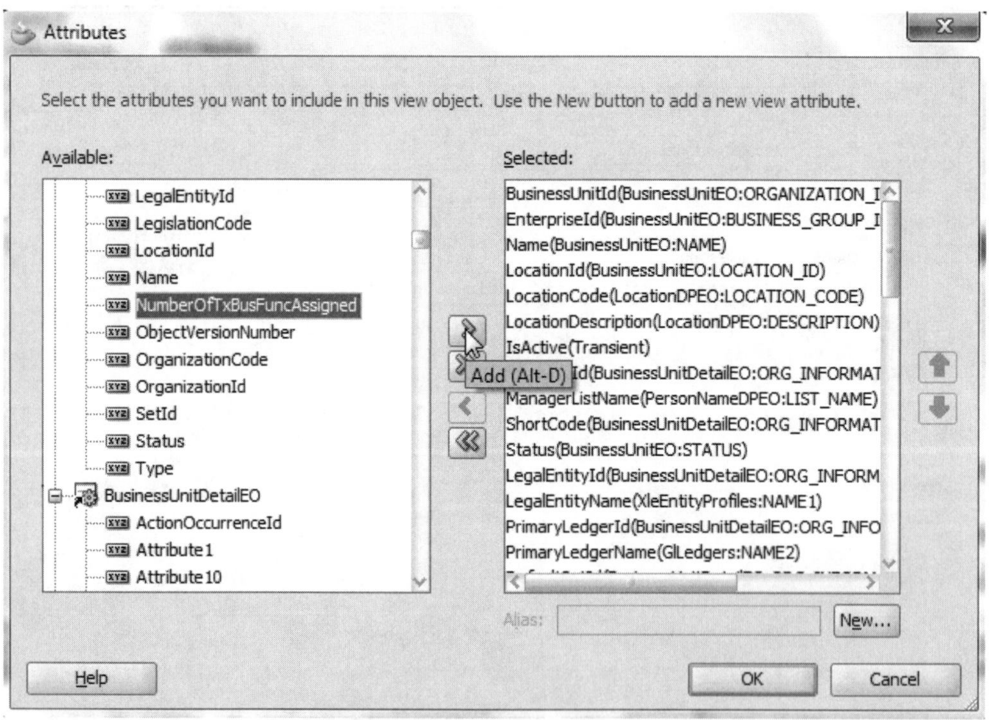

FIGURE 7-23. *Selecting an EO attribute to be added to the VO*

5. Open BuSearch.jsff and BuSearchPageDef in customization mode. Expand the Data Control page and look for BusinessUnit VO under FinFunBusinessUnitsUsageSetupAMDataControl as shown in Figure 7-24. If you do not see this data control, select Tools | Preferences | Business Components: General and check the box Display Imported ADF Libraries in Data Control Palette. Close the Preferences dialog and then refresh the Data Control Palette.
6. Drag the NumberOfTxBusFuncAssigned field and drop it as a read-only ADF column in the business unit search result table as shown in Figure 7-25.

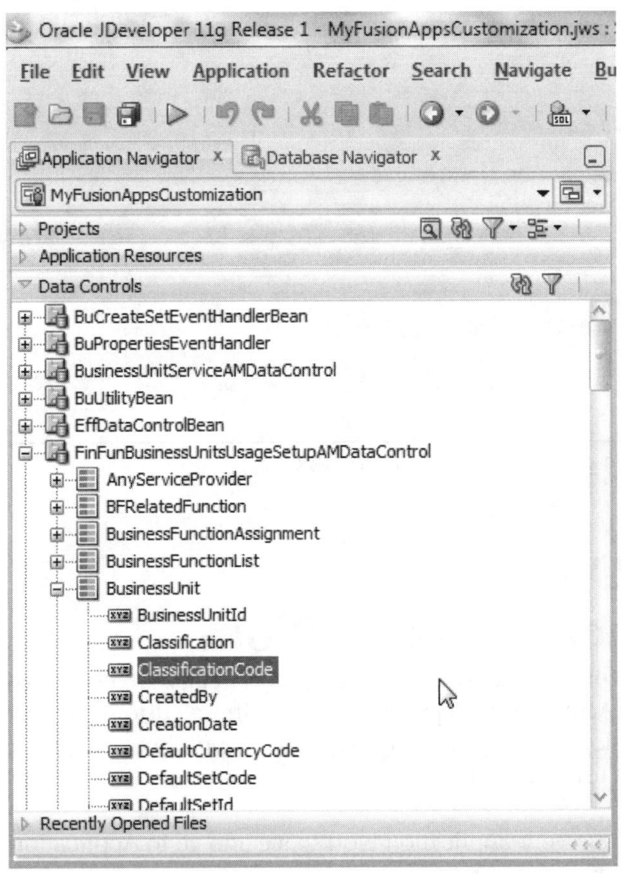

FIGURE 7-24. *Finding the view object in data control*

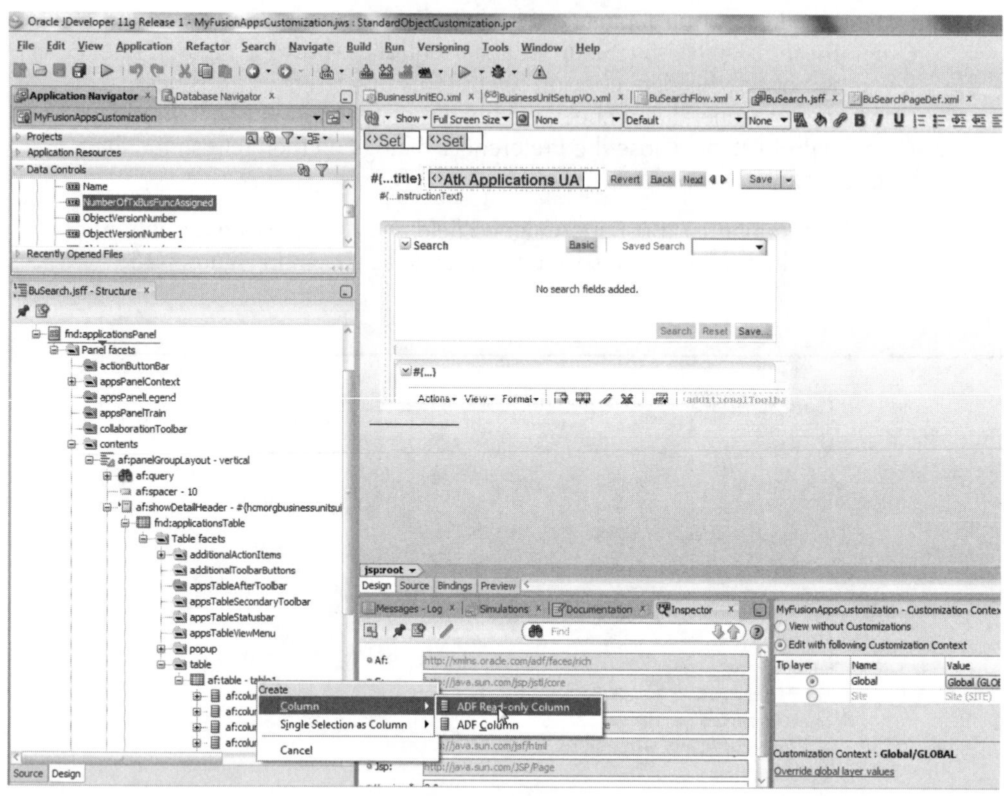

FIGURE 7-25. *Adding a new attribute on the page*

How to Deploy JDeveloper Customizations

When customizations are made to existing artifacts in an ADF library, you need to use the Metadata Achieve (MAR) profile to deploy those customizations to a deployed application. This is a standard deployment profile option in Fusion Applications built using JDeveloper.

1. Right-click on your application workspace and go to Application Properties from the context menu.

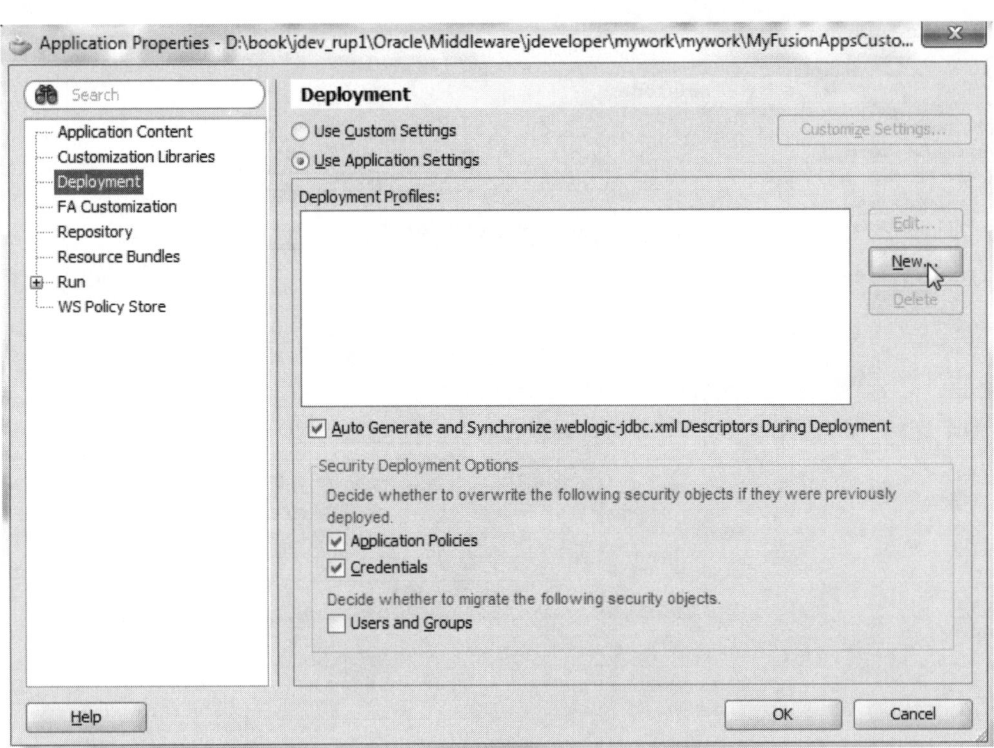

FIGURE 7-26. *Creating a new deployment profile for an application*

2. Select the Deployment link and click the New button to create a new deployment profile for this application as shown in Figure 7-26.
3. Select the Archive Type as MAR and click OK.
4. In the MAR profile properties, make sure that all necessary directories are selected for ADF Library Customization as shown in Figure 7-27. Also make sure that User metadata and HTML root directories do not have anything selected.

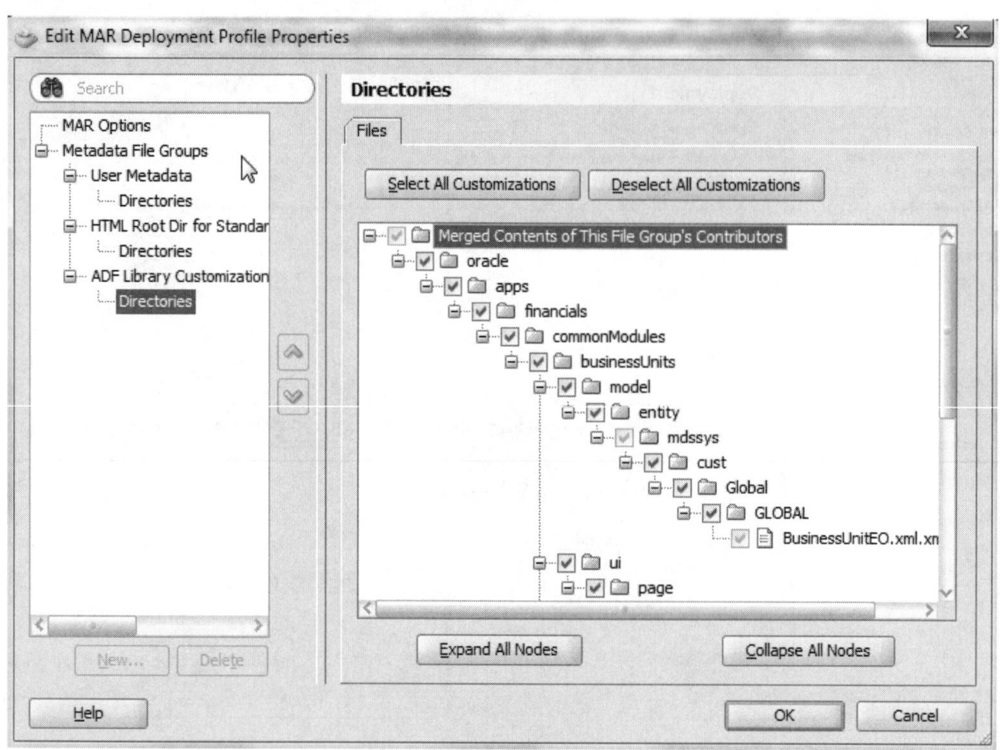

FIGURE 7-27. *Examine the content included in the MAR deployment profile.*

5. Right-click on the application and select Deploy | metadata1 as shown in Figure 7-28.
6. Select the Export to Deployed Application option to upload the customizations to an already deployed application on a server and follow the wizard to complete the deployment.

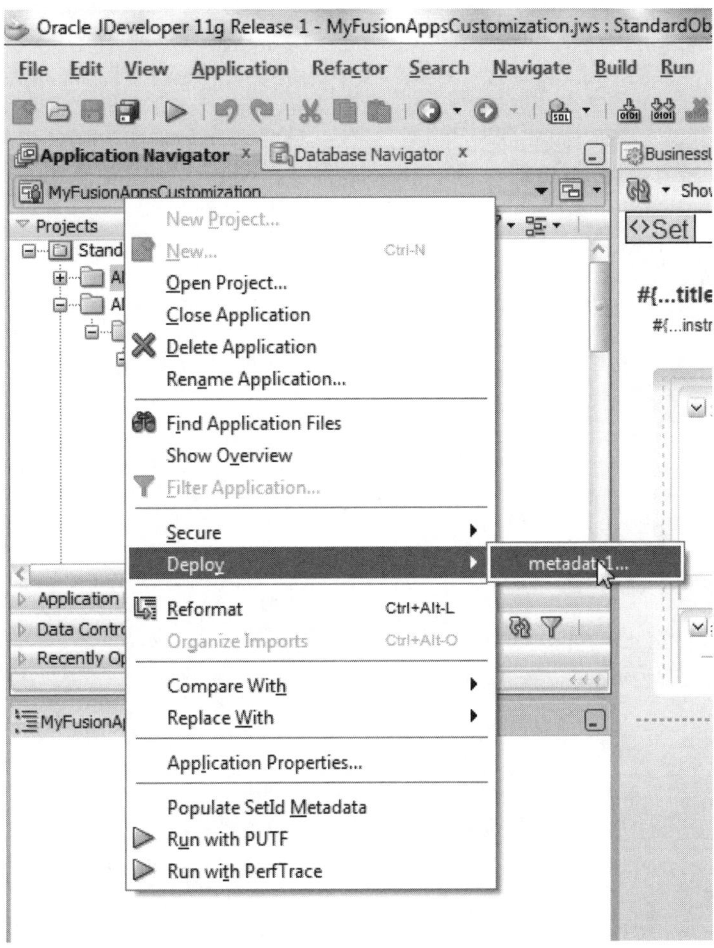

FIGURE 7-28. *Deploying the customizations using the MAR profile*

Summary

In this chapter, we discussed how to set up Oracle JDeveloper for customizations of Fusion Applications. We discussed what roles to use for customizations and how to identify artifacts to be customized from the run-time application. We covered several use cases for JDeveloper customization, such as modifying LOV, adding new business validation, modifying the search page, and adding a new attribute to an application page. At the end we explained how to deploy these customizations to an existing running application server.

CHAPTER 8

Building a New User Interface with ADF

In Chapter 6, we discussed how to define a new custom object and its workarea pages and integrate with CRM applications. If you have a requirement to add any non-CRM custom object, you will need to use JDeveloper. You may also want to deploy your custom application to non-CRM containers, and in that case, you will need to use JDeveloper to build this new application. In this chapter, we will discuss basic steps to create a new object and its simple workarea pages and integrate it with an existing application.

At a high level, you will need to do the following tasks to build a Fusion Application extension:

1. Create a new Fusion Application workspace with model and view controller projects and import the necessary libraries to use the Fusion Application base classes.
2. Define a database schema for your extension application.
3. Define ADF business components on your database schema for create, read, update, and delete operations using your application user interfaces.
4. Define validations, lists of values, labels, and business rules in your business components.
5. Define bounded task flows and declarative navigations for your application flow and interactions.
6. Add pages to your bounded task flows and add UI components per your business needs.
7. Build the page with a UI Shell template and include the task flows in your page using menus.
8. Enable security on your application and add deployment to a WebLogic server to make it accessible to users.

How to Create a New Custom Application

You must set up JDeveloper following the steps in Chapter 7 before you begin building a new application. Open JDeveloper in the "Fusion Applications Developer Role."

1. Click File | New and select Fusion Web Application (ADF) as shown in Figure 8-1.
2. Complete the Application Creation Wizard by giving the model project name as **ServiceRequestModel** and the UI project name as **ServiceRequestUi**.

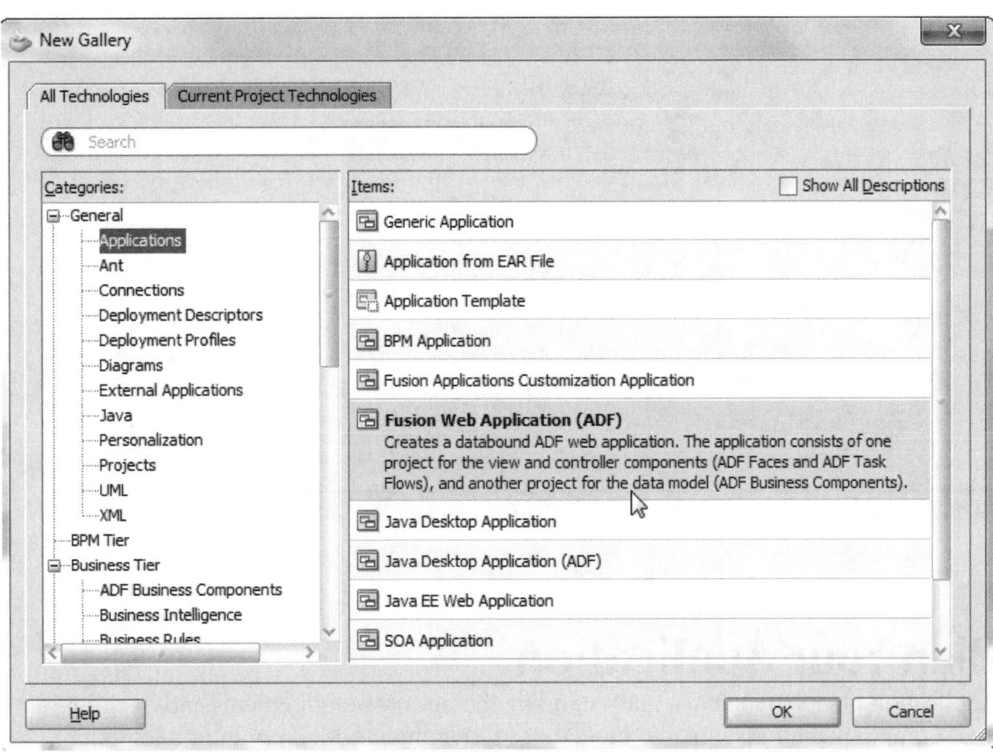

FIGURE 8-1. *Creating a new Fusion Web Application*

Define the default package for model project as **my.custom.apps.sr.model** and UI project as **my.custom.apps.sr.ui**. The new application is created in JDeveloper with these projects as shown in Figure 8-2.

3. The application overview page in JDeveloper helps you plan and guide building your application artifacts and helps track the progress. There are several steps in completing a Fusion Application extension, starting from planning what you will be building to database schema, business components, and model logic, UI flows, security, testing, and deployment of your application.

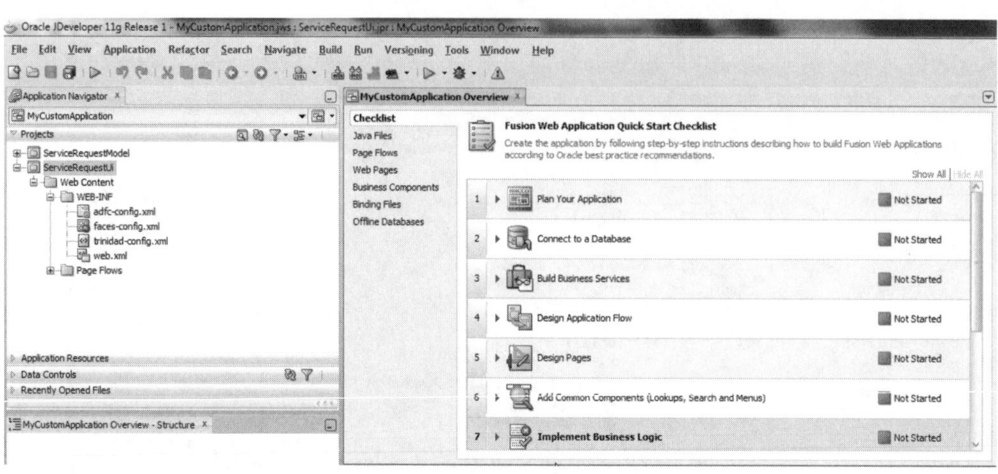

FIGURE 8-2. *New application with model and UI projects in JDeveloper*

Plan Your Application

Application planning includes understanding the business requirements and deciding on the implementation choice to meet those requirements. It is very important that you first make sure that there is no way to configure out-of-the-box Fusion Application functionality to meet the requirement. You should also first make sure that simple customizations do not meet your business needs. Once you have concluded that you must build your own custom application, do careful planning of the application extension before you start building it.

In this chapter, we will build a service request object, similar to what we created using CRM Application Composer in Chapter 6. We will build a service request object with its search, create, and edit UI using JDeveloper. We will need to define a new database table, new entity object, view object, application module, and new ADF task flows for the UI and navigations. As you make progress on these components, you can start marking this in the application overview page.

How to Define a New Schema

JDeveloper provides you with the necessary tools to build your database schema. You can build your schema as an offline database and then apply that to any real database that you deploy your application to. We will service a request and response schema that will be used to build the sample application.

1. Select File | New and choose the Offline Database option as shown in Figure 8-3.
2. Give the offline database a name and give the default schema as **FUSION**.

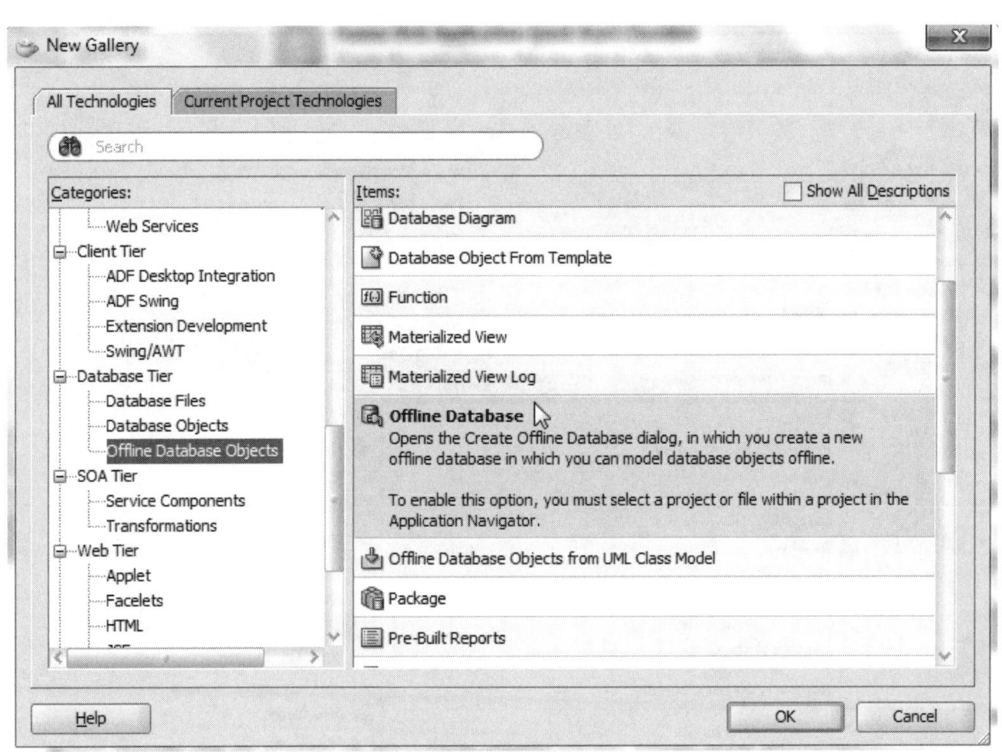

FIGURE 8-3. *Defining a new offline database schema*

3. Right-click on the FUSION schema and select the New Database Object | New Table option as shown in Figure 8-4.
4. Give your custom table name as **XM_SERVICE_REQUEST** and add the columns as shown in Figure 8-5.
5. Click the Advanced check box to go to the Detail Table wizard and add an index on the SERVICE_REQUEST_NAME and REQUEST_DATE column so that it can be used for search, as shown in Figure 8-6.
6. Once you save this offline database table, you need a database connection in your application where you want to apply this schema. Choose the Create A Database Connection option as shown in Figure 8-7. Give the details for the connection such as username, password, host, port, and SID.

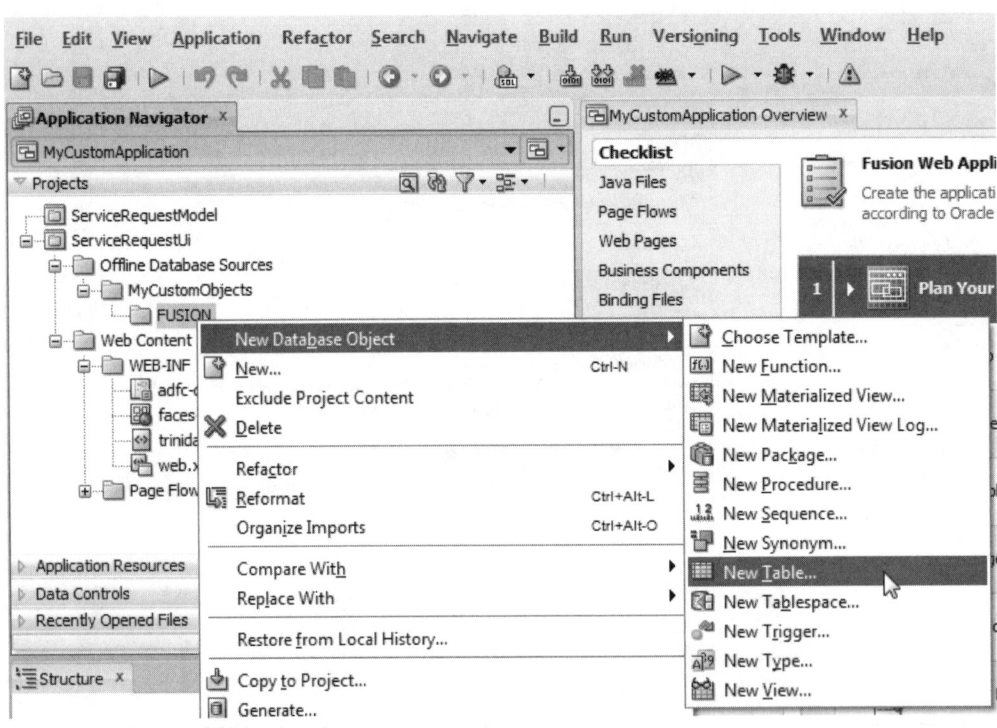

FIGURE 8-4. *Creating new schema objects*

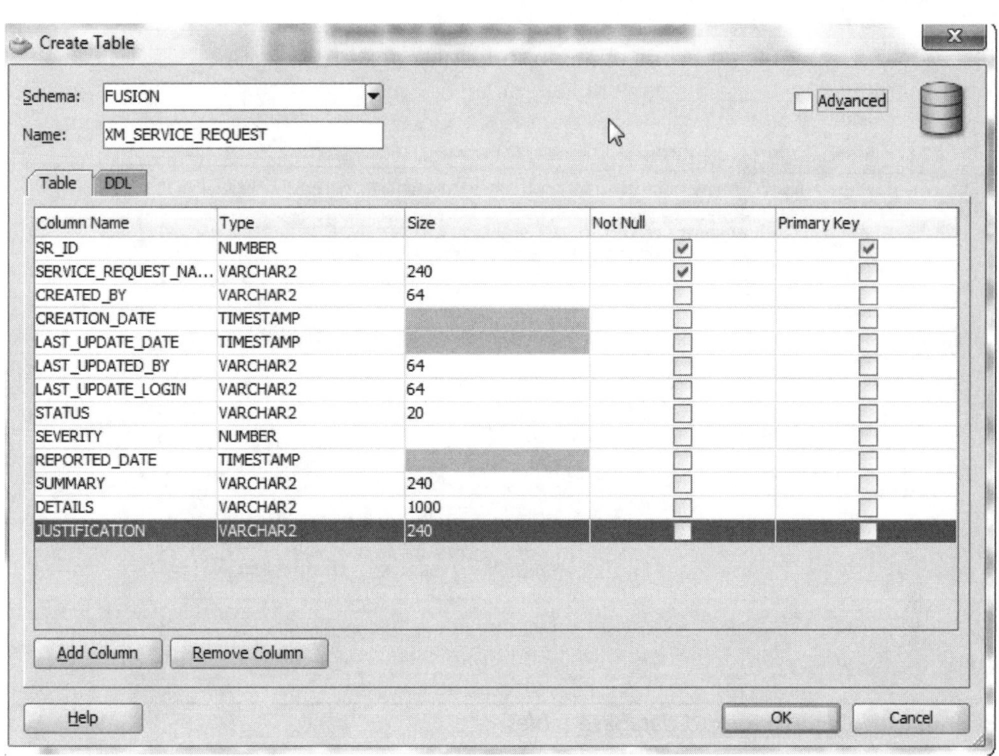

FIGURE 8-5. *Create a new database table and columns for service request.*

7. Right-click on the offline table file and choose Generate To | ApplicationDB to apply to the database connection defined earlier, as shown in Figure 8-8. This will generate the new table in the database specified by the connection.

8. Similarly, define a service response table as shown in Figure 8-9 and apply to your application database. Add an index on the SERVICE_REQUEST_ID, SERVICE_RESPONSE_NAME, and RESPONSE_DATE columns.

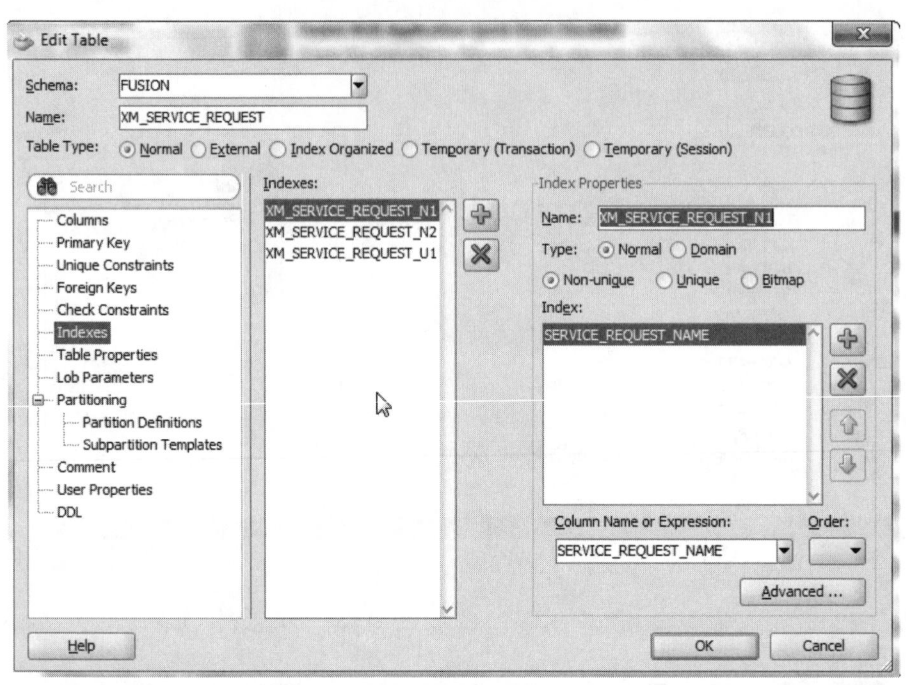

FIGURE 8-6. *Adding an index to database tables*

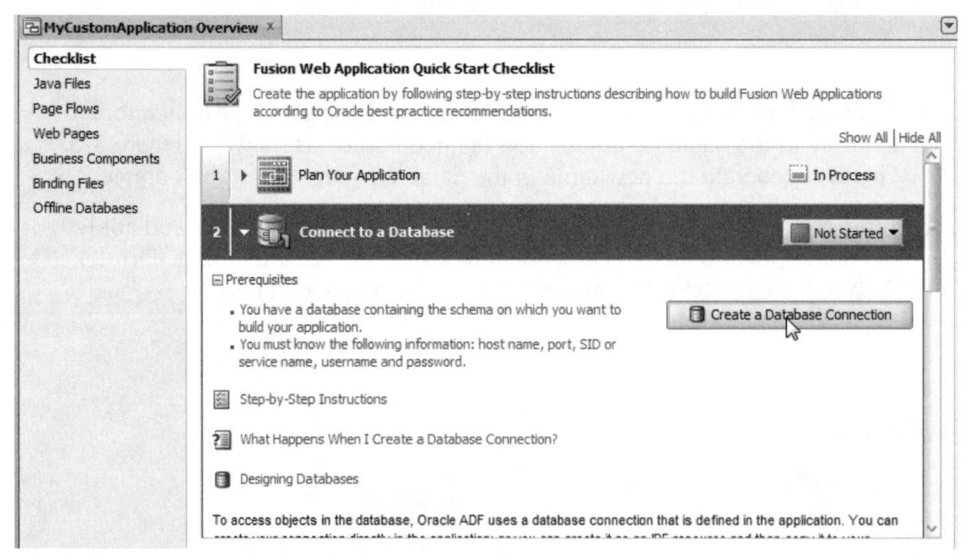

FIGURE 8-7. *Defining a new database connection*

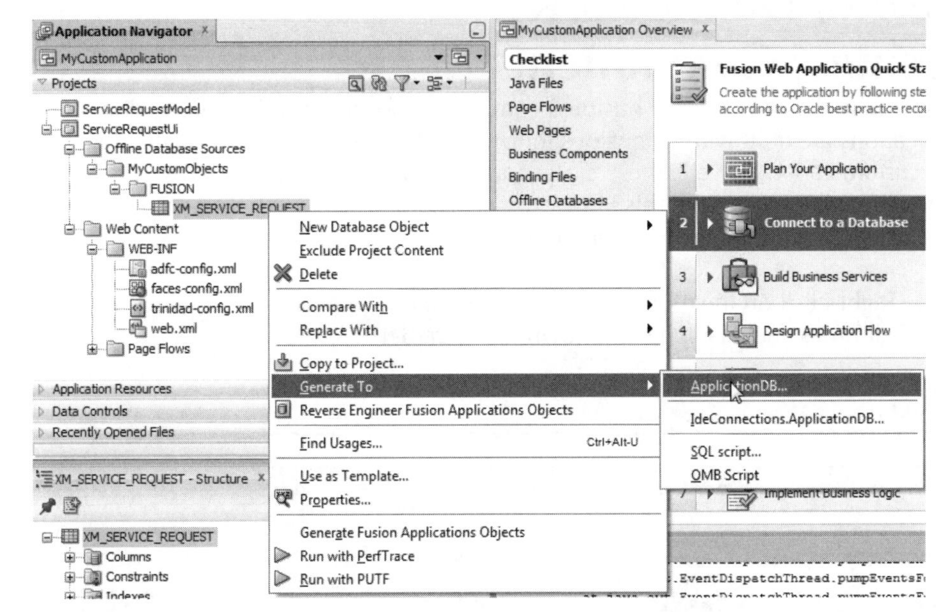

FIGURE 8-8. *Deploying offline schema artifacts to the database*

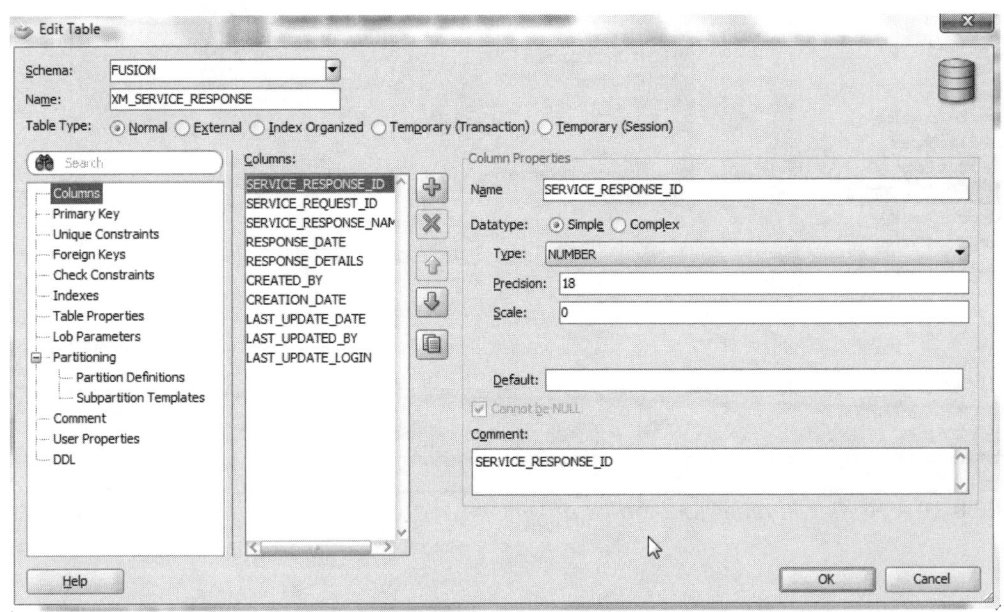

FIGURE 8-9. *Create a service response database table.*

How to Define New Business Components

We will now define new ADF business components for this application. Fusion Applications are built with extensions for base ADF classes and are available for your customization as well. These classes are available in the Application Core library. We will need to add this library to our model project to use it as the base class for our new ADF business components.

1. Right-click on the model project, go to Project Properties, and select Libraries and Classpath as shown in Figure 8-10.

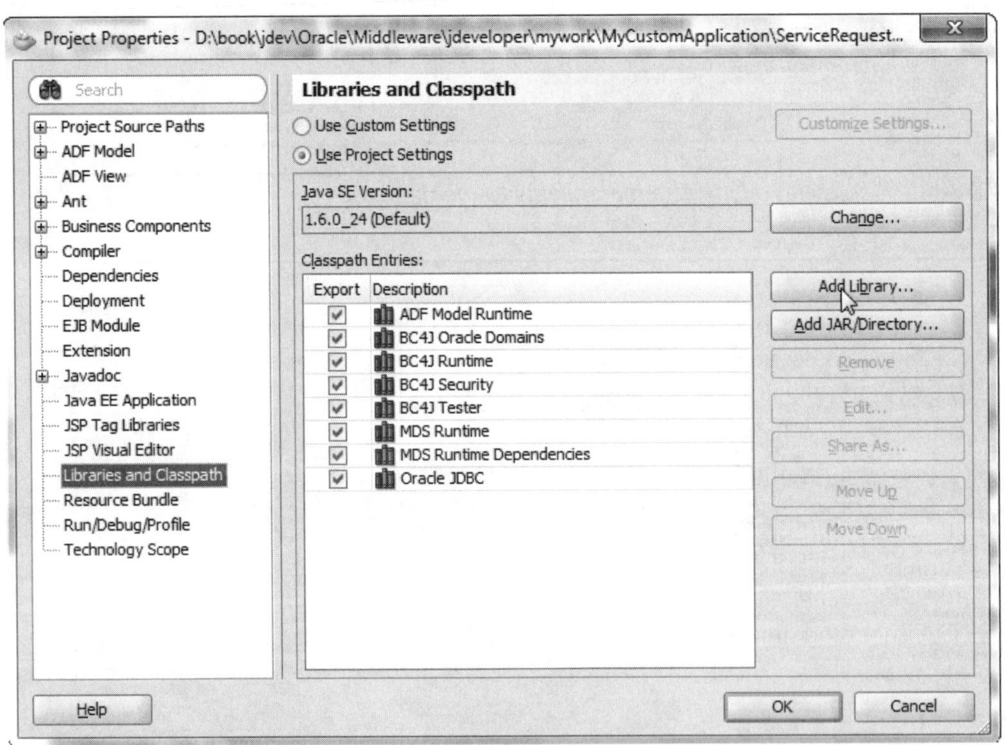

FIGURE 8-10. *Adding libraries to a model project*

2. Click the Add Library button and choose Applications Core to add this library to our model project as shown in the following illustration. Similarly, add library BC4J Client and BC4J Service Runtime.

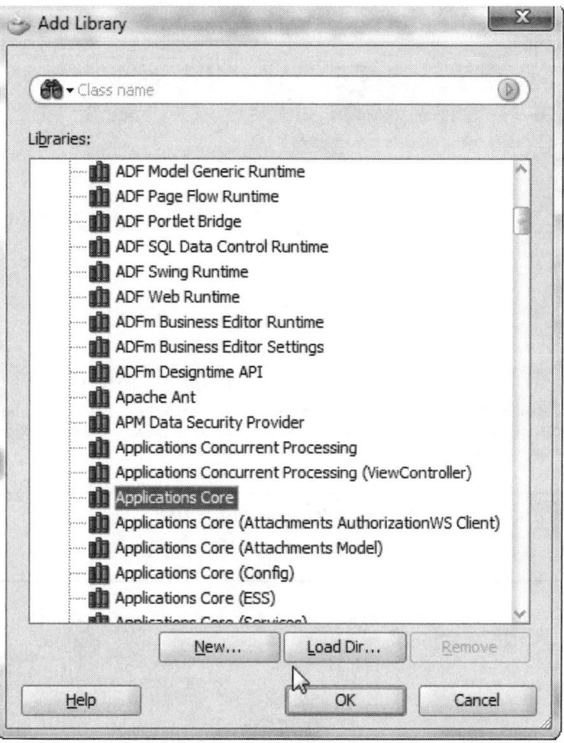

3. From the application overview, click Go To Subtasks from the Build Business Services task. Click the Create Entity Objects and Associations button as shown in Figure 8-11. The other option is to use File | New | Business Components | Business Components from Database Table.

4. Follow the wizard and select the database connection and then search for the two new tables we defined earlier, as shown in Figure 8-12.

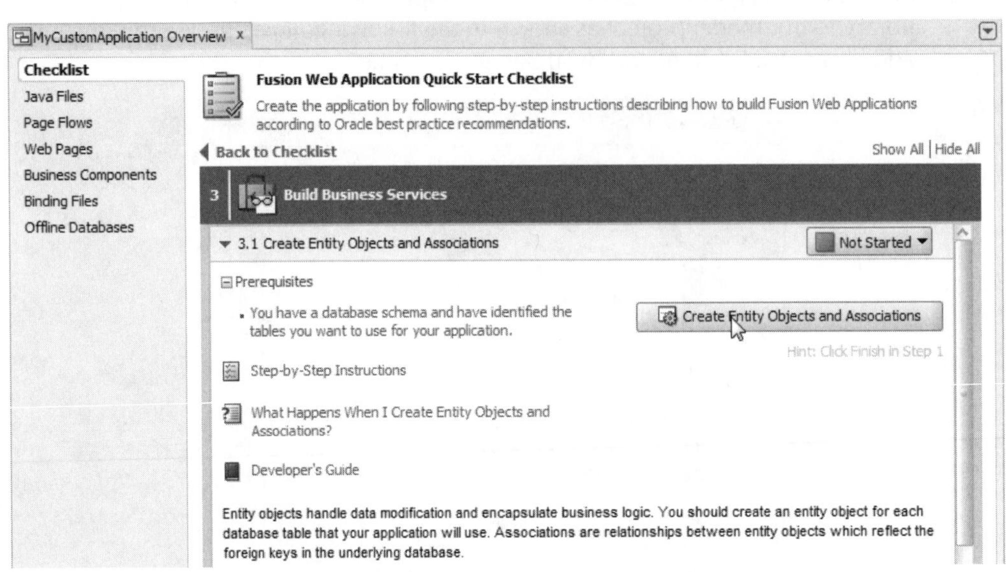

FIGURE 8-11. *Creating entity objects and associations*

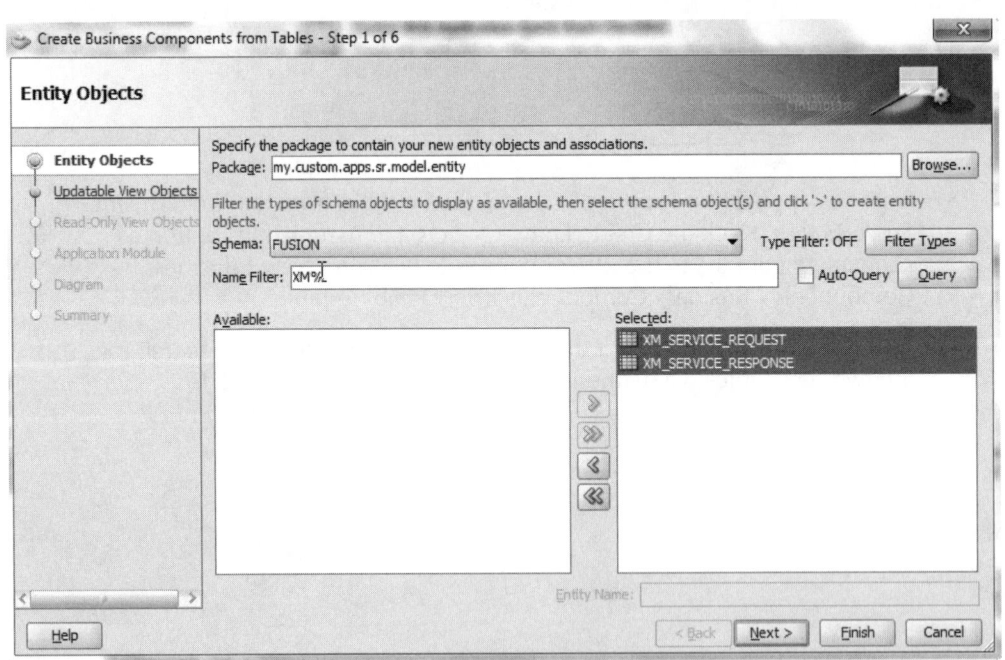

FIGURE 8-12. *Select database tables to create entity objects.*

5. Do not select the view object and application module for now. Choose to define the Business Components diagram as shown in Figure 8-13, and complete the wizard.

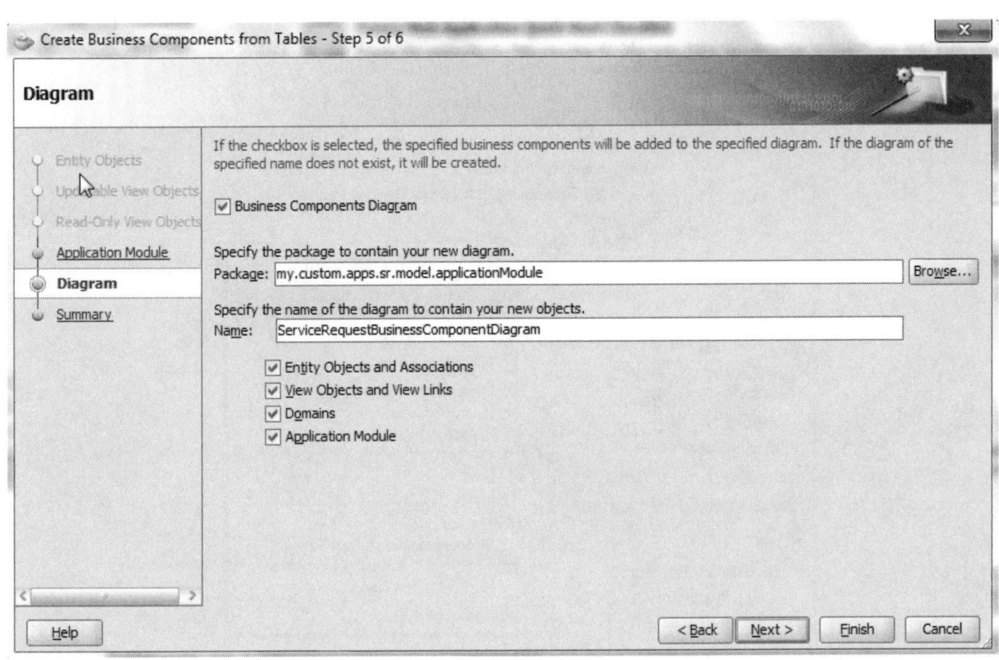

FIGURE 8-13. *Create a Business Components diagram.*

6. Right-click on the EO and choose the New Default View Object option to create a new editable VO for a given EO as shown in the following illustration. Do this for both of the EOs.

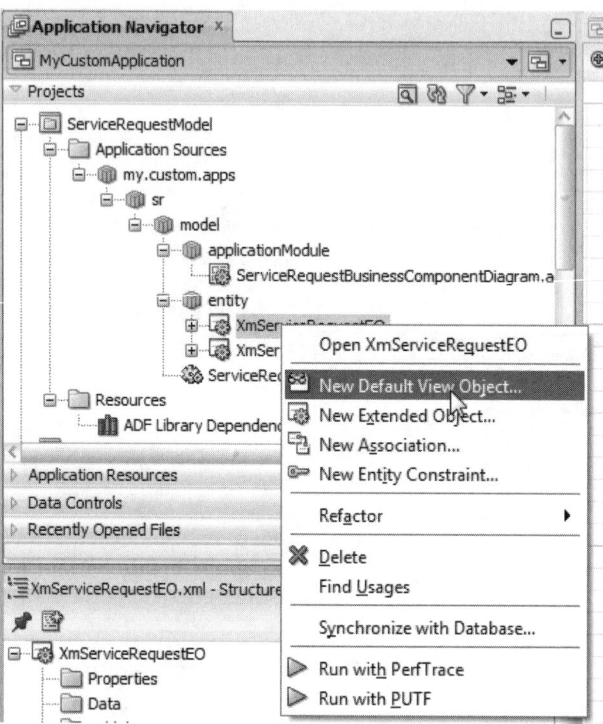

7. Right-click on the entity package and choose the New Association option. Give the name of the association as **XmServiceRequestEOToXmServiceResponseEO**. Select the cardinality as 1..* and join on ServiceRequestId as shown in Figure 8-14.

8. Choose to expose the accessor in both sides of the association and mark the association as composite (check the Composition Association check box), as shown in Figure 8-15.

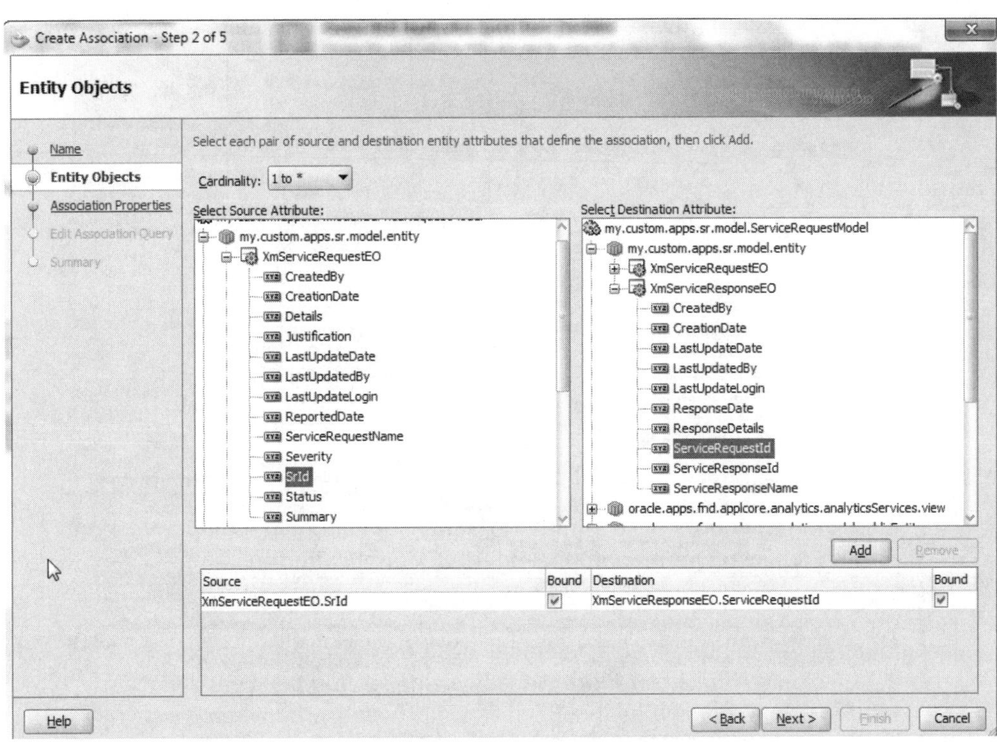

FIGURE 8-14. *Create an entity association.*

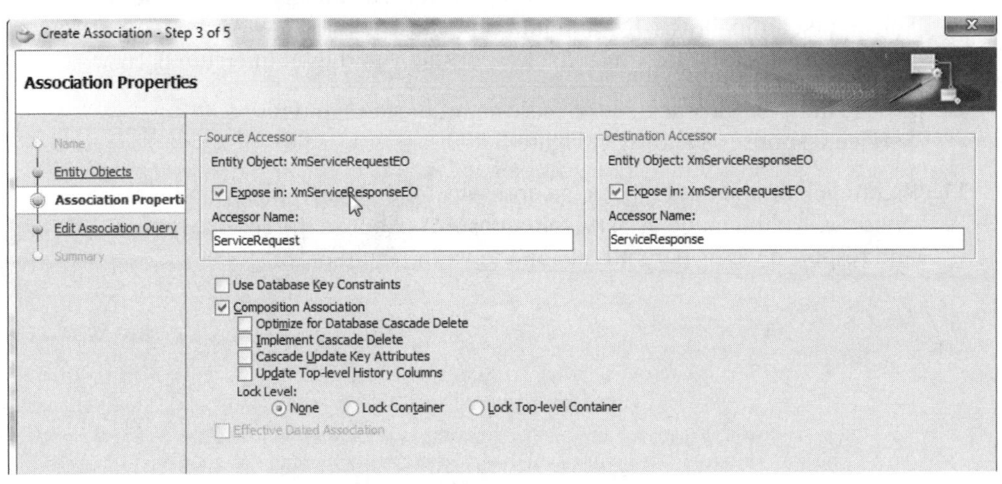

FIGURE 8-15. *Specify association accessors and other properties.*

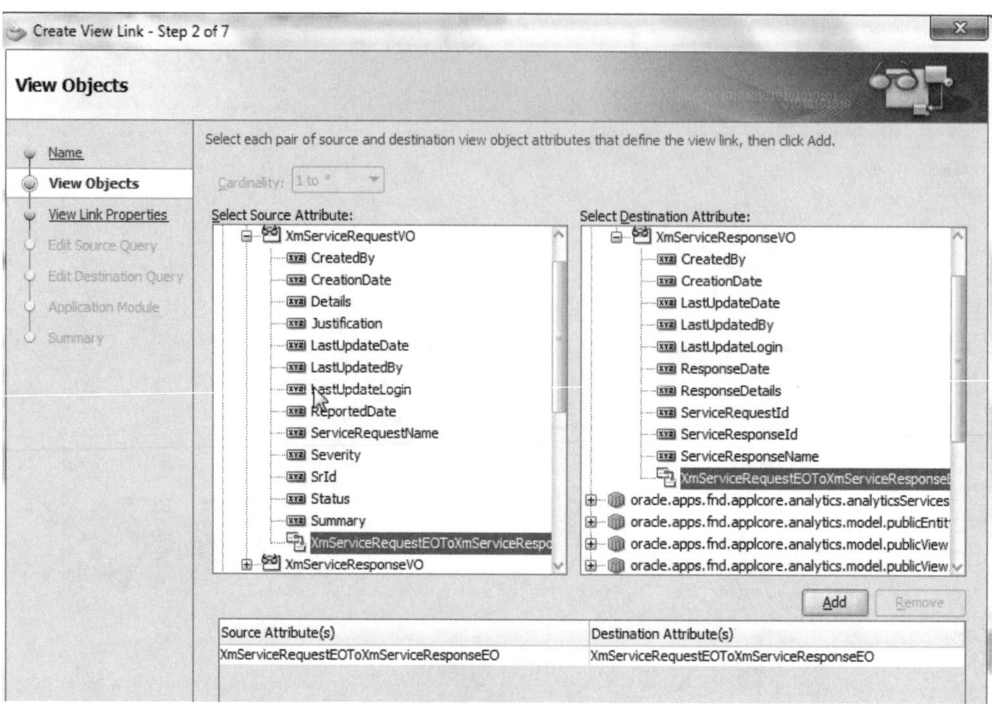

FIGURE 8-16. *Create a view link based on association.*

9. Right-click on the view package and choose the New View Link option. Give the Name To View link as **XmServiceRequestVOToXmServiceResponseVO**. Select the cardinality as 1..* and join on the association XmServiceRequestEOToXmServiceResponseEO as shown in Figure 8-16.

10. Expose the view link accessor in service request VO and name it **ServiceResponse** as shown in Figure 8-17.

11. Right-click on the model package and select the New Application Module option. Give the name as **ServiceRequestAM**. Choose the service request and response VO as parent-child as shown in Figure 8-18.

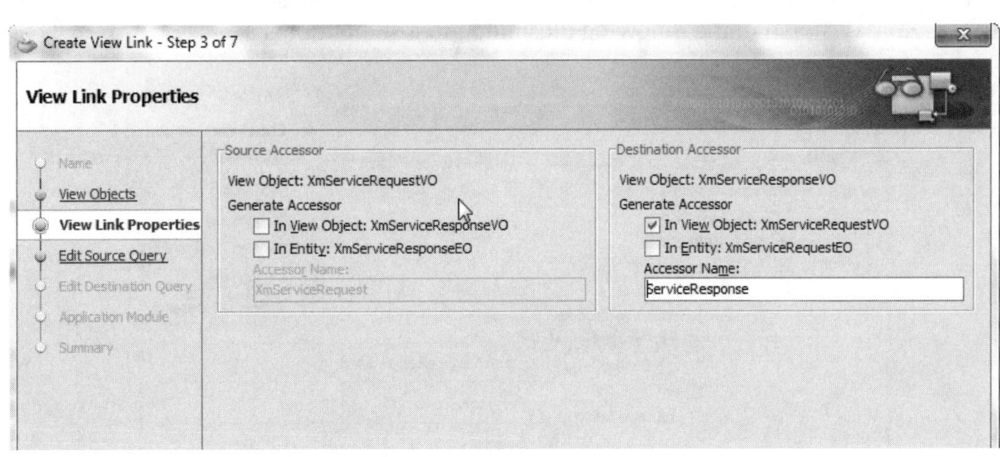

FIGURE 8-17. *Specify the view link accessor.*

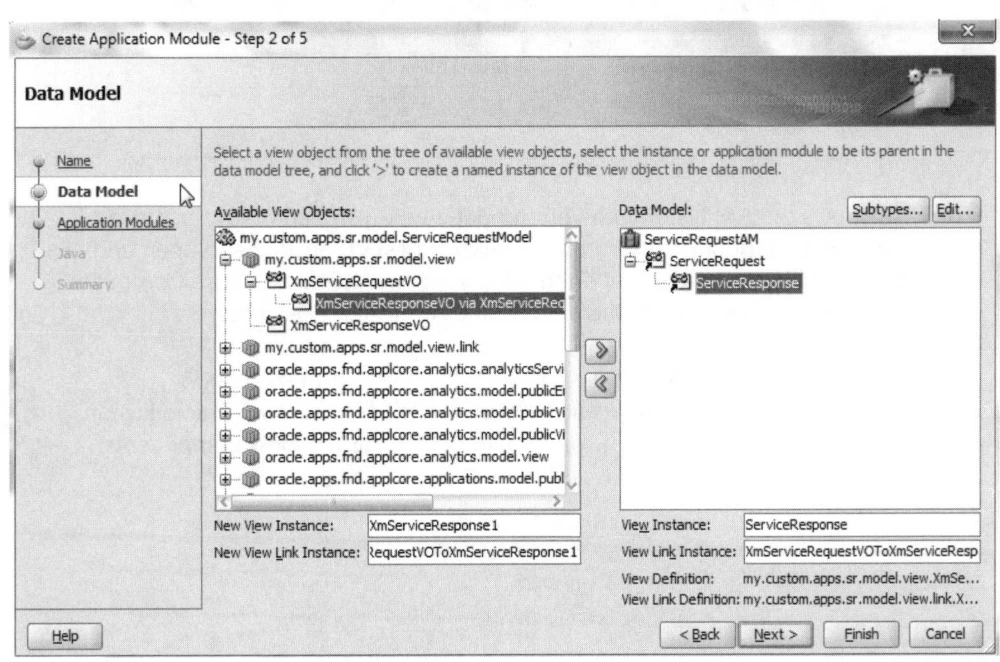

FIGURE 8-18. *Create a new application module and select view object instances.*

12. Build the model project. Right-click on the ServiceRequestAM and choose Run as shown in the following illustration to test the model.

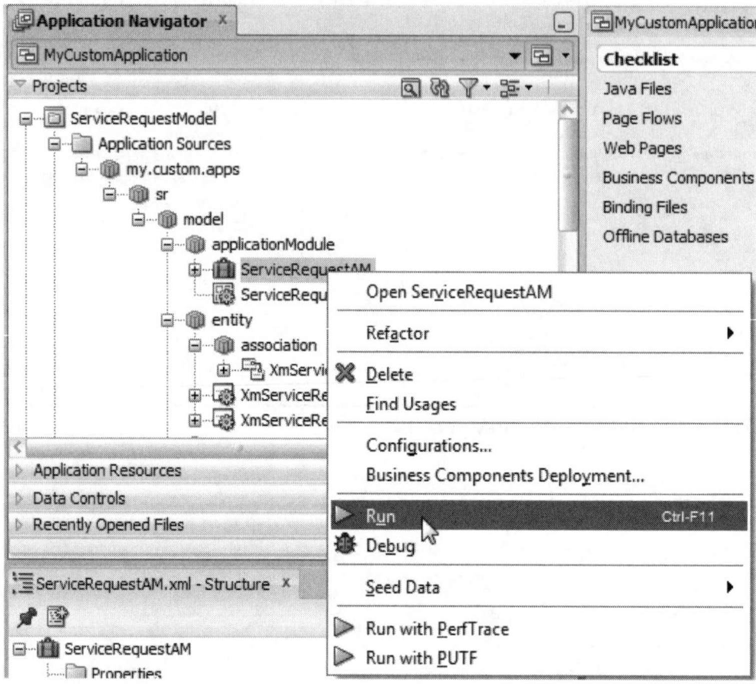

13. This shows the AM tester with your model where you can query, create, and update data. Double-click on the ServiceRequest VO instance to open and see data. Click the green + icon to add new rows. Click Database Commit to save changes. Figure 8-19 shows what the AM tester looks like.

Please read the "Building Your Business Services" section in the *Fusion Developer's Guide for Oracle Application Development Framework* (Oracle Fusion Applications Edition) for more details on how to build your business components.

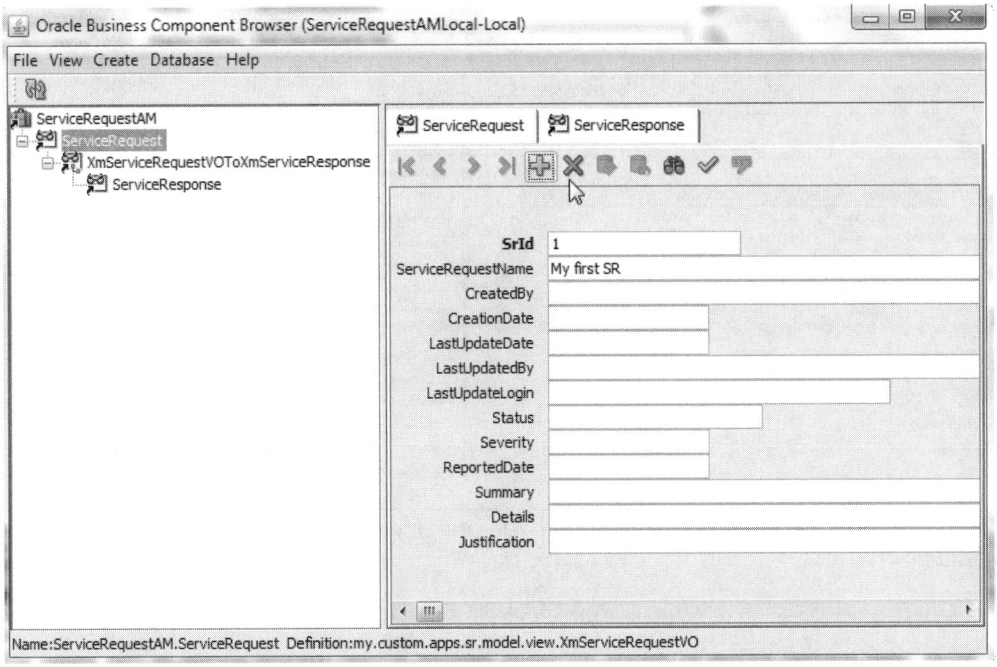

FIGURE 8-19. *Application module tester*

How to Implement Business Logic

In Fusion Applications, most of the business logic is implemented in EO. In this section, we will discuss how to generate primary key attribute values from a Fusion unique ID generation scheme, how to set system columns, how to define validations, how to define hints for attributes, and how to define a list of values for attributes that will be used on UI.

1. Open XmServiceRequestEO and go to the Attributes tab. Select the primary key attribute SrId from the property inspector for the attribute, and set Application Unique ID to true as shown in Figure 8-20. Set this property for the other EO primary key as well.

2. Now select the attribute CreatedBy and click the Edit icon, or double-click to open and edit the attribute properties. Check the History Column check box and select Created By from the list of values as shown in Figure 8-21. Similarly, set this property for other WHO columns, such as CreationDate, LastUpdateDate, LastUpdatedBy, and LastUpdateLogin. Set this for both of the EOs.

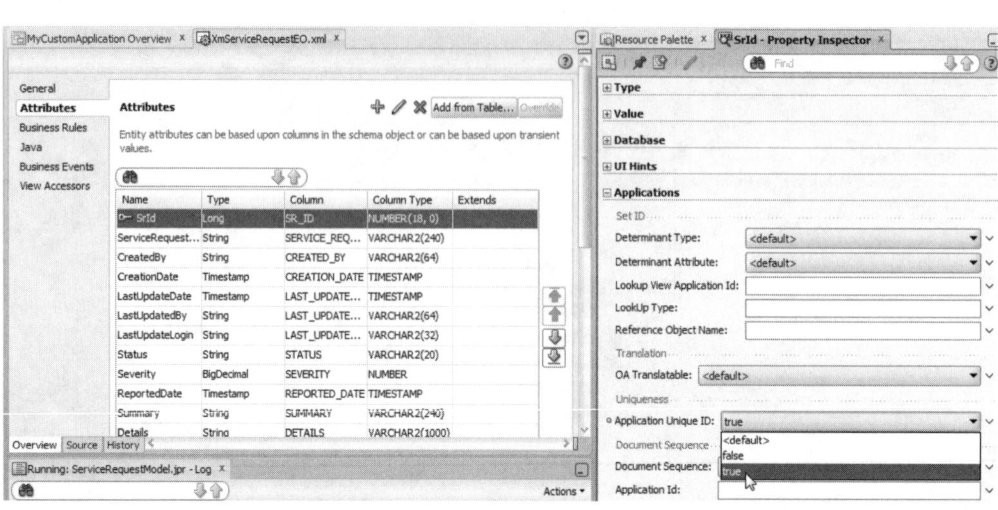

FIGURE 8-20. *Specify properties to generate the primary key with Fusion unique ID generation.*

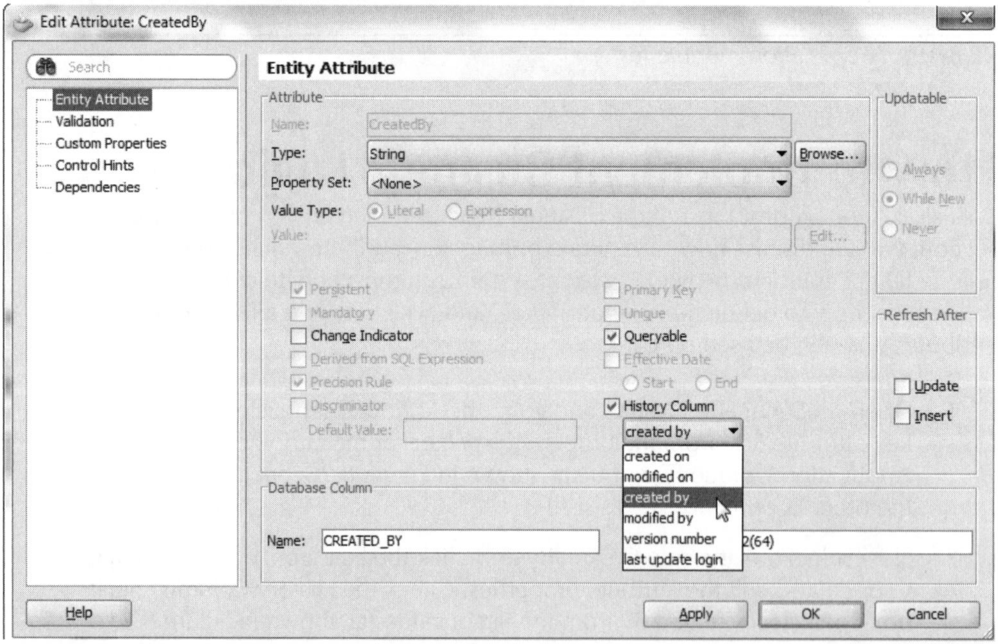

FIGURE 8-21. *Set history attribute properties.*

3. Now we will set default values for some of the attributes. Open the ReportedDate attribute, set the Value Type as Expression, and provide Value as **adf.currentDateTime** as shown in Figure 8-22. Mark the attribute as Mandatory as well.
4. Similarly, set the default value of attribute Status to literal value OPEN and set the default value of attribute severity to literal value 3.

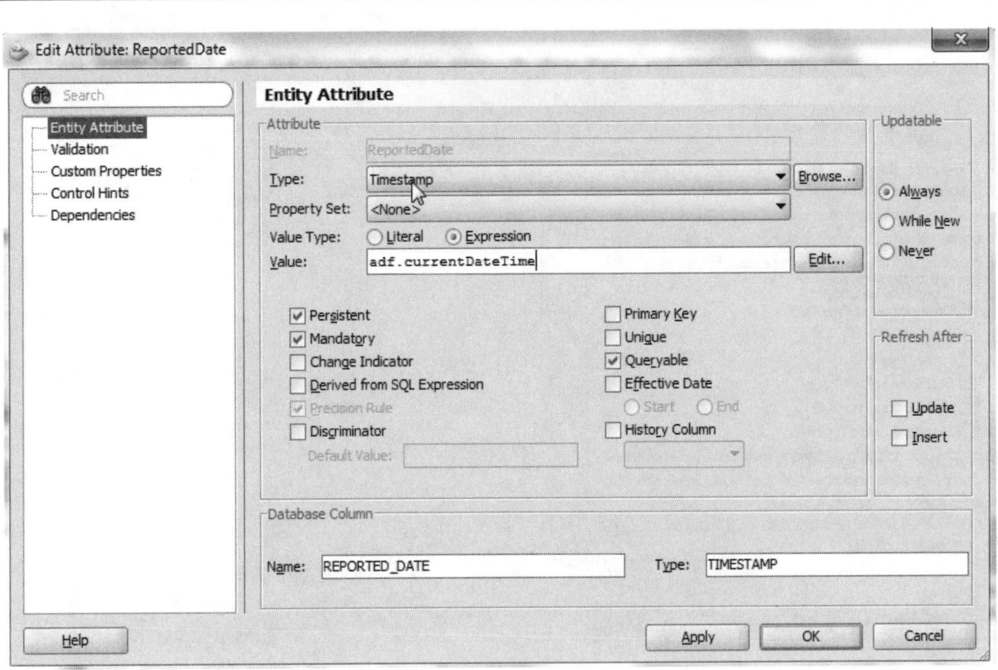

FIGURE 8-22. *Specify the default value for an entity attribute.*

5. Now we will define a rule to validate the value of attribute Status against the lookup XM_SR_STATUS. Open the EO and go to the View Accessors tab. Click the Add icon to create a new view accessor. Select CommonLookupPVO from the Available View Objects list and name it StatusLookup. Shuttle it to the View Accessors list as shown in Figure 8-23.

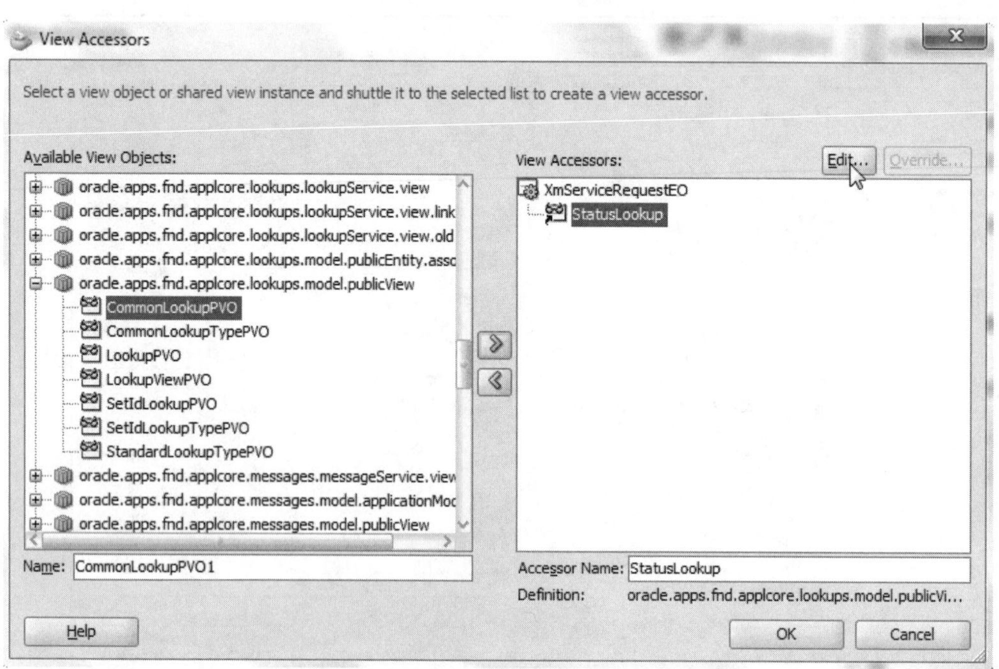

FIGURE 8-23. *Add a new view accessor in entity object for validation.*

6. Click the Edit icon and shuttle the ByLookupType View Criteria from the Available list to the Selected list. Give the BindLookupType bind parameter value "XM_SR_STATUS". Give Order By as MEANING as shown in Figure 8-24.

7. Open the EO and go to the Business Rules tab. Click the Create New Validator icon to add a new business rule.

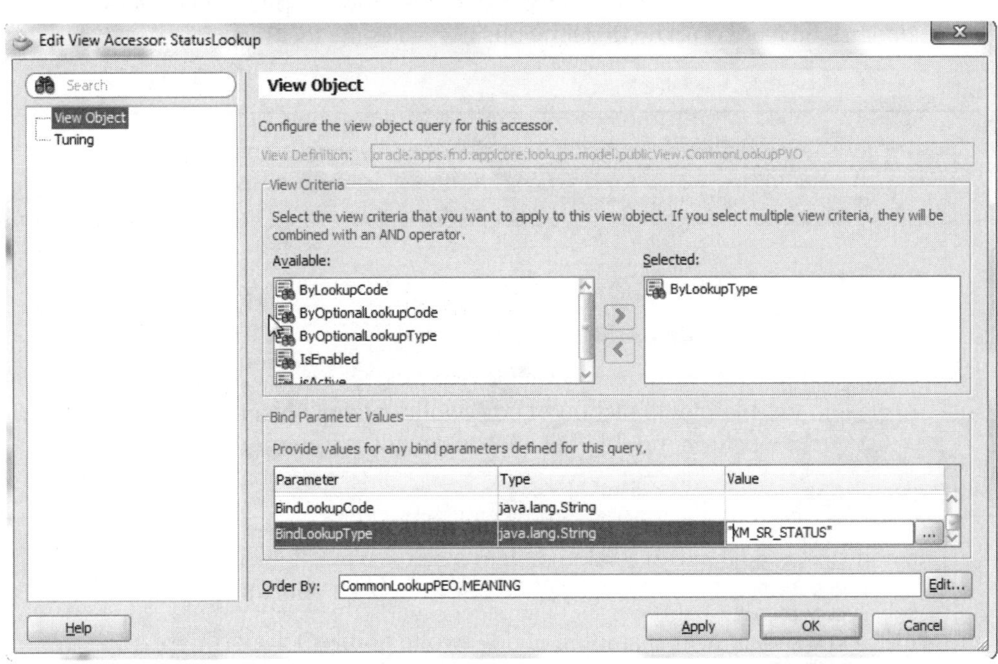

FIGURE 8-24. *Specify bind variable values for view accessor.*

8. In the Add Validation Rule dialog, select Type as List. Select the attribute as Status, Operator as In, and List Type as View Accessor Attribute. Choose the attribute LookupCode from the list of available attributes from the view accessor StatusLookup created earlier as shown in Figure 8-25. This rule means that at run time, the value given for attribute Status will need to be one in the list returned by a query generated by CommonLookupPVO where LookupType is XM_SR_STATUS. Similarly, you can define other validations based on your business rules. Please read the chapter "Defining Validation and Business Rules Declaratively" in *Fusion Developer's Guide for Oracle Application Development Framework* (Oracle Fusion Applications Edition) to understand more on how to define business rules.

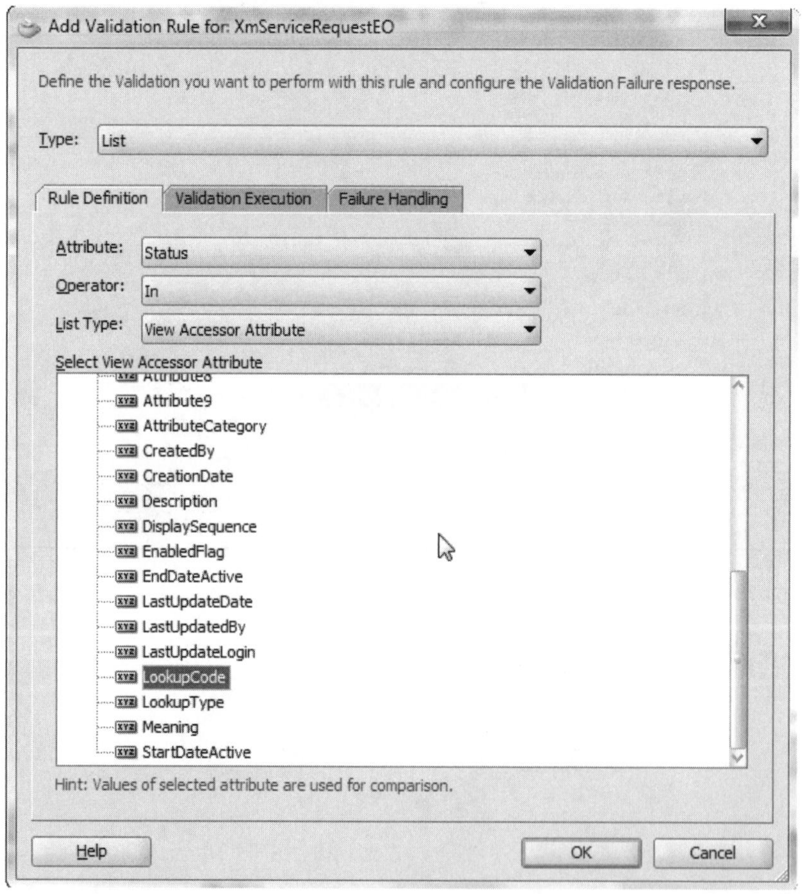

FIGURE 8-25. *Create a List type validation rule using view accessor.*

9. Go to the Failure Handling tab and click the Search icon for Failure Message. Select Application Messages and search for **%LOOK%**. We are picking an existing application message in this validation. You can define your own message using the Manage Application Messages task in FSM. Select a message as shown in Figure 8-26.

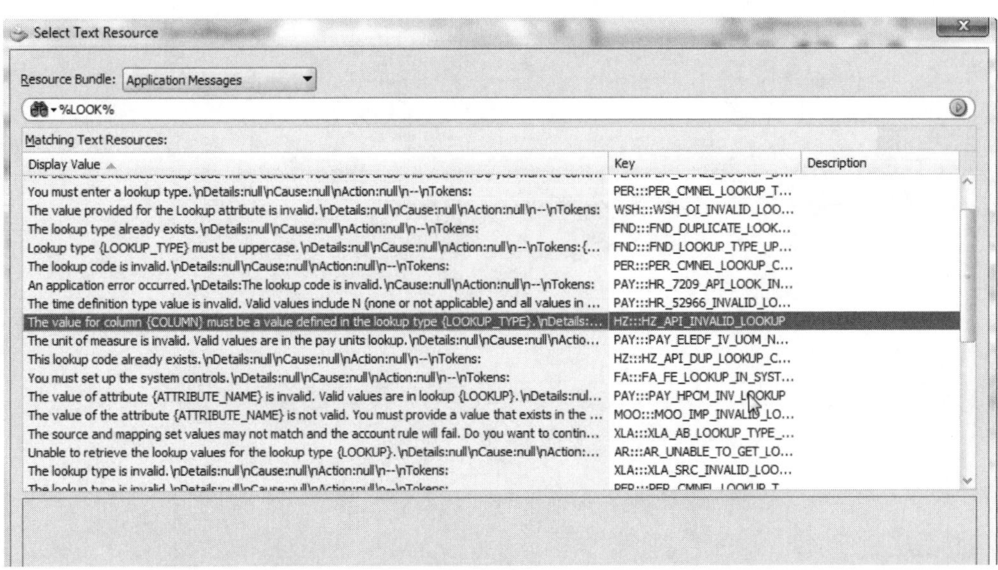

FIGURE 8-26. *Specify a validation error message.*

10. Provide the values of the token in the message. Give the lookup type as "XM_SR_STATUS" and column as source.hints.Status.label so that at run time, the validation message will show the user-defined label for the Status column as shown in Figure 8-27.

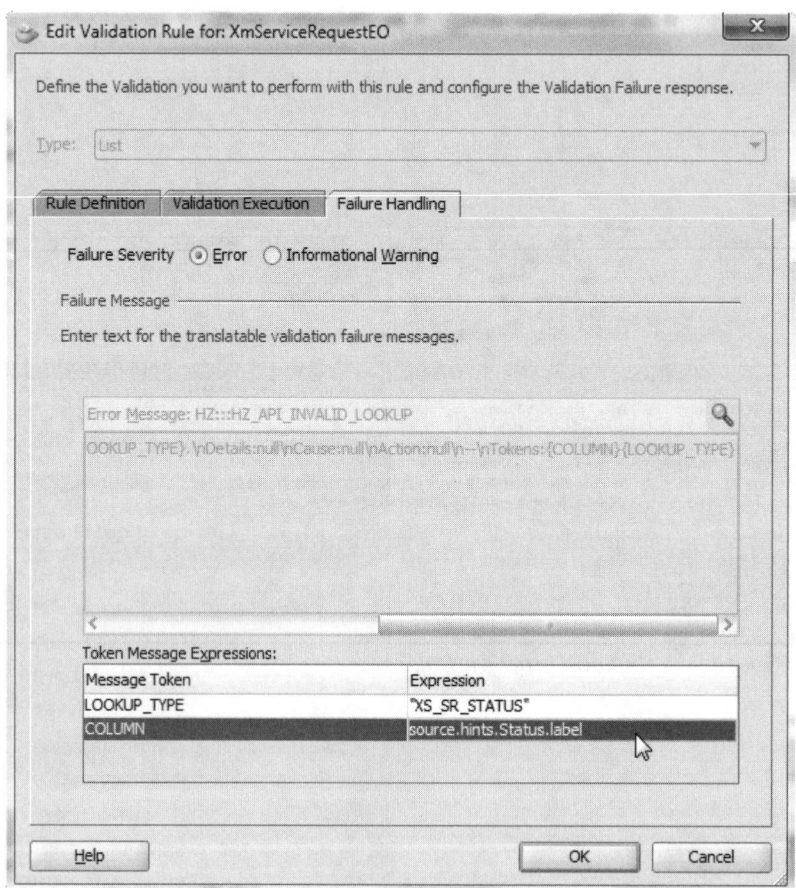

FIGURE 8-27. *Specify token values for the validation error message.*

11. Run the AM tester again and create a new Service Request row. Notice that it defaults to the attribute values as defined earlier. Change the Status attribute to OPEN_test, and save. This will throw a validation error message as shown in Figure 8-28.

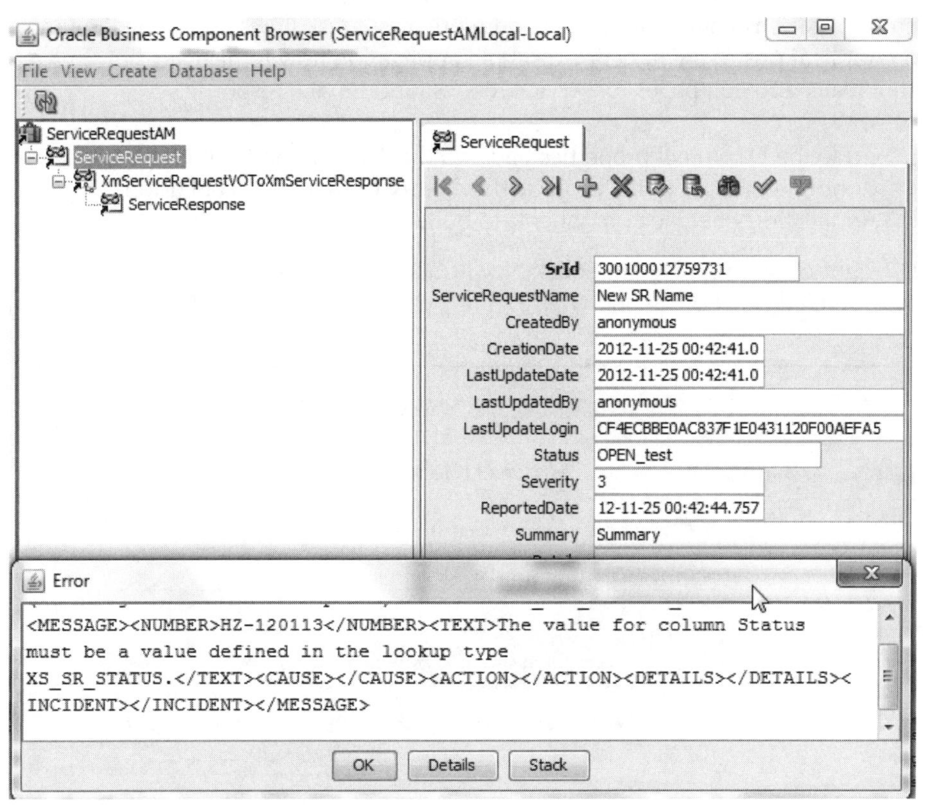

FIGURE 8-28. *Test the validation and error message using the application module tester.*

How to Define the Application Navigation Flow

In this section, we will discuss how to define your application navigation flow. Fusion Applications are built using bounded task flows, and navigations are defined declaratively in the task flow. Please read the "Creating ADF Task Flows" section in *Fusion Developer's Guide for Oracle Application Development Framework* (Oracle Fusion Applications Edition) to understand more about task flows and navigation in Fusion Applications. We will define a simple application flow to navigate between search, create, and edit pages for service request and service response.

1. Go to the UI project properties and add the Application Core (View Controller) library to the project. This library is needed to get Fusion Application–specific components to build the application pages.
2. Right-click on Project and click New. Choose ADF Task Flow to create a new bounded task flow as shown in Figure 8-29.

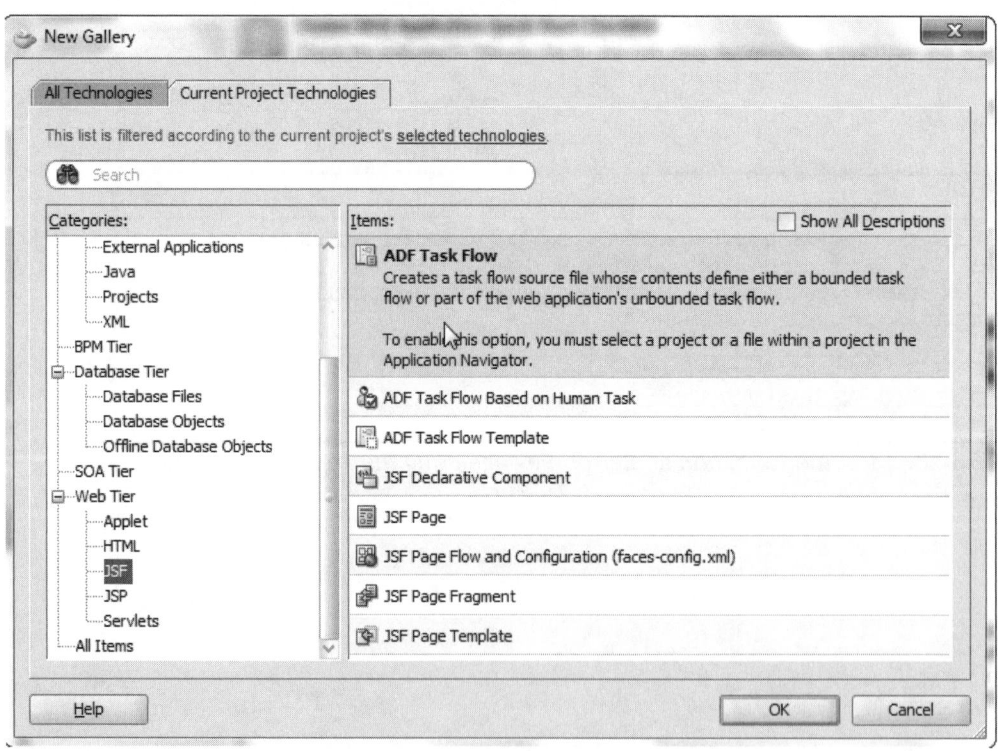

FIGURE 8-29. *Create a new ADF task flow.*

3. Name the TF as XmServiceRequestSearchTF and give the right package. Keep the default options for Bounded Task Flow and Page Fragments, as shown here.

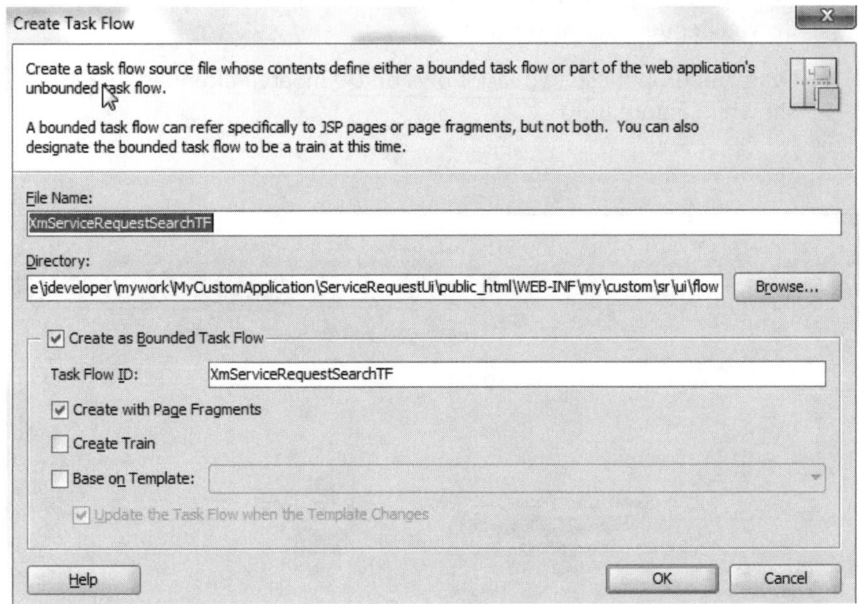

4. From the Component palette, drag and drop View activity on the task flow and name it **ServiceRequestSearch** as shown in the following illustration. This is the first page in our flow to search the service requests.

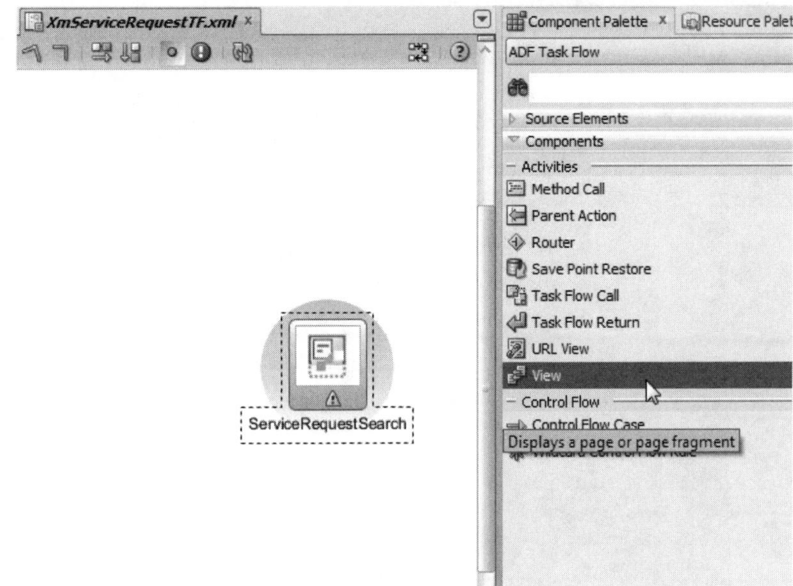

5. Similarly, create a new task flow XmServiceRequestCreateTF and XmServiceRequestEditTF for create and edit. Drag and drop view activity in each of these task flows, and name them **ServiceRequestCreate** and **ServiceRequestEdit** respectively.

   Drag and drop these two task flows onto XmServiceRequestSearchTF as shown in Figure 8-30.

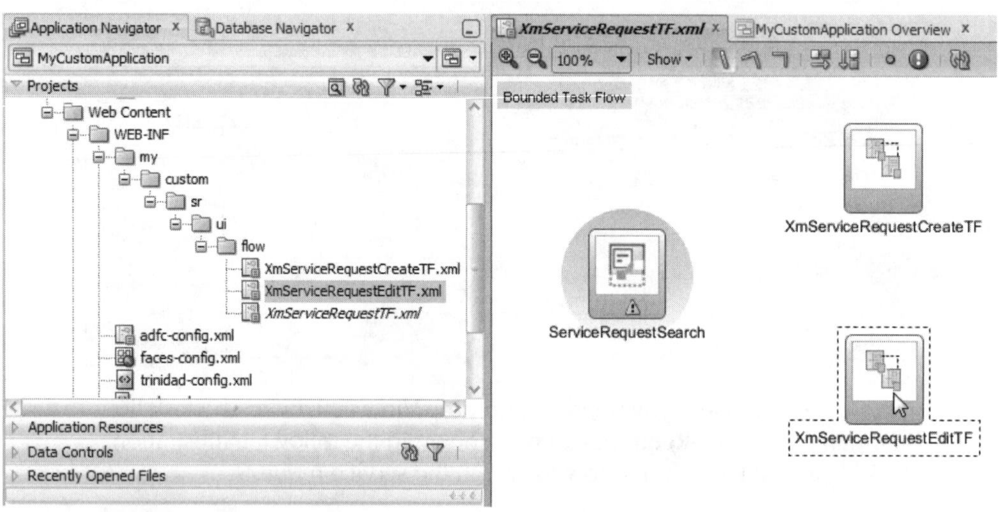

FIGURE 8-30. *Add task flow call activities for create and edit on search task flow.*

6. From the Component palette, select Control Flow Case. Click on the ServiceRequestSearch activity in the task flow and then click on CreateTF Activity as shown here.

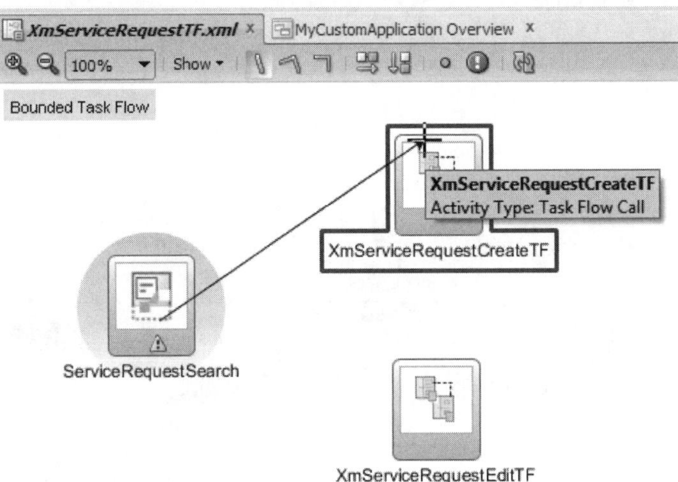

7. Name the navigation case as **create**. Similarly, define the control flow between search and edit activity and name it **edit**. Now define the control flow from create to search and edit to search activity, name those as **return**, and save as shown here.

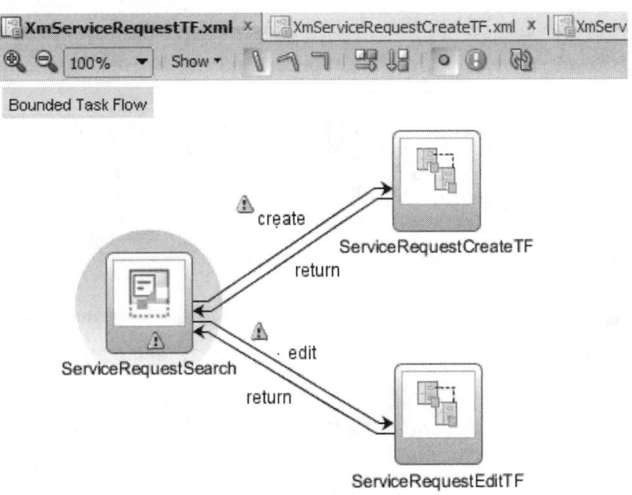

8. Open the Create TF and drag and drop the Task Flow Return Activity and name it **cancel**.

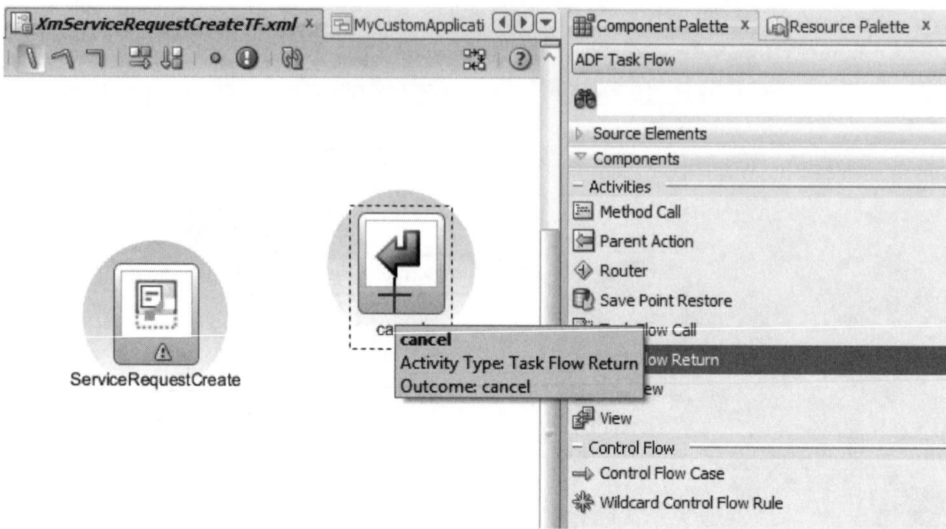

9. Add another TF return activity and name it **save**. Add control flow from the create activity to cancel and save TF return activity and name it accordingly as shown in the following illustration. The Outcome for the save return activity is "save" so when that return navigation happens, the Search TF will use "save" control flow navigation.

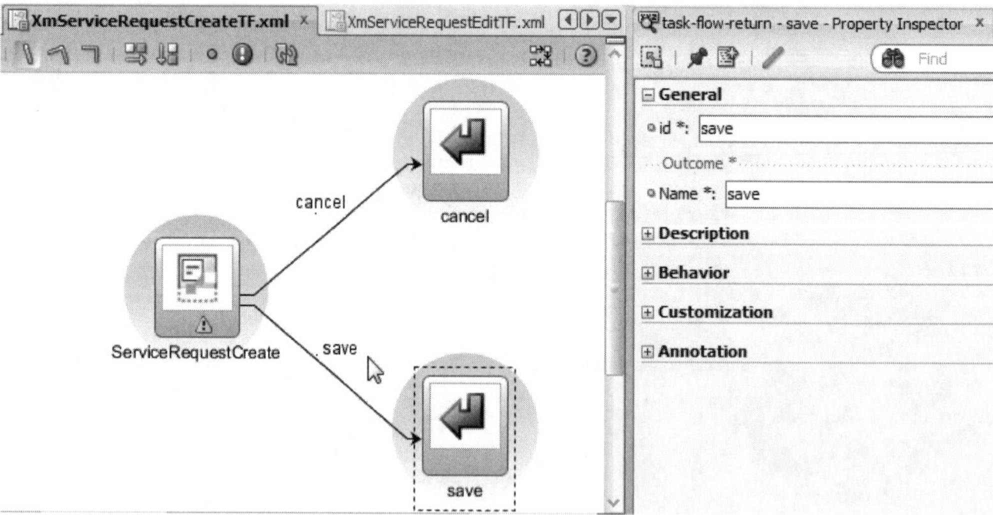

10. Now we will set the properties on the task flows for their transaction behavior. There are two properties that dictate how the task flows behave. The transaction property decides if the TF will start a new transaction or participate in an existing transaction. The data control property decides if the TF will share the data with the caller page or not. Set the transaction to "Always Begin New Transaction" and "Share Data Controls with Calling Task Flow" for the search TF as shown here.

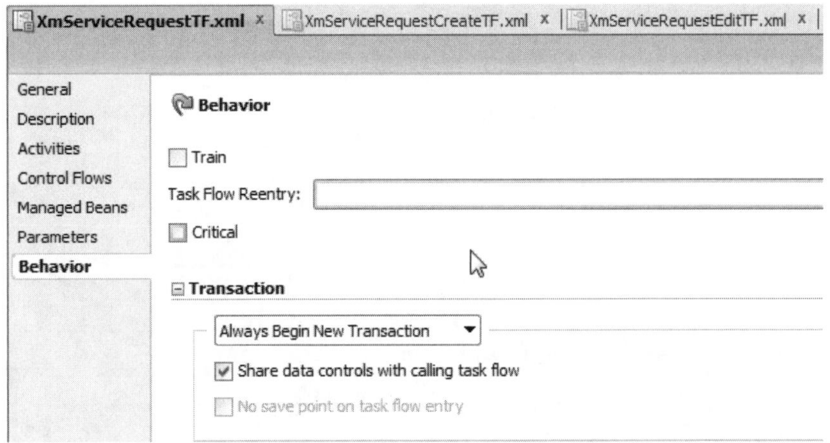

11. Set the new transaction and uncheck Share Data Controls with Calling Task Flow.

12. Set the existing transaction with shared data control for edit TF.

13. Now that we have defined the task flow transaction behavior, we will define the behavior on TF return. Select the cancel return activity and set the End Transaction property to rollback as shown in Figure 8-31. Select the save return activity and set the end transaction to commit. This means when the TF is ended with either cancel or save navigation return, the changes made in the TF will be either discarded or saved.

14. Similarly, we need to add commit and rollback logic to Edit TF. We have set up Edit TF to share the transaction so the TF commit and rollback happens only when the parent TF does the commit or rollback. Drag and drop commit and rollback.

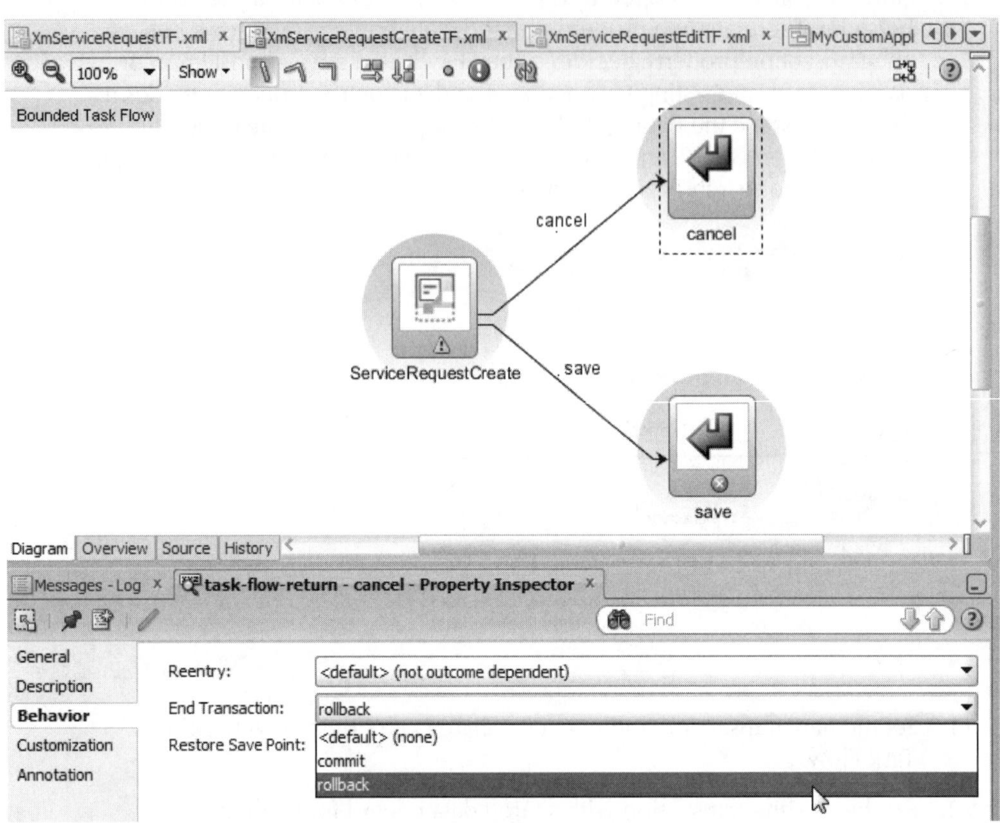

FIGURE 8-31. *Setting task flow end transaction behavior on return activities*

How to Define Application Pages

In this section we will define the pages inside the task flow. We have added a view activity in each TF and we will add content to that. Please read the chapter "Creating a Databound Web User Interface" in *Fusion Developer's Guide for Oracle Application Development Framework* (Oracle Fusion Applications Edition).

1. The application pages inherit several UI hints from the model such as label, display width, and so on. You can specify these at the UI layer as well, but it is recommended that you do it at the model so that every UI gets it automatically. Open the ServiceRequestName attribute in the EO and go to Control Hints. Provide the Label Text as **Request Name** and Display Width as **30** as shown in Figure 8-32.

2. Similarly, set the display width and label for all attributes that will be shown on the UI.

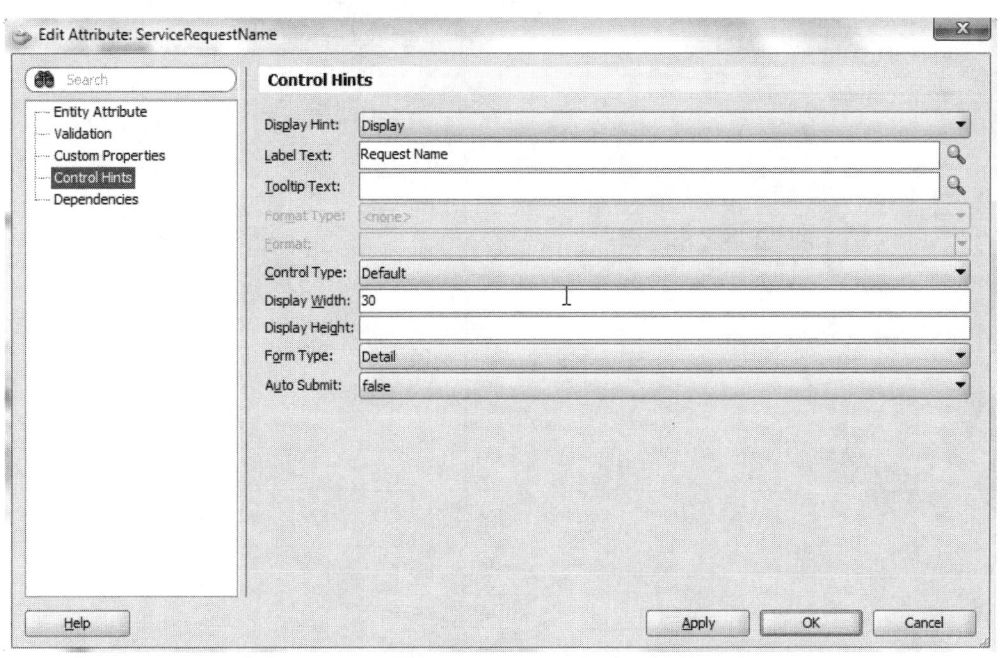

FIGURE 8-32. *Specifying control hint properties for an entity attribute*

3. Now we are ready to define the UI page. First we will build the search page. The search page is declaratively built using view criteria and an ADF query component. Open the service request VO and define a view criteria with attributes that you want to enable search on as shown in Figure 8-33.

4. Go to the UI Hints tab and give the Display Name as Search Service Request for the view criteria. Check the Show in List box. This will show up in a saved search at run time on the search page.

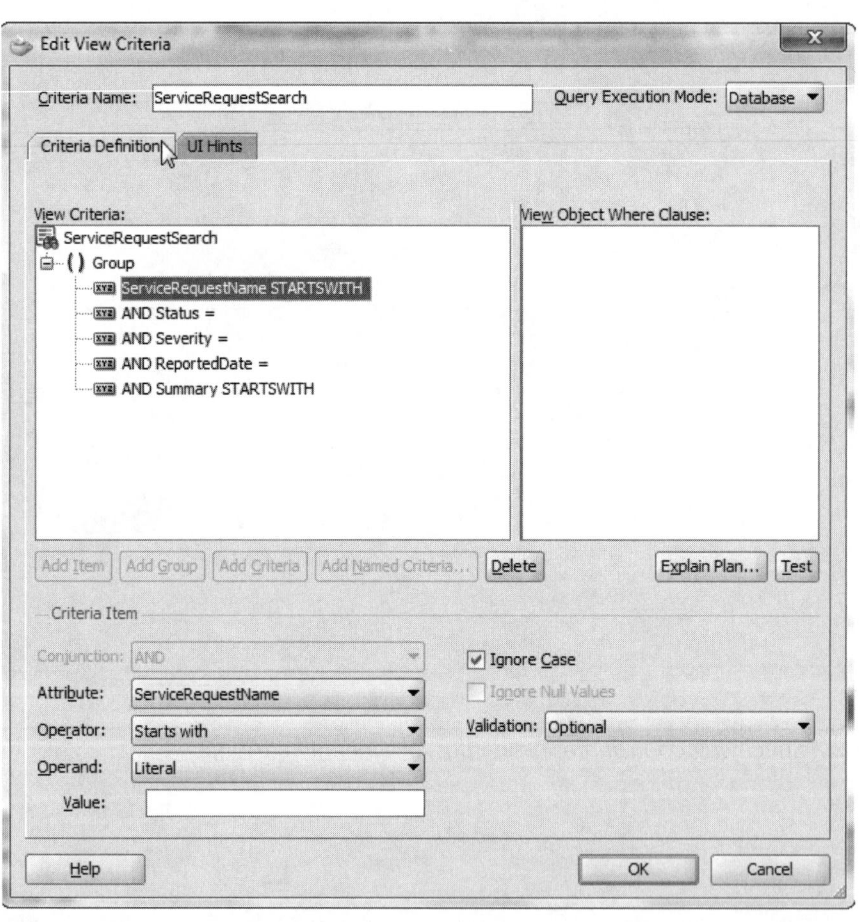

FIGURE 8-33. *Create a view criteria for the search page.*

5. Now we will define a List of Values for the Status attribute so that the UI presents an LOV to the user to pick the values from. Define a view accessor StatusLOV to CommonLookupsPVO as we defined on the EO, and bind the right parameters. Go to the Status attribute in service request VO and click the Add List of Values button as shown in Figure 8-34.

6. Select the List Data Source as StatusLOV and List Attribute as LookupCode as shown in Figure 8-35.

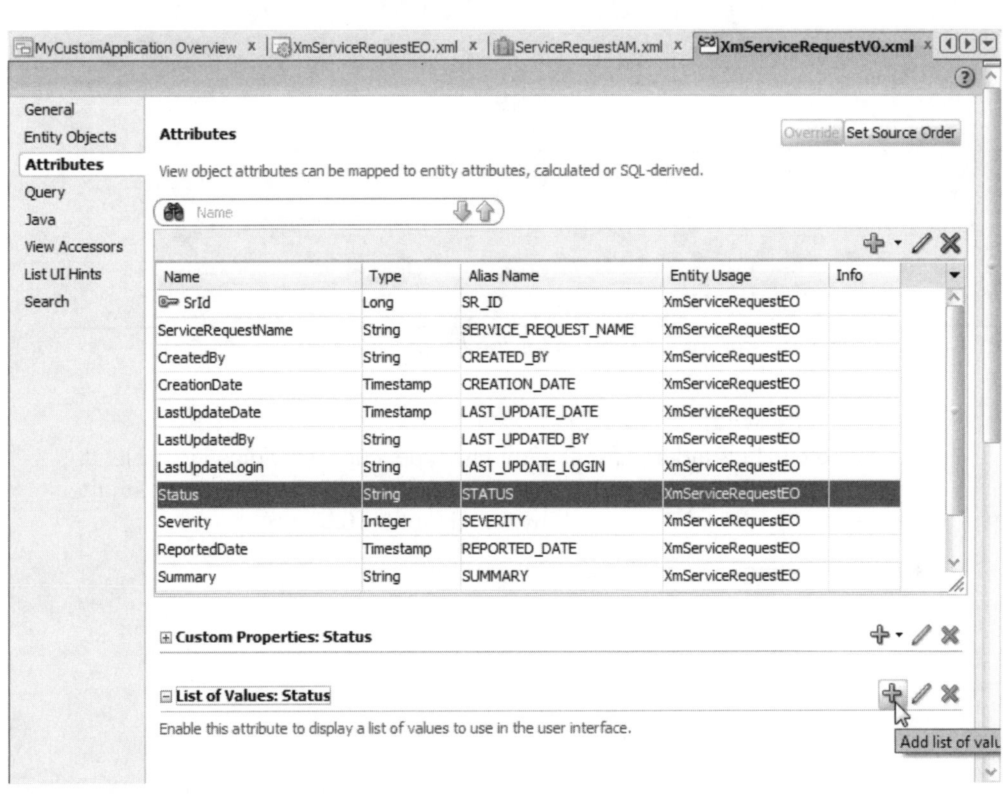

FIGURE 8-34. *Adding a list of values to an attribute in a view object*

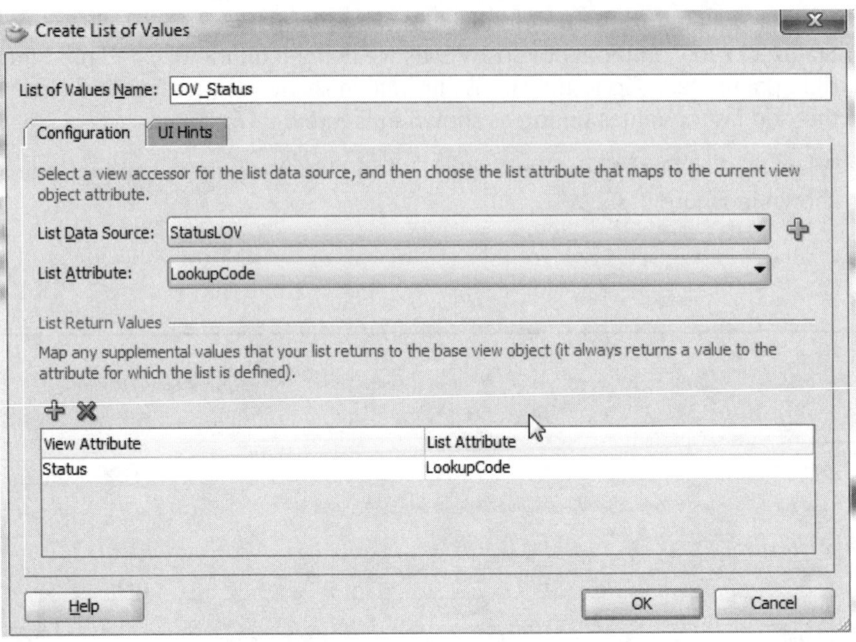

FIGURE 8-35. *Specifying attribute mappings for the list of values*

7. Go to the UI Hints tab and for Default List Type, choose Choice List. Select the display attribute as Meaning so that a user-friendly value is shown on the UI instead of internal code, as shown in Figure 8-36.

8. Similarly, define LOV on the severity attribute.

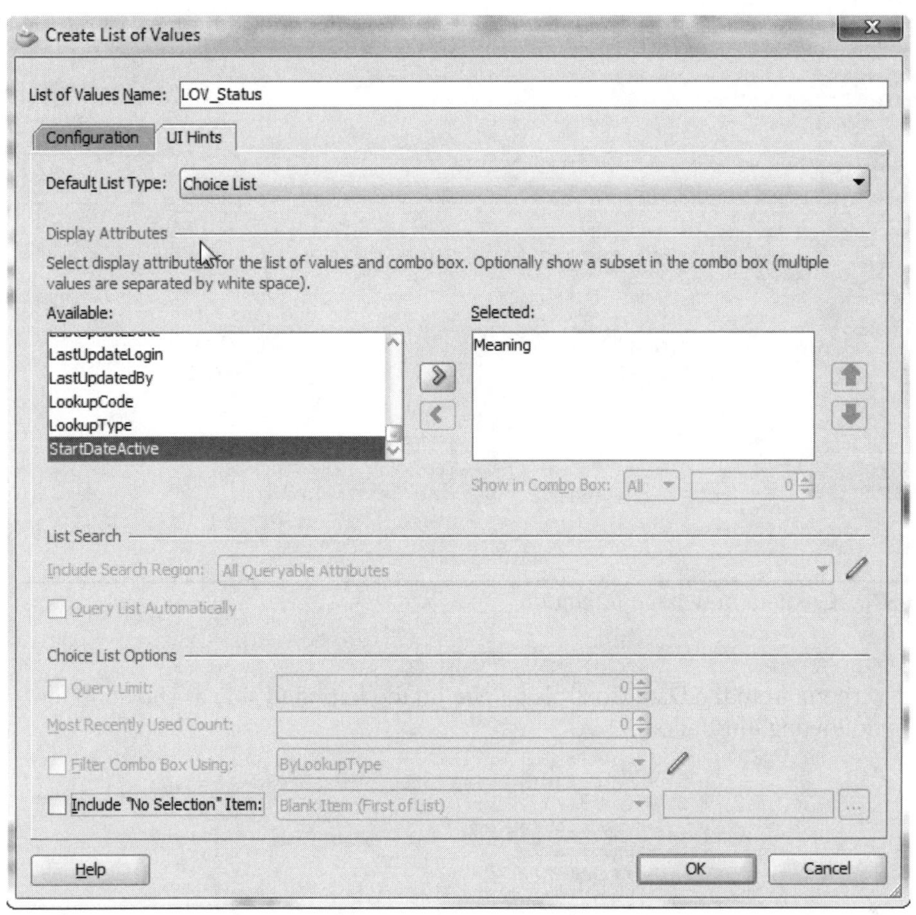

FIGURE 8-36. *Specifying UI hints for list of values definition*

9. Now double-click on the ServiceRequestSearch view activity in the search TF. Give the name and directory path for the JSFF as shown in Figure 8-37. This will create an empty page where we will add content for the search page.

10. To build the page and bind it to the model, ADF makes the AM available as data control by default. You can select the ServiceRequestSearch view

FIGURE 8-37. *Create a new page fragment.*

criteria from the Data Controls palette on the left-hand side as shown in the following illustration.

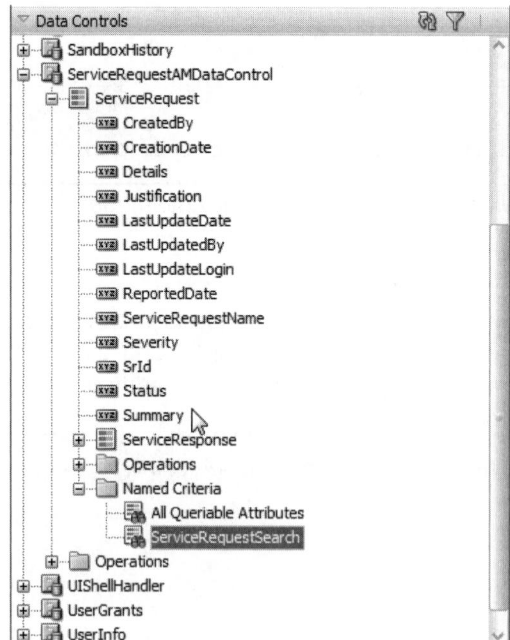

11. Drag and drop this view criteria on the JSFF. Choose the ADF Query Panel option to build the search page.

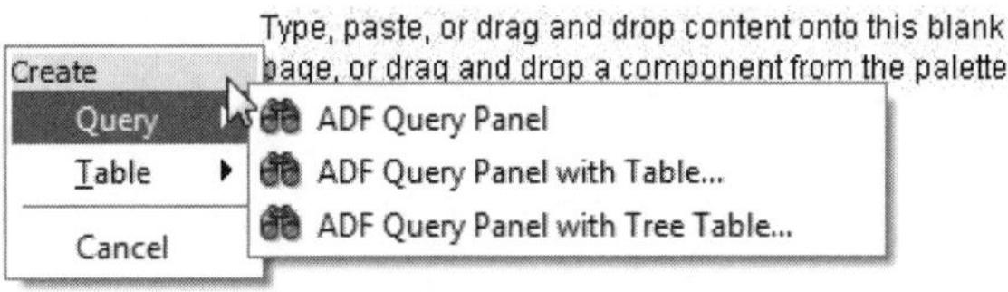

12. Now drag and drop the ServiceRequest VO instance from data control on the page and choose the Applications | Table option.

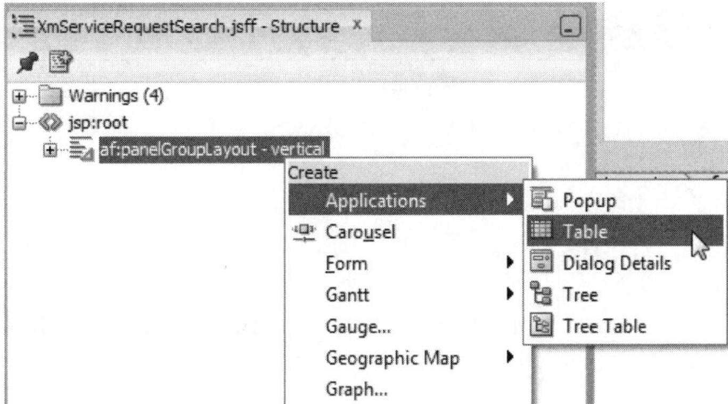

13. From the Create Table dialog, enable single-row selection, sorting, and filtering. Mark it as a read-only table. Remove the attributes that you do not want to show on the result table using the Delete icon as shown in the following illustration. Change Status and Severity to ADF Select One Choice so that the UI shows user-friendly meaning and click the Continue button.

Once the page is created, set the property readonly = true for the Status and Severity fields.

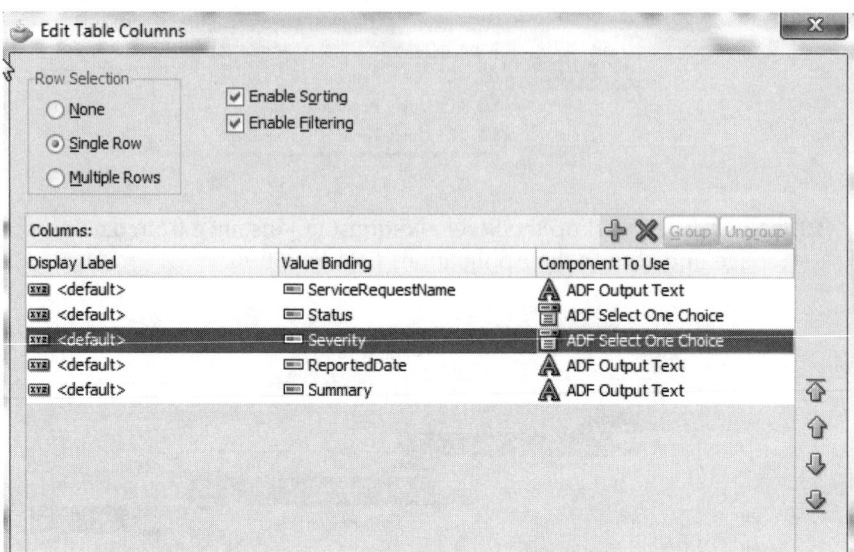

14. In the Configure Table Patterns dialog, enable Create and Edit with Page pattern and enable Export.

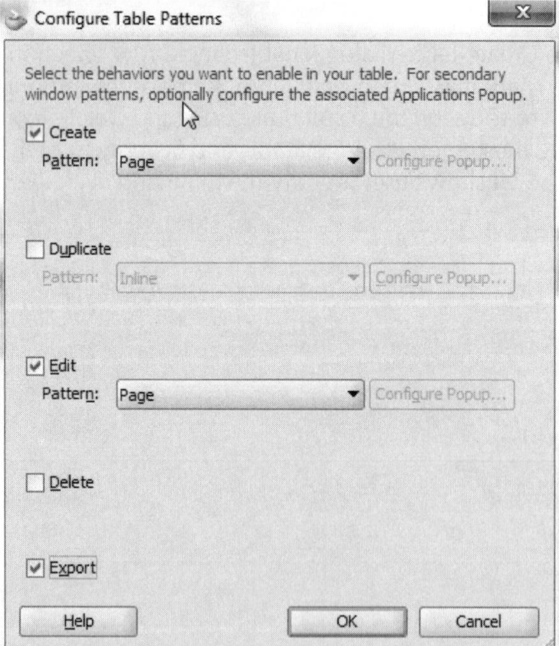

15. Select the query component in the structure window and move it out of the extra af:panelHeader component. Move the fnd:applicationsTable component under the af:panelHeader. Change the query component Header Text property to "Search Service Request" and the af:panelHeader text property to Results. The components should look like the following illustration.

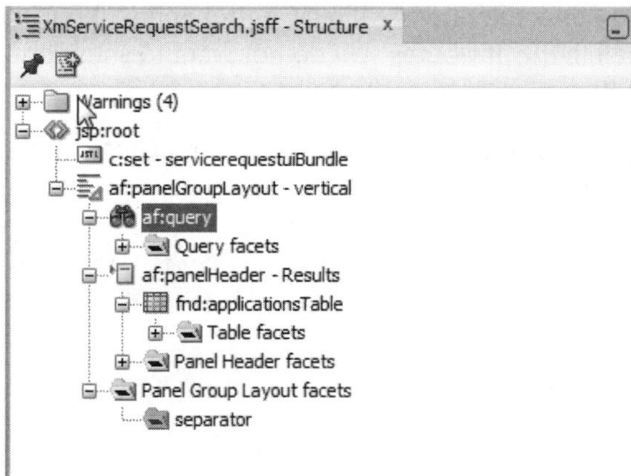

16. Select the query component and select Edit for ResultComponentId as shown in the following illustration. Select the af:table from the editor so that the search and result are connected on the UI.

17. Similarly, double-click on the view activity on create and edit TF to create the JSFF. Right-click on the JSFF root in the structure window and select the Insert Inside | Applications | Panel option as shown in Figure 8-38.

18. From the Application Panel dialog, give the Panel Title as "Create Service Request" and click Next. On the Components page, check Bind Data Now and select ServiceRequestAMDataControl.ServiceRequest from the Browse menu. Delete the attributes you do not want to show on the UI as shown in Figure 8-39.

19. In the Page Buttons section, choose Save and Close for the Submit slot and Cancel for the Cancel slot.

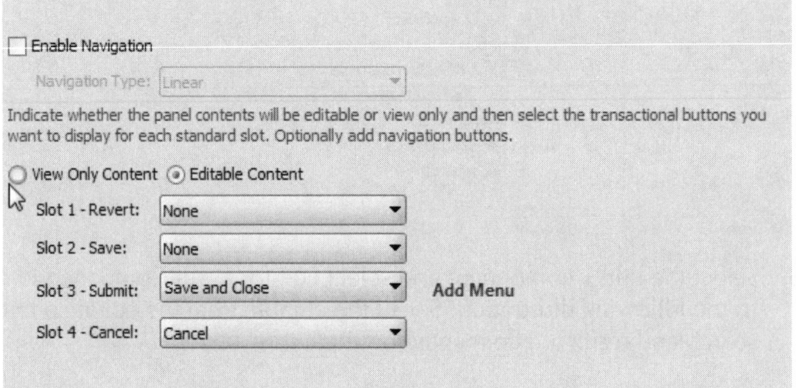

20. Complete the wizard and select the application panel on JSFF or the structure window. Go to properties and scroll down to the Page Buttons section. Go to slot 3 and select the Save and Close button. Select the Action value as "save" from the drop-down as shown in Figure 8-40. This is the value we have defined in the create TF for navigation to TF return with commit. Similarly, select the cancel action for the Cancel button from slot 4.

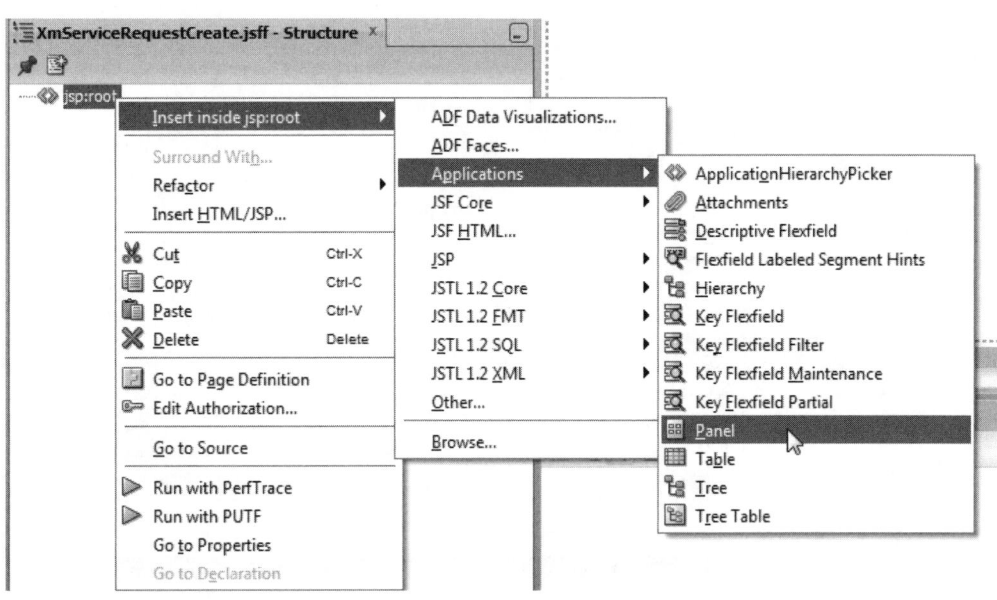

FIGURE 8-38. *Add applications panel to create a service request page.*

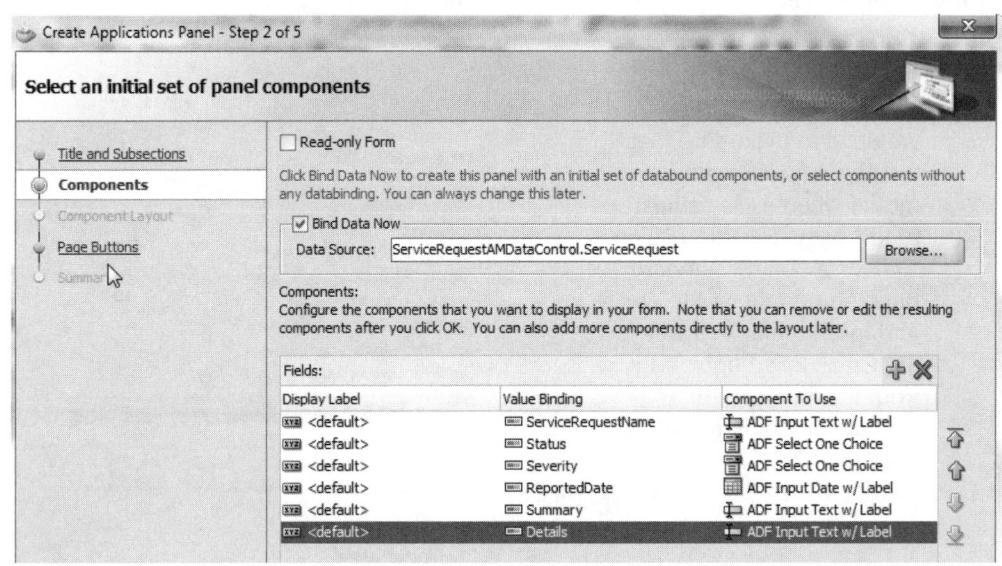

FIGURE 8-39. *Specify a create service request page attribute.*

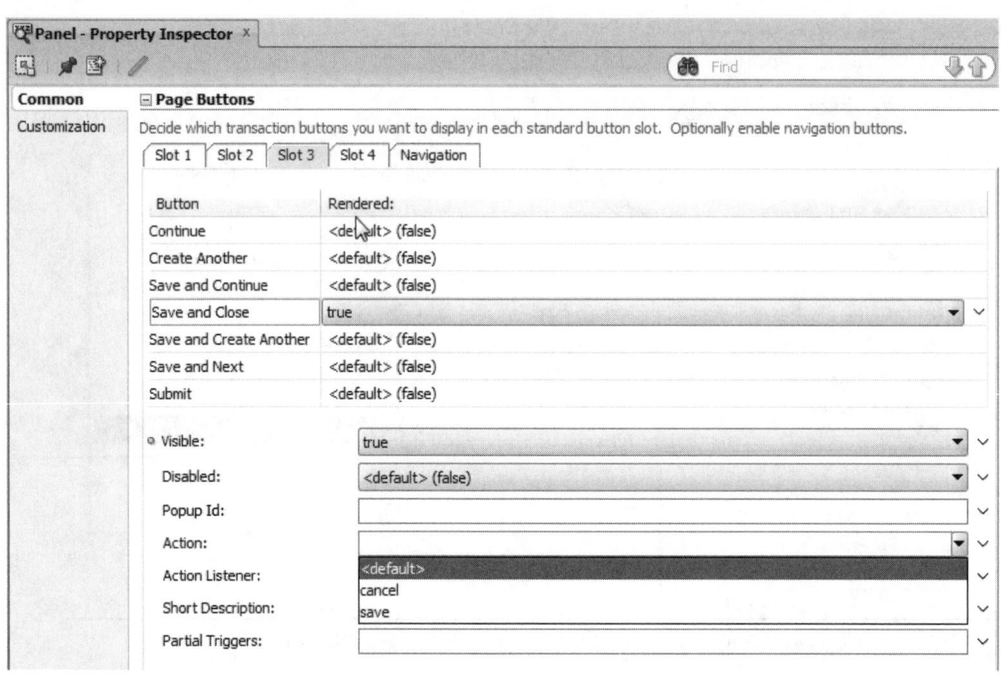

FIGURE 8-40. *Specify action values for buttons in application panel.*

21. Now that the page is defined, we need to make sure that the new row is created in the model when users navigate to this page. For this, use an ADF data control standard operation on the VO to create and insert a blank row. Select the CreateInsert operation from the data control as shown here and drop it on the Create TF.

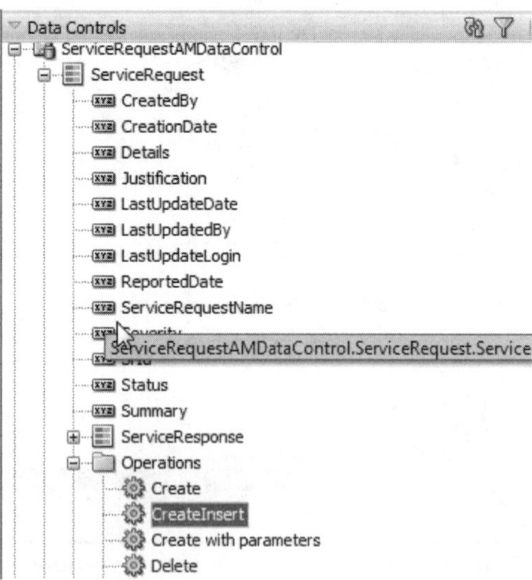

22. Define a Control Flow Case between the CreateInsert method activity and the ServiceRequestCreate view activity. Select the CreateInsert method activity and make it a default activity for this TF so that it is executed first when TF is loaded as shown here.

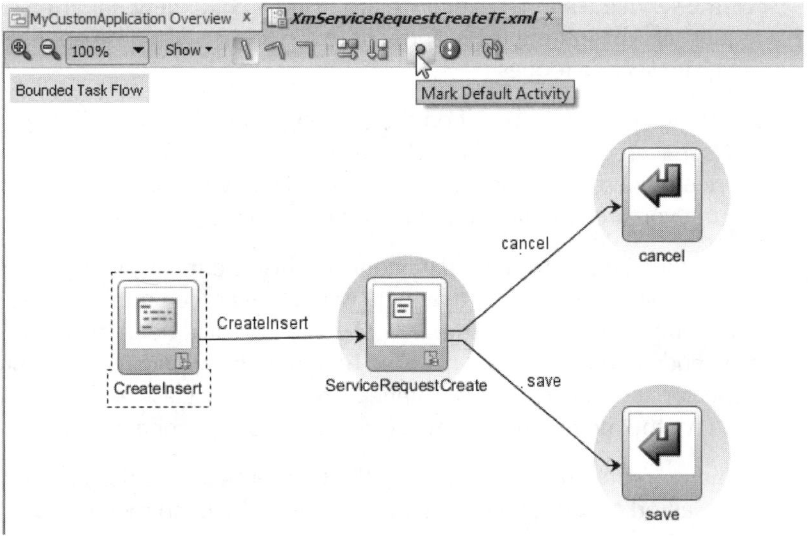

23. Similarly, define the edit page and add an application panel with Save and Close and Cancel buttons. Add a new af:panelHeader below af:panelformLayout where we will add a service response child table. From the data control, select the ServiceResponse child of ServiceRequest and drop it inside af:panelHeader as Application Table as shown at right. Complete the wizard by selecting the attributes you want to show. Do not mark this as a read-only table. Enable create and edit pattern as inline on this table.

24. For the edit page, we do not need to do any model query execution in this TF because the edit TF shares the transaction and data control with the parent TF. So, when the user searches and selects a row to edit, the page on edit TF will show the currently selected row in the VO from search page. For the service response, since we are using a child view link from service request, it will automatically show only the service response applicable for the given service request.

25. Select the application panel on the edit page and change the Title property to #{servicerequestuiBundle.EDIT_SERVICE_REQUEST}: #{bindings.ServiceRequestName.inputValue}. This will show the name of the service request you are editing in the title of the edit page.

26. We defined edit TF to share data control. This also means that the commit and rollback from the return activity will not get saved until the parent data control frame calls commit or rollback. We will need to add managed bean code to do this. Select the Save button in the applicationPanel property inspector and specify Action Listener. Create a new class, ServiceRequestEdit, and give the method name Save. Choose the bean scope as request.

27. Similarly, define Action Listener for the Cancel button to the same bean class and method called Cancel. Set the content of the bean method as follows.

```
package my.custom.sr.ui.bean;

import java.util.Map;
import javax.faces.context.FacesContext;
import javax.faces.event.ActionEvent;
import oracle.adf.model.BindingContext;
import oracle.adf.model.DataControlFrame;

public class ServiceRequestEdit {
    public ServiceRequestEdit() {
    }
    public void save(ActionEvent actionEvent) {
        DataControlFrame dcFrame = getDataControlFrame();
        dcFrame.commit();
        dcFrame.beginTransaction(null);
    }
    public void cancel(ActionEvent actionEvent) {
        DataControlFrame dcFrame = getDataControlFrame();
        dcFrame.rollback();
        dcFrame.beginTransaction(null);
    }
    public static DataControlFrame getDataControlFrame() {
        Map sessionMap =
            FacesContext.getCurrentInstance().getExternalContext().getSessionMap();
```

```
        BindingContext context =
            (BindingContext)sessionMap.get(BindingContext.CONTEXT_ID);
        String currentFrameName = context.getCurrentDataControlFrame();
        DataControlFrame dcFrame =
            context.findDataControlFrame(currentFrameName);
        return dcFrame;
    }
}
```

28. Go to the Overview tab on the task flow and go to Managed Beans. Notice the new Java class you defined for the listeners is registered as request scope managed bean on this task flow.

How to Integrate with UI Shell

The application flow is built using bounded task flows, and you cannot run the bounded TF directly. Now that we have application pages along with model integration and navigation flow defined, we need to define a page that can be set as run target. The ADF application needs a JSPX page to be set as run target. Fusion Applications come with a UI Shell template that you can use for your JSPX page so that other common features of the Fusion Application such as Navigator menu, preferences, logout link, and so on, are available on your page when it is integrated with existing Fusion Application deployment. Please read the chapter "Implementing the UI Shell" in the *Fusion Applications Developer's Guide*.

1. Open the adfc-config.xml file and add a View activity from the Component palette and name it **ServiceRequestWorkarea**. Double-click on the view activity to create a JSPX page. Choose the right package and select a page template as UI Shell as shown in Figure 8-41.

2. This JSPX page is just the container for the UI Shell template. All other page content items, such as the regional, local, and contextual area flows and the task list, are defined independently. At run time, the menu definition assembles the content in various regions on the page. All task flows are loaded into a page created with the UI Shell template by configuring the Menu file.

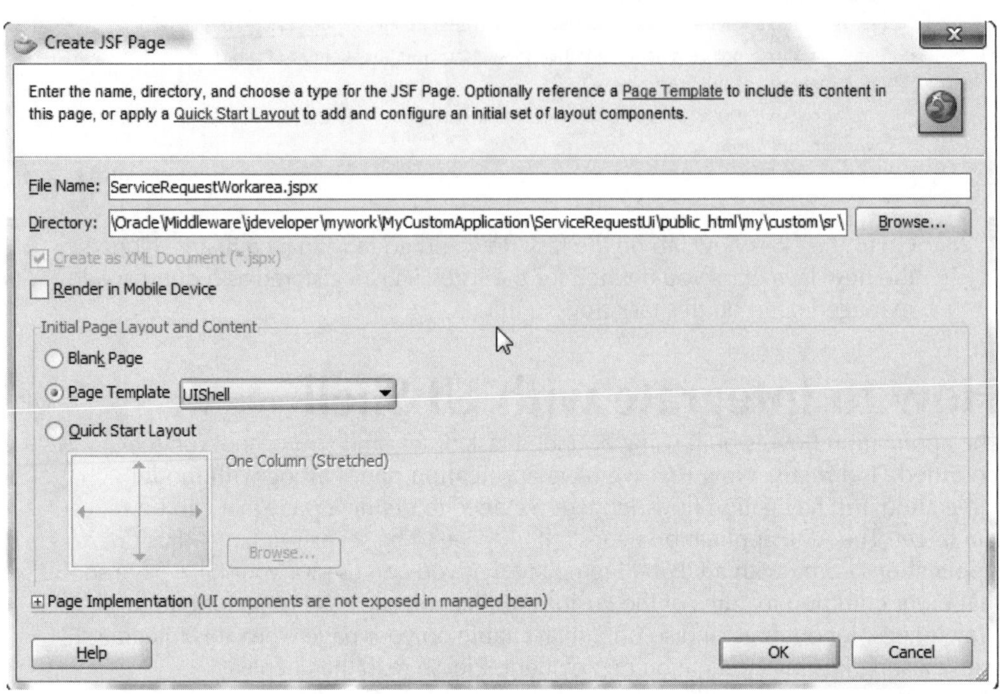

FIGURE 8-41. *Define a page using UI Shell template.*

3. Right-click on the JSPX page in the application navigator and choose the Create Applications Menu option as shown in Figure 8-42. This creates an empty menu file that we will use to put details about the content for the actual application workarea pages.

4. Right-click on the itemNode in the menu file and choose the Insert Inside itemNode option.

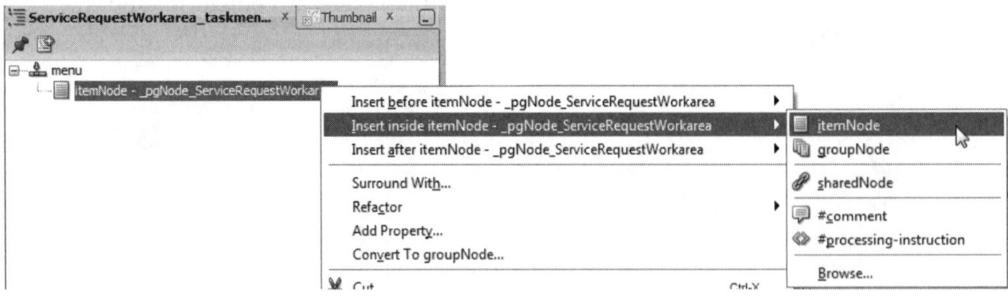

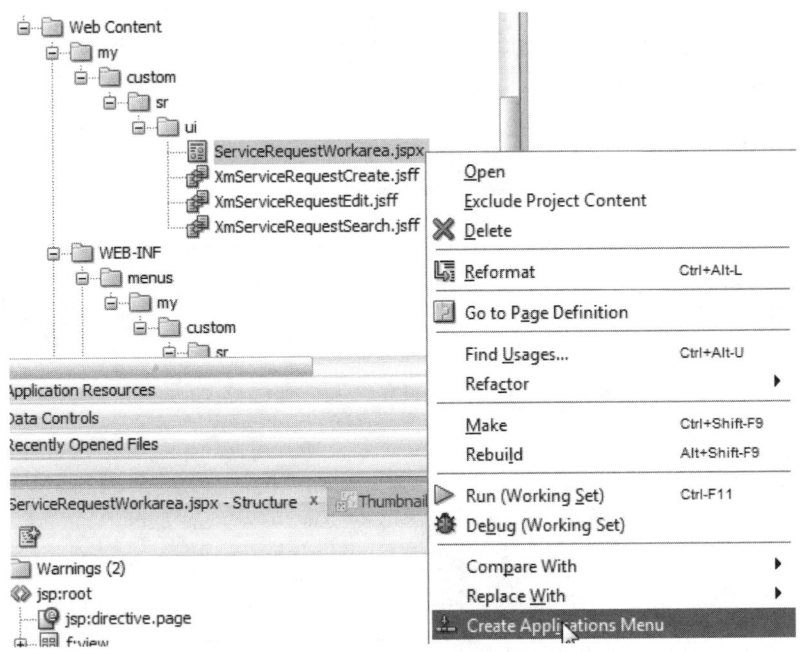

FIGURE 8-42. *Create an applications menu and associate with the page.*

5. Provide the id as ServiceRequestWorkarea_search and choose focusViewId as /ServiceRequestWorkarea.
6. Select this newly created item node and go to the property inspector. Set the properties label = Service Requests, Task Type = defaultMain, Task Flow Id = select XmServiceRequestTF.xml using the browser icon as shown in Figure 8-43.
7. Right-click on the adfc-config.xml file and choose Run. This will show the search service request page and you can navigate to create and edit service request pages from there.

Applications
ADF
Customization

id *: ServiceRequestWorkarea_search
focusViewId *: /ServiceRequestWorkarea
action:
label: Service Requests
rendered: <default> (true)

Advanced

Web Application:
Preferences For Applications:
Set attribute values for either Task or Page level item nodes.

Task | Page

Task Type: defaultMain
Page Title:
Tooltip:
Inflexible Height:
Task Flow Id: /WEB-INF/my/custom/sr/ui/flow/XmServiceRequestTF.xml#XmServiceRequestTF
Disclosed: default <false>
Reuse Instance: default <true>

FIGURE 8-43. *Specify the default task flow to be used for the page.*

8. You can add a task pane in the menu by inserting a new itemNode and move it as the first child above the dynamicMain itemNode. Set the Id and focusViewId as before. Set the label as label="#{applcoreBundle.TASKS}" and Task Type="defaultRegional", taskFlowId="/WEB-INF/oracle/apps/fnd/applcore/patterns/uishell/ui/publicFlow/TasksList.xml#TasksList", parameters List="fndPageParams=#{pageFlowScope.fndPageParams}".

9. Now add a new itemNode and set the label = Create Service Request, Task Type = dynamicMain, and specify the XmServiceRequestCreateTF. This adds a link under the task pane and will open the create service request page when you click on the link at run time. When you run the application now and click the Search button, the run-time page looks like the example in Figure 8-44. You can go to the create and edit pages and make changes.

10. You can adjust the application page and field look and feel and layout per your needs following the *Fusion Applications Developer's Guide*.

11. Similarly, you can add more itemNodes and give a TF Id if you want to add more regional areas. Each node creates a new regional area section. You specify the Task Type as defaultRegional for the itemNode.

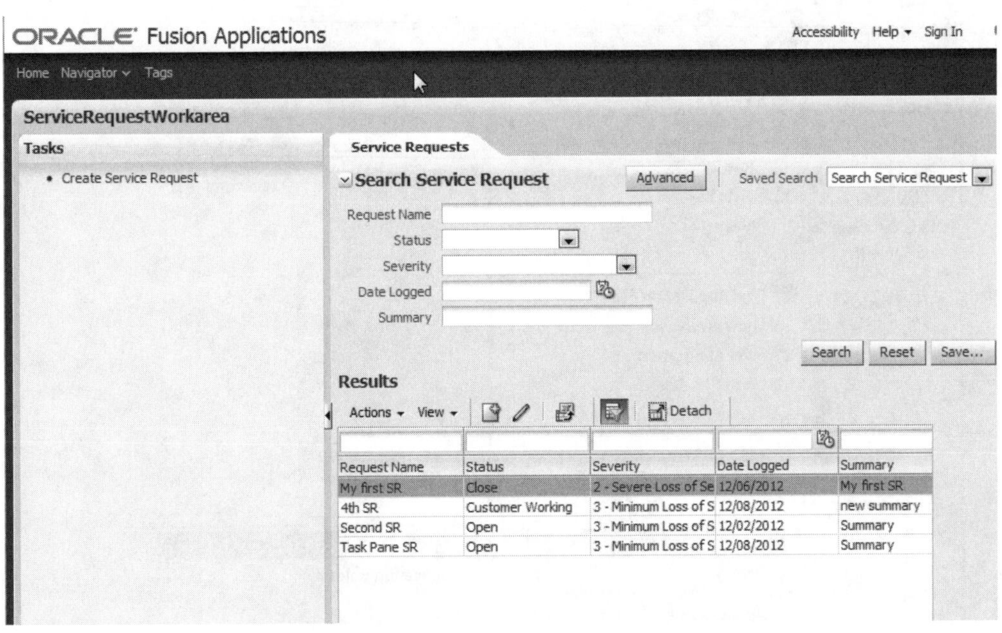

FIGURE 8-44. *Service request workarea run-time page*

How to Secure the Application

Fusion Applications are secured and you need an authenticated user with applicable roles to access the application flows. There are two main tasks to secure your new custom application so that it works seamlessly with existing Fusion Applications.

Enable Security

The new Fusion Application you built in JDeveloper is not secured by default. To enable security on your application, follow these steps.

1. Select the Application menu and select the Secure | Configure ADF Security menu option as shown in Figure 8-45.

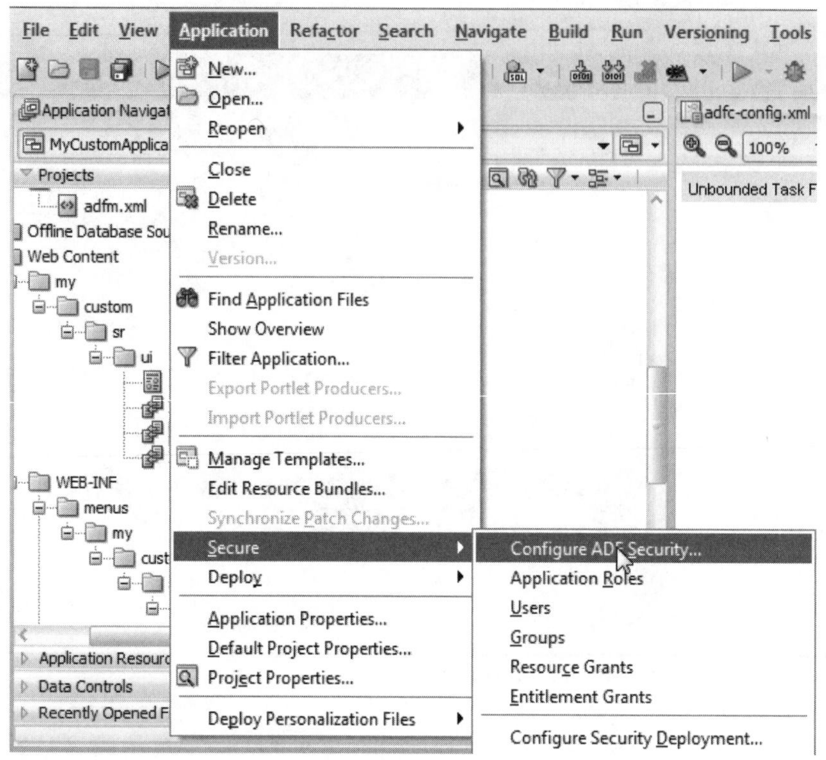

FIGURE 8-45. *Securing the ADF Web application*

2. Choose ADF Authentication and Authorization on Step 1 as shown in the following illustration.

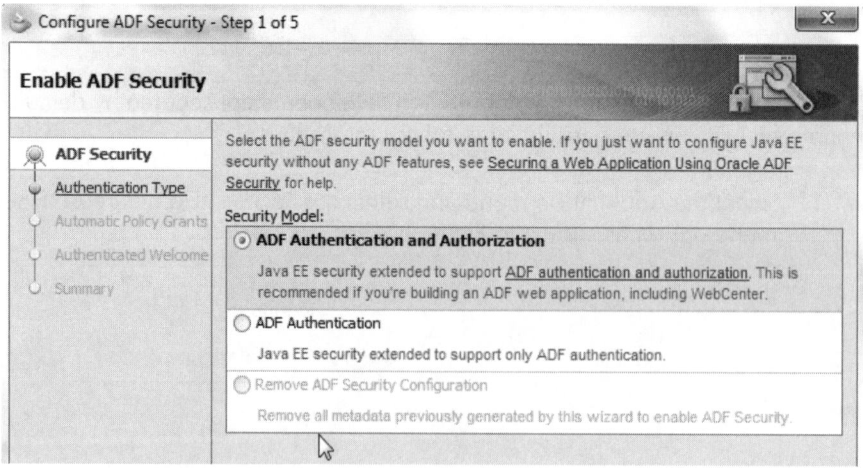

3. Choose your UI project from the Web Project drop-down and HTTP Basic Authentication for Authentication Type on Step 2.

4. Select No Automatic Grants on Step 3.

5. Do not select Redirect on Step 4.

6. Complete the wizard. This enables security on your application and all the task flow and JSPX on your application are now secured. The wizard modifies several configuration files such as adf-config.xml, jps-config.xml, and jazn-data.xml to include these security configurations.

Add Permissions

How to customize Fusion Application security is discussed in Chapter 4 of this book. You will need to use some of the concepts discussed in that chapter to add permissions for your application artifacts so that they can be accessed by end users. You need to define necessary privileges, duties, and roles to access your application flows. Then use those privileges to give permission to the task flow and JSPX pageDef. There are two ways to add these permissions and propagate them to run-time Fusion Application deployment, using Application Policy Manager or using XML-based security policy store.

Using Applications Policy Manager

Once you have used APM to define necessary privileges for your application, you can add the permissions to your artifacts in APM. You first need to define the resource for the task flows and JXPS pageDef. Once these resources are defined, you need to add entitlements to these resources under appropriate roles. Please read *Oracle Fusion Middleware Oracle Authorization Policy Manager Administrator's Guide* (Oracle Fusion Applications Edition) to understand more about how to execute these steps.

Using jazn-data.xml

The Fusion Applications are configured with an active LDAP for authentication and authorizations. Your applications administrator can extract the policy store from the LDAP server into an XML-based policy store called jazn-data.xml. Read more information about how to generate this file in the "Securing Oracle Fusion Applications" chapter of the *Oracle Fusion Applications Administrator's Guide*. Once you have the jazn-data.xml file from your Fusion Applications, you can use the security editor in JDeveloper to add necessary permissions. Once these permissions are defined in JDeveloper, the administrator will need to export these changes to the policy store to merge it with existing Fusion Applications policies.

How to Deploy and Integrate with Fusion Applications

Every Fusion Application is deployed as an Enterprise Achieve (ear) file on the application server. To incorporate your new custom application along with an existing Fusion Application deployed on a server, you need to package these artifacts into an ADF library jar file and place the jar files in the proper location within the application. To define an ADF library, go to the project property for your model and UI project and choose Deployment. Define a new ADF Library jar file and give it a name such as XmAdfServiceRequestUi as shown in Figure 8-46.

Right-click on your project and choose the Deploy option to generate the ADF Library jar file. Once you have generated both model and UI jar files, your administrator needs to put these jar files in the existing Fusion Application deployed ear location. The ADF library jar for the new model artifacts should be placed into the <ExplodedEarDirectory>/APP-INF/lib directory (for example, /fusionapps/applications/hcm/deploy/EarHcmCore.ear/APP-INF/lib/ XmAdfServiceRequestModel.jar). The ADF Library jar for the new UI artifacts should be placed in the <ExploadedWarDirectory>/WEB-INF/lib directory.

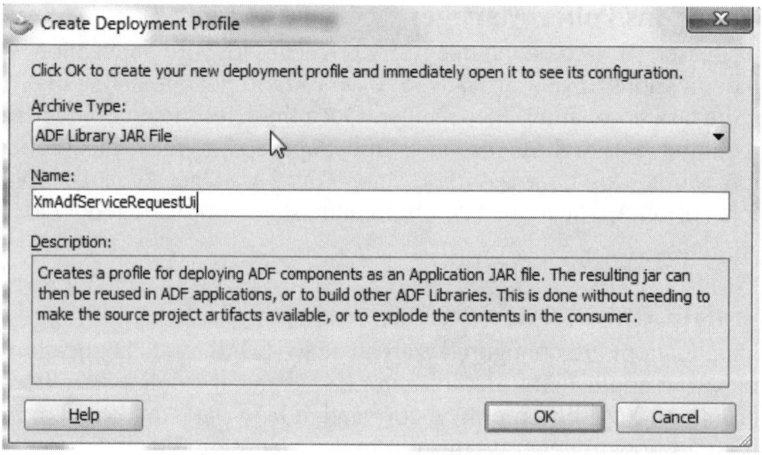

FIGURE 8-46. *Defining a deployment profile of type ADF Library jar file*

Once this is done, you can integrate your application by adding a new menu entry in the Navigator menu using the setup task "Manage Menu Customizations" from Functional Setup Manager accessed via the Setup and Maintenance link from the Navigator menu under the Tools category.

Summary

In this chapter, we discussed how to design a custom Fusion Application and what are the building blocks of such an application. We started with defining a database schema for the application, and we built ADF business components such as EO, VO, and application modules. We defined business logic and validations and discussed how to set UI hints and other attribute properties. We discussed how to define application navigation flows and incorporate application pages with content. We defined a JSPX page with UI Shell template and configured menu. Finally we discussed how to secure Fusion Applications and deploy them.

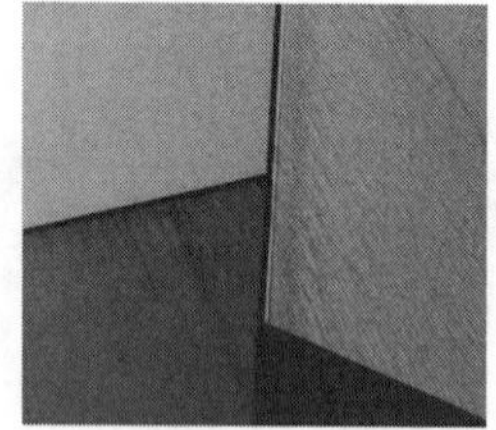

CHAPTER 9

Business Process Management (BPM) in Fusion Applications

Oracle Business Process Management (BPM) Suite is yet another Oracle Fusion Middleware technology that is used in Fusion Applications, albeit on a very small scale in the current releases. As the name suggests, BPM is all about making efficient, agile, and optimized business processes and workflows, and Oracle BPM Suite supports the full lifecycle of business processes including design, modeling, implementation, deployment, administration, and monitoring.

Most ERP and CRM products deployed in the cloud or at a customer site (on-premise) require the capability to deliver streamlined business processes that often incorporate human tasks through various types of notifications and messages such as approval e-mails and automated activities for retrieving approval hierarchies or expense report limits from an application's database. In Oracle E-Business Suite, it is the Oracle Workflow product that allows users to visually capture business processes that are mapped to various functions within E-Business Suite, while in Fusion Applications in the current releases (up to and including 11.1.6), it is the products from Oracle SOA rather than the Oracle BPM product offering that are most often used to manage business process orchestration and integration.

The reasons for the prevalent use of Oracle SOA in favor of Oracle BPM in Fusion Applications probably lie in the recent history of the global mergers and acquisitions activity in the IT sector, in which Oracle Corporation played a very active role. In 2004, Oracle announced the acquisition of Collaxa and the intention to incorporate its business process automation software into Oracle middleware products such as Application Server 10*g*. Collaxa was one of the first companies to build its product around Business Process Execution Language (BPEL), which after acquisition became known as Oracle BPEL Process Manager. Even today the BPEL Process Manager is still one of the key components of Oracle SOA Suite 11*g*. In 2008, Oracle acquired BEA Systems, which had its own BPM product called Aqualogic BPM, based on BPMN (Business Process Model and Notation). By the time Oracle managed to incorporate BEA's BPM tool into Oracle's Fusion Middleware product offering, the effort of building Fusion Applications from the ground up was well under way.

With that said, in this chapter we going to cover use cases for Oracle BPM customization very briefly, as there are only a couple of BPM processes in the Human Capital Management (HCM) product family shipped with the current releases of Fusion Applications, as opposed to hundreds of Oracle SOA-based composites, which are covered in the next chapter in proportionately more detail.

Oracle BPM in Fusion Applications: Architecture and Tools Overview

As far as run-time architecture is concerned, both Oracle SOA and BPM share the same server infrastructure based on Service Component Architecture (SCA). In fact, Oracle BPM 11*g* is installed on top of Oracle SOA 11*g*, and BPM leverages SOA

Suite components such as Human Workflow and Business Rules. The use of interrelated modeling components is made possible by unifying all of the components into a single run-time service infrastructure inside Oracle Fusion Middleware.

In addition to the run-time environment, Oracle BPM provides the following design-time tools:

- **BPM Studio** Offers modeling and development capability and is installed as a plug-in to JDeveloper
- **Process Composer** Web-based modeling interface targeted to be used by business analysts for high-level process modeling

The diagram in Figure 9-1 provides an overview of the system components and actors involved, which most noticeably features BPM Meta Data Repository (MDS) and run-time engines including the BPMN service engine in addition to design-time tools like BPM Studio and BPM Process Composer.

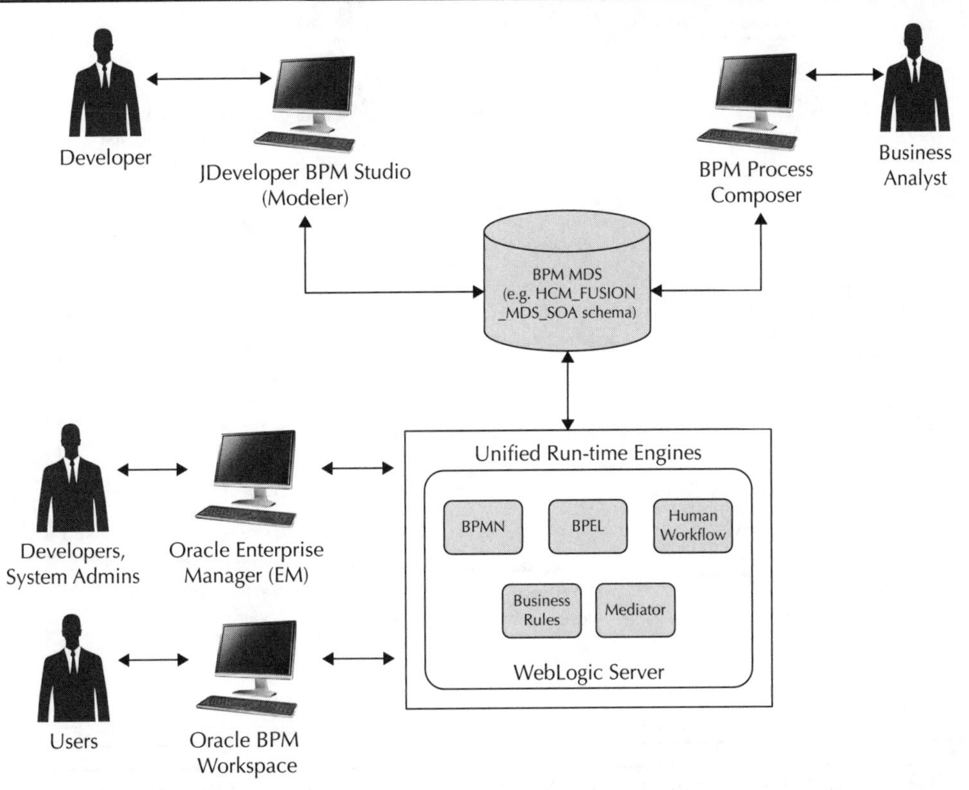

FIGURE 9-1. *Oracle BPM design tools, BPM, and SOA run-time engines*

We'll now further examine the run-time architecture and guide readers on how to access and look for BPM processes in Fusion Applications.

BPMN Component Run-time Environment

As illustrated in Figure 9-1, both BPMN and BPEL engines execute within one unified environment inside the WebLogic server built on top of Service Component Architecture (SCA). SCA is an open standard managed by OASIS (http://www.oasis-opencsa.org), which is embraced by Oracle and helps promote open standards in implementing services. There are many ways and methodologies to implement services, and they range from vendor-specific implementations like Tuxedo, to SCA, the open standard for SOA-style implementations. SCA provides a model for service composition and their reuse; therefore, BPMN components are deployed as part of the SOA composite and at run time appear just like any SOA composite component (Figure 9-2).

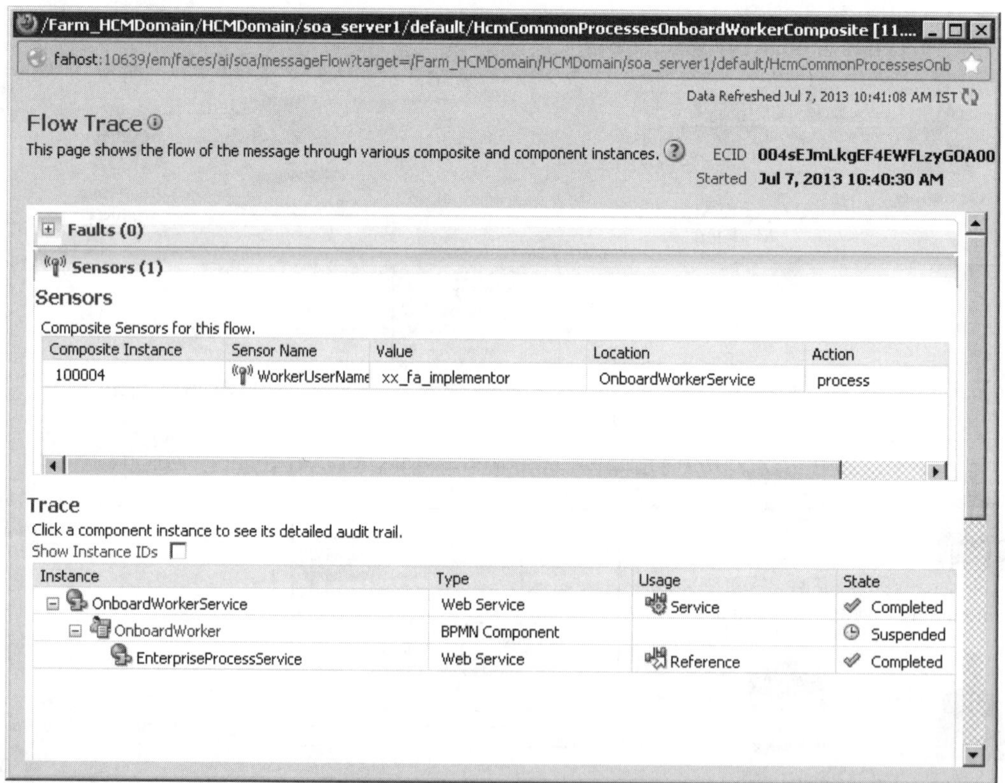

FIGURE 9-2. *Flow trace of a running BPMN component in Enterprise Manager*

In Chapter 1, we mentioned that each application pillar or product family like Human Capital Management (HCM) has its own SOA server cluster inside its domain. Therefore, all the running instances of the BPMN processes and deployed SOA composites can be found by accessing Enterprise Manager Fusion Applications Control for the corresponding domain (http://host:port/em).

NOTE
BPEL and BPMN service engines share a common process core for shared components that handle instance dehydration, service invocation, timer scheduling, and so forth.

BPMN Design Tools

Oracle BPM offers two modeling tools for the design of BPMN processes:

- **BPM Studio** Plug-in to JDeveloper, normally used by technical developers to create service catalogs, provide service implementations, create and extend BPM templates, and so forth
- **BPM Process Composer** Process modeling geared toward business analysts and the business process owner type of end user

In order to facilitate the collaborative modeling and design approach between implementation detail, usually performed by BPMN/SOA developers using the JDeveloper tool, and high-level business process design performed by business analysts, the BPM tooling architecture is connected by a central Meta Data Services (MDS) component called BPM MDS, as shown in Figure 9-3.

The BPM MDS repository is a BPM project-sharing enabler that allows bottom-up and top-down approaches in the designing and modeling of business processes. For example, developers can create a BPM process catalog of services and business rules and publish it via BPM MDS as a template, which could subsequently be used by the business analysts and process owners to create BPMN diagrams and processes inside the BPM Process Composer tool. On the other hand, in the top-down design approach, the process owners could first design the outline of the business process using BPM Process Composer, and publish (save) it into the BPM MDS repository for sharing with IT, that is, process-implementation developers who will later provide the concrete implementation for the BPMN activities that require wiring with the Web and other services deployed on the server.

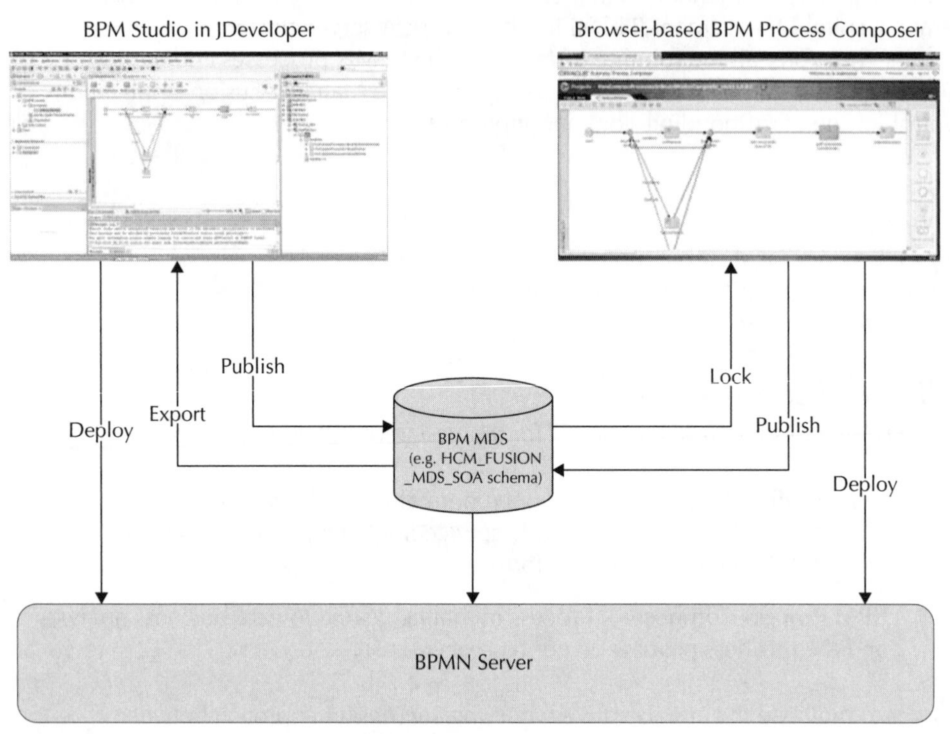

FIGURE 9-3. *BPM design tools and BPM MDS repository*

Connecting to BPM MDS Repository from JDeveloper

The BPM MDS repository partition is called Oracle BPM Meta Data Service or OBMP MDS. As already mentioned, BPM MDS provides integration and sharing capabilities between the two main design and modeling tools: JDeveloper and BPM Business Process Composer. In order to access the repository partition from JDeveloper via BPM MDS Navigator, we first need to create a BPM MDS connection to it. However, the prerequisite to a BPM MDS connection is to have available an SOA MDS connection as well as the connection to the "soainfra" server deployed in the WebLogic domain of interest, for example, HCMDomain.

NOTE
As always when working with Fusion Applications, we use JDeveloper with Fusion Applications Extensions, which is set up as explained in Chapter 7.

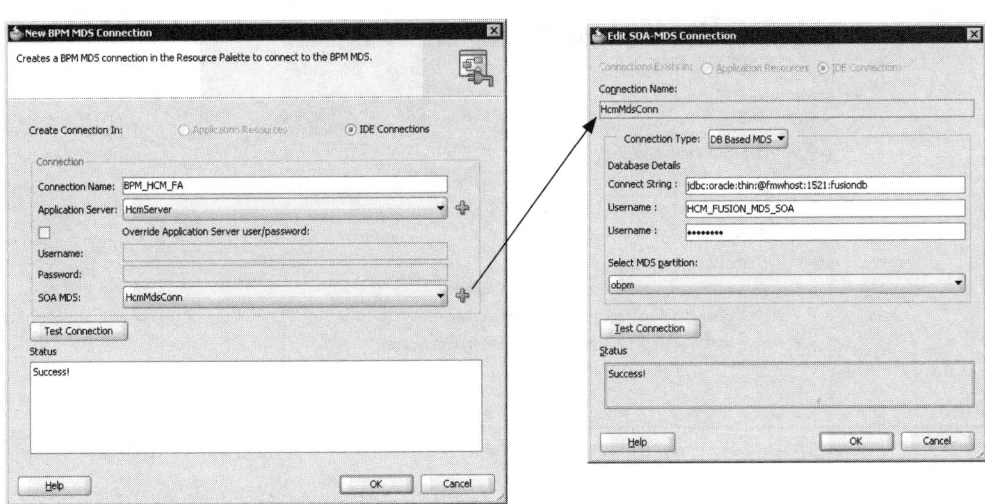

FIGURE 9-4. *Creating a BPM MDS Connection in JDeveloper*

Figure 9-4 shows the two main steps required to connect to the BPM MDS. Note that at the current time only the HCM product family has one BPM process deployed at run time and three BPM templates published in the BPM MDS repository. Following is a summary of the steps required to create a BPM MDS connection to the HCM WebLogic domain:

1. Create a database connection in the Resource Palette: select View | Resource Palette from the main menu, right-click New Connection, and then select Database. Here we specify the HCM_FUSION_MDS_SOA database user name and corresponding password along with other parameters required to connect to the database (hostname, port, and DB SID).
2. Create an SOA MDS connection, give it a name like HcmMdsConn, choose the database connection from the previous step, and make sure to select **obpm** as MDS partition.
3. In the Resource Palette, create a new BPM MDS connection by selecting the SOA MDS connection HcmMdsConn created in the previous step.

It is possible to create a BPM MDS connection using a different sequence of steps, but what matters is that we can view the content of the BPM MDS repository as illustrated in Figure 9-5.

Generally, developers create BPM implementation-ready templates that include fully designed and developed implementation artifacts and publish them into a BPM MDS repository so that business process owners can use them to further model

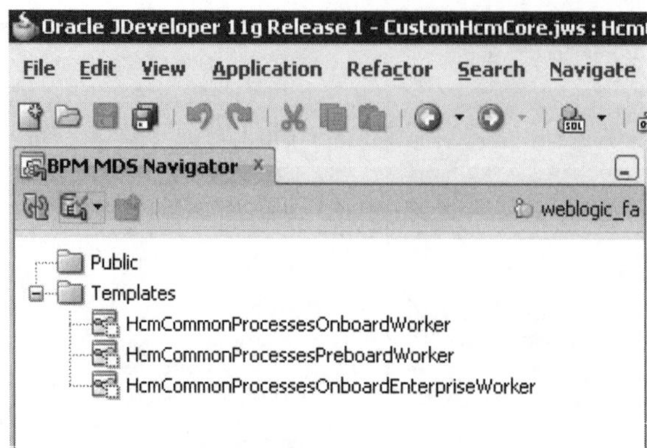

FIGURE 9-5. *HCM product family BPM templates available in BPM MDS Navigator*

processes via a business analyst–friendly BPM Composer tool. The published templates are available in the Templates root folder in the BPM MDS Navigator (Figure 9-5).

NOTE
The current Fusion Applications Extensibility Guide *suggests that developers can customize and extend project templates when it is necessary to customize and extend business catalog components that are part of the default project templates. However, the* Extensibility Guide *also stresses that when customizing a project template, developers must first make a copy of the existing template using JDeveloper to avoid overwriting the project templates previously published into the BPM MDS repository.*

Accessing BPM Process Composer in Fusion Applications

BPM Process Composer is intended for use by business analysts and process owners who are familiar with BPMN modeling notation. It is a browser-based tool that allows users to design BPM processes that use standard BPMN activities, business rules, and human tasks.

At the current time there are only three BPM templates shipped with Fusion Applications:

- HcmCommonProcessesOnboardWorker
- HcmCommonProcessesPreboardWorker
- HcmCommonProcessesOnboardEnterpriseWorker

You've already gathered that all three are from the HCM product family and they all relate to the Worker Hiring business process area in HCM.

To access BPM Process Composer, we go to http://host:port/bpm/composer and log in as a user who has access to it. Once logged in to BPM Composer, the analysts can explore deployed run-time projects as shown in Figure 9-6, view projects owned by them, and most importantly, they can create new projects based on published BPM templates or even without templates.

In the next section we take a look at a simple example of BPM process customization using BPM Business Process Composer.

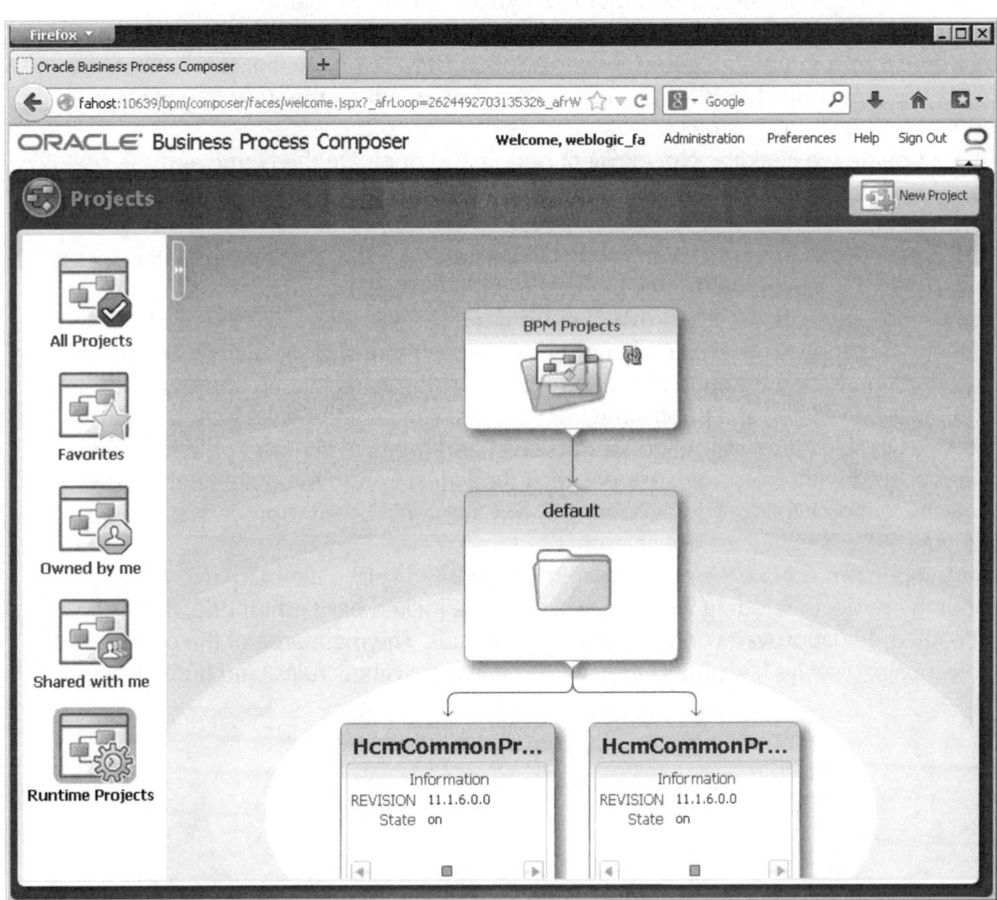

FIGURE 9-6. *BPM Process Composer home page*

Example of BPM Process Customization Based on an Existing Template in Process Composer

Suppose that the process owner in the Human Resources department wants to create a customized BPMN process based on the HcmCommonProcessesOnboardWorker template in the development Fusion Applications instance for testing purposes by adding BPMN script activity to default the legislation code to a certain value. As mentioned in the previous section, in order to be able to access the BPM Composer screens, the process owner needs to have adequate user privileges such as Application Implementation Consultant assigned to their username.

We've also mentioned that the Fusion Applications HCM product family ships with the HcmCommonProcessesOnboardWorker BPM template that can be used to create the new project in BPM Composer. We'll now outline the summary of steps required to create such project.

First of all, we click the New Project button and populate the Name and Description text fields with an appropriate name and a description of the project as shown in Figure 9-7.

Because we want our custom project to be based on the existing template, we also need to make sure to tick the Use Template check box and select HcmCommonProcessesOnboardWorker from the list. We then click the Next button, which opens the Deployment Options screen (not shown), where we specify the value **None** for the Approval Workflow field. This means that no approval will be required when saving and publishing this process. Clicking the Next button again allows us to select the visibility of our process, and here we choose Public visibility so it is shared with everyone. Last, we click the Finish button to complete the New Project Creation Wizard, which opens our XxOnboardWorker01 process as shown in Figure 9-8.

An open project like the one shown in Figure 9-8 displays summary information about the project including whether the project is locked or in edit mode, if sharing is enabled, the approval workflow, and other details. The main area of the open project page displays key project artifacts: processes, business rules, and human tasks.

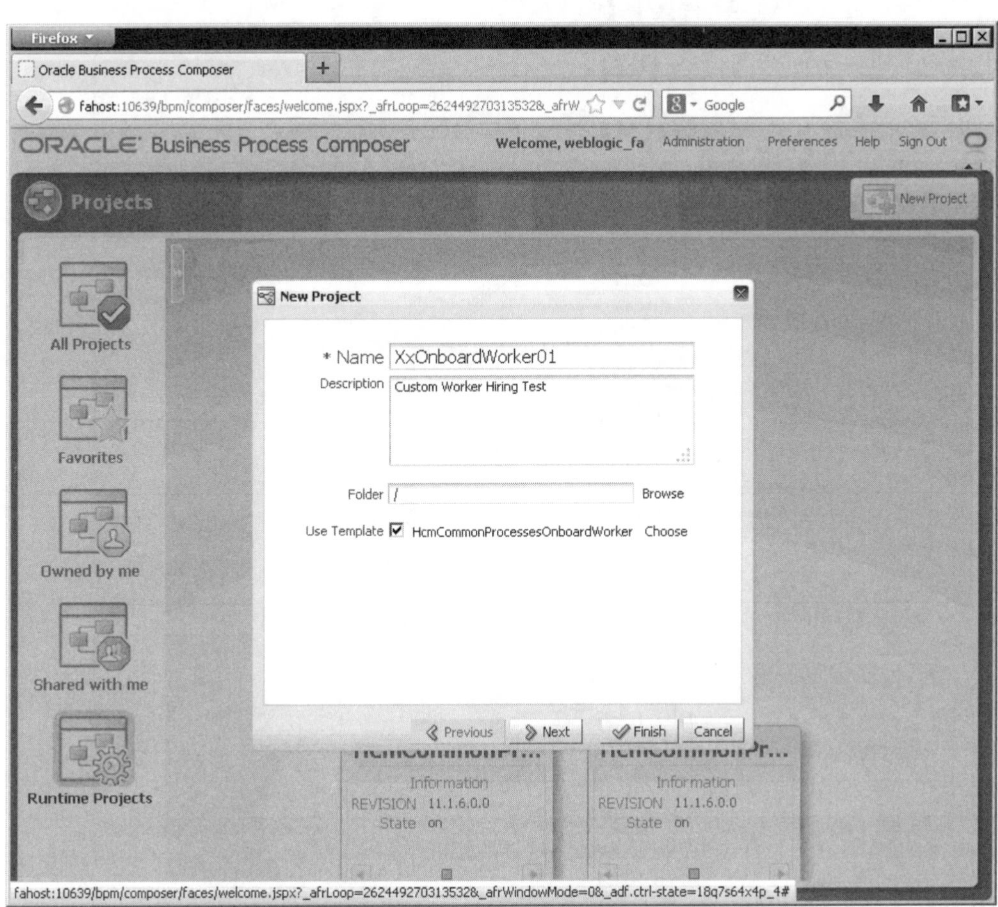

FIGURE 9-7. *Creating a new project based on an existing template*

We can see that our project based on the HcmCommonProcessesOnboardWorker template has one process called OnboardWorker that we want to customize, and because the project is in the edit mode, we should be able to customize the process by clicking on it. Our requirement was to default the legislation code to a fixed value when the process is launched, and to achieve that, we drag and drop at the first transition in the process a script activity that we called XxSetLegislation. At this point we can validate our design in BPM Composer by clicking the Validate button in the top menu. Figure 9-9 shows the BPM process with added XxSetLegislation script activity and confirmation of the successful process validation.

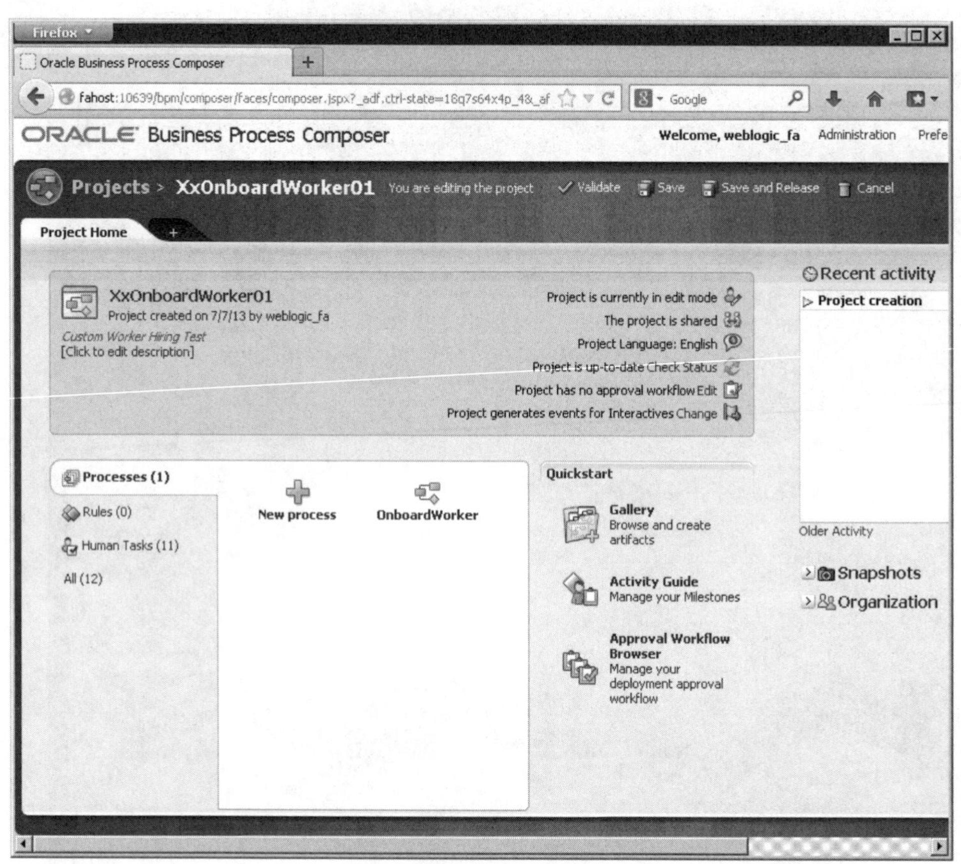

FIGURE 9-8. *Custom BPM process opened in Process Composer*

Now we click the Save and Release button, which will make our project available to be shared with IT for further work on this process; for example, they would need to create appropriate data mappings between the process input object and the added script activity XxSetLegislation.

Once the development cycle is completed by deploying the BPMN process as a running composite inside HCMDomain's soa_server cluster, we need to find a mechanism for invoking it by an appropriate function in a deployed HCM application. There is no hard and fast rule as to what is the best way to do this; the best practice is to review the product documentation including the implementation guides for a

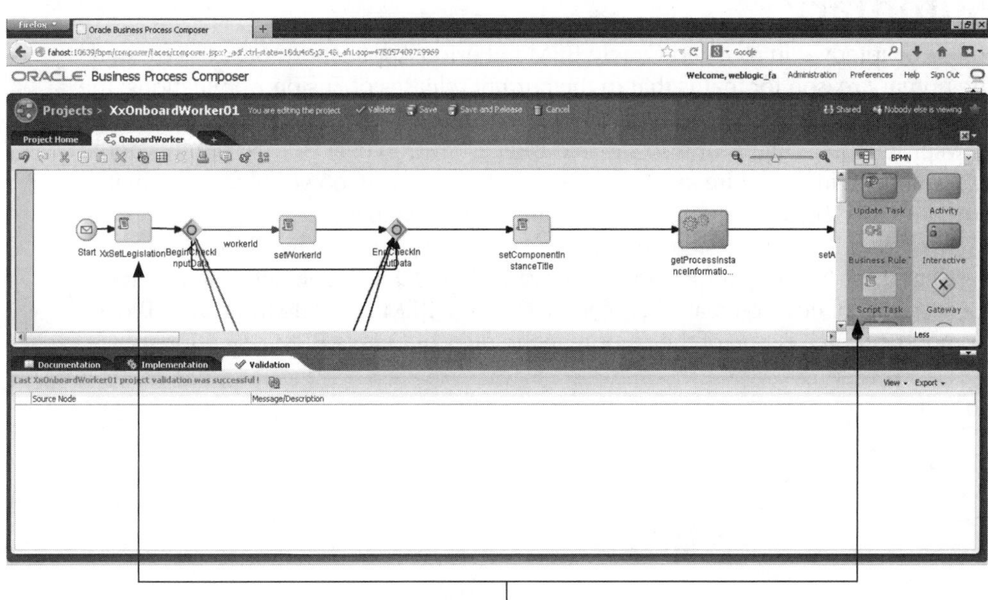

Drag and drop BPMN script activity on the first transition in the process, name it XxSetLegislation, and click the Validate button.

FIGURE 9-9. *Validation successful after adding script activity*

clue on how to invoke this process at run time by an application. For example, there is nothing to stop us from deploying an SOA composite that contains the customized BPMN using the same composite name but a different revision ID; however, obviously this makes configuration management more complex and has other disadvantages. Careful observers would also notice that in HCM there is a task accessible from Functional Setup Manager (FSM) that allows registering a custom Workforce business process. However, in the current *Oracle Fusion Applications Workforce Deployment Implementation Guide*, there is no mention of how to use it.

Alternatively, most Fusion Applications products raise business events through SOA EDN (Event Delivery Network), and that is one of the best ways to initiate a custom process, as start activity in Oracle BPM can be based on an event. We'll cover events in more detail in subsequent chapters, most notably Chapter 10 and Chapter 15.

Summary

In this chapter we introduced Oracle BPM in Fusion Applications only briefly, and the primary reason for that is that in the current releases of Fusion Applications, the main orchestration tools are coming from Oracle SOA 11*g* rather than the Oracle BPM product offering. That is to say that BPEL is favored over BPMN, but this could easily change in the future as Oracle BPM has some really powerful features that we are sure could be used in Fusion Applications quite effectively.

We listed the BPM design and modeling tools available, went through some detail on how to set up a BPM modeler available in JDeveloper, and also provided an overview of how to create a project based on a BPM template from BPM Process Composer, which is one of the favorite techniques of Oracle BPM practitioners.

CHAPTER 10

Run-time and Design-time Customizations of SOA Components in Fusion Applications

Service-oriented architecture (SOA) is often described as a strategy for developing and integrating systems through interoperable standards-based services. Fusion Applications leverage the capabilities of Oracle SOA Suite 11*g* to provide service-enabled enterprise applications that can be integrated into SOA.

Oracle SOA Suite 11*g* consists of a number of processing service engines, and in this chapter we are going to focus on the customization and extension aspects of the following:

- Human task implementations that execute inside the Human Workflow Engine
- Business rules implementations that execute inside the Business Rules Engine
- BPEL process implementations that execute inside the BPEL Engine
- Mediator implementations that execute inside the Mediator Engine

Other components such as Business-to-Business (B2B) engine, Complex Event Processing (CEP), Business Activity Monitoring (BAM), and others are not discussed in this book as we look to home in on the key usages of Oracle SOA in Fusion Applications, while Business Process Management (BPM) is covered in Chapter 9.

In addition to the default set of core components, Oracle SOA 11*g* features the Event Delivery Network (EDN) component, which provides Fusion Applications with a mechanism to publish system and business events to which other composite applications can then subscribe; the raised events can trigger execution of composite applications when something of interest such as purchase order creation or new employee hire occurs in the system. We cover this topic in detail in Chapter 15 along with a worked example on how to use EDN to integrate to and from Fusion Applications. But before we start exploring the customization and extension methods, let us have a look at some of the most common scenarios and interaction patterns that involve SOA components and service engines in Fusion Applications.

Typical Interaction Patterns with SOA Composites in Fusion Applications

Oracle SOA tools and methodologies are used extensively in Fusion Applications. We have already mentioned the event processing use case, but there are many others like the use of the Human Workflow component typically in approvals and other notification-driven tasks, the use of the Mediator component to enable edge integration with third-party systems, the use of BPEL as an asynchronous programming technique

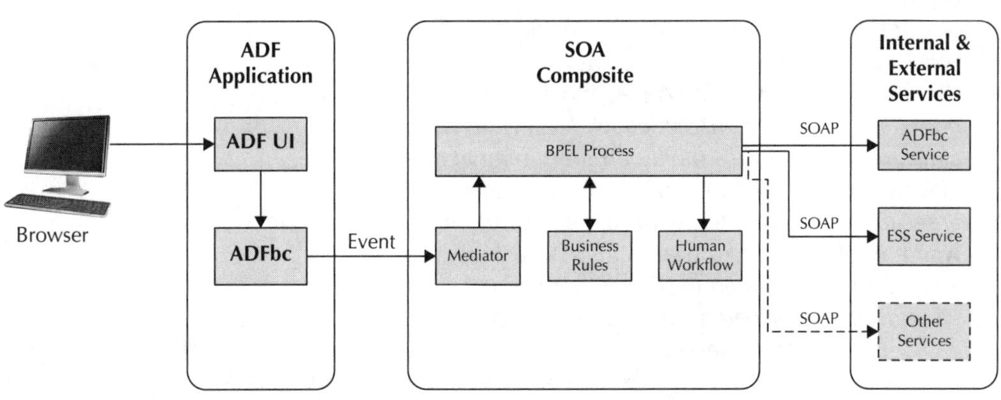

FIGURE 10-1. *An example of event-driven integration between SOA and ADF applications*

in long-running BPEL batch jobs, the use of BPEL in process flows, the use of the Business Rules component in Approval Management Extensions (AMX), and so forth.

Figure 10-1 shows an example of an interaction scenario involving an SOA composite.

In this example an end user interacts with an application's user interface (ADF UI) and at some point, for example, when a button to confirm some action is clicked, a business event is raised from Oracle ADFbc (ADF Business Component), which in turn is consumed by the Mediator component in the SOA composite that is subscribed to that event.

Every event has a unique name and associated data structure that describes the event. Developers and application designers can use different techniques including Java and PL/SQL APIs to raise a business event when something interesting happens in their application and they want other applications to be able to subscribe to them. This approach was also exploited in Oracle E-Business Suite, but in Fusion Applications you'll quite often see that the entity object (EO) in an underlying ADFbc component is configured to publish business events, and this happens at run time when an EO data row instance is created, updated, or deleted.

Figure 10-1 also shows the interaction between BPEL process and external or internal services such as Enterprise Scheduler Service (ESS) and ADFbc services. Of course, this is just an example use case, and both BPEL and Mediator components can interact with a wide variety of other services such as Web services that implement a Service Data Object (SDO) interface, services based on Oracle SOA adapters like file, database, Java Messaging Service (JMS) adapters, and so on.

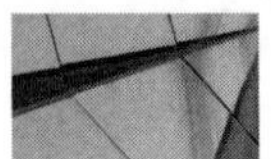

NOTE
The Service Data Object (SDO) specification for programming data architecture was originally developed by IBM and BEA (see more details at http://www.jcp.org/en/jsr/detail?id=235). Its main aims are to unify and simplify programming across different data sources. In Fusion Applications, SDOs are usually implemented with ADFbc components, which implement SDO specification interfaces. They are easily created in JDeveloper using ADFbc wizards and deployed as an ADFbc service interface archive to WebLogic Server.

Some of the other interaction patterns that are not shown in Figure 10-1 are invocation of SOA (BPEL) synchronous composites via JAX-WS client applications, BPEL orchestration of remote ADFbc services, using BPEL entity variables to update data in a Fusion Applications database, invoking a BPEL process from Enterprise Scheduler (ESS) Java jobs, interaction with Oracle Data Integrator (ODI), and many others.

Instead of just providing a seemingly endless list of SOA components' usages in Fusion Applications, let us take a deeper look into a typical SOA composite application that provides a key application functionality, examine its components, and describe its main interaction patterns.

An Example: Introducing General Ledger Journal Approvals

We have chosen the General Ledger (GL) Journal Approval process to demonstrate the use of SOA components simply because most people can associate it with the underlying business process and one of its main requirements, to be able to route approval notifications through a desired approval hierarchy. From a functional perspective, the implementation guide for Fusion Applications Financials only describes how to manage journal approval rules, but from the technical perspective we are interested what is happening under the hood of this process at both run time and design time.

Accessing and Exporting an SOA Composite

The SOA composite that drives the GL Journal Approval process is called *FinGlJrnlEntriesApprovalComposite* and it can be accessed by logging in to Enterprise Manager (EM) Fusion Applications Control for Financials Domain. Remember we mentioned in Chapter 1 that each WebLogic domain in Fusion Applications contains its own SOA server cluster; therefore, all SOA composites that relate to the Financials product offering are deployed inside the Financials WebLogic domain.

Developers, system integrators, and business analysts alike can use export functionality to download the composite of interest on their desktops as shown in Figure 10-2 and open it in JDeveloper. For readers with E-Business Suite background, this would be an equivalent of opening an Oracle Workflow item type in the Oracle Workflow Builder desktop tool for analysis, extension, and customization.

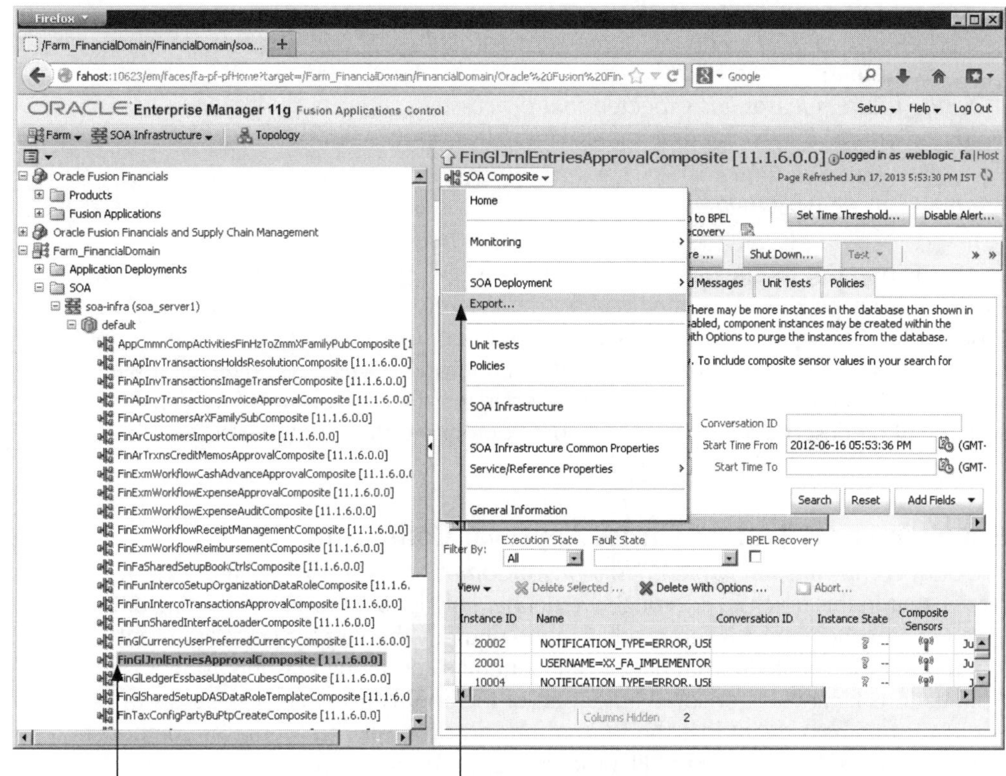

1. Highlight FinGlJrnlEntriesApprovalComposite.

2. Expand the SOA Composite menu and click the Export option to open the Export Composite page.

FIGURE 10-2. *Accessing the SOA Export Composite page from Enterprise Manager console*

NOTE
Oracle supports both BPEL and BPMN notations for describing and executing business processes. While BPEL is a part of the Oracle SOA Suite and BPMN is supported by Oracle BPM Suite, they seamlessly complement each other by sharing the same development tool (JDeveloper), Service Component Architecture (SCA) model, deployment techniques (SCA ant scripts), and management and monitoring infrastructure (Enterprise Manager console). In the current release of Fusion Applications 11.1.6, we find the use of BPEL to be the dominant approach to drive business processes, although we anticipate that in the future releases it is expected that processes based on BPMN will become more widespread in applications that require workflow and business processes orchestration.

The Export Composite page shown in Figure 10-3 provides different options for exporting a snapshot of a running composite. We select Option 1: Export with All Post-Deploy Changes and click the Export button to download the composite.

The composite can be opened with SOA Editor in JDeveloper; however, if we want to extend the composite using JDeveloper, we need to follow a few steps, which will be described later in this chapter, before we start applying design-time extensions.

Examining a GL Journal Entries Approval Composite

The SOA composite *FinGlJrnlEntriesApprovalComposite* is shown in Figure 10-4. Notice that in this quick walkthrough we deliberately ignore the error-handling branch of the composite, which is removed from the figure. When a user posts a journal batch using the Create Journal page from General Accounting Dashboard in Fusion Applications Financials, or some other part of the application that triggers a Journal Approval business event like the Journal Import process, the Mediator component *JournalApproval* launches the BPEL process *JournalApprovalDriverProcess,* which will in turn decide whether to invoke the approval BPEL process (*JournalApprovalProcess*) or post the journal batches directly (*JournalDirectPostingProcess*) without the approval depending on the decision criteria. The actual posting occurs when *EssWebService* is invoked from the composite and the *FinGlJournalApproval* human task handles

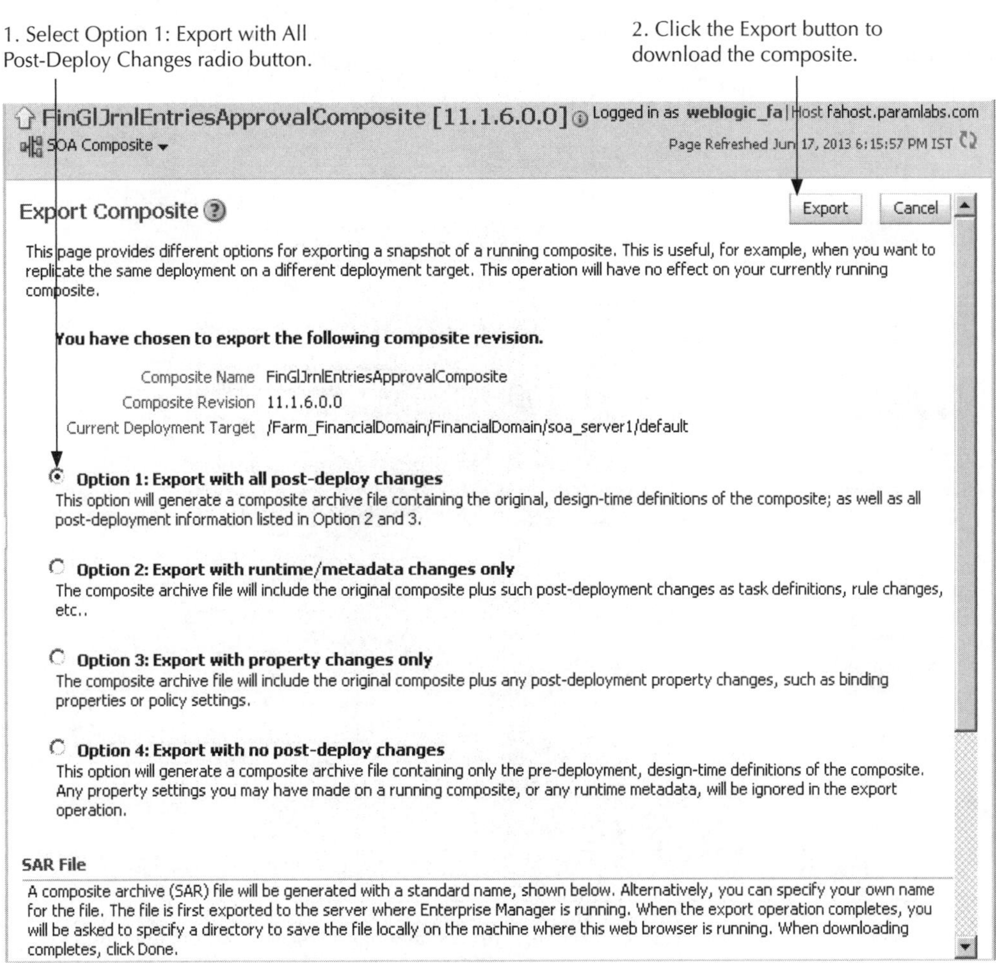

FIGURE 10-3. *Exporting an SOA composite*

interaction with end users when approval is required. Whether the journal batches require approval or not is determined by the application setup and can be observed by checking the value of the ENABLE_JE_APPROVAL_FLAG and JOURNAL_APPROVAL_FLAG columns in the GL_LEDGERS and GL_SOURCES_B tables respectively in the Fusion Applications database.

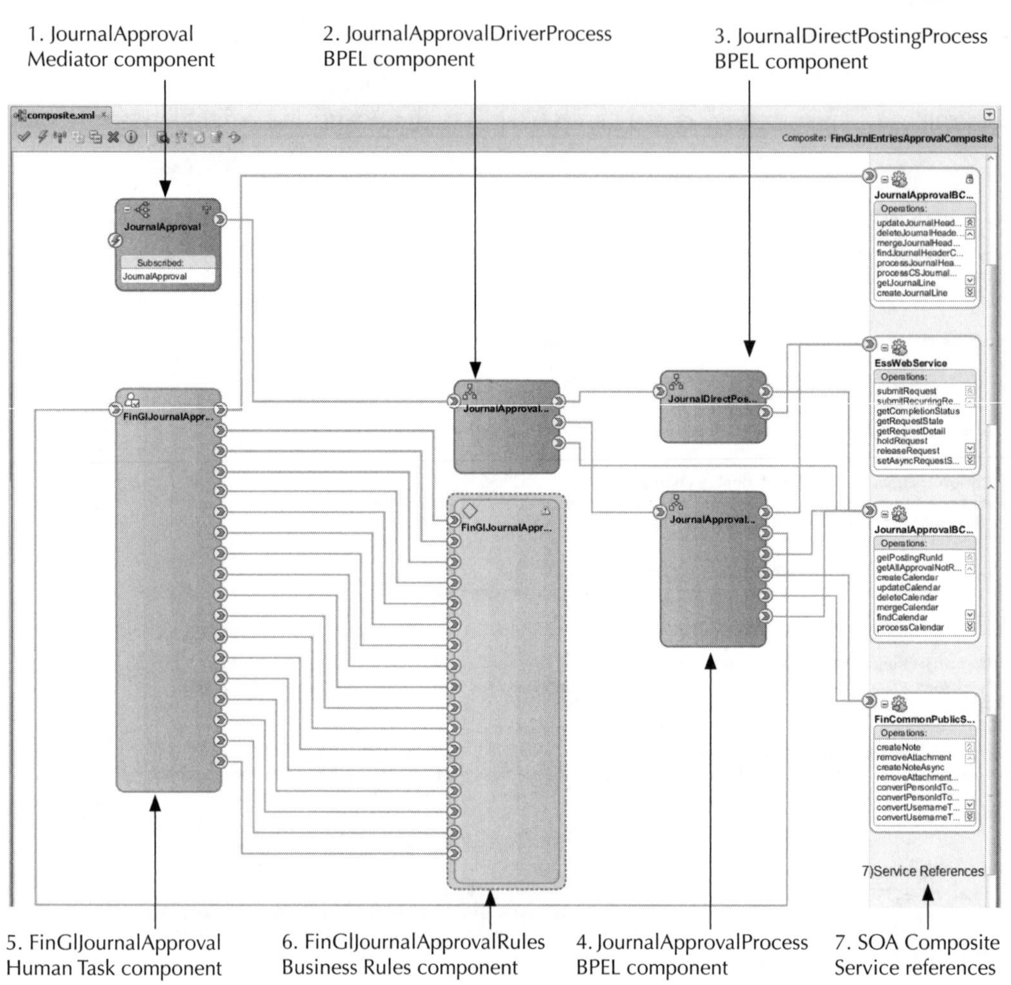

FIGURE 10-4. *GL Journal Entries Approval SOA composite*

The main part of the process consists of the Mediator, BPEL, Business Rules and Human Task components listed in Table 10-1.

Figure 10-5 shows the run-time flow trace in Enterprise Manager for an instance of *FinGlJrnlEntriesApprovalComposite* that went through the batch approval process.

Component Name	Type	Purpose
JournalApproval	Mediator	Subscribes to the JournalApproval event and initiates the process; enables event processing; and provides loose coupling by subscribing to the business events that can be raised from various sources such as ADF UI, PL/SQL, Java, and so on.
JournalApprovalDriverProcess	BPEL	Driver process flow, which accepts journalApprovalRequestMessage as input that contains references to journal batches through the batchId, batchName, action, and ledgerId attributes. Essentially, the process makes a check if an action attribute is equal to ONLY_POSTING, in which case a particular journal batch is processed and posted without the approval.
JournalApprovalProcess	BPEL	Similar to the driver BPEL process, this process also accepts journalApprovalRequestMessage. The process counts the number of journal batches in the input message and spawns that many parallel flows, which in turn execute *JournalBatchApprovalProcess* where all the action that requires approval happens. The process updates Journal Batch status code and a GL Journal Approval human task is invoked. Depending on the outcome of the approval, for example, approved or rejected, the journal batch status is again updated by invoking the *JournalApprovalBCService* ADFbc service. This same helper service is invoked to generate a Posting Run Id value just before the batch is posted by invoking the *EssWebService* service.

TABLE 10-1. *Main Components in FinGlJrnlEntriesApprovalComposite (Continued)*

Component Name	Type	Purpose
JournalDirectPostingProcess	BPEL	This process is quite similar to *JournalApprovalProcess*, but in this case the GL Journal Approval human task is not invoked on this occasion and batches are posted without going to the approval human task.
FinGlJournalApproval	Human Task	This component provides Human Workflow approval capability to the composite. The main source of data for this task is obtained by invoking JournalApprovalBCServiceForHWF service operation getJournalBatch, which provides the details about the journal batches such as Journal Header, Ledger, MaxJournalAmount, JournalSource, and so on. The task also defines a rules-based assignment of approval process participants and approval task outcome such as APPROVE or REJECT.
FinGlJournalApprovalRules	Business Rule	This component allows evaluation of dynamic decisions during the process execution such as creating a supervisory list of journal batch approvers at run time, for example, which is used by the FinGlJournalApproval human task to derive the list of approval participants on the fly. Rules are implemented as IF-THEN structures grouped into rule sets and provide human task assignments based on policies such as Supervisory Hierarchy, Job Level Hierarchy, Position Hierarchy, or even a custom Approval Group defined by a system integrator in charge of designing an approval hierarchy.

TABLE 10-1. *Main Components in FinGlJrnlEntriesApprovalComposite*

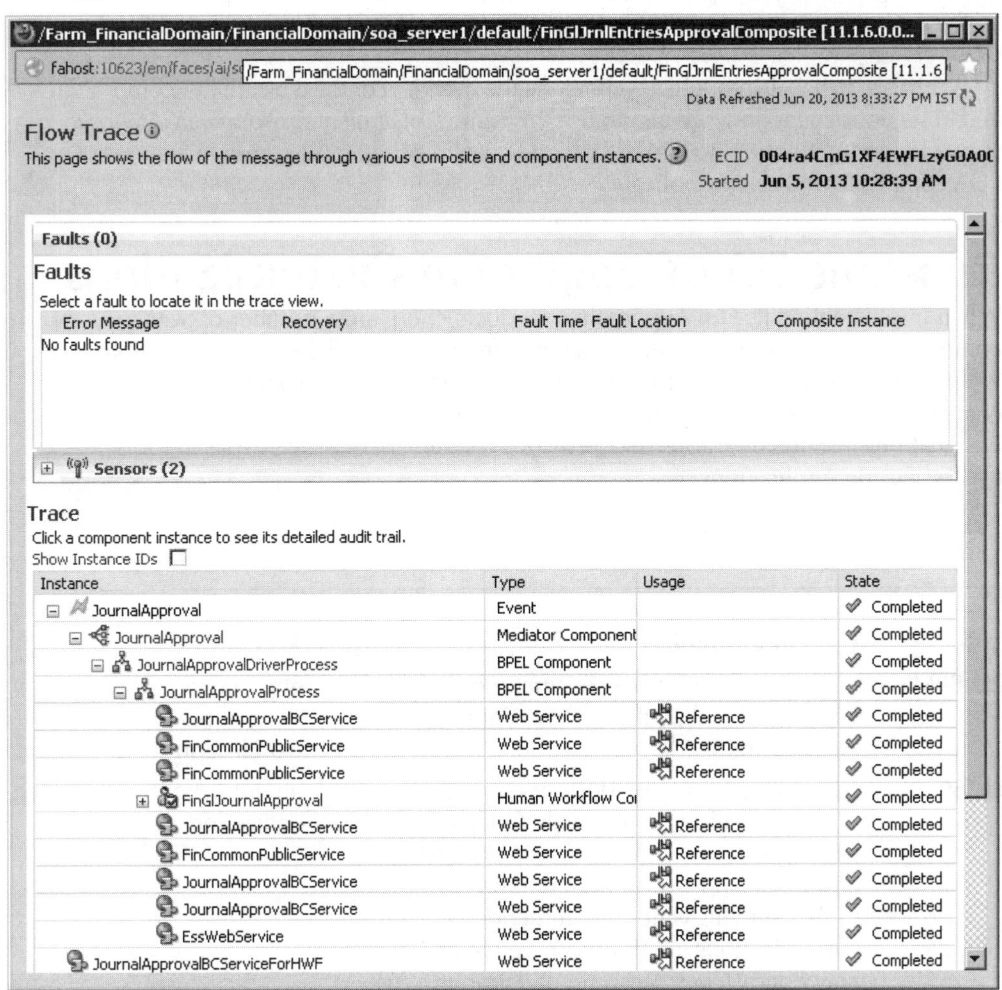

Instance	Type	Usage	State
JournalApproval	Event		Completed
JournalApproval	Mediator Component		Completed
JournalApprovalDriverProcess	BPEL Component		Completed
JournalApprovalProcess	BPEL Component		Completed
JournalApprovalBCService	Web Service	Reference	Completed
FinCommonPublicService	Web Service	Reference	Completed
FinCommonPublicService	Web Service	Reference	Completed
FinGlJournalApproval	Human Workflow Co		Completed
JournalApprovalBCService	Web Service	Reference	Completed
FinCommonPublicService	Web Service	Reference	Completed
JournalApprovalBCService	Web Service	Reference	Completed
JournalApprovalBCService	Web Service	Reference	Completed
EssWebService	Web Service	Reference	Completed
JournalApprovalBCServiceForHWF	Web Service	Reference	Completed

FIGURE 10-5. *FinGlJrnlEntriesApprovalComposite instance flow trace*

The flow of SOA components execution in the trace hierarchy for this instance of the process run shows *JournalApproval* event as initiator of the process at the very top; *JournalApprovalDriverProcess* invoking *JournalApprovalProcess*; a number of invocations to Web services to update the batch approval status, for example (*JournalApprovalBCService*), and to derive additional Financials data required for the business process (*FinCommonPublicService*); and Enterprise Scheduler Service

EssWebService to post the journal batches. Human task *FinGlJournalApproval* is aided by the data provided as a result of invoking the *JournalApprovalBCServiceForHWF* Web service.

With this brief walkthrough, we conclude the overview of the typical SOA composite and in sections that follow, we aim to use this same *FinGlJrnlEntriesApprovalComposite* to provide instructions on how to extend and customize the most common features of SOA composites in Fusion Applications.

Run-time SOA Component Customizations

When implementing Fusion Application products, there are a number of SOA components that can be customized using different browser-based customization tools at run time. By referring to run-time customizations, we mean applying changes to a deployed application on a WebLogic server that belongs to a Fusion Applications installation. Table 10-2 provides a summary of browser-based tools used in Fusion Applications.

Tool	Used to Customize	Access URL
Oracle BPM Worklist	Business rules in processes that require approvals configuration and assignment rules to be customized.	http://host:port/integration/worklistapp
Oracle SOA Composer	Non-approval-related business rules and SOA application domain value maps (lookup values). Although it is possible to customize approvals configuration in SOA Composer, this is not recommended because customizations are not preserved after applying patches. Recommendation is to use Oracle BPM Worklist application for approvals configuration and customizations.	http://host:port/soa/composer
Enterprise Manager (Fusion Applications Control)	Web service endpoint properties in SOA composite applications, Web Services Manager (WSM) security policies, and Web Services binding properties.	http://host:port/em

TABLE 10-2. *Tools for SOA Component Customizations at Run Time*

We'll now take a closer look at configuration of custom approval assignment rules, which is an activity commonly performed by system integrators and implementation consultants when implementing Fusion Applications products, but also business analysts after a project goes live and changes are required to meet new business needs.

Approvals Management, Configuration, and Assignment Rules in Fusion Applications

The approval management in Fusion Applications is no different than the approval management in Oracle SOA Suite, which is a part of its Human Workflow services—a component responsible for human interactions within a business process. Sometimes in the Fusion Applications and Oracle SOA Suite documentation, the approval management features within Oracle SOA Human Workflow services are referred to as Approval Management Extensions or AMX for short.

The main purpose of AMX is to enable routing of human tasks primarily for the purposes of approvals in business processes such as GL Journal Approval, described in the previous section. AMX supports different levels of approval complexity from a simple static list of approvers to various types of multistage patterns of approval hierarchies that include supervisory, position-based, dynamic approval groups and so on. AMX is the successor to the E-Business Suite Approvals Management (AME) and PeopleSoft Approval Workflow (AWE) engines, and it has functionality similar to that of R12 AME and PeopleTools AWE.

Fusion Applications developers use the Human Task editor in JDeveloper at design time to define a human task input data, task outcomes such as ACCEPTED or REJECTED, escalation rules, and notification delivery mechanism like an e-mail or even instant messenger. They also define task routing (approval) stages used in the approval process along with approval list builders, which are used to assign tasks at run time. Following are typical approval list builders found in Fusion Applications as described in *Fusion Middleware Modeling and Implementation Guide for Oracle BPM*:

- **Approval Groups** Includes predefined approver groups in the approver list. Approval groups can be static or dynamic.
- **Job Level** Ascends the supervisory hierarchy, starting at a given approver and continuing until an approver with a sufficient job level is found.
- **Position** Ascends the position hierarchy, starting at a given approver's position and continuing until a position with a sufficient job level is found.
- **Supervisory** Ascends the primary supervisory hierarchy, starting at the requester or at a given approver, and generates a chain that has a fixed number of approvers in it.

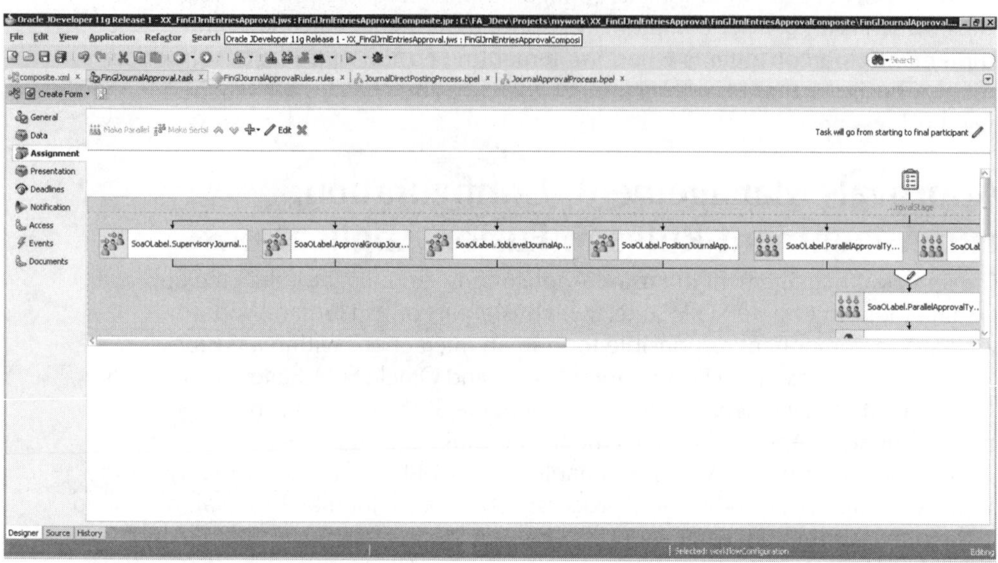

FIGURE 10-6. FinGlJournalApproval *task assignment definition in JDeveloper*

Figure 10-6 shows *FinGlJournalApproval* task and its Assignments tab when opened in JDeveloper. We can see that this task has just one stage defined as a combination of a number of sequential and parallel task participants.

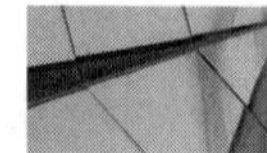

TIP

Supervisory- and position-level hierarchies are defined through Human Capital Management (HCM) configuration. If the hierarchy for a user who is expected to participate in the approval process is not set up correctly or hierarchy list builders used in rules are not providing the expected results, Fusion Applications system administrators can manually invoke HierarchyProviderService, *which is a part of the* HcmCore *application to troubleshoot the issues. The WSDL files are deployed to HCM Domain at http://host:port/hcmEmploymentCoreApprovalHierarchy/HierarchyProviderService?wsdl for supervisory hierarchy and http://host:port/hcmTreesModel/HierarchyProviderService?wsdl for position hierarchy.*

The creation of approval rules is one of the key activities during the product implementation phase, and in the next sections, we will provide simple but practical examples on how to customize business rules for approval assignments. It must also be noted that the readers who didn't have previous exposure to the approval management techniques in Oracle SOA Suite 11*g* would probably find this topic a little abstract; therefore, the best thing to do is to walk through a couple of examples.

Example 1: Creating and Using a Static Approval Group in the GL Journal Approval Process

As previously mentioned, AMX comes with a number of list builders to manage approval lists in Fusion Applications. Currently, the GL Journal Approval process comes with just one out-of-the-box predefined approval rule, and that is ManagerApprovalRule based on Supervisory list builder, which is defined as Supervisory_JournalApprovalRuleSet within the FinGlJournalApprovalRules.rules Business Rules component in *FinGlJrnlEntriesApprovalComposite* at design time. The Supervisory list builder uses Human Resources (HR) hierarchies set up in the Human Capital Management (HCM) module. For example, if a user enters and posts a journal, it will go to his manager for an approval, and this can continue for a number of levels. The number of approval levels, starting and top participant can be configured through the Task Configuration page in the BPM Worklist tool.

In our example we will use the Approval Group list builder, which is usually used for approvals and decision making outside of the managerial chain. Also, if you are working with a brand new installation of Fusion Applications, the chances are that HR hierarchies are not set up yet, but you may still need to be able to demonstrate the approval process, and by configuring and customizing JournalApprovaGroupRule, you may be able to achieve just that. Let's walk through a step-by-step example of setting up a simple static approval group.

Step 1: Ensure That Ledger Is Enabled for Approvals Functional or implementation consultants usually define journal approval for a ledger. The options that enable journal approval at the ledger level and by journal source are configured by accessing the following tasks through Functional Setup Manager (FSM) in Fusion Applications:

- *To enable journal approval for a ledger:* In FSM, search for and open the Specify Ledger Options task and check the Enable Journal Approval check box for the ledger.
- *To enable journal sources for journal approval:* In FSM, search for and open the Manage Journal Sources task and check the Require Journal Approval check box for the source to enable journal approval.

You can also validate this by querying the ENABLE_JE_APPROVAL_FLAG and JOURNAL_APPROVAL_FLAG columns in the GL_LEDGERS and GL_JE_SOURCES_B Fusion Applications database tables respectively.

Step 2: Access BPM Worklist Running on Financials WebLogic Domain to Disable Default Rule Set Oracle BPM provides the BPM Worklist application, which allows system administrators, implementation consultants, business analysts, and others to administer, configure, and customize approval and nonapproval business rules. A user needs to be assigned an appropriate role such as Financial Application Administrator (FUN_FINANCIAL_APPLICATION_ADMINISTRATOR) to be able to access the BPM Worklist application. The task customization is performed from the Task Configuration tab, which can be accessed by logging on to http(s):// :<FinancialsDomain_Host>/:<FinancialsDomain_Port>/integration/worklistapp and navigating to it by clicking the Administration link and Task Configuration tab. In the Task Configuration tab we select the FinGlJournalApproval task and click the Rules subtab, which opens a page with the heading Data Driven Configuration as shown in Figure 10-7.

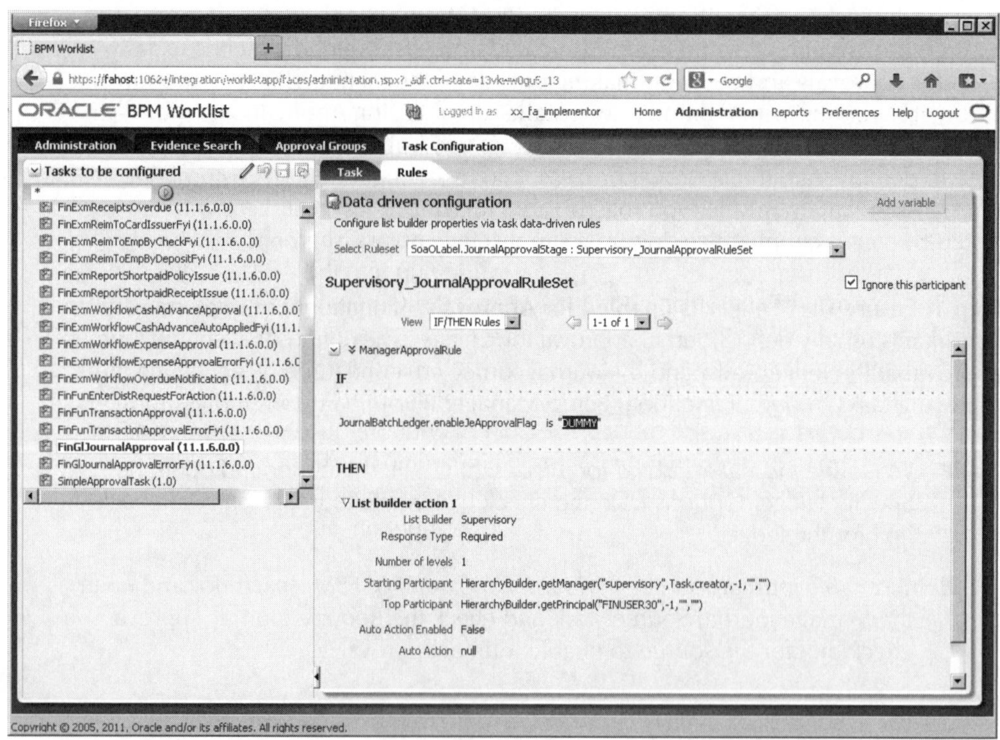

FIGURE 10-7. *Customizing a task in BPM Worklist application*

As mentioned earlier in this chapter, Supervisiory_JournalApprovalRuleSet is configured out of the box, and if your Fusion Applications instance HR Supervisory Hierarchy is not configured, an attempt to run an approvals task will result in error. Therefore, we are going to disable it by checking the Ignore This Participant check box for Supervisiory_JournalApprovalRuleSet.

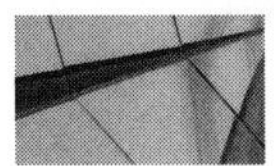

TIP
If you find that the default rule ManagerApprovalRule as part of the Supervisory rule set is still "firing" when Journal Batch needs to be approved even if the Ignore This Participant check box is checked, set the condition in the IF section of the rule that always evaluates to 'false'; for example, `JournalBatchLedger .enableJeApprovalFlag is "DUMMY"` *to work around the issue, before addressing it through Oracle Support if need be.*

Step 3: Create a Static Approval Group Approval groups are created by accessing the Approval Groups tab in the BPM Worklist application as shown in Figure 10-8 and saving it to the database by clicking the Apply button.

Okay, our static approval group that we called XxGlStatic_ApprovalGroup is very simple and it consists of only one member user called xx_gl_approver. This is hardly a requirement you will find in real-life implementation, but we are merely demonstrating the principles here.

Step 4: Assigning a Custom Approval Group to Approval Group List Builder Now when we have saved our custom static approval group into the database, we can use it in Approval Group List Builder within ApprovalGroup_JournalApprovalRuleSet as demonstrated in Figure 10-9.

Notice that we have also set a business rule test inside JournalApprovaGroupRule to evaluate at run time if JournalBatchLedger.enableJeApprovalFlag is set to a value of "Y" (you need to surround the letter Y with the double quotes as shown in Figure 10-9). In addition to that, the Ignore This Participant check box is unchecked to enable our rule, and also we need to commit the changes by clicking the Commit Task button, which is situated to the right of the Save button, after which the following pop-up message will be displayed:

"The Rules defined for the list builders of this task are committed successfully"

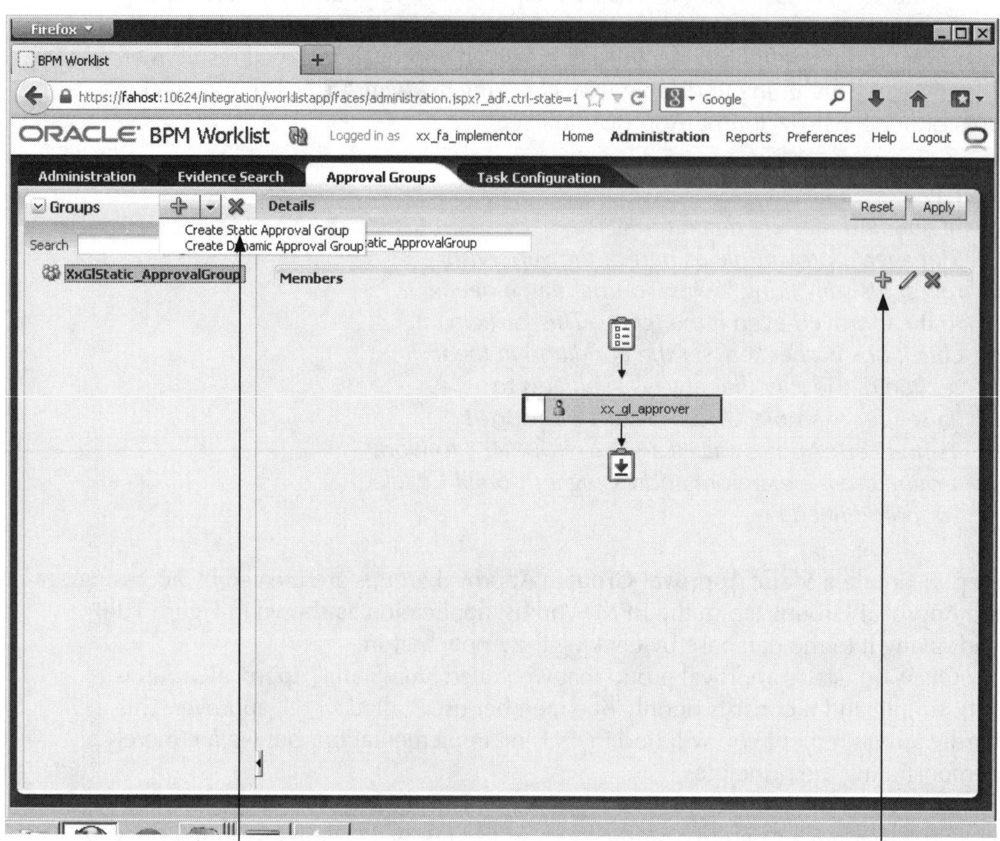

FIGURE 10-8. *Creating a static approval group*

Now we can proceed to test whether the changes we introduced have produced the desired effect; for example, we are expecting the xx_gl_approver user to be assigned an approval task after successfully submitting a journal batch for approval.

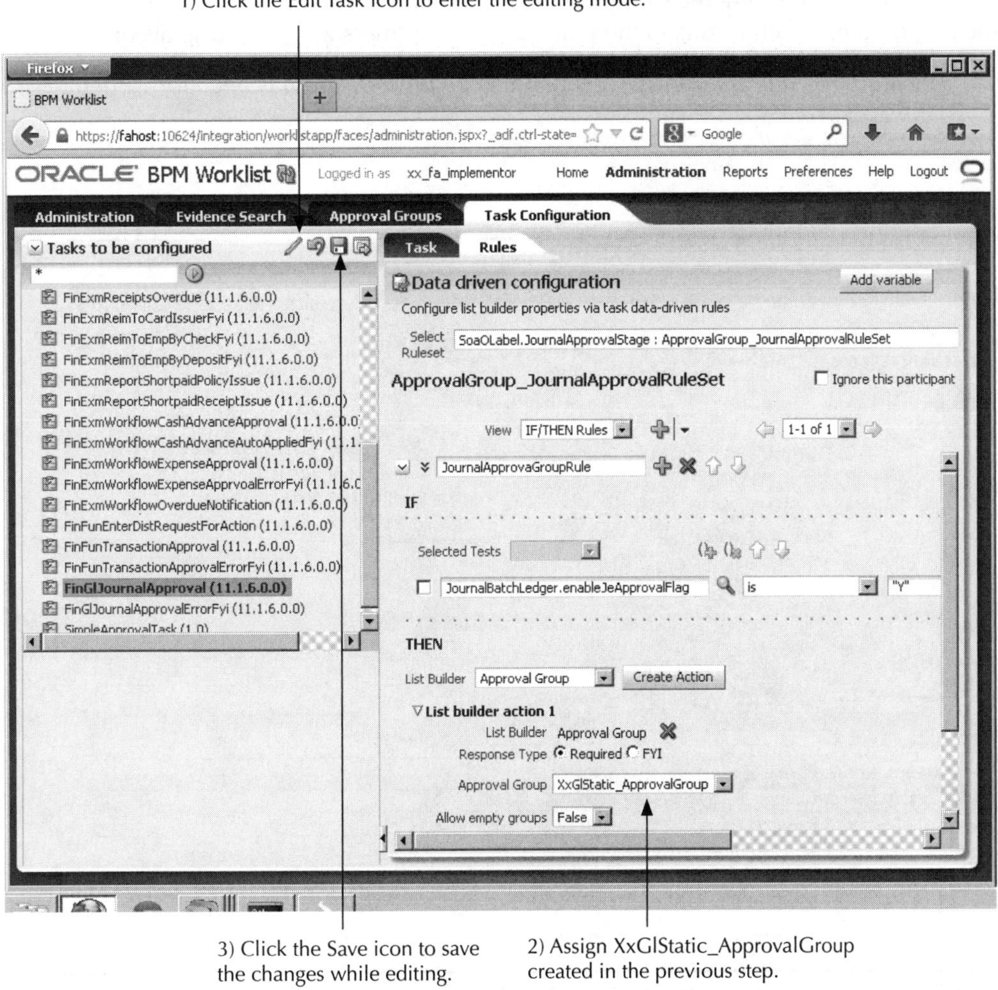
1) Click the Edit Task icon to enter the editing mode.
3) Click the Save icon to save the changes while editing.
2) Assign XxGlStatic_ApprovalGroup created in the previous step.

FIGURE 10-9. *Customizing ApprovalGroup_JournalApprovalRuleSet*

Step 5: Submitting a Journal Batch for Approval and Verifying the Approval Rules Changes In this step we log in to Fusion Applications as a user who has access to the Create Journal screen from, say, the General Accounting Dashboard. In our case that is the XX_FA_IMPLEMENTOR user and we enter the journal batch as demonstrated in Figure 10-10.

Before posting the journal batch named Test 005 in Figure 10-10, we first need to complete it by clicking the Complete button and then post the journal by clicking the Post button, which results in the following pop-up message being displayed:

> *"The journal requires approval before it can be posted, and has been forwarded to the approver."*

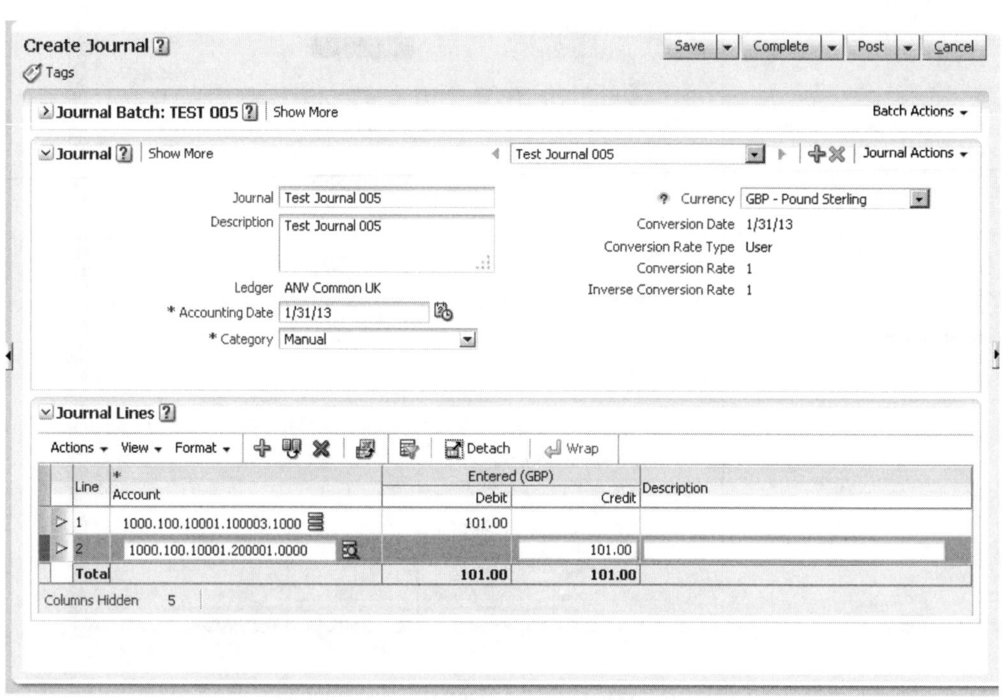

FIGURE 10-10. *Creating a sample journal for approval*

If we now log in as the XX_GL_APPROVER user, we should see in the home page application a notification informing us about the pending task that needs to be actioned, as illustrated in Figure 10-11. Clicking the Journal Batch TEST 005 for the XX_FA_IMPLEMENTOR link in the Worklist region will open a task page, which will allow us to review the journal batch details before approving or rejecting it (shown in Figure 10-12).

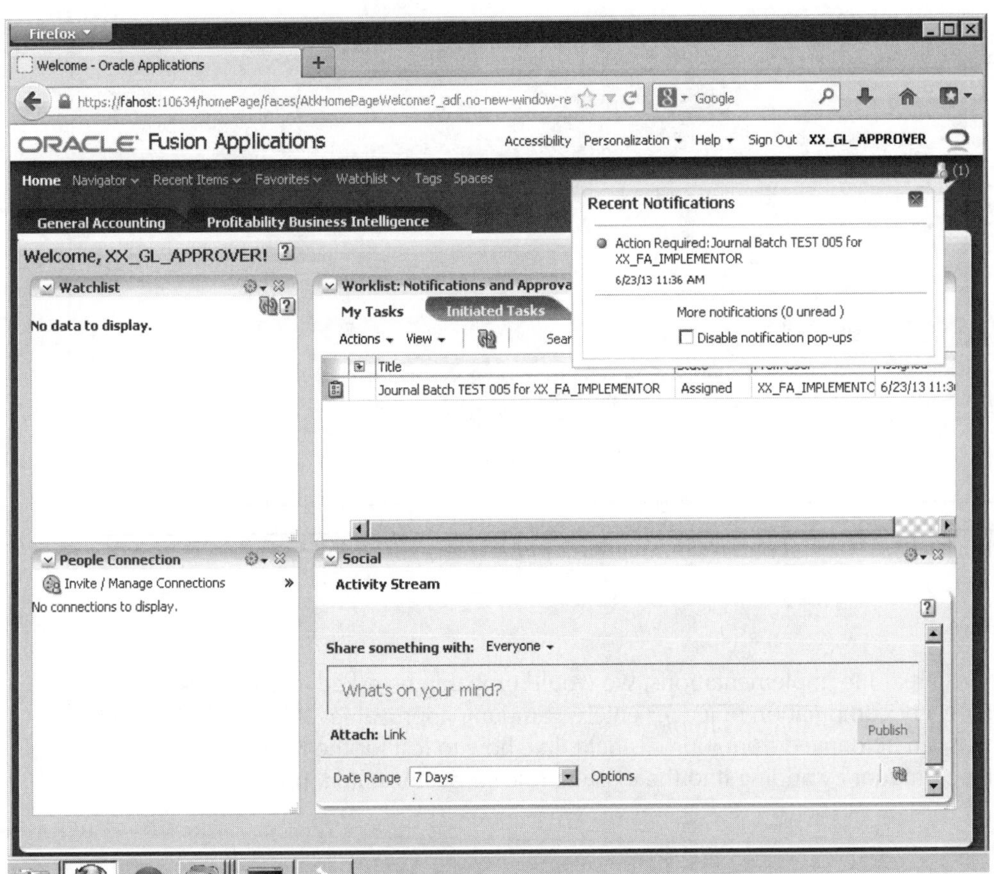

FIGURE 10-11. *Approver as defined in custom approval group is assigned approval task.*

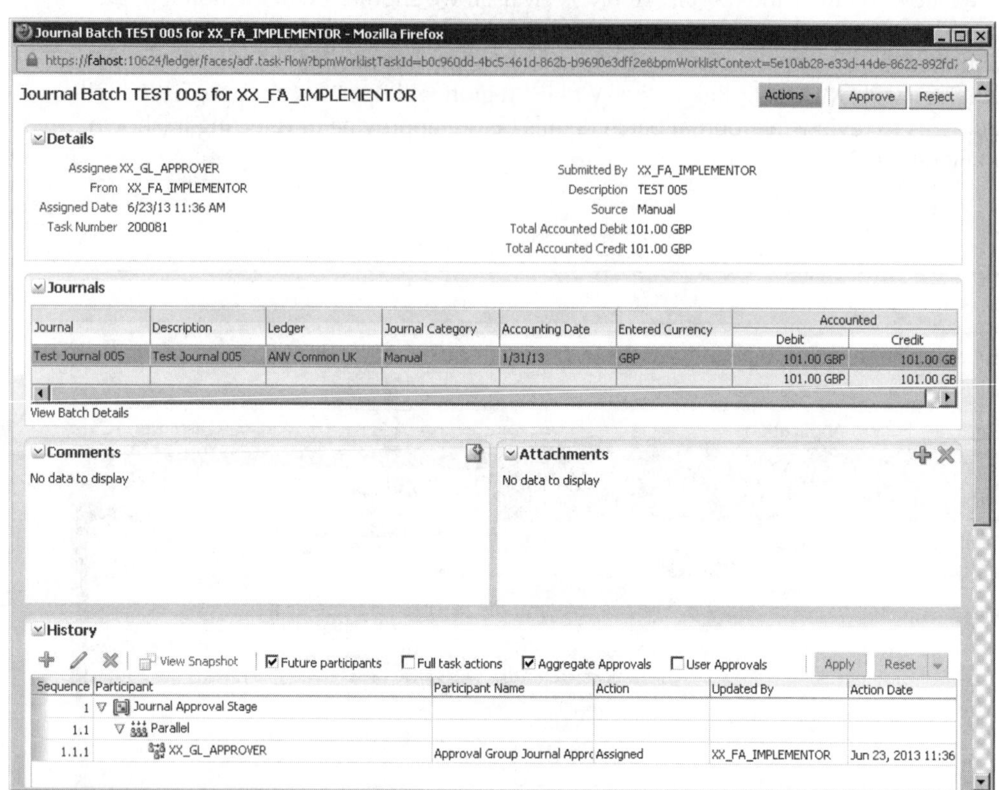

FIGURE 10-12. *Journal Batch approval task in BPM Worklist application*

In real-life implementations, we would probably be asked to build custom rules for every combination of ledger entered amount, approval level, and other attributes that can be derived from journals data, like how to test for the Maximum Journal Line Amount by adding it to the existing rule set as illustrated in Figure 10-13.

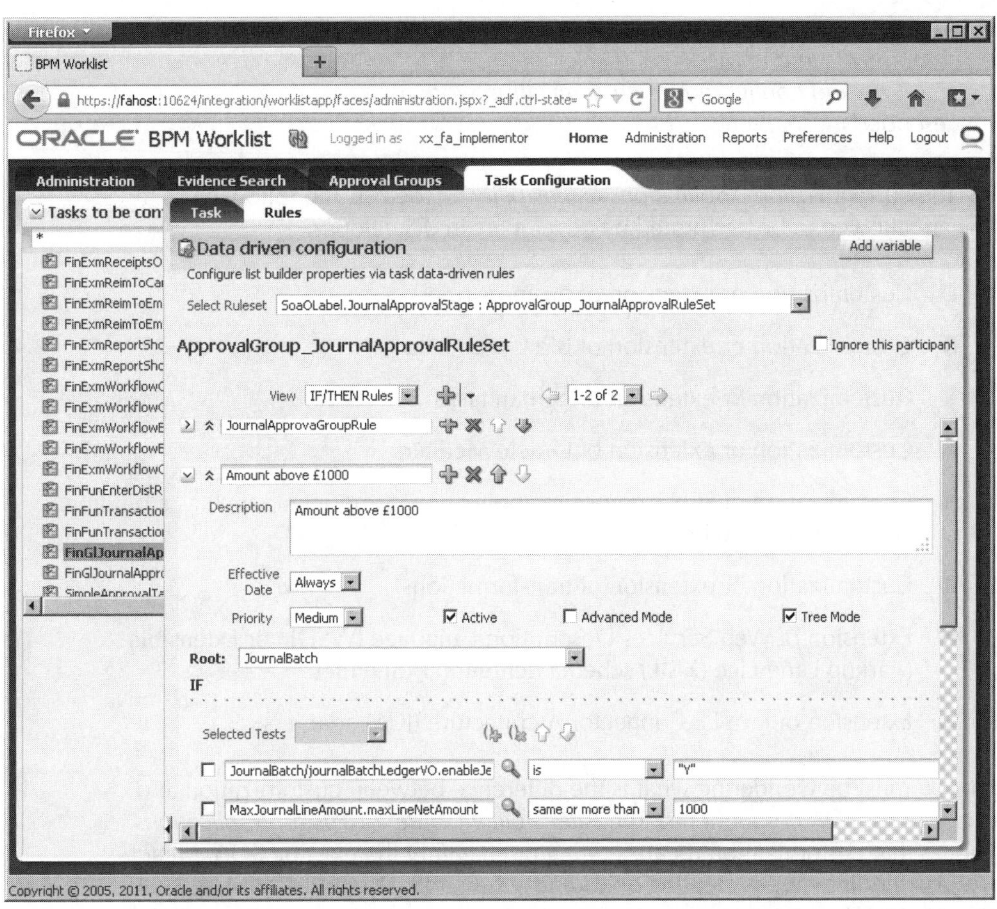

FIGURE 10-13. *Adding rule tests and conditions*

Design-time Customizations

The design-time customizations and extensions are performed by developers in the JDeveloper tool. At design time, developers have far more options for what to customize or extend; for example, while BPEL and Mediator components can't be customized and extended with run-time tools, it is possible to do so with JDeveloper at design time.

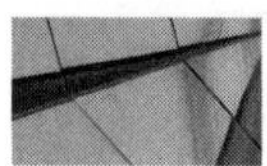

NOTE
To perform design-time customizations of SOA components and composites, JDeveloper needs to be set up and configured for customization work as described in Chapter 7.

The current *Fusion Applications Extensibility Guide* lists the following as tasks that are allowed to be performed by developers in JDeveloper:

- Customization or extension of business rules
- Customization or extension of BPEL processes
- Customization or extension of human tasks
- Customization or extension of Oracle Mediator
- Customization of SOA composite application components such as a binding component and wire
- Customization or extension of transformations
- Extension of Web Services Description Language (WSDL) or Extensible Markup Language (XML) schema definition (XSD) files
- Extension of Java EE Connector Architecture (JCA) adapters

So, you must be wondering what is the difference between customization and extension of SOA components? The *Extensibility Guide for Fusion Applications* implies that customization means editing or changing the existing SOA artifact, while extending means creating or adding a new artifact into the existing SOA composite. We are not going to get into the semantics of this; instead, we'll take a look at an example in which we'll set up JDeveloper to work with SOA customizations at design time and provide some examples.

Setting Up JDeveloper to Customize and Extend SOA Composites

Prior to starting work on customization or extension of SOA composites, it is important to understand that JDeveloper with Fusion Applications extensions must be set up as explained in Chapter 7. We'll work on *FinGlJrnlEntriesApprovalComposite* as it was the case so far in this chapter, and what follows is the list of steps we need to perform in order to get ready for SOA composite customizations in JDeveloper.

Step 1: Export the FinGlJrnlEntriesApprovalComposite

We have already covered this step in the section "Accessing and Exporting an SOA Composite" (see the earlier Figure 10-3). Just as a reminder, we need to log in to the Enterprise Manager Fusion Application Control console in the relevant WebLogic Server domain, which in our example is the Financials domain. Here we can expand the SOA folder under Farm_FinancialsDomain and select *FinGlJrnlEntriesApprovalComposite* for export by right-clicking on it. We select Option 1: Export with All Post-deploy Changes as shown in Figure 10-3 and we also make sure to select the Export With Default Archive Name option under the SAR File heading.

Once we have the exported archive file on our desktop, we are ready to open it in JDeveloper and proceed with the next step. The version of this composite on our installation is sca_FinGlJrnlEntriesApprovalComposite_rev11.1.6.0.0.jar.

Step 2: Import the Composite into JDeveloper for Customization

Open JDeveloper configured for Fusion Applications customizations and select the Oracle Fusion Applications Developer role.

NOTE
You'll usually get prompted during the startup to select the role in JDeveloper, but if that is not the case, you can go to Preferences | Roles to select the appropriate role when working in JDeveloper. JDeveloper will ask you to restart it after you select the new role from the Preferences window.

Create a generic application called XXFIN_FinGlApprovalComposite, for example. We don't need any projects configured in this application, as we'll create it from the SOA composite archive as shown in Figure 10-14.

3) When the Import SOA Composite wizard opens, give **FinGlJrnlEntriesApprovalComposite** as the Project Name, and this should match the name of the composite we are customizing. Click the Next button.

4) Use the Browse button to find the exported SOA composite sca_finGlJrnlEntriesApprovalComposite_rev11.1.6.0.0.jar. Make sure that Composite Name is set to FinGlJrnlEntriesApprovalComposite and that Import For Customization is checked.

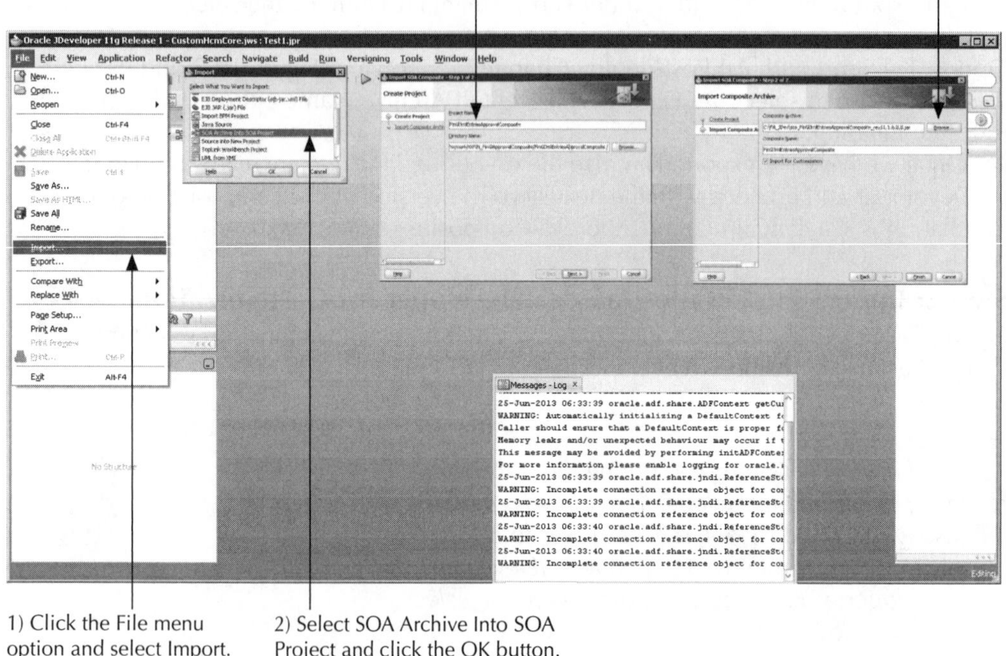

1) Click the File menu option and select Import.

2) Select SOA Archive Into SOA Project and click the OK button.

FIGURE 10-14. *Importing the composite into JDeveloper for customization*

In JDeveloper go to File | Import, and in the Import pop-up window, select SOA Archive Into SOA Project and click the OK button. This action will launch the Import SOA Composite wizard, which allows us to create the FinGlJrnlEntriesApprovalComposite project. Click the Next button to progress to the second step in the wizard where we browse for the exported sca_finGlJrnlEntriesApprovalComposite_rev11.1.6.0.0.jar file from the Enterprise Manager console in the earlier step and give **FinGlJrnlEntriesApprovalComposite** as the composite name. We must be sure to check the Import For Customization box as illustrated in the figure.

JDeveloper should open the composite in the editor, but we need to switch the role from Oracle Fusion Applications Developer to Oracle Fusion Applications

Administrator Customization by going to Tools | Preferences | Roles from the JDeveloper menu or restarting JDeveloper and selecting Oracle Fusion Applications Administrator Customization on startup.

Step 3: Configure adf-config.xml

Before we configure adf-config.xml, we'll add the Applications Core library to the project as shown in Figure 10-15.

Now we proceed with configuring adf-config.xml to include the MDS Connection details and enable customizations. Normally, the adf-config.xml can be configured

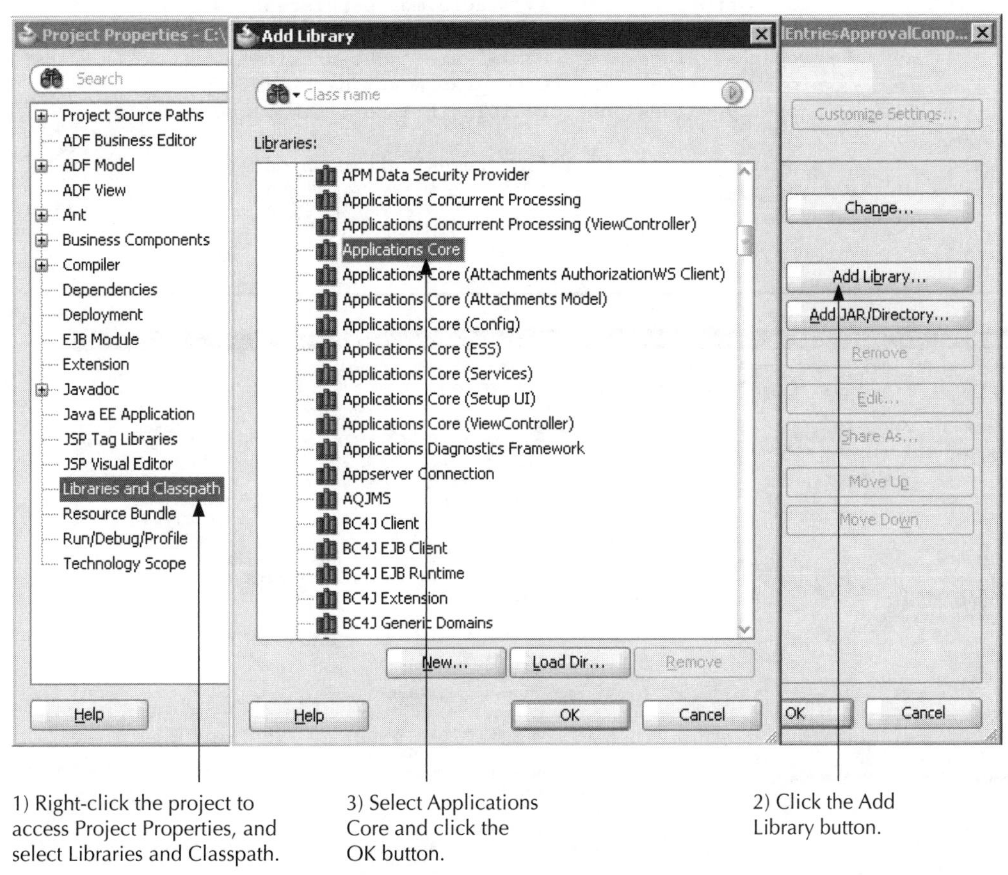

FIGURE 10-15. *Adding the Applications Core library to the FinGlJrnlEntriesApprovalComposite project*

through the user-friendly interface in JDeveloper, but to add MDS connection details, we need to perform this task by modifying the XML source directly. Access adf-config.xml through Application Navigator | Application resources | Descriptors (see Figure 10-16).

The /apps path needs to be added to the MDS configuration section by adding the following line in adf-config.xml:

```
<namespace path="/apps" metadata-store-usage="mstore-usage_2"/>
```

Inside the <metadata-store-usages> tag, we need to add the following:

```
</metadata-store-usage>
           <metadata-store-usage id="mstore-usage_2">
            <metadata-store class-name="oracle.mds.persistence.stores
.db.DBMetadataStore">
              <property value=<MDS_SCHEMA> name="jdbc-userid"/>
              <property value="<MDS_SCHEMA_PASSWORD> name="jdbc-password"/>
              <property value="jdbc:oracle:thin:@<host_name>:<port>:<SID>
name="jdbc-url"/>
              <property value="soa-infra" name="partition-name"/>
            </metadata-store>
          </metadata-store-usage>
```

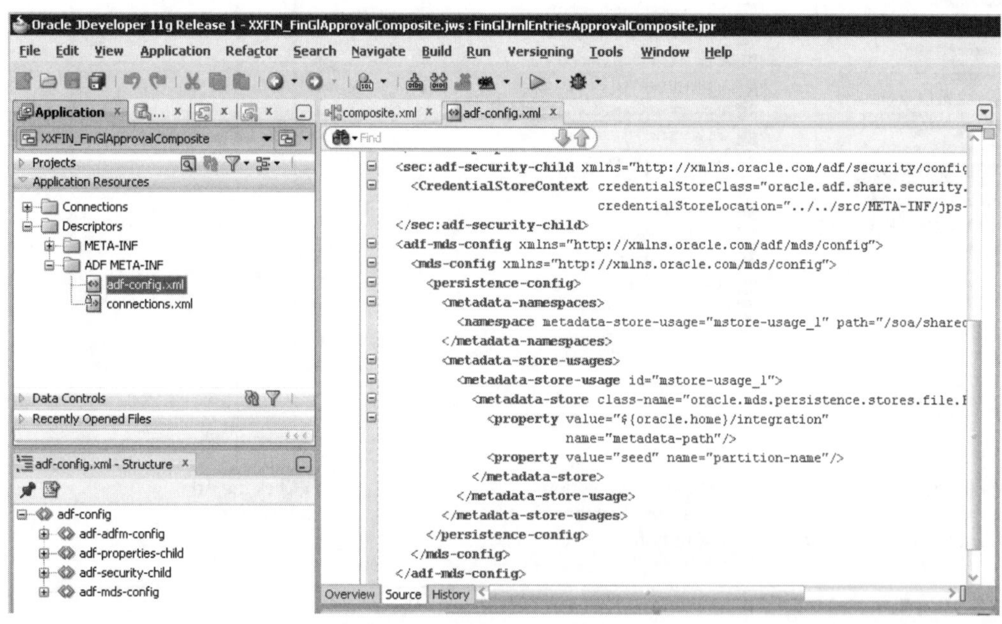

FIGURE 10-16. *Configuring adf-config.xml in JDeveloper*

where <MDS_SCHEMA> is the name of the Oracle database schema, for example, FIN_FUSION_MDS_SOA; <MDS_SCHEMA_PASSWORD> is the password for that schema; and <host_name>:<port>:<SID> are the details related to the JDBC connect string for the database where the MDS schema is installed.

Here is an example for your reference of our adf-config.xml file in the following listing:

```
<?xml version="1.0" encoding="UTF-8" ?>
<adf-config xmlns="http://xmlns.oracle.com/adf/config"
            xmlns:config="http://xmlns.oracle.com/bc4j/configuration"
            xmlns:adf="http://xmlns.oracle.com/adf/config/properties"
            xmlns:sec="http://xmlns.oracle.com/adf/security/config">
  <adf-adfm-config xmlns="http://xmlns.oracle.com/adfm/config">
    <defaults useBindVarsForViewCriteriaLiterals="true"
              useBindValuesInFindByKey="true"/>
    <startup>
      <amconfig-overrides>
        <config:Database jbo.locking.mode="optimistic"/>
      </amconfig-overrides>
    </startup>
  </adf-adfm-config>
  <adf:adf-properties-child xmlns="http://xmlns.oracle.com/adf/config/properties">
    <adf-property name="adfAppUID" value="XXFIN_FinGlApprovalComposite-5647"/>
  </adf:adf-properties-child>
  <sec:adf-security-child xmlns="http://xmlns.oracle.com/adf/security/config">
    <CredentialStoreContext credentialStoreClass="oracle.adf.share.security.providers
.jps.CSFCredentialStore"
                            credentialStoreLocation="../../src/META-INF/jps-config
.xml"/>
  </sec:adf-security-child>
  <adf-mds-config xmlns="http://xmlns.oracle.com/adf/mds/config">
    <mds-config xmlns="http://xmlns.oracle.com/mds/config">
      <persistence-config>
        <metadata-namespaces>
          <namespace metadata-store-usage="mstore-usage_1" path="/soa/shared"/>
          <namespace path="/apps" metadata-store-usage="mstore-usage_2"/>
        </metadata-namespaces>
        <metadata-store-usages>
          <metadata-store-usage id="mstore-usage_1">
            <metadata-store class-name="oracle.mds.persistence.stores.file
.FileMetadataStore">
              <property value="${oracle.home}/integration"
                        name="metadata-path"/>
              <property value="seed" name="partition-name"/>
            </metadata-store>
          </metadata-store-usage>

           <metadata-store-usage id="mstore-usage_2">
            <metadata-store class-name="oracle.mds.persistence.stores
.db.DBMetadataStore">
```

```
                <property value="FIN_FUSION_MDS_SOA" name="jdbc-userid"/>
                <property value="Param123" name="jdbc-password"/>
                <property value="jdbc:oracle:thin:@192.168.1.151:1521:fusiondb"
name="jdbc-url"/>
                <property value="soa-infra" name="partition-name"/>
              </metadata-store>
            </metadata-store-usage>
          </metadata-store-usages>
        </persistence-config>
      </mds-config>
    </adf-mds-config>
</adf-config>
```

Now when we are connected to MDS, we need to add a customization class to the MDS configuration. To do that, in the Overview tab we click the plus (+) icon to add or edit customization classes. We search for GlobalCC and add the oracle.apps .fnd.applcore.customization.GlobalCC class as shown in Figure 10-17.

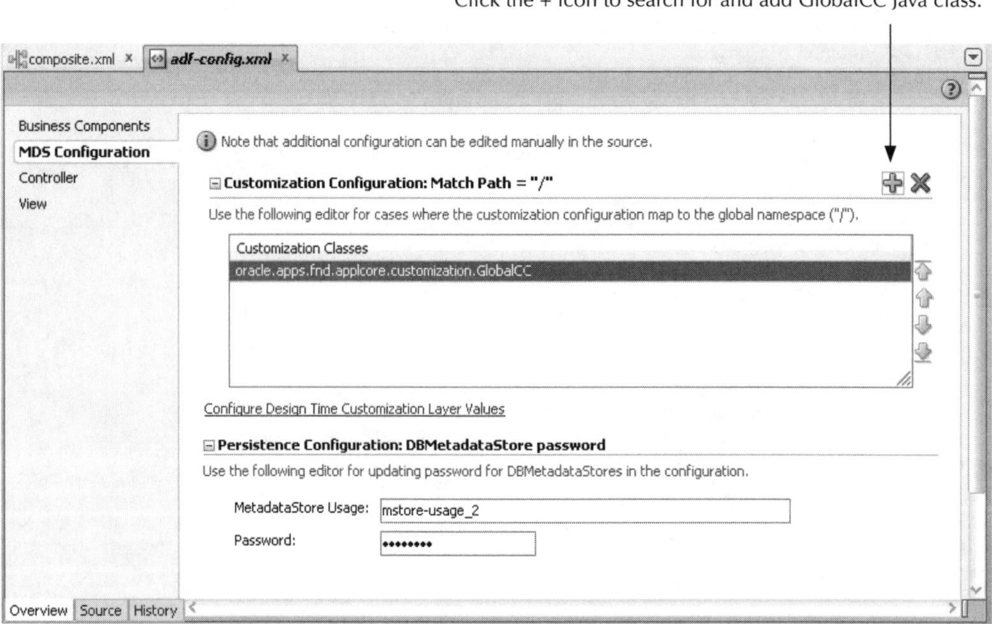

FIGURE 10-17. *Adding GlobalCC customization class to MDS configuration*

NOTE

Oracle Fusion Middleware applications such as ADF and SOA use the Meta Data Services (MDS) framework to create customizable applications. This allows customers to make changes and modifications that suit their particular business or other needs on different levels (global, site, industry and so on). Fusion Applications provide customization classes and layers to support the customizations of metadata content. To customize SOA composites, developers that perform customizations must specify the customization layer and its value, which allows them to be recognized by JDeveloper. Customization features are only enabled when working in the Oracle Fusion Applications Customizations Administrator JDeveloper role. A customized SOA application contains base SOA composite as well as customized metadata content, which is fetched at run time so that customizations can be applied.

After restarting JDeveloper in the Oracle Fusion Applications Administrator Customization role, we are ready to start customizing when we select the customization context by going to the View menu option in JDeveloper, clicking on Customization Context, and selecting Customization Context, which is Global in our case (Figure 10-18).

An Example of Extending and Customizing SOA Components

Fusion Applications provides a summary of what SOA components render themselves for customization or extensions. For example, we should be able to add (extend) JCA File Adapter to the existing (base) SOA composite and wire it to a Mediator component, which is part of the base composite. Creating this wire between the file adapter and Mediator component will automatically add a static routing rule in the existing mediator (customization) as demonstrated in Figure 10-19.

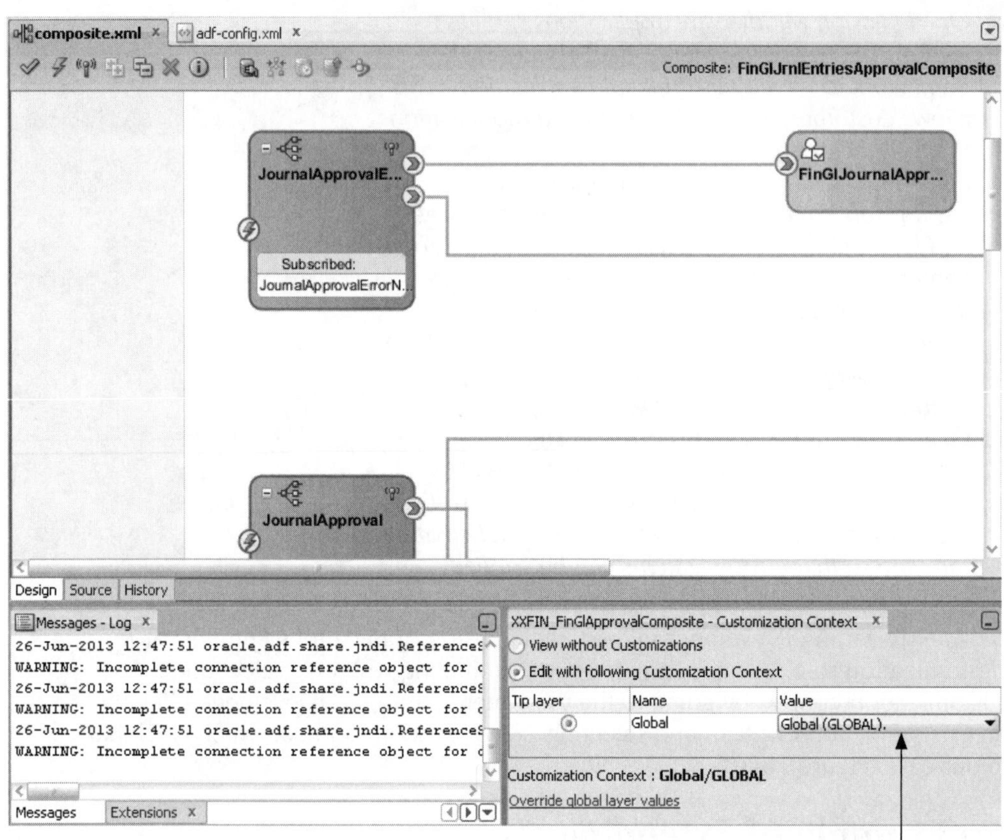

FIGURE 10-18. *Selecting a customization context in JDeveloper*

If we hover above the little star icon inside the added static routing rule, it will inform us that it is created by the current customization context. For the full list of components that are either customizable, extensible, or both, it is best to consult Oracle's *Extensibility Guide for Fusion Applications* as this is an official product documentation and any customizations outside the scope of this document are not supported.

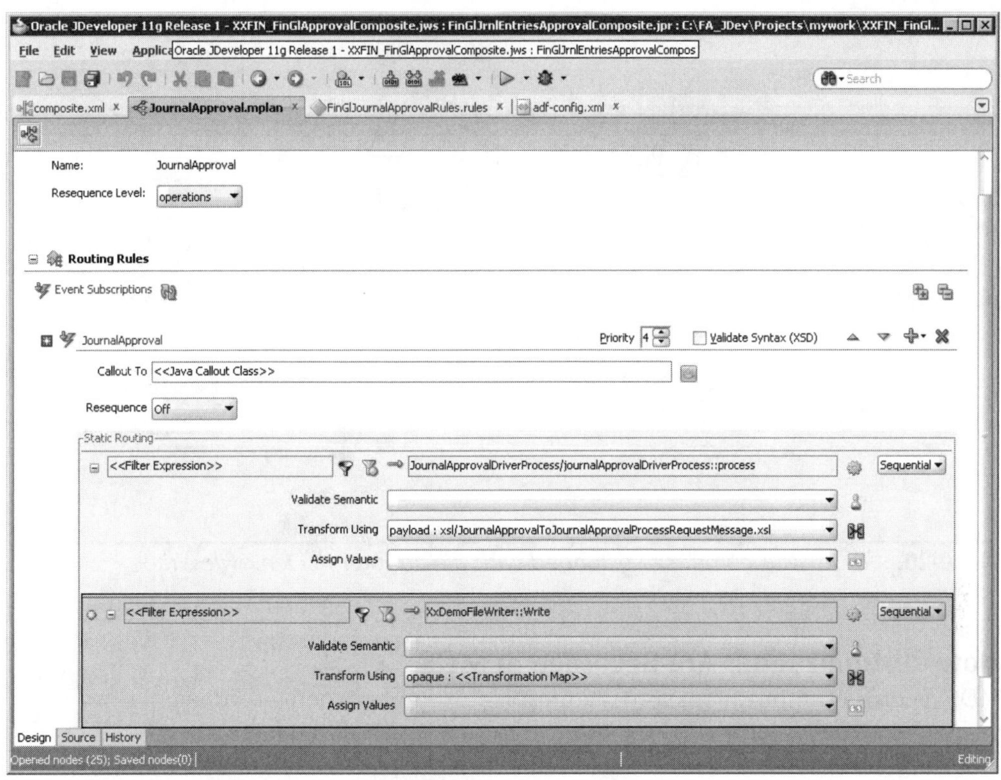

FIGURE 10-19. *Customizing a Mediator component*

In this example we have added XxDemoFileWriter to the FinGlJrnlEntriesApprovalComposite and configured it to write the data passed to it into the /tmp directory on the server where SOA Server is running. Figure 10-20 shows the wiring between the mediator JournalApproval that receives business events when journals are posted to the general ledger.

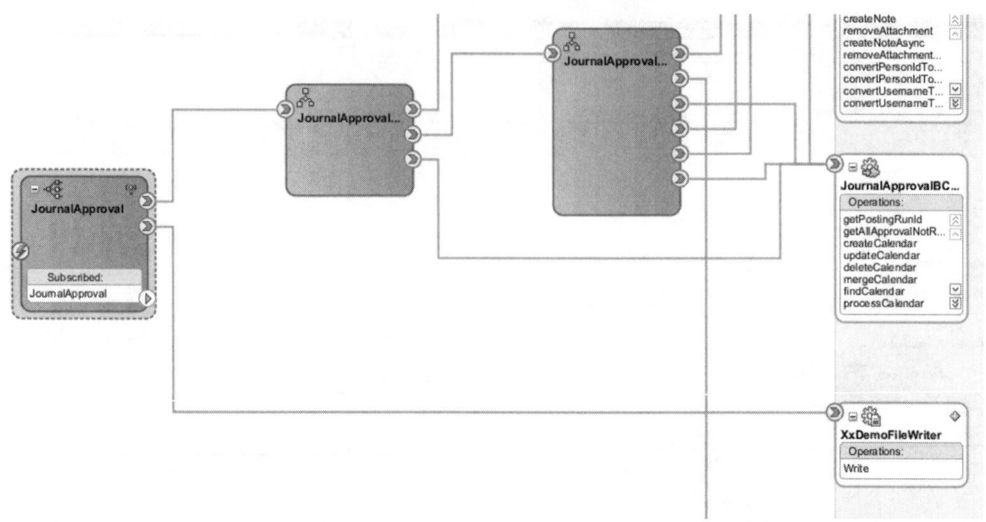

FIGURE 10-20. *Base SOA composite extended with file adapter XxDemoFileWriter*

How Customizations Are Recorded in MDS

MDS records customizations as delta files. For example, when we added the XxDemoFileWriter and wired it to the JournalApproval mediator, the following files are created under the XXFIN_FinGlApprovalComposite\FinGlJrnlEntriesApprovalComposite\mdssys\cust\Global\GLOBAL project directory by JDeveloper:

- composite.xml.xml
- JournalApproval.componentType.xml
- JournalApproval.mplan.xml

Notice that we are performing the changes in the global customization context, but it could be site, industry, or others. These delta files document the changes introduced by performing the customization of the base composite, and here is their content:

```
composite.xml.xml
<mds:customization version="11.1.1.63.91"
                   xmlns:mds="http://xmlns.oracle.com/mds">
  <mds:insert after="id_85" parent="id_1">
    <reference name="XxDemoFileWriter" ui:wsdlLocation="XxDemoFileWriter
.wsdl"
```

```
               xml:id="Global_186" xmlns="http://xmlns.oracle.com/sca/1.0"
               xmlns:ui="http://xmlns.oracle.com/soa/designer/">
      <interface.wsdl interface="http://xmlns.oracle.com/pcbpel/adapter/
file/XXFIN_FinGlApprovalComposite/FinGlJrnlEntriesApprovalComposite/
XxDemoFileWriter#wsdl.interface(Write_ptt)"
                      xml:id="Global_187"/>
      <binding.jca config="XxDemoFileWriter_file.jca" xml:id="Global_188"/>
    </reference>
  </mds:insert>
  <mds:insert after="id_29" parent="id_1">
    <import namespace="http://xmlns.oracle.com/pcbpel/adapter/file/XXFIN_
FinGlApprovalComposite/FinGlJrnlEntriesApprovalComposite/XxDemoFileWriter"
            location="XxDemoFileWriter.wsdl" importType="wsdl"
            xml:id="Global_185" xmlns="http://xmlns.oracle.com/sca/1.0"/>
  </mds:insert>
  <mds:insert parent="id_1" position="last">
    <wire xml:id="Global_189" xmlns="http://xmlns.oracle.com/sca/1.0">
      <source.uri xml:id="Global_190">JournalApproval/XxDemoFileWriter</
source.uri>
      <target.uri xml:id="Global_191">XxDemoFileWriter</target.uri>
    </wire>
  </mds:insert>
</mds:customization>

JournalApproval.componentType.xml
<mds:customization version="11.1.1.63.91"
                   xmlns:mds="http://xmlns.oracle.com/mds">
  <mds:insert parent="id_1" position="last">
    <reference name="XxDemoFileWriter" ui:wsdlLocation="XxDemoFileWriter.
wsdl"
               xml:id="Global_4" xmlns="http://xmlns.oracle.com/sca/1.0"
               xmlns:ui="http://xmlns.oracle.com/soa/designer/">
      <interface.wsdl interface="http://xmlns.oracle.com/pcbpel/adapter/
file/XXFIN_FinGlApprovalComposite/FinGlJrnlEntriesApprovalComposite/
XxDemoFileWriter#wsdl.interface(Write_ptt)"
                      xml:id="Global_5"/>
    </reference>
  </mds:insert>
</mds:customization>

JournalApproval.mplan.xml
<mds:customization version="11.1.1.63.91"
                   xmlns:mds="http://xmlns.oracle.com/mds">
  <mds:insert parent="id_3" position="last">
    <case executionType="direct" name="XxDemoFileWriter.Write"
          xml:id="Global_10" xmlns="http://xmlns.oracle.com/sca/1.0/
mediator">
      <action xml:id="Global_11">
        <invoke reference="XxDemoFileWriter" operation="Write"
               xml:id="Global_12"/>
```

```
      </action>
    </case>
  </mds:insert>
</mds:customization>
```

Deploying a Customized and Extended SOA Composite

Before we can deploy our customized version of the SOA composite, we need to create a SAR file locally in JDeveloper by right-clicking on the FinGlJrnlEntriesApprovalComposite project and selecting the Deploy option. If successful, the Deployment.log file in JDeveloper will show something like this:

```
[03:10:52 PM] ----  Deployment started.  ----
[03:10:52 PM] Target platform is  (Weblogic 10.3).
[03:10:52 PM] Running dependency analysis...
[03:10:52 PM] Building...
[03:11:38 PM] Deploying profile...
[03:11:38 PM] Updating revision id for the SOA Project
'FinGlJrnlEntriesApprovalComposite.jpr' to '11.1.6.0.0'..
[03:11:58 PM] Wrote Archive Module to C:\FA_JDev\Projects\mywork
\XXFIN_FinGlApprovalComposite\FinGlJrnlEntriesApprovalComposite\deploy\
sca_FinGlJrnlEntriesApprovalComposite_rev11.1.6.0.0.jar
[03:11:58 PM] Elapsed time for deployment:  1 minute, 7 seconds
[03:11:58 PM] ----  Deployment finished.  ----
```

The compiled SOA archive file sca_FinGlJrnlEntriesApprovalComposite_rev11.1.6.0.0.jar can now be deployed using Enterprise Manager in the Financials WebLogic domain. Of course, when deploying composites from other product pillars such as Human Capital Management (HCM), we need to use the corresponding WebLogic server's Enterprise Manager to deploy the composite.

If we are to put one journal through the Financials Dashboard, we should observe that the newly deployed and customized version of *FinGlJrnlEntriesApprovalComposite* is invoking the custom XxDemoFileWriter file adapter as shown in Figure 10-21.

Patching and Upgrade Considerations

Finally, we want to mention patching and upgrading. Oracle recommends using OPatch because it preserves run-time customizations and merges a new patch update into an SOA composite application that was customized in JDeveloper at design time and run time using SOA Composer and BPM Worklist tools. OPatch is a standard tool for upgrade and patching of various Oracle system components.

However, if customizations performed in JDeveloper at design time are not supported by OPatch, patches will fail to apply to a running WebLogic server instance. There are a number of steps that Oracle recommends to preserve SOA composite JDeveloper customizations before applying the patch, and they are documented in the *Oracle Fusion Applications Patching Guide* in the section "Patching Oracle Fusion Applications Artifacts."

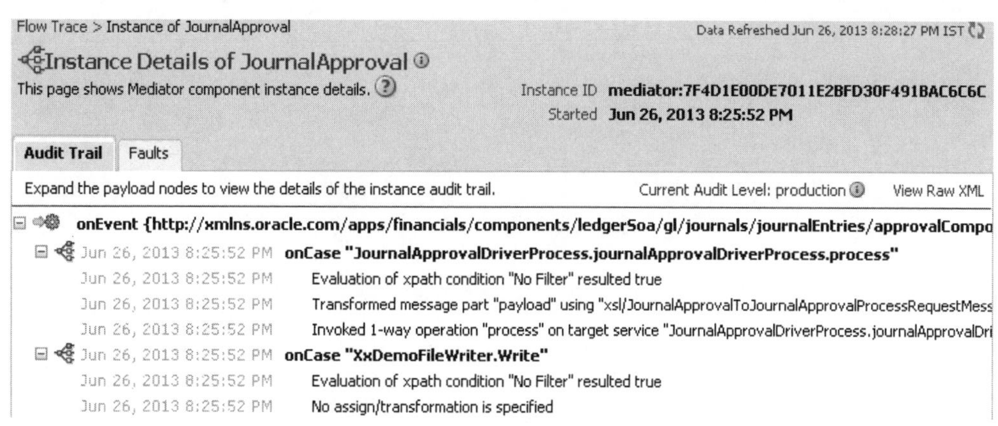

FIGURE 10-21. *Run-time audit trail from customized Mediator component*

NOTE

We should stress that developers and implementors must be fully familiar with all the recommendations outlined in the section "Patching Service-Oriented Architecture (SOA) Composites" of the Oracle Fusion Applications Patching Guide *in order to minimize the impact on system configuration that could potentially occur when customizing and extending SOA artifacts.*

Summary

In this chapter we have given an overview of the most typical interaction patterns related to SOA composites in Fusion Applications. We had a brief walkthrough of SOA tools and methodologies with emphasis on the most common ones such as Approval Management Extensions (AMX). We then introduced the General Ledger Journal Approvals process to demonstrate customization and extensibility techniques, which in our view is a fairly straightforward business process that most of us can relate to.

CHAPTER 11

Reports

In Fusion Applications it is possible for implementers to write reports with negligible programming effort. This reporting is possible on data that resides either inside Fusion Applications Oracle Database or in an external source via a Web service, or a variety of other methods.

When compared to Oracle E-Business Suite, the BI Publisher report creation process is quite different in Fusion Applications. Oracle Business Intelligence Enterprise Edition (OBIEE) comes integrated with Oracle Fusion Applications and it provides various ways to generate reports. For developers with a background in Oracle Reports Writer, the data model designer concept in Fusion Applications is very similar to the data model for the Oracle Reports tool. Both Oracle Reports and Fusion Applications allow you to create groups based on SQL statements and define relationships between groups. However, in the case of Fusion Applications, the data model builder can be accessed from the browser, which means that you do not need the database connection credentials for developing reports because SQL queries can be designed straight into the browser-based data model editor. Another key difference is that the Oracle Reports data model editor can only connect to an Oracle database for sourcing the data; however, the data model builder in Fusion Applications can source the data from a variety of sources, as discussed later in this chapter.

In this chapter you will learn the architecture and the steps for developing BI Publisher reports. This technique for developing BI Publisher reports can be applied to both SaaS (Software as a Service) and On Premise implementations of Fusion Applications.

BI Publisher Report Architecture in Fusion Applications

Conceptually, the creation of BI Publisher reports is the same regardless of the platform used, whether Fusion Applications or Oracle E-Business Suite, but the physical steps are quite different. At the back end there needs to be a source that returns the data, which is converted into valid XML; in the middle is a report template that contains the design and presentation logic; and on the front end is the BI Publisher report output in one of the supported formats. Figure 11-1 shows the architecture of the data generation using BI Publisher Report in Fusion Applications.

The three main components of BI Publisher reporting in Fusion Applications are data model, layout template, and report output as explained in the following sections.

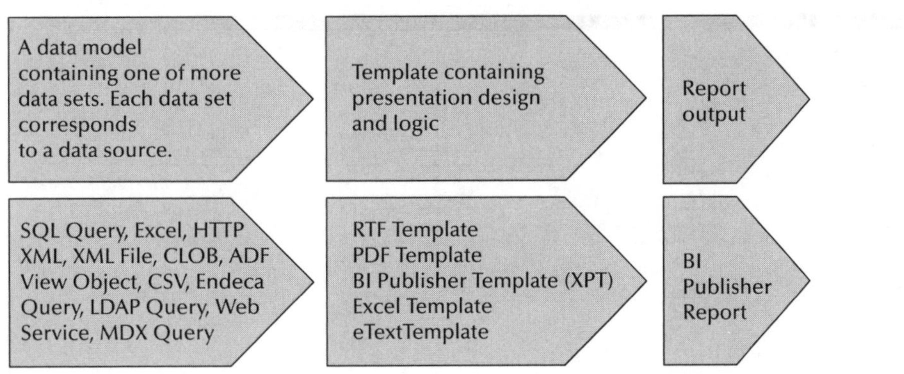

FIGURE 11-1. *Basic architecture of Fusion reporting and comparison with Oracle E-Business Suite reports*

Data Model

A data model is where the data that is to be presented in the report output is designed. You must be assigned a BI Administrator Application Role to access the data model editor in Fusion Applications. A data model contains one or more data sets. Each data set corresponds to a source of data such as SQL query, Excel, CSV, and so on. In other words, a data set contains the logic to retrieve data from the data source. Given that a data set can retrieve data from a variety of data sources, it is therefore possible for a single report to contain data from a SQL query and also from a Web service. This data returned from the source can either already be in XML format or be converted into XML format by the Fusion Applications reporting engine. In Oracle Fusion Human Capital Management, you can also generate data using product-specific functionality, such as HCM Extract, which can then be presented in a BI Publisher report.

The data model also allows you to link the data by defining master-detail relations between the data sets. This allows developers to build a hierarchical data model. You can also perform calculations and create group level totals and subtotals to aggregate the data using the data model editor. Figure 11-2 shows the data model editor in Fusion Applications when it is accessed via URL similar to http://host:port/analytics. Click the New menu, and then select a report type, following which you get the option of using an existing data model or creating a new data model or the option of uploading a data model from Excel.

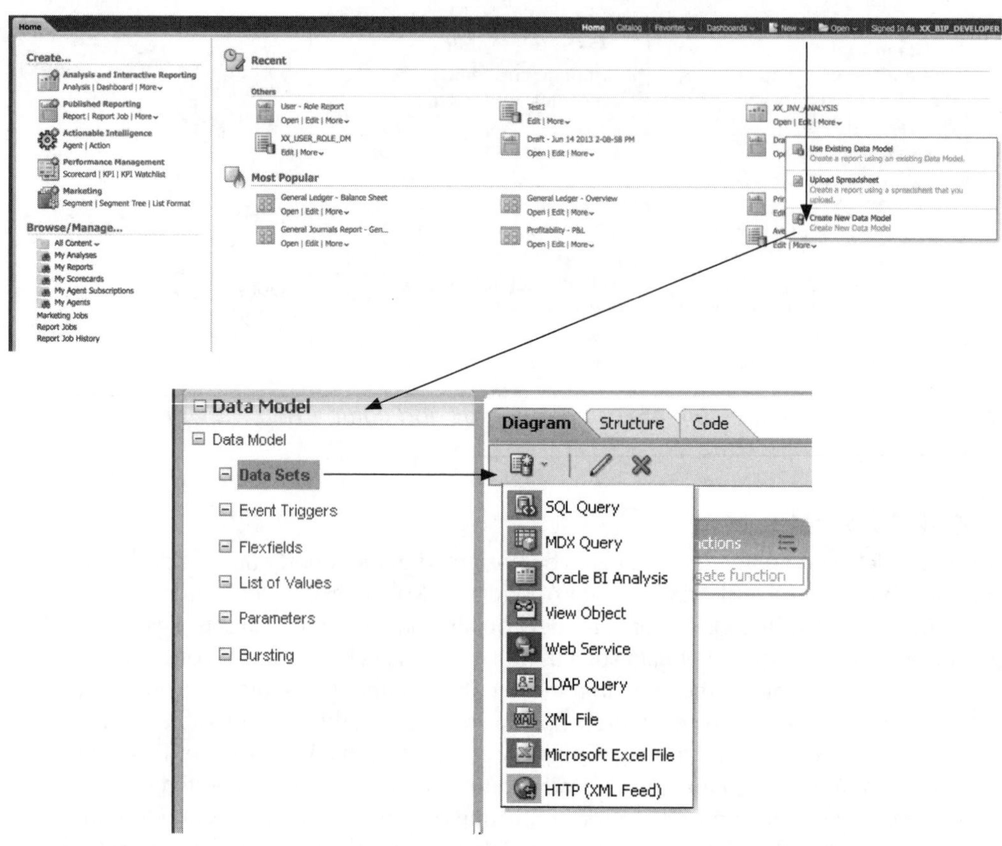

FIGURE 11-2. *Data model editor in Fusion Applications*

As shown in Figure 11-2, the components of the data model are

- Data Sets
- Event Triggers
- Flexfields
- List of Values
- Parameters
- Bursting

Data Source and Data Set

A data set is based on a data source that is responsible for fetching the desired data for reporting. Therefore, a BI Publisher data source may need to be configured by your administrator before you can begin using the data set. The list of data sources that can be created are shown in the following list. By default the data source for the Fusion Transaction Database is preconfigured for Financial Supply Chain Management, HCM, and CRM. Therefore you will notice that the data sources ApplicationDB_FSCM, ApplicationDB_HCM, and ApplicationDB_CRM are configured out of the box in Fusion Applications. A data source for the OBIEE server is also configured out of the box for developing BI Publisher reports in Fusion Applications. Your administrator can configure further data sources depending on the list of source systems from which you wish to report data in a Fusion Applications BI Publisher report. The following types of data sources can be created:

- **JDBC Connection** The connect string, userid, and password of the database are required to configure this connection. When using third-party JDBC drivers, the corresponding JDBC driver must be installed by your Administrator and should be available in the WebLogic Server classpath.
- **Database Connection Using a JNDI Connection Pool** A connection pool is set up in the application server and is identified by Java Naming and Directory Interface (JNDI). You can specify the JNDI name to create the data source.
- **LDAP Server Data Source** In order to prepare BI Publisher reports to produce data from an LDAP server, you first need to configure the connection to that LDAP server. This can be done by configuring hostname, port, username, password, and JNDI Context Factor Class.
- **OLAP Data Source** In order to connect to an OLAP server, its connect string, username, password, and OLAP type must be entered when creating the data source.
- **File Data Source** If you want BI Publisher reports to be written directly on top of Excel files, CSV files, or XML files, then the directory containing those files must be configured as a data source. The full directory path on the server should be entered and it should be given a user-friendly name.

To configure data sources, log in to http://host:port/xmlpserver, click Administration in the top-right corner, and you will then find a section to configure Data Sources in the top-left section of the page.

For each data source, you can specify the roles that have access to that particular data source. For example, you may want only a particular role to be allowed for developing reports in Microsoft Excel or XML files from a specific folder that contains strategic finance or annual performance bonus data. Alternatively, you can enable the public access to the data source by enabling the Allow Guest Access check box. This will allow any Fusion Applications role to use that data source for reporting.

A data set can be created after the data source has been either identified or configured. In Oracle Fusion Applications, BI Publisher supports various types of data sets, as shown in Table 11-1.

Data Set Based On	Description
SQL Query	Allows you to write a SQL query for retrieving data from the Fusion Applications Oracle Database. It is also possible to use the Query Builder option for constructing the SQL queries. Query Builder presents you with a GUI to design in the data model editor without you having to write the SQL query. The implementers can select tables and required columns from those tables and build joins without being SQL experts.
MDX Query	These are the queries written against an OLAP database. This type of query allows you to query multidimensional objects such as cubes and return multidimensional cellsets that contain cube data.
BI Analysis	Allows usage of the Oracle Business Intelligence Presentation catalog as a data source. The BI analysis internally issues a SQL query against Oracle BI Server. Fusion Applications comes prepackaged with BI analysis reports for a list of predefined objects. This allows analysis of data objects, and this analysis is sometimes referred as BI Answers. Parameters and list of values are inherited from the BI analysis and they display at run time.
ADF View Objects	The view objects defined in ADF can be used as a data source for BI Publisher reports. The advantage of using this approach is that the data security policies defined in Oracle Authorization Policy Manager can be applied at the time of retrieving the data. In order to select the view objects, you first need to enter the full path of the Application module such as xx.apps.hcm.entity.applicationModule.AppraisalAM and then click the Load View Objects link to select the view object. Finally, you can create and map parameters for each bind variable.
Web Service	You can specify the WSDL of the Web service along with the method name that returns the XML data to be presented in a BI Publisher report. Parameters can be added and the response from the Web service can be tested in real time from the data model editor by selecting Get XML Output.

TABLE 11-1. *Different Data Sets Supported by Fusion Applications BI Publisher* (*Continued*)

Data Set Based On	Description
LDAP Query	You can write queries against Lightweight Directory Access Protocol (LDAP) data sources by specifying the LDAP attribute names to be reported on, along with filter conditions.
XML File	When setting up the data sources, you can define a file directory as a data source. XML files can be placed in that folder and then be used for developing BI Publisher reports to report against the XML data.
Microsoft Excel File	In a manner similar to XML files, Excel files can be used as the data source for BI Publisher reports.
HTTP (XML Feed)	You can develop BI Publisher reports on the data returned by RSS feed by creating a data set for RSS feed. In order to create this data set, you need to select the feed URL, Method=GET, and optionally enter the username, password, realm, and parameters.

TABLE 11-1. *Different Data Sets Supported by Fusion Applications BI Publisher*

NOTE
In addition to the data sets listed in Table 11-1, Oracle also has added capabilities for reporting from CSV and Endeca-based data sources. An Oracle Endeca data source can be used for running queries to extract meaningful information from unstructured data. These features were added in the 11.1.1.7 version of BI Publisher 11g and we anticipate they will soon be available in Fusion Applications.

SQL queries and the BI analysis are the most commonly used data sets for developing reports in Fusion Applications. The prepackaged data sources used for running SQL queries against the Fusion database connect to a schema named FUSION_RUNTIME.

Event Triggers

You can conditionalize the execution of a scheduled report based on an event. To implement this option, you can define an event trigger of type=Schedule. This event trigger can be associated with a SQL query. If this SQL query returns no record, then a scheduled run of the report will not be executed. Therefore, just prior to running the scheduled job, the associated SQL in the event trigger is executed. If no data is returned from the SQL, then the report job run instance is skipped. If data is returned, the job instance runs as scheduled. One example of this feature is where you wish to e-mail the exceptions of a nightly batch process. If there are no exceptions in the error table, then you can skip the running of the exception listing report. On similar lines, you may wish to skip the execution of a scheduled import process if there is no data in the corresponding interface table.

You can also write your custom PL/SQL code to be executed before or after the execution of data. The Before Data trigger is executed before the data set is executed, and the After Data trigger is executed after the BI Publisher engine has generated the XML from all the data sets within the data model. The PL/SQL function used for these triggers must return a Boolean. In an SaaS-based environment, the customers are not allowed to write their own PL/SQL, and therefore there is a restriction on the usage of before and after event triggers for SaaS customers for their custom reports.

Flexfields

Flexfields allow customers to create new fields for either a code combination such as an accounting code combination or to capture additional information. A flexfield can have various structures, with each structure representing the different field combinations. The data model editor supports retrieving data from flexfield values using a lexical tag &LEXICAL_TAG. For example, to display General Ledger Accounting Flexfield segment values in a BI Publisher report, you will create a flexfield named XX_ACCT_FLEX in the data model under the Flexfields node as shown in Figure 11-3. Next you will assign Application Short name=GL, and ID Flex Code=GL# with the "ID Flex Number" being assigned from a parameter passed to the report at run time. To display all the segments of the flexfield in the report, enter **Segments =ALL** and **Output Type=Value**. Next, in the SQL statement of the data model, you will enter `select &XX_ACCT_FLEX,....from...where....` On similar lines, the Flexfield lexical value can also be used in the WHERE clause or the ORDER BY clause of the SQL statement, as shown in Figure 11-3.

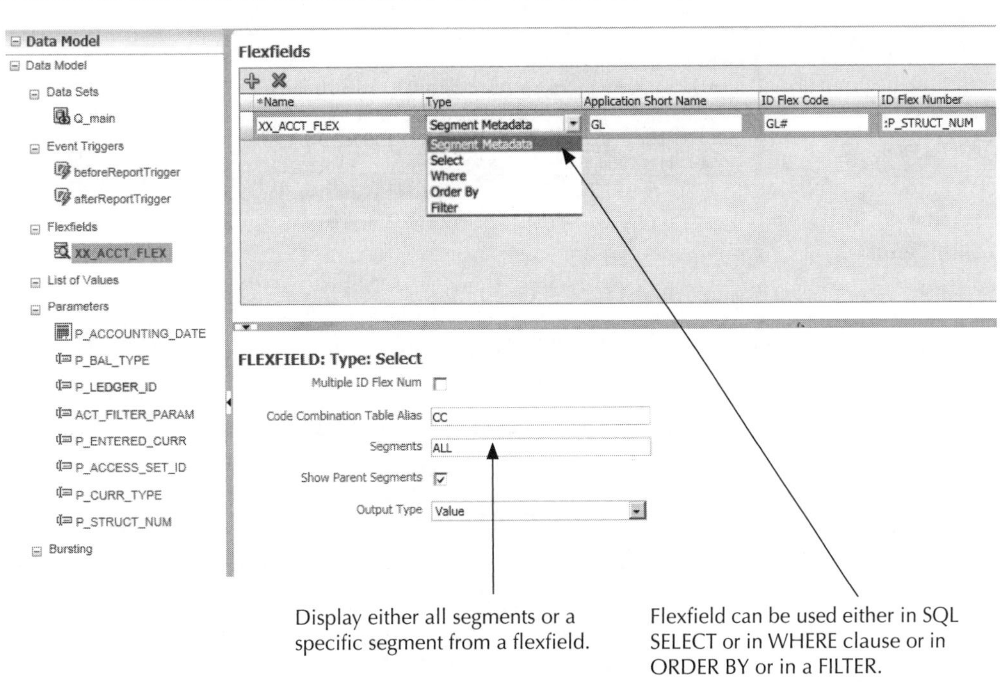

FIGURE 11-3. *Using a flexfield in reporting data model*

Lists of Values

A list of values can be created from a SQL query as shown in Figure 11-4. You can write a SQL query to retrieve data or you can provide static values to a list of values. A list of values is generally used for report parameters if you want to restrict the user from entering a wrong value into the parameter.

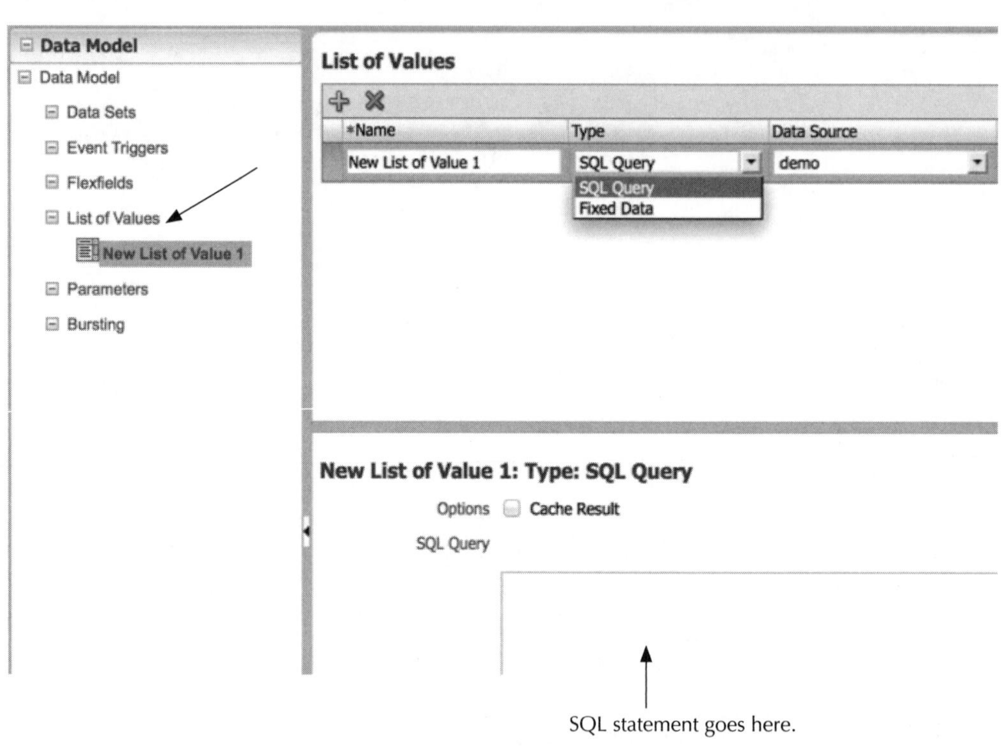

FIGURE 11-4. *List of values can be defined to be used by report parameters.*

Parameters

A parameter is used to pass values to the report at run time. A parameter can be of three types, Text, Menu or Date, as shown in Figure 11-5. When the parameter type is set to Menu, then you will be prompted to enter the name of the List of Values defined as per Figure 11-5.

Parameter Type Text You can enter any free text value if you create a text type of parameter. You can restrict the number of characters to be entered in the text field using the "Text Field Size" field if you want validation of text length.

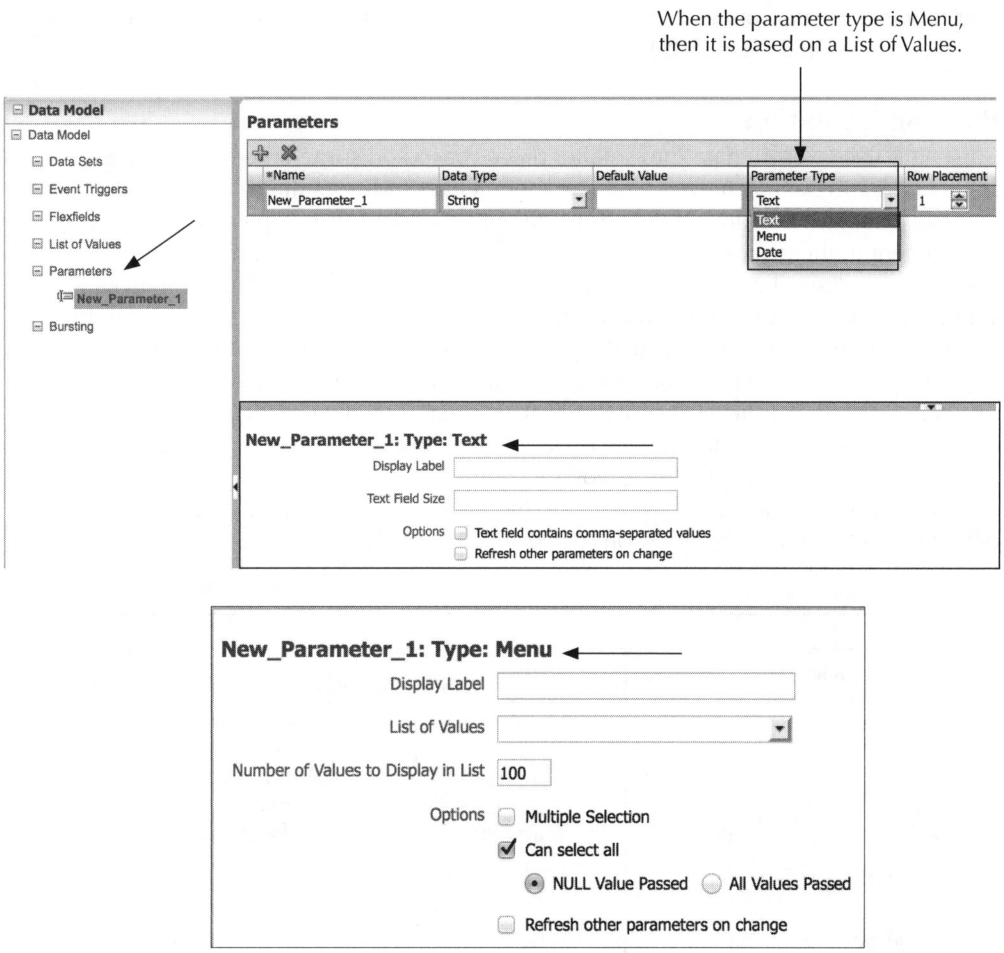

FIGURE 11-5. *Define the parameter for the report.*

Parameter Type Menu If you choose the Parameter Type menu, then you will have the option to choose a list of values. There is an option to choose multiple values from a list of values in parameter if you check the Multiple Selection check box. You can also restrict number values to be displayed in the list as shown in Figure 11-5.

Parameter Type Date You can create a date type parameter when you want the user to select a date from a calendar. To default the system date in the date type parameter, enter **{$SYSDATE()$}** in the Default value field.

Bursting Definitions

Bursting is used to split data into smaller pieces based on some criteria. After the split of data has been achieved, you can then deliver those smaller pieces of data to multiple locations. Bursting definitions contain instructions for splitting data, generating a document in the desired format for each split section, and then delivering the output to the desired destination using a desired mechanism. For example, you can split the remittance advice in payables remittance print, so that each supplier can be e-mailed the relevant payments that have been made to them. Further to that, bursting gives you the option of applying a different layout template and delivery mechanism to each split section of the XML generated by data model. In other words, there is an option for you to use a different layout for certain key suppliers. Figure 11-6 explains how bursting works.

As you might notice from Figure 11-6, the most important aspect of bursting definitions is to answer the questions listed in Table 11-2.

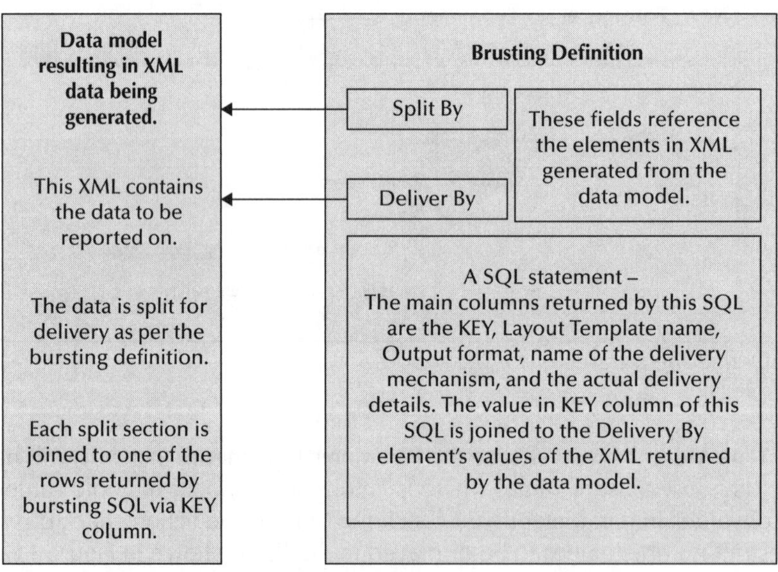

FIGURE 11-6. *Bursting architecture*

Question	Answer
How will the output be split for delivery?	By using the XML element name in the field Deliver By.
How does the system decide whether the output will be e-mailed or delivered by fax or by FTP?	The bursting definition SQL query will return a column named DEL_CHANNEL. For example, you could write a SQL query to pick the delivery channel from the supplier definition.
The data model generates an XML output. How is it joined to the SQL present in the bursting definition?	The Delivery By field in a bursting definition tells you which element of the data model XML is used for splitting the output for delivery. For example, in a remittance advice this could refer to VENDOR_ID. The SQL in the bursting definition will contain an alias named KEY for the VENDOR_ID column. For example, the value in the Delivery By XML element from the data model's data will be joined to the value in the KEY column of the bursting SQL. The corresponding record from the bursting SQL will then decide the delivery mechanism of the output.
In this example, can each supplier record have its own formatting and its own delivery mechanism?	Yes, it is possible. For example, the bursting SQL can be made to return one single record for each supplier. That record can return a different delivery mechanism and different layout format for each supplier.
FAX, e-mail, printing, and FTP require different types of values for delivery to their corresponding destination. How is this done?	The bursting SQL has a generic set of up to 10 parameters. For each delivery channel, the parameters represent a different value. When the delivery channel is e-mail, the parameter values are PARAMETER1: E-mail address PARAMETER2: cc PARAMETER3: From PARAMETER4: Subject PARAMETER5: Message body PARAMETER6: Attachment value ('true' or 'false') PARAMETER7: Reply-To PARAMETER8: Bcc PARAMETER9 & 10: Should be left blank for e-mail When the delivery channel is Fax, the parameter values are PARAMETER1: Fax Server PARAMETER2: Fax Number PARAMETER3 to 10: Should be left blank for fax. For a complete list of parameters for each delivery channel, see the Fusion Applications BI Publisher documentation on http://docs.oracle.com

TABLE 11-2. *FAQ on bursting in BI Publisher*

Figure 11-7 shows an example of the bursting definition. It must be noted that the example in the figure derives the delivery mechanism from the attribute columns of the supplier tables, which may not be the same for your implementation.

You can send data to the user in different ways, which are e-mail, printer, fax, WebDAV, file, FTP, or SFTP. E-mail and FTP are the most frequently used options. The column OUTPUT_FORMAT specifies the type of output that is generated for the burst data. The list of valid values for OUTPUT_FORMAT is shown in Table 11-3.

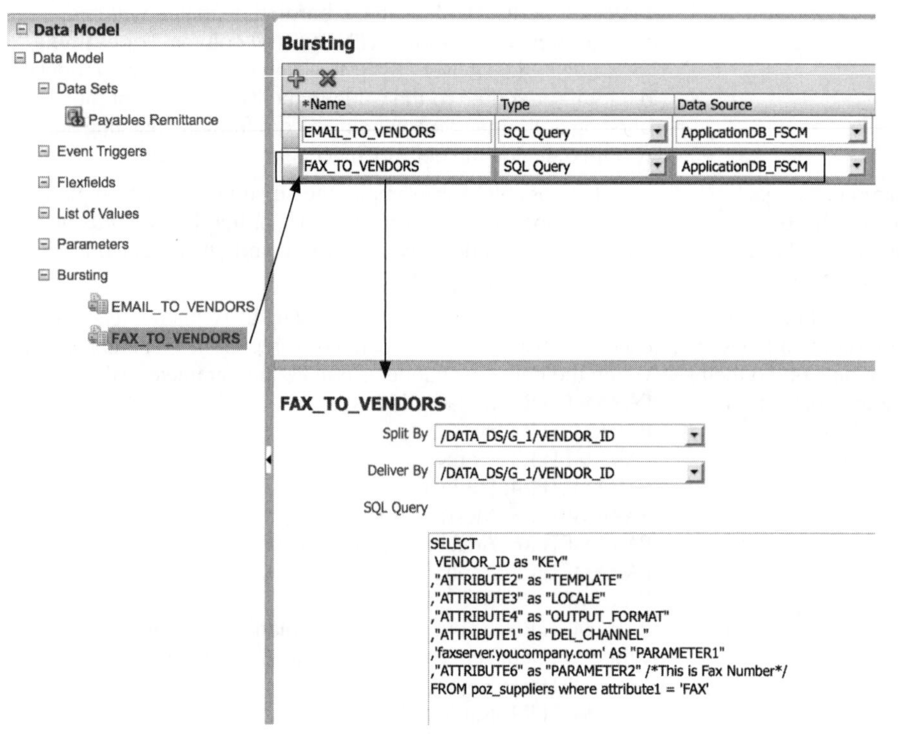

FIGURE 11-7. *Bursting definition in data model*

Output Format	OUTPUT_FORMAT in Bursting SQL Query
Interactive	Not supported for bursting
HTML	html
PDF	pdf
RTF	rtf
Excel	excel for mhtml, excel2000 for html, xslx for xslx
PowerPoint	ppt or pptx
PDF	pdfa for PDF/A, pdfx for PDF/X, and pdfz for zipped PDF
FO Formatted XML	xslfo
XML	xml
Comma Separated	csv
Text	text
Flash	flash

TABLE 11-3. *List of Formats Supported by Oracle BI Publisher*

Template

Templates are used to format the data for presentation. Oracle BI Publisher provides an add-in to Microsoft Office to facilitate the coding of layout instructions into Office documents. Most of the templates delivered in Oracle Fusion Applications are RTF templates. An RTF template is a Rich Text Format file that contains the layout instructions for BI Publisher to use when generating the report output. RTF templates are created using Microsoft Word. Oracle Fusion Applications also come with an embedded template builder tool that can be used for generating interactive HTML-based reports.

Report Output

A report is the final output where the user can view the data in the desired format. Some of the key output formats supported by BI Publisher are listed in Table 11-3. The complete list can be found in Oracle product documentation, as Oracle can add new supportable formats.

BI Publisher Report Example

In this section you will find a step-by-step approach to create a data model, template, and report with example. Fusion Applications BI Publisher environment can be accessed using a URL similar to https://<host:port>/analytics//. In this simple example, a report will be developed to list the users in Fusion Applications and the role assigned to those users. The steps for developing this report are:

1. First we need to create the data model. To extract the data for Fusion Applications users and their roles, we can either write a single SQL query joining the user and role tables, or we can write two separate SQL queries and join the results of the User query to the Role query. In this example we will write two separate queries and link them together.
2. Create a user named XX_BIP_DEVELOPER and assign the roles: Application Implementation Consultant, Business Intelligence Applications Worker, and Transactional Business Intelligence Worker.
3. Next, log in as XX_BIP_DEVELOPER user and click navigation New | Data Model. Enter a value in the description field and select the default data source as ApplicationDB_FSCM as shown in Figure 11-8.

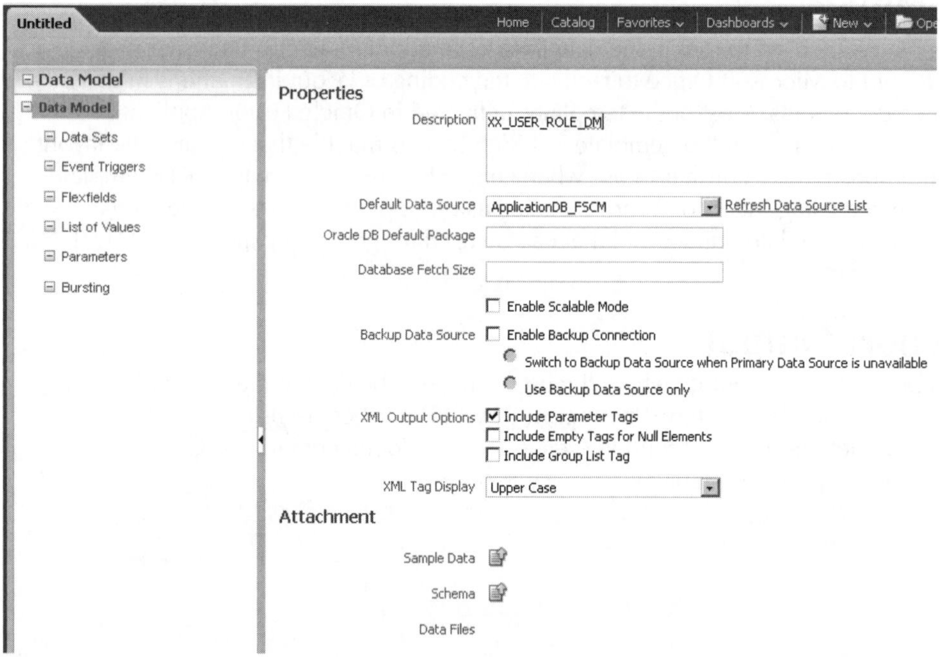

FIGURE 11-8. *Create data model.*

4. Click the Save button to save the data model. At this point the system will prompt you to select the data model location. Given that this is a custom data model, select the folder structure /Shared Folders/Custom/Financials, as shown in the following illustration. Don't save your data model in "My Folders," as it will only be visible to the user from which it is created.

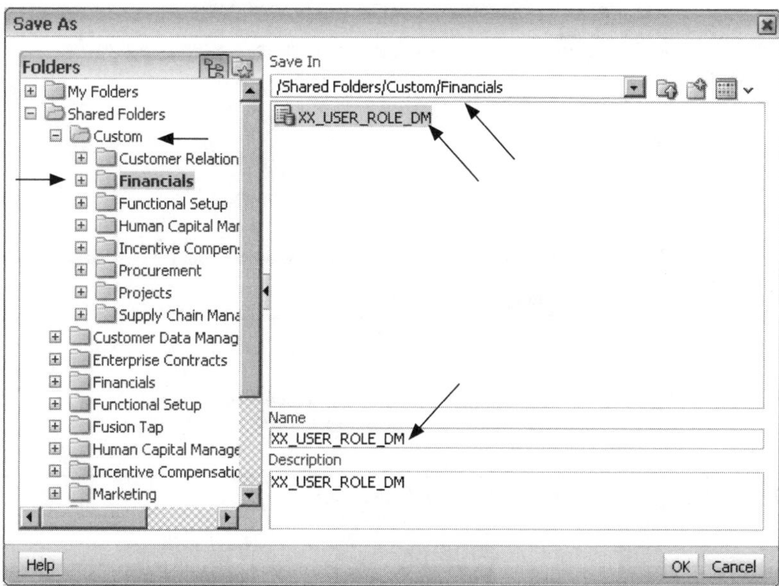

5. Next, create a Text type parameter as shown in Figure 11-9 for retrieving User and Role information based on the User Name passed as parameter.

6. Now go to the data set node and create two data sets using the following queries :

Query for User data set:

```
select user_id ,username, to_char(creation_date,'DD-MON-RRRR')
creation_date from per_users pu where username=nvl(:p_user_
name,username)
```

Query for Role data set:

```
select pur.user_id role_user_id ,pur.role_id, prdt.role_name,
prdt.description, to_char(pur.start_date,'DD-MON-RRRR') Start_
```

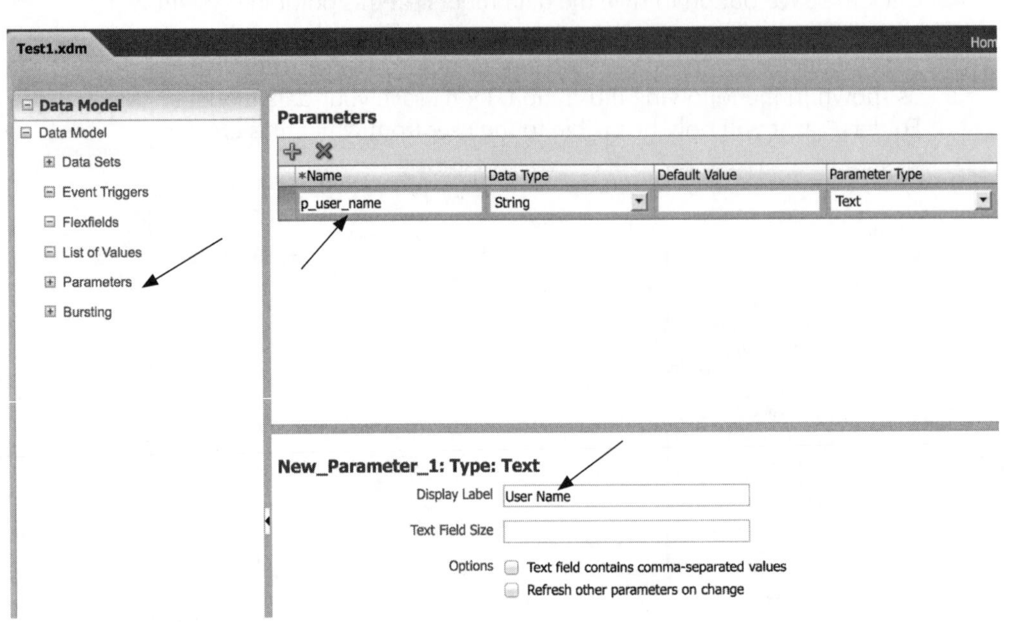

FIGURE 11-9. *Add a parameter to the User Role listing report.*

```
date from per_user_roles pur,per_roles_dn_tl prdt where pur.
role_id=prdt.role_id and prdt.language='US'
```

These data sets will be of type SQL Query as shown in the following illustration.

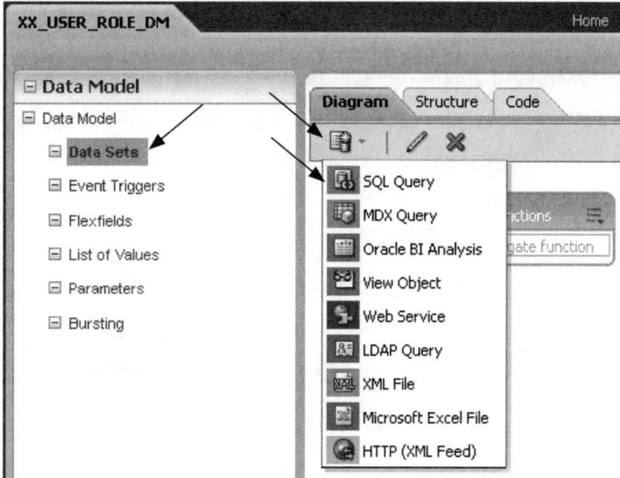

7. Create a "User" data set as shown here.

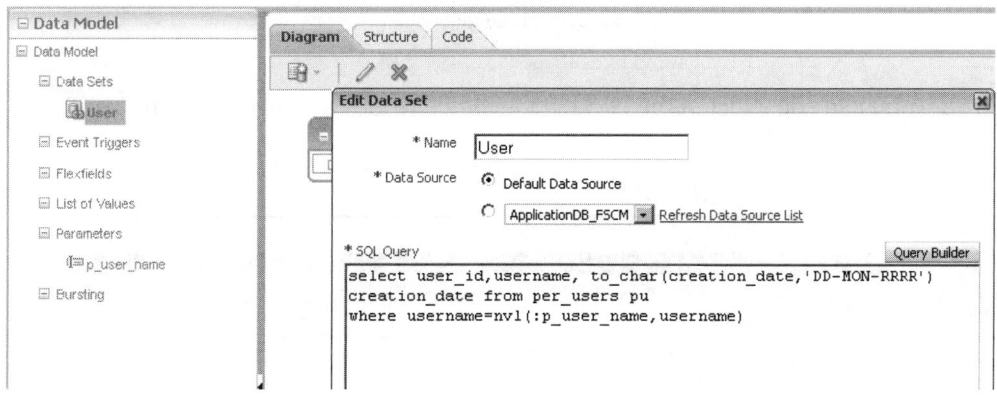

8. Create a "Roles" data set using the query as shown here.

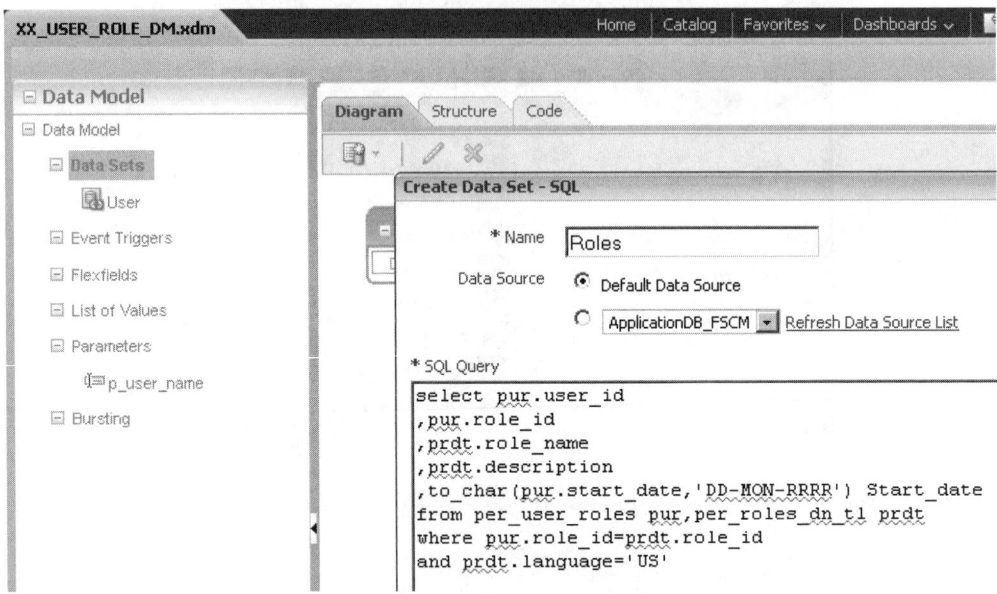

9. You can edit structure by clicking the Structure tab as shown in Figure 11-10.

Data Source	XML Tag Name	Sorting	Value If Null	Display Name	Data Type
Report Data					
Data Structure	DATA_DS				
User	G_USER			G_USER	
USER_ID	USER_ID			USER_ID	999
USERNAME	USERNAME			USERNAME	abc
CREATION_DATE	CREATION_DATE			CREATION_DATE	abc
Roles	G_ROLE			G_ROLE	
USER_ID	USER_ID_1			USER_ID	999
ROLE_ID	ROLE_ID			ROLE_ID	999
ROLE_NAME	ROLE_NAME			ROLE_NAME	abc
DESCRIPTION	DESCRIPTION			DESCRIPTION	abc
START_DATE	START_DATE			START_DATE	abc

FIGURE 11-10. *Optionally amend the structure of the XML to be generated by navigating to the Structure tab.*

10. Link both the datasets by joining the Primary key of the User data set with the foreign key of the Roles data set by clicking >> beside the USER_ID in the first group and selecting Create Link. Linking the data set can be done by dragging one data set's key value and dropping it on another data set's key value so that both data sets will be joined as shown in Figure 11-11. Save using the Save button.

11. Click the Get XML Output button to see the XML output. Enter the user name parameter value and click Run Report so that the XML file can be generated as shown in Figure 11-12.

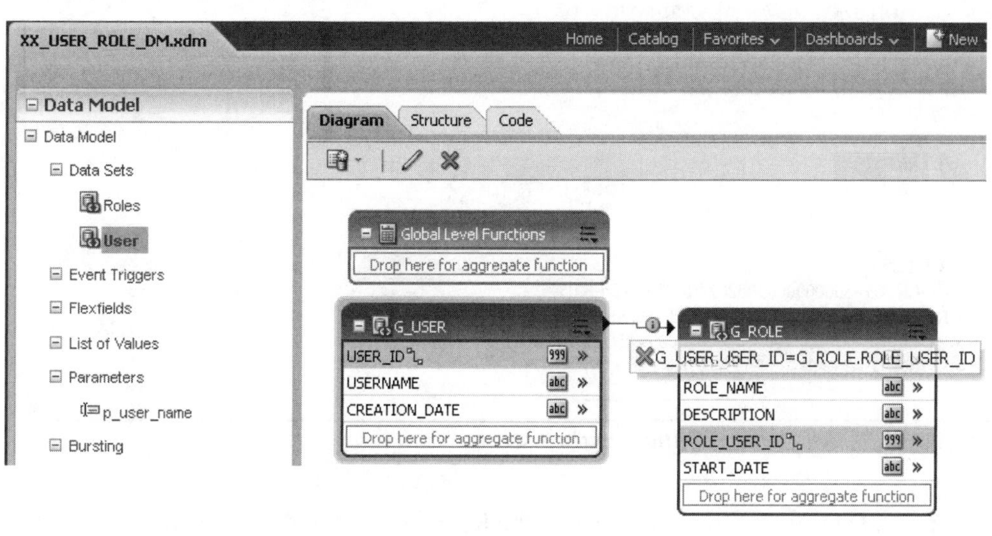

FIGURE 11-11. *Link the User and Roles data sets.*

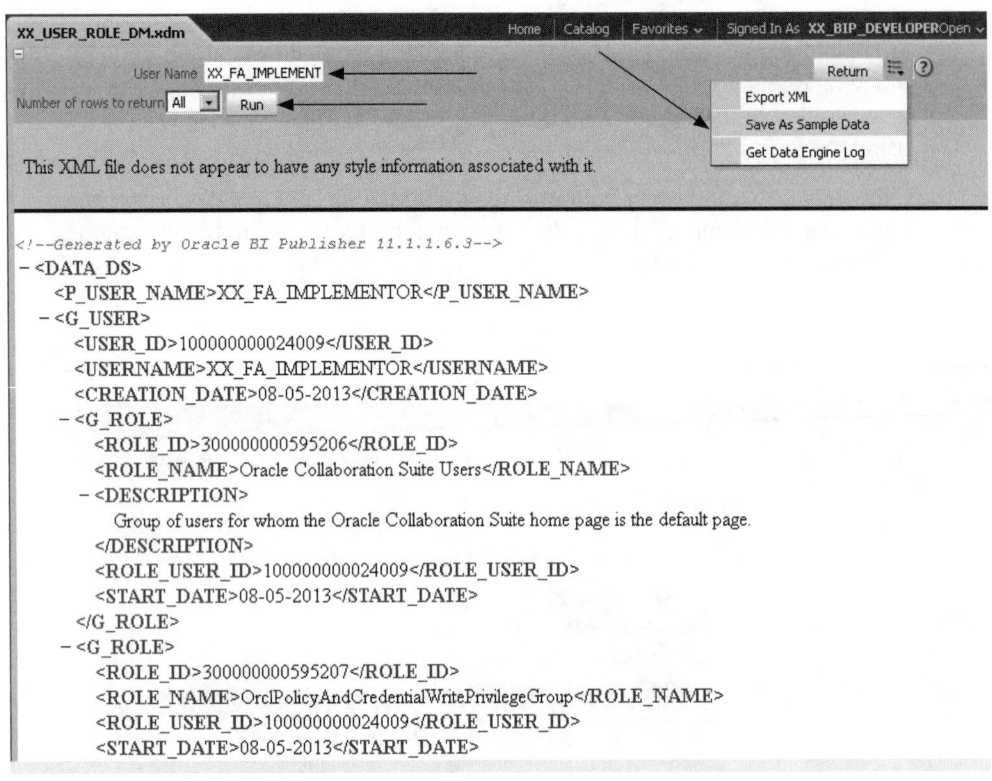
XX_USER_ROLE_DM.xdm
Home | Catalog | Favorites | Signed In As XX_BIP_DEVELOPER Open
User Name XX_FA_IMPLEMENT
Number of rows to return All Run
Return
Export XML
Save As Sample Data
Get Data Engine Log
This XML file does not appear to have any style information associated with it.
<!--Generated by Oracle BI Publisher 11.1.1.6.3-->
- <DATA_DS>
<P_USER_NAME>XX_FA_IMPLEMENTOR</P_USER_NAME>
- <G_USER>
<USER_ID>100000000024009</USER_ID>
<USERNAME>XX_FA_IMPLEMENTOR</USERNAME>
<CREATION_DATE>08-05-2013</CREATION_DATE>
- <G_ROLE>
<ROLE_ID>300000000595206</ROLE_ID>
<ROLE_NAME>Oracle Collaboration Suite Users</ROLE_NAME>
- <DESCRIPTION>
Group of users for whom the Oracle Collaboration Suite home page is the default page.
</DESCRIPTION>
<ROLE_USER_ID>100000000024009</ROLE_USER_ID>
<START_DATE>08-05-2013</START_DATE>
</G_ROLE>
- <G_ROLE>
<ROLE_ID>300000000595207</ROLE_ID>
<ROLE_NAME>OrclPolicyAndCredentialWritePrivilegeGroup</ROLE_NAME>
<ROLE_USER_ID>100000000024009</ROLE_USER_ID>
<START_DATE>08-05-2013</START_DATE>

FIGURE 11-12. *XML output for the two data sets*

12. Next click the icon to the right of the Return button, and select Save As Sample Data. Save the sample data file as XX_USER_ROLE_SAMPLE_DATA.xml. Now we can proceed with creation of the report. Click New | Report as shown here.

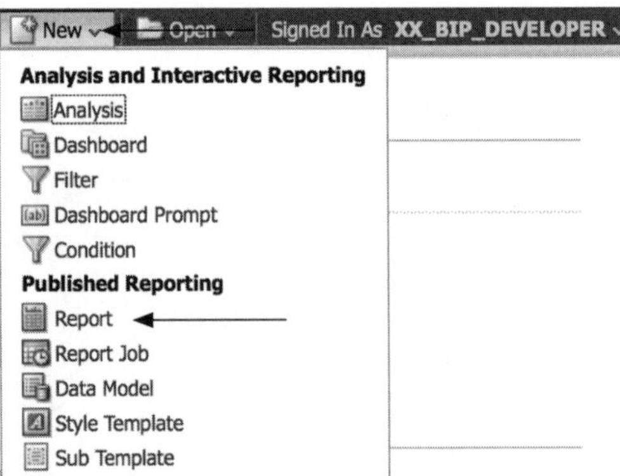
New
Open
Signed In As XX_BIP_DEVELOPER
Analysis and Interactive Reporting
Analysis
Dashboard
Filter
Dashboard Prompt
Condition
Published Reporting
Report
Report Job
Data Model
Style Template
Sub Template

13. At this stage, the system will prompt you to select an existing data model or to create a new data model. In response to that, click Use Existing Data Model and select the data model that you have created earlier from the Custom folder/Financials, as shown in the following illustration.

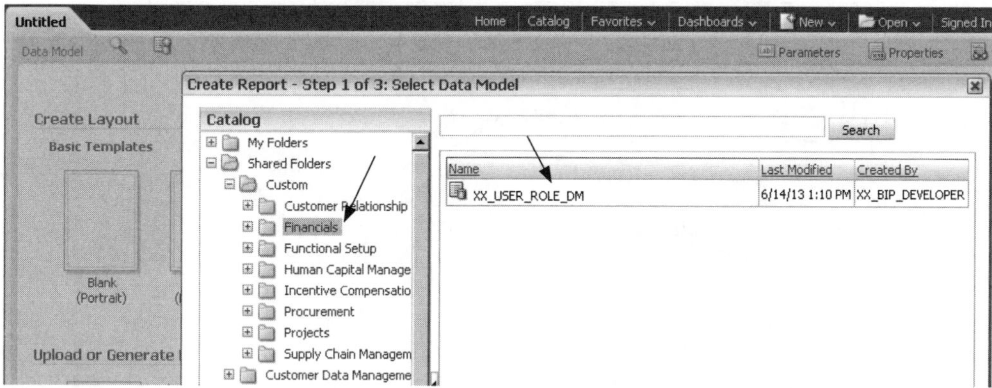

14. Now click the Next button and click the Use Report Editor radio button.

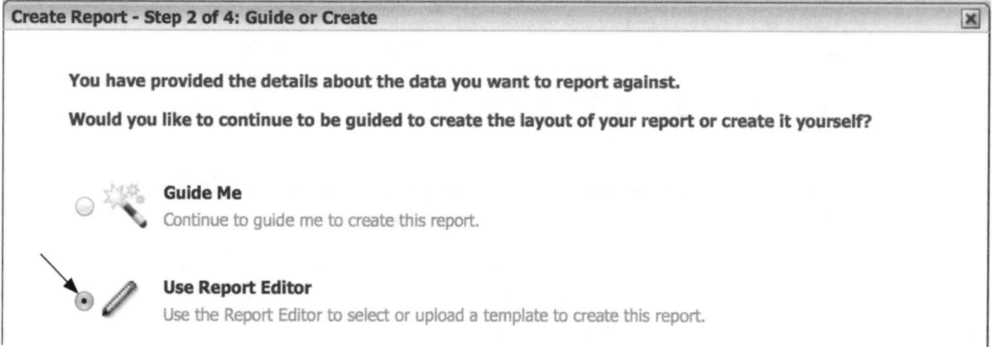

15. When you click Finish, you will be prompted to save the report as shown in the following illustration. In this example, we will save the report in the same directory where we saved the data model.

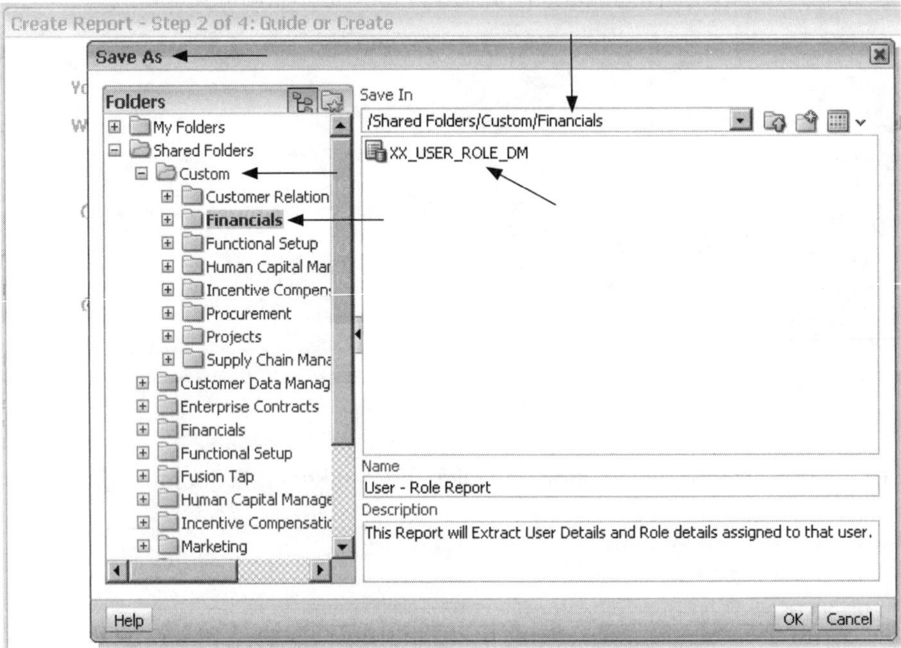

16. When you click the OK button, you will be presented with a window for creating or uploading a template, as shown in Figure 11-13.

Here you can either use the built-in report editor of Fusion Applications or you can upload a BI Publisher Template. The Basic Templates provide a few basics in built layout formats for building the report. In this example we will first create the template using the Embedded Template Builder. In order to do so, click on the

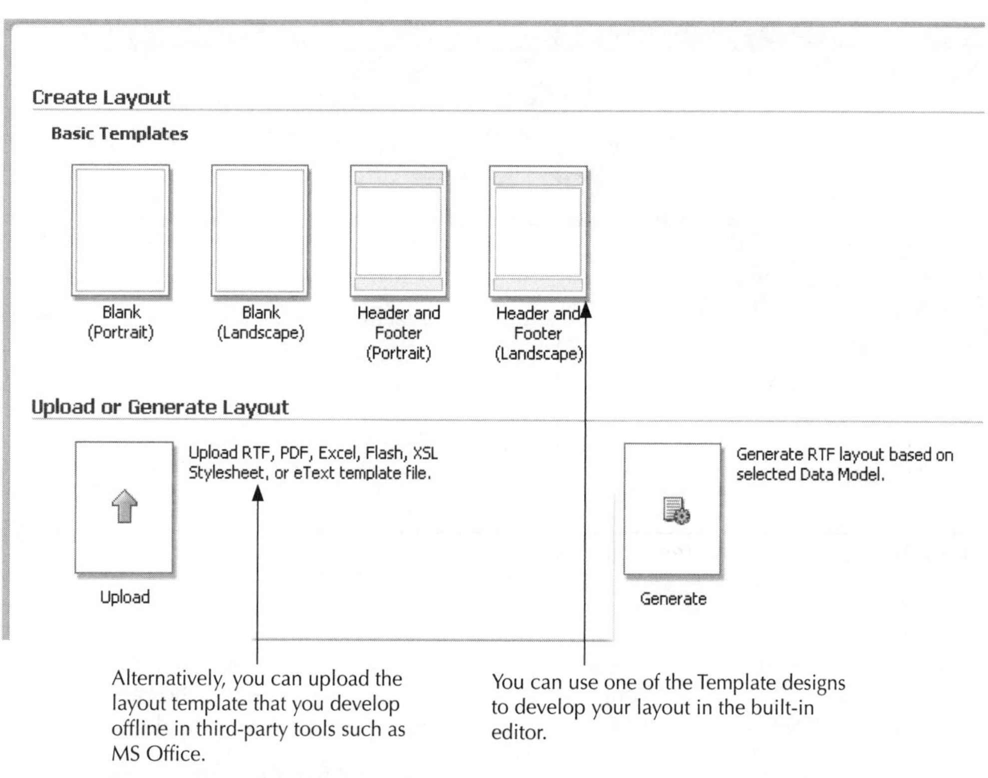
Create Layout
Basic Templates
Blank
(Portrait)
Blank
(Landscape)
Header and
Footer
(Portrait)
Header and
Footer
(Landscape)
Upload or Generate Layout
Upload RTF, PDF, Excel, Flash, XSL
Stylesheet, or eText template file.
Upload
Generate RTF layout based on
selected Data Model.
Generate
Alternatively, you can upload the
layout template that you develop
offline in third-party tools such as
MS Office.
You can use one of the Template designs
to develop your layout in the built-in
editor.

FIGURE 11-13. *Create or upload template.*

"Header and Footer(Landscape)" template as shown in Figure 11-13. You will now be presented with a Embedded Template Builder interface as shown in Figure 11-14.

1. Click the Insert tab and then click Data Table. Alternatively, from the left-hand pane Components section, click Data Table. This will create a placeholder for a data table in your layout.

2. Now, from the left-hand pane under the section Data Source, drag and drop USERNAME followed by CREATION_DATE from G_USER into the placeholder for the data table. Select the USERNAME column in the data table, and select Group Left within the Grouping section.

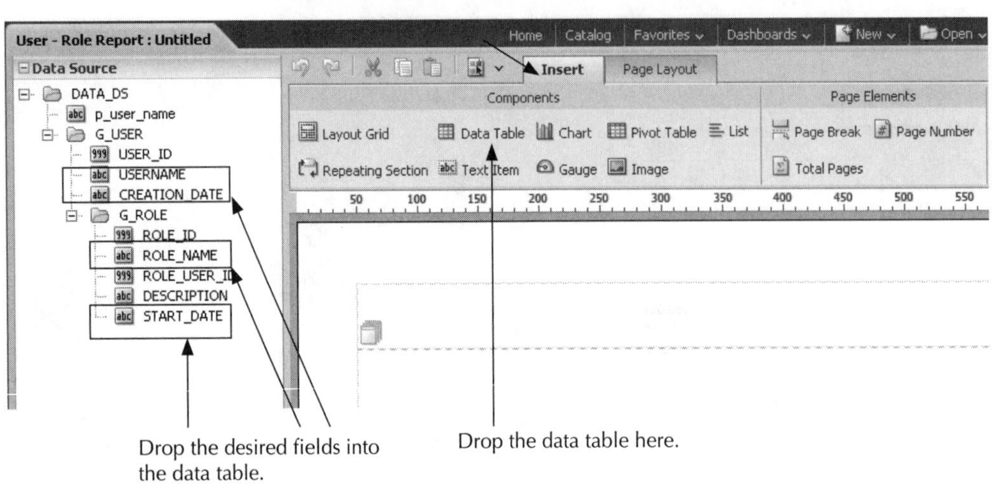

FIGURE 11-14. *BI Embedded Template Builder*

3. Next, select the CREATION_DATE column in the data table, and again select Group Left within the Grouping section. Doing so will ensure that the values for USERNAME and CREATION_DATE will not repeat with every single record.

4. Now drag Role Name and Description from G_ROLE in the Data Source beside the CREATION_DATE in the data table.

5. Save this layout by clicking the Save button and give the name **XX_ USER_ ROLE_TEMPLATE** to the layout.

A single user can have more than one role attached to them. Therefore, we need to apply the grouping USERNAME and CREATION_DATE columns as shown in Figure 11-15. Click the Save button and then click the Return button.

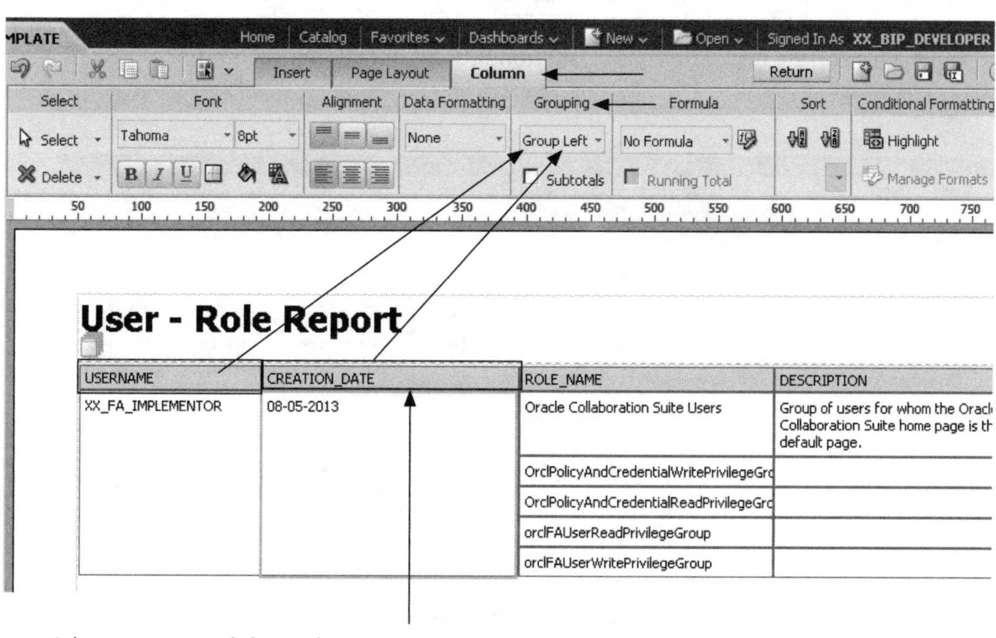

FIGURE 11-15. *Create the layout and define a grouping of columns.*

Now the Layout Template has been created. Click View Report to see the actual output of the report.

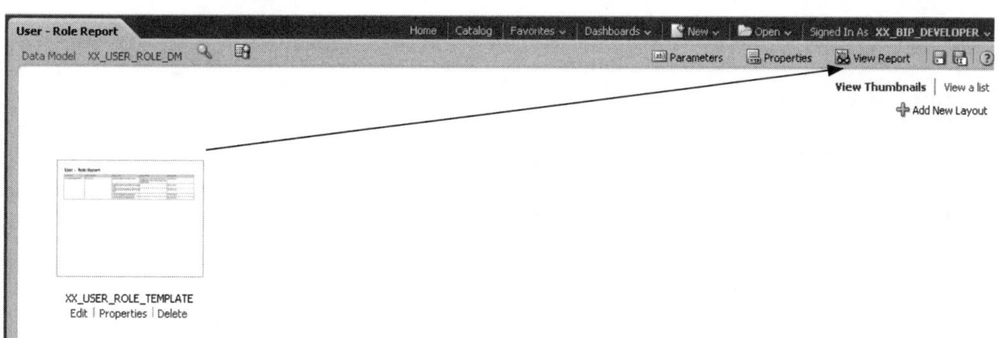

Enter the value of the username parameter and click the Run button to run the report. You will able to see the output as shown in the following illustration. You can also perform sorting and other basic functionality on data as shown here.

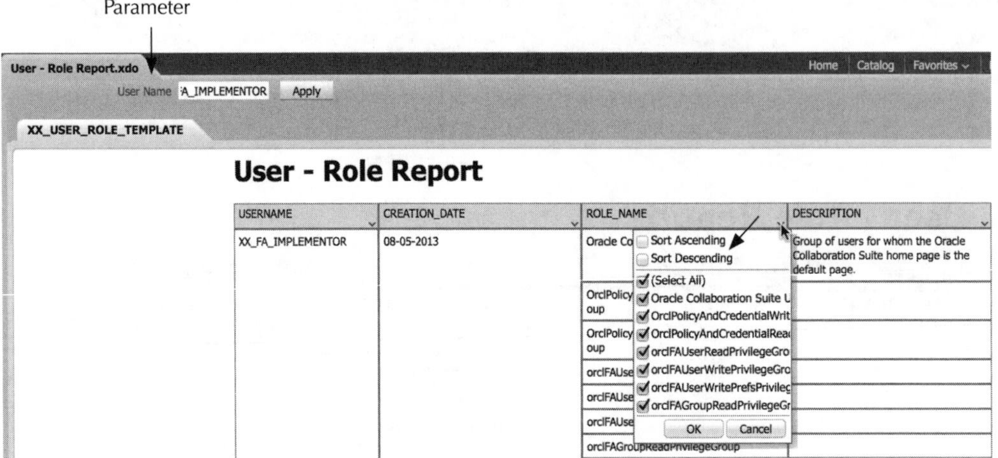

The example shown in the preceding steps was a very simple example to build the reports using the built-in layout editor of Fusion Applications. You can use this technique to build reports using interactive charts, pivot tables, and so on as shown in Figure 11-16.

You can also create a layout template using the BI Template builder plugin in Microsoft Word as shown in Figure 11-17. To do so, it is assumed that you have already downloaded and installed the BI Publisher plugin for MS Office, which can be downloaded from the Oracle Web site. After developing your template, save it as an RTF file in Microsoft Word.

Using the built-in layout editor, you can embed charts, pivot tables, and so on, to give drill-down to data.

During run time, the output can be exported to these formats.

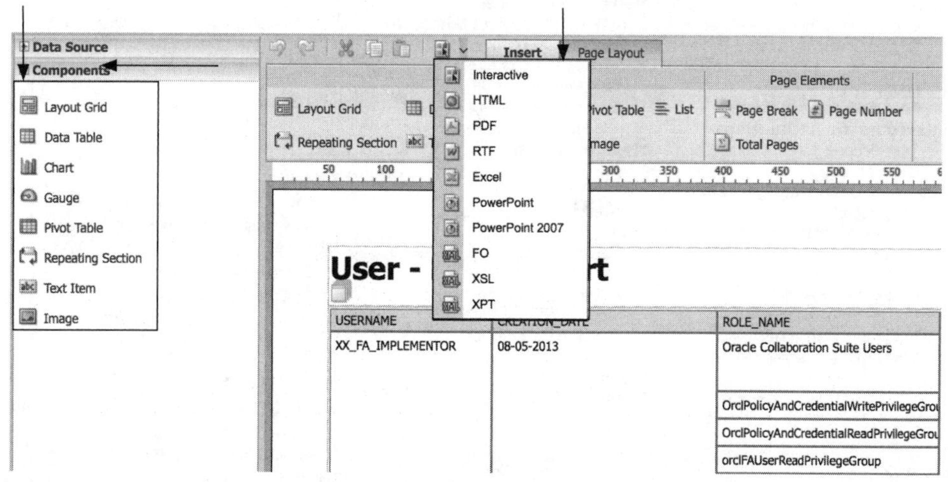

FIGURE 11-16. *Other component types and export formats supported in the built-in layout editor*

After the BI publisher plug-in for MS Office is installed…

You can preview the output offline based on the sample XML data.

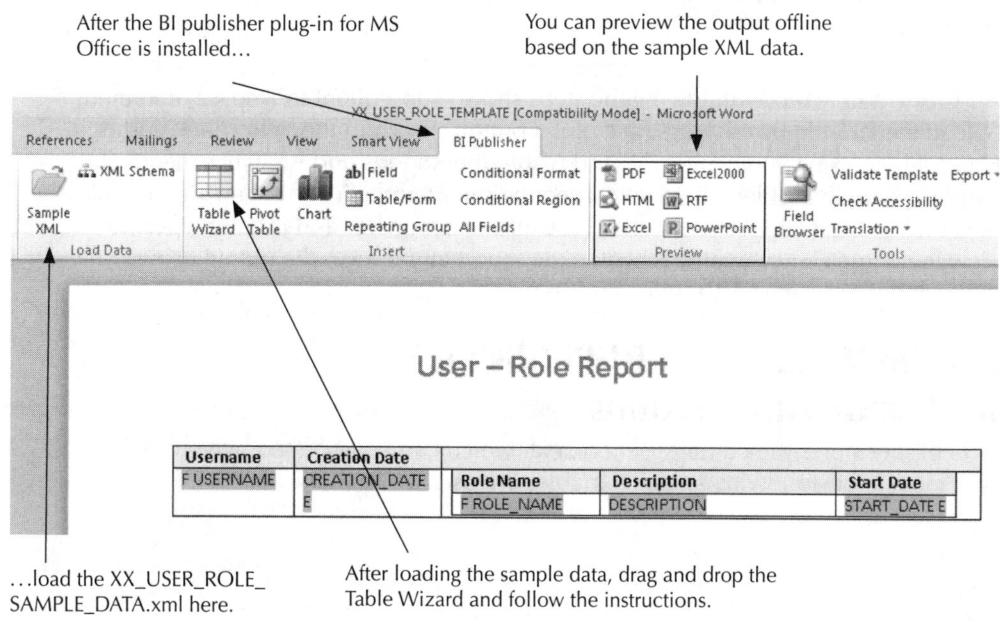

…load the XX_USER_ROLE_SAMPLE_DATA.xml here.

After loading the sample data, drag and drop the Table Wizard and follow the instructions.

FIGURE 11-17. *Create template using MS Office.*

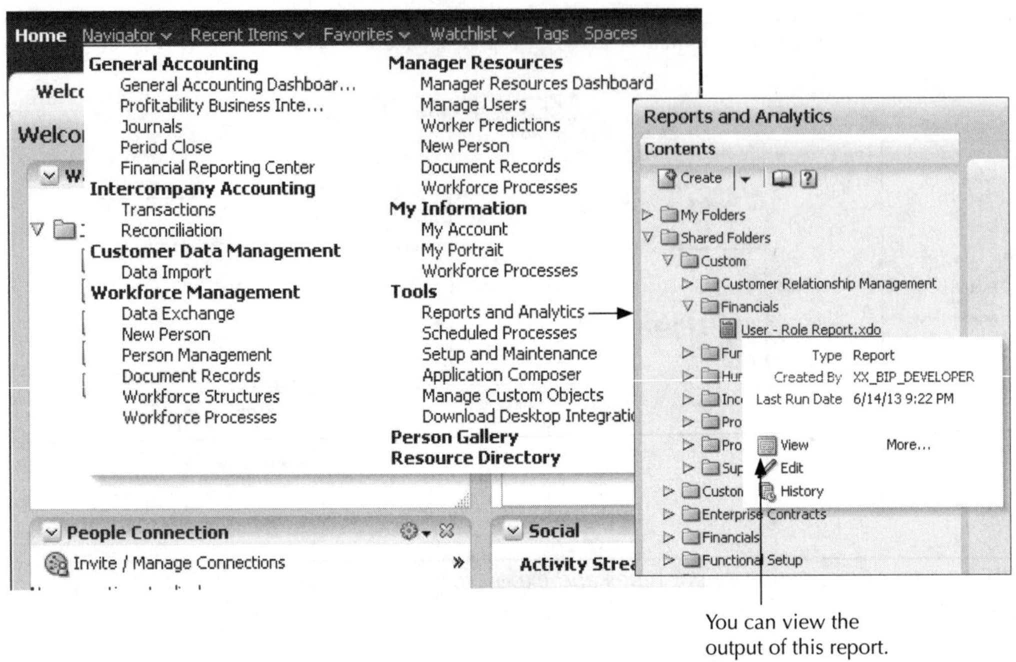

FIGURE 11-18. *Run the report from the menu.*

Create a new report following the steps shown subsequent to Step 12, and then upload the RTF file by clicking the Upload button shown in the bottom-left corner in Figure 11-13. Next you can log in, and within the Reports and Analytics menu, you can search for the folder where you saved the report and click the View Report link as shown in Figure 11-18. Enter the value for the parameter and run the report to view the output. You can also schedule the report and deliver the output using different options such FTP, e-mail, and so on.

System Variables in BI Publisher for Fusion Applications

BI Publisher stores the current user context, which can be accessed by your report data model. The following system variables are used by BI Publisher.

System Variable	Description
xdo_user_name	UserID of the user submitting the report. For example: Administrator
xdo_user_roles	Roles assigned to the user submitting the report. For example: XMLP_ADMIN, XMLP_SCHEDULER
xdo_user_report_oracle_lang	Report language from the user's account preferences. For example: ENG
xdo_user_report_locale	Report locale from the user's account preferences. For example: en-US
xdo_user_ui_oracle_lang	User interface language from the user's account preferences. For example: US
xdo_user_ui_locale	User interface locale from the user's account preferences. For example: en-US

To add the user information to your data model, you can define the variables as parameters and then define the parameter value as an element in your data model. Or, you can simply add the variables as parameters and then reference the parameter values in your report. The following example returns only those expense reports that were created by the user running the report:

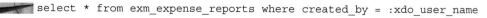

```
select * from exm_expense_reports where created_by = :xdo_user_name
```

Customizing the BI Publisher Layout Templates

It is very common in implementation projects to modify the template for changing the layout or design of a report. Typical tasks are adding, modifying, or deleting fields or columns or moving the fields in the layout. After you have modified the template, it must be published to the Oracle BI Publisher server for the changes to take effect.

The steps to modify the BI Publisher Layout Template are as follows:

1. Download and rename the template.
2. Modify and upload the template.

These steps are explained in the following section, citing the example for customization of the Printable Expense Report Template.

Download and Rename the Template

To download the Printable Expense Report Template, perform the following steps:

1. In Oracle BI Publisher Enterprise, log in as a user with Administrator access.
2. In the toolbar, click the Catalog menu.
3. In the Catalog pane, open Shared Folders and then open the Financials folder.
4. Select the Expenses folder and then select the Printable Expense Report Template icon and click the Edit link. The Printable Expense Report Template tab appears.
5. In the Printable Expense Report Template tab, click the Edit link. This will prompt you to save FinExmExpenseTemplate.rtf to your desktop. Save the Printable Expense Report Template locally.
6. To create a copy of the Printable Expense Report Template by renaming it, click the View a List link in the upper-right corner of the page. The Layout region appears.
7. In the Layout region, change the template name in the Name field from FinExmExpenseTemplate to **xxFinExmExpenseTemplate.**
8. To save the name change, click the Save icon in the toolbar.
9. Rename the RTF file to xxFinExmExpenseTemplate.rtf before making the changes.

Modify and Upload the Template

To modify the Printable Expense Report Template, you can open the RTF file that was downloaded. Your change may be to just change the Submission text in the header section of the template so as to specify the address for sending the original expense receipts to the Payables department. Next, repeat Steps 1 to 4 as listed for downloading the template, and perform the following steps.

- In the Printable Expense Report Template tab, click the View Thumbnails link in the upper-right corner of the page and then click the Add New Layout icon. The Printable Expense Report Template tab appears.
- In the Upload or Generate Layout region, click the Upload icon. The Upload Template File dialog box appears.
- In the Layout Name field, enter **xxFinExmExpenseTemplate**.

- In the Template File field, browse to and select the locally saved template to which you made changes.
- In the Type field, select RTF Template.
- In the Locale field, select English (United States).
- To upload the modified Printable Expense Report Template to the Oracle BI Publisher Enterprise server, click the Upload button.
- To save the changes to the Printable Expense Report Template, click the Save icon in the toolbar.

Further Information on Reporting in Fusion Applications

Reporting is a vast area in Fusion Applications. The preceding sections present you with one of the commonly used reporting techniques in the implementation projects using the BI Publisher. There are various other tools and techniques supported by Fusion Applications to generate reports. See Chapter 12 to understand the finer details of analytical reporting in Fusion Applications.

Other Reporting Techniques in Fusion Applications

Given that Fusion Applications leverages OBIEE, it therefore opens up various other reporting techniques that are supported by the OBIEE technology. Oracle Business Intelligence Enterprise Edition (OBIEE) is an industry-leading enterprise business intelligence tool that includes a scalable and efficient query and analysis server, an ad-hoc query and analysis tool, interactive dashboard infrastructure, proactive intelligence and alerts functionality, and an enterprise-reporting engine.

Furthermore, Fusion Applications comes prepackaged with Essbase, which further allows tools such as Financial Reporting Studio and Smart View to be used for reporting.

- **Analysis Editor** Can be accessed via menu Navigator | Tools. It is a subcomponent of OBIEE and is also known as BI Answers. It lets you explore and interact with data by presenting data in tables, graphs, pivot tables, and so on.
- **Oracle Transactional Business Intelligence (OTBI)** A predefined set of OBIEE repository (.rpd) and Web catalog are supplied with Fusion Applications. These reports are typically based on the ADF view objects. These reports are designed to report on operational data from the Fusion transaction database in real time.

- **BI Composer** BI Composer is a wizard-based tool to generate analyses based on subject areas. It allows users to modify the embedded analytics in Fusion Applications, such as adding content from the BI Catalog, as well as extending existing content such as adding new analysis columns, creating alternative views of data, sorting and filtering the data, and applying conditional formatting.
- **Mobile BI** Reports can be made available to the mobile platform using Application Composer in Fusion Applications. To develop reports for a mobile platform, log in to Fusion Applications, and click the Application Composer link. Select the application from the drop-down list, and click the link for Manage Mobile Report. Here you will be able to create a new report using predefined analytics as shown in Figure 11-19.

Next, you need to save the report and add it to the ADF Mobile springboard. The report then becomes available on the mobile platform as shown in Figure 11-20.

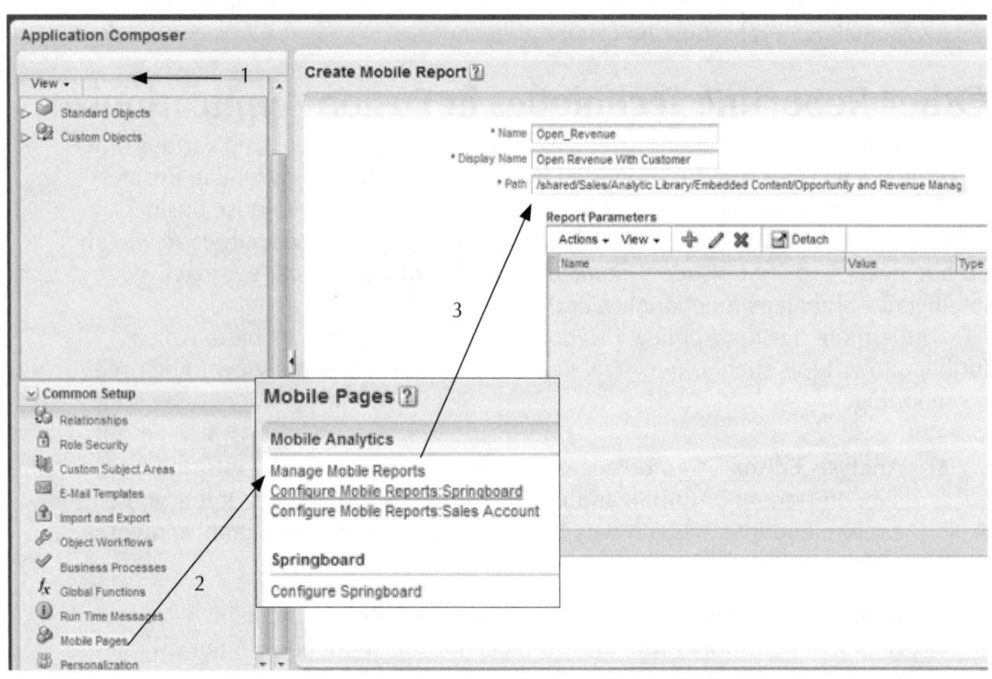

FIGURE 11-19. *Create a report for a mobile platform.*

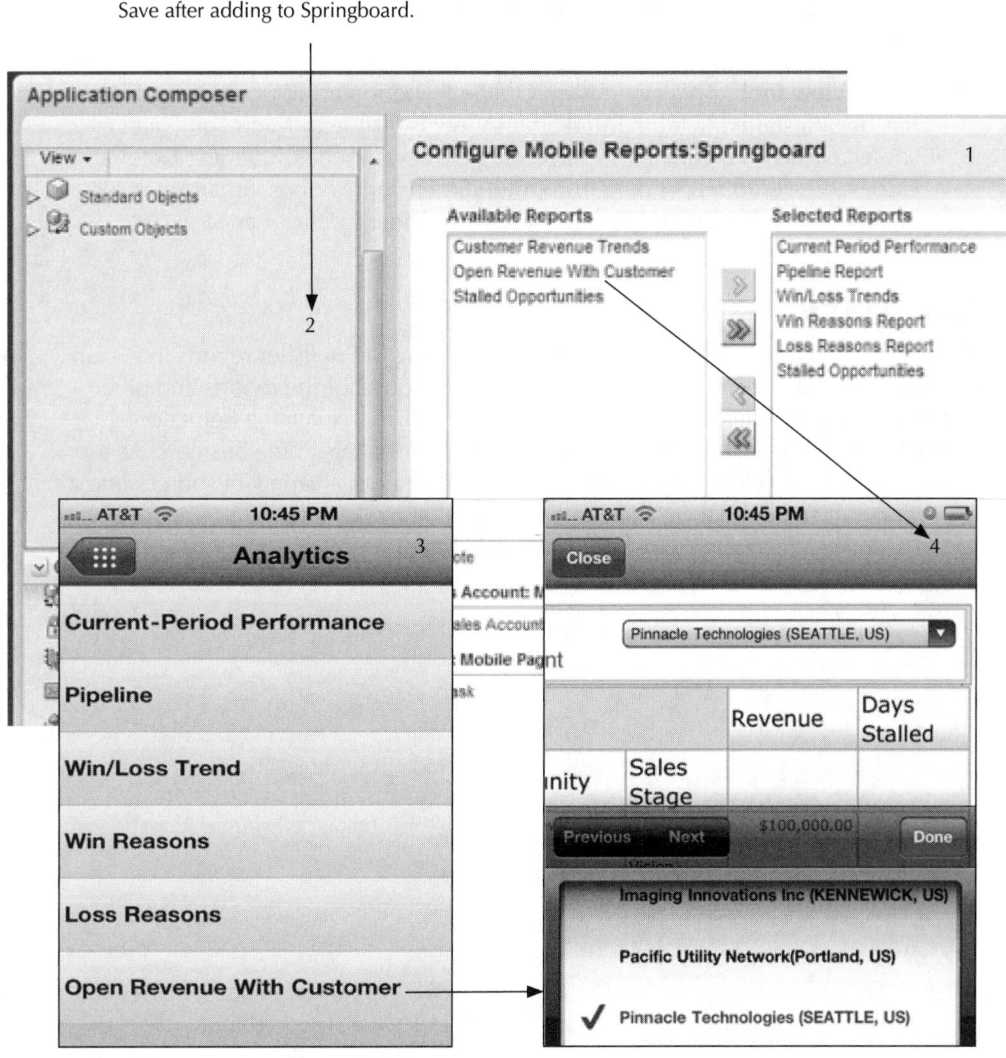

FIGURE 11-20. *Making the Fusion Applications report available on mobile platform*

- **Financial Reporting Studio** This is an Oracle Hyperion tool installed on your desktop and it allows you to develop reports primarily on Essbase database.
- **Smart View tool** This again is an Oracle Hyperion tool. Once the tool has been installed, a tab named Smart View is visible in Microsoft Excel as shown earlier in Figure 11-17. This plugin allows users to connect Excel to Essbase Server to report data from multidimensional cubes. Smart View also allows data to be entered into Essbase using the Excel front end.

Summary

In this chapter you learned the techniques for developing BI Publisher reports in Fusion Applications. You also learned the customization techniques for the reports and other reporting techniques. After reading this chapter, you will appreciate the tremendous potential the reporting architecture in Fusion Applications offers to the business. As a developer you can develop reports that can display data from a variety of sources into a single report, which allows the management to get all the relevant information for a report in a single place, which can be presented in real time.

CHAPTER 12

Analytics in Fusion Applications

Oracle Fusion Applications provides various mechanisms to report on your data. The nature of the reporting technique that you use depends on the reporting requirement. The three key techniques are BI Publisher, Oracle Business Intelligence Applications (OBIA), and Oracle Transactional Business Intelligence (OTBI). In addition, some products in Fusion Applications leverage the Oracle Hyperion suite that comes with Financial Reporting Studio and the Smart View tools that can also be used for reporting.

The BI Publisher–based reports are explained in Chapter 11.

OBIA is a technique that extracts the transactional data from Fusion Applications' transactional database and places it into a data warehouse. OBIA is mainly used for trending, historical analysis, and strategic reporting with drill-down capabilities. OBIA comes out of the box with a prepackaged data warehouse for Oracle EBS, PeopleSoft, JD Edwards, Siebel, and Fusion Applications.

OTBI allows business users to report and analyze transactional data in self-service or ad-hoc mode in real time and therefore it does not require a data warehouse. One of the key aspects of OTBI is that it retains the transactional data security roles applicable for the user. For example, if a business user cannot create purchase orders for a specific organization unit, then OTBI can ensure that the very same user cannot report on the purchase orders for that organization. This is made possible because OTBI leverages the same data security as used by ADF screens. For the details of data security, please refer to Chapter 4. In this chapter we will present the OTBI architecture and will describe the steps involved in developing analytic reports using OTBI.

OTBI Architecture and Concepts

OTBI leverages the Oracle OBIEE (Oracle Business Intelligence Enterprise Edition) technology for querying and reporting. Therefore, in order to understand OTBI, it is important to first understand the underlying OBIEE concepts from a developer perspective.

Introduction to OBIEE

OBIEE comes with a Windows-based tool to develop the contents for reports. This tool is also known as the OBIEE client tool or Oracle BI Administration Tool. The instructions for downloading the correct version of this tool for your Fusion Applications version can be found in Oracle Support Note 1446674.1.

The purpose of the tool is to allow developers to collate the data sources and to design and develop the contents of the reports. The repository that contains the metadata for contents of the report in OBIEE is a file with an extension of .rpd. This is also referred to as the RPD or the repository file. Oracle Fusion Applications comes shipped with an RPD file. which can be opened by accessing the file by FTP from

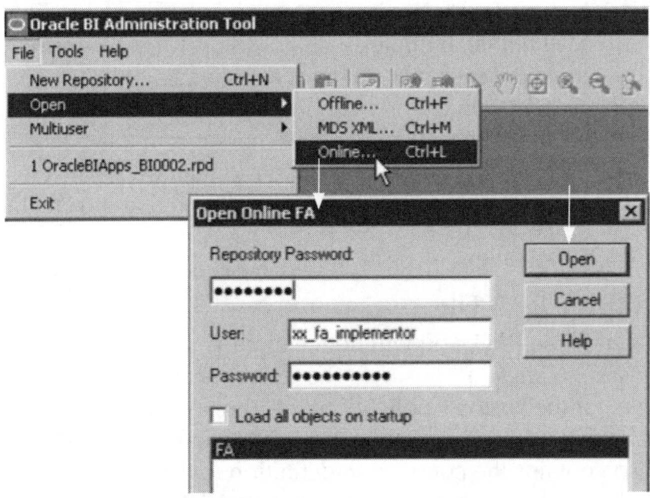

FIGURE 12-1. *Opening the OBIEE repository for Fusion Applications in online mode*

the Fusion Applications server, or the RPD can be opened in online mode by connecting to the Fusion Applications BI Server. You can refer to Oracle Support Note 1452102.1 to know the location of the RPD file on the server.

After the OBIEE Administration Tool has been installed in your Windows environment, you can open the Fusion Applications RPD in online mode as shown in Figure 12-1. The connection name FA in Figure 12-1 is an ODBC data source that you must define in your Windows environment where the OBIEE Administration Tool is installed. To install this data source, go to Control Panel, and add a data source to connect to Oracle BI Server using the WebLogic username and password for the Business Intelligence domain.

Dimensions and Facts

In the analytics and data warehouse world, it is very common to hear the words dimensions, facts, and measures. *Dimensions* are used to narrow down a set of data. For example, you may wish to report your global sales on regions such as by continent or by countries or by states or cities within the states. In this case, a region is a dimension, and a dimension hierarchy is required to report for sales at any level in the region hierarchy. Some other common dimensions are customer, line of business, time, product, and so on. Using these dimensions, you can measure the activity within an organization at relevant levels. In other words, it provides who, what, when, and why for the transactional facts. These dimensions have a dimension table that has a unique column known as a *surrogate key*. For example, in a data warehouse, a CustomerRowID can be a surrogate key in a customer dimension table. This dimension table can have further attributes such as customer name, customer number competitor flag, country code, customer status, and so on.

Measures belong to a fact table. For example, columns such as UnitPrice, QuantityOrdered, and QuantityDelivered are the measures in a fact table named POR_REQUISITION_LINES_ALL. Unlike the dimension tables, the fact tables can have a huge number of records, and therefore you will find that the fact tables are normalized.

Layers in the OBIEE RPD File

After you have opened the RPD, you will notice that there are three layers in the repository. These are the Physical, Business Model and Mapping, and Presentation layers. These layers for the Fusion Applications are shown in Figure 12-2.

The Physical layer contains the references to the actual tables and columns of a data source. It also contains the connection definition to that data source. In this layer some of the key activities that you perform are to define joins, primary keys, and foreign keys. It must be noted that the Physical layer does not contain any data; it merely contains the pointers to the data sources, and the connection to those data sources is established using the connection pool for that data source.

The Business Model and Mapping layer is where you create an abstract business layer on top of referencing the physical layer. You can also combine the data from various sources of the Physical layer. For example, a large organization grown by acquisitions might have Siebel in one business unit, and Oracle EBS in another business unit. Using this Business layer, you can create a common business entity for

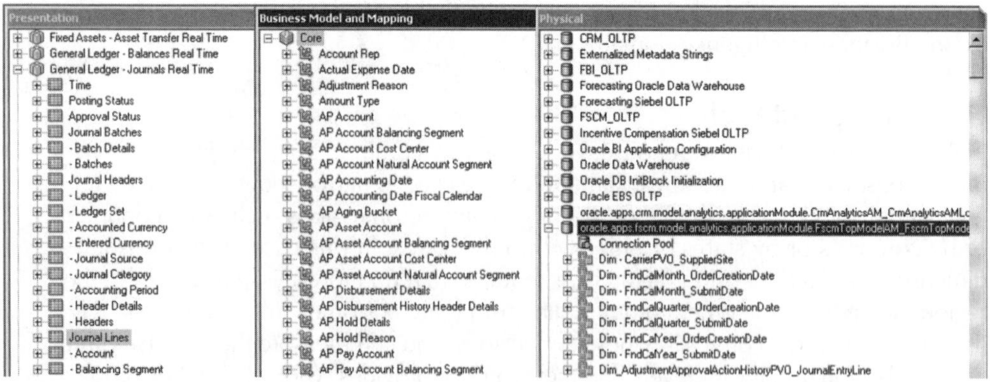

FIGURE 12-2. *RPD file for Fusion Applications*

a customer that collates the sales orders from the Oracle EBS tables and the Siebel sales tables. Therefore, in this example, the Business layer of RPD helps us to present a unified view of sales orders across the enterprise. The ability to stitch together the data from multiple physical sources is also known as *federated querying*.

As seen in Figure 12-2, RPD for Oracle Fusion Applications contains a predefined business model named Core. This contains all the logical tables, logical columns, logical joins, and dimension hierarchies for reporting on data in Fusion Applications. A logical table source defines the mapping from a single logical table to one or more physical tables. For example, a logical table for GL Journals Real Time is sourced from three data sources, that is, JournalBatchPVO, JournalHeaderPVO, and JournalLinePVO as shown in Figure 12-3.

The Presentation layer consists of subject areas, which represents the content of the Business layer for the end users. The subject areas organize content for users in such a manner as to map to their business needs for reporting and analysis requirements. The subject areas are further divided into presentation tables, which organize columns into

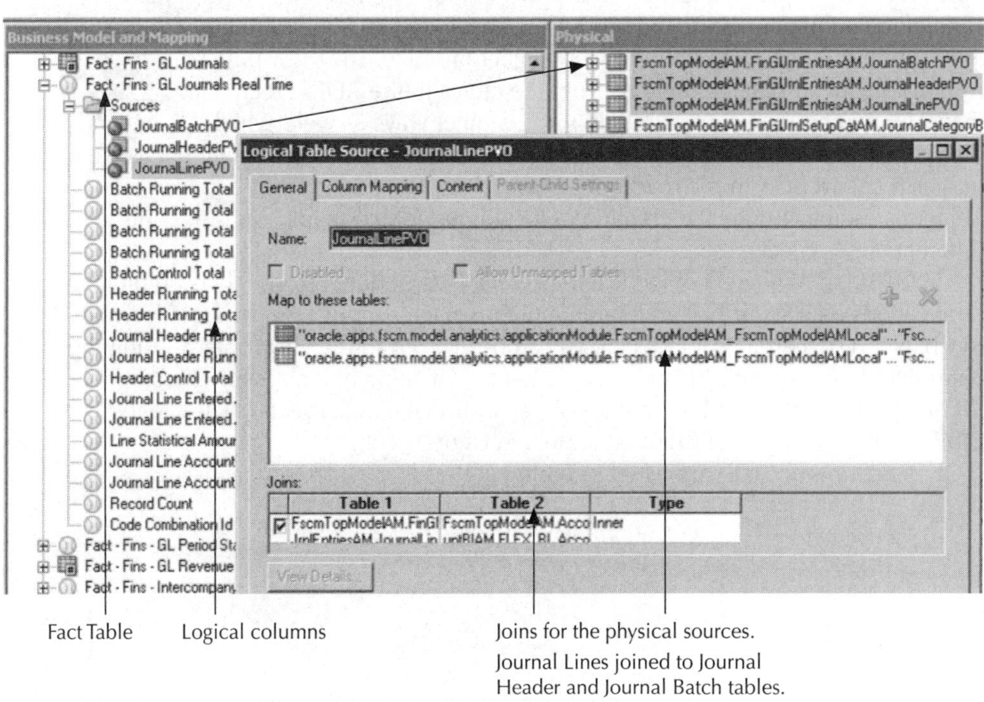

FIGURE 12-3. *One logical table can be mapped to more than one physical source object.*

categories of business data. Further down are the presentation columns, which are mapped to the Business Model and Mapping layer. It is a normal practice to present a different name to the presentation column by overriding the Logical Column Name. This is done to ensure that the column names are user-friendly, because the business users running the reports are agnostic to the underlying data structures in physical and logical layers. As shown in Figure 12-2, all the subject areas that have their names ending with the word "Real Time" are the OTBI subject areas.

Leveraging OBIEE in Fusion Applications

OTBI uses OBIEE as the query and reporting tool, and uses browser-based Oracle BI Dashboard as an end-user tool to give business users an easy-to-use interface to perform a current state analysis of their business applications. When the user runs an OTBI report, the constructed queries are executed in real time against the transactional schema referenced by ADF (Application Development Framework) view objects.

For those not familiar with Oracle ADF business components, it is worth noting that an entity object represents a database table, and an instance of an entity object represents a record in the entity object. A view object is a wrapper around the entity object. A view object is encapsulated in an Application module that manages the state of the ADF page at run time. The encapsulation of a view object into the application module gives rise to a view object instance. The view object instance is responsible for displaying the data from the tables in the ADF screen. Having said that, ADF screens can source data in various other ways as well, which are beyond the scope of this chapter. The view object can be based on a SQL statement as well, in which case it becomes a read-only view object. The relationship between view objects is established by the creation of view links, which helps join the results of different view objects.

In OTBI, an ADF view object can represent facts or dimensions tables, implement applications data security, and handle multilanguage support. As you have learned in Chapter 4, dynamic WHERE clauses can be applied to the view objects using the data security framework. This data security for ADF view objects is inherited by OTBI reporting because the same set of transactional view objects is used in the OBIEE's Physical layer for OTBI, as shown in Figure 12-2.

Key features of OTBI are listed in Table 12-1.

Feature	Description
Self-service ad-hoc analysis	Business users can easily access, analyze, and use the transactional information in their reporting.
Access real-time data	OTBI allows creating reports with real-time transactional data without any latency, with data reported directly from Oracle Fusion Applications tables.
Seamless integration with Oracle Fusion Applications	Leverages the Fusion Applications login and password. OTBI also uses the same data security as Oracle Fusion applications, with no separate data security setup required. Any changes done on Oracle Fusion Applications data security are immediately available in OTBI as well.
Speed of report development	The user interface screens already contain view objects that have all the desired joins to bring back the necessary data to be displayed in the Fusion Applications screens. In traditional BI development, you have to remodel those joins in the BI development tool, and the BI developer needs to understand the joins of the operational database. With OTBI, the report developer simply reuses those joins by importing the ADF view objects that contain the necessary joins to the tables. Not only that, the view links joining the different view objects can also be automatically imported and automatically created into complex joins in OBIEE. This reduces the time for developing reports.
Report-building capability	Oracle BI Answers is used as the interface to build and modify reports for ad-hoc analysis. You can also use BI Composer to build and modify reports.
Flexible and extensible	Leverages Oracle Fusion Applications concepts such as flexfields, trees, single sign-on, embedded content, and multilanguage. It is easy to add additional attributes, measures, or reports.

TABLE 12-1. *Key Features of OTBI*

Development Process for OTBI Reports

As shown in Figure 12-4, the OTBI uses the ADF view objects and Essbase cubes as a source for data in the Physical layer.

The OBIEE is integrated with ADF Business Components to generate reports on transactional data. The OBIEE RPD in Fusion Applications comes preconfigured with database sources for CRM, Financials & Supply Change Management, and Oracle Fusion HCM. These OBIEE data sources connect to the ADF business components via

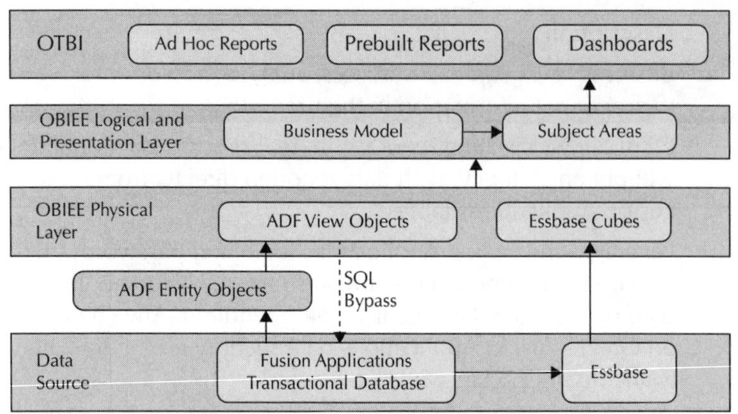

FIGURE 12-4. *OTBI architecture*

OBIEE Broker as shown later in the URL field of Figure 12-6. Each of these applications has its respective parent ApplicationModules, which encapsulate all the transactional view objects for reporting. The Oracle Fusion RPD file comes shipped with these Applications Modules imported for OTBI reporting.

To generate new OTBI reports based on ADF view objects, first you need to import the ADF View Objects metadata into the OBIEE Physical layer using the Administration Tool, then map the data from the Physical layer to the Business Model and Mapping layer and then to the Presentation layer. After you restart the Oracle BI Server and reload the metadata into Oracle BI Presentation Services, you can log in to Oracle BI Answers and drag and drop the columns to generate a report on the imported metadata.

During the import of the ADF view objects into the physical layer of OBIEE, the required physical table representations are automatically created for the view objects. Likewise, the joins in physical layers are automatically created for the view links as shown in Figure 12-5. View links are used to create the master-detail relationship between different view objects in ADF. These get automatically converted into complex joins during the import of ADF, as shown in Figure 12-5. Note that the External Expression field in the Complex Join dialog for ADF data sources is populated with the join condition defined in the view link.

The name of the automatically generated joins follows a naming convention similar to ViewObjectName1_ViewObjectName2 (for example, AppModuleAM.AP_VO1_ AppModuleAM_BU_VO1). The ViewLink instance name appears in the ViewLink Name field of the Complex Join dialog. The complex joins are only created automatically if a ViewLink instance is available. In Oracle ADF, when the view link

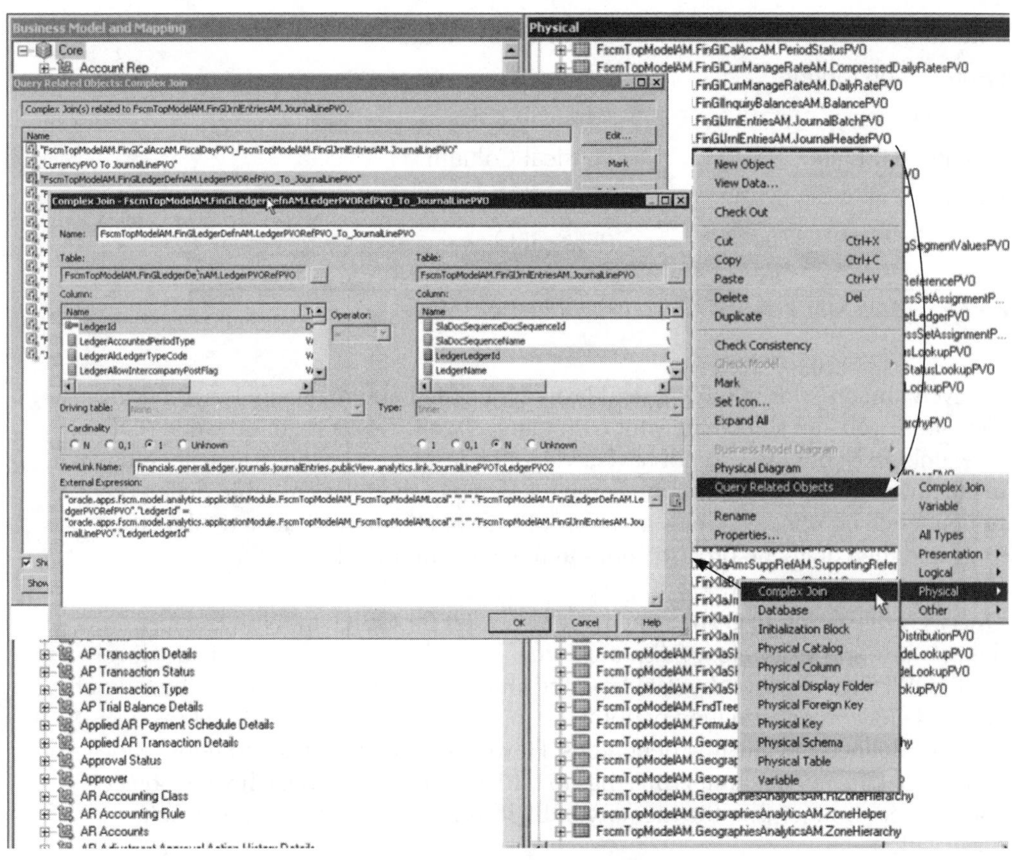

FIGURE 12-5. *Complex joins created for view object links in OBIEE*

or view object is included within an Application Module, it then becomes a view link or view object instance respectively. The complex joins are not created for ViewLink definitions that do not have an instance with an Application Module. Joins for these ViewLink definitions must be created manually. To do this, you can specify the ViewLink definition name in the ViewLink Name field of the Complex Join dialog. Be sure to use the fully qualified VO instance names for the source and destination VOs, as well as the fully qualified package name for the ViewLink definition.

After the import, the ADF Metadata gets modeled into OBIEE as shown in Table 12-2.

ADF Metadata	Imported BI Metadata
Root Application Module	Database
View Objects	Physical Tables
View Object Attribute	Physical Column
View Object Key	Physical Key
View Links	Physical Joins

TABLE 12-2. *ADF Metadata Modeled in OBIEE*

Even though joins in the Physical layer are created automatically for you using view links, you can still create your own joins as well. This is required when ADF view links exist but they do not have a view link instance created. To create joins manually, you can either click the Foreign Key tab of the Physical Table dialog box, or right-click on selected tables and select Physical Diagram | Selected Object(s) Only and then drag and drop the links in the diagram modeler.

Query Optimization in OTBI There are two ways for OBIEE to retrieve data from the database. For example, to display journal lines along with journal header level fields, OBIEE can retrieve the data from the Journal Lines view object and the Journal Headers view object and then perform the joins between the two data sets as per the joins defined in view link definitions. However, this mechanism to retrieve the data is not efficient because OBIEE has to retrieve the data from each view object and then perform joins in the memory of BI Server to collate the desired results for presentation.

To ensure that data is retrieved for such scenarios from journal lines and journal header tables in a single SQL execution, OTBI uses the OBIEE feature called SQL Bypass. This feature is enabled in Fusion Applications via the connection pool definition that connects OBIEE to the ADF Application Modules as shown in Figure 12-6.

In this scenario, when a business user runs an OTBI report on the "General Ledger - Journals Real Time" Subject area, the Oracle BI server at run time creates a composite view object that contains the joins between the Journal Header and Journal Lines tables. The resultant SQL statement of this composite view object is then executed directly in the database to return a single data set for the desired data. This means that only one SQL statement with all the necessary joins is executed for the desired results across multiple database tables, rather than executing multiple SQL statements for each view object in the physical layer. When implementing SQL Bypass, the Oracle BI server ensures that the data security conditions for the logged-in

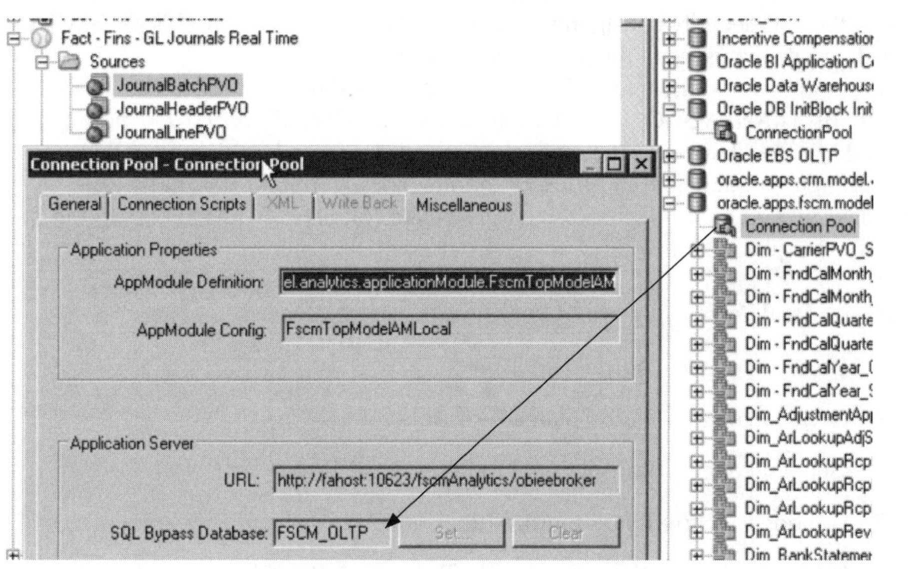

FIGURE 12-6. *SQL Bypass allows a query with joins to be executed directly in the database.*

users are retained. Further to that, the BI server also prunes out the unneeded view objects and the ADF Composite view object API prunes out the unneeded entities, so that the bare minimum set of database tables is queried to retrieve the columns desired by the user's reports.

Security in OTBI

The OTBI Security model consists of users, job roles, duty roles, and privileges. A user can be assigned to one or more job roles. A job role is descriptive of the user's job function, such as General Ledger Clerk or Accounts Payable Manager. A user is granted a job role and a job role has one or more associated duty roles. A job role can span all the applications, whereas a duty role is specific to an application. Job roles are grouped hierarchically to reflect lines of authority and responsibility. Privileges allow specific access to an application or reporting objects and data sets; for example, read access to a report, or read access to a table, and so on. Privileges are associated with duty roles. As soon as a user logs in to Fusion Applications, the system knows the function and data security applicable for that logged-in session. For example, when a department manager views a headcount of staff using an OTBI report, the manager will only see the count of staff that report to them in their supervisor hierarchy. However, when an HR Administrator runs the same report, given their data access security, they will be able to see the complete staff headcount. This is made possible because the OTBI respects the data security constraints on the underlying view objects. This security is applied despite the usage of the SQL Bypass feature.

To ensure that the users are enabled for baseline OTBI reporting access, a role named FBI_TRANSACTIONAL_BUSINESS_INTELLIGENCE_WORKER must be assigned to a user. Further to that, the relevant duty roles can be assigned to the users for granting them access to a group of reports. For example, OTBI Duty Role FBI_GENERAL_LEDGER_ TRANSACTION_ANALYSIS_DUTY has access to the following subject areas:

- General Ledger - Balances Real Time
- General Ledger - Journals Real Time
- General Ledger - Period Status Real Time
- General Ledger - Transactional Balances Real Time
- Subledger Accounting - Journals Real Time
- Subledger Accounting - Supporting References Real Time

OTBI Function Security Job roles and their associated duty roles and privileges are assigned to users of Oracle Fusion Applications. The implementation team usually indicates which users can access which application menu or page. This level of security is known as *function security*. This function security also secures access to OTBI reporting objects by assigning BI-specific duty roles to BI-specific job roles.

In Fusion Applications, you will find that for every given subject area, usually a single BI duty role is defined, using the naming convention "<xyz>Analysis Duty". Some examples are Account Analysis Duty and Expense Analysis Duty roles. The BI duty role can be mapped to the subject area using the RPD file as shown in Figure 12-7, by clicking the button labeled Permissions in the Subject Area property window.

In order to know the list of roles for the desired subject areas, it is possible to run a report in the OBIEE Administration Tool. To run this report, execute the following steps:

1. Log in to the OBI Administration Tool and connect offline to the Fusion Repository.
2. In the Presentation layer, multiselect the desired subject areas for which a Permission Report is required.
3. Right-click and select Permissions Report.
4. This will list each select subject area, along with the duty role that has been granted read access to that area. If you wish to save this output in a CSV file, then click the Save As button and save the file in CSV format.

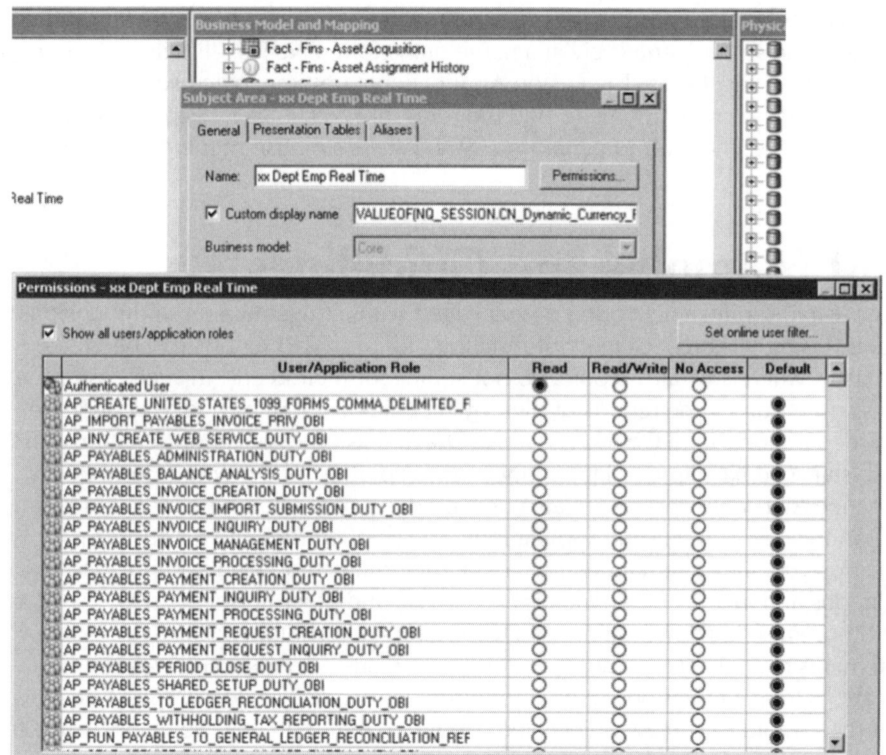

FIGURE 12-7. *Use RPD to map a subject area to a duty role in the Presentation layer.*

OTBI Data Security OTBI data security relies heavily on the Oracle Fusion Applications concepts of data security. Oracle Fusion Applications data security is based on data security roles and privileges stored in a table named FND_GRANTS. This content encodes the role (which spans all applications); the application-specific privileges, which indicate which action can be performed against which entity (where an entity is a logical business object that may be made up of multiple Fusion Applications tables); and a specification of the actual tables and SQL WHERE clause that filters the database rows constituting the logical entity. Privileges are assigned to job roles in FND_GRANTS. This security implementation model means that the same privilege can be specified by any number of roles for any number of row sets (which define the logical entities).

The ADF view object enforces transaction data security by looking up its security specification at run time, from FND_GRANTS. An existing FND_GRANTS security specification is referenced indirectly through an ADF view criteria object attached to the ADF view object. In other words, the view criteria acts as a security filter of the view object and such criteria is given a name of the form FNDDS__Privilege/Action__ObjectName__ObjectAlias. The Fusion Applications run-time logic uses the ADF view object's view criteria name to find the relevant FND_GRANTS specification and uses that specification to generate a SQL WHERE clause that enforces data security.

OTBI Examples and Guidelines

Oracle Fusion Applications comes prepackaged with a huge number of dimensions and facts. Using this prepackaged information, ad-hoc OTBI reports can be created by the users where standard reports do not suffice for their needs. In such cases, the business users can define reports of their own choice without having to depend on their IT department. To make this possible, Oracle Fusion Applications contains prebuilt star schemas designed for analysis and reporting. The prebuilt Business Intelligence ADF view objects are also delivered out of the box for a large number of operational tables in Fusion Applications. The shipped RPD file for Fusion Applications contains premapped metadata, including embedded best practice calculations and metrics for financial, executives, and other business users.

In on-premise implementations of Fusion Applications, the business requirements may dictate the necessity of creating custom tables and custom applications to meet their operational requirements. In such cases there is a need to import the custom ADF view objects into OBIEE so that those can be made available for ad-hoc OTBI reporting by the users.

The implementation team can also configure some descriptive flexfield segments that might have to be exposed to the business users for ad-hoc reporting via OBIEE. In such cases, the ADF view objects associated with flexfields need to be imported into OBIEE and made available to the subject area.

A Simple Analysis Report with Graph

In this simple example we will see how a business user can create a report that displays the list of posted and unposted journals with their debit amounts. The results will be displayed in a tabular format and also will be displayed in a graphical format. Using this report, a business user can get an idea of the number of journals that remain unposted in General Ledger. In order to develop this report, we will be using a preshipped subject area in OTBI. The sequence of steps followed will be to firstly create a new analysis report, and then select the desired columns from the subject area and then define a graphical view for the output.

Log in as the XX_FA_IMPLEMENTOR user that was defined in Chapter 4 using the URL https://<hostname>:<portname>/analytics. Click New | Analysis as shown in the following illustration. At this point in time, you will be prompted to select a subject area. Select "General Ledger - Journals Real Time" as your subject area.

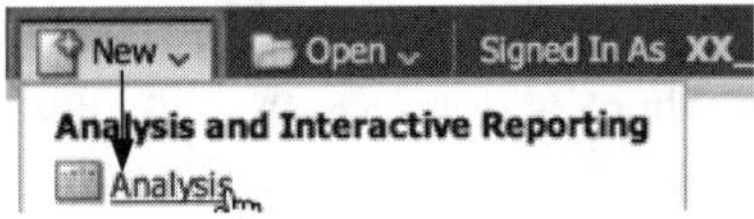

You will notice that by default a Criteria tab will be presented to you. Within the subject area you will be presented with the dimensions and the facts, with dimensions being presented on the top. This subject area has Time, Posting Status, Approval Status, Journal Batches, Journal Headers, and Journal Lines as dimensions and facts.

Expand the Time dimension tree and double-click on Accounting Period Name. By doing so, this column will become a selected column for your ad-hoc report. Expand the Posting Status dimension tree and double-click on Posting Status Meaning to be included. Within Journal Headers, expand Ledger and double-click Ledger Name. Expand Headers and double-click Running Total Accounted DR. The report design will look similar to the image shown in Figure 12-8.

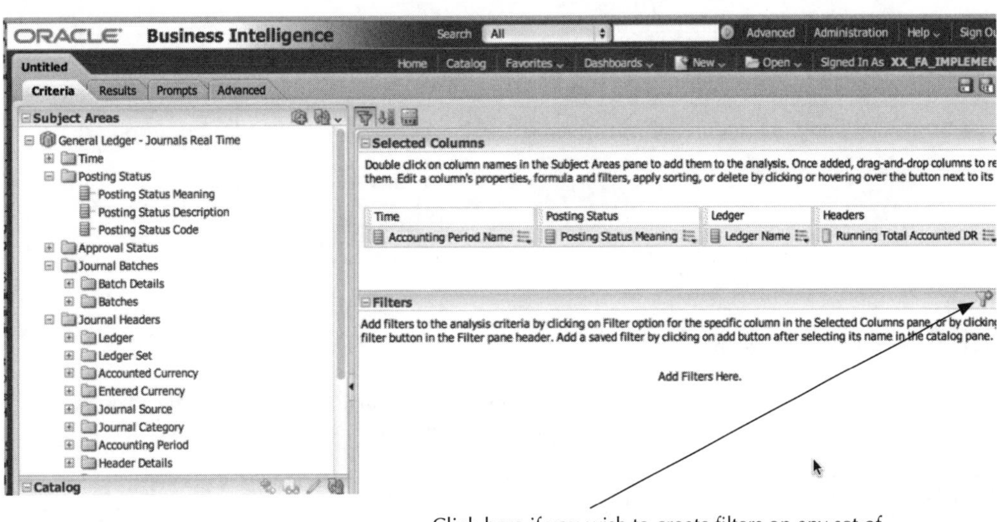

FIGURE 12-8. *Create a report using an existing subject area.*

Click the Results tab, which is displayed in Figure 12-8, to see the results in tabular format. Next, click the New View (+) icon that is to the right of the refresh icon and select Graph | Pie. This will display the default graph region. Click the Edit Pencil icon in the Graph region and drag and drop the Posting Status Meaning column into the Pies and Slices region as shown in Figure 12-9.

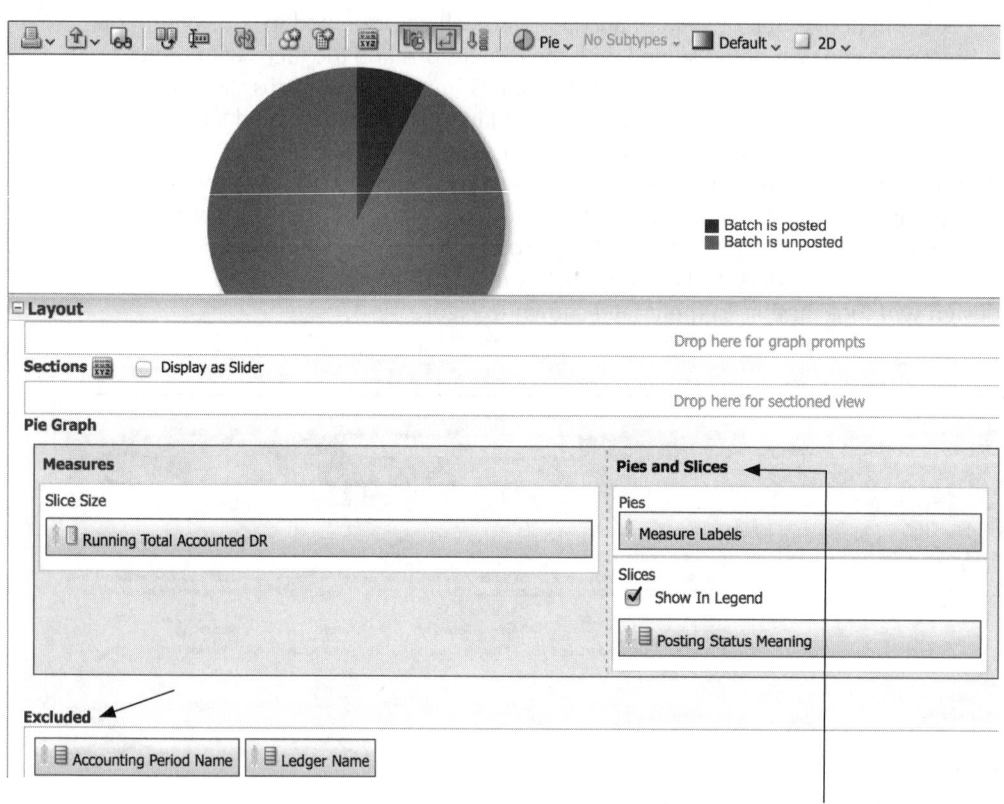

FIGURE 12-9. *Include Posting Status to slice the graph.*

Next, click the Done button to see the report as shown in the following illustration.

Accounting Period Name	Posting Status Meaning	Ledger Name	Running Total Accounted DR
Jan-13	Batch is posted	ANV Common UK	361
	Batch is unposted	ANV Common UK	3362

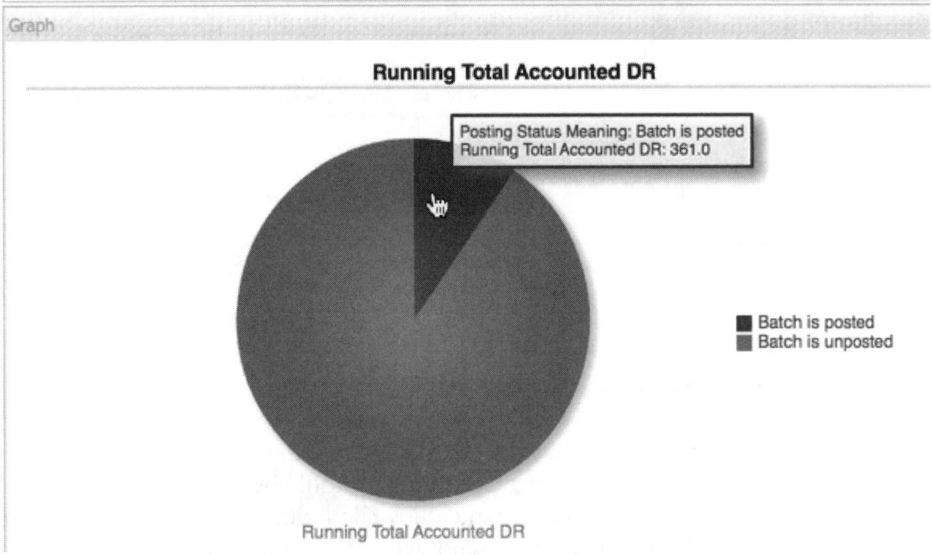

Graph

Running Total Accounted DR

Posting Status Meaning: Batch is posted
Running Total Accounted DR: 361.0

Batch is posted
Batch is unposted

Running Total Accounted DR

As you can see, a business user has the capability to create a new report with a few mouse clicks. After finalizing the report, the user can save the report to a desired custom folder or their own folder if they are the only person to ever run this report in the future.

Importing Custom Objects into OBIEE for OTBI Reporting

Custom objects are required when you make extensions to the product. For those extensions you may create new database tables. These database tables may also have some data security applied to them via view objects and APM. In such cases, you may wish to grant the user the control to generate ad-hoc reports on those custom tables in a secured manner.

In this example we will see the steps that are involved in making these custom view objects available to the OBIEE Physical layer. After these objects have been imported into the OBIEE Physical layer, you can then create a business model and mapping and the subject area in the Presentation layer. The subject area can be granted read permissions to a duty role. If a user has been granted that duty role via a job role, then they will be able to create ad-hoc reports on the custom tables.

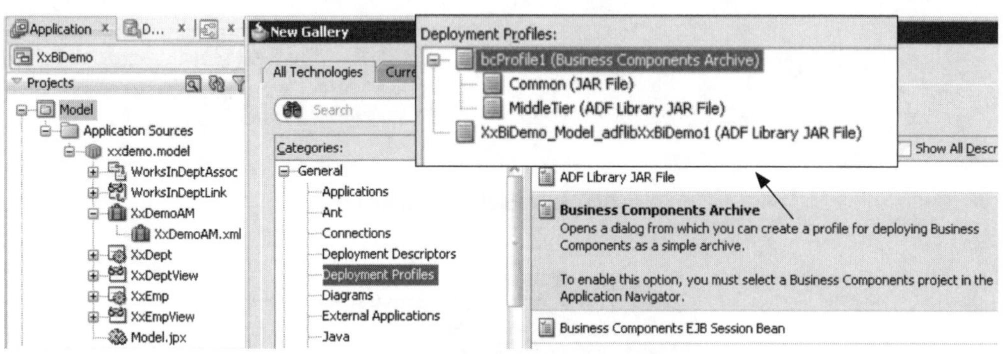

FIGURE 12-10. *Create a deployment profile for your model project with custom view objects.*

Let us assume that you have already created a BC4J (Business Components For Java) model for Department and Employee View Objects in a project named Model.jpr in an application named XxBiDemo. After creating the Application Module, View Object, and View links, create a Deployment profile by selecting the Model.jpr project in JDeveloper, and on the menu, click File | New. In the New Gallery window, select the All Technologies tab, and within the General category, select Deployment Profiles. In the right-hand side pane, select Business Components Archive. Accept the default and this will result in a default deployment profile bcProfile1 getting created as shown in Figure 12-10.

Next, we need to make custom ADF view objects available for the OBIEE Broker Servlet, so that using the OBIEE Broker Servlet, the OBIEE's Physical layer can connect to these custom BC4J objects. Again in JDeveloper, create a new Web Project using File | New | General | Projects, and then in the right-hand pane, select Web Project. We have given the name OBIEEBroker to this project for convenience, but you may select any another name. At this stage the wizard will prompt you to select a Web Application Version and select Servlet 2.5\JSP2.1 (Java EE 1.5) as the servlet type and click Next. For Page Flow Technology, select the option "None" in the wizard. Click Next again to skip the selection of Tag Libraries, and then in the Web Project Profile window of the wizard, override the Java EE Web Application Name and Java EE Context Root by OBIEEDemo. Note that this root context name will appear in the URL of the OBIEEBroker that you will use to connect to ADF objects from the OBIEE Administration tool.

After having created this Web project, we need to include the libraries for BI Integration and applcore into this project. To do so, select the OBIEEBroker.jpr project, and in the Application Resources section of JDeveloper, expand Descriptors | META-INF and double-click weblogic-application.xml. Select Libraries in the left-hand pane, and in Shared Library References, add two libraries as shown in Figure 12-11.

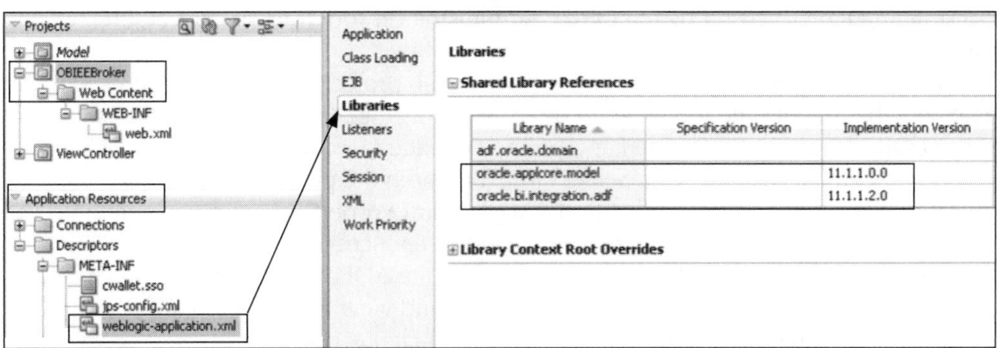

FIGURE 12-11. *Add the applcore and BI libraries to the Web project.*

In the Projects section for OBIEEBroker, within WEB-INF, double-click web.xml and edit the web.xml file to include a reference to the OBIEE Servlet class. Also, map that servlet to a URL pattern /obieebroker as shown in the servlet-mapping node of the following web.xml snippet:

```
<?xml version = '1.0' encoding = 'windows-1252'?>
<web-app xmlns:xsi="http://www.w3.org/2001/XMLSchema-instance"
         xsi:schemaLocation="http://java.sun.com/xml/ns/javaee http://java.sun.com/
xml/ns/javaee/web-app_2_5.xsd"
         version="2.5" xmlns="http://java.sun.com/xml/ns/javaee">
  <context-param>
  <description>This holds the Principals (CSV) that a valid end user should
have (at least one) in order to query the ADF layer from BI.</description>
  <param-name>oracle.bi.integration.approle.whitelist</param-name>
  <param-value>DISABLE_BI_WHITELIST_ROLE_CHECK</param-value>
</context-param>
<filter>
  <filter-name>ServletADFFilter</filter-name>
  <filter-class>oracle.adf.share.http.ServletADFFilter</filter-class>
</filter>
<filter-mapping>
  <filter-name>ServletADFFilter</filter-name>
  <servlet-name>OBIEEBroker</servlet-name>
  <dispatcher>FORWARD</dispatcher>
  <dispatcher>REQUEST</dispatcher>
</filter-mapping>
<servlet>
  <servlet-name>OBIEEBroker</servlet-name>
  <servlet-class>oracle.bi.integration.adf.v11g.obieebroker.OBIEEBroker
  </servlet-class>
</servlet>
<servlet-mapping>
  <servlet-name>OBIEEBroker</servlet-name>
  <url-pattern>/obieebroker</url-pattern>
</servlet-mapping>
</web-app>
```

The URL pattern can be any text instead of obieebroker, and that text is used for constructing the URL used by the OBIEE Administration Tool to connect to OBIEE Broker.

Finally, before we deploy the model and the Web project, we need to build an assembly that stitches the model and Web project together. Remember that the Web project OBIEEBroker.jpr is created as a proxy reference to allow connection to BC4J objects by OBIEE Broker Servlet. Select OBIEEBroker in the projects section and click the JDeveloper menu Application | Application Properties. Here you can configure our OBIEEBroker Web Project to include references to the BC4J components jar files so that OBIEE Broker Servlet can reference the ADFbc components, which are the custom application module, view objects, and view links in this case. The instructions for building this assembly are shown in Figure 12-12.

Next, deploy the entire application XxBiDemo to the CRM domain of Fusion Applications. This can be done via JDeveloper as well for your development environment. After the application has been deployed, navigate to the Enterprise Manager for the Oracle Fusion CRM using a URL similar to http://<host>:<Port>/em, and make a note of the URL for OBIEE Broker Web App as shown in Figure 12-13.

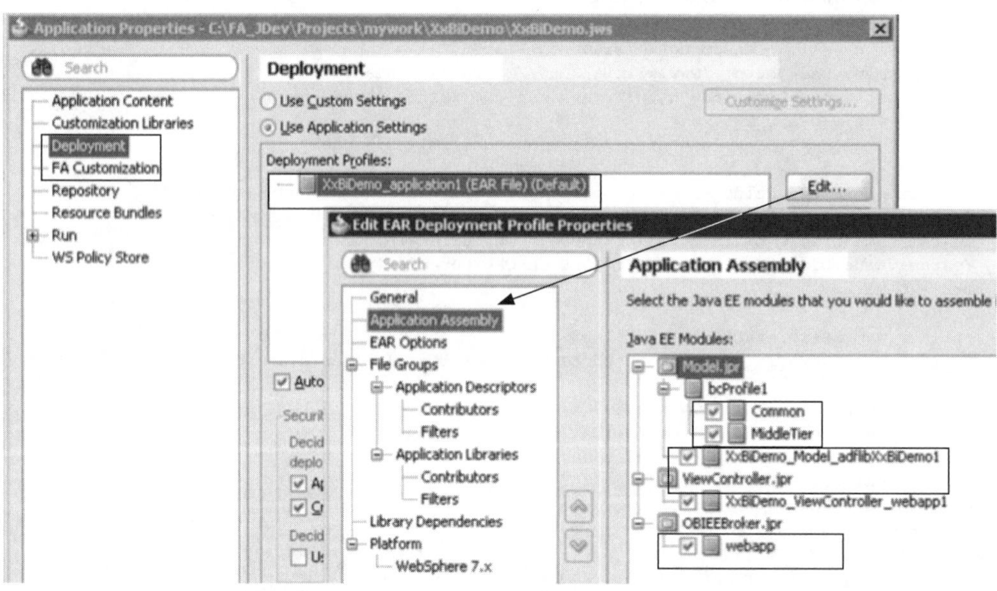

FIGURE 12-12. *Create an assembly that includes BC4J Project and OBIEE Broker Web App.*

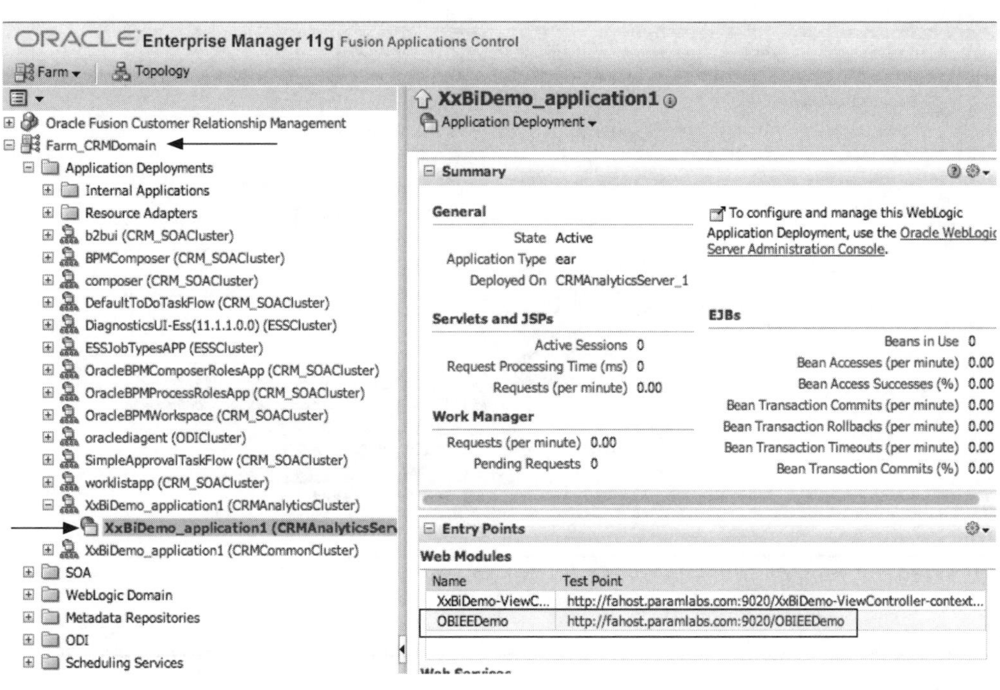

FIGURE 12-13. *Deployed Web App URL for OBIEE Broker*

To this URL, append the servlet mapping URL Pattern from web.xml and make a note of the complete URL, which will look similar to http://fahost.com:9020/OBIEEDemo/obieeebroker.

In the OBIEE Administration Development Tool, on the menu, click File | Import Metadata and this will present you with a wizard with which you can import the ADF objects into the Physical layer. Select Import Type = OracleADF_HTTP. Create a New Connection as shown in Figure 12-14. Please note that the URL will be pointing to the OBIEE Broker Servlet instance that gives you access to your custom BC4J objects.

The password for username FUSION_APPS_BI_APPID is generated by the system during the install of Fusion Applications, and your DBA should be able to provide you with that password. Alternatively, use the wlst command `listCred` to obtain this password in free text:

```
listCred(map="oracle.apps.security", key="FUSION_APPS_BI_APPID-KEY")
```

Shuttle the desired objects into the Physical layer of OBIEE as shown in Figure 12-15 and click Finish to complete the import.

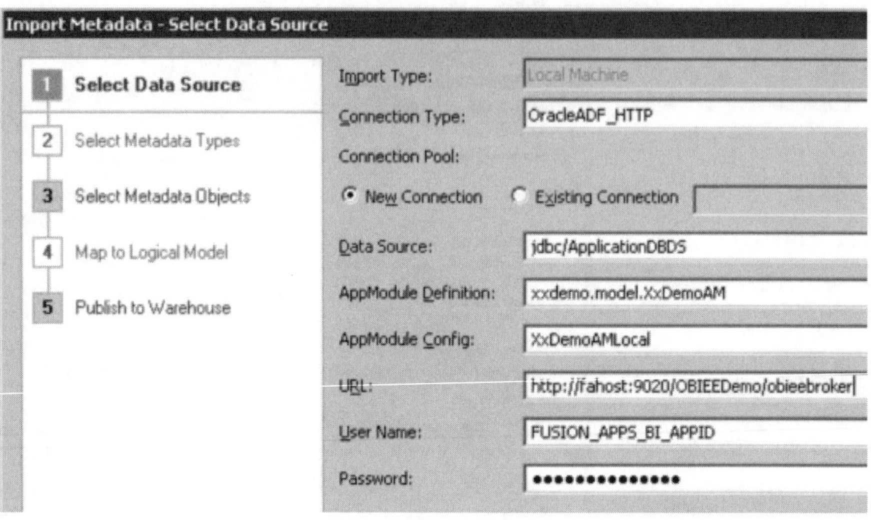

FIGURE 12-14. *Connect OBIEE to OBIEE Broker Servlet to import ADF objects.*

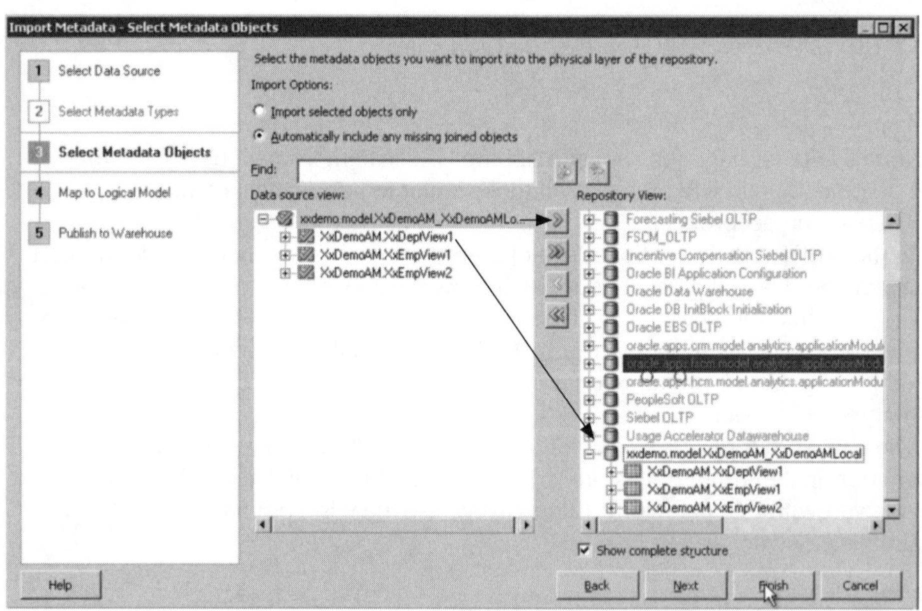

FIGURE 12-15. *Import the Application Module, View Object, and View links to the physical layer.*

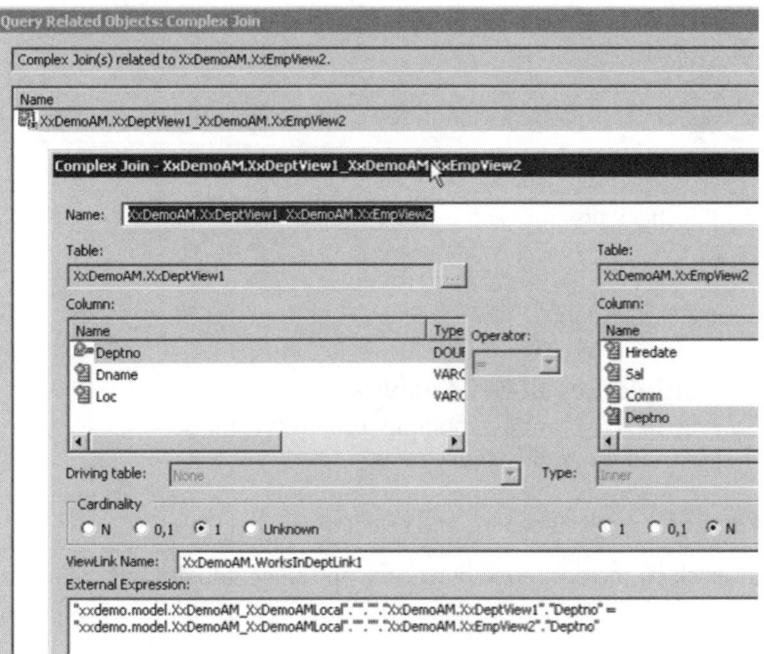

FIGURE 12-16. *Complex joins created for view links*

As shown in Figure 12-16, you will notice that the complex joins are created automatically in the Physical layer for the view link that was created in JDeveloper.

After the import of the ADF objects into OBIEE, you can then proceed to build the Business Model and Mapping layer, followed by the subject area to make the custom objects available for OTBI reporting.

Joining Two Subject Areas into a Single Report

In BI Answers, there are two ways to create cross–subject area queries:

1. Creating a single-result set by combining data from multiple subject areas.
2. Combining multiple result sets using Set Operators (such as Union, Union All, Intersection, and Difference).

Creating a Single-Result-Set Analysis

Use the following steps to create a single-result set by combining data from multiple subject areas:

1. Create a new Analysis report, and select the Criteria tab.
2. Right-click on the desired Subject Area and select Add/Remove Subject Areas.
3. Select the check box for each needed subject area.
4. Click OK.
5. Select the Results tab.

Creating a Multiple-Result-Set Analysis

Use the following steps to combine multiple result sets using set operators, therefore reporting on data from multiple subject areas:

1. Create a new Analysis report, and select the Criteria tab.
2. Right-click on the desired Subject Area and select the desired column.
3. Click OK.
4. Repeat Steps 1 and 2 for each subject area and column to use in the cross-subject area analysis.
5. Select the Results tab.

Restrictions in Using Cross-Subject Analysis

The following restrictions apply when using cross-subject analysis:

- You can create a query joining only subject areas within your security access.
- A cross–subject area query is limited by the underlying schema relationship and is only possible through common dimensions shared by the selected subject areas.
- Degenerate dimensions are not supported. A "degenerate dimension" is a local dimension that exists only in the selected subject area. If additional attributes are added, the query does not return correct data.
- Nonconforming dimensions are not supported. "Conforming dimensions" are those dimensions that exist in all subject areas selected for the query. Therefore a "nonconforming" dimension is the one that does not exist in all subject areas selected for the query.

Steps for Including Flexfields in OTBI

The descriptive flexfields allow implementers to add new fields to the user interfaces. These fields are mapped to database columns, and therefore, often there is a need to report on the flexfield segments in the OTBI. The registration process of a descriptive flexfield has a flag named BI Enabled. Also, you can enable the desired segments for BI by setting the BI Enabled flag for that segment in the descriptive flexfield. Next, when you deploy the descriptive flexfield, it generates new view objects with the view attributes that correspond to flexfield segments that are BI Enabled. These changes to the view objects can be imported into the Physical layer of OBIEE. You can follow the step-by-step instructions shown in Oracle Support Note 1513020.1 to import descriptive flexfield segments into OBIEE.

The key flexfields also have a BI Enabled flag for their segments. The value sets attached to the key flexfield segments may have a hierarchy. The values in the value set hierarchy can be flattened using the task Manage Trees and Tree Versions. The view objects are generated for the flexfield value set values during the deployment. These view objects can be imported as dimension tables in OBIEE. For a detailed step-by-step example for implementing GL Accounting Key Flexfield into OTBI, please read Oracle Support Note Oracle Fusion Financials OTBI Set-Up - Addendum - Accounting Role Playing Dimensions (Doc ID 1355653.1). This support note contains an attached zipped field containing a document named "Release Notes Addendum AccountKFF_PreReqSetupSteps.docx". This document gives detailed step-by-step instructions for importing Accounting key flexfields into OBIEE.

Summary

In this chapter you have learned about the key features of Oracle Transactional Business Intelligence, which allows the analysis of data in an ad-hoc and secured manner. At the heart of this technology is the integration of OBIEE with ADF view objects. Given that the view objects already contain the relevant joins between different tables, it therefore avoids the need for the report developer to understand in depth the relationships between various transactional tables. This not only reduces the time it takes for report development but also ensures that the data security of the operational systems is replicated in the OTBI Reporting used in Fusion Applications.

CHAPTER 13

Enterprise Scheduler Jobs and Processing

Oracle Enterprise Scheduler is a new Fusion Middleware component that provides the capability to run PL/SQL, Java, host scripts, and binary executables on time-based schedules. In Fusion Applications, Oracle Enterprise Scheduler takes the role of the Concurrent Processing component, available in Oracle E-Business Suite, and readers with an Oracle E-Business Suite background should be able to make direct comparisons between Oracle Enterprise Scheduler and Concurrent Processing components.

Although the growing need to process and consume information in real time or near-real time through the event-driven architecture approach is becoming increasingly prevalent, we still require the capability to run large jobs on a scheduled basis outside of normal working hours such as the large import of invoices or any other bulk data transfers that are usually executed outside of normal working hours. Additionally, the scheduling capabilities of Oracle Enterprise Scheduler could also be used to complement, or even replace in simple integration scenarios, the use of other tools from the technology stack such as Oracle SOA, BPM, and so forth.

In this chapter, we'll touch on the architecture, security, and monitoring aspects of Oracle Enterprise Scheduler, but most importantly, we'll go through a practical example to show us what it takes to create and set up a custom Oracle Enterprise Scheduler job in Fusion Applications.

Enterprise Scheduler in Fusion Applications

From now on we'll refer to Enterprise Scheduler in Fusion Applications as Enterprise Scheduling Service or ESS for short. We already mentioned that ESS provides the capability to schedule the running of jobs at some predefined time, and if needed in some predefined order too. When we say *jobs*, think of units of work or programs that need to be performed within certain constraints such as time windows for execution, system resources like available Java threads on the server, and so forth.

Fusion Applications system administrators and developers usually focus on somewhat different aspects of system components, and ESS is not an exception. In the next two sections we'll provide a summary of available tools for administration as well as an overview of ESS architecture from the custom ESS job developer's angle.

Overview of ESS for System Administrators

Whether we think of ESS as an application for batch processing or time-based scheduling application that provides callbacks to client applications to run their jobs (programs) as described in Oracle documentation, in technical terms ESS is just a JEE application named ESSAPP deployed to a WebLogic server as a part of Oracle Fusion Middleware technology stack. The ear file for ESSAPP JEE application is located at <middleware_home>/atgpf/ess/archives/ess-app.ear.

ESS Administration Pages

For readers familiar with E-Business Suite, what is markedly different between Concurrent Processing in E-Business Suite and the ESS component in Fusion Applications is that the former existed as a single component (Concurrent Manager) shared across all modules in E-Business Suite while ESS is a part of each product offering in Fusion Applications, and therefore all products offering WebLogic domains like FinancialsDomain, CRMDomain, and HCMDomain have ESS deployed separately in each of them.

For example, to access ESS administration tasks for the Financials product family, we go to Enterprise Manager for FinancialsDomain via http(s)://<fin_domain_host>:<fin_domain_port>/em to access ESS administration pages.

The following list, together with corresponding annotations on Figure 13-1, presents a summary of the functionality available in the current releases of Fusion Applications:

1. Admin tasks are accessed by navigating to Scheduling Services from the EM navigation pane and selecting the ESSAPP component.
2. Selecting the Scheduling Service menu opens a list of ESS admin options.
3. The Home Page is used as a starting point for ESS administration and monitoring. It provides page sections that display information like top ten long-running jobs (requests), scheduler components, jobs (requests)

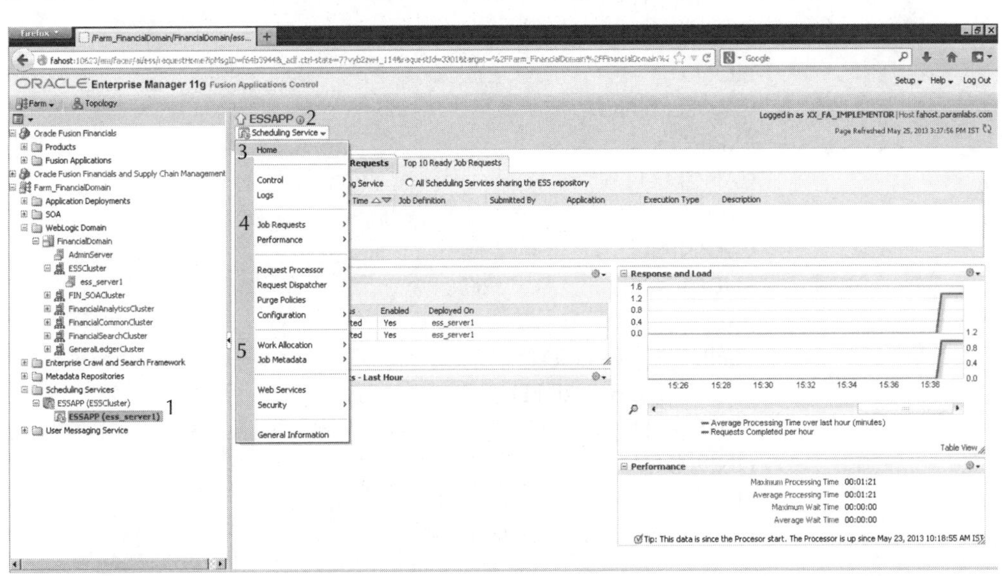

FIGURE 13-1. *ESS Administration pages in Enterprise Manager for Financials domain*

completed in the last hour, response and load page region, and overall performance summary.

4. Job requests can be scheduled, submitted, searched, and viewed from the Job Requests menu option. Selected requests can be cancelled, held, or resumed depending on their current status. The full list of ESS job states is listed in Table 13-1.

5. Job definitions are accessed by clicking on Job Metadata | Job Definitions (submenu not shown in Figure 13-1). After we select an application that we are interested in, the list of all available job definitions is presented, and clicking any of them will allow us to access the details for that job such as type of the job (PL/SQL, Java, and so on), display name, path, parameters, user properties, and so forth. We'll examine job definitions more closely when we present a worked example later in this chapter.

ESS jobs can have the states listed in Table 13-1.

Job State Number	Job State
1	WAIT
2	READY
3	RUNNING
4	COMPLETED
5	BLOCKED
6	HOLD
7	CANCELLING
8	EXPIRED
9	CANCELLED
10	ERROR
11	WARNING
12	SUCCEEDED
13	PAUSED
14	PENDING_VALIDATION
15	VALIDATION_FAILED
16	SCHEDULE_ENDED
17	FINISHED
18	ERROR_AUTO_RETRY
19	ERROR_MANUAL_RECOVERY

TABLE 13-1. *ESS Job States*

Request Log and Output Files

Similar to applications in E-Business Suite, jobs can be coded to generate log and output information and save it in the corresponding log and output files. From both administration and development perspectives, we need to know where they get generated and what happens to them at runtime. According to Oracle Support portal and its article "Where Are the Log and Output Files for ESS Jobs Stored?" [ID 1401648.1], the log files are temporarily created in the following locations:

- RequestFileDirectory/<request_id>/log/
- RequestFileDirectory/<request_id>/out/

The following SQL query helps identify the full paths:

```
select processgroup,logworkdirectory,outputworkdirectory
from fusion_ora_ess.request_history
where requestid = <request_id>;
```

The support note also states that once the entire log is written out, it is uploaded to the Universal Content Management server and deleted from the temporary location.

The question most system administrators would ask is: how is this behavior controlled and is it possible to change it for development, testing, or other purposes? The answer to this is that the location of the log and output files is defined by the FilePersistenceMode and RequestFileDirectory parameters within the connections.xml file, which can be found in the ess-app.ear/ adf / META-INF directory. Actually, the modifications to this file must not be done manually but through the System MBean Browser functionality in Enterprise Manager as shown in Figure 13-2. Here is how to do it:

1. Navigate to WebLogic Domain and select the Oracle Enterprise Scheduler server.
2. From the WebLogic Server menu, select System MBean Browser and expand Application Defined MBeans.
3. Expand oracle.adf.share.connections as shown in Figure 13-2.

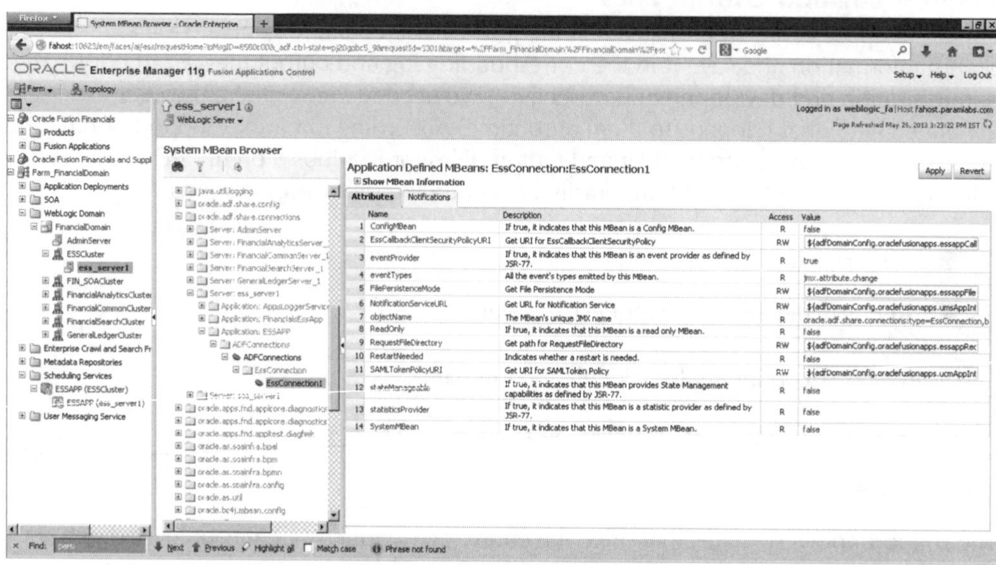

FIGURE 13-2. *FilePersistenceMode and RequestFileDirectory parameters in Enterprise Manager*

Depending on the FilePersistenceMode parameter value at runtime, the behavior that affects the location of the log and output files is as follows:

- **Value set to content** When set to **content**, the files will be stored as an attachment in Universal Content Management (UCM), in which case they are removed from the file system and uploaded to the UCM server under the default folder contribution Folders/Attachment/ESS_REQUEST_HISTORY/<request_id>, where <request_id> is a unique job request identifier.

- **Value set to file** If parameter is set to **file**, the value of the RequestFileDirectory parameter will determine the full path of the job request's log and output directory on the file system.

NOTE
Do not confuse ESS Server Logging with Job Request log and output files. The ESS Server Logging configuration is defined by navigating to the ess_server1 menu from the expanded WebLogic Domain tree in the navigation pane and selecting Logs | Log Configuration. The Log Configuration page that opens allows you to configure different log levels for various loggers such as oracle.apps.fnd.applcp, oracle.as.ess, oracle.as.scheduler., oracle.ess.*, and others. The ESSAPP log files can be accessed from the Scheduling Service menu for ESSAPP and selecting Logs | View Log Messages.*

Later in the chapter we'll discuss what APIs are available for developers to produce and populate output and log files.

ESS Database Schema FUSION_ORA_ESS

A schema in Oracle Database where ESS tables and packages reside is called FUSION_ORA_ESS. My Oracle Support portal has a useful note (ID 1347299.1), which lists ESS tables along with their description as shown in Table 13-2.

ESS Table	Description
ESS_CONFIG	Table for general ESS configuration parameters for the ESS schema.
REQUEST_HISTORY	ESS request history table.
REQUEST_METADATA	ESS runtime metadata store.
JOB_INCOMPATIBILITY	Incompatibilities referenced by a job/jobset definition.
INCOMPATIBILITY_LOCK	Incompatibility lock table.
REQUEST_INCOMPATIBILITY	Incompatibilities used (acquired/released) during lifetime of a request.
REQUEST_PROPERTY	Application-specified request parameters. May also contain scoped system parameters for jobsets.
REQUEST_CONSTRAINT	Request parameters that have been flagged as read-only.
EVENT_FILTER	Event filter information used for trigger-based requests.
REQUEST_SEC_PRINCIPAL	Table for security principals used for execution of a request. This information is used by CP for PL/SQL runAs and possibly other CP tasks.
REQUEST_CP	Table for storing miscellaneous information used by CP.

TABLE 13-2. *ESS Database Tables (Continued)*

ESS Table	Description
WAIT_QUEUE	ESS wait queue.
ESS_COORD	Table for basic coordination between ESS instances.
ESS_APP_REGISTRATION	Table that lists applications with active endpoints in a given instance.
CONFIGURED_BINDINGS	Work assignment to processor bindings for all ESS instances using this schema. The bindings are managed by EM.
OPERATIVE_BINDINGS	Bindings that are in effect for all ESS instances using this schema. If an instance is down, it will not have any rows in this table. For each instance, this table provides a cache of the configured bindings it last read, plus state on those bindings.
ASYNC_THROTTLE	Each type of async job (plsql, async java) can be limited for a (work assignment, workshift) within a process group. This table contains the limit and current allocation for work assignments that are so limited. The limit is the maximum number of jobs that can be executing, meaning within initialize to finalize stages. A limit of –1 means no limit. The allocation is the number of jobs that are currently executing.
CHANGED_WA_METADATA	Contains, for each instance, metadata IDs of work assignment metadata that have changed and may need to be reloaded.
ESS_WS_ASYNC_INFO	Table that stores information used for Web service asynchronous callbacks.
SCRATCH_QUERY_PRINCIPAL	Table used for security principal information for query request operation.
COMMAND_WORK	Table for async commands/operations issued from PL/SQL interface.
WORK_UNITS	Used to track work, usually relating to request processing. It is the cornerstone of ESS processing. Work is checked out from this table, stages are tracked for optimal recovery, and so on.
EVENT_WORK	ESS events table.
NOTIFY_REGISTRATION	Notification support for work units, events.
FAILED_EXECUTION_HISTORY	ESS failed execution history table. Contains history of failed past execution attempts for requests that are being or have been retried (automatically or manually). Each row contains information copied from request_history before the request_history row is reset for retry. Note that dispatcher and processor are the servername, not the instance ID.
RECOVERY_DELETE	Stores information for manual recovery scenarios when deleting instances, for example, removal of an entire process group.

TABLE 13-2. *ESS Database Tables*

The information stored in ESS tables is particularly useful for troubleshooting purposes; for example, the REQUEST_HISTORY table allow us to query all available data for a particular job that was run or is still running.

Overview of ESS for Fusion Applications Developers

The ESS administration pages discussed in the previous sections help system administrators and developers alike manage the lifecycle of a job definition, such as scheduling, distribution, and monitoring. In the sections that follow we are going to introduce the ESS architecture and development aspects of the job definition along with tools and techniques available to Fusion Applications developers in order to create custom ESS jobs.

Oracle Enterprise Scheduler Architecture Overview

The product documentation defines Oracle Enterprise Scheduler as an application that provides time- and schedule-based callbacks to other applications to run their jobs, which means that Oracle Enterprise Scheduler is not aware of the details for a particular job request; in other words, Oracle Enterprise Scheduler is decoupled from an application that schedules and runs the job request. In ESS, an application that submits the job requests is called a client application.

Although Oracle Enterprise Scheduler does not provide a UI for the end user to interact with it directly, in Fusion Applications the end user normally interacts with the prebuilt applications that are part of the product offering. The names of the applications that launch job requests depend on which product is used: FinancialsEssApp, HcmEssApp, CrmEssApp, ProjectFinancialsEssApp, and ProcurementEssApp are some examples.

NOTE
In Fusion Applications, to define custom ESS jobs and their associated metadata such as job type, Java executable name, PL/SQL procedure name, and others, we can use Manage Custom Enterprise Scheduler Jobs taskflow from the Setup and Maintenance menu available to users with administrator Functional Setup Manager privileges. We can also use the ESS administration page in Enterprise Manager as shown in Figure 13-1 (Job Metadata menu option). Although the Oracle Fusion Applications Developer's Guide for Oracle Enterprise Scheduler *suggests using Oracle JDeveloper to create an Oracle Enterprise Scheduler executable class and Oracle Enterprise Scheduler–specific metadata for job executables, we actually use the existing job hosting applications such as FinancialsEss and EarHcmEss and an existing job submission application without the need to build the client UI from scratch. This will be demonstrated in a worked example later in the chapter.*

Figure 13-3 shows system interactions within individual ESS components:

1. User submits a request from a Web browser using client application.
2. Client application sends the request to Enterprise Scheduler to schedule the job.
3. Enterprise Scheduler reads the metadata for the request.
4. Enterprise Scheduler puts the request in a wait queue (table) in FUSION_ORA_ESS schema, along with the metadata.
5. At the scheduled time, Enterprise Scheduler sends a callback message to the client application with all the request parameters and metadata captured at the time of the job request submission.
6. Client application performs the jobs and returns a status.
7. Enterprise Scheduler updates the history with the job request status in the REQUEST_HISTORY table.

It is possible to have Client Application and Enterprise Scheduler in a split configuration where submitting and hosting application reside on different WebLogic servers.

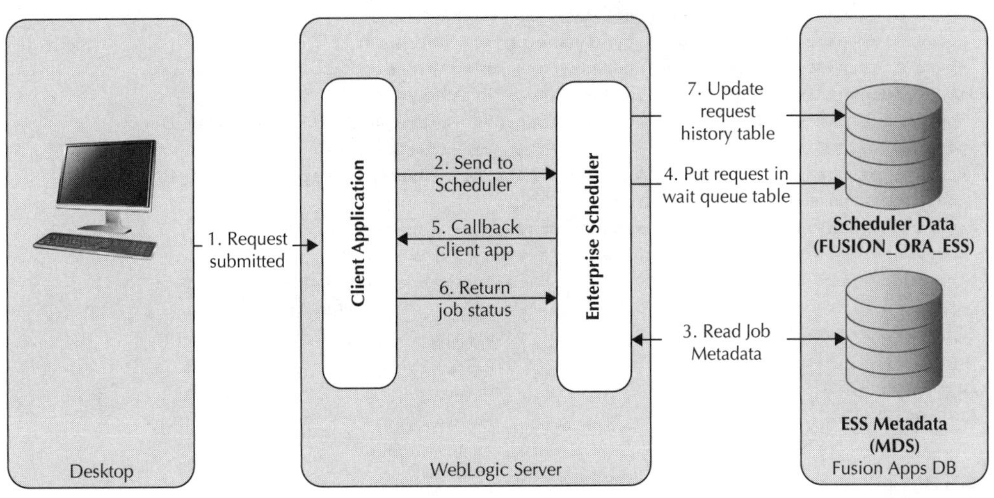

FIGURE 13-3. *ESS components*

ESS Metadata Services

Metadata Services, also called MDS, is used in almost all components of Fusion Middleware, and ESS is no exception. ESS MDS is used to store the application level of metadata, such as job type, job definition, job set, and other application-level metadata. Additionally, MDS also stores global metadata such as schedules, work shifts, and work assignments.

The data in MDS is organized hierarchically, similar to file directory structures on Windows or Linux operating systems. For example, the custom job definition XxInterfaceCount that we define in our example presented in the next section is stored under the following path in MDS: /oracle/apps/ess/custom/ledger/interface/Jobs and has the following content:

```
<?xml version="1.0" encoding="UTF-8"?>
<job-definition xmlns="http://xmlns.oracle.com/scheduler"
             job-type="/oracle/as/ess/ext/JobType/PlsqlJobType.xml"
             name="XxInterfaceCount"
             xmlns:xsi="http://www.w3.org/2001/XMLSchema-instance">
<description>Demo: Custom PL/SQL ESS job</description>
<display-name>XX Interface Count</display-name>
<parameter-list>
  <parameter name="SYS_procedureName" data-type="string">XxCustomLedger
.InterfaceCount</parameter>
  <parameter name="SYS_priority" data-type="integer"/>
  <parameter name="jobDefinitionApplication" data-type="string">CustomGL</parameter>
  <parameter name="EXT_PortletContainerWebModule" data-type="string">Ledger</
parameter>
```

```
  <parameter name="SYS_application" data-type="string"/>
  <parameter name="SYS_retries" data-type="integer"/>
  <parameter name="srsFlag" data-type="string">Y</parameter>
  <parameter name="parametersVO" data-type="string">sessiondef.oracle.apps.atk.
essMeta.XxInterfaceCountAtkEssParamaterViewDef</parameter>
  <parameter name="SYS_effectiveApplication" data-type="string">FinancialsEss</
parameter>
  <parameter name="SYS_product" data-type="string">CustomGL</parameter>
  <parameter name="SYS_requestCategory" data-type="string"/>
  <parameter name="SYS_request_timeout" data-type="integer"/>
  <parameter name="ParameterTaskflow" data-type="string"/>
  <parameter name="SYS_allowMultPending" data-type="boolean">false</parameter>
  <parameter name="Program.FMG" data-type="string">L.XML,O.PDF</parameter>
  <parameter name="defaultOutputExtension" data-type="string">txt</parameter>
  <parameter name="numberOfArgs" data-type="string">1</parameter>
</parameter-list>
</job-definition>
```

TIP

The MDS repository can be exported from Oracle Database into a file system directory on a local machine where a browser is running. For example, to export MDS from FinancialsEssApp log in to Enterprise Manager for Financials Domain, expand the Fusion Applications folder under the root Oracle Fusion Financials node, select FinancialsEssApp (ess_server1), click the Fusion J2EE Application menu button under FinancialsEssApp, and select MDS Configuration Option. From here you can export MDS that belongs to the globalEss partition from the database in the flat files.

We'll shortly discuss how MDS namespaces and paths are used to secure ESS resources and allow only users with the correct privileges to be able to define and run ESS jobs.

Custom ESS Job Worked Example

The best way to get familiar with the concepts relating to creation and configuration of custom ESS jobs is to go through a hands-on example. Fusion Applications support the following types of job types and their corresponding programs or executables:

- SQL Loader programs
- SQL Plus scripts
- PL/SQL procedures
- Perl scripts
- Java classes
- Host programs (shell scripts)
- C programs (C executables)
- BIP (Business Intelligence Publisher Reports)

In our step-by-step example we are going to look at how to set up and configure a simple custom PL/SQL job. Before we begin our custom job definition steps, we'll create a custom application and assign correct access privileges to the users.

Creating a Custom Application

A custom application can be added by accessing the Setup and Maintenance page (Navigator | Setup and Maintenance) and searching for the Manage Taxonomy Hierarchy task.

In the Manage Taxonomy Hierarchy task page, expand all the nodes, select Oracle Fusion (1), and click on the Create Child Module button (2) as indicated in Figure 13-4.

In the Child Module Details region, set the Product Line field to Fusion, Module Type to Family, Module Name to Custom, Alternative ID to some unique number such as 10001 in our case, and set Usage Type to Installed (see Figure 13-5). Click the Save button to save a newly added record into the database.

After saving the Custom family, the Manage Taxonomy Hierarchy page should refresh and the newly added Custom family will appear under Oracle Fusion hierarchy. Now we can click on our Custom module and add a custom application by selecting it and clicking the Create New Module button. This will open a page that will allow us to populate values and create XX Custom Ledger App as shown in Figure 13-6 after saving the record to the database.

We now should be able to specify XX Custom Ledger App as an application when defining our custom ESS jobs.

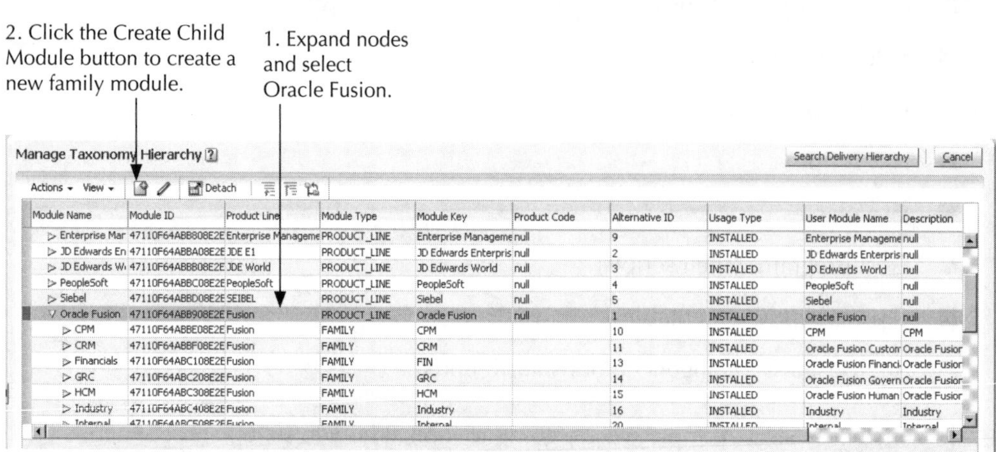
2. Click the Create Child Module button to create a new family module.
1. Expand nodes and select Oracle Fusion.
Manage Taxonomy Hierarchy
Search Delivery Hierarchy
Cancel
Actions
View
Detach

Module Name	Module ID	Product Line	Module Type	Module Key	Product Code	Alternative ID	Usage Type	User Module Name	Description
▷ Enterprise Mar	47110F64ABB808E2E	Enterprise Manageme	PRODUCT_LINE	Enterprise Manageme	null	9	INSTALLED	Enterprise Manageme	null
▷ JD Edwards En	47110F64ABBA08E2E	JDE E1	PRODUCT_LINE	JD Edwards Enterpris	null	2	INSTALLED	JD Edwards Enterpris	null
▷ JD Edwards W	47110F64ABBB08E2E	JDE World	PRODUCT_LINE	JD Edwards World	null	3	INSTALLED	JD Edwards World	null
▷ PeopleSoft	47110F64ABBC08E2E	PeopleSoft	PRODUCT_LINE	PeopleSoft	null	4	INSTALLED	PeopleSoft	null
▷ Siebel	47110F64ABBD08E2E	SIEBEL	PRODUCT_LINE	Siebel	null	5	INSTALLED	Siebel	null
▽ Oracle Fusion	47110F64ABB908E2E	Fusion	PRODUCT_LINE	Oracle Fusion	null	1	INSTALLED	Oracle Fusion	null
▷ CPM	47110F64ABBE08E2E	Fusion	FAMILY	CPM		10	INSTALLED	CPM	CPM
▷ CRM	47110F64ABBF08E2E	Fusion	FAMILY	CRM		11	INSTALLED	Oracle Fusion Custom	Oracle Fusion
▷ Financials	47110F64ABC108E2E	Fusion	FAMILY	FIN		13	INSTALLED	Oracle Fusion Financi	Oracle Fusion
▷ GRC	47110F64ABC208E2E	Fusion	FAMILY	GRC		14	INSTALLED	Oracle Fusion Govern	Oracle Fusion
▷ HCM	47110F64ABC308E2E	Fusion	FAMILY	HCM		15	INSTALLED	Oracle Fusion Human	Oracle Fusion
▷ Industry	47110F64ABC408E2E	Fusion	FAMILY	Industry		16	INSTALLED	Industry	Industry

FIGURE 13-4. *Manage Taxonomy Hierarchy task page*

Manage Taxonomy Hierarchy

Parent Module Details

Module ID 47110F64ABB908E2E040449823C60DB6
Product Line Fusion
Module Type PRODUCT_LINE
Module Name Oracle Fusion
Module Key Oracle Fusion
Product Code
Alternative ID 1
Usage Type INSTALLED
Is Seed Data Allowed N

Child Module Details

* Module ID DDAFB718B6C263A1
* Product Line Fusion
* Module Type Family
* Module Name Custom
* Module Key CUSTOM
* Alternative ID 10001
* Usage Type Installed
User Module Name
Description
Is Seed Data Allowed NO
Logical Domain

FIGURE 13-5. *Create a Custom family in Taxonomy Hierarchy*

Manage Taxonomy Hierarchy

Module ID DDAFB718B6C263A1E0439701A8C048D0
Product Line Fusion
Module Type FAMILY
Module Name Custom
Module Key CUSTOM
Product Code
Alternative ID 10001
Usage Type INSTALLED
Is Seed Data Allowed N

Module Details

Module ID DDAFB718B6C463A1E0439701A8C048D0
* Product Line Fusion
* Module Type Application
* Module Name CustomGL
* Module Key CUSTOM_GL
* Product Code XXGL
* Alternative ID 9999
* Usage Type Installed
User Module Name XX Custom Ledger App
Description XX Custom Ledger App
Is Seed Data Allowed YES

FIGURE 13-6. *Creating a custom application in Taxonomy Hierarchy*

NOTE
The process of creating custom applications in Fusion Applications is not fully documented in user manuals at the time of writing of this book (Release 11.1.6). We suggest consulting with an Oracle Support representative for further details, as we understand that the product documentation is going to be updated with more details.

For more details on application taxonomy, we suggest that you read the *Oracle Fusion Applications Product Information Management Implementation Guide* available from the product documentation page on OTN.

Configuring Metadata Security for a Custom ESS Job

In Chapter 3, we discussed how to create a super user with admin privileges and we are going to use the same XX_FA_IMPLEMENTOR user to create a custom ESS job.

Our XX_FA_IMPLEMENTOR user has Application Implementation Consultant, Application Implementation Manager, and IT Security Manager among other roles assigned to it. This should generally be sufficient for developers to be able to define a custom ESS job and access Functional Setup Manager tasks. In addition to Functional Setup Manager tasks, we also need an access to Authorization Policy Manager (APM), which is a graphical interface tool to manage application authorization and access policies, as discussed in Chapter 3.

Metadata Services Namespace for Custom ESS Jobs

Data in Metadata Services (MDS) is organized in hierarchical fashion similar to Unix and Windows file systems. Instead of directories, MDS uses namespaces or package names to locate a file. ESS stores its metadata under the globalEss partition with namespace /oracle/apps/ess and each application family and offering have their own namespace such as /oracle/apps/ess/hcm for Human Capital Management.

Custom ESS jobs should be defined under the /oracle/app/ess/custom path. How we organize the path under /oracle/app/ess/custom is entirely up to us and should be part of the build standards that all developers adhere to in a particular organization. For example, we could have a parent hierarchy /oracle/app/ess/custom /generalLedger/interface under which we have custom ESS jobs that relate to General Ledger interfaces in Financials. The best practices have still not emerged in terms of naming conventions, but the important thing is that each organization must adopt its own standards and stick to them.

In our example, we'll make sure that Application Implementation Manager has correct privileges and access to /oracle/app/ess/custom/* hierarchy:

1. Log in to Authorization Policy Manager (APM) via http(s)://<common_domain_host>:<common_domain_port>/apm url. Once logged in, select an application, which in our exercise is called fscm and then click the New link under the Resources heading as shown in Figure 13-7 (1).

   When the Untitled tab opens, choose ESSMetadataResourceType and enter the following values as shown in Figure 13-7:

   - **Display Name** oracle.apps.ess.custom.*
   - **Name** oracle.apps.ess.custom.*
   - **Description** Path for custom jobs

   Click Save to persist the record in the database and close the tab.

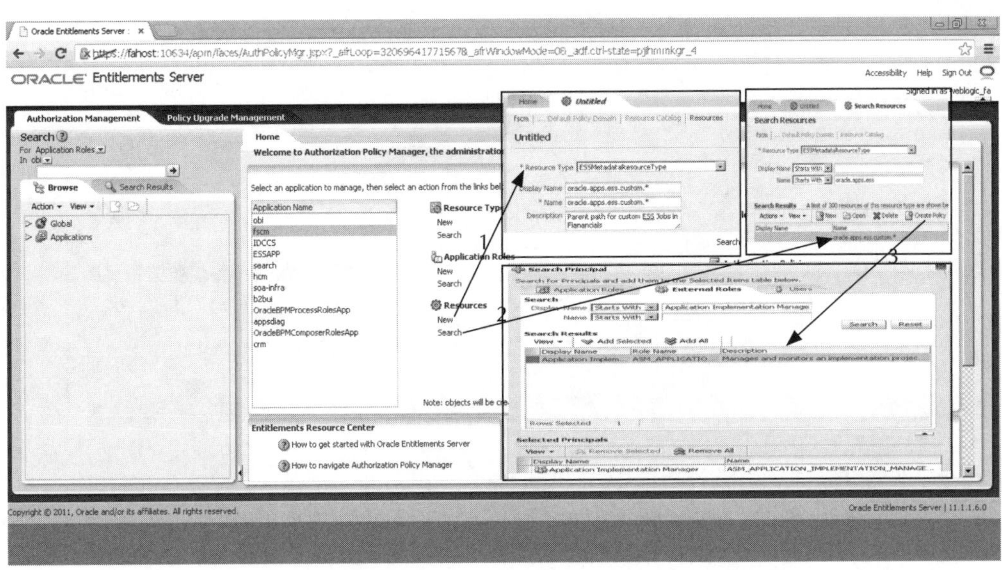

FIGURE 13-7. *Defining a resource for a custom ESS job*

NOTE
We used a wildcard "" to define a resource for all nodes under /oracle/apps/ess/custom hierarchy.*

2. Go back to the main screen, make sure that the fscm application is selected, and click the Search link under the Resources heading. This will open the Search Resources tab where we again select ESSMetadataResourceType from the drop-down list and search for the resource that has a name that starts with oracle.apps.ess as shown in Figure 13-7 (2). Hopefully our resource oracle.apps.ess.custom* that we created in the previous step will show up in the results table.

3. We now select the row with the oracle.apps.ess.custom* resource and click the Create Policy button as shown in Figure 13-7 (3). The new tab will now open, in which we click on the Add Principal button, which will open a search pop-up to search for users, external roles, and application roles. Search for Application Implementation Manager under the External Roles tab.

4. Enable Update, Delete, Create, Execute, and Read actions as demonstrated in Figure 13-8.

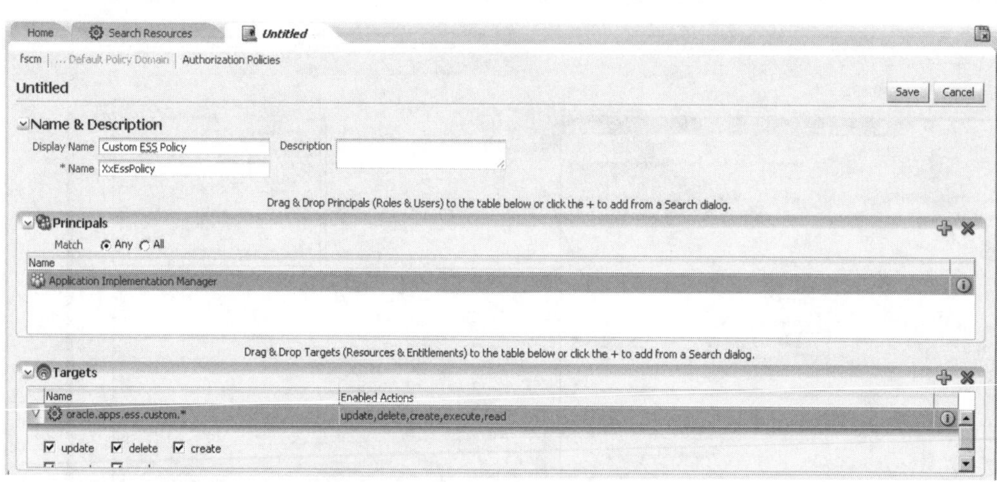

FIGURE 13-8. *Enabling and granting required actions for custom ESS jobs*

Remember that we have already assigned the Application Implementation Manager role to our XX_FA_IMPLEMENTOR user and now we are ready to create a custom ESS job as that user.

Creating a Custom PL/SQL ESS Job

The steps to create a custom PL/SQL job broadly consist of creating the PL/SQL procedure in Oracle Database where the ESS schema resides, that is, the Fusion Application database, and creating a custom PL/SQL job definition using Functional Setup Manager tasks.

Note that the current *Oracle Fusion Applications Developer's Guide for Oracle Enterprise Scheduler* states that for PL/SQL jobs we have to do the following:

- Create or obtain the PL/SQL stored procedure that you want to use with Oracle Enterprise Scheduler.
- Load the PL/SQL stored procedure in the Oracle Database, grant the required permissions, and perform other required DBA tasks.
- Use Oracle JDeveloper to create job type and job definition objects and store these objects with the Oracle Enterprise Scheduler application metadata.
- Use Oracle JDeveloper to create an application with Oracle Enterprise Scheduler APIs that runs and submits a PL/SQL stored procedure.

However, the good news is that in Fusion Applications we don't have to use JDeveloper to create job type and job definition objects or create an application that runs and submits the PL/SQL stored procedure. Instead, we can use out-of-the-box functionality as demonstrated in our next example.

Step 1: Create a PL/SQL Stored Procedure

For the purposes of this exercise we'll create a simple PL/SQL procedure in Fusion Applications FUSION database schema with the correct signature and one parameter *ledgerId*:

```
create or replace package XxCustomLedger AUTHID Current_USER AS

Procedure InterfaceCount (
       errbuf out NOCOPY varchar2,
       retcode out NOCOPY varchar2,
       ledgerId in number );
END XxCustomLedger;
/
create or replace package body XxCustomLedger as

procedure InterfaceCount (
       errbuf out NOCOPY varchar2,
       retcode out NOCOPY varchar2,
       ledgerId in number  )
is
 v_intCount number;
  begin
   fnd_file.put_line(fnd_file.log, 'PL/SQL Procedure InterfaceCount running.');
    fnd_file.put_line(fnd_file.log, 'User Name: ' || fnd_global.user_name);
     select count(*) into v_intCount
     from gl_interface;
    fnd_file.put_line(fnd_file.output, ' Job Request Id:  ' || fnd_job.request_id);
    fnd_file.put_line(fnd_file.output, ' |----------------------------------|');
    fnd_file.put_line(fnd_file.output, '  GL Interface Row Count:  ' || v_intCount);
    fnd_file.put_line(fnd_file.output, ' |----------------------------------|');
    errbuf := fnd_message.get_string ('fnd', 'Normal Completion');
  retcode := 0;
  end InterfaceCount;
end XxCustomLedger;
/
```

NOTE
Using the FUSION database schema for custom ESS jobs is consistent with recommendations provided in the Oracle Fusion Applications Developer's Guide for Oracle Enterprise Scheduler *(Part Number E10142-01).*

The procedure InterfaceCount, which is contained inside the XxCustomLedger PL/SQL package, simply counts a number of rows in the GL_INTERFACE table and uses FND_FILE.PUT_LINE, FND_FILE.OUTPUT, and FND_FILE.LOG to write text to the output and log files. The mandatory parameters *errbuf* (error buffer) and *retcode* (return code) must exists in the procedure signature and *retcode* should return 0, 1, 2, or 3 values, representing SUCCESS, WARNING, FAILURE, or BUSINESS ERROR statuses.

After creating the procedure, we need to assign a correct grant to it by issuing the following statement:

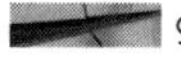

```
grant execute on XxCustomLedger to fusion_apps_execute;
/
```

Step 2: Access Task to Manage Custom ESS Jobs

We log in as XX_FA_IMPLEMENTOR, go to the Setup and Maintenance (Navigator | Setup and Maintenance) page, and search for Manage Custom Enterprise Scheduler Jobs for Ledger and Related Applications task. We select this task and click the Go to Task button, which opens the task in which we manage job definitions as shown in Figure 13-9.

Click the Create button to define a custom job.

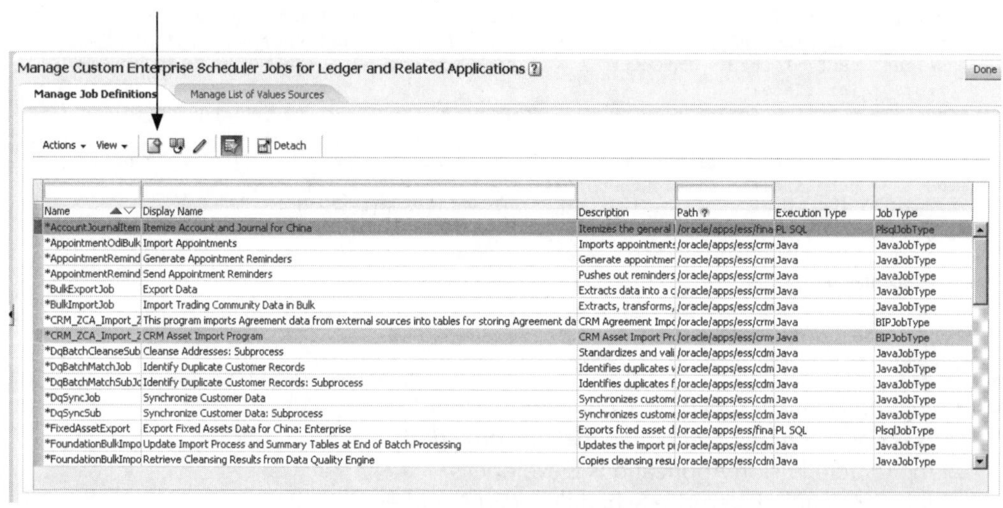

FIGURE 13-9. *Task to manage custom ESS jobs*

We chose the Manage Custom Enterprise Scheduler Jobs for Ledger task for this exercise, but you can also use other tasks to manage custom ESS jobs.

Step 3: Define a Custom PL/SQL Job

In the Manage Custom Enterprise Scheduler Jobs for Ledger task, we click the Create button as indicated in Figure 13-9 and populate the Job Definition page region with the following values:

- **Display Name** Custom Interface Count
- **Name** XxInterfaceCount
- **Path** /oracle/apps/ess/custom/ledger/interface
- **Application** XX Custom Ledger App
- **Description** Demo: Custom PL/SQL ESS job
- **Job Application Name** FinancialsEss
- **Job Type** PlsqlJobType
- **Procedure Name** XxCustomLedger.InterfaceCount
- **Default Output Format** TXT

We also check the Enable Submission from Enterprise Manager and Enable Submission from Scheduled Processes boxes. This will enable us to submit our job from both Enterprise Manager and Scheduled Processes central ESS UI app pages.

For PL/SQL programs we must define the numberOfArgs property under the User Properties tab (see Figure 13-10). This property identifies the number of job submission arguments excluding the mandatory arguments *errbuf* and *retcode*.

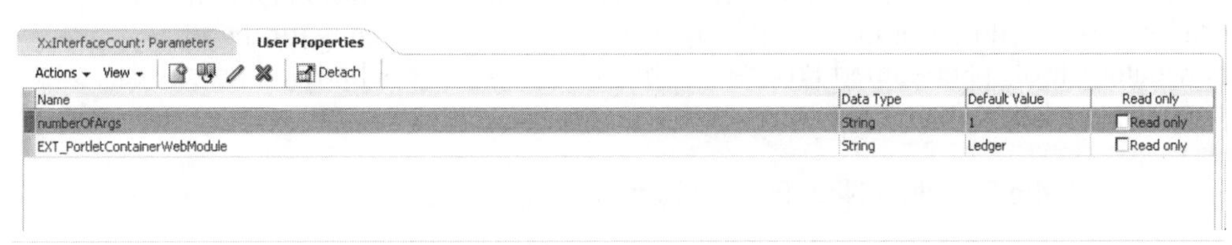

FIGURE 13-10. *Mandatory Number of Arguments (numberOfArgs) property for PL/SQL jobs*

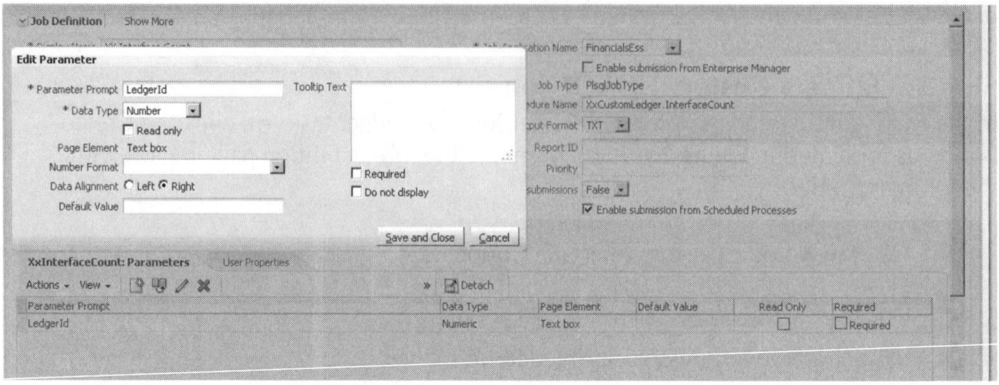

FIGURE 13-11. *Creating or editing job parameters*

Lastly we define our arguments, which in our case is just one: Ledger Id. We click the XxInterfaceCount: Parameters tab and click the Create button, which in turn will allow us to populate the Create (Edit) Parameter pop-up screen as shown in Figure 13-11.

The values we enter in our example are

- **Parameter Prompt** LedgerId
- **Data Type** Number
- **Page Element** Text Box

Save and close the Edit Parameter pop-up screen.

Step 4: Scheduling and Running an ESS Custom Job

We are going to use an ESS Central UI App deployed to the Common Domain to search and schedule our custom job by using the following navigation path: Navigator | Tools | Scheduled Processes. This will launch the Scheduled Processes page (Figure 13-12) where we:

1. Click the Schedule New Process button.
2. Search for our XX Interface Count Custom PL/SQL job.

We click the OK button to select it, and this in turn launches the Process Details pop-up screen (not shown) where we populate parameters (LedgerId in our case) and click the Submit button to run our PL/SQL program.

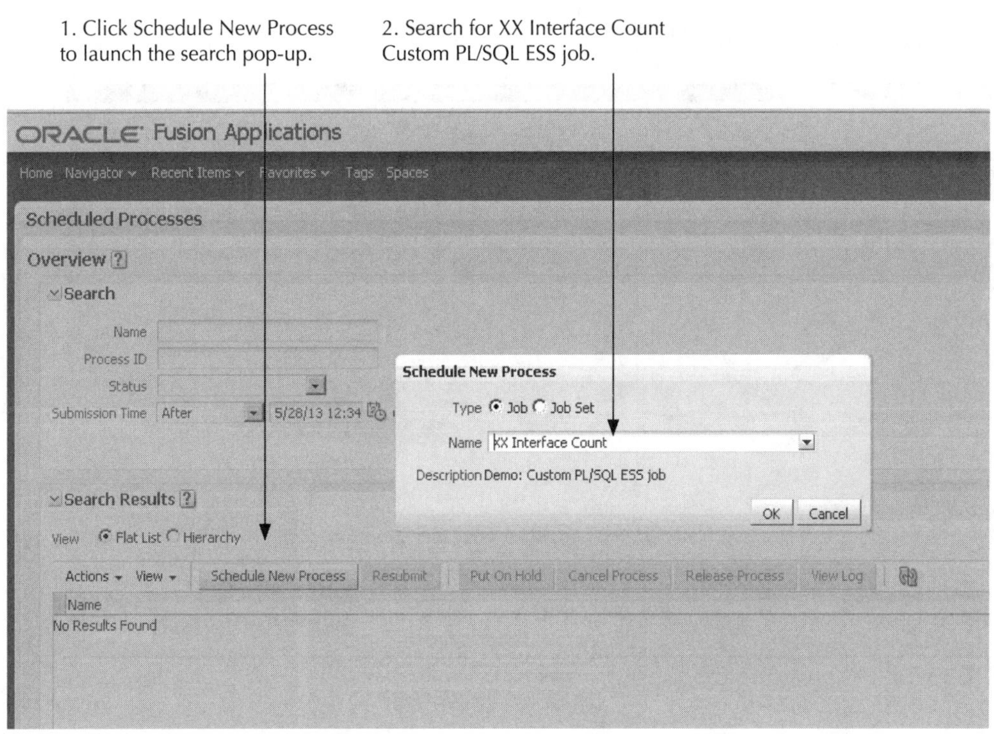

FIGURE 13-12. *Searching for jobs in ESS Central UI app*

An Information dialog box should pop up with the Request Number informing us about successful submission after which we can search for that request in the Scheduled Processes ESS Central UI App. Our request has completed successfully and has produced both log and output files, which are available as attachments as marked in Figure 13-13.

The data security is not implemented in this example; for more details on that topic, read Function and Data Security in Fusion Applications (Chapter 3), which discusses how security works in Fusion Applications including Oracle Fusion Data Security.

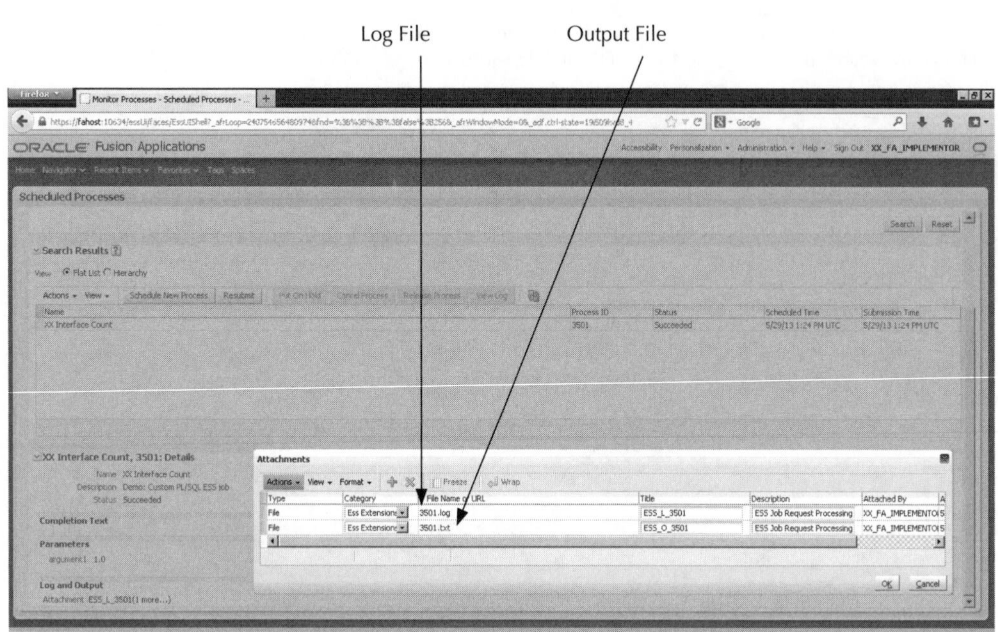

FIGURE 13-13. *Monitoring ESS jobs (processes)*

Summary

In this chapter we have introduced the basics of Enterprise Scheduler processing in Fusion Applications and its architecture components.

We have also:

- Learned how to create a custom application in Taxonomy Hierarchy
- Learned how to configure metadata security for custom ESS jobs
- Explained how MDS namespaces work for custom ESS jobs
- Learned how to schedule and monitor ESS jobs

More importantly, we have gone through the worked example of creating a custom PL/SQL ESS job, and we should now feel more comfortable to explore other types of ESS jobs available in Fusion Applications.

CHAPTER 14

Custom Look and Feel with ADF Skinning

An enterprise application quite often requires having corporate branding applied to it when deployed along other IT systems in an organization. Even more important is the capability to customize the default out-of-the-box user interface (UI) appearance for externally facing applications, which are exposed outside the perimeter of the corporate network.

Oracle Fusion Applications offer a wide variety of approaches to change the default application look and feel. As we discovered in other parts in this book, you can use the Page Composer tool to change properties that control the appearance and behavior of UI page components. Oracle JDeveloper can be used to customize the UI Shell template; change and customize home page, preferences, and Navigator menus in Oracle Applications; and the text can be customized by overriding the resource bundle.

In this chapter, we'll cover a specific technique of application branding and styling in Oracle Fusion Applications commonly referred to as *skinning*. In fact, this technique is made available through Oracle Application Development Framework (ADF) and from now on we'll refer to it as ADF skinning. In the next few sections, we'll provide a brief introduction to the ADF skinning framework, explain how it relates to Cascading Style Sheets (CSS), and provide step-by-step instructions on how to create and deploy a custom skin in Oracle Fusion Applications.

Introduction to ADF Skinning

Readers who are familiar with Oracle E-Business Suite will recognize that Oracle Applications (OA) Framework, the presentation layer in releases R11*i* and R12, was built on Oracle's now-deprecated UIX (User Interface XML) technology. Oracle UIX enabled developers to create applications with a consistent look and feel; it also allowed customers to use its look-and-feel customization framework, often referred to as CLAF (Custom Look and Feel), to change the appearance of Oracle's Web-based products by applying UIX Custom Style Sheets and UIX Custom Icons, and creating UIX Custom Renderers for ultimate control over the look of UI.

In the current version of Oracle ADF, or more specifically ADF Faces Rich Client (often called just ADF Faces) in JDeveloper 11*g*, the skinning framework is still largely based on the UIX CLAF framework, although it is considerably enhanced in the present day. ADF Faces is a set of JavaServer Faces (JSF) components that provide rich functionality to browser-based applications, client- and server-side programming models, and among numerous other features, it offers the skinning feature through a rich JSF component render kit. The component renderers are Java classes that handle HTML content and corresponding client-side components, and also expose component-style selectors used in skinning.

NOTE
ADF component-style selectors should not be confused with the standard W3C-defined selectors. In the ADF skinning framework, we use component selectors to directly transform the appearance of a specific component rather than rendered HTML, which will ultimately also change but indirectly as a consequence of applying skin through ADF Faces component-style selectors. We'll expand on this further in the sections that follow.

Since ADF skinning is based on CSS, in the next sections we'll provide a very concise summary of the CSS style sheet language and how it relates to ADF Faces.

A Very Brief Overview of Cascading Style Sheets (CSS)

The goal of CSS is to provide a simple, flexible, and declarative language for adding style to Web documents. HTML and XHTML are the most common types of documents to which CSS gets applied, although it can easily be applied to XML and other document types. Web documents such as HTML Web pages contain elements that are the basis of document structure, and styles define how to display HTML elements. Often, the elements in HTML play a part in the presentation of a document and CSS allows us to separate its content from presentation.

Consider the following HTML markup:

```
<p><font color="red" size="+2">This is a paragraph</font></p>
```

To style the text "This is a paragraph" and display it in red and in a certain size, the `<font>` tag and its attributes `color` and `size` are mixed with the actual content of the HTML markup. This approach created problems for Web developers and administrators of large Web sites when such tags were introduced in HTML.

The World Wide Web Consortium (W3C) came up with CSS to resolve this problem by introducing style sheets, which consist of rules in CSS syntax. Here is an example of such a CSS rule:

```
p {
    color:red;
    font-size:8px;
  }
```

The main parts of a CSS rule are

- **Selector** Element to which style applies, such as p for paragraph in our example.
- **Declaration** Property and value pairs such as color:red and font-size:8px.

The following snippet demonstrates how to set HTML element style:

```
<html>
 <head>
  <style>
   p {
      color:red;
      font-size:8px;
     }
  </style>
 </head>
<body>
 <p>This is a styled paragraph.</p>
</body>
</html>
```

In CSS it is quite common to set styles to user-defined selectors called id and class.

With the id selector we define a style for a single document element as shown next:

```
<html>
 <head>
  <style>
  #mypar
  {
  color:red;
  font-size:8px;
  }
  </style>
 </head>
<body>
 <p id="mypar">This is a styled paragraph</p>
 <p>This paragraph is not affected by any style.</p>
</body>
</html>
```

The styling rule applied to the HTML element with attribute id="mypar" and other paragraph elements were not affected by the rule.

Similarly, we use the `class` selector to define a style for a group of document elements as shown next:

```
<html>
 <head>
  <style>
  .smallred
   {
   color:red;
   font-size:8px;
    }
 </style>
 </head>
<body>
 <h1 class="smallred">This is a styled header</h1>
 <p class="smallred">This is a styled paragraph</p>
</body>
</html>
```

In the previous example, all elements with `class="smallred"` will have a style applied to them. Additionally, we can also specify what particular elements are affected by the style:

```
h1.smallred { color:red; font-size:8px; }
```

We have only scratched the surface, and there are numerous rules on how document elements can be styled, but this is outside the scope of this book and we mention it here only as an introduction to ADF skinning.

Lastly, we should mention that there are three ways of inserting a style sheet and styles:

- **Inline styles** Applied by using the `style` attribute within the HTML tag itself. Inline styles mix together content and presentation; therefore, they are not considered to be the best practice and they indeed defeat the purpose of CSS to some degree.
- **Internal style sheet** Defined in the HEAD section of an HTML document inside the `<style>` tag, as we did in our previous examples. This is generally used only for documents that have a unique and specific style.
- **External style sheet** Defined when styling applies to the whole Web site, application, or multiple documents. HTML pages are linked to the external style sheet using the `<link>` tag inside the HEAD section.

Here is an example of how an external style sheet example.css is linked to an HTML document:

```
<head><link rel="stylesheet" type="text/css" href="example.css"></head>
```

The CSS specification from W3C specifies the order of precedence if rules are defined at multiple levels for an element. The details can be found at www.w3.org/TR/CSS21/cascade.html#cascading-order, but generally the cascading order of precedence is such that an inline style would override a style inside the document's HEAD tag, external, and browser default styles. Likewise, the external style has higher precedence than browser default values. All the other rules, exceptions, and in-depth details can be found at www.w3.org.

About ADF Faces Skinning

ADF is based on JSF architecture and, similar to component renderers in JSF, ADF renderer Java classes take care of how components are displayed on a specific device. The key difference between working with standard CSS selectors as described in the previous section and the style selectors in ADF is that the latter use ADF Faces component renderers to expose component-specific selectors, and this is what we work with when skinning ADF-based applications. In other words, rather than operating on HTML output directly such as `h1.smallred`, we use ADF component selectors like `af|calendar`, which is the selector on the root DOM element of the calendar ADF Faces component.

Oracle ADF documentation defines skins as style sheets based on CSS 3.0 syntax that are specified in one place for an entire application. Skinning allows developers and designers to change the styles, icons, properties, and text of ADF Faces components, which means that a skin consists of a CSS file, images, and localized strings. All ADF applications including Oracle Fusion Applications have a default skin; when we decide to introduce a custom skin for an application, we must select a parent skin that we are extending so that components that are not affected by our style definitions can inherit styles from the parent skin.

NOTE
The skin document in the current releases of Oracle ADF uses CSS 3 syntax only for styling rules for the ADF Faces components, which at run time get converted into a CSS 2 style document by the skinning framework. It is the generated CSS 2 document that is added to the final HTML document, which is rendered in the end user's browser.

Skin Keys and Selectors

Oracle documentation related to skinning, such as Oracle Fusion Middleware Tag Reference for Oracle ADF Faces Skin Selectors, documents available component selectors and skin keys. These terms are used interchangeably, but the most important thing to understand is that in order to be successful in styling an ADF application, one has to be very familiar with the available skin selectors. For example, to style the ADF Input Text Component, we can use the following selector:

```
af|inputText{color:green}
```

Generally, skin keys begin with `af|` followed by the component name we want to skin, and optionally can also be followed by a specific part of the component we want to skin, such as `label` in the following example:

```
af|inputText::label{color:orange}
```

Some ADF Faces component selectors also have pseudo-classes similar to those in HTML such as `:active`, `:disabled`, `:selected:`, `:hover`, while other components have ADF Faces–specific pseudo-classes. Apart from pseudo-classes, ADF Faces allow access to the component-specific areas via pseudo-elements.

There are three main types of selectors available in ADF Faces, and a summary of their role in the skinning framework is as follows:

- **Style classes** Used to create custom global selectors, and can also be referenced in the `styleClass` component attribute. They are usually prebuilt, such as `.AboutPageText`, which comes with the Application Core extension in Fusion Applications. If referenced in the `styleClass` attribute, the style class rules are applied to the component root element.
- **Global selectors** Affect multiple components at the same time. In ADF Faces component selectors implement global selector names, which allows us to reuse the styles in our custom skin rather than repeating their definition for each component.
- **Component selectors** Affect a single type of a component because in the ADF Faces skinning framework, all components implement the skin component selectors `af|`<*`component name`*>, where <*`component name`*> is the name of the component, such as *`inputText`*.

If you are new to skinning, working with ADF selectors can appear to be a bit difficult to digest initially, but the good news is that apart from the official product documentation, there are lots of resources out there, such as the *Oracle Fusion Developer Guide* from Oracle Press, that cover this subject in some detail.

Skinning Tools and Important Resources

In comparison to Custom Look And Feel (CLAF) skinning in earlier releases of ADF 10*g* based on User Interface XML (UIX) and E-Business Suite 11*i* and R12, Oracle has made it much easier for developers to create and design their own skins in ADF 11*g*, and in the case of Oracle Fusion Applications, to extend and customize the default skin that is shipped with applications. While previous releases had little documentation and publicly available resources related to skinning, Oracle Fusion Middleware documentation covers this topic in some detail now, and on top of it, a tool has been provided to help customize existing or create brand new skins. In the next sections, we'll take a look at this tool as well as other resources available to skin developers to help them change the appearance of Fusion Applications.

ADF Skin Editor and an Extension for Fusion Applications

The most important tool that offers skin development support is the Skin Editor. While the recent releases of JDeveloper 11*g* Release 2 have an built-in skin editor, the current release of Oracle Fusion Applications 11*g* Release 6 (11.1.6) at the time of writing this book is built with JDeveloper 11.1.1.6, which doesn't have an built-in skin editor. To use the skin editor in this release of Fusion Applications, use a stand-alone skin editor available for download from the ADF downloads page at Oracle Technology Network (OTN) at www.oracle.com/technetwork/developer-tools/adf/downloads/index.html.

Installing the stand-alone skin editor is very simple; just follow the simple instructions provided at the same download page. For Fusion Applications skinning, we also need to update the skin editor with the Fusion Applications Skin Extension Bundle by going to Help | Check for Updates in the Editors menu. In the Updates source screen, check the Official Oracle Extensions and Updates tick box, click the Next button, and search for the word *skin* as demonstrated in the following illustration.

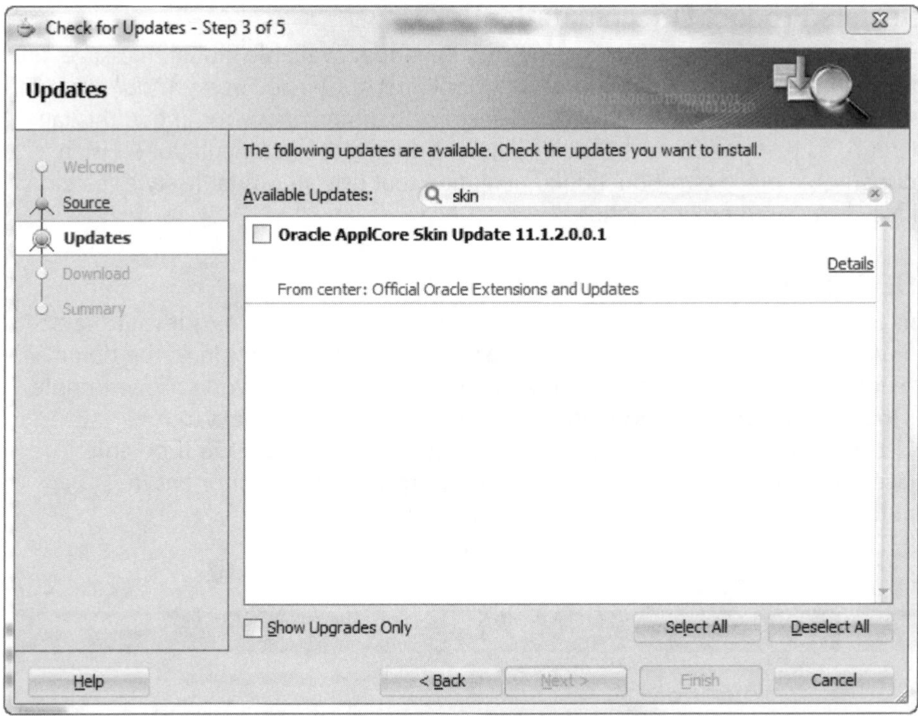

Install the latest release of Oracle ApplCore Skin Update extension and restart the skin editor.

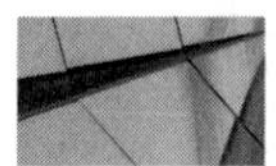

NOTE

The product documentation at present doesn't appear consistent with regard to the extension name. It refers to Fusion Applications Skin Extension Bundle rather than Oracle ApplCore Skin Update. We suspect the name for Fusion Applications Skin Extension could change in future updates.

Now we are ready to start creating custom skins for Fusion Applications, but before we turn our attention to it, let's have a look at other resources available to us.

Reference Documentation, Browser Tools, and Other Resources

In the next few sections we are going to list some of the most important publicly available resources that provide a great deal of support to developers when skinning Oracle Fusion Applications.

Selectors Product Documentation

If you are asking where to look for information about available global, message, and component selectors and pseudo-classes, look first at *Oracle Fusion Middleware Tag Reference for Oracle ADF Faces Skin Selectors* documentation. You'll find this tag reference as part of standard Oracle Fusion Middleware documentation. It is an indispensable piece of product documentation that lists all available style selectors with a corresponding description.

ADF Faces Rich Client Demos

This is another freely available demo hosted by Oracle at http://jdevadf.oracle.com/adf-richclient-demo/faces/index.jspx. The skinning section of the demo provides an interactive guide on how component skinning works. For example, for the `inputText` component, if we click the check box next to `af|inputText::content{background-color:red}`, we'll be able to see how it affects the appearance of the `inputText` component in real time without having to refresh the screen:

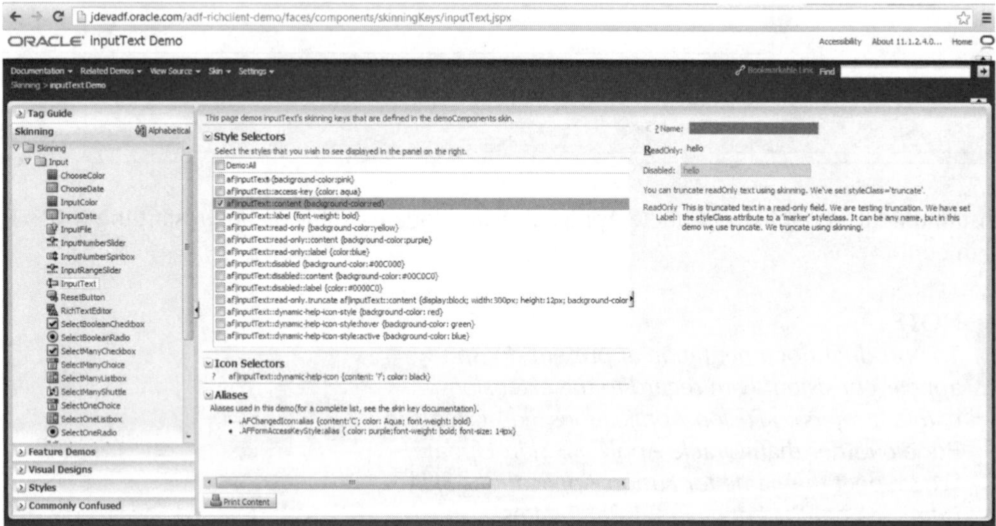

As we can see from this example, if applicable, the icon selectors and aliases (style classes) are also shown in the demo. This is a great way to start learning about ADF skinning.

Browser Tools and Add-Ons

Browsers and their add-ons do not provide any ADF-specific tools for skinning; however, Firefox add-ons like Firebug and Firefox's inspect element feature do provide extensive capability to inspect HTML documents and modify their style at run time for development purposes.

Apart from being very helpful for debugging purposes, these tools allow you to view and visualize CSS, change their definitions on the fly, and explore the component DOM tree in the browser. In the context of ADF skinning, the element inspection feature allows developers to discover the names of the ADF skin selectors for a particular component.

The element inspection feature is available in most modern browsers, and the following screen shot shows the output from Firefox's inspection plugin, which is accessible by right-clicking on the page and selecting Inspect Element from the context menu.

You'll notice in Figure 14-1 that the style class names are obfuscated and show up in HTML output as .xf1 and .xb7 for performance reasons in production environments. During development or debugging, the feature that compresses style class names can be switched off in the application's web.xml file, and this will allow us to see the full names of ADF style classes:

```
<context-param>
  <param-name>
    org.apache.myfaces.trinidad.DISABLE_CONTENT_COMPRESSION
  </param-name>
  <param-value>true</param-value>
</context-param>
```

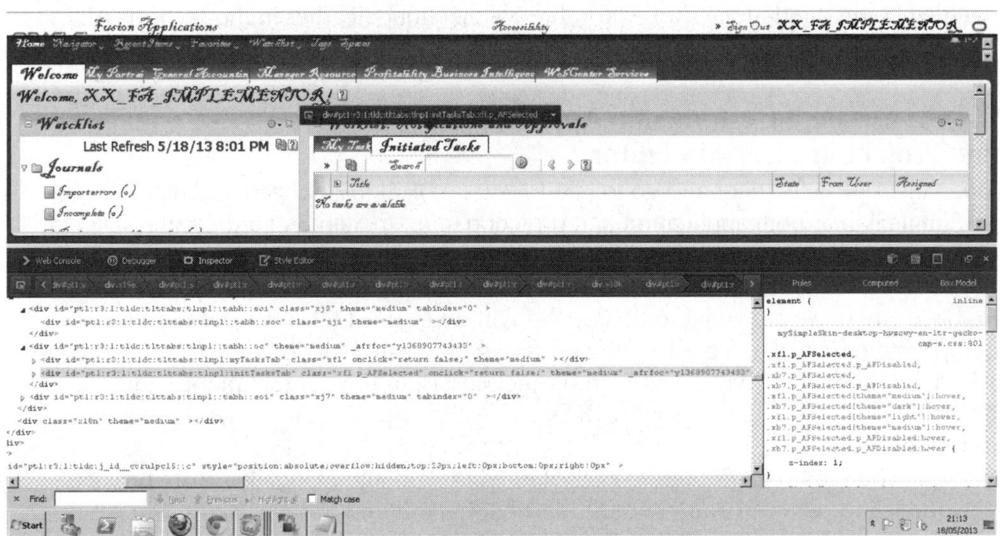

FIGURE 14-1. *Output from Firefox's Inspect Element tool*

TIP
To familiarize yourself with available component selectors, create an empty ADF page in JDeveloper, add a component of interest, disable decompression, and run the page inside JDeveloper's integrated WebLogic server. Use Firebug or a similar tool to inspect generated HTML output.

Deploying and Setting Up a Custom Skin in Fusion Applications

The principles of Fusion Applications skinning are no different than in any other ADF application. In the next sections we'll provide a step-by-step guide on how to deploy a custom skin into a Fusion Applications instance. We'll also discuss the deployment options as well as profile options available to administrators to control who and what applications are affected by the custom skin.

Creating and Deploying a Custom Skin Example

The skin that we are going to create and deploy in the example that follows is very simple, and its purpose is not to teach you the nuts and bolts of ADF skinning, but to show you the process and outline what it takes to create and deploy a custom skin in Oracle Fusion Applications. With that said, let's go through the steps starting with opening of the stand-alone skin editor that we mentioned earlier in the section "ADF Skin Editor and an Extension for Fusion Applications."

Step 1: Create a Custom Skin Application and Project in ADF Skin Editor

Open the ADF Skin Editor and go to File | New | ADF Skin Application. Enter **MySimpleSkin** as both application and project names. In Step 2 of the Create ADF Skin Application Wizard, set Target Application Release to match the release version of Fusion Applications, which in our case is 11.1.1.6 since our Fusion Applications instance where we are going to deploy the skin is version 11.1.6. Click Finish to complete the wizard and project structures will be created for you.

Right-click on the MySimpleSkin project and from the context menu, add mySimpleSkin by going to New | ADF Skin File and populate the values as shown in Figure 14-2.

After you click the OK button, ADF Skin Editor will automatically create project structures and required entries in trinidad-config.xml and trinidad-skins.xml configuration files under the WEB-INF directory.

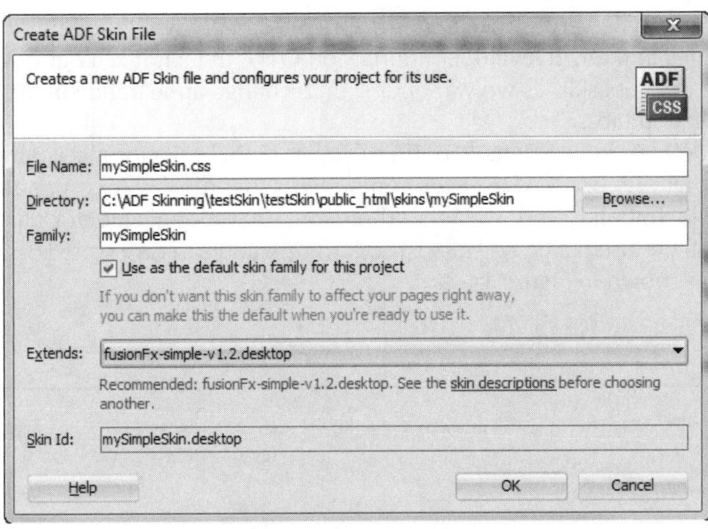

FIGURE 14-2. *Create ADF Skin File dialog*

The trinidad-config.xml file will contain the skin family name mySimpleSkin, which is the name we are going to use when configuring Fusion Applications later on:

```
<?xml version="1.0" encoding="windows-1252"?>
<trinidad-config xmlns="http://myfaces.apache.org/trinidad/config">
  <skin-family>mySimpleSkin</skin-family>
  <skin-version>default</skin-version>
</trinidad-config>
```

Similarly, the trinidad-skins.xml file will contain the skin id, skin family name, name of the parent skin we are extending, render kit, and the location of the style sheet mySimpleSkin.css relative to the location of the configuration directory:

```
<?xml version="1.0" encoding="windows-1252"?>
<skins xmlns="http://myfaces.apache.org/trinidad/skin">
  <skin>
    <id>mySimpleSkin.desktop</id>
    <family>mySimpleSkin</family>
    <extends>fusionFx-simple-v1.2.desktop</extends>
    <render-kit-id>org.apache.myfaces.trinidad.desktop</render-kit-id>
    <style-sheet-name>skins/mySimpleSkin/mySimpleSkin.css</style-sheet-name>
    <bundle-name>resources.skinBundle</bundle-name>
  </skin>
</skins>
```

Step 2: Design Your Custom Skin

Our skin is going to be very simple and is inspired by a very well-known Princess skin that features in many JDeveloper tutorials on OTN. In fact, it is a cut-down version of the Princess skin as we want our skin to change appearance of the default font and navigation tabs.

Our skin defines the .AFDefaultFontFamily:alias global selector alias, which sets a default font family for all ADF Faces components that display text. We also set .AFDefaultBoldFont:alias and .AFDefaultBoldFont:alias global selector aliases. In addition to that, we also define `af|navigationPane` and `af|navigationTabbed` components as shown in Figure 14-3.

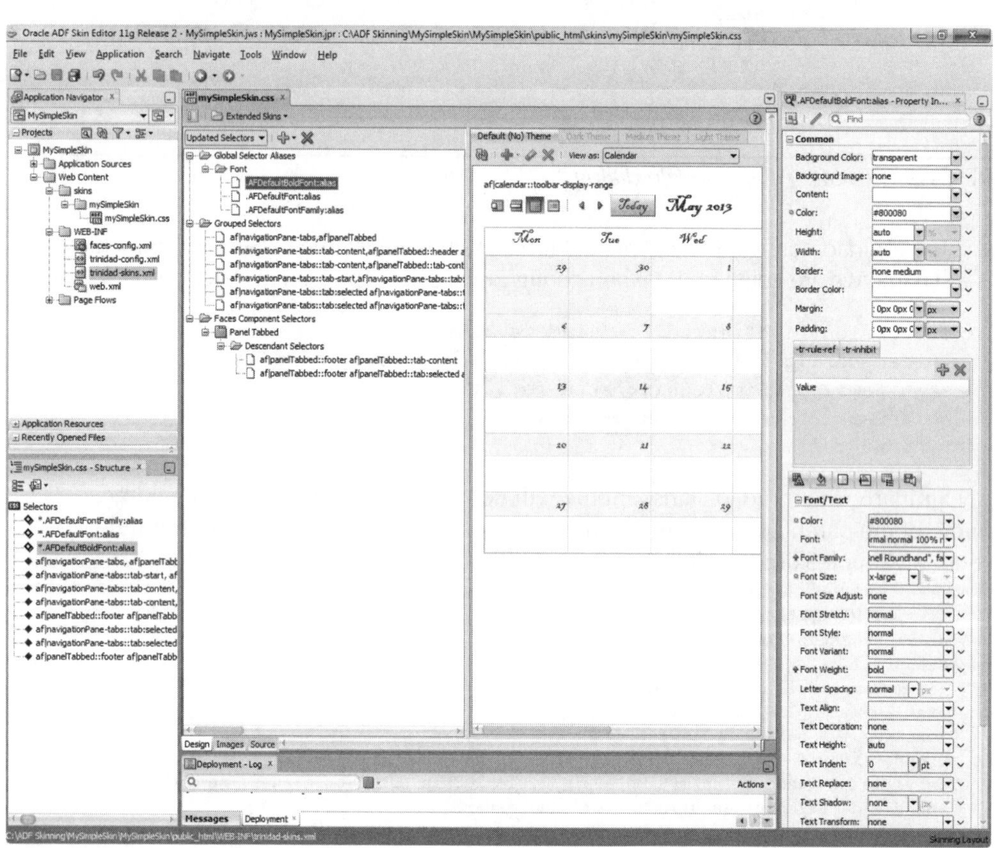

FIGURE 14-3. *Global, Grouped, and Component selectors in a simple custom skin*

If we click the Source tab, the mySimpleSkin.css has the following selectors defined:

```
/**ADFFaces_Skin_File / DO NOT REMOVE**/
@namespace af "http://xmlns.oracle.com/adf/faces/rich";
@namespace dvt "http://xmlns.oracle.com/dss/adf/faces";
@namespace af "http://xmlns.oracle.com/appcore";

.AFDefaultFontFamily:alias {
  font-family: "Blackadder ITC", "Monotype Corsiva", "Apple Chancery", "Snell
Roundhand", fantasy;
}
.AFDefaultFont:alias {
  font-size: large;
  color: #800080;
}
.AFDefaultBoldFont:alias {
  color: #800080;
  font-size: x-large;
}
/* Enable themes for specific components */
af|navigationPane-tabs,
af|panelTabbed {
  -tr-enable-themes: true;
}
/* tab-start and tab-end do not render anything in the princess skin */
af|navigationPane-tabs::tab-start,
af|navigationPane-tabs::tab:selected af|navigationPane-tabs::tab-start,
af|navigationPane-tabs::tab-end,
af|navigationPane-tabs::tab:selected af|navigationPane-tabs::tab-end,
af|panelTabbed::tab-start,
af|panelTabbed::tab:selected af|panelTabbed::tab-start,
af|panelTabbed::tab-end,
af|panelTabbed::tab:selected af|panelTabbed::tab-end {
  border-width: 0px;
  width: 0px;
}
/* unselected tabs */
af|navigationPane-tabs::tab-content,
af|panelTabbed::tab-content {
  background-color: #CFDFF9;
  border-left: 1px solid purple;
  border-right: 1px solid purple;
  padding: 0px 10px;
}
af|navigationPane-tabs::tab-content,
af|panelTabbed::header af|panelTabbed::tab-content {
  border-top: 1px solid purple;
}
af|panelTabbed::footer af|panelTabbed::tab-content {
  border-bottom: 1px solid purple;
}
/* selected tabs */
af|navigationPane-tabs::tab:selected af|navigationPane-tabs::tab-content,
af|panelTabbed::tab:selected af|panelTabbed::tab-content {
  background-color: white;
```

```
  border-left: 1px solid black;
  border-right: 1px solid black;
}
af|navigationPane-tabs::tab:selected af|navigationPane-tabs::tab-content,
af|panelTabbed::header af|panelTabbed::tab:selected af|panelTabbed::tab-content {
  border-top: 1px solid black;
}
af|panelTabbed::footer af|panelTabbed::tab:selected af|panelTabbed::tab-content {
  border-bottom: 1px solid black;
}
```

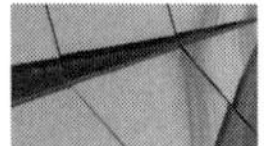

TIP
Prior to the 11.1.6 release, to customize a logo we had to change UIShell, usually in JDeveloper. As of the 11.1.6 release, a custom logo can be updated through skin definition using the `.AFBrandingBarLogo` *style class.*

Step 3: Deploy a Project to an ADF Library Jar File

In Java Enterprise Edition (JEE), a common deployment package is a jar file containing configuration files in the META-INF and WEB-INF directories. In the case of an ADF skinning project, the configuration files are under the WEB-INF directory.

We create the deployment profile by right-clicking on the MySimpleSkin project and selecting Deploy | New Deployment Profile. When selecting the name for the deployment profile, we need to make sure that it starts with "Xx_"; for example, in our case Xx_MySimpleSkin. This is just a naming convention specific to Fusion Applications and will ensure that the custom skin deployment is upgrade-safe. When creating the new deployment profile, we can specify a local directory where the jar file is going to be generated and saved. As we are running the Skin Editor on a Windows machine, we selected the C:\ADF Skinning\MySimpleSkin\MySimpleSkin\deploy directory to be the target directory where Xx_mySimpleSkin.jar is saved.

Step 4: Deploy a Generated Skin Jar File to Fusion Applications

Once the jar file is generated, we need to transfer it to the Fusion Applications middle tier where individual applications are deployed to run inside the WebLogic server. Prior to this point, we should have exercised a little bit of planning to decide which applications and users should be affected by our custom skin. For the purposes of this exercise we are going to deploy mySimpleSkin into the HomePageApp, which is the first page we are presented with after a successful login.

We use the WinSCP tool to copy Xx_mySimpleSkin.jar from the desktop machine into the exploded directory /app/fusion/fusionapps/applications/atf/deploy/EarAtkHomePage.ear/EarAtkHomePage.war/WEB-INF/lib onto the middle tier machine, which happens to be Linux.

CAUTION

For releases prior to 11.1.6, in addition to a custom skin jar file, you may also need to place the adf-richclient-fusion-simple-11.1.1.5.0.jar file found in Skin Editor's jlib directory and the XxApplCoreSkin.11.1.1.5.jar file found on OTN and java.net into the application's WEB-INF/lib directory.

Step 5: Set Profile Option FND_CSS_SKIN_FAMILY

Fusion Applications use the native capability of the ADF skinning framework to be able to dynamically set and switch arbitrary skin definition at run time. This is achieved by setting the FND_CSS_SKIN_FAMILY profile option by logging in as FA System Administrator, or any other user with an appropriate role assigned to them to access Functional Setup Manager, and navigating to the profile options task by selecting Navigator | Setup and Maintenance (Tools) | All Tasks (Tab) and searching for Manage Administrator Profile Values.

Click Go To Task and in the Manage Administrator Profile Values task, search for the FND_CSS_SKIN_FAMILY profile option code and set our mySimpleSkin as Profile Value for a user, product, or site, as demonstrated in Figure 14-4.

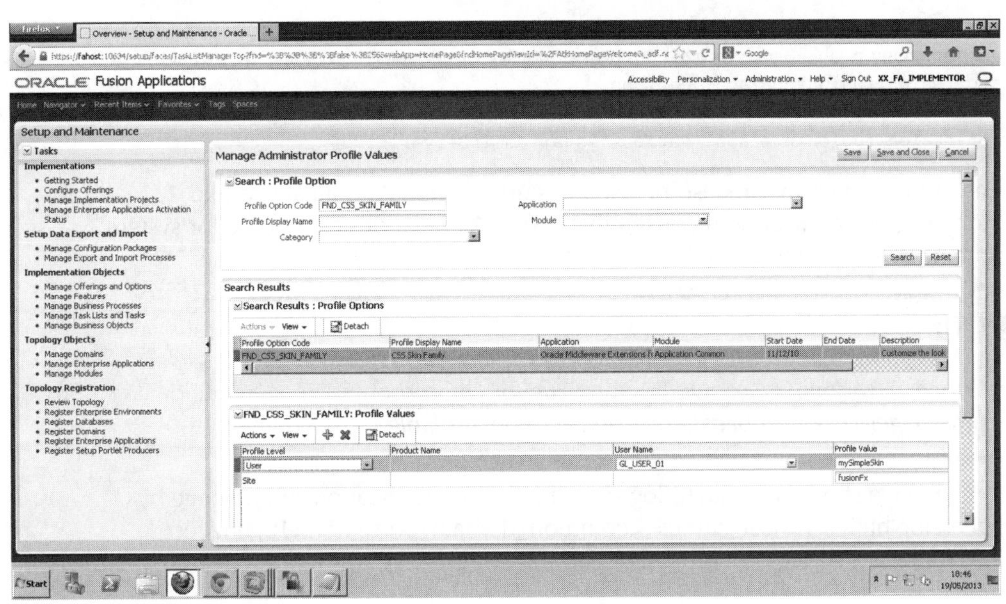

FIGURE 14-4. *Setting a profile option value for FND_CSS_SKIN_FAMILY profile option*

Step 6: Bounce HomePageApp in WebLogic Common Domain

While the profile option to set a skin family value can be set before or after restarting of HomePageApp, one thing we must do for the changes to take effect is to restart the affected applications. To bounce this HomePageApp, follow these steps:

1. Log in to the Common Domain Enterprise Manager Fusion Applications Control. The URL pattern looks like http(s)://<hostname>:<common_domain_port>/em.
2. Expand nodes under Farm_CommonDomain | WebLogic Domain | CommonDomain and select HomePageCluster. Click the WebLogic Cluster button located just under the HomePageCluster label in the right-hand side panel and navigate to Control | Shut Down. Once the cluster is stopped, go back to Control | Start Up to restart the cluster.
3. Verify that the HomePageApp is up and running by clicking on HomePageCluster in the navigation tree on the left-hand side panel inside Fusion Applications Control.

An alternative method is to use the fastartstop utility available to system administrators. For example, to bounce the whole Common Domain including HomePageApp, we issue the following commands:

```
cd /app/fusion/fusionapps/applications/lcm/ad/bin
./fastartstop.sh -Stop -domains CommonDomain -username weblogic_fa -appbase /
app/fusion/fusionapps/applications
./fastartstop.sh -Start -domains CommonDomain -username weblogic_fa -appbase /
app/fusion/fusionapps/applications -startAdminServer true
```

The fastartstop utility can also be used to start individual applications like HomePageApp. You should consult the Fusion Applications user guide for system administrators for more details.

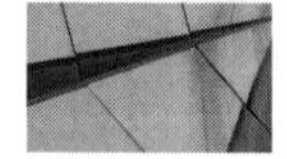

TIP
Make sure that WebLogic domains are started with the -startAdminServer switch set to true for Enterprise Manager Fusion Applications Control to be available.

Now we should be able to log in to the Fusion Applications home page by accessing http(s)://<host_name>:<common_domain_port>/homePage/faces/AtkHomePageWelcome.

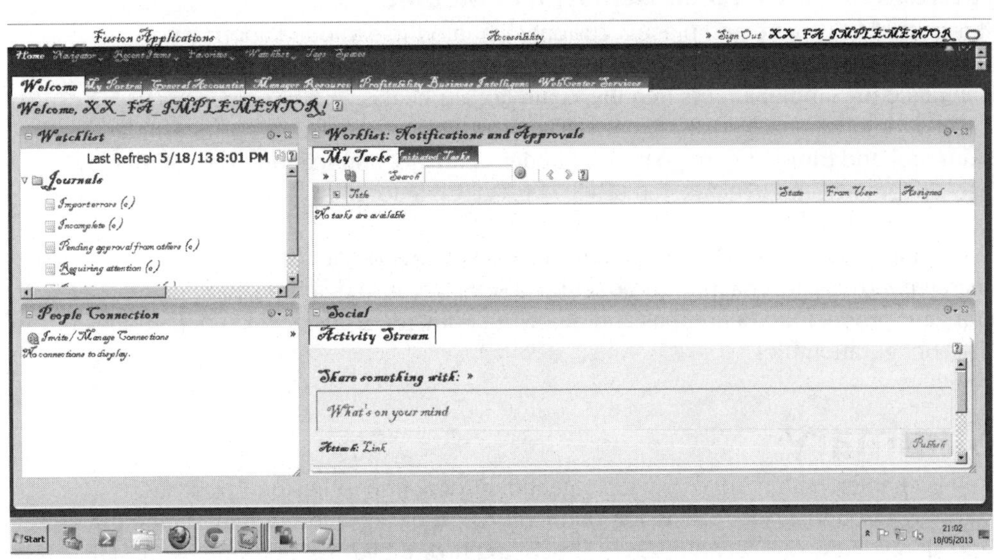

FIGURE 14-5. *Custom skin applied to Fusion Applications Home page*

We now see as illustrated in Figure 14-5 that our custom skin mySimpleSkin is applied to the Home Page application and that it looks markedly different from the default fusionFx skin that ships with Fusion Applications.

NOTE

If a user for whom the custom skin has been set up navigates away from the Home Page application, he or she will notice that the custom skin is not applied. Instead, Fusion Applications will apply a simple skin, and this is because we deployed our custom skin only to HomePageApp. Rather, we need to make sure to apply the custom skin to all applications that are affected or will be accessed by the end users. This is quite different from applying CLAF skins in E-Business Suite where we needed to do this only in one place for all applications. This is a price that has to be paid for having modular applications architecture.

Alternative Custom Skin Deployment Method

It is possible to create and place a custom skin into the exploded applications directory directly without creating an ADF skin deployment jar file. For example we can place mySimpleSkin.css into the <path_to_applications_dir>/atf/deploy/EarAtkHomePage.ear/EarAtkHomePage.war/css directory, and update the trinidad-skins.xml and trinidad-config.xml files under <path_to_applications_dir>/atf/deploy/EarAtkHomePage.ear/EarAtkHomePage.war/WEB-INF to point to our mySimpleSkin custom skin family.

While this may be OK in certain development environments, we do not recommend this approach for production servers because patches can update standard product file definitions and overwrite pointers to custom skin definitions in the configuration files.

Summary

In this chapter we aimed to provide a gentle introduction to Fusion Applications skinning through a brief discussion of the historical background of ADF skinning, and an overview of Cascading Style Sheets and how they relate to skinning in ADF and Fusion Applications. While the simple skin we presented in our hands-on exercise won't help you learn how to create pretty-as-a-picture Fusion Applications styles, it is good enough to show you the concepts behind skinning, what it takes to create one, and how to deploy custom skins into Fusion Applications environments.

CHAPTER 15

Integration with Fusion Applications

Fusion Applications are completely built from scratch and you have to implement them from the ground up. You will find that the features and functions in Fusion Applications may not be exactly the same as what you are using in other legacy applications such as Oracle E-Business Suite, PeopleSoft, Siebel, or any other non-Oracle application suite. Most of the time, you cannot simply shut down your existing applications and immediately move to use Fusion Applications in a production instance. Sometimes you may not find all necessary functions and products in Fusion Applications and you may have to continue to use your legacy application and Fusion Applications at the same time. You have to migrate your data from existing systems to a new Fusion Applications instance. All of this means that there is a need to integrate Fusion Applications with other non-Fusion applications or other systems. In this chapter, we will discuss some of the integration patterns and best practices of how you can integrate with Fusion Applications.

You can integrate with Fusion Applications to exchange data both inbound and outbound. You can also integrate using real-time or batch mode to exchange information. Different products have different capabilities, but the general strategy for integration remains the same. For inbound, you will use Web services or bulk import tools, and for outbound, you will use business events or bulk export tools. You can use your choice of middleware for integrations because Fusion Applications are built on standards-based Fusion Middleware. The following diagram illustrates the general interaction pattern for Fusion Applications along with Fusion Middleware.

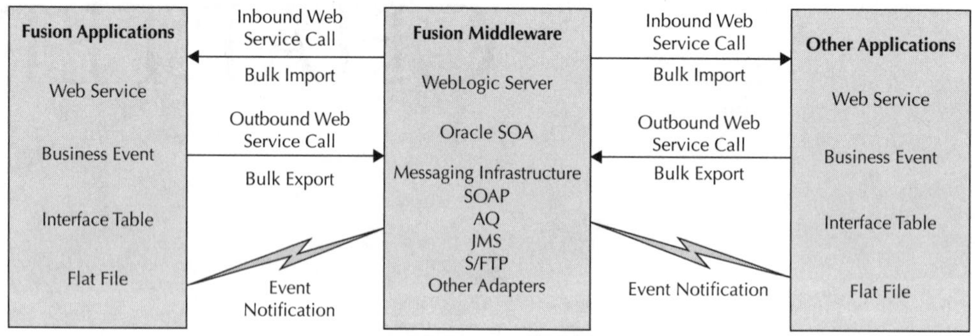

What Is Oracle Enterprise Repository (OER)?

Fusion Applications document all the integration artifacts or assets in Oracle Enterprise Repository (OER). You can use OER as a single source of integration information. It provides visibility into lifecycle and support details about a given asset. Each asset is marked with the level of compatibility supported by Oracle. You can discover all assets in OER, including the ones that are not supported.

Fusion Applications are designed with Service Oriented Architecture in mind. There are many services in Fusion Applications, but not all of them are suited for integration purposes. You should only use assets that are marked as Compatibility = "Supported – Backward Compatibility Assured" for integrations so that upgrades or patches do not break your code. The services in OER are also marked with the keyword EXTERNAL to indicate that the service end point is visible to external clients. Table 15-1 explains the intended usage of assets with a given compatibility.

Compatibility	Keyword	Usage
Supported	EXTERNAL	Services are available to external clients. Services can be used by customers and partners to extend and integrate with Fusion Applications.
Supported	INTERNAL or not specified	Services cannot be accessed by external clients but can only be accessed by custom composites that are deployed in Fusion Applications SOA domains.
Not Supported	EXTERNAL	These series are accessible to external clients but not designed to be used for integration purposes by customers or partners. Such services are made external for specific out-of-the-box integration Fusion Applications may have as part of standard functionality. Oracle can change the interfaces at any time without notice to customers.
Not Supported	INTERNAL or not specified	Services cannot be accessed by external clients and should not be used even by custom composites that are deployed in Fusion Applications SOA domains. Oracle can change the interfaces at any time without notice to customers.

TABLE 15-1. *Customization Layers*

What Are the Different Types of Assets in OER?

OER documents all Fusion Applications assets. In this section, we will describe some of the important types of these assets that you will use for integration purposes.

Web Services

Fusion Applications use standards-based Web services to allow inbound integrations. Any development environment or tool that is compliant with Web service standards can be used to invoke Fusion Applications Web services. Fusion Applications expose two types of Web services depending on their underlying implementation. Both the services are exposed in OER—ADF Services and SOA Composite services.

ADF Services

ADF Services are built on Fusion Applications business components. These services expose standard Create, Read, Update, and Delete (CRUD) type of operations to manipulate the data for a given object. ADF Services also expose special operations to do a specific business function such as convert a lead to an opportunity or promote an employee. These services allow you to access the data using Service Data Object (SDO) where the entire object structure is exposed to the service interface using a schema (XSD). The standard SDO-based ADF service for a given object will have create, update, delete, get, find, and merge operations that you can use to query and manipulate the data for a given object. The merge operation is a combination of insert and update in which the data is created if the row is not found for the given identifier. The find operation is a very powerful tool to return the data based on your filter conditions as well as attributes that you like to see in the output of the service invocation. All the operations and input/output schema for a given service are documented in OER and can be seen from the Web service definition file (WSDL) as well.

SOA Composite Services

A composite service typically represents a complete business flow such as order fulfillment. This service might be triggered by certain actions or functions within Fusion Applications or can be invoked explicitly by a program or client. Composite services may be non-object-based and represent an end-to-end back-end process that spans multiple objects and orchestrates other ADF Services, human task workflow, or business rules. The composite services are also described by WSDL and XSD and can be invoked by any standard Web service client, similar to the way you invoke

ADF Services. Fusion Applications use composite services when there is an out-of-the-box integration between different functions and the integration needs to be loosely coupled between those applications. Typically these composites are triggered by raising business events in one application and use ADF Services to communicate between these applications.

Business Events

Fusion Applications business objects publish business events to the Event Delivery Network (EDN). Business events are a way to notify any subscriber about any change to a given business object. Every object in Fusion Application does not raise business events; you can check product-specific documentation to find out if there are events that are not documented in OER. The business events for a given object could be raised on create, update, or delete of a given instance of the business object. There are business process–specific events such as bulk import as well that are available in Fusion Applications.

Scheduled Processes

Fusion Applications use Enterprise Scheduler Services (ESS) for background processing. You can find these ESS programs in OER and understand details such as their use, parameters required to run the process, and so on. Some of the ESS programs are exposed as a task in FSM so that the administrator does not need to understand the details behind it. Some are invoked internally from the UI or from SOA composites. Please read Chapter 13 for more details on ESS.

Tables and Views

All the physical tables and views for Fusion Applications are available in OER. These tables are used to store the transaction, setup, and configuration data. OER exposes all important information such as the table description, columns, column description, index, constraints on the table, and so on. Most of the important Fusion Applications objects support bulk import, which is useful for initial data load or migration or periodic bulk updates. Typically, data loads are done through interface tables where you populate the data in raw format and then the Fusion Applications import program will move the data into transaction tables. In the process, it will apply the necessary data conversions and validation rules to make sure there are no data integrity issues. You can load the interface tables in a variety of ways such as Oracle Data Integrator (ODI), a database adapter in Oracle SOA Suite, or SQL commands or loaders.

Data Model Diagrams

In addition to physical table information, OER also exposes data model diagrams. You can find the diagram for a given logical area. The diagram shows relationships between physical tables and helps you understand internal implementation. OER exposes both a logical data model diagram and a physical relational data model diagram.

How to Discover Integration Assets in OER

To view OER on your deployment, navigate to http:/host:port/oer where you have installed OER. This gives you information based on the Fusion Applications release you have provisioned and gives you a concrete URL for WSDL and XSD. You can also go to the public OER hosted by Oracle at https://fusionappsoer.oracle.com if you just want to discover assets. This publicly hosted OER is for the latest Fusion Applications release that is available for download from Oracle e-Delivery. You can log in to OER, either as a guest or with an authenticated account as shown in Figure 15-1.

Once you log in to OER, you can find what is new in the current release, how to find documentation for various products, and how to search assets in OER as shown in Figure 15-2.

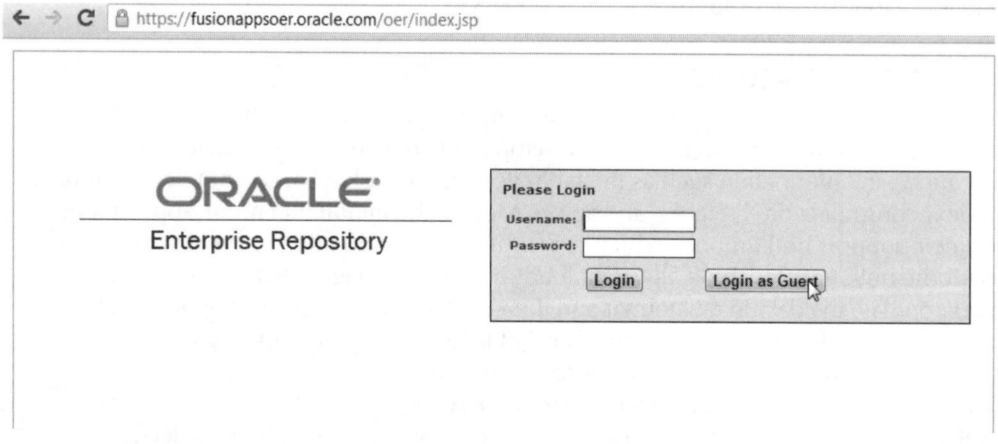

FIGURE 15-1. *OER login screen*

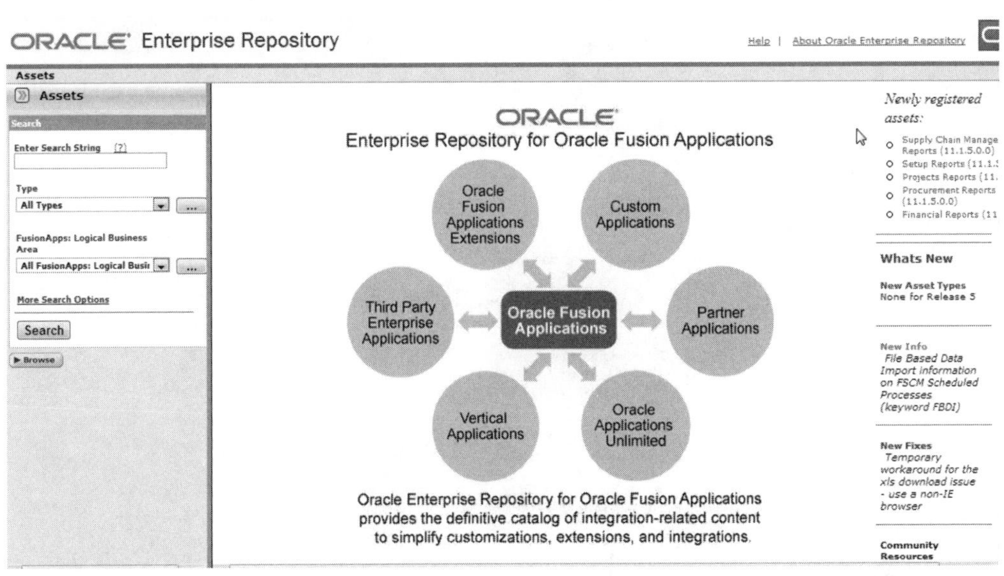

FIGURE 15-2. *OER home page*

We will search for a Web service to manage location data in the customer data management module using OER in this section.

1. From the Assets search window on the left-hand side, select Type as ADF Service as shown in the following illustration.

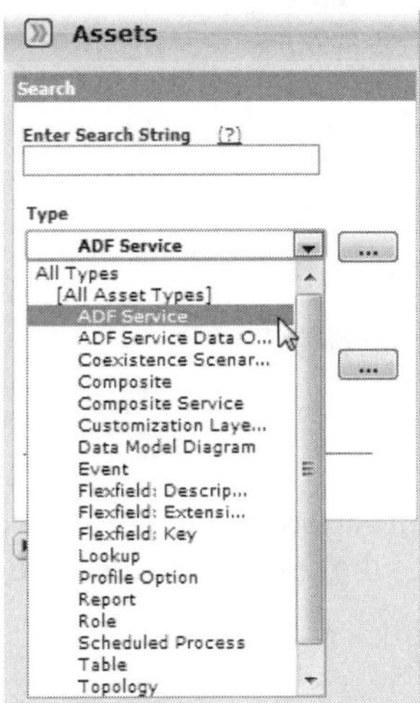

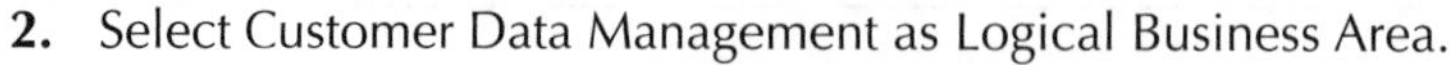

2. Select Customer Data Management as Logical Business Area.

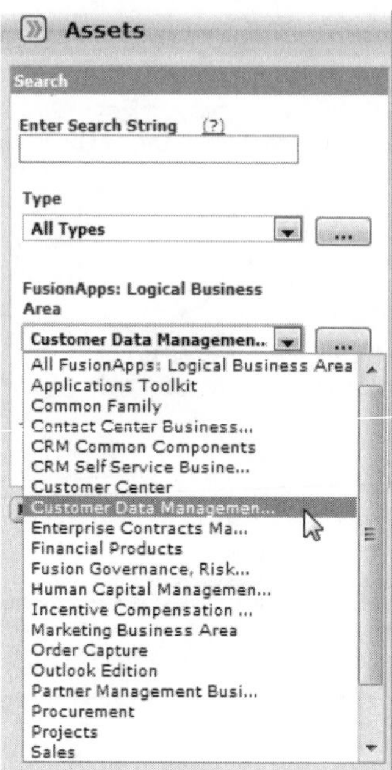

3. Provide the search string as **location** and click the Search button. This will return the matching services for the given criteria as shown here.

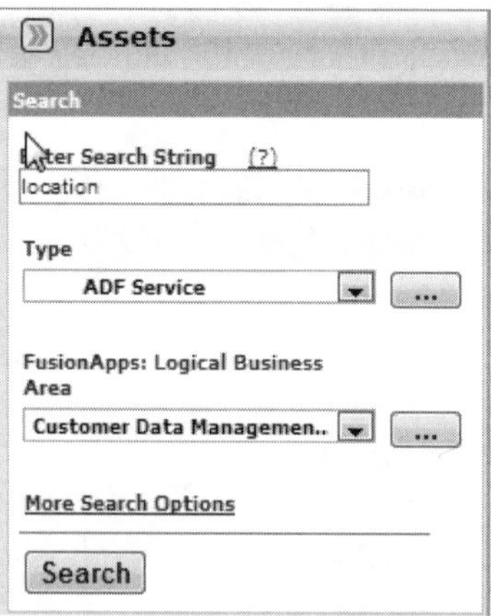

4. You can examine the details about the selected service on the Overview tab. It provides a description of the service, its lifecycle, and compatibility details as shown in Figure 15-3.

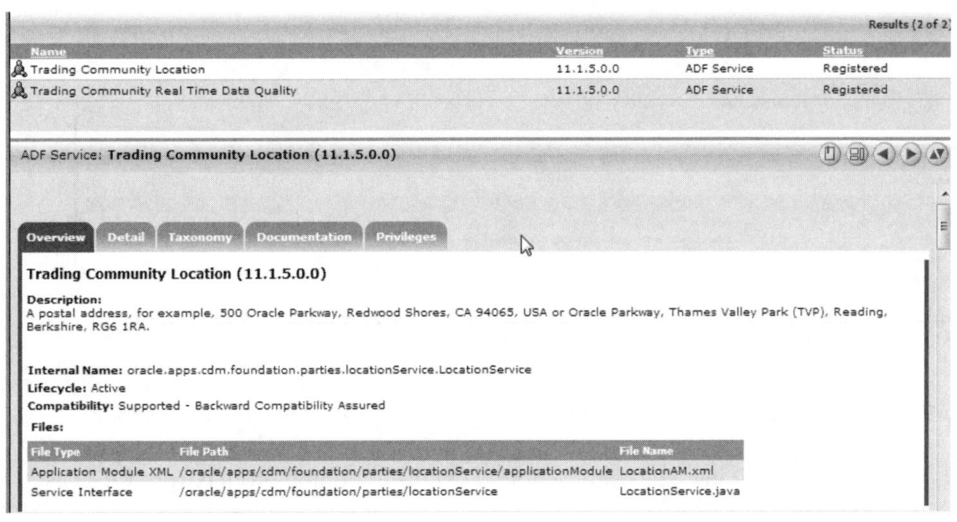

FIGURE 15-3. *Location service details*

5. You can examine the operations, their description, and input and output parameters for this service on the Detail tab, as shown in Figure 15-4.

6. The Detail tab also shows you the WSDL location for this service as shown here.

Service Path: http://<HostName:PortNumber>/foundationParties/LocationService?WSDL
Abstract WSDL URL: rep://FUSIONAPPS_HOSTEDREP/oracle/apps/cdm/foundation/parties/locationService/LocationService.wsdl

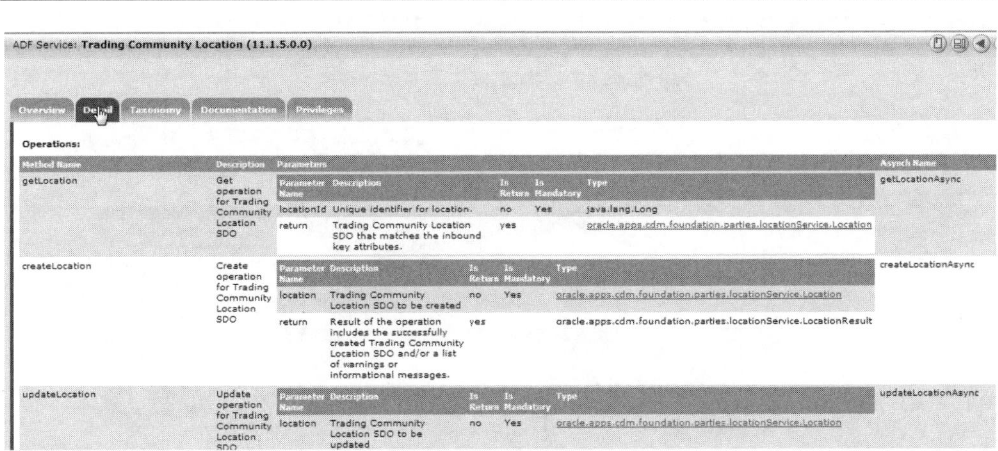

FIGURE 15-4. *Location service operations*

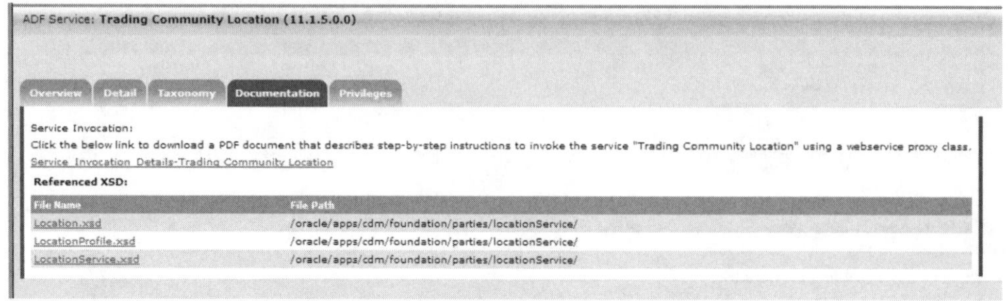

FIGURE 15-5. *Location service documentation*

7. The Documentation tab allows you to check the XSD for this Web service and its operations. It also provides you a link to the cookbook on how the service can be invoked and complete details about the service from OER, as shown in Figure 15-5.

8. The Privileges tab gives details about what privileges and roles the user will need to access the service and its operations, as shown in Figure 15-6.

9. Similarly, you can search for other types of assets and examine all the details about the artifact and how you can use that for your integrations using OER.

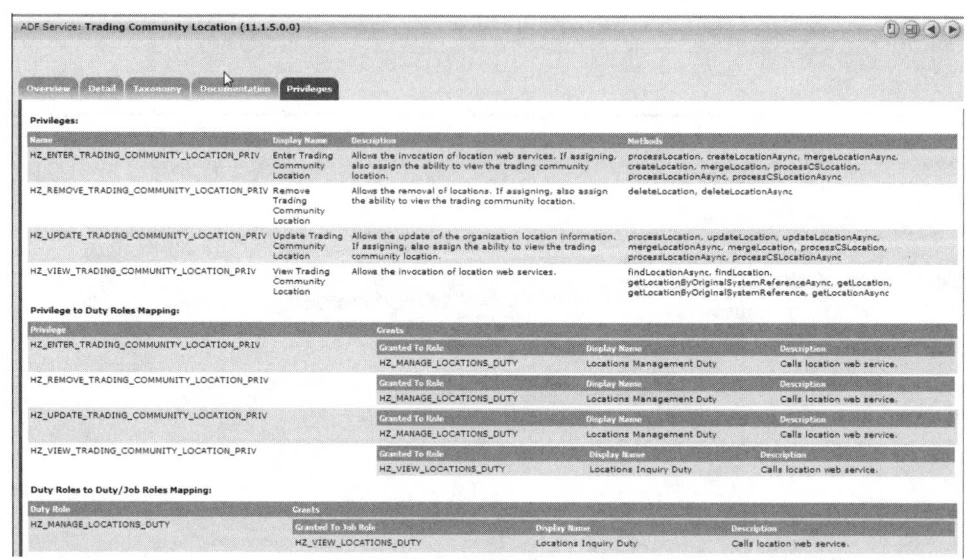

FIGURE 15-6. *Location service security*

Outbound Integration Patterns with Fusion Applications

You may need to call out to other applications from Fusion Applications when your business requirements span multiple applications. Outbound calls may be needed for a totally new business process or as a customized or extended process to Fusion Applications. Different precuts in Fusion Applications provide different capabilities to do outbound integrations. We will briefly discuss these options in the following section.

Object Workflow

CRM Application Composer provides you a feature called Object Workflow as discussed in Chapter 6. This feature allows you to define your own events and triggers on several out-of-the-box objects in CRM. In response to the event you define, you can choose an outbound service call as an action. You need to first use OER or product-specific documentation to find out the Web service interface for a given object for outbound call and then build your own WS that takes the same XSD as input. Once you have your own service that take a CRM object as input, you register that service with a CRM object workflow outbound call in response to the event for that object. At run time, when the condition specified in Object Workflow is satisfied, it will call out the Web service you registered. Your Web service will need to do whatever action you may need per your requirement to take the object details and communicate to other applications. The CRM Object Workflow is the only mechanism that lets you do real-time outbound integration with Fusion Applications in SaaS deployment mode. This option works for On-Premise customers as well.

Business Events

Fusion Applications provide many business events on several objects. These events are raised on Fusion Applications SOA domain EDN for a given product family such as CRM or HCM. Since these events are raised within the Fusion Application domain, SaaS customers cannot subscribe to these events. You can consume these events if you have access to middleware domains in your On-Premise deployment. You can use OER to find out what business events are available for a given area. Some events may not be documented, so you may have to read product-specific documentation for that. Once you find out the event details, you can create an SOA Composite With Mediator that will subscribe to the event using the Event Definition Language (EDL) file. The event payload should give you enough information to then get more details about the object and do necessary processing with that data in your composite. If there are no existing events that meet your needs, you can use JDeveloper as discussed in Chapter 7 to add your own custom events and subscribe to them in your Mediator. Business events are the standard and recommended approach to do outbound integration with Fusion Applications.

Bulk Export

There are certain Fusion Applications products that provide Bulk Export interfaces, which allow you to extract the data out of Fusion Applications. Fusion CRM applications have a "Schedule Export Processes" FSM task that allows you to select an object you want to export, the filter criteria, the attributes to export, and the scheduling frequency. You can use this task to get the data out of CRM applications either on SaaS or On-Premise deployment. Figure 15-7 shows an example of exporting location data with a few selected attributes.

Similarly, HCM applications have a Bulk Extract interface that allows you to specify data blocks to be extracted for given logical entity. It allows you to specify extract parameters, delivery options, delivery schedule, and other mappings that you can use for reporting purposes. You can access the HCM extract UI using the FSM task "Define Extracts." Figure 15-8 shows an example payroll extract. Please read HCM product documentation for more details on all the configuration and extract options and capabilities.

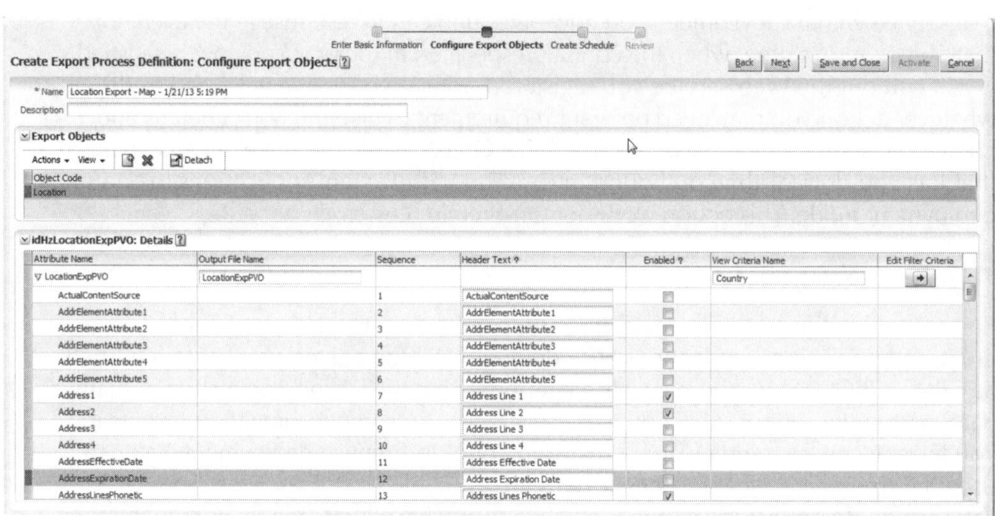

FIGURE 15-7. *Bulk Export configuration*

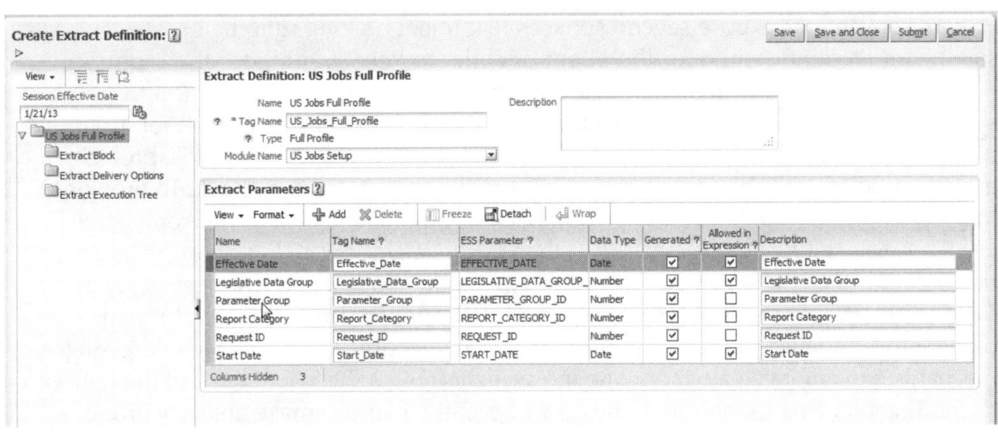

FIGURE 15-8. *HCM export definition*

Inbound Integration Patterns with Fusion Applications

Similar to outbound integration, you may need to do inbound integration with Fusion Applications to bring in data or take certain actions based on the changes happening in your other applications. Most of the products in Fusion Applications support both real-time and batch integration capabilities. We will discuss some of the common integration points in this section for inbound calls to Fusion Applications.

Calling Web Services

Invoking ADF service from a client can be done in various ways. You can use Web service binding or BPEL entity variables if you are using BPEL, or use a proxy class if it is a Java client or any other tool to call a service. You can invoke the service as synchronous request-response invocation or asynchronous request-reply invocation.

Making a Synchronous Service Call

Fusion Applications expose synchronous services. You will use synchronous service calls when you expect the call to return very quickly. These services return the response to the caller, and until the response is returned, the caller will keep waiting as shown in the following illustration.

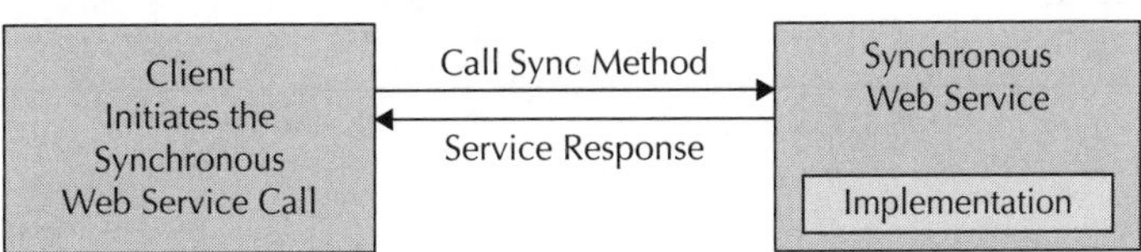

Making an Asynchronous Service Call

Fusion Applications expose several services that might be long-running or take a significant amount of time for the client or caller to keep waiting for the reply. Fusion ADF Services typically expose asynchronous interfaces in addition to synchronous for a given service operation. You can find the details in OER for a given service. The asynchronous service call can be easily made from a BPEL process, and the process will wait for the response from the service to come back. To provide this asynchronous interface and right callback to waiting clients, Fusion Applications use the Advance Queue (AQ) feature in the Fusion database. The Fusion Applications database has these AQs per product family to handle request and response, such as CRM_AsyncWS_Request and CRM_AsyncWS_Response. The administrator can monitor these queues for diagnostics. The SOA run time uses a Web service addressing mechanism to automatically correlate the asynchronous service call back to the right client. The following list describes the flow of events when you make an asynchronous service call, as shown in Figure 15-9.

1. The client calls an asynchronous method.
2. The asynchronous Web service receives the request and stores it in the request queue.
3. The asynchronous Web service sends a receipt confirmation to the client.

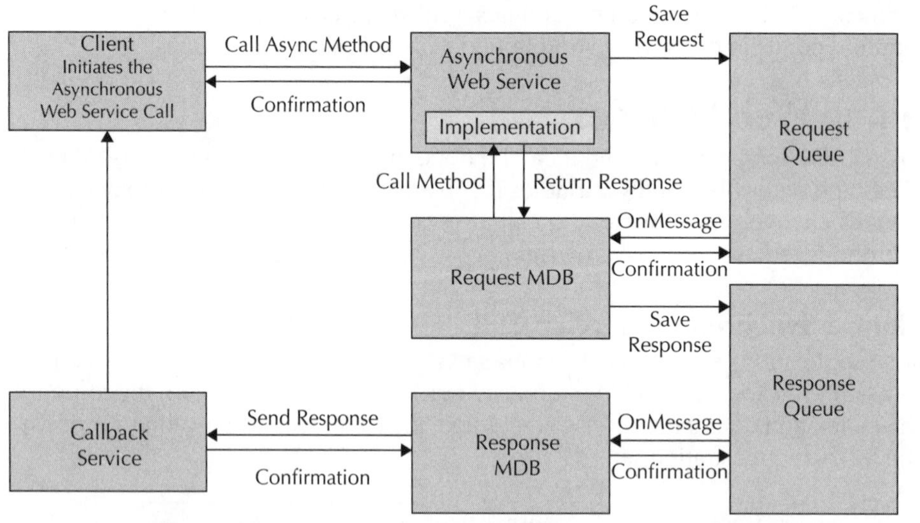

FIGURE 15-9. *Asynchronous service call*

4. The MDB listener on the request queue receives the message and initiates processing of the request.
5. The request MDB calls the required method in the Web service implementation.
6. The Web service implementation returns the response.
7. The request MDB saves the response to the response queue.
8. The request MDB sends a confirmation to the request queue to terminate the process.
9. The onMessage listener on the response queue initiates processing of the response.
10. The response MDB, acting as the callback client, returns the response to the callback service.
11. The callback service delivers the response to the client that initiated the request if the client was waiting for the response.
12. The callback service returns a receipt confirmation message.
13. The response MDB returns a confirmation message to the response queue.

Primary Key Management

When integrating using Web services, the ADF Services typically need the caller to pass the surrogate primary key of the object to identify the data to be updated. Sometimes the services also expose the user-friendly alternative keys in the service interface and the caller can pass those alternative keys to identify rows to be updated instead of surrogate primary key values. In both cases, you will need a way to cross-reference the keys between Fusion Applications and your other external application that you integrate with Fusion Applications. There are four ways in which you can achieve this cross-referencing.

Cross-Reference in Fusion In this approach, Fusion Applications store the cross-reference to external system keys. Some Fusion Applications such as Customer Data Management have a built-in infrastructure to store such cross-references. It simply maps the Fusion surrogate primary key to the external system keys that you will have at hand when you get the event originated in the external system. You can then query Fusion Applications using those external keys to get Fusion surrogate key values to be used for calling the service.

Cross-Reference in External Systems In this approach, the cross-reference to Fusion Applications entities is stored in your external system. It is very similar to the first approach, but the mapping is stored in an external system. When you want to call the Fusion Applications Web service, you will need to look up the cross-reference in your external system to identify the surrogate keys and then use those keys to call the service.

Cross-Reference in Middleware The Fusion Middleware SOA Suite has built-in cross-reference functionality that you can use to manage the cross-reference between your external applications and Fusion Applications. You may choose to use this approach if you want to maintain this cross-reference outside of your applications and be able to use it for many cross-application integrations. You will use this middleware cross-reference map to look up keys before calling necessary services.

Using Alternative Keys Some of the Fusion Applications services allow you to pass alternative business keys in addition to surrogate primary key values. In such cases, when you create the data, you can populate these alternative key attributes in Fusion with exact values from your external or source system. When you need to update the data in future, you can simply pass the value of these keys as you get them from your external system without any lookup. Note that this approach works only for one-to-one system integration. If you had multiple systems with different values for these alternative keys, this approach will not work and you will have to keep the cross-reference for each system by following one of the three options discussed earlier.

Security

Fusion Applications Web services are secured using Oracle Web Service Manager (OWSM), which follows Web service security standards. Different services implement different security policy on the server side. The clients need to use appropriate client-side policy accordingly in order to make a successful service call. You can examine the security policy on a given service either in the WSDL or in the Enterprise Manager where the service is deployed. The administrator can modify the out-of-the-box security on a service using Enterprise Manager. Please read the *Oracle Fusion Middleware Security and Administrator's Guide for Web Services* to understand more about the security and how to call services with different policies.

Bulk Import

Many Fusion Applications provide bulk import capabilities that you can use to do initial loads or migrate data from your legacy or external applications. To bulk-import data, you will first need to load the raw data in the interface tables. Then run the background processes from Fusion Applications to load the interface data into the

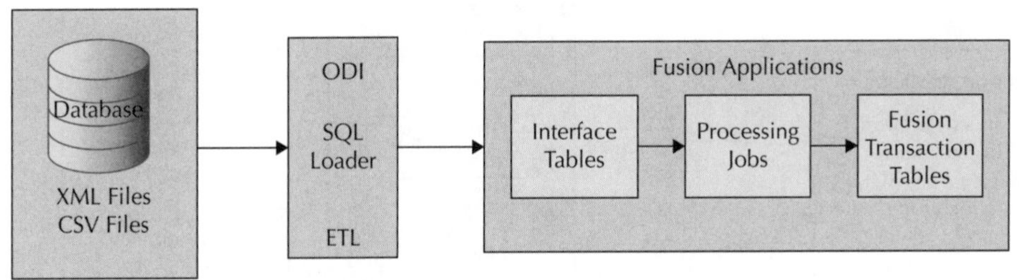

FIGURE 15-10. *Bulk import data flow*

transaction tables. Please read product-specific documentation to understand what capabilities are provided to load specific object data. The typical bulk import flow looks like Figure 15-10.

File Import

Some of the Fusion Applications, such as CRM and HCM, provide utilities to import data from files from end users. The tools take files in formats such as CSV, XML, and XLS as input from the desktop of the user or from a network-accessible location. The tool then uses the regular interface tables and kicks off the import processing. These loaders also provide user interfaces to monitor and review the progress of the process and inspect the errors. You can use the Manage Import Activities task to use a file import interface for CRM applications. You can choose the object from this UI that you want to import and then use the mapping tool to specify what attribute from your input file format maps to the object attribute and submit the batch to start the import process. Please read product-specific documentation to understand more about the specific capabilities of the file import.

An Example Integration Using Standard Patterns

In this section, we will discuss a sample integration using some of the patterns discussed in this chapter. We will use SOA Composite and Web services to do both outbound and inbound integration with Fusion Applications. The high-level integration flow looks like the chart in Figure 15-11. Note that in this example, we are using Fusion Applications as a source of both outbound and inbound integration. The event is originated in Fusion Applications when you create a new location using a page, and you get the outbound message in the form of business event in the SOA

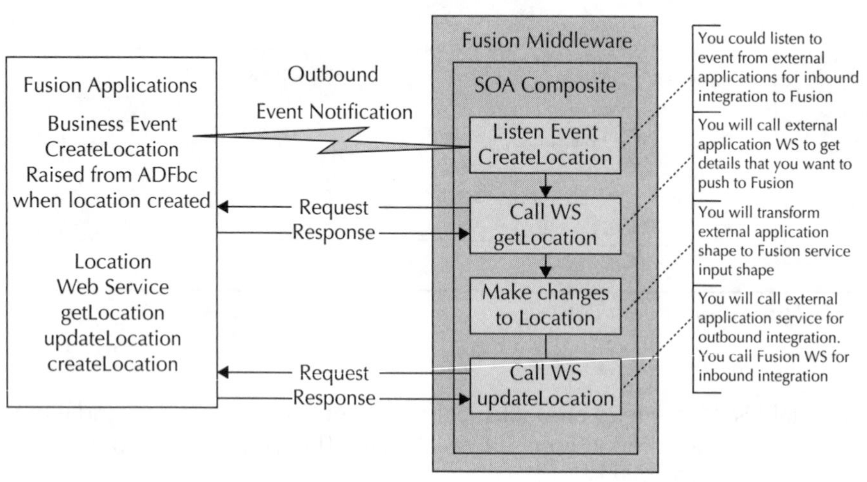

FIGURE 15-11. *Typical integration pattern between applications*

composite. You will then use a synchronous Web service operation to get the details of the location created out of the Fusion Application. And then make an inbound service call to the same Fusion Application to make some changes to the location. In real integration scenarios, the application on the other side will be your external application that you want to integrate with Fusion Applications.

To build this integration, we will need to follow several sets of tasks.

Define a Connection to MDS Repository to Find an Event Definition

Once you have identified the name of the business event that you need to listen to, either using OER or from product documentation, you can discover the event definition and schema using the SOA MDS repository on your environment.

1. Go to JDeveloper and view the Resource Palette. Select New Connection: SOA MDS as option to create a new connection to your Fusion Applications SOA MDS repository.

2. Give your connection a name, select Connection Type as DB Based MDS, provide database connection details for the CRM_FUSION_MDS_SOA schema user, select MDS partition as soa-infra, and test that the connection is successful.

3. Once the connection is created, you can expand the connection and find out the event definition for the create location at oracle.apps.cdm.foundation.parties.publicModel.locations.entity.events as shown in Figure 15-12.

FIGURE 15-12. *Finding a location event in MDS connection*

Define a New SOA Composite Application and Subscribe to Events

In this section, we review the steps to define a new SOA composite and subscribe to the event that is raised when a new location is created.

1. Select the New Application option, give it the name **FusionAppsLocationIntegration**, and choose the SOA Application template as shown in Figure 15-13.
2. Click Next and name the project as **LocationIntegration**. Click Next, give the composite name **LocationIntegration**, choose template Composite With Mediator as shown in Figure 15-14, and click Finish to complete the wizard.
3. In the Create Mediator dialog, give it the name LocationCreate and choose the template Subscribe to Events. Now click the Add icon to subscribe to a new event as shown in Figure 15-15.

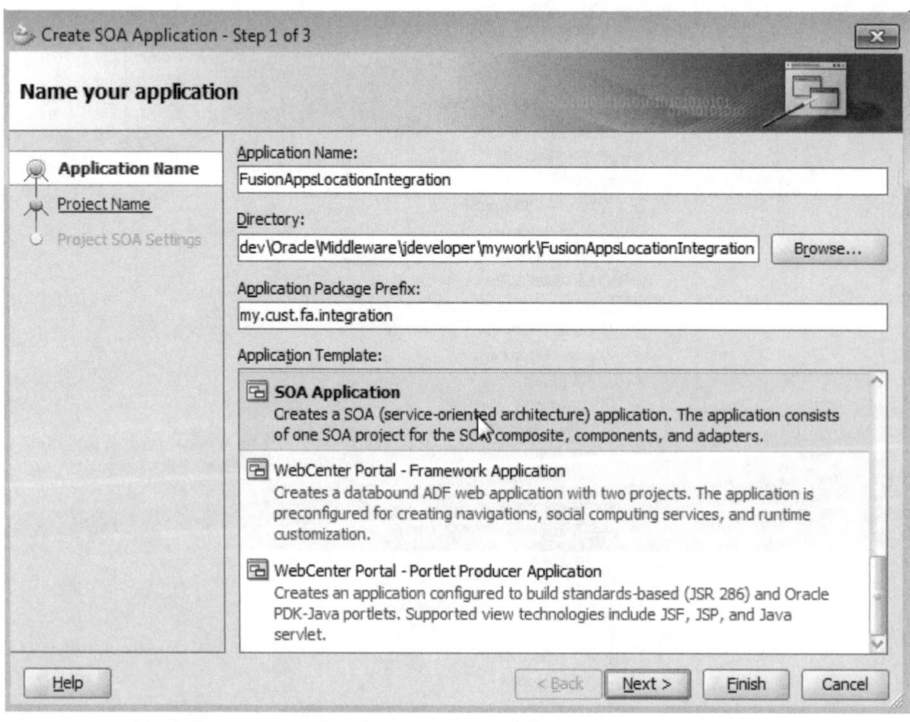

FIGURE 15-13. *Creating a new application*

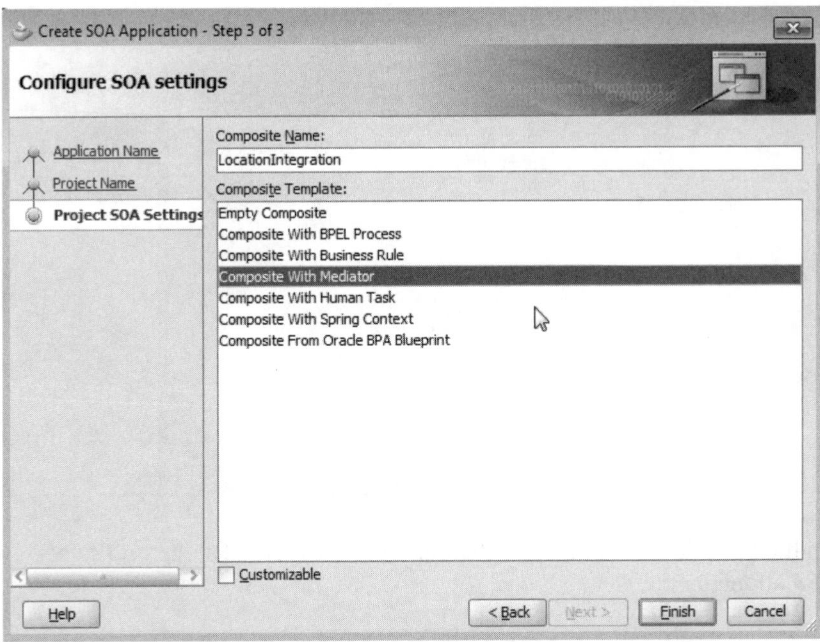

FIGURE 15-14. *Creating a new SOA Composite With Mediator project*

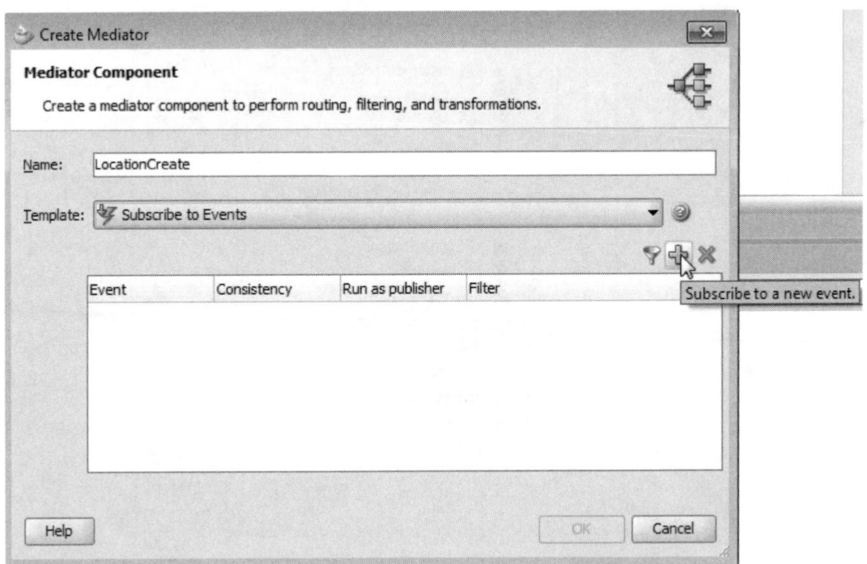

FIGURE 15-15. *Subscribe to an event using Mediator*

4. Click the browse icon for picking the event definition file for the Location Creation event.

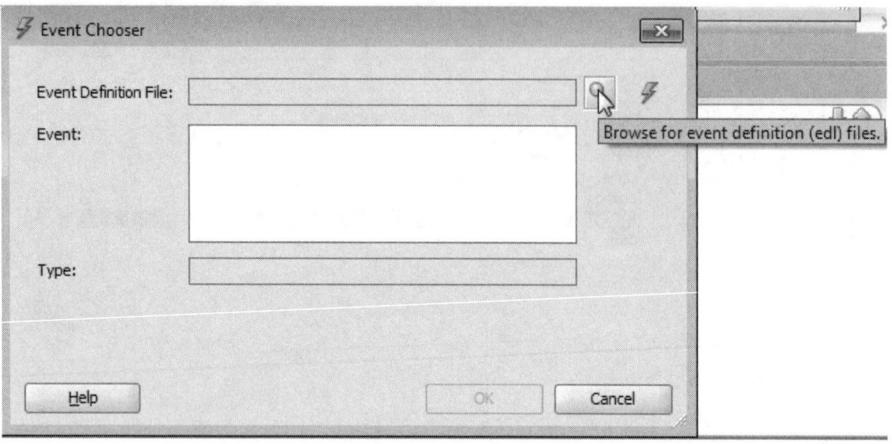

5. In the SOA Resource Browser dialog, select Resource Palette and select LocationEO.edl.

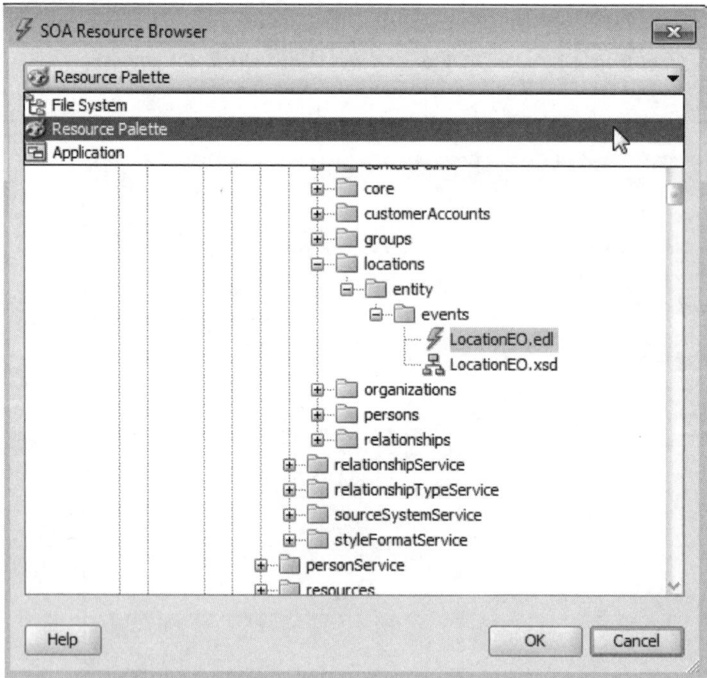

6. Choose CreateLocation as the event name in the Event Chooser dialog and click OK to complete the wizard.

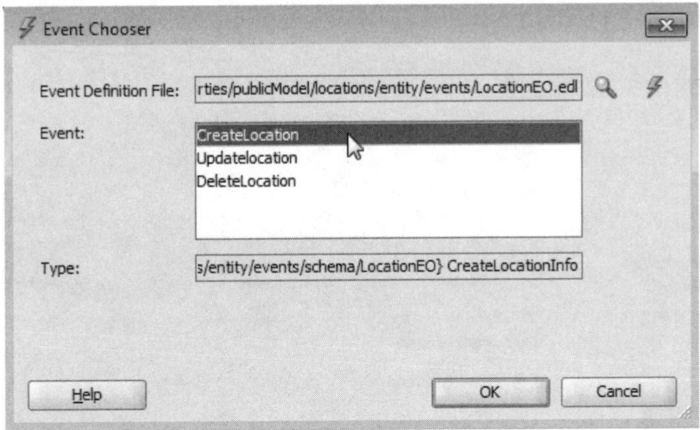

Create a BPEL Process and Route the Event to the Process

In this section, we define a new BPEL process that will orchestrate our flow for integration and route the incoming event from the SOA composite to the BPEL process.

1. Select File | New from the menu and choose to create a new BPEL Process as shown in Figure 15-16.
2. Name the BPEL process as ProcessLocation. Choose the Synchronous BPEL Process template and set the transaction to requiresNew as shown in Figure 15-17.

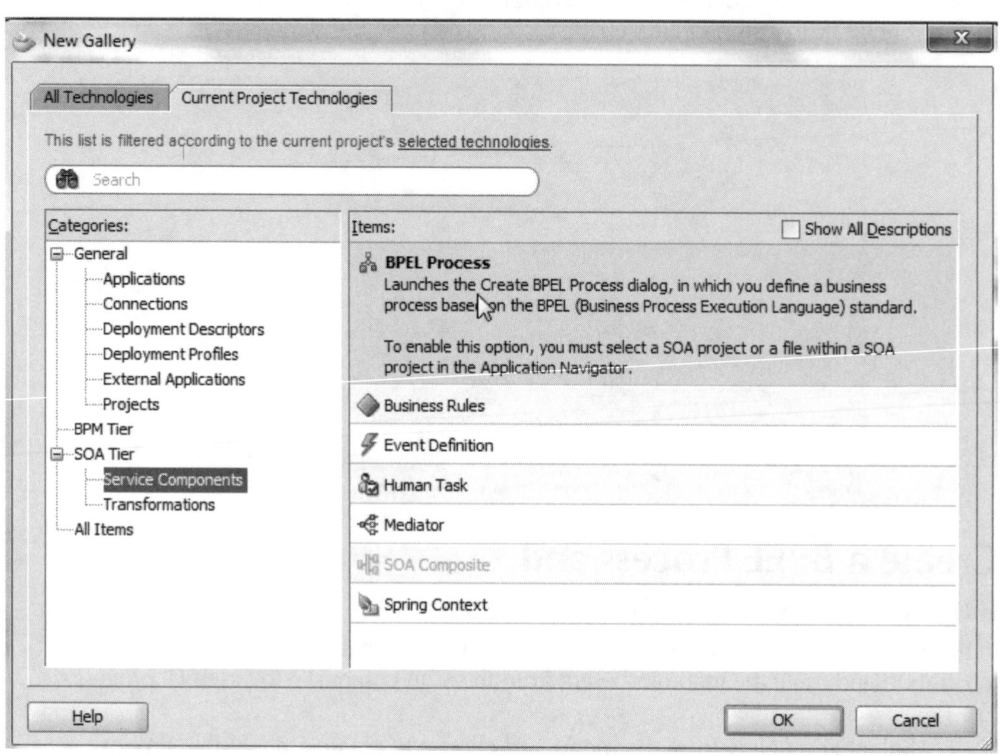

FIGURE 15-16. *Creating a new BPEL process*

3. This illustration shows the SOA composite.

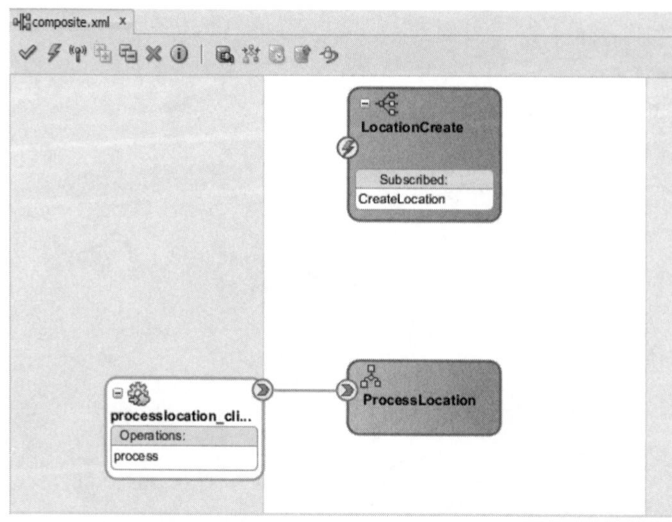

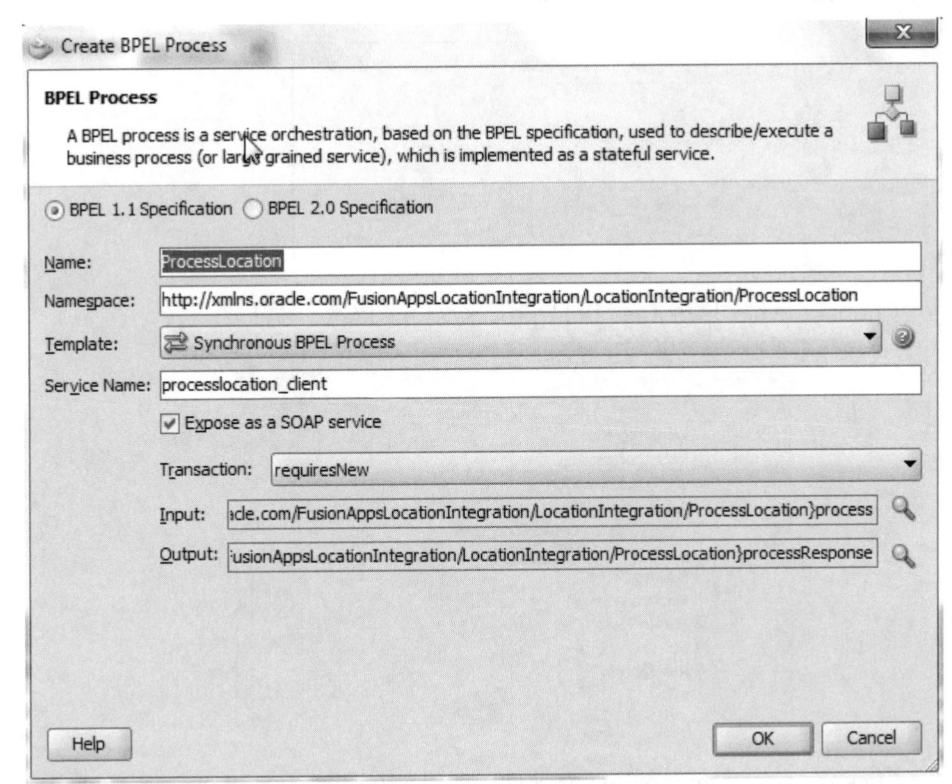

FIGURE 15-17. *Configure BPEL process properties.*

4. Now double-click on the LocationCreate mediator. Click the green add icon (+) to define a new routing rule that will route the event to a BPEL process as shown here.

Routing Rules
Event Subscriptions
CreateLocation
Priority 4
Validate Syntax (XSD)
static routing rule
Callout To <<Java Callout Class>>
Resequence Off

5. Select Service as the routing rule target type.

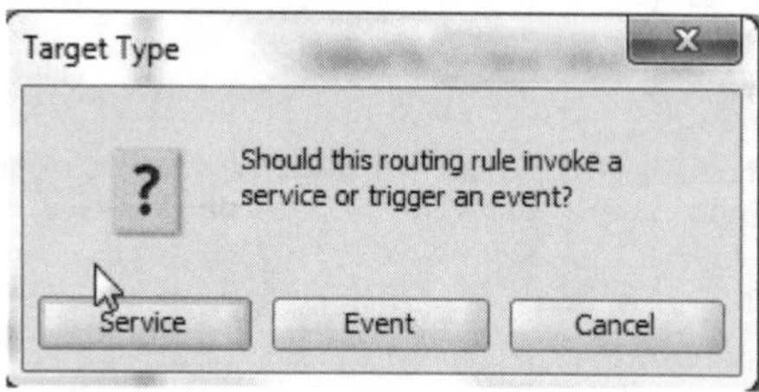

6. Choose the newly defined BPEL process as the target service.

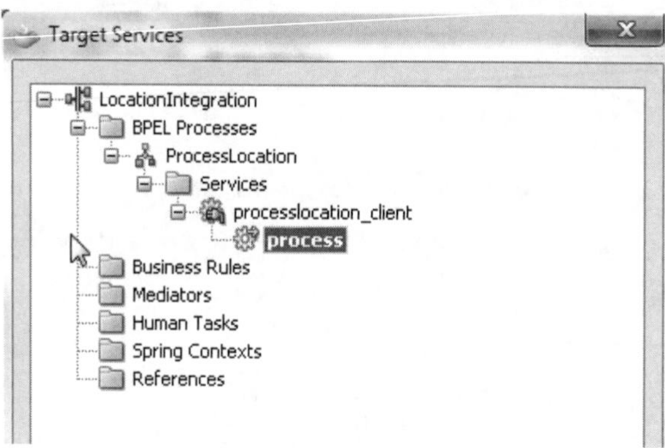

7. Click the Transform icon to pass the LocationId value from the event to the BPEL process.

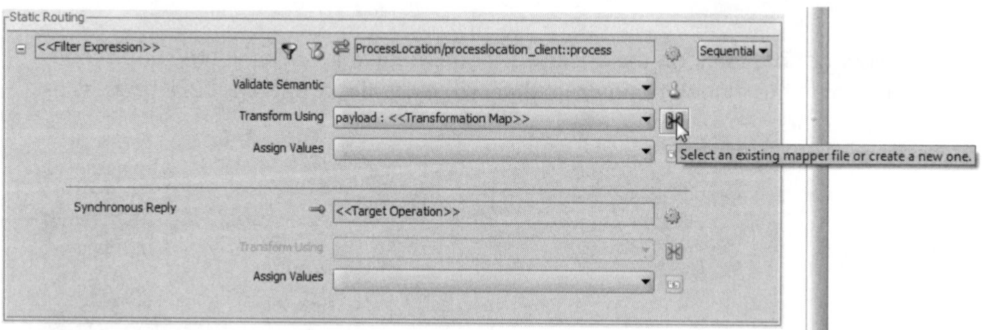

8. Choose the Create New Mapper File option in the Event Transformation Map dialog.

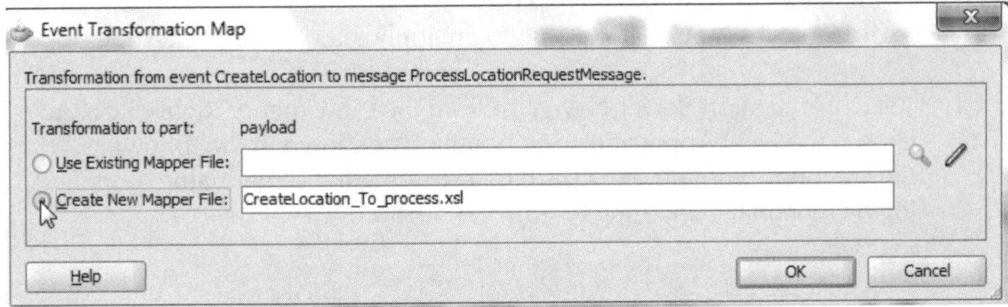

9. On the XSLT transformation, map the LocationId : newValue : value field to the BPEL process input field by drag and drop.

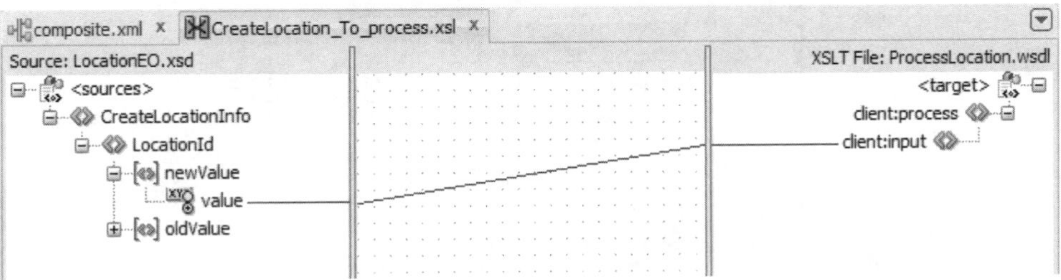

10. The SOA composite after this routing rule looks like Figure 15-18.

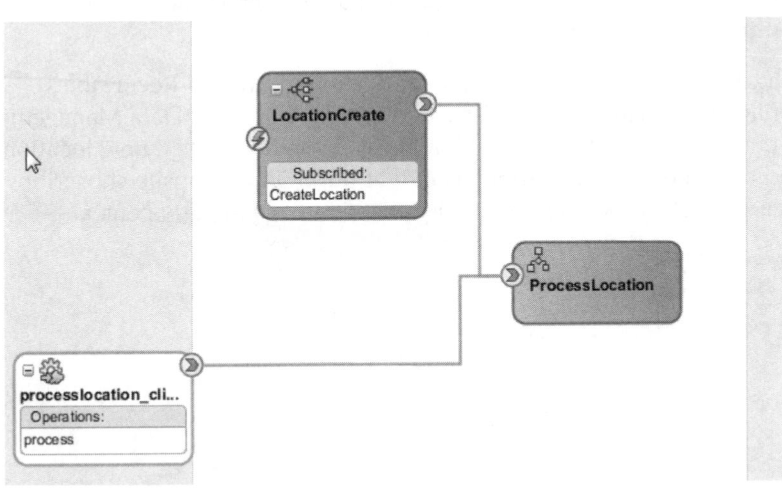

FIGURE 15-18. *SOA Composite With Mediator routing to BPEL process*

Deploy to Application Server and Test Event Subscription

Now we will deploy this SOA composite to an application server for testing.

1. Select Application Server Navigator from the View menu. Right-click and choose the New Application Server option as shown in the following illustration. Complete the wizard by providing the server name, port, and login credentials, and then test the connection.

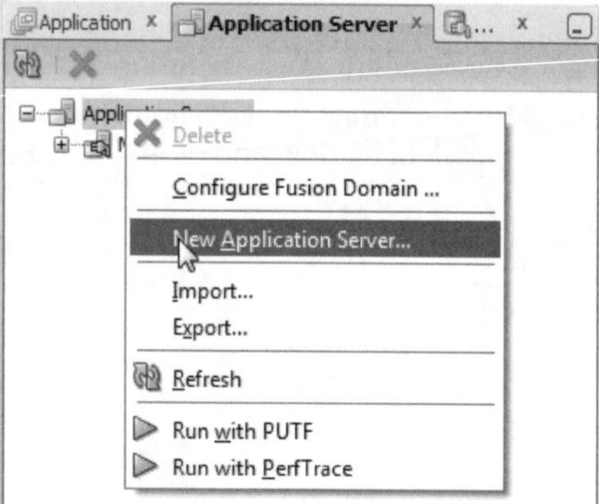

2. Right-click on the LocationIntegration project and choose the Deploy: LocationIntegration option. In the Deployment Action dialog, choose the Deploy to Application Server option as shown in Figure 15-19. Choose the application server connection created in Step 1 and complete the wizard to deploy the SOA composite to the server.

3. You can use the Customer Center application in CRM or Receivables application in Financials or Party Center from Customer Data Management to create a new party along with address. This will create a new location and raise the CreateLocation event that our SOA composite subscribes to. Figure 15-20 shows the Create Organization page in party center.

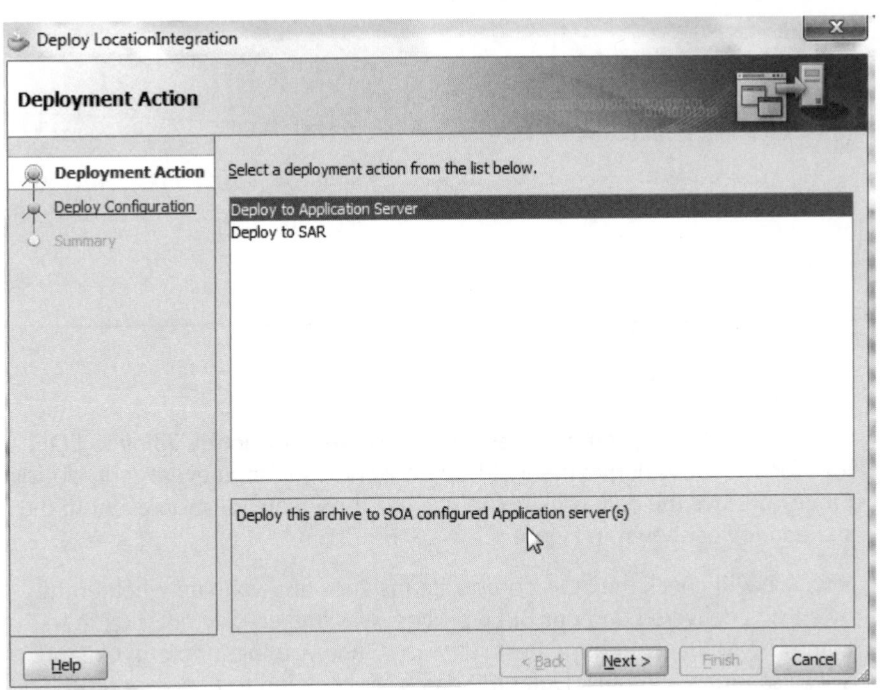

FIGURE 15-19. *Deploying SOA composite*

Create Organization
* Organization Name: Location Event Organization
* From Date: 5/17/13
* Usage: Party of Interest
D-U-N-S Number
Registry ID: CDRM2_241027
URL
Phone + 1
Fax + 1
Preferred Contact Method
* Country: United States
* Address Line 1: Location Event
Address Line 2
Address Line 3
City: REDWOOD SHORES
State: CA
ZIP Code: 94065

FIGURE 15-20. *Create Organization application user interface*

```
        <parameter>
            <name>USER_DISPLAY_NAME</name>
            <namespace>FND$SECURITY</namespace>
            <value>Hunter Robinson</value>
        </parameter>
    </fmw-context>
  </context>
  <tracking>
    <ecid>29ea7a02aaeed5a2:61b22679:13eb4f9342c:-8000-000000000000d5e9</ecid>
  </tracking>
  <content>
    <CreateLocationInfo xmlns="/oracle/apps/cdm/foundation/parties/publicModel/locations/entity/events/schema/LocationEO">
        <LocationId>
            <newValue value="300100020683800"/>
        </LocationId>
    </CreateLocationInfo>
  </content>
</business-event>
 [@17-MAY-2013 10:30:15]
```


FIGURE 15-21. *Business event in EDN log*

4. You can check if a given business event was raised or not by going to EDN logs for your SOA deployment at http://host:port/soa-infra/events/edn-db-log. Once you save the data on UI, you can see the CreateLocation event in the soa edn log as shown in Figure 15-21.

5. Now we will check the SOA composite instance and validate whether the event was delivered and our BPEL process was triggered or not. Log in to the Enterprise Manager at http://host:port/em. Once you log in to em, expand SOA : soa-infra and click Default. Search for Location to find your SOA composite as shown in the following illustration.

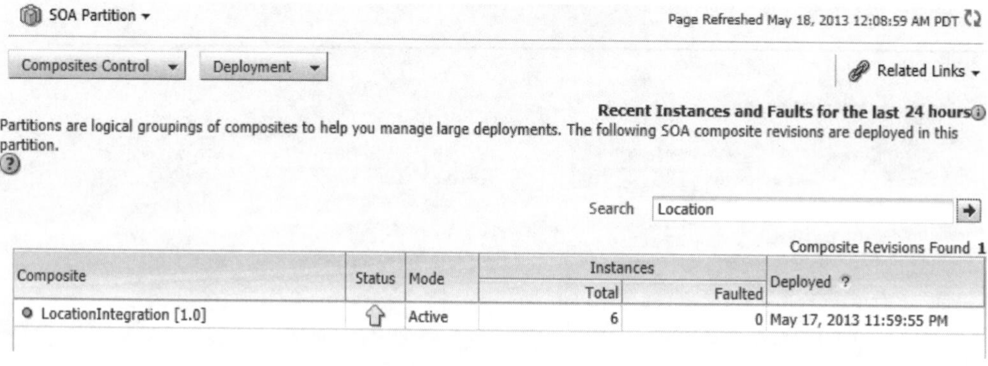

6. Click on LocationIntegration composite to check all instances of this SOA composite. Click on the first Instance ID as shown in the following illustration to see details.

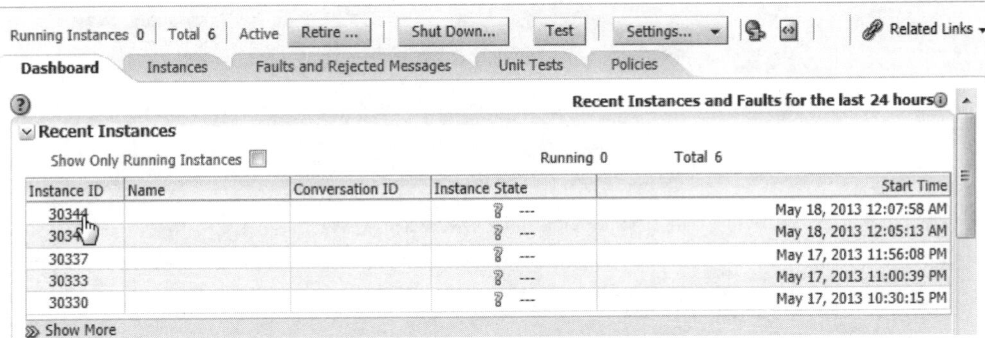

7. This launches the composite Flow Trace window. You can see that the composite received the CreateLocation event that was received by LocationCreate mediator and routed to ProcessLocation BPEL process as shown in Figure 15-22.

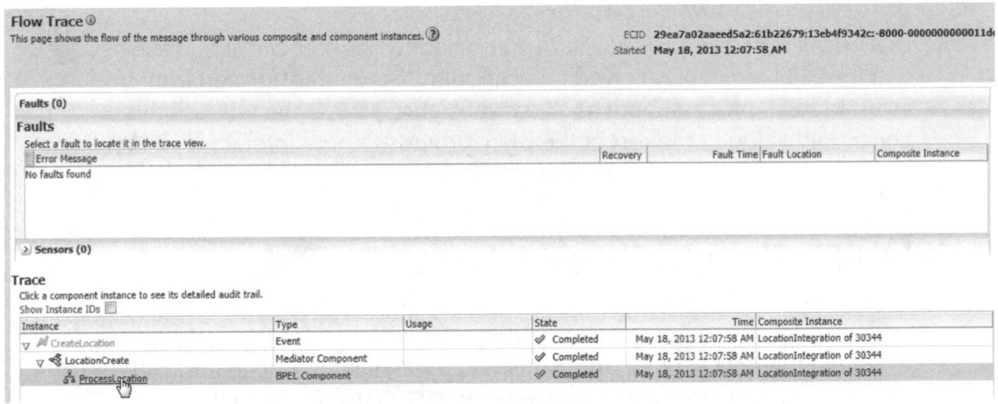

FIGURE 15-22. *SOA composite instance flow trace*

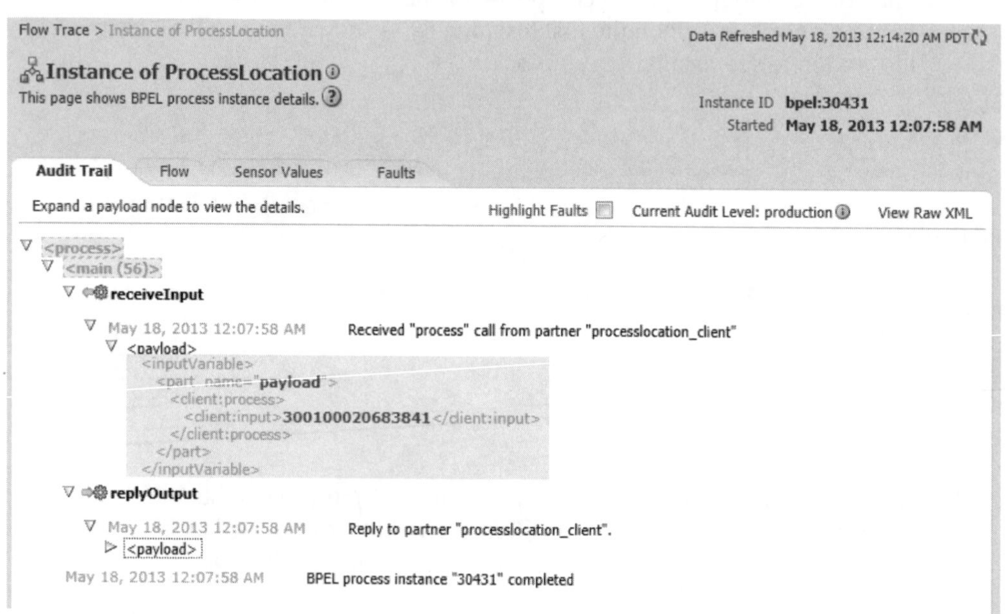

FIGURE 15-23. *Empty BPEL process instance audit trail.*

8. This opens the BPEL process Audit Trail window. As you can see, it shows that the BPEL process received a LocationId that we transformed from the event to BPEL process input as shown in Figure 15-23. We will use this LocationId value in the rest of the BPEL process to now interact with Web services.

Build BPEL Flow to Process Location Data

Now that we have an SOA composite that successfully instantiates on a business event, we will add processing logic in the BPEL. We will first use the getLocation service to get the full details of the location and then make an update and call updateLocation service to make changes and validate that using the UI.

1. Open the BPEL process in the editor. Drag and drop Partner Link from the Component Palette onto the BPEL process as shown in Figure 15-24.

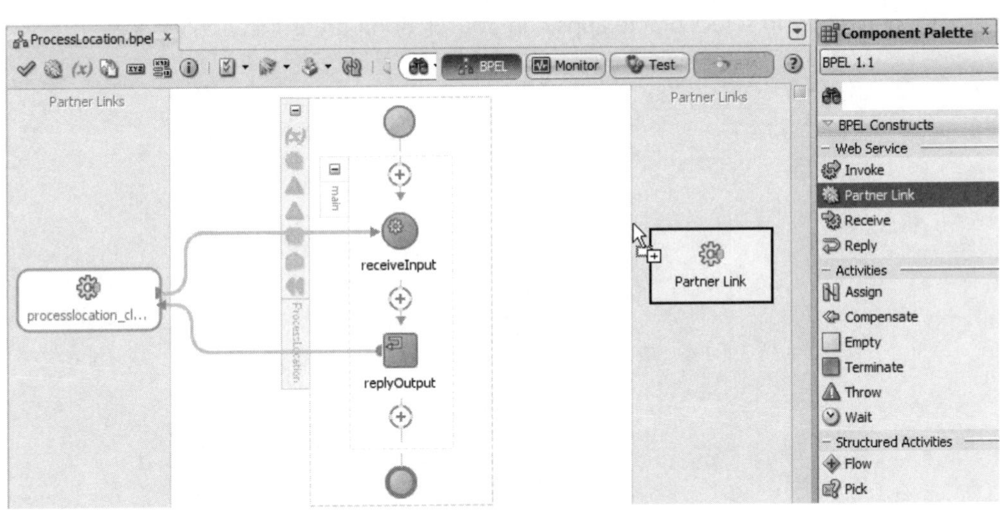

FIGURE 15-24. *Adding a partner link to BPEL process*

2. Give it the name **LocationService** and click on SOA Resource Browser as shown here.

3. In the browser window, select Resource Palette and browse your SOA MDS connection to select oracle.apps.cdm.foundation.parties.locationService.

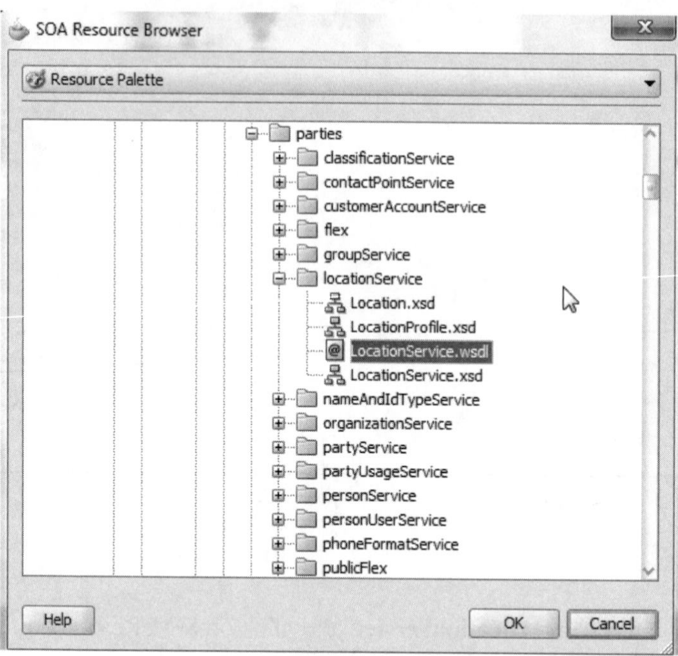

4. Choose the Partner Link Type and My Role as shown in the following illustration and click OK.

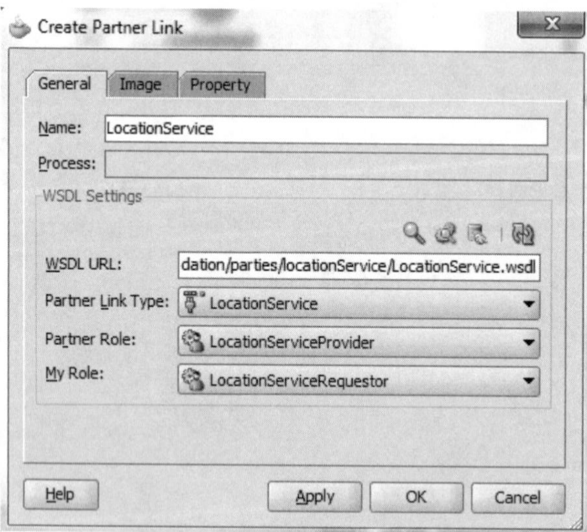

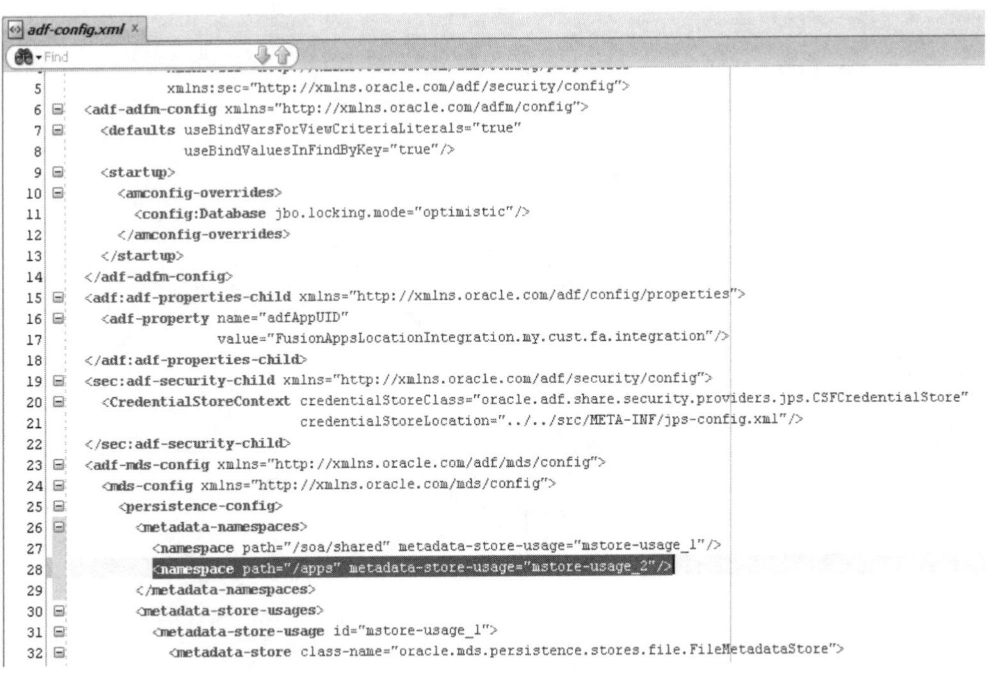
adf-config.xml
Find
xmlns:sec="http://xmlns.oracle.com/adf/security/config">
<adf-adfm-config xmlns="http://xmlns.oracle.com/adfm/config">
<defaults useBindVarsForViewCriteriaLiterals="true"
useBindValuesInFindByKey="true"/>
<startup>
<amconfig-overrides>
<config:Database jbo.locking.mode="optimistic"/>
</amconfig-overrides>
</startup>
</adf-adfm-config>
<adf:adf-properties-child xmlns="http://xmlns.oracle.com/adf/config/properties">
<adf-property name="adfAppUID"
value="FusionAppsLocationIntegration.my.cust.fa.integration"/>
</adf:adf-properties-child>
<sec:adf-security-child xmlns="http://xmlns.oracle.com/adf/security/config">
<CredentialStoreContext credentialStoreClass="oracle.adf.share.security.providers.jps.CSFCredentialStore"
credentialStoreLocation="../../src/META-INF/jps-config.xml"/>
</sec:adf-security-child>
<adf-mds-config xmlns="http://xmlns.oracle.com/adf/mds/config">
<mds-config xmlns="http://xmlns.oracle.com/mds/config">
<persistence-config>
<metadata-namespaces>
<namespace path="/soa/shared" metadata-store-usage="mstore-usage_1"/>
<namespace path="/apps" metadata-store-usage="mstore-usage_2"/>
</metadata-namespaces>
<metadata-store-usages>
<metadata-store-usage id="mstore-usage_1">
<metadata-store class-name="oracle.mds.persistence.stores.file.FileMetadataStore">

FIGURE 15-25. *Specify namespace in the adf-config file.*

5. Modify the adf-config file from the Application Resources: Descriptors: ADF META-INF folder to use namespace /apps instead of /apps/oracle as shown in Figure 15-25.

6. Now drag and drop the Invoke activity onto the BPEL process between receiveInput and replyOutput. Connect the Invoke activity to LocationService as shown in Figure 15-26.

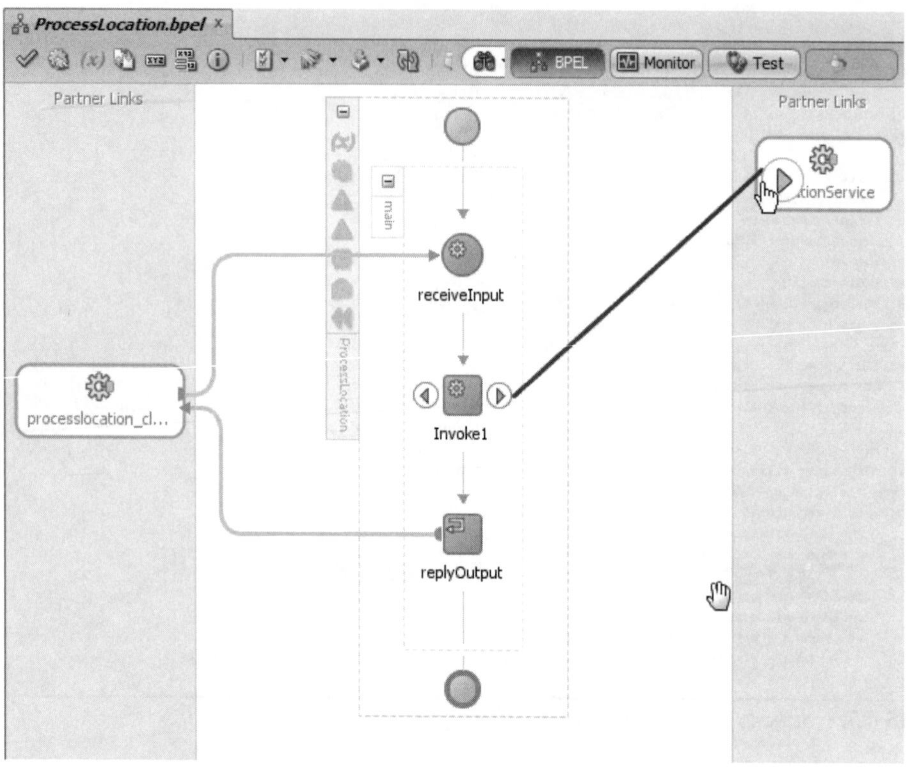

FIGURE 15-26. *Adding Invoke activity for get location service*

7. In the Edit Invoke dialog, provide the name **InvokeGetLocation**. Select getLocation as the Operation. Click the green plus icon to automatically generate input and output variables that will be used for this service call as shown in Figure 15-27.

8. The getLocation service needs the LocationId input parameter. Our BPEL process gets the LocationId as input. We will pass the input of BPEL to the input of the WS invoke variable. Drag and drop the Assign activity on the BPEL process between the receiveInput and InvokeGetLocation activities. Name this activity as AssignLocationId. Double-click on the assign activity and go to the Copy Rules tab. Map the inputVariable input to InvokeGetLocation_getLocation_InputVariable locationId variable as shown in Figure 15-28.

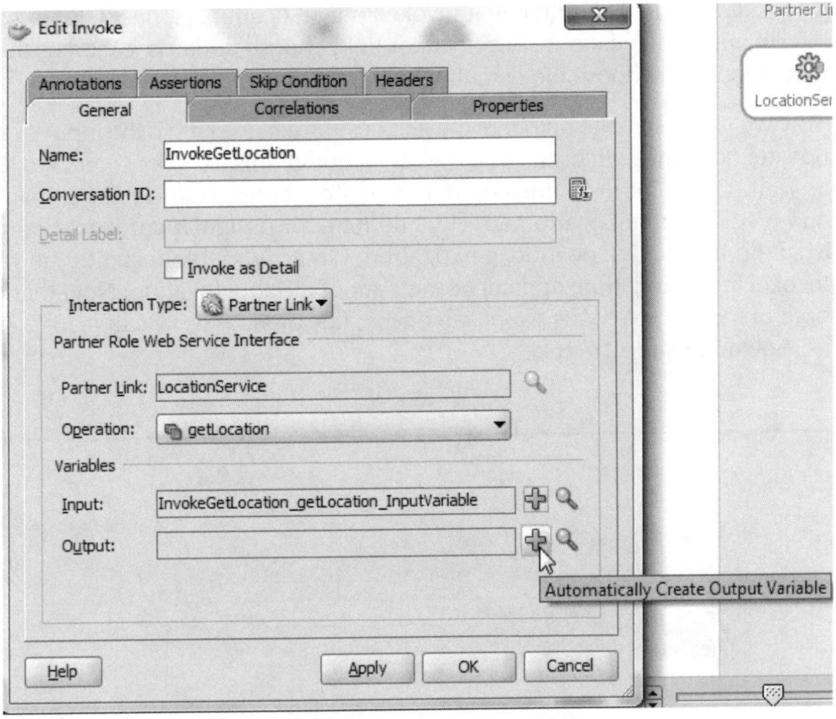

Edit Invoke

Annotations | Assertions | Skip Condition | Headers
General | Correlations | Properties

Name: InvokeGetLocation
Conversation ID:
Detail Label:
Invoke as Detail
Interaction Type: Partner Link
Partner Role Web Service Interface
Partner Link: LocationService
Operation: getLocation
Variables
Input: InvokeGetLocation_getLocation_InputVariable
Output:
Automatically Create Output Variable

Help | Apply | OK | Cancel

Partner Li
LocationSe

FIGURE 15-27. *Defining operation to invoke and variables*

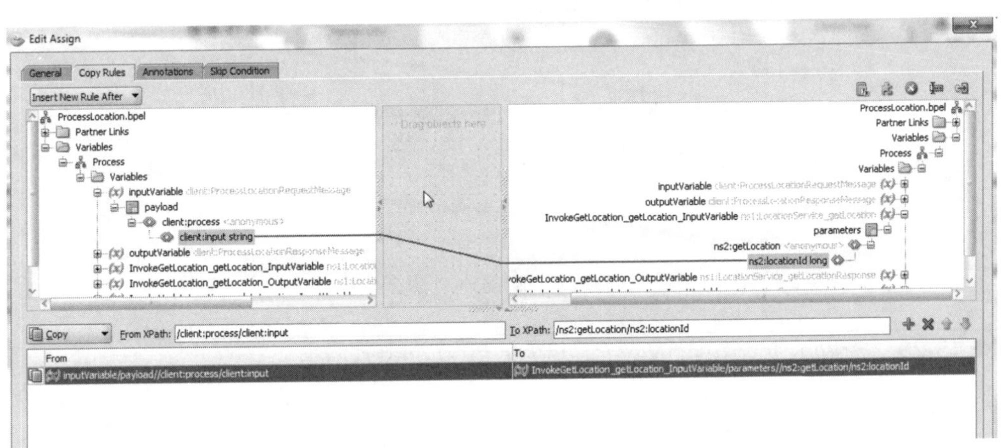

FIGURE 15-28. *Adding Assign activity to pass input variable to a service call*

9. Drag and drop the invoke activity between InvokeGetLocation and replyOutput activity and name it InvokeUpdateLocation. Connect this invoke with the LocationService Partner link, choose updateLocation as the Operation, and choose the default variables as shown in Figure 15-29.

10. Now we will assign the output of the getLocation service call to the input of the updateLocation service call. Later we will modify this to make some updates as well. Drag and drop the assign activity between InvokeGetLocation and InvokeUpdateLocation activity and name it **AssignUpdateLocation**. Map the InvokeGetLocation_getLocation_OutputVariable result to the InvokeUpdateLocation_updateLocation_InputVariable location. Note that both of the variable parts are of same type, Location, and we can map them as shown in Figure 15-30.

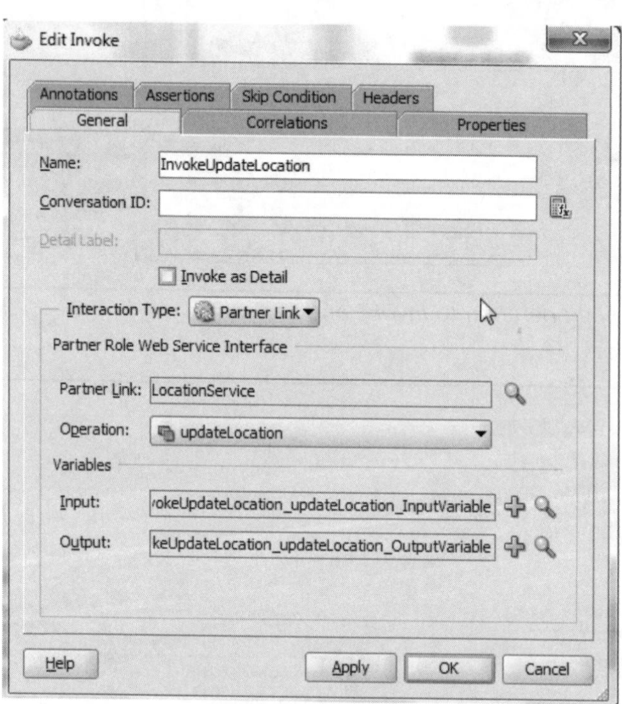

FIGURE 15-29. *Adding Invoke activity for update location service*

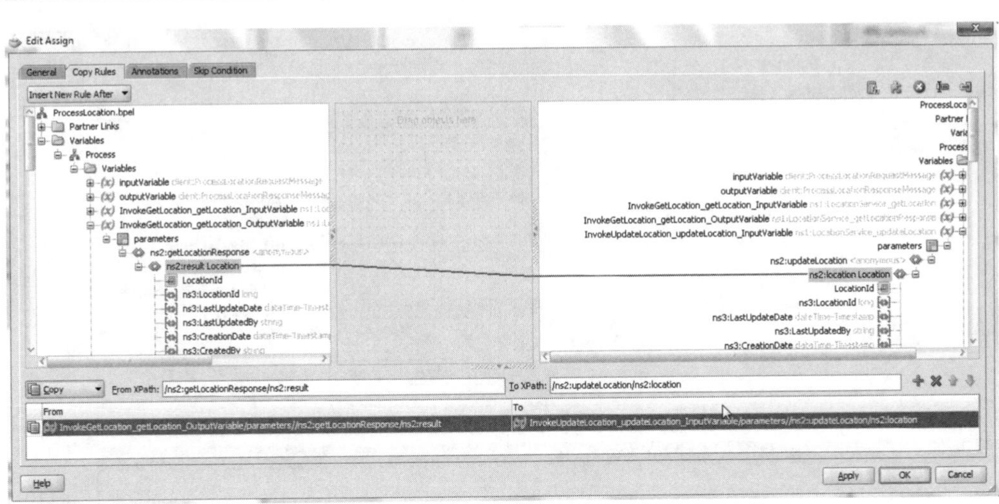

FIGURE 15-30. *Add Assign activity for update location input variable.*

11. Now we will modify address line 1. Right-click on the middle section and choose an expression as shown in the following illustration. Type **Update Address 1** and click OK.

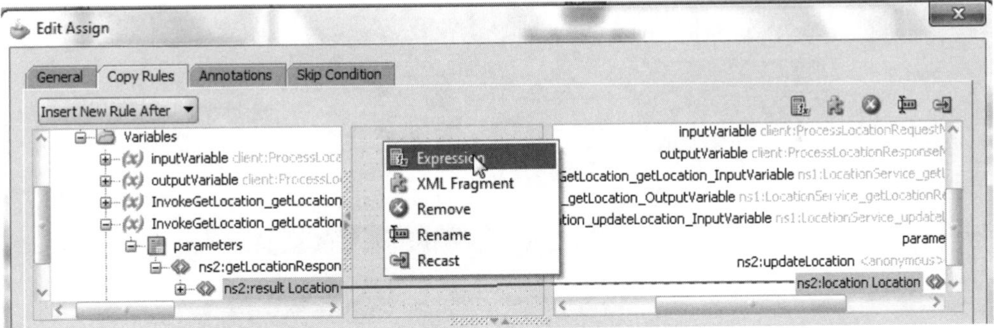

12. Connect this expression to Address1 in the variable InvokeUpdateLocation_updateLocation_InputVariable as shown in Figure 15-31.

13. Now we will need to add appropriate security policies to the service that we are calling from the composite. You can find supported security policies for a given service from OER. Right-click on the service reference in your composite.xml file and choose Configure WS Policies | For Request as

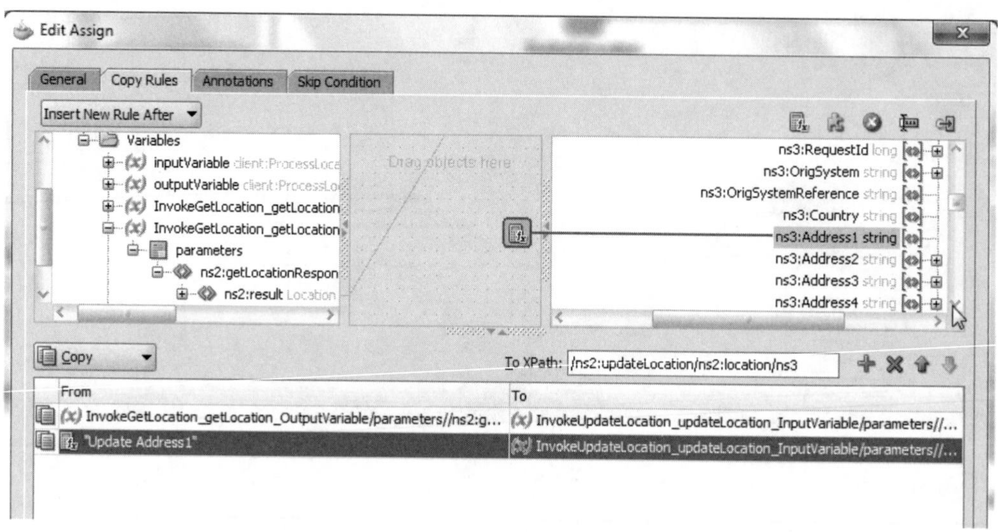

FIGURE 15-31. *Assign the modified value to update the location input variable.*

shown in the following illustration. Click the Add Security Policies button under the Security section and choose the security policy oracle/wss11_saml_token_with_message_protection_client_policy.

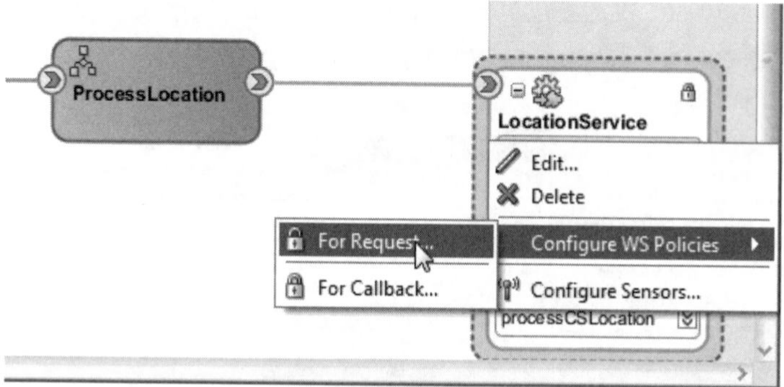

14. Similarly, configure Callback security policy and choose oracle//wss11_saml_or_username_token_with_message_protection_service_policy.

15. Validate that you have a service reference in the composite.xml file as shown in the following code. If it is missing, please add manually.

```
  <reference name="LocationService"
           ui:wsdlLocation="oramds:/apps/oracle/apps/cdm/foundation/parties/
locationService/LocationService.wsdl">
    <interface.wsdl interface="http://xmlns.oracle.com/apps/cdm/foundation/parties/
locationService/applicationModule/#wsdl.interface(LocationService)"
                    callbackInterface="http://xmlns.oracle.com/apps/cdm/foundation/
parties/
locationService/applicationModule/
#wsdl.interface(LocationServiceResponse)"/>
    <binding.ws port="http://xmlns.oracle.com/apps/cdm/foundation/parties/
locationService/applicationModule/
#wsdl.endpoint(LocationService/LocationServiceSoapHttpPort)"
    location="oramds:/apps/oracle/apps/cdm/foundation/parties/
locationService/LocationService.wsdl">
      <wsp:PolicyReference URI="oracle/wss11_saml_token_with_message_
protection_client_policy"
                             orawsp:category="security" orawsp:status="enabled"/>
    </binding.ws>
    <callback>
      <binding.ws port="http://xmlns.oracle.com/apps/cdm/foundation/parties/
locationService/applicationModule/
#wsdl.endpoint(LocationService/LocationServiceResponse_pt)">
        <wsp:PolicyReference URI="oracle//wss11_saml_or_username_token_with_message_
protection_service_policy"
                               orawsp:category="security"
                               orawsp:status="enabled"/>
      </binding.ws>
    </callback>
  </reference>
```

16. Make sure the following wiring information is in the composite.xml file for this service reference to BPEL process as shown here.

```
    <wire>
      <source.uri>processlocation_client_ep</source.uri>
      <target.uri>ProcessLocation/processlocation_client</target.uri>
    </wire>
    <wire>
      <source.uri>LocationCreate/ProcessLocation.processlocation_client</source.uri>
```

```
    <target.uri>ProcessLocation/processlocation_client</target.uri>
  </wire>
  <wire>
    <source.uri>ProcessLocation/LocationService</source.uri>
    <target.uri>LocationService</target.uri>
  </wire>
```

Deploy the SOA Composite with Concrete Service URL

In this section, we will deploy our SOA composite such that the service reference in the composite points to the right service URL.

1. The SOA composite service reference points to the WSDL location in the MDS connection we used. We need to use a configuration plan so that this reference service location gets updated with a concrete service URL during deployment. Save the following content as an FADeployPlan.xml file. Replace the host and port in the file to point to the real host and port where your service is deployed.

```
<?xml version="1.0" encoding="UTF-8"?>
<SOAConfigPlan xmlns="http://schemas.oracle.com/soa/configplan">
  <composite name="LocationIntegration">
    <reference name="LocationService">
      <binding type="ws">
        <attribute name="location">
          <!--replacing node for portType {http://xmlns.oracle.com/apps/cdm/
foundation/parties/
locationService/applicationModule/}LocationService-->
<replace>http://host:port/foundationParties/LocationService?WSDL</replace>
        </attribute>
      </binding>
    </reference>
  </composite>
</SOAConfigPlan>
```

2. Select the SOA composite project and build it.
3. Right-click on the project and select LocationIntegration.
4. Select Deploy to Application Server from Deployment Action.
5. Choose this file as deployment plan as shown in Figure 15-32.
6. Choose your application server in the next step and complete the deployment wizard.

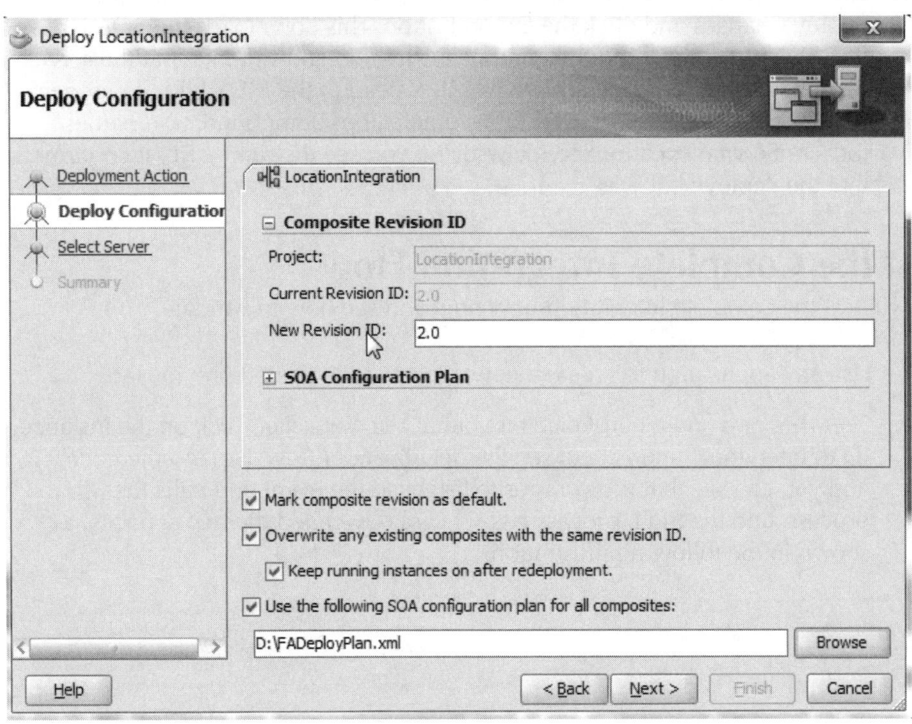

FIGURE 15-32. *Using SOA configuration plan for deployment*

7. Go to Enterprise Manager for your deployment at http://host:port/em and navigate to SOA: soa-infra: default and click on your SOA composite LocationIntegration.

8. Click on the SOA Composite drop-down and select the Export option.

9. On the Export Composite page, choose Option 1: Export with All Post-deploy Changes and click the Export button. This downloads the SOA jar file. Unzip the file, open the composite.xml file, and validate that the service reference is updated to a concrete URL instead of the MDS URL you see in JDeveloper: location="oramds:/apps/oracle/apps/cdm/foundation/parties/locationService/LocationService.wsdl". If you see the right URL, it confirms that the deployment was accurate.

Test the Complete Integration Flow

We will test the complete integration flow now and see how to validate.

1. Use any application to create a new address as indicated previously.
2. Go to EM and find the instance for your SOA composite. Click on the instance ID to open the composite to see the details of our flow. Expand the trace and you can see that the composite listens to the event and calls the BPEL process, and the BPEL process has successfully called the two services, as shown in the following illustration.

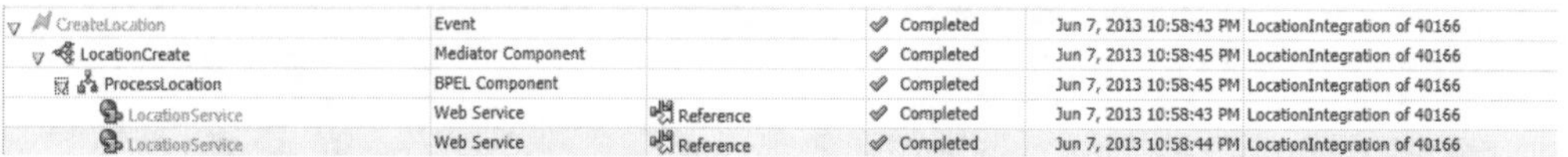

CreateLocation	Event		Completed	Jun 7, 2013 10:58:43 PM	LocationIntegration of 40166
LocationCreate	Mediator Component		Completed	Jun 7, 2013 10:58:45 PM	LocationIntegration of 40166
ProcessLocation	BPEL Component		Completed	Jun 7, 2013 10:58:45 PM	LocationIntegration of 40166
LocationService	Web Service	Reference	Completed	Jun 7, 2013 10:58:43 PM	LocationIntegration of 40166
LocationService	Web Service	Reference	Completed	Jun 7, 2013 10:58:44 PM	LocationIntegration of 40166

3. Click the ProcessLocation link to open the BPEL process and examine the Audit Trail.
4. You can expand each step in the flow and see the data being processed as shown in Figure 15-33.

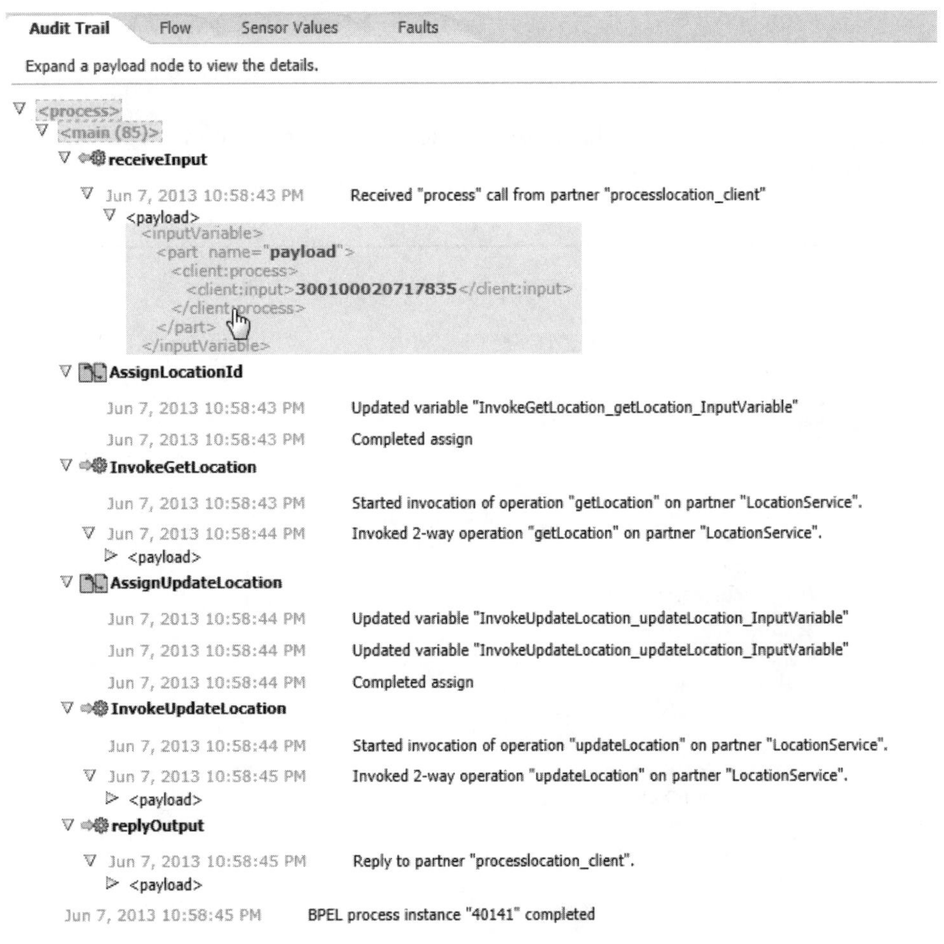

FIGURE 15-33. *Examine the BPEL process audit trail.*

How to Test Fusion Applications Web Services

You can test Fusion Applications Web Services using Enterprise Manager. You can use OER to identify what role is needed to access a given service. Once you identify the role, you can then create a user and assign that particular role to that user and invoke the service with that user for testing. For our example, we will need a user who has the Master Data Management Application Administrator role, which gives access to Location Service.

1. Log in to EM where your service is deployed.
2. Right-click on the server that hosts your service and select the Web Services menu option as shown in Figure 15-34.

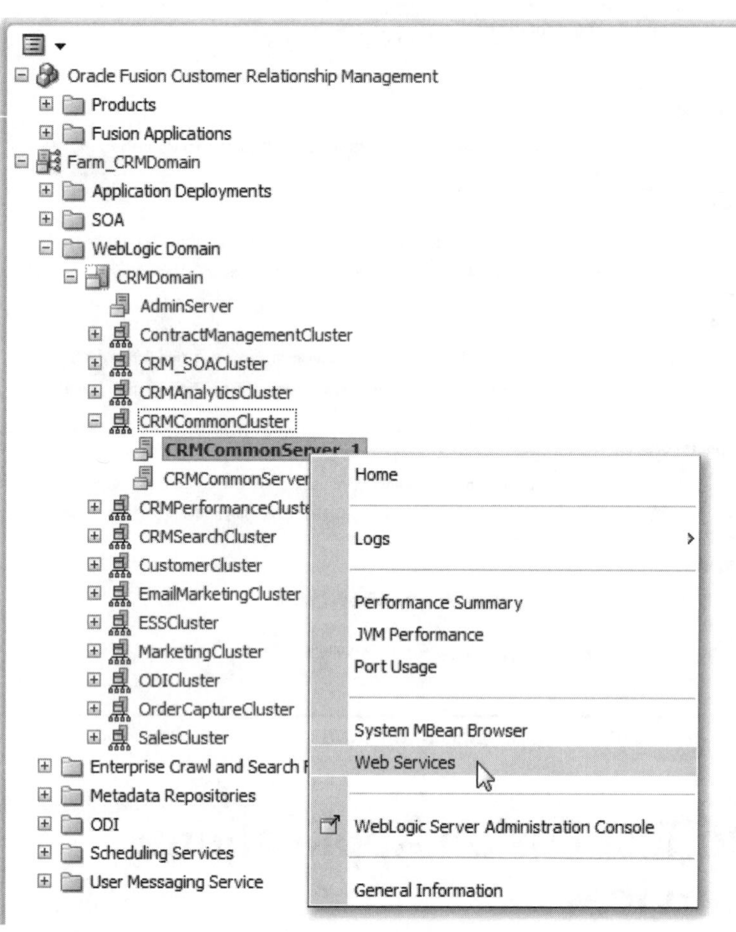

FIGURE 15-34. *Web services in Enterprise Manager*

3. Locate the service you are interested in testing from the list and click on the service as shown in the following illustration. We will use location service as an example.

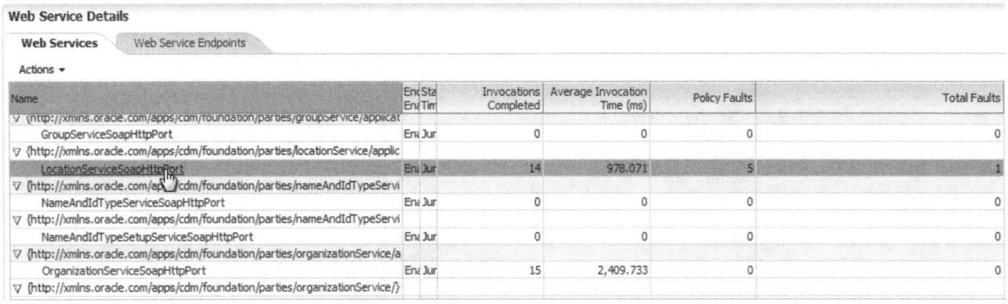

4. The service page shows details about the service, such as operations, the security policy used by the service, and other configuration details. You can click on the Web Services Test link at the top of the page as shown in Figure 15-35.

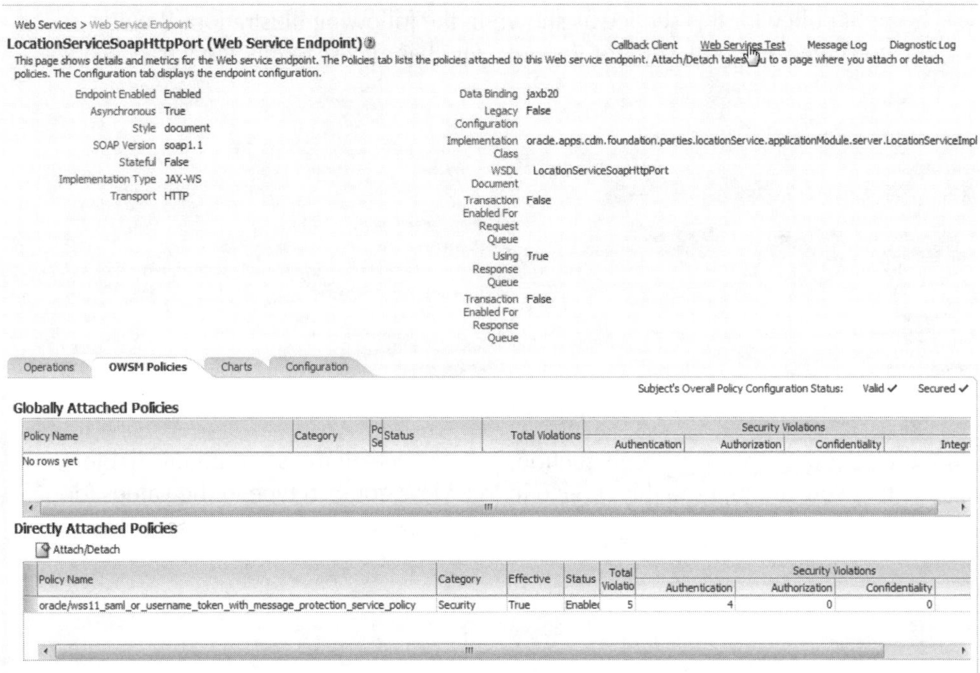

FIGURE 15-35. *Getting to the test service page in Enterprise Manager*

5. On the service test page, choose the Operation createLocation.

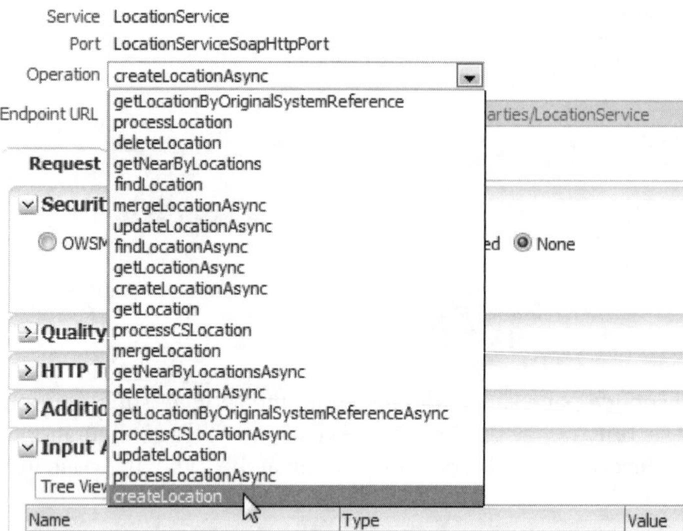

6. Under the security section, choose OWSM Security Policies and select the right policy for this service as shown in the following illustration. Provide a username and password for the user who has access to this service.

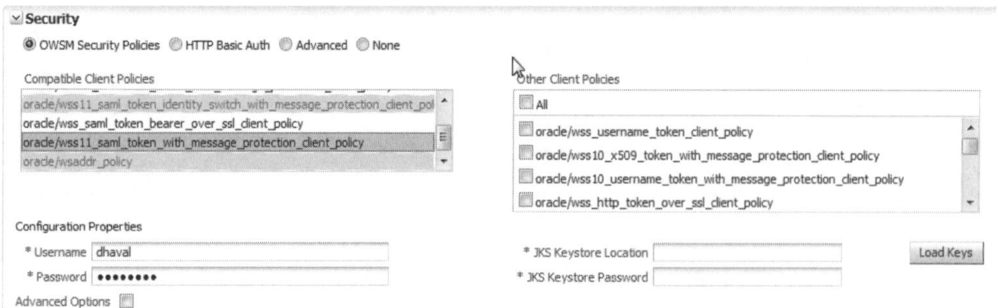

7. Under the input arguments section, you can see all the attributes available that you can input to this service in tree view. You can type in the values for

mandatory attributes per documentation. You can switch to XML view and enter the following input payload.

```
<soap:Envelope xmlns:soap="http://schemas.xmlsoap.org/soap/envelope/">
    <soap:Body>
        <ns1:createLocation xmlns:ns1="http://xmlns.oracle.com/apps/cdm/foundation/
parties/
locationService/applicationModule/types/">
            <ns1:location xmlns:ns2="http://xmlns.oracle.com/apps/cdm/foundation/
parties/
locationService/">
                <ns2:Country>IN</ns2:Country>
                <ns2:Address1>Address1</ns2:Address1>
                <ns2:City>City</ns2:City>
                <ns2:PostalCode>PostalCode</ns2:PostalCode>
                <ns2:CreatedByModule>AMS</ns2:CreatedByModule>
            </ns1:location>
        </ns1:createLocation>
    </soap:Body>
</soap:Envelope>
```

8. Click the Test Web Service button from the top or bottom-right corner of the page. This will invoke the service with the given username and provide the result in the Response tab as shown here.

```
<env:Envelope xmlns:env="http://schemas.xmlsoap.org/soap/
envelope/" xmlns:wsa="http://www.w3.org/2005/08/addressing">
      <env:Header>
      <env:Body xmlns:wsu="http://docs.oasis-open.org/wss/2004/01/
oasis-200401-wss-wssecurity-utility-1.0.xsd" wsu:Id="Body-2Tplx6O0WK501GGh6ijVKw22">
            <ns0:createLocationResponse xmlns:ns0="http://xmlns.oracle.com/apps/cdm/
foundation/parties/locationService/applicationModule/types/">
                  <ns2:result xmlns:ns0="http://xmlns.oracle.com/adf/svc/types/"
xmlns:ns1="http://xmlns.oracle.com/apps/cdm/foundation/parties/
locationService/" xmlns:ns2="http://xmlns.oracle.com/apps/cdm/foundation/parties/
locationService/applicationModule/types/" xmlns:ns3="http://xmlns.oracle.com/apps/
cdm/foundation/parties/
partyService/" xmlns:ns4="http://xmlns.oracle.com/apps/cdm/foundation/parties/
flex/location/" xmlns:tns="http://xmlns.oracle.com/adf/svc/errors/"
xmlns:xsi="http://www.w3.org/2001/XMLSchema-instance"
 xsi:type="ns1:LocationResult">
                        <ns1:Value>
                              <ns1:LocationId>300100020720793</ns1:LocationId>
                              <ns1:LastUpdateDate>2013-06-08T00:37:48.183-07:00
</ns1:LastUpdateDate>
                              <ns1:LastUpdatedBy>DHAVAL</ns1:LastUpdatedBy>
                              <ns1:CreationDate>2013-06-08T00:37:48.009-07:00
</ns1:CreationDate>
```

```
                              <ns1:CreatedBy>DHAVAL</ns1:CreatedBy>
            <ns1:LastUpdateLogin>DEA07C1FD59B2F9EE0431120F00A6EA0
</ns1:LastUpdateLogin>
                              <ns1:RequestId xsi:nil="true"/>
                              <ns1:OrigSystem xsi:nil="true"/>
<ns1:OrigSystemReference>300100020720793
</ns1:OrigSystemReference>
                              <ns1:Country>IN</ns1:Country>
                              <ns1:Address1>Address1</ns1:Address1>
                              <ns1:Address2 xsi:nil="true"/>
                              <ns1:Address3 xsi:nil="true"/>
                              <ns1:Address4 xsi:nil="true"/>
                              <ns1:City>City</ns1:City>
                              <ns1:PostalCode>PostalCode</ns1:PostalCode>
                              <ns1:State xsi:nil="true"/>
                              <ns1:Province xsi:nil="true"/>
                              <ns1:County xsi:nil="true"/>
                              <ns1:AddressStyle xsi:nil="true"/>
                              <ns1:ValidatedFlag>false</ns1:ValidatedFlag>
                              <ns1:AddressLinesPhonetic xsi:nil="true"/>
                              <ns1:PostalPlus4Code xsi:nil="true"/>
                              <ns1:Position xsi:nil="true"/>
                              <ns1:LocationDirections xsi:nil="true"/>
                              <ns1:AddressEffectiveDate xsi:nil="true"/>
                              <ns1:AddressExpirationDate xsi:nil="true"/>
                              <ns1:ClliCode xsi:nil="true"/>
                              <ns1:Language xsi:nil="true"/>
                              <ns1:ShortDescription xsi:nil="true"/>
                              <ns1:Description xsi:nil="true"/>
                              <ns1:SalesTaxGeocode xsi:nil="true"/>
                  <ns1:SalesTaxInsideCityLimits>1</ns1:SalesTaxInsideCityLimits>
                              <ns1:FaLocationId xsi:nil="true"/>
                              <ns1:ObjectVersionNumber>1</ns1:ObjectVersionNumber>
                              <ns1:CreatedByModule>AMS</ns1:CreatedByModule>
                              <ns1:ValidationStatusCode xsi:nil="true"/>
                              <ns1:DateValidated xsi:nil="true"/>
                              <ns1:DoNotValidateFlag xsi:nil="true"/>
                              <ns1:Comments xsi:nil="true"/>
                              <ns1:HouseType xsi:nil="true"/>
                              <ns1:EffectiveDate>2013-06-08</ns1:EffectiveDate>
                              <ns1:AddrElementAttribute1 xsi:nil="true"/>
                              <ns1:AddrElementAttribute2 xsi:nil="true"/>
                              <ns1:AddrElementAttribute3 xsi:nil="true"/>
                              <ns1:AddrElementAttribute4 xsi:nil="true"/>
                              <ns1:AddrElementAttribute5 xsi:nil="true"/>
```

```
                    <ns1:Building xsi:nil="true"/>
                    <ns1:FloorNumber xsi:nil="true"/>
                    <ns1:StatusFlag>true</ns1:StatusFlag>
                    <ns1:InternalFlag>false</ns1:InternalFlag>
                    <ns1:TimezoneCode xsi:nil="true"/>
                </ns1:Value>
            </ns2:result>
        </ns0:createLocationResponse>
    </env:Body>
</env:Envelope>
```

How to Change the User in SOA Composite to Call Services

In our example in the preceding section, we did not specify any user when we called the service from the BPEL process in the SOA composite. By default, SOA composites do identity propagation; that is, the composite will invoke the service with the exact same user identity that resulted in the instantiation of the composite. In our example, the SOA composite is instantiated by a Create Location event, which is raised when a user created data in the application UI. The service from the SOA composite is called with the exact same user. In our example, we are calling the service from the same Fusion Applications installation, so the integration works seamlessly. You will be faced with situations many times where you will need to switch the identity of the user before making the service call from the SOA composite because the systems you are integrating are not the same. There are two ways to do this identity switch in the SOA composite.

Using a Hard-Coded Username and Password

If you know the username and password for a user who has access to call a given service from a given application, you can simply pass that fixed username and password for calling the service. You can specify the values as properties in the SOA composite service reference as shown here.

```
    <binding.ws port="http://xmlns.oracle.com/apps/cdm/foundation/parties/
locationService/applicationModule/
#wsdl.endpoint(LocationService/LocationServiceSoapHttpPort)"
    location="oramds:/apps/oracle/apps/cdm/foundation/parties/
locationService/LocationService.wsdl">
      <wsp:PolicyReference URI="oracle/wss11_saml_token_with_
message_protection_client_policy"
                           orawsp:category="security" orawsp:status="enabled"/>
      <property name="basicHeaders">credentials</property>
      <property name="basicUsername">dhaval</property>
      <property name="basicPassword">Welcome1</property>
    </binding.ws>
```

Using Keystore Configuration

The hard-coded way to pass the username and password may not sound secure, and you may want to use a more robust mechanism to do the user switch. Please read *Oracle Fusion Middleware Security and Administrator's Guide for Web Services* to understand how to generate the csf-key to use with a Web service. This is a standard way to generate secured tokens that can be used to call a service, and it will work only for a given server configuration. Once you have the csf-key generated from your security administrator, you can use it in your SOA composite as shown here.

```
    <binding.ws port="http://xmlns.oracle.com/apps/cdm/foundation/parties/
locationService/applicationModule/
#wsdl.endpoint(LocationService/LocationServiceSoapHttpPort)"
    location="oramds:/apps/oracle/apps/cdm/foundation/parties/
locationService/LocationService.wsdl">
      <wsp:PolicyReference URI="oracle/wss11_saml_token_with_message_protection_
client_policy"
                          orawsp:category="security" orawsp:status="enabled"/>
      <property name="csf-key" many="false">your-csf-key</property>
    </binding.ws>
```

Summary

In this chapter, we discussed the different integration options available for Fusion Applications for inbound and outbound interaction. We discussed how to discover the assets using OER. We discussed various service options available in Fusion Applications and how the service-oriented architecture can be used to do integrations using business events and Web services. We also walked through a complete end-to-end example of integrating two applications for data sync. We examined how to deploy the SOA composite and how to test and examine the flow using Enterprise Manager. Finally, we talked about how to switch users for calling services from the SOA composite and how to test Fusion Applications Web services.

Index

A

C

M

N

O

P

Q

R

S

T

U

V

W

X

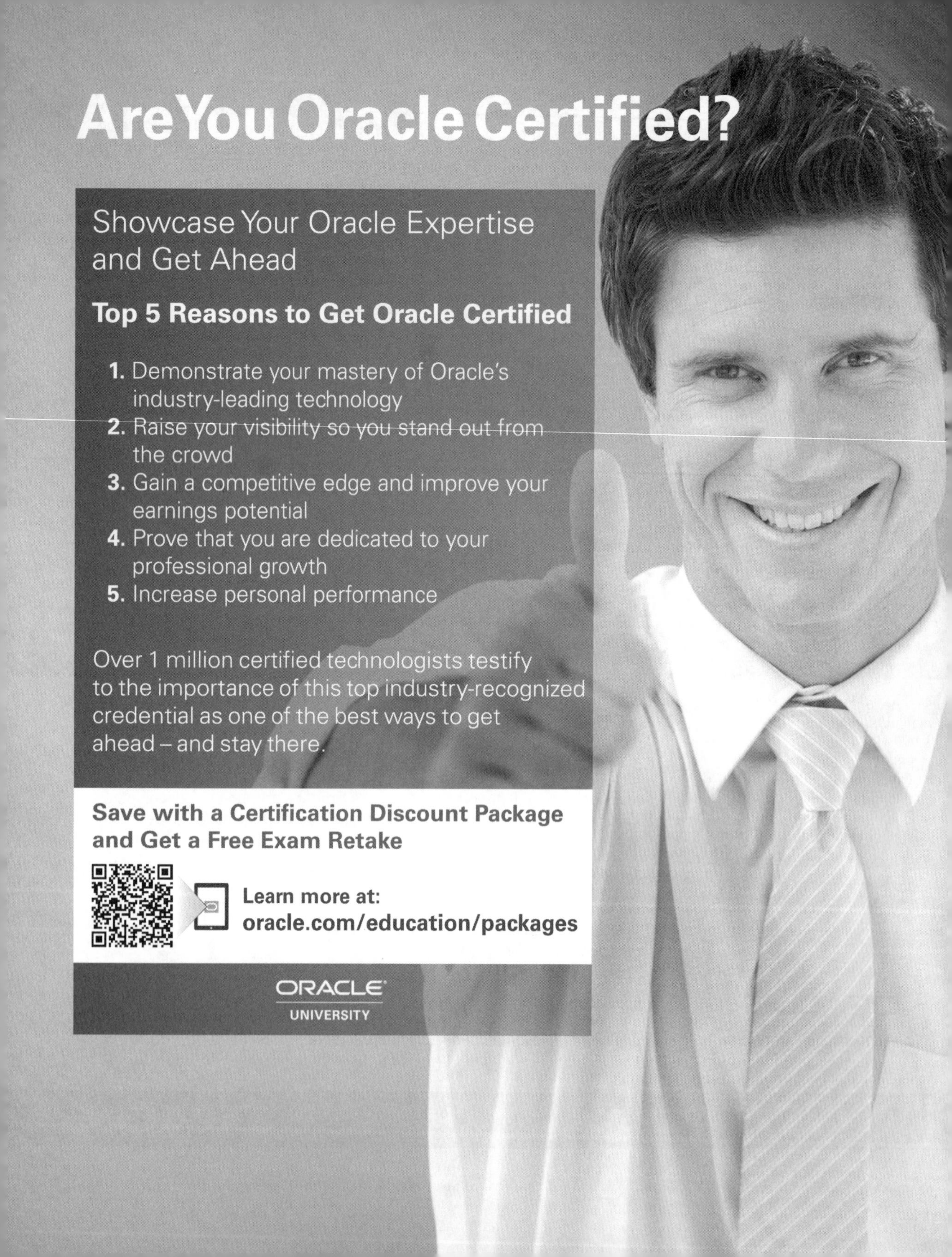
Are You Oracle Certified?
Showcase Your Oracle Expertise and Get Ahead
Top 5 Reasons to Get Oracle Certified
1. Demonstrate your mastery of Oracle's industry-leading technology
2. Raise your visibility so you stand out from the crowd
3. Gain a competitive edge and improve your earnings potential
4. Prove that you are dedicated to your professional growth
5. Increase personal performance
Over 1 million certified technologists testify to the importance of this top industry-recognized credential as one of the best ways to get ahead – and stay there.
Save with a Certification Discount Package and Get a Free Exam Retake
Learn more at:
oracle.com/education/packages
ORACLE
UNIVERSITY